PIETY AND POLITICS

PIETY AND POLITICS

The Dynamics of Royal Authority in
Homeric Greece,
Biblical Israel, and
Old Babylonian Mesopotamia

Dale Launderville

William B. Eerdmans Publishing Company
Grand Rapids, Michigan / Cambridge, U.K.

Wm. B. Eerdmans Publishing Co.
2140 Oak Industrial Drive N.E., Grand Rapids, Michigan 49505 /
P.O. Box 163, Cambridge CB3 9PU U.K.

Printed in the United States of America

08 07 06 05 04 03   7 6 5 4 3 2 1

Library of Congress Cataloging-in-Publication Data

Launderville, Dale.
   Piety and politics : the dynamics of royal authority in Homeric Greece,
biblical Israel, and old Babylonian Mesopotamia / Dale Launderville
      p.   cm.
   Includes bibliographical references (p.) and index.
   ISBN-10: 0-8028-4505-3 / ISBN-13: 978-0-8028-4505-4 (pbk. : alk. paper)
   1. Kings and rulers — religious aspects. 2. Greece — Kings and rulers —
   Religious aspects. 3. Israel — Kings and rulers — Religious aspects.
   4. Babylonia — Kings and rulers — Religious aspects. 5. Divine right
   of kings.   I. Title.

BL325.K5 L38   2002
291.1' 77' 093 — dc21

                                        2002029497

www.eerdmans.com

CONTENTS

CONTENTS

PREFACE

> *Polis* is usually translated as city or city-state. This does not capture the full meaning. *Polis* means, rather, the place, the there, wherein and as which historical being-there is. The *polis* is the historical place, the there in which, out of which, and for which history happens.
>
> Martin Heidegger, *Introduction to Metaphysics*[1]

A meaningful life can be gained only through engagement with other humans, with nature, and with God or the gods. This place of engagement is the locus where harmony and conflict converge, where integration and fragmentation counterpoint each other, where mind and heart meet. The "sense of place" that wells up within a person when such engagement happens is captured in the statement: it is good that we are here. The creating or "authoring" activity that leads to this "sense of place" manifests the authority essential to human community. Heidegger refers to the *polis* as this treasured place in which humans create themselves and their world. This primordial sense of *polis* is not simply a geographical location but much more profoundly and elusively a place of convergence of the spiritual and the material, of the social and the natural. Such convergence is a new beginning that must be gained over and over again. The thinking, the acting, and the existing involved in sustaining such a place of new beginnings constitute political thinking in its most basic sense.

The peoples who created and lived within the worlds and traditions of Homeric Greece, biblical Israel, and Old Babylonian Mesopotamia were political

---

1. Martin Heidegger, *Introduction to Metaphysics* (New York: Doubleday, 1959), p. 128.

thinkers in this basic sense. They were concerned about maintaining order in their communities and finding their place within a cosmos ruled by God or the gods. Their political thinking addressed topics spanning heaven and earth and saw authority as a gift of God or the gods that required careful attention and diligent effort to receive. This book explores this fundamental human quest for a meaningful home in a world in which kings claimed a privileged relationship with God or the gods. The authority exercised by a king had credibility to the extent that the king's rule created a sense of place, a point of convergence where life made sense.

The dynamics of royal authority within these three cultures will be unfolded through the comparison of texts drawn from each of the three cultures. Triptych after triptych of texts — each arranged according to a topic or theme — will show aspects of how these peoples fashioned the worlds in which they lived. In the interplay between these individual texts, the living political, social, and theological questions that engaged these ancient peoples — and persist into the present — emerge. My juxtaposition of texts of these three cultures has brought me into conversation with the voices of their traditions and their interpreters. I hope that this conversation across disciplines will introduce new questions and new ways of reading the texts within the disciplines of Homeric, biblical, and ancient Near Eastern studies.

The topic of this book and initial stages of research can be traced to my doctoral dissertation, which I wrote in the mid-1980s at The Catholic University of America under the title, *A Comparative Study of Kingship in Homeric Greece, Biblical Israel, and Old Babylonian Mesopotamia.* My director, Brother Aloysius Fitzgerald, F.S.C., provided careful and wise guidance and predicted that this topic would require many more years of research and reflection on my part. Since that time, chapters of this book have gone through numerous recensions in seminars with my students at the School of Theology of Saint John's University in Collegeville, Minnesota. I am grateful for their engagement with the material and their insightful, searching questions. My faculty colleagues in the School of Theology have been invaluable conversation partners on this topic of royal authority for the past fifteen years. Their criticism and encouragement not only took the form of ideas significant for the composition of this book but also consisted of practical instruction on the dynamics of authority in an academic setting where I served as their academic dean for ten years.

The members of the Old Testament Colloquium, who meet for a three-day seminar annually at Conception Abbey in Conception, Missouri at the invitation of Abbot Gregory Polan, have examined various versions of this work over the past ten years. Their guidance has been a vital source for its growth and development. I am especially grateful to S. Irene Nowell, O.S.B., for reading the entire manuscript in its penultimate form, recommending significant improvements, and offering wise guidance on a number of issues. I also wish to thank Mary Beth Banken, and Carol Johannes for their generous assistance with technical details.

I am particularly indebted to Dr. Jay Semel, his staff, and faculty colleagues at the Obermann Center for Advanced Studies at the University of Iowa. They created an ideal environment for research and reflection during my sabbatical year in 1999-2000 when I composed the first draft of this book. The Center lived up to its billing as "the Magic Mountain." I am especially grateful to Dr. John F. Garcia of the Department of Classics at the University of Iowa for reading portions of the manuscript and for providing strategic advice in the revision of the manuscript. The hospitality of Fr. Ed Fitzpatrick and his staff at the Catholic Student Newman Center in Iowa City rivaled that of Eumaeus.

I am indebted to Professor David Noel Freedman for his careful attention to this text and numerous suggestions for refining my ideas and my prose. I am grateful to Allen Myers and his staff at Eerdmans for including this work in the Bible in Its World Series and seeing it through the publication process.

To Abbots Timothy Kelly and John Klassen of Saint John's Abbey and Brother Dietrich Reinhart, president of Saint John's University, I am grateful for the sabbatical and released time over the past two years that have enabled me to bring this project to a completion. My life as a Benedictine monk under the rule of an abbot for the past twenty-five years has no doubt shaped many of the values that come to expression in my interpretation of the ancient texts of this study. I have learned that obedience to a monarch works best when there are engagement and care by all parties involved. In this model of authority, criticism and protest have an important role but are by no means solely responsible for the manifestation of truth.

I have tried to avoid privileging the texts of any one of these three traditions: Homeric Greece, biblical Israel, and Old Babylonian Mesopotamia. Yet I have been raised in the Christian tradition that is grounded in the biblical tradition of Israel; therefore, throughout this book I have consistently capitalized "God" when referring to YHWH.

The chronology for each of the traditions is based on the following: the chronology for the Dark and Archaic Ages in Greece is drawn from Ian Morris, *Archaeology as Cultural History* (Oxford: Blackwell, 2000), p. 7; the chronology for biblical Israel is taken from John Bright, *A History of Israel* (Philadelphia: Westminster, 1981), pp. 465-74; the chronology for Mesopotamia is based upon that provided by Dominique Charpin, "The History of Ancient Mesopotamia: An Overview," *Civilizations of the Ancient Near East*, ed. Jack Sasson (New York: Scribner, 1995), pp. 807-29.

The translations of the texts from Homer, the Bible, and the various Mesopotamian texts are my own unless otherwise indicated. My translations of texts from the *Iliad* and the *Odyssey* are based on the following critical texts: David B. Monro and Thomas W. Allen, eds., *Homeri Opera: Iliad I–XII* and *Iliad XIII–XXIV,* 3rd ed., 2 vols. (Oxford: Clarendon, 1920); and Thomas W. Allen, *Homeri Opera: Odyssey I–XII* and *Odyssey XIII–XXIV,* 2nd ed., 2 vols. (Oxford: Clarendon, 1917, 1919).

I dedicate this work to my parents, Leon Francis and Mary Maxine Launderville, whose care and love taught me to cherish the gift of authority for its indispensable role in engaging the world and searching along with others to find a meaningful home within it.

DALE LAUNDERVILLE, O.S.B.
Saint John's University
Collegeville, Minnesota
February 2002

ABBREVIATIONS

AbB	*Altbabylonische Briefe*
ABD	*Anchor Bible Dictionary*
ANET	J. B. Pritchard, ed., *Ancient Near Eastern Texts*
ARM	*Archives royales de Mari*
BASOR	*Bulletin of the American Schools of Oriental Research*
Bib	*Biblica*
BO	*Bibliotheca Orientalis*
BTB	*Biblical Theology Bulletin*
CAD	*Assyrian Dictionary of the Oriental Institute of the University of Chicago*
CAH	*Cambridge Ancient History*
CBQ	*Catholic Biblical Quarterly*
CH	*Code of Hammurapi*
CRRA	*Compte rendu, Rencontre Assyriologique Internationale*
ETR	*Etudes théologiques et religieuses*
GKC	*Gesenius' Hebrew Lexicon*, ed. E. Kautzsch and A. E. Cowley
HTR	*Harvard Theological Review*
HUCA	*Hebrew Union College Annual*
IDB	*Interpreter's Dictionary of the Bible*
Int	*Interpretation*
JANES	*Journal of the Ancient Near Eastern Society*
JAOS	*Journal of the American Oriental Society*
JBL	*Journal of Biblical Literature*
JCS	*Journal of Cuneiform Studies*
JHS	*Journal of Hellenic Studies*

JNES	*Journal of Near Eastern Studies*
JNSL	*Journal of Northwest Semitic Languages*
JQR	*Jewish Quarterly Review*
JSOT	*Journal for the Study of the Old Testament*
JSS	*Journal of Semitic Studies*
LBA	Late Bronze Age
LXX	Septuagint
NABU	*Nouvelles assyriologiques brèves et utilitaires*
OB	Old Babylonian Period (2003-1595 B.C.)
OLP	*Orientalia Louvaniensia Periodica*
Or	*Orientalia*
PEQ	*Palestine Exploration Quarterly*
PW	Pauly-Wissowa, *Real-Encyclopädie der klassichen Altertumswissenschaft*
RA	*Revue d'assyriologie et d'archéologie orientale*
RIME	*The Royal Inscriptions of Mesopotamia, Early Periods*
RLA	*Reallexikon der Assyriologie*
SJOT	*Scandinavian Journal of the Old Testament*
Vg.	Vulgate
VT	*Vetus Testamentum*
ZA	*Zeitschrift für Assyriologie*
ZAW	*Zeitschrift für die alttestamentliche Wissenschaft*

For additional abbreviations, see the *Chicago Assyrian Dictionary* or the journal *Orientalia* for topics on ancient Mesopotamia and *Old Testament Abstracts* or *Elenchus Bibliographicus Biblicus* for biblical Israel.

Biblical Israel

Beirut

Sidon

PHOENICIA

Litani R.

Abana R.

Damascus

Mt. Hermon

Pharpar R.

ARAM

Tyre

Dan

Kedesh

J. Jarmuk

Hazor

Acco

Sea of Galilee

Ashtaroth

Mt. Carmel

Mt. Tabor

Mediterranean Sea

Kishon

Mt. Moreh

Yarmuk R.

Edrei

Megiddo

Ramoth-gilead

Taanach

R.

Mt. Gilboa

Beth-shan

Ibleam

Jabesh-gilead?

Jordan R.

Tirzah

Samaria

Mt. Ebal

Succoth?

Penuel?

Mahanaim?

Yarkon R.

Mt. Gerizim

Shechem

Jabbok R.

Joppa

Aphek

Shiloh

ISRAEL

Bethel

Jericho

Rabbah (Amman)

AMMON

Gezer

Ashdod

Ajalon

Jerusalem

Mt. Nebo

Heshbon

Gath

Bethlehem

Medeba

Ashkelon

Mareshah

Gaza

Hebron

Dibon

Gerar

JUDAH

Dead Sea

Arnon R.

Raphia

Besor Br.

Beer-sheba

MOAB

Kir-hareseth

PHILISTIA

Zered Br.

WILDERNESS

W. el-Aris

Region periodically contested by Judah and Edom

Bozrah

EDOM

Kadesh-barnea

0   10   20   30   40 miles

0 10 20 30 40 kilometers

WILDERNESS

©MAPQUEST.COM

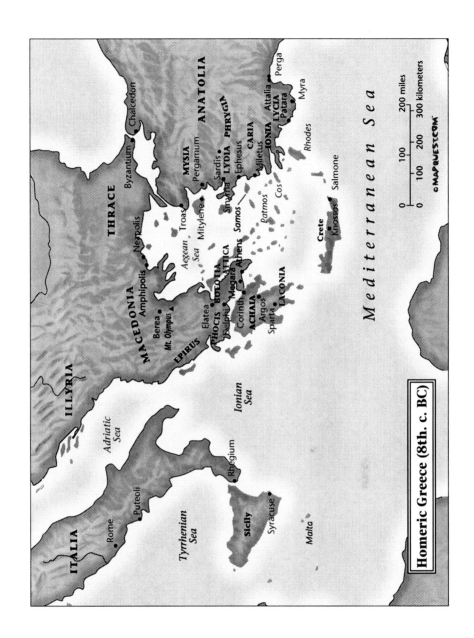

Homeric Greece (8th. c. BC)

ITALIA
Rome
Puteoli
Tyrrhenian Sea
Rhegium
Syracuse
Sicily
Malta
Ionian Sea
Adriatic Sea
ILLYRIA
EPIRUS
MACEDONIA
Berea
Mt. Olympus ▲
Amphipolis
Neapolis
THRACE
Byzantium
Chalcedon
ANATOLIA
MYSIA
Pergamum
Troas
Mitylene
Aegean Sea
Delphi
Elatea
PHOCIS
BOEOTIA
ATTICA
Megara
Athens
Corinth
ACHAIA
Argos
Sparta
LACONIA
Samos
Patmos
Cos
Sardis
Smyrna
LYDIA
PHRYGIA
Ephesus
Miletus
CARIA
IONIA
Attalia
Patara
LYCIA
Myra
Perga
Rhodes
Salmone
Crete
Knossos
Mediterranean Sea

0   100   200 miles
0   100   200   300 kilometers
©MAPQUEST.COM

The Traditional Pattern for Legitimating Royal Authority in Homeric Greece, Biblical Israel, and Old Babylonian Mesopotamia

W hy would anyone obey a king's command? Compliance in the face of coercion does not constitute a form of obedience, for obedience is a freely chosen response. Obviously every response is conditioned by a number of circumstances, but in the end the individual's choice counts. If a king rules with authority, then his commands will influence the choices that individuals make. There is a point at which a king could abandon persuasion and rule only by physical force, but then the king would have become a tyrant without real authority. How royal authority arose and operated in Homeric Greece, biblical Israel, and Old Babylonian (OB) Mesopotamia (2003-1595 B.C.) and how it manifested similar, different, and analogous dynamics in these three cultures of the eastern Mediterranean basin in the first two millennia B.C. will be the foci of this study.

Royal authority in the ancient Near East was revered as a gift from the gods to increase the well-being of the community by strengthening the quality of relationships between the ruler and the ruled. The king, as the recipient of this gift of authority, was the earthly agent who exercised sovereign rule in a community on behalf of the king of the gods. Yet the people's reception of the king and his decisions was integral to the dynamics of the king's authority. As a relational reality, royal authority existed between the king and the people. How the people perceived the king was important to the king's effectiveness. To cultivate the loyalty of the people, the kings in Homeric Greece, biblical Israel, and OB Mesopotamia drew heavily upon the traditions of each community in shaping royal rhetoric promoting the legitimacy of the king's rule. Such traditional thought and rhetoric for the legitimation of a king's rule not only promoted obedience on the part of the people but also provoked scrutiny of the justice of the king's ways. An important factor in whether or not the people obeyed a directive from the king was their perception of the king as one obedient to and empowered by God or the gods. Royal authority itself was not a possession of the king but rather a gift on loan from the gods. The king who divorced piety from politics ran the risk of self-aggrandizement and the illusion that he was accountable to no one, whereas the king who tried to integrate piety and politics wrestled with the decisions and sacrifices required of him in caring for the people entrusted to his rule.

This promonarchical view of royal authority might strike one as sheer ideology propagated by the royal establishment. It is true that, in practice, such a view of royal authority could support the machinations of the tyrant as well as the self-sacrificing objectives of the just king, but no form of government can guarantee that abuses will not creep into its operations. The antimonarchical skeptic might go further and question even the type of rule exercised by moderate royal rulers, for in his estimation even moderate royal rule generates a greater measure of obedience to a central authority and a greater passivity toward the possibilities of life than the human condition requires.[1] It is important to note, however, that fundamental to the worldviews of these ancient communities of Homeric Greece, biblical Israel, and OB Mesopotamia was the conviction that God or the gods ruled over heaven and earth. These ancient peoples' reflections on authority in their communities necessarily involved speaking about God or the gods, which means that their political reflections took the form of political theologies, rhetorically shaped by metaphors, symbols, and narratives, rather than the form of political theories, composed primarily to meet the expectations of reasoned argument.[2]

Authority is indispensable to every human community. If a community is to be a home where the members find their places and their roles, then the cooperative and competitive ways that individuals interact need to be coordinated. Certain individuals assume the role of legitimately coordinating social relations so that the community or social system can function. As defined by the anthropologist Ronald Cohen, "authority is legitimate power" in a community; it is a highly valued subset of power within the community but is not the sum total of that power. The interplay between power and authority in social relations defines these relations as "political." So, even relations within a family can be seen to have a political aspect. Yet since a community consists of a number of families, groups, and individuals, the proper locus for the term "politi-

---

1. Cf. Peter W. Rose, *Sons of the Gods, Children of Earth: Ideology and Literary Form in Ancient Greece* (Ithaca: Cornell University Press, 1992), p. 36.

2. Cf. Paul Ricoeur, *Freud and Philosophy: An Essay on Interpretation* (New Haven: Yale University Press, 1970), p. 54.

cal" is the set of social relations involving power and authority in this larger network known as a community.[3]

Tyrants maintain their rule by coercion and not by authority, for authority requires the support of the people and of God or the gods. Communities torn by internal dissension yearn for stability and security, even that afforded by a strong king, whereas communities flourishing in times of peace often work to remove constraints placed on individual projects by the tradition or other authority structures. Where to draw the line between the legitimate activities of the individual and the individual's responsibilities toward the common good is a perennial question in all human communities. The monarchical form of government emphasizes the importance of collective action and support for the common good as symbolized in the person of the king. In the ancient communities of Homeric Greece, biblical Israel, and OB Mesopotamia, God or the gods played a pivotal role in the integrity of such collective efforts.

This comparative study examines the character and dynamics of the rhetoric and ideas that the kings of Homeric Greece, biblical Israel, and OB Mesopotamia used to legitimate their rule. This is a work in comparative political theology. A recurring pattern within the royal rhetoric of these political theologies described the king as a ruler chosen by the king of the gods to care for the people. This pattern concerning the divine election of the king and his accountability before the sovereign deity is illustrated by the following texts drawn from each of these three cultures:

a. from Homer's *Iliad* in the passage that describes the lineage of the scepter of Argos:

Lordly Agamemnon stood with the scepter in hand which Hephaestus had laboriously crafted. Hephaestus gave it to lord Zeus, the son of Kronos, and then Zeus gave it to the runner Argeiphontes, and lord Hermes gave it to Pelops, driver of horses, and then Pelops in turn gave it to Atreus, shepherd of people. When Atreus died, he bequeathed it to Thyestes, owner of many sheep. Then Thyestes in turn bequeathed it to Agamemnon to bear and rule over many islands and all of Argos. (*Il.* 2.100-8)

b. from Psalm 78, which narrates a version of Israel's salvation history culminating in the election of David as king:

He [the Lord] chose David, his servant,
   and brought him from the sheepfolds,

---

3. Ronald Cohen, "The Political System," in *Handbook of Method in Cultural Anthropology*, ed. R. Naroll and R. Cohen (New York: Columbia University Press, 1970), p. 488.

From tending the ewes he brought him,
   in order to shepherd Jacob, his people,
   and Israel, his possession.
He shepherded them with all his heart,
   and with skillful hands he led them. (Ps. 78:70-72)

c. from a Mesopotamian inscription of the OB Babylonian king Samsuiluna (1749-1712 B.C.):

When Anum and Enlil, the kings of heaven and earth, looked joyfully upon Marduk, the first-born son of Ea, gave him an exalted name among the Annunaki, gave him dominion over the four regions of the world, (and) made firm for him the foundation of Babylon like (that of) heaven and earth; at that time, Marduk, the chief god of his land, the god who creates wisdom, gave to me, Samsuiluna, the king of his longing, all the lands to shepherd. Indeed he instructed me in a grand fashion to bring about the settling of the pastures of his land and lead forever his widespread people in peace.[4]

The common pattern instanced in these three texts from Homeric Greece, biblical Israel, and OB Mesopotamia is summarized in the shepherd metaphor: the king of the gods, who owned the sheep, entrusted them to the care of the earthly king who was empowered to tend them.

This simple pattern embodied within the person of the king a dynamic between heaven and earth that unfolded in various genres of texts within the traditions of each of the three cultures. This pattern and dynamic of royal legitimation mapped out in symbolic form the interplay of divine and human power in the politics of a monarchic community. This divine-human interplay was cooperative and conflictual, affirming and demanding; it was a continuous process within the divine-human relationship where authority came to birth. The pattern functioned symbolically by bringing together two different spheres of reality, the divine and the human, and relating them so that the lesser known divine sphere and the better known human sphere could be seen as influencing and illuminating one another. The places and times in which authority fostered communal bonds and collective action were moments of grace in which the interplay of divine and human actors brought the community into harmony with the larger world order. This epiphanic moment, fleeting though it might be,

---

4. Douglas Frayne, *RIME 4*, E4.3.7.5, lines 1-24. Victor Hurowitz ("Literary Structures in Samsuiluna A," *JCS* 36 [1984]: 204) argues on the basis of a comparison of this inscription and Hammurapi's clay-nail inscription (Frayne, *RIME 4*, E4.3.6.2) that the Mesopotamian scribes composed royal inscriptions from widely shared patterns and literary devices.

could shape the outlook of the king and the people to work for the common good over the long term.

The logic of this traditional pattern demanded that the divine actors be taken as seriously as the human actors. In the hard-nosed practices of the political arena, the piety of such a pattern may appear to have been a ploy by the royal establishment to increase its hold on power by mystifying the causes of its rise to power. Yet the understanding of the divine world and the image of the pious king in the traditional pattern were framed so as to take into account the shadow side of politics as well as its more presentable aspects. Knowledge of and communication with the divine took place within and not apart from the context of human experience. The interplay between the shadow and presentable sides of politics was no more subject to resolution than that between the divine and the human; both dualities called not only for acceptance but also for questioning, for truth was manifested in the confluence and contrast of light and shadow: the chiaroscuro effect. The revelation of such truth was short-circuited if piety was removed from politics.

The term "theology" is derived from *theos*, "God," and *logos*, "word, gathering together," and so it can be translated as "God-talk." Such a translation can free theology from the expectation of a systematic treatment of God or the gods and highlight the metaphorical nature of knowledge about the divine. In each tradition, God or the gods were named and treated as agents; there is no question that the authors of these texts talked about God or the gods regardless of whether or not they believed in the existence of such divine beings. Since the traditional pattern for legitimating royal authority treated the divine sphere as an integral part of its structure and dynamic, there are grounds for labeling those texts in the Homeric, Israelite, and OB texts that incorporated this pattern as texts of political theology. This pattern typically unfolded in narrative form; it was embodied in texts that used metaphors, symbols, and figurative speech drawn from the community's tradition. So, this form of political theology appeared as poems and narratives, both literary and historical, rather than as tracts in philosophy where reasoning from first principles set the agenda for the structure and style of the composition.

I argue that these narrative and poetic texts as political theologies exemplify a form of early political thinking. Questions of a political nature arise in these texts that incorporate the traditional pattern for legitimating royal authority embodied in the shepherd metaphor. Some genres allow such questions a direct airing (e.g., Did Agamemnon misuse his royal authority against Achilles in chapter 1 of the *Iliad?*) while in others one can only infer that suspicions or questions were raised about the claims made in the texts (e.g., the self-adulation of the king in the OB royal inscriptions). Examples of important political topics addressed in these texts include: the right of possessing a plot of land, the meaning of going to battle on behalf of the community, and the way in which leaders of the community kept or failed to keep their promises. Whether reflection on such topics took place in a popular assembly at the city gate or in the workplace does not define such questions as political.[5] Rather, it is the nature of the topics addressed in such reflection that determines whether or not the label "political" is appropriate. That is, do these reflections address issues of power and authority in social relations that shape the community?[6] So, in these texts where reflection was triggered on issues of the right ordering of the community through the exercise of royal authority given by God or the gods, such reflection was a form of political thinking that operated according to poetic and narrative modes rather than according to the dictates of a type of philosophical discourse that came to define itself over against poetry.[7] A

5. In contrast, Paul Cartledge ("Writing the History of Archaic Greek Political Thought," in *Archaic Greece: New Approaches and New Evidence,* ed. N. Fisher and H. van Wees [London: Duckworth, 1998], p. 385) emphasizes the connection between the "civic space" in the middle of the "collective life" and the development of politics that he defines as: "communal and collective decision-making, in public, effected after substantive discussion among more or less equals, on issues of principle as well as purely technical, operational matters." Such a definition describes the process of decision making initiated in cities of fifth century B.C. Greece, but it hardly provides a sufficient definition of the "political" *per se.* Keith Michael Baker ("Introduction," in *The French Revolution and the Creation of Modern Political Culture,* vol. 1: *The Political Culture of the Old Regime,* ed. K. M. Baker [New York: Pergamon, 1987], p. xii) defines politics more broadly as "the activity through which individual groups in any society articulate, negotiate, implement, and enforce the competing claims they make one upon another."

6. See Sally C. Humphreys, "Diffusion, Comparison, Criticism," in *Anfänge politischen Denkens in der Antike: Die nahöstlichen Kulturen und die Griechen,* ed. Kurt Raaflaub and Elisabeth Müller-Luckner (Munich: R. Oldenbourg, 1993), pp. 3-5; Cohen, "The Political System," p. 488; Kurt Raaflaub, "Homer and the Beginnings of Political Thought," *Proceedings of the Boston Area Colloquium in Ancient Philosophy* 4 (1988): 4-7. In contrast, Christian Meier ("Emergence of an Autonomous Intelligence among the Greeks," in *The Origins and Diversity of Axial Age Civilizations,* ed. S. N. Eisenstadt [Albany, N.Y.: SUNY Press, 1986], pp. 70, 75; idem, *The Greek Discovery of Politics* [Cambridge, Mass.: Harvard University Press, 1990], pp. 29, 36, 45) claims that no genuine political thinking occurred prior to that of the Greek city-states of the fifth century B.C.; he claims that politics arose in Greece because of the absence of a monarchy and the need to use thought rather than directives from a sovereign as a means of ordering their communities. To define the "political" as does Claude Mosse ("Inventing Politics," in *Greek Thought: A Guide to Classical Knowledge* [Cambridge, Mass.: Harvard University Press, 2000], p. 147) as a process in which an assembly debates issues and then makes decisions unnecessarily limits from the outset the types of reflection, communication, and practice in a community that can be regarded as political.

7. Glenn Most ("The Poetics of Early Greek Philosophy," in *The Cambridge Companion to Early Greek Philosophy,* ed. A. Long [Cambridge: Cambridge University Press, 1999], pp. 22-23)

"demystifying mentality"[8] could have engaged these texts of political theology and in the process of trying to debunk them would have addressed questions of the legitimate exercise of royal power and thereby would have contributed to the tensive dynamic at the heart of the traditional pattern for legitimating royal authority.

The Comparative Method

The purpose of the comparative dimension of this study is to identify similar, different, and analogous aspects of the rhetoric and thought used to legitimate royal authority in Homeric Greece, biblical Israel, and OB Mesopotamia.[9] The traditional pattern for legitimating royal authority has been drawn from texts in each of the three cultures and provides a general grid of the relationships among God or the gods, the king, and the people in these communities. Aspects of these political, theological, and social relationships have been identified as themes or topics that texts from each of the three traditions address. On a particular theme, a text from Homer will be discussed, followed by a text from biblical Israel and then a text from OB Mesopotamia. By reason of their selection, the texts address a similar theme or topic, but the ways in which they do so reflect their different historical and cultural circumstances and, to varying extents, analogies in their royal practices and traditions. The comparisons based on these texts are made between the traditions of these three cultures where each tradition is treated as a distinct whole. So, the Homeric tradition, the Israelite tradition, and the OB tradition are regarded as distinct environments to be compared. The comparisons do not rest on dating each text to a particular time and place within the Homeric world or within Mesopotamian or Israelite history even though such historical information — insofar as it is known — is taken into account in the interpretation of each text.

I aim first to identify the ways and the extent to which the dynamics of authority in each of the three cultures were isomorphic. Were similar political questions regarding royal authority addressed in these three cultures? My next aim is to discover what were the similar, dissimilar, or analogous ways in which

---

explains that Aristotle and his student Theophrastus were the first to differentiate early Greek poets from early Greek philosophers. Cf. Ricoeur, *Freud and Philosophy*, pp. 41-42.

8. A term that G. E. R. Lloyd (*Demystifying Mentalities* [New York: Cambridge University Press, 1990], pp. 8-9, 143) used to describe the critical spirit in legal, philosophical, and scientific contexts that required proof by rational argumentation in order to persuade an audience.

9. Paul Ricoeur (*Time and Narrative*, vol. 3 [Chicago: University of Chicago Press, 1985], p. 154) argues that "our relation to the reality of the past has to pass successively through the filters of the Same, the Other, and the Analogous."

these political questions were discussed. This comparative methodology can be categorized as a typological approach rather than as a historical-genetic approach: that is, aspects of the dynamics of royal authority can be seen to form types or categories that appear in each of the three cultures at an appropriate level of generalization, but I do not try to prove that one culture was the source of an idea or practice for one of the other cultures compared.[10] As distinct as each of these three cultures was geographically and chronologically, the people within them nevertheless lived on the same planet, and so at an appropriate level of generalization common ground can be found between these three cultures. Nevertheless, the distinctiveness of the dynamics of royal authority in each culture is to be given as much if not more attention in the comparison. This typological approach is thus two-pronged: comparative and contrastive. Such a typological approach has heuristic value:[11] it allows us to see the texts of each culture from new perspectives and to gain new understandings of the political questions with which they wrestled.

The format of an outline communicates well the basic logic of the comparative-contrastive exercise undertaken in this study: the main items of the outline (e.g., #1 and #1a) that are at a higher level of generalization communicate aspects of royal rule shared by each of the three cultural traditions of royal rhetoric; then the subordinate items (e.g., #1a.1, 1a.2, and 1a.3) give specific instances of this aspect in each culture. It is usually in the latter category of subordinate items that the distinctive features of kingship in each culture come to the fore. The distinctive feature is demonstrable from the text cited, but the comparative context in which this feature is framed sheds light on how this feature functions within the traditional pattern of authority. For example, to understand Agamemnon's confiscation of Achilles' trophy as an instance where Agamemnon ignored the power of traditional authority in his divine election raises important questions that can be applied to the ways David and Hammurapi understood their divine election and how this influenced the justice of their rule. The aim then is to show that similar questions about royal authority were addressed in each of the three traditions in distinctive ways according to specific texts of

---

10. Meir Malul, *The Comparative Method in Ancient Near Eastern and Biblical Legal Studies,* AOAT 227 (Neukirchen: Neukirchener Verlag, 1990), p. 53; Marc Bloch, "Two Strategies of Comparison," in *Comparative Perspectives: Theories and Methods,* ed. A. Etzioni and F. Dubow (Boston: Little, Brown and Company, 1970), pp. 40-41; Abraham Malamat, *Mari and the Bible* (Leiden: Brill, 1998), p. 3; Hans Barstad, "Comparare necesse est? Ancient Israelite and Ancient Near Eastern Prophecy in Comparative Perspective," in *Prophecy in Its Ancient Near Eastern Context: Mesopotamian, Biblical, and Arabian Perspectives,* SBL Symposium Series 13 (Atlanta: Society for Biblical Literature, 2000), pp. 5-7.

11. Malul, *The Comparative Method in Ancient Near Eastern and Biblical Legal Studies,* p. 64.

each tradition. So, the outline format describes the organizing principle of this study: the historical interpretation of specific texts from each tradition selected because they address a particular aspect of kingship.[12]

On a macro-level, there are five recurring aspects of kingship that thread their way horizontally through the seven chapters of this study and form a backdrop against which distinctive aspects of kingship in each of the three cultures can be identified: (1) the king as the chief redistributor of material and symbolic goods in the community; (2) the king as a symbol centralizing the community; (3) the king's responsibility to be attentive to the divine world; (4) the justice of royal rule according to the ethical world order; and (5) the role of the prophet and the popular assembly in challenging the king and promoting just royal rule.

In juxtaposing texts from Homeric Greece, biblical Israel, and OB Mesopotamia, I aim to bring the voices of the three cultures together, without privileging any one of them, to address perennial political questions. I do not try to trace the historical diffusion of rhetoric, ideas, and practices from one culture to another.[13] Rather, I identify isomorphisms and unique aspects in royal rhet-

12. One might object that my selection of specific texts is highly subjective. Numerous historiographers have argued that the subjective element is not only unavoidable in history writing but is also integral to its rigor (cf. Frank Ankersmit, *History and Tropology: The Rise and Fall of Metaphor* [Berkeley: University of California Press, 1994], pp. 168, 206, 218). I have selected particular texts on the basis of each one addressing a theme or aspect of the traditional pattern of authority exemplified in the texts quoted above on pages 3-4. The organization of this study is thematic, but the heart of the study is the comparison and contrast carried out at the level of the particular texts. The texts may be compared to pictures in a gallery. The successful exhibit is one that enhances the significance of the individual pictures, not one that highlights each picture as an example of a more general type. The framing of the exhibit plays an indispensable role, yet the point of the exhibit is to present the individual pictures. For more on this way of distinguishing between a modern and postmodern understanding of history writing, see Frank Ankersmit, "Historicism, Post-Modernism and Epistemology," in *Post-Modernism and Anthropology: Theory and Practice* (Assen: Van Gorcum, 1995), p. 26.

13. However, the recovery of artifacts from the second half of the second millennium and the first millennium b.c. from each of these cultures in the archaeological sites of the others demonstrates that there were interaction and exchange by traders, scribes, artisans, and so forth. See Eric H. Cline, *Sailing the Wine-Dark Sea: International Trade and the Late Bronze Age Aegean*, BAR International Series 591 (Oxford: Tempus Reparatum, 1994), pp. xvi-xviii; Mario Liverani, "The Collapse of the Near Eastern Regional System at the End of the Bronze Age: The Case of Syria," in *Centre and Periphery in the Ancient World*, ed. M. Rowlands et al. (Cambridge: Cambridge University Press, 1987), pp. 66-73; Jane C. Waldbaum, "Greeks *in* the East or Greeks *and* the East? Problems in the Definition and Recognition of Presence," *BASOR* 305 (1997): 12; Walter Burkert, *The Orientalizing Revolution: Near Eastern Influence on Greek Culture in the Early Archaic Age* (Cambridge, Mass.: Harvard University Press, 1992), pp. 21, 25, 120; Stephanie Dalley, "The Influence of Mesopotamia on Israel and the Bible," pp. 57-83, and Stephanie Dalley

oric and practices in these three cultures in order to understand better their reflection and thought about community life under the rule of a king authorized by God or the gods.

Overview of the Study

The first chapter provides an overview of the rhetoric, dynamics, and meaning of the traditional pattern for legitimating royal authority. The king of the gods issued a command to the earthly king that empowered the king to make authoritative statements. This pattern had at its core an authoritative command. The chain of command in this pattern viewed the heavenly world "as if" it functioned the way the earthly kingdoms did. This form of metaphoric truth was also operative in symbols and narratives that produced structures in the king's political and social circumstances that set the stage for the effectiveness of his words and so played a fundamental role in enhancing the king's authority. The king's production of political and social structures could not have been explained without recourse to metaphoric, symbolic truth that disposed people to look beyond appearances for an intuitive truth that explained their experience and offered them reason to hope. This truth beyond appearances had a stabilizing effect that tended to slow the rate of change by making change appear superficial and ephemeral. Conservation and integration were higher values in the traditional pattern of royal legitimation than were innovation and diversity.

The accountability of the earthly king to the king of the gods was central to the pattern of legitimation. On the basis of the guarantee that the king was accountable to God or the gods, the community was able to take the risk of shaping its identity around the king. How this pattern for the legitimation of royal authority could have avoided functioning as sheer ideology to shore up the king's hold on power depended on the vitality of the metaphors, symbols, and narratives which delegitimated an unjust king just as they legitimated a just one. The vitality of figurative language in its communication of metaphoric and symbolic truth was most favorably generated in a performative context where truth emerged in the interaction and dialogue of the participants. Metaphoric truth played a key role in freeing theology from the grasp of wooden ideology.

The second chapter focuses on the dynamics of the speech-acts of the king

---

and A. T. Reyes, "Mesopotamian Contact and Influence in the Greek World," pp. 85-106, in *The Legacy of Mesopotamia*, ed. S. Dalley (Oxford: Oxford University Press, 1998); Norman Gottwald, *The Politics of Ancient Israel* (Louisville: Westminster/John Knox, 2001), pp. 206-7.

in the context of his social, political, and historical circumstances. The authoritative speech-acts of Odysseus in chapter 2 of the *Iliad* are compared to those of David in 1 Samuel 25 and to those of Hammurapi in his clay-nail inscription from Sippar. Essential to the king's rhetorical effectiveness were the support and power provided by the royal household. The relationships within that household also served as a cooperative model for forging relationships with other kings and notables outside the kingdom. So, the speech of the king operated within but also shaped the sociopolitical context in which he ruled.

Chapter three addresses the ways in which the person and actions of the king served as a central symbol of the community's identity. The king was the chief redistributor of material and symbolic goods in the community that exerted a centripetal force on the practices of the community so that they were shaped within the field mapped out by royal authority. This field of royal authority consisted of a number of binary oppositions addressing the primary concerns of the community. The process of negotiating these oppositions created the space within which individuals pressed their limits, encountered the divine, and so found a measure of integration within the community stretching between heaven and earth. The centripetal force of the symbol of the just king provided a reference point for holding these binary oppositions in the force field of divinely bestowed royal authority. I examine the following binary oppositions in chapter three: the civilized versus the savage, nature versus culture, the aristocrat versus the commoner, life versus death, and the divine versus the human. Each of these binary oppositions can be imagined to have been the foci of an ellipse that created a field whose boundaries were the circumference of the ellipse. The resulting ellipses can be seen as intersecting with the divinely elected king at the center where the common identity of the members of the community was succinctly stated by the royal metaphor: the king "is" the people (see the illustration on p. 12).

Chapter four examines ways in which a king shaped his authority by remembering the tradition. Narrating from memory was a practice that rescued shared values and experiences in a community from oblivion and incorporated them into the ways that the future was imagined. Remembering the name of God or the gods and the name of heroes and ancestors was a way of honoring them and keeping them alive in the community. In other words, remembering was a vehicle for acknowledging their higher status and immortality. The king grounded his authority in the command of the king of the gods; therefore, his remembering God or the gods and heroes was essential to the persuasiveness of how he legitimated his authority according to the traditional pattern. Such remembering of the hierarchy of gods and humans created a visionary context within which to understand innovations within the continuity of the tradition.

The King as the Centralizing Symbol of the Community

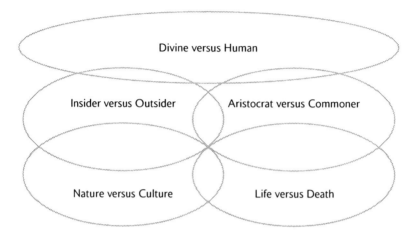

Chapter five explores how a king received and discerned divine communications to guide him through crises and to discern future courses of action. The authoritative king did not simply receive his divine election at the beginning of his reign and then report back to the king of the gods at the end of his reign. Rather, he called upon prophets, diviners, and sages to assist him in gaining direction from God or the gods. The ambiguity of such divine communications and the politics of their reception and interpretation provided ample grounds for skepticism and questioning. The king was expected to make sacrifices for the well-being of the community; heroes likewise were supposed to give of themselves in return for the honor by which they would be remembered in the tradition. Yet the case was also made in certain communities that it was better for the king to survive against formidable odds by his cleverness and practical wisdom than to give himself courageously over to death in a memorable burst of glory. What was the combination of oracular knowledge and clever discernment that was necessary for the king to lead the community into the future with authority?

Chapter six examines how crises within a community cast doubt on the justice of a king's rule and the reality of his divine election. In extreme crises where an individual or a community saw no practical solution at hand to resolve their difficulties, they cried out to God or the gods in lament. Lamentations and supplications exemplify a genre that seeks a resolution of an unbearable tension through the act of crying out. In some situations, crying out could have resulted in efforts to reform a situation by moving beyond contradictions that were previously regarded as unresolvable tensions or antinomies. Discernment of the nature of a crisis spawned by the unjust rule of a king (e.g., the withdrawal of Achilles from the Achaean coalition led by Agamemnon or the secession of the Israelite northern tribes at the time of Rehoboam) could have led to the conviction that regicide in a particular case was legitimate. From the king's perspective, the revolutionaries were probably to be regarded as opportunists. The criteria for assessing the legitimacy of revolts against royal rule arose from the traditions and customary laws of the people insofar as they reflected an underlying ethical world order.

Chapter seven deals with the response of the communities of Homeric Greece, biblical Israel, and OB Mesopotamia to the need for an ideal king who would rule like a god. Visions of ideal kings in the form of the Phaeacian king Alcinous in the *Odyssey,* the messianic king in Isaiah 11, and the ruling kings honored in the OB royal inscriptions emphasized the potential of kingship to bring harmony to an earthly community. Such visions also created models for criticizing ruling kings. The king's position midway between heaven and earth presented the possibility that a king might have transgressed the boundary between gods and humans so that he had become a rival of the gods. The piety of the king was an important antidote to such hubris. To keep such piety alive, the king cultivated practices of prayer, attentiveness to traditions, and care for the sanctuaries of God or the gods. The ideal just king maintained order in the community according to the divine will and so brought the community into harmony with the ethical world order.

The Texts of the Study

Homer's *Iliad* and *Odyssey* are traditional oral compositions that were put in written form anywhere from the middle of the eighth century to the end of the sixth century B.C. The later tradition attributed these epics to a single composer or bard, yet the nature of the material indicated that parts of it stemmed from oral performances stretching back over a number of generations.[14] Almost no one questions whether the *Iliad* and the *Odyssey* were originally oral compositions, but the point at which writing began to influence their shape is a highly contested issue. Gregory Nagy argues that the *Iliad* and the *Odyssey* reached

---

14. Gregory Nagy, *Homeric Questions* (Austin: University of Texas Press, 1996), p. 92; idem, *Poetry as Performance* (Cambridge: Cambridge University Press, 1996), p. 61; John Miles Foley, "Individual Poet and Epic Tradition: Homer as Legendary Singer," *Arethusa* 31 (1998): 149-50. Cf. Ian Morris, "The Uses and Abuses of Homer," *Classical Antiquity* 5 (1986): 83-85.

their present shape through generations of oral performances from the late eighth century to the middle of the sixth century B.C.[15] The bards traveled to the various cities and performed for Greek audiences who were gradually coming to an awareness of their shared identity with other peoples who spoke Greek and lived in the cities of the Peloponnese, Attica, Thebes, Ionia, and so forth. Oral performers typically took themes and developed them creatively in response to their audience. The need to maintain the integrity of the story in performances before audiences in various Greek cities contributed to the fixation of the story: a form of oral textualization.[16] As the *Iliad* and the *Odyssey* were repeatedly performed throughout Greece, the need to maintain the story line probably reduced the freedom of individual bards to improvise and draw fully on the traditions of the local audience. So, according to Nagy's model for the oral composition of the Homeric epics, the poems were entirely composed by the bards in performance contexts. The scribes became preservers of a fully developed text when they began to write down the epics in the late sixth century.[17] In contrast, a number of other scholars (Henry Wade-Gery, Richard Janko, Ian Morris, David Tandy, Peter Rose) would see the introduction of writing in the structuring and communication of the epics in the latter half of the eighth century B.C.[18]

15. Gregory Nagy, "An Evolutionary Model for the Making of Homeric Poetry: Comparative Perspectives," in *To the Ages of Homer*, ed. Jane Carter et al. (Austin: University of Texas Press, 1995), p. 174; Nagy, *Homeric Questions*, p. 42.

16. Nagy, "An Evolutionary Model for the Making of Homeric Poetry," p. 165; Nagy, *Homeric Questions*, pp. 39, 109. However, Richard Janko ("The Homeric Poems as Oral Dictated Texts," *Classical Quarterly* 48 [1998]: 12, n. 63) argues for the opposite effect of performing the epics for audiences in various Greek cities: such wider diffusion of the performance of the epics would have introduced more differences.

17. Nagy, *Homeric Questions*, p. 42; see also Richard Seaford, *Reciprocity and Ritual: Homer and Tragedy in the Developing City-State* (Oxford: Clarendon, 1994), pp. 153, 189; Egbert Bakker, *Poetry in Speech: Orality and Homeric Discourse* (Ithaca: Cornell University Press, 1997), pp. 26-27. Mogens Herman Hansen ("Introduction: *Polis* as a Citizen-State," in *The Ancient Greek City-State*, ed. M. T. Hansen [Copenhagen: Munksgaard, 1993], p. 11) claims that the absence of archaeological remains of anything approximating a Homeric *polis* may call for dating the final form of the epics to the seventh century B.C., a date long argued for by Martin West ("The Date of the Iliad," *Museum Helveticum* 52 [1995]: 203) and also held by Kurt Raaflaub ("A Historian's Headache: How To Read 'Homeric Society'?" in *Archaic Greece: New Approaches and New Evidence*, ed. N. Fisher and H. Van Wees [London: Duckworth, 1998], pp. 187-88).

18. Henry Wade-Gery, *The Poet of the Iliad* (Cambridge: Cambridge University Press, 1952), p. 39; Morris, "The Uses and Abuses of Homer," p. 93; David Tandy, *Warriors into Traders: The Power of the Market in Early Greece* (Berkeley: University of California Press, 1997), p. 11; Peter W. Rose, "Ideology in the *Iliad*: Polis, Basileus, Theoi," *Arethusa* 30 (1997): 171. Joseph Russo ("Oral Theory: Its Development in Homeric Studies and Applicability to Other Literatures," in

In their final form, the *Iliad* and the *Odyssey* sing the exploits of Greek heroes who fought in the Trojan War and then sought to return home. The main themes of the *Iliad* are the wrath of the dishonored Achilles and the restoration of his honor through divine intervention and human struggles in the Trojan War. The warrior-king Agamemnon confiscated a previously awarded war trophy, the woman prisoner of war Briseis, from Achilles and signaled thereby as an authority figure that he did not value Achilles' heroic exploits. Zeus's intervention was necessary to restore Achilles' honor, but this came about only through ten years of warfare at Troy. The main theme of the *Odyssey* is the return of Odysseus to his royal household and kingdom in Ithaca. The adventures and trials of his lengthy return voyage are paralleled by the disarray and conflicts in Ithaca due to his twenty-year absence.

Historically, the Trojan War appears to have taken place sometime between 1250 and 1140 b.c.[19] If the stories were to preserve the memories of these Mycenaean historical figures, then such accounts would have been passed on orally for almost four to five centuries. However, anthropologists and scholars of oral traditions claim that three generations is the outer limit for an oral memory to retain its original shape before alterations and adaptations in the telling of the story have rendered it in a new form from which the original cannot be recovered and whose content cannot be verified.[20] The possibility that some traces of Mycenaean heroes were preserved is possible, but the last remnants of the Mycenaean way of life in central Greece had vanished by 1000 b.c.[21] What was remembered about a Mycenaean hero such as Agamemnon was a mental model of "what he must have been like" that was shaped by the communal telling and retelling of stories about Agamemnon.[22] The retelling of

---

Mesopotamian Epic Literature: Oral or Aural? ed. Marianna E. Vogelzang and Herman L. J. Vanstiphout [Lewiston, N.Y.: Edwin Mellen, 1992], p. 18) argues that Homer has a style that mixed oral and written modes of communication; cf. Foley, "Individual Poet and Epic Tradition," pp. 149-50. Janko ("The Homeric Poems as Oral Dictated Texts," pp. 11-13) sees the texts of the *Iliad* and the *Odyssey* as we have them as transcripts of dictations of the epics as performed in royal courts in the eighth century b.c.

19. Walter Burkert, "Lydia Between East and West or How to Date the Trojan War: A Study in Herodotus," in *The Ages of Homer*, ed. Jane Carter et al. (Austin: University of Texas, 1995), p. 140.

20. Raaflaub, "A Historian's Headache," pp. 175, 184; Jan Vansina, *Oral Tradition as History* (Madison: University of Wisconsin Press, 1985), pp. 193, 196; Tandy, *Warriors into Traders*, p. 13; John Miles Foley, *Homer's Traditional Art* (University Park: Pennsylvania State University Press, 1999), pp. xii-xiii.

21. Ian Morris, *Archaeology as Cultural History* (Oxford: Blackwell, 2000), p. 198.

22. Cf. Maurice E. F. Bloch, *How We Think They Think: Anthropological Approaches to Cognition, Memory, and Literacy* (Boulder, Colo.: Westview, 1998), p. 123.

these epics as found in our written versions reflects the values, outlooks, and social and political institutions of the late Dark Age (1075-700 B.C.)[23] and Archaic Age (700-480 B.C.), but primarily those of the late eighth century B.C.[24] The collective memories recorded in the epics engaged audiences in the Archaic Age to shape their own mental models of what the Mycenaean heroes were like and what happened at the Trojan War. Such collective imagining of what it must have been like was an activity fundamental to the emergence of a Panhellenic consciousness in the Archaic Age.[25]

The dialogues of the epics repeatedly raise questions about the king's use of power and authority, the means for sustaining collective action, the role of the public assembly, and so forth.[26] The political genius of the epics as products of a performative setting is their capacity to raise perennial political issues and spark reflection on them among aristocrats and commoners alike without ever pretending to bring closure to the political questioning and reflection with a doctrinal or logically reasoned answer.[27] Important truths for the right ordering of the community emerged through the engagement of the audience with these political questions. The narratives of the two epics addressed many insoluble issues that linked them together with similar issues in other myths and narratives of the tradition.[28] The performance of the *Iliad* and the *Odyssey* in the Panhellenic festivals and other festivals of the Archaic Age made these epics an important means for shaping a worldview with its competing and shared

23. Moses Finley, *The World of Odysseus,* rev. ed. (New York: Viking, 1978), p. 48. The dates for the Dark Age and Archaic Age are those given by Morris, *Archaeology as Cultural History,* p. 7.

24. Morris, *Archaeology as Cultural History,* p. 173; Raaflaub, "A Historian's Headache," p. 181; Hansen, "Introduction," p. 11; cf. James Whitley, *Style and Society in Dark Age Greece: The Changing Face of a Pre-literate Society 1100-700 BC* (Cambridge: Cambridge University Press, 1991), pp. 35-37.

25. Gregory Nagy, *Greek Mythology and Poetics* (Ithaca: Cornell University Press, 1990), pp. 37-38; Seaford, *Reciprocity and Ritual,* pp. 182-83; Karl-Joachim Hölkescamp, *Schiedsrichter, Gesetzgeber und Gesetzgebung im archaischen Griechenland,* Historia 131 (Stuttgart: Franz Steiner, 1999), p. 283; Morris, *Archaeology as Cultural History,* pp. 190-91; Bloch, *How We Think They Think,* p. 123.

26. Rose, "Ideology in the *Iliad,*" p. 184; Dean Hammer, "'Who Shall Readily Obey?': Authority and Politics in the *Iliad,*" *Phoenix* 51 (1997): 2.

27. Oswyn Murray, "Cities of Reason," in *The Greek City from Homer to Alexander,* ed. Oswyn Murray and Simon Price (Oxford: Clarendon, 1990), pp. 19-20; Claude Calame, "The Rhetoric of *Muthos* and *Logos,*" in *From Myth to Reason?* ed. Richard Buxton (Oxford: Oxford University Press, 1999), pp. 137-41; Dean Hammer, "The Politics of the *Iliad,*" *Classical Journal* 94 (1998): 9-11; Rose, "Ideology in the *Iliad,*" p. 185.

28. Richard Buxton, *Imaginary Greece* (Cambridge: Cambridge University Press, 1994), p. 213.

values of the Greeks of that time.[29] Poets and philosophers of subsequent generations had to contend with the authority of the Homeric epics when they sought to propound their own views on aspects of the Greek *Weltanschauung*.[30]

The texts from the Israelite tradition quoted in this study include passages from the Historical Books, the Psalms, the Prophets, and the Pentateuch. These texts were selected because they addressed a particular theme or aspect of royal authority that could be compared with the same theme or aspect in texts selected from the Homeric and OB Mesopotamian traditions. The selected Israelite texts consist of various genres including historical reports, hymns, laments, oracles, and teachings. The recitation and reading of these various texts contributed in distinctive ways to shaping the Israelite tradition and worldview. The oral and written dimensions of these compositions aimed to engage an audience so as to create the rhetorical space within which the divine will might be made manifest.

The narratives from the Historical Books are traditional compositions of anonymous authorship. The final editor of the books of First and Second Samuel and First and Second Kings had written and oral sources available in his writing of the history of the monarchy in Israel and Judah from its introduction to its collapse.[31] These narratives include both pro- and antimonarchic voices that reflect a double-mindedness of the Israelites toward earthly kingship among them. These narratives present a more strongly royalist position in some chapters (e.g., 1 Sam. 9:1–10:12) and a more prophetic position in others (e.g., 1 Samuel 8).[32] The juxtaposition of these affirming and critical ap-

---

29. Nagy, *Greek Mythology and Poetics*, pp. 37-38; Jean-Pierre Vernant, *Mortals and Immortals* (Princeton: Princeton University Press, 1990), pp. 278-79; Bruno Gentili, *Poetry and Its Public in Ancient Greece: From Homer to the Fifth Century* (Baltimore: Johns Hopkins University Press, 1988), pp. 4-8; Seaford, *Reciprocity and Ritual*, pp. 152-53, 183-84; Rose, *Sons of the Gods, Children of Earth*, pp. 139-40; Morris, *Archaeology as Cultural History*, p. 32.

30. Calame, "The Rhetoric of *Muthos* and *Logos*," pp. 128, 135; Walter Nicolai, "Gefolgschaftsverweigerung als politisches Druckmittel in der Ilias," in *Anfänge politischen Denkens in der Antike: Die nahöstlichen Kulturen und die Griechen*, ed. Kurt Raaflaub and Elisabeth Müller-Luckner (Munich: R. Oldenbourg, 1993), p. 328; Margalit Finkelberg, *The Birth of Literary Fiction in Ancient Greece* (Oxford: Clarendon, 1998), pp. 6-11; Richard Klonoski, "The Preservation of Homeric Tradition: Heroic Re-Performance in the 'Republic' and the 'Odyssey'," *Clio* 22 (1993): 253, 256.

31. For an overview of theories and studies on the Deuteronomistic history, see: Gary Knoppers, "Introduction," in *Reconsidering Israel and Judah: Recent Studies on the Deuteronomistic History*, ed. G. Knoppers and J. G. McConville (Winona Lake, Ind.: Eisenbrauns, 2000), pp. 1-18; Erik Eynikel, *The Reform of King Josiah and the Composition of the Deuteronomistic History*, OTS 33 (Leiden: Brill, 1996), pp. 7-31.

32. Baruch Halpern, "The Uneasy Compromise: Israel Between League and Monarchy," in *Traditions in Transformation*, ed. B. Halpern and J. Levenson (Winona Lake, Ind.: Eisenbrauns,

proaches to kingship contributes in no small measure to the air of "objectivity" surrounding these narratives.[33] The narratives promote the view that the truth about the kingship could not be determined in the abstract but had to be worked out in the particular political dynamics of the community through succeeding generations. Promonarchical narratives (e.g., 1 Samuel 25) often left ample room for criticizing a king, even if such criticism in monarchical times could often have emerged safely only within the privacy of one's reflections. The dialogue and debate engendered by these narratives perpetuated an important dynamic within Israel's historical memory: one that not only demystified the monarchical institution but also entertained the possibility of a more ideal king in the near or distant future.

The Psalms are lyric compositions that address typical human experiences.[34] The particular historical circumstances of a psalm and the date of its composition are usually difficult to recover since most often there are few historical allusions embedded in a psalm's poetry. The Psalms quoted in this study are primarily royal psalms (e.g., Psalms 18, 20, 72, 89, 101, 132), so-called because their content addresses royal issues and not because they are similar in form or genre.[35] For example, Psalm 18 is a hymn of thanksgiving, whereas Psalm 89 is a lament that contains a hymn (vv. 6-16) and an oracle (vv. 20-38) within it. Hymns support the status quo; laments express strong criticism of it; thanksgiving psalms proclaim reconciliation with a changed status quo.[36] The psalmist's expressions to God of praise, disappointment or anger, and thanksgiving are analogous to statements and requests made to an earthly king. The personal issues addressed by these psalms demonstrate how individual ex-

---

1981), pp. 79-80; Marc Brettler, "Biblical Literature as Politics: The Case of Samuel," in *Religion and Politics in the Ancient Near East,* ed. A. Berlin (Bethesda: University Press of Maryland, 1996), pp. 88-92.

33. Albrecht Alt, "The Formation of the Israelite State in Palestine," in *Essays on Old Testament History and Religion* (Garden City, N.Y.: Doubleday, 1968), pp. 244-45. John Van Seters (*In Search of History: Historiography in the Ancient World and the Origins of Biblical History* [New Haven: Yale University Press, 1983], p. 355) contends that only when the nation itself took precedence over the king in its self-understanding could history-writing — an activity in which one critically analyzes sources — take place; he understands the Deuteronomistic history to be a single composition in the Exilic period influenced by ways of thinking shared by the later Greek historian Herodotus.

34. Claus Westermann, *Praise and Lament in the Psalms* (Atlanta: John Knox, 1981), pp. 24, 25-35.

35. Scott Starbuck, *Court Oracles in the Psalms: The So-Called Royal Psalms in Their Ancient Near Eastern Context,* SBLDS 172 (Atlanta: Scholars, 1999), pp. 22, 36, 46.

36. Walter Brueggemann, *The Message of the Psalms* (Minneapolis: Augsburg, 1984), pp. 19-23.

periences occur within and have an impact on the structure and dynamics of royal authority within the community: an authority that spans both heaven and earth and promotes the integration of the individual within the community and the order of creation.

The texts quoted from the prophetic corpus in this study complement the prophetic viewpoint expressed in many of the historical narratives. The judgment oracles of Ezekiel 28, the messianic oracle of Isaiah 11, and Hezekiah's psalm of thanksgiving in Isaiah 38 are passages that highlighted the potential of the kingship for good and for ill: the character and the practices of a particular king would determine which it would be. A particular king like Hezekiah had a transformative effect on the Israelite community and its future, but yet he was also found wanting in prophetic circles (Isa. 39:1-8; cf. 11:1-9).[37] According to the Book of Isaiah, it was Hezekiah's practice of intercessory prayer that spared Jerusalem from the Assyrians (Isa. 37:14-21). Yet Isaiah 11:1-9 says that it would take an even more ideal king than Hezekiah to deliver Jerusalem and rule it according to the divine will; such a godlike king would be suffused with the Lord's spirit.[38] An oracular utterance demanded an immediate hearing and acceptance, followed by interpretation and adaptation; the structure of a prophetic book through its collection and arrangement of oracles testified to this interpretive dynamic operative in the prophetic tradition.[39] The interplay between docility and criticism was essential to the discernment of the ways in which divine power worked through or against the earthly king.

The two texts quoted from the Pentateuch (Exod. 3:1-5; Deut. 17:14-17) are narratives that highlight particular aspects of the royal rule of the Lord or of the earthly king. The genre and tradition history of each of these passages pointed to the ways in which the royal characteristics and practices addressed (divine incomparability in Exod. 3:1-5; royal attentiveness to tradition and law in Deut. 17:14-17) were honored and critiqued in the tradition. The collective memory communicated by these texts attested to truths that needed to be searched out and rethought repeatedly if such truths were to remain alive in the community.[40]

---

37. Peter Ackroyd, "Isaiah I–XII: Presentation of a Prophet," in *Congress Volume: Göttingen 1977*, VTSup 29 (Leiden: Brill, 1978), pp. 43-46.

38. Hans Wildberger, *Isaiah 1–12* (Minneapolis: Fortress, 1991), p. 469.

39. Ackroyd, "Isaiah I–XII," pp. 44-48; Hans Barstad, "No Prophets? Recent Developments in Biblical Prophetic Research and Ancient Near Eastern Prophecy," *JSOT* 57 (1993): 56-60; cf. Karel van der Toorn, "Mesopotamian Prophecy between Immanence and Transcendence: A Comparison of Old Babylonian and Neo-Assyrian Prophecy," in *Prophecy in Its Ancient Near Eastern Context: Mesopotamian, Biblical, and Arabian Perspectives*, SBL Symposium Series 13 (Atlanta: Society for Biblical Literature, 2000), pp. 74-77.

40. Frank Moore Cross, *From Epic to Canon: History and Literature in Ancient Israel* (Balti-

The Akkadian royal inscriptions of the Old Babylonian period (2003-1595 B.C.) form the primary corpus of Mesopotamian texts for this study. In terms of recovered cuneiform texts, the OB period is one of three best-attested time frames in Mesopotamian history, along with the Ur III period (2103-2004 B.C.) and the late Neo-Assyrian and Neo-Babylonian periods (ca. seventh-sixth centuries B.C.).[41] Because kingship in Mesopotamian cities in the OB period did not achieve the status of imperial rule with control over distant provincial holdings, such as Assyria and Babylonia did in the first millennium B.C., the structure and dynamics of OB kingship with rule over the smaller territories of a city or of a particular people manifest clearer analogies with the kingships of Homeric Greece and biblical Israel. Since an important objective of the typological approach of this comparative study is to identify isomorphisms in the structure and dynamics of royal authority in the traditions of Homeric Greece, biblical Israel, and Mesopotamia rather than diffusion of concepts and practices, the local or regional character of royal rule in the OB period is a more appropriate representative of the Mesopotamian tradition than are the Neo-Assyrian (744-612 B.C.) and Neo-Babylonian (612-539 B.C.) periods. Another reason for using texts from the OB period is that the scribes who composed the OB royal inscriptions were probably influenced more by oral tradition and the ways in which the king communicated with the people than were the scribes of the first millennium who had increasingly separated themselves from society as they focused more upon the interpretation of written texts.[42]

The OB royal inscriptions were first-person royal proclamations written on stone monuments, clay tablets, or other clay objects such as cones or nails.[43] The stone monuments were visible to the public and aimed to make an impression by their iconography and the mystery associated with cuneiform writing, which only the scribes or a small minority in the land could read.[44] The capacity of a text

more: Johns Hopkins, 1998), pp. 28-29, 38-40; Ernest Nicholson, *Pentateuch in the Twentieth Century: The Legacy of Julius Wellhausen* (Oxford: Clarendon, 1998), p. 268. On the multivoiced character of the text of Genesis, see David Carr, *Reading the Fractures of Genesis* (Louisville: Westminster/John Knox, 1996), p. 293.

41. Marc Van de Mieroop, *Cuneiform Texts and the Writing of History* (New York: Routledge, 1999), p. 106.

42. Cf. Piotr Michalowski, "Presence at Creation," in *Lingering over Words: Studies in Ancient Near Eastern Literature in Honor of William L. Moran,* ed. T. Abusch et al., HSM 37 (Atlanta: Scholars, 1990), p. 395.

43. A. Kirk Grayson, "Assyria and Babylonia," *Or* 49 (1980): 144-45.

44. Sabina Franke, *Königsinschriften und Königsideologie: Die Könige von Akkade zwischen Tradition und Neuerung* (Münster: LIT, 1995), p. 238; Joan Goodnick Westenholz, "Thoughts on Esoteric Knowledge and Secret Lore," in *Intellectual Life of the Ancient Near East,* ed. Jiří Prosecký, CRRA 43 (Prague: Oriental Institute, 1998), p. 456; Irene Winter, "Royal Rhetoric and

and that of an image to get a point across or to make an impression overlap greatly: for example, a warning can often be given with a gesture or visual sign just as effectively as with an utterance.[45] Still, the message proclaimed by the king in writing was no doubt conveyed orally to the people as a whole or to their elders.[46] In OB times, kings such as Hammurapi and his son Samsuiluna composed (or directed scribes to compose) building inscriptions in which they celebrated the successful completion of a divinely willed construction project. Such projects included the construction or reconstruction of temples, walls, canals, or irrigation and flood-control works. Building inscriptions were typically buried in the foundations of the structure to testify to future generations and to the gods that a particular king had built the structure in response to a divine command.[47]

A. K. Grayson has labeled these inscriptions as "commemorative inscriptions" and has identified three categories: (1) The narrative of the inscription identified the king, including titles and epithets, and then described his accomplishments as a builder. (2) The narrative first identified the deity to whom a structure or building project was dedicated. The divine titles and epithets included here communicated the status and particular characteristics of the god. Then the king was identified through titles — indicating the extent of his territorial rule — and through epithets — celebrating his unique characteristics and often linking him to the gods honored in the inscription. Finally, the accomplishment itself was described. (3) The third category of commemorative inscriptions was distinctive to the OB period. The inscription began with a temporal clause, then a report of the king's commission to carry out a project, and finally the statement of its accomplishment.[48] Only a few of the inscriptions concluded with blessings and curses designed to preserve the structures and their inscriptions to perpetuity through sacral sanctions. Many inscriptions also included reports of battles (e.g., inscriptions of Samsuiluna) or foreign campaigns (e.g., inscriptions of Yaḫdun-Lim). These stylized narratives, designed to exalt the name of the king, contain important historical data.

---

the Development of Historical Narrative in Neo-Assyrian Reliefs," *Studies in Visual Communication* 7 (1981): 12-13; Jacob Klein, "On Writing Monumental Inscriptions in the Ur III Scribal Curriculum," *RA* 80 (1986): 1, 6-7.

45. W. J. T. Mitchell, "Ekphrasis and the Other," in *Picture Theory: Essays on Verbal and Visual Representation* (Chicago: University of Chicago Press, 1994), p. 160.

46. Winter, "Royal Rhetoric," pp. 12-13; cf. Jack M. Sasson, "King Hammurabi of Babylon," in *Civilizations of the Ancient Near East*, ed. J. Sasson (New York: Scribner, 1995), pp. 907-8.

47. William W. Hallo, "The Royal Inscriptions of Ur: A Typology," *HUCA* 33 (1962): 10; cf. Richard S. Ellis, *Foundation Deposits in Ancient Mesopotamia* (New Haven: Yale University Press, 1968), pp. 69-71, 159.

48. Grayson, "Assyria and Babylonia," pp. 160-61.

The OB Akkadian royal inscriptions were influenced by the style and conventions of votive inscriptions and battle reports of earlier Sumerian and Old Akkadian rulers.[49] The structure of the third category of commemorative inscriptions, which is distinctive to the OB royal inscriptions, exhibits what I have referred to as the pattern of the traditional account for legitimating royal authority: the king was commissioned by the gods to carry out a particular task that benefited the people and the community. This form of the royal inscription was a frequent means by which the royal court proclaimed the legitimacy of the king's rule, for it emphasized how he maintained his place within the cosmic chain of command.

An important subset of the royal inscription was the *narû* inscription. This type of royal composition was inscribed on a stele with the intention of instructing subsequent rulers on particular lessons that the king learned in order to help them avoid similar errors.[50] The *Cuthean Legend* of Naram-Sin is a composition from the OB period that exemplifies this genre. The most famous *narû* inscription is the *Code of Hammurapi* (*CH* XLVII:75; XLVIII:9, 15, 66, 79, 84; XLIX:4, 20). This collection of exemplary royal verdicts is introduced by a prologue celebrating Hammurapi's care for the sanctuaries of Mesopotamia and concludes with an epilogue proclaiming the justice of Hammurapi's rule and sealing this royal inscription against alteration with blessings and curses.[51]

The uniformly royalist perspective of the royal inscriptions only occasionally allows one to hear the voices of other constituencies in the kingdom. The voices of prophets, priests, poets, and people at large can better be heard, although still indirectly, through the Akkadian literary works of the *Epic of Gilgamesh*, the story of *Atraḫasis*, and the *Enuma Elish*.[52] These narratives allow criticism of royal rule to be expressed obliquely. Another important source on the daily activities of a Babylonian kingdom, which will be quoted as needed, is

49. Johannes Renger, "Königsinschriften B. Akkadisch," *RLA* 6:68; Franke, *Königsinschriften und Königsideologie,* pp. 19, 238.

50. J. G. Westenholz, *Legends of the Kings of Akkade* (Winona Lake, Ind.: Eisenbrauns, 1997), pp. 264-66, 296; Tremper Longman III, *Fictional Akkadian Autobiography: A Generic and Comparative Study* (Winona Lake, Ind.: Eisenbrauns, 1991), pp. 147-48, 228; Gerdien Jonker, *The Topography of Remembrance: The Dead, Tradition, and Collective Memory in Mesopotamia,* Studies in the History of Religions 68 (Leiden: Brill, 1995), pp. 91, 95.

51. Victor Hurowitz, *Inu Anum Ṣīrum: Literary Structures in the Non-Juridical Sections of Codex Hammurabi,* Occasional Publications of the Samuel Noah Kramer Fund 15 (Philadelphia: University of Pennsylvania Museum, 1994), pp. 13, 51-52; cf. Tikva Zadok, "The Distribution of the Temporal Sentences in the Old Babylonian Royal Inscriptions," *JANES* 24 (1996): 113-14.

52. Even though the composition of the *Enuma Elish* is dated to the late second millennium B.C., it drew on the traditions of the earlier parts of the second millennium and stemmed from a Babylonian milieu whose kings were not imperial rulers.

the royal correspondence. Even though most of the extant letters were written to or for a king, this less formal genre provides a wealth of information about the lives of a wide range of people in OB society. One Sumerian composition, *The Lament for Ur*, is drawn upon to exemplify how OB kings expressed their piety and their solidarity with a community recovering from great suffering.

With these texts from Homeric, biblical Israel, and OB Mesopotamia, the stage is set for our examination of how royal authority functioned in these ancient communities and traditions.

CHAPTER ONE

Poetic Truth and the Manifestation of the Divine Source of Royal Authority

W ithin the political theologies of Homeric Greece, biblical Israel, and OB Mesopotamia, it is axiomatic that God or the gods rule over heaven and earth. Sovereign authority is wielded by the king of the gods: Zeus in Homer, the Lord in Israel, and Enlil in OB Mesopotamia. The traditional pattern for legitimating royal authority is anchored in the authoritative decree of the king of the gods who commissions an earthly king to share in his sovereign rule. The outline of this traditional pattern is simple and straightforward: the king of the gods commissions the earthly king to rule over a people who belong to the king of the gods; the earthly king accepts and thereby takes responsibility for the well-being of the people. This pattern can be developed into a narrative or woven into another narrative as an element of its plot. This traditional pattern, which functions within the rules and practices of the literary, theological, and political discourse of these three cultures, played a central role in increasing the vitality and well-being of a community. It supplied a map for how the voice of royal authority in the community was to stay in touch with the authorities in heaven and on earth. How this pattern operates is fundamental to understanding the legitimacy of royal rule.

The Revelatory Power of Metaphors, Symbols, and Narratives in Theological Discourse

Language is integral to human life. By its capacity to name and order human experience, language enables human agents to learn about and adapt to their environments. This awareness of language as an important tool or instrument shows how we are able to participate in and use language, a reality that was a constitutive part of our person and environment before we willed anything. So, language is first of all a gift that we humans receive, and without which conscious life would hardly be possible. This language, whether it be English, Greek, or Hebrew, is given to us in a form that has been shaped by a culture and that in turn shapes our consciousness. We do not start from ground zero. We are possessed by the language we receive and then participate in it and unfold its potential throughout our lives. We are called to be attentive, or obedient, to this linguistic reality in which we share.

Language is indispensable for the communion that individuals experience with other humans and their environment, yet such a communion is only partial and is usually subject to change.[1] Even our most literal statements about an inanimate object only approximate the reality of that object. Such a partial, shifting knowledge about life and the world has led humans to try to find a way out of this impasse of instability and incompleteness. Yet there is no way out, no once-and-for-all exit from this alienation. Despite the pervasiveness of language — its constitutive role in human consciousness, social relations, and cultural production — it is unable to bring an individual into harmony with all that exists. Nevertheless, we can live more honestly within such a linguistically relative world by responding to the revelatory potential such language offers.[2]

A metaphor brings together two distinct persons, objects, or categories of reality and suggests that they are the same.[3] The statement "Hammurapi is a wild bull" is metaphorical. On a literal level, Hammurapi does not have four legs and two horns and weigh over a thousand pounds; however, on a figurative level, he appears to have such a high level of strength and physical power. The truth of the metaphor arises through the tension and the interplay between the literal and figurative meanings of the terms.[4]

Metaphors are indispensable for describing the gods and their actions. In Mesopotamia, a royal inscription identifies the sun god Shamash as "the war-

---

1. John Gumpertz and Stephen Levinson ("Introduction: Linguistic Relativity Re-examined," in *Rethinking Linguistic Relativity,* ed. J. Gumpertz and S. Levinson [Cambridge: Cambridge University Press, 1996], pp. 1-18) note that language is largely unconscious, but that the grammar of a particular language structures and categorizes reality in a way not shared by observers who speak another language.

2. Gumpertz and Levinson, "Introduction," p. 8; Richard Kearney, *Modern Movements in European Philosophy,* 2nd ed. (Manchester: Manchester University Press, 1994), pp. 124-25; Jonathan Culler, *The Pursuit of Signs* (Ithaca: Cornell University Press, 1981), p. 41.

3. Paul Ricoeur, *The Rule of Metaphor: Multidisciplinary Studies of the Creation of Meaning in Language* (Toronto: University of Toronto Press, 1977), p. 235.

4. Ricoeur, *The Rule of Metaphor,* pp. 212-15.

rior, the hero."[5] Here the sun god Shamash both *is* and *is not* a warrior. As an invisible being, the sun god does not take up his armor and go to battle, but he may defend a king against aggressive foes where it seems "as if" Shamash has gone into battle. In the Hebrew Psalter, metaphors abound in the description of the Lord — for example, "smoke ascended from his nostrils, and consuming fire from his mouth" (Ps. 18:9[8]). Homer occasionally describes the excellence of a heroic action by saying that a protector deity has intervened: for example, Diomedes strikes down Pandaros with the throw of a spear and claims that Athena guided the spear (*Il* 5.290-93). The anthropomorphic description of the gods in all three traditions is metaphoric.

The gods are invisible. If they are conceived as real actors in a narrative, they must be named and described as humanlike beings, existents who have character traits and ways of acting that are understandable to their human audiences. The literary critic Northrup Frye claims that "gods are ready-made metaphors, a metaphor being a statement of identity of the type 'A is B,' where personality and natural object are said to be the same thing, although they remain two different things."[6] Yet to say that a god *is* a metaphor is itself a metaphorical statement that "is" and "is not" true.[7] If the structure and dynamics of a metaphor tell us important things about a god, they obviously do not provide us with a literal, sufficient definition.

If a metaphor resonates with us, it will engage us and stimulate interaction and communion with the world around us.[8] Metaphors bring us into relationship with important realities but do not supply us with the information that would allow us to control them. Manipulation and control are antithetical to the dynamics of a metaphor. The knowledge communicated through a metaphor is bestowed upon the receptive listener. Such knowledge is never absolute; it is a form of knowledge accessible to finite humans. If there is a mismatch in the formulation of a metaphor for an audience, its communicative power will be limited or nonexistent.

In the culturally mediated language bestowed upon us, we also received symbols. In the *Iliad*, Agamemnon holds a scepter whose heritage can be traced back three generations and ultimately to Zeus. It brings to mind the relationships among the Achaeans and their common identity and calls those in the community to acknowledge and respond to their common bonds. Yet for those who are outside the community or on the margin, the scepter may function

---

5. Douglas Frayne, *RIME 4*, E4.3.7.3, line 26.

6. Northrup Frye, *Words with Power* (San Diego: Harcourt Brace Jovanovich, 1990), p. 71.

7. Ricoeur, *The Rule of Metaphor*, pp. 247-48.

8. George Lakoff and Mark Johnson, *Philosophy in the Flesh: The Embodied Mind and Its Challenge to Western Thought* (New York: Basic Books, 1999), pp. 72-73.

simply to pass on information about the Achaean community without generating a sense of belonging. How the symbol speaks to the various individuals depends on how they feel a part of the fabric of the community.[9]

Religious or political symbols evoke a system of associations that calls people to join a group or community. The American flag, particularly in times of national crisis, reveals and strengthens the bonds among the citizens of the United States. Those hostile to or alienated from the United States as a nation or as a government sometimes express their dissent through the symbolic action of flag burning. Between the two poles of devotion to the nation and hostile dissent, citizens express varying degrees of patriotism. Essential to the evocative power of a symbol is its polyvalence: the signifier dances around the signified with multiple, complementary meanings. If the signifier is seen to communicate fully the reality of the signified, then the religious or political symbol is broken.[10] How this symbol resonates with a person's experience determines how vital this symbol is within the community.[11] The reception of a political or religious symbol can be seen as an action homologous to the reception of a metaphor: the truth of a symbol, like that of a metaphor, becomes manifest when individuals or groups respond and resonate with it. Unlike the abstract symbols of systems of formal logic, the interplay with human experience is essential to the integrity of religious or political symbols.[12]

The desire to remember the past and to imagine further into the future spurs on the development of symbols and the symbolic. The corporeality of the symbol gives it stability within our embodied world. The trace of the symbol can extend the boundaries of our experience and the way we reflect on it. For example, writing is a series of symbols that puts words in a visible medium. A written page also allows one to skip forward and backward and so to examine the text in its totality rather than to be forced to get the point of an oral presentation by listening to a sequence of phrases or sentences.[13] However, the reading of a fixed written text does not permit the immediacy of en-

9. Robert Cummings Neville, *The Truth of Broken Symbols* (Albany, N.Y.: SUNY Press, 1996), pp. 61-62; Louis-Marie Chauvet, *Symbol and Sacrament: A Sacramental Reinterpretation of Christian Existence* (Collegeville, Minn.: Liturgical, 1995), pp. 112, 115-16.

10. Neville, *The Truth of Broken Symbols*, p. 62; Paul Ricoeur, *Freud and Philosophy: An Essay on Interpretation* (New Haven: Yale University Press, 1970), pp. 11-12; Douglas McGaughey, "Ricoeur's Metaphor and Narrative Theories as a Foundation for a Theory of Symbol," *Religious Studies* 24 (1988): 424-25.

11. Ricoeur, *Freud and Philosophy*, p. 31.

12. Ricoeur, *Freud and Philosophy*, pp. 48-49.

13. Anthony Giddens, "Structuralism, Post-Structuralism and the Production of Culture," in *Social Theory Today*, ed. Anthony Giddens and Jonathan Turner (Cambridge: Polity, 1987), p. 218.

gagement afforded in an oral exchange between a speaker and a hearer.[14] Spoken metaphors would seem to be less likely to gloss over the experience of the audience, whereas symbols can be employed to cover over, reshape, or even do violence to the experience of those addressed. Symbols can become a source of alienation for members of a community if they sustain conventional structures and practices in a community with little connection to the primary concerns of the people.[15]

Metaphors and symbols can be significant components of narratives. A narrative configures a sequence of actions and events so that there are a beginning, middle, and an end.[16] The characters and the circumstances are related and explained through the plot. Symbols and metaphors used to describe characters and circumstances point beyond the surface of the narrative to ways in which the world of the narrative relates to a world beyond it. The plot of the narrative forms a coherent whole that can resonate with episodes in the lives of the people who listen to or read the narrative. The story of Adam and Eve has shaped the imaginations of countless generations of readers through its capacity to address fundamental existential questions (Gen. 2:4–3:24). Narrative truth has the same "as if" structure as metaphoric truth: if the story line resonates with one's experience, it is revelatory; if it does not, then it will be lifeless or meaningless. The "as if" character of narrative truth is helpful in providing insights on action, whereas the "as if" character of metaphoric truth casts light on the qualities of people and things and their relationships.[17]

---

14. Giddens, "Structuralism, Post-Structuralism and the Production of Culture," p. 219; Roy Rappaport, *Ritual and Religion in the Making of Humanity* (Cambridge: Cambridge University Press, 1999), p. 444; Luc Brisson, *Plato the Myth Maker* (Chicago: University of Chicago Press, 1998), pp. 136-37; Walter Ong, *Orality and Literacy: The Technologizing of the Word* (New York: Methuen, 1982), pp. 6-7, 79-81; cf. Bruce Lincoln, *Theorizing Myth: Narrative, Ideology, and Scholarship* (Chicago: University of Chicago Press, 1999), p. 26.

15. Ricoeur, *The Rule of Metaphor*, pp. 252-54; Pierre Bourdieu, "The Production and Reproduction of Legitimate Language," in *Language and Symbolic Power*, ed. John B. Thompson (Cambridge, Mass.: Harvard University Press, 1991), p. 51; Rappaport, *Ritual and Religion*, p. 55; Zdzislaw Mach, *Symbols, Conflict, and Identity: Essays in Political Anthropology* (Albany, N.Y.: SUNY Press, 1993), p. 108; Jonathan Hart, *Northrup Frye: The Theoretical Imagination* (New York: Routledge, 1994), p. 241.

16. Paul Ricoeur, *Time and Narrative*, vol. 1 (Chicago: University of Chicago Press, 1984), pp. 65-66; Brigitte Groneberg, "Toward a Definition of Literariness as Applied to Akkadian Literature," in *Mesopotamian Poetic Language: Sumerian and Akkadian*, ed. M. Vogelzang and H. Vanstiphout, Cuneiform Monographs 6 (Groningen: Styx, 1996), p. 71.

17. Ricoeur (*Time and Narrative*, p. xi) explains that the creative function of metaphor is paralleled by that of the plot of a narrative. He sees the sphere of metaphor to be primarily that of "sensory, emotional, aesthetic, and axiological values," whereas plots primarily create new meaning "in the field of action and its temporal values."

Narratives also can address the temporal dimension of human experience, aspects of which are the incomplete or fragmentary character of experience and the rate of change within one's experience and environment. The confusion that Cain must have experienced over God's acceptance of Abel's offering and not of his own brought him face-to-face with the challenge of rivalry and jealousy (Gen. 4:1-7). Some intractable problems for individuals and communities (i.e., antinomies), such as rivalry, can best be dealt with by projecting them into narrative form where fictional characters can bring about a resolution and the narrative can become a voice for rationality and justice.[18] How one imagines one's place in the world with the assistance of metaphors, symbols, and narratives is indispensable for coming to terms with the fragmentary, yet dynamic, processes of life.

Royal Rhetoric and the Engagement of the Popular Mind

The peoples of Homeric Greece, biblical Israel, and OB Mesopotamia drew heavily upon the resources of metaphor, symbol, and narrative to assist them in coming to terms with their histories and environments and so to help them make their worlds inhabitable. The realities of disease, war, famine, and death made inescapable the acknowledgment of the finitude of human existence. The primary way in which these ancient peoples talked about the limits of human life was to compare human life with divine life.[19] How they understood limitations on human freedom and possibilities was most often expressed through the interaction of humans with God or the gods. Stories in which God or the gods and humans interacted explored baffling issues of human existence that would beset generation after generation.[20] These stories arose in the oral tradition of these communities and complemented and supplemented one another. Contradictions among accounts were worked out in the process of retelling without discarding any of the accounts.[21] This decentralized, inter-

18. Fredric Jameson, *The Political Unconscious: Narrative as a Socially Symbolic Act* (Ithaca: Cornell University Press, 1981), pp. 80, 183.

19. Karl Reinhardt, "The Adventures in the *Odyssey*," in *Reading the Odyssey: Selected Interpretive Essays,* ed. Seth Schein (Princeton: Princeton University Press, 1996), p. 64.

20. Richard Buxton, *Imaginary Greece: The Contexts of Mythology* (Cambridge: Cambridge University Press, 1994), p. 213.

21. Marcel Hénaff, *Claude Levi-Strauss and the Making of Structural Anthropology* (Minneapolis: University of Minnesota Press, 1998), pp. 181-82, 217-18, 230; Carlo Brillante, "History and the Historical Interpretation of Myth," in *Approaches to Greek Myth,* ed. Lowell Edmunds (Baltimore: Johns Hopkins University Press, 1990), p. 96. Cf. Fredric Jameson, *The Seeds of Time* (New

locking world of tales played an important role in the traditions of Homeric Greece, biblical Israel, and OB Mesopotamia where allusions to characters and themes triggered connections among the myths and wove together a cultural world.[22]

We are heirs to the Greek tradition in which poets as early as Homer began to label these traditional narratives that address baffling problems of human existence as *mythos*, "myths." Walter Burkert argues that most of these traditional tales have an imperative at the beginning of the plot.[23] These narratives are concerned about action: about the possibility of taking or refraining from action. They address problems from a practical rather than a theoretical perspective.[24] An imperative statement that initiates action is an example of authority in action: a manifestation of authority in its purest and simplest form. Yet obedience to a command does not occur in a vacuum. What are the circumstances that lead a son to obey his father or a servant to obey his master? An array of social, economic, political, historical, and religious reasons converge to make a command bear weight or be authoritative.[25]

A narrative with an imperative at the beginning of its action will give an account from which one can deduce how social, political, historical, and religious factors affect the configuration of the narrative, and thus one can come to a better understanding of how authority functions and becomes manifest. Bruce Lincoln has argued that in texts prior to Heraclitus an oppositional discourse of the marginalized *(logos)* developed alongside the authoritative discourse of leaders *(mythos)* where the rational tactics of this marginalized discourse *(lo-*

York: Columbia University Press, 1994), pp. 4-5; Margalit Finkelberg, "*Timē* and *Aretē* in Homer," *Classical Quarterly* 48 (1998): 27; idem, *The Birth of Literary Fiction in Ancient Greece* (Oxford: Clarendon, 1998), pp. 136-37.

22. Gregory Nagy, *Homeric Questions* (Austin: University of Texas Press, 1996), pp. 130-31; Piotr Michalowski, "Sumerian Literature: An Overview," in *Civilizations of the Ancient Near East*, ed. Jack Sasson (New York: Scribner, 1995), pp. 2284-85; John Rogerson, *Myth in Old Testament Interpretation*, BZAW 114 (New York: Walter de Gruyter, 1974), pp. 124-27; Laura Slatkin, *The Power of Thetis: Allusion and Interpretation in the "Iliad"* (Berkeley: University of California Press, 1991), pp. xv-xvi, 5-6, 101-2, 118.

23. Walter Burkert, *Structure and History in Greek Mythology and Ritual* (Berkeley: University of California Press, 1979), p. 16.

24. Burkert (*Structure and History*, p. 22) defines myth as a traditional tale applied, and its relevance and seriousness stem largely from this application. Cf. Paul Ricoeur, "Practical Reason," in *From Text to Action*, trans. Kathleen Blamey, ed. John B. Thompson, Essays in Hermeneutics 2 (Evanston, Ill.: Northwestern University Press, 1991), p. 199.

25. Jürgen Habermas, "Comments on John Searle's 'Meaning, Communication, and Representation' (1988)," in *On the Pragmatics of Communication* (Cambridge, Mass.: MIT Press, 1998), p. 264.

gos) included deception, seduction, and lying.[26] *Logos* and *mythos* are two different forms of discourse that vie with one another and define one another within such opposition. Another way to characterize this opposition between *logos* and *mythos* in Archaic Greece is that *logos* was a form of discourse focused upon persuading an assembly, whereas *mythos* was discourse linked with the authority of a wisdom figure.[27]

Emerging Greek philosophical discourse defined its own sphere of authority as reasoned argument over against the imaginative tales of poets and bards: *logos* was pitted against *mythos,* which led in the fourth century B.C. to the unfortunate definition of *mythos* as a false or imaginary fabrication, which is the dominant meaning of the term "myth" to the present day.[28] Yet even those philosophers who attacked *mythos* as false needed to draw upon metaphor and narrative to explain aspects of human experience in their discourses or treatises.[29] The interplay between *mythos* and *logos* in the traditional tales of the oral tradition persisted in the oral and written dialogues of pre-Socratic and classical philosophers.[30] Furthermore, the inquiries of the demystifying mentality of the pre-Socratics were not without precedent in the questioning and searching that led generations of Greeks to repeat tales about baffling aspects of human existence.[31] It was the tendency of pre-Socratics to refrain from personifying the causes of the phenomena they

26. Lincoln, *Theorizing Myth,* pp. 10, 17-18; see also Nagy, *Homeric Questions,* p. 125; Claude Calame, "The Rhetoric of *Muthos* and *Logos,*" in *From Myth to Reason?* ed. Richard Buxton (Oxford: Oxford University Press, 1999), pp. 122, 140-41; Ricoeur, *The Rule of Metaphor,* pp. 15-16; Gerard Naddaf, "Translator's Introduction," in Luc Brisson, *Plato the Myth Maker* (Chicago: University of Chicago Press, 1998), pp. vii-xi.

27. Sitta von Reden, "Re-evaluating Gernet: Value and Greek Myth," in *From Myth to Reason?* ed. Richard Buxton (Oxford: Oxford University Press, 1999), pp. 65, 69.

28. Calame, "The Rhetoric of *Muthos* and *Logos,*" p. 137; Brisson, *Plato the Myth Maker,* p. 90.

29. For example, Plato draws upon the shepherd metaphor to describe the good ruler (*Republic* 1.343-45). See Richard Billows, *Kings and Colonists: Aspects of Macedonian Imperialism,* Columbia Studies in the Classical Tradition 22 (Leiden: Brill, 1995), p. 66; Hannah Arendt, *Between Past and Future: Six Exercises in Political Thought* (New York: Viking, 1961), pp. 107-9, 119; Brisson, *Plato the Myth Maker,* p. 11; Lincoln, *Theorizing Myth,* p. 39; Finkelberg, *The Birth of Literary Fiction in Ancient Greece,* p. 121.

30. Calame, "The Rhetoric of *Muthos* and *Logos,*" p. 137. Glenn Most, "From *Mythos* to *Logos,*" in *From Myth to Reason?* ed. Richard Buxton (Oxford: Oxford University Press, 1999), p. 29.

31. Walter Nicolai, "Gefolgschaftsverweigerung als politisches Druckmittel in der *Ilias,*" in *Anfänge politischen Denkens in der Antike: Die nahöstlichen Kulturen und die Griechen,* ed. K. Raaflaub and E. Müller-Luckner (Munich: Oldenbourg, 1993), pp. 327-28; G. E. R. Lloyd, *Demystifying Mentalities* (New York: Cambridge University Press, 1990), pp. 140-41.

sought to explain that distinguished their explanations from the poets and sages before them.[32]

If *mythos* is defined as an authoritative utterance, then such a command, for which no rationale has been given, has the force to bring about obedience because of the person who uttered it and the circumstances in which it was uttered.[33] Reasoned argument cannot take the place of intuitive truth in all circumstances: the limitations of the human mind and insufficient data often render useless any projections about the future. Yet in the first two millennia B.C. humans acted upon intuitions or hunches. An authoritative leader was one who made decisions and issued commands on the basis of partial information and intuitive knowledge and took responsibility for his decisions. Simple imperatives, however, wielded little authority if the leader was not well known or did not shore up his commands with explanations and demonstrations from the traditions of his community and from his own track record. Such explanations were essential to effective leadership, for then as now legitimate authority was not mute. It was in such explanations that *logos* joined together with *mythos* to make a case for following the lead of an authority figure.[34]

The traditional pattern for legitimating the rule of a king was embodied in narratives and encapsulated in symbols that aimed to persuade an audience to join together and see their common identity under the king's leadership. Persuasion was part of every king's repertoire. Convincing an audience to follow the lead of an authority figure had been part of royal rhetoric in Homeric Greece and in the traditions of the ancient Near East long before the sixth century B.C. The king's poets and scribes aimed to increase the king's authority by making his decisions appear more intelligible and just. They did so primarily by praising the king and defending his actions in narratives communicated orally or incorporated into public monuments such as stelae. For example, in Mesopotamia, the *Code of Hammurapi* was inscribed on stelae and placed in a public space in the Esagila temple in Babylon, in Nippur, in Sippar, and probably in

32. G. E. R. Lloyd, "Greek Cosmologies," in *Methods and Problems in Greek Science* (Cambridge: Cambridge University Press, 1991), p. 150. Glenn Most ("The Poetics of Early Greek Philosophy," in *The Cambridge Companion to Early Greek Philosophy*, ed. A. Long [Cambridge: Cambridge University Press, 1999], p. 352) notes that in the fifth century B.C. Xenophanes entered in the poetic competitions with the bards but did not recite such canonical compositions as Homer and Hesiod. Instead, he introduced a new content whose truth was not based on corresponding "to the legendary past of a specific contingent people, but to a fundamental and permanent structure necessarily valid for the whole world."

33. Pierre Bourdieu, "Authorized Language: The Social Conditions for the Effectiveness of Ritual Discourse," in *Language and Symbolic Power*, ed. John B. Thompson (Cambridge, Mass.: Harvard University Press, 1991), p. 111.

34. Calame, "The Rhetoric of *Muthos* and *Logos*," p. 142.

other cities;[35] in biblical Israel, the story of David's rise to power in 1 Samuel 16:14–2 Samuel 5:10 was probably written in the courts of David and Solomon to fend off criticism and garner support. Yet in texts extant from OB Mesopotamia and biblical Israel, public debates between relative equals appear rarely and then indirectly (e.g., the debate of the elders at the city gate in Gilgamesh and Aka;[36] the debate between the younger and older counselors of Rehoboam in 1 Kings 12). This distinctive trait of popular assemblies of Greek cities beginning in the sixth century B.C. is foreshadowed in a few instances in the *Iliad* where rhetorical combats between relative equals in royal courts (*Il.* 9.30-49, 225-306) arose in situations where a weak king was unable to respond to a crisis facing the community.[37]

In the debates in the law courts and popular assemblies of sixth century B.C. Greece, a new form of persuasion was cultivated: the practice of reasoned argument where one was expected to supply a logical proof for one's position. This type of reasoning then spread into the spheres of medicine, cosmological speculation, and rhetoric.[38] The traveling pedagogues, later known as sophists, competed with one another in attracting students; their authority rose and fell upon the persuasiveness of the reasoned arguments in their teachings.[39] The term *logos* came to be associated primarily with such reasoned argument, the use from which our term "logic" is derived. In earlier times, oppositions such as right/wrong, hot/cold, dry/moist, and mortals/immortals were listed and categorized so as to produce explanations of realities that were clear, consistent, and comprehensive.[40] Yet a new stage of reasoning emerged in the development of what we have come to know as "logic"; G. E. R. Lloyd describes this development as "the evolution of ideas on the nature of opposites qua opposites, and in

35. Victor Hurowitz, *"Inu Anum Sīrum": Literary Structures in the Non-Juridical Sections of Codex Hammurabi*, Occasional Publications of the Samuel Noah Kramer Fund 15 (Philadelphia: University of Pennsylvania Museum, 1994), p. 10.

36. Thorkild Jacobsen, *The Harps That Once . . . Sumerian Poetry in Translation* (New Haven: Yale University Press, 1987), pp. 346-47.

37. Nicolai, "Gefolgschaftsverweigerung als politisches Druckmittel in der *Ilias*," pp. 321-23; Hans Van Wees, *Status Warriors: War, Violence and Society in Homer and History* (Amsterdam: J. C. Gieben, 1992), pp. 77, 84.

38. G. E. R. Lloyd, "The Social Background of Early Greek Philosophy and Science," in *Methods and Problems in Greek Science* (Cambridge: Cambridge University Press, 1991), p. 131.

39. Oswyn Murray, "Cities of Reason," in *The Greek City from Homer to Alexander*, ed. O. Murray and S. Price (Oxford: Clarendon, 1990), p. 17; Jean-Pierre Vernant, *Mortals and Immortals* (Princeton: Princeton University Press, 1990), p. 307; Werner Jaeger, *Paideia: The Ideals of Greek Culture*, 2nd ed., 3 vols. (New York: Oxford University Press, 1945), pp. 292-93.

40. G. E. R. Lloyd, *Polarity and Analogy: Two Types of Argumentation in Early Greek Thought* (Cambridge: Cambridge University Press, 1966), pp. 41, 46, 49, 83.

particular the gradual clarification and analysis of the distinctions between the different modes of opposition."[41]

The fitness of a king to rule could only be intuited beforehand and could be verified only after the fact. The king's claim to be divinely elected could gain credibility only through his accomplishments.[42] Mesopotamian kings from the early third millennium B.C. understood the importance of capitalizing on their accomplishments and so inscribed their heroic deeds on stone monuments, votive objects, and clay tablets in order to make known to the gods, their contemporaries, and future generations that they were carrying out their divine mandates. The impact of such visual symbols of royal authority upon the popular imagination should not be underestimated.[43] While a small elite were probably the only ones able to read the cuneiform inscriptions, the writing itself carried an aura that probably captured the attention of the people at large.[44] Promotion of the king's charisma and skill was important for the mobilization of the population in supporting and assisting in building projects and military campaigns. In many cases, the people were probably manipulated by economic and military factors, but, even in those circumstances where coercion was strong, the people's willingness to follow a king's commands was not a negligible factor in accomplishing the project. The people's intuition of the king's fitness to rule and the wisdom of his decisions was influenced by the metaphors, symbols, and narratives of traditional Mesopotamian royal rhetoric. The more successful the king was, the more authority he exercised among those who benefited from his rule.[45]

The truth of metaphors, symbols, and narratives is highly sensitive to the context in which they are communicated.[46] The similarities and dissimilarities manifested in the tensive juxtaposition of two different persons, things, or categories of reality in a metaphor are dynamics capable of responding to the inter-

---

41. Lloyd, *Polarity and Analogy*, p. 86.

42. Sabina Franke, *Königsinschriften und Königsideologie: Die Könige von Akkade zwischen Tradition und Neuerung* (Münster: LIT, 1995), p. 118; cf. Mario Liverani, *Prestige and Interest: International Relations in the Near East ca. 1600-1100 B.C.* (Padova: Sargon SRL, 1990), p. 48.

43. Irene Winter, "Royal Rhetoric and the Development of Historical Narrative in Neo-Assyrian Reliefs," *Studies in Visual Communication* 7 (1981): 11-13.

44. Joan Goodnick Westenholz, "Thoughts on Esoteric Knowledge and Secret Lore," in *Intellectual Life of the Ancient Near East*, ed. J. Prosecký, CRRA 43 (Prague: Oriental Institute, 1998), pp. 452, 455-56; Jean-Jacques Glassner, "The Use of Knowledge in Ancient Mesopotamia," in *Civilizations of the Ancient Near East*, ed. J. Sasson (New York: Scribner, 1995), p. 1818; cf. Roy Harris, *Signs of Writing* (London and New York: Routledge, 1995), p. 34.

45. Cf. Franke, *Königsinschriften und Königsideologie*, pp. 25, 118-19; A. Kirk Grayson, "Assyria and Babylonia," *Or* 49 (1980): 159-64.

46. Ricoeur, *The Rule of Metaphor*, pp. 254-55.

play of light and shadow in human experience. The multiple interpretations that a symbol is capable of fielding testify to its capacity to mobilize a community in all its diversity and idiosyncrasies. The reasons of the heart — or of the "cognitive unconscious" — are usually more significant in making political decisions than are the logical arguments supplied by reason — a dimension of the human psyche that pretends to be disembodied.[47] So, royal rhetoric appeals to the heart and intuition of the people such that they are inclined to follow the king's lead because it seems to make sense, even though they may not be able to articulate why they have decided to follow him.[48]

Success speaks loudly. Past accomplishments provide a concrete basis on which a king can appeal to the people to follow his commands. In times of crisis, whether induced from within or without, the king has the opportunity to increase his authority, for, if the people take the risk of following him and he is successful, they will naturally place greater confidence in his rule. So, those situations in which chaos threatens and risk is involved are prime contexts in which royal authority can grow — or diminish. In such ambiguous situations at the boundaries where the forces of chaos and order stand in tension, the point of the anthropologists' adage rings true: the power is in the dirt.[49]

Insights into the manner in which authority should create structure in a community can be gained from reflections on how routine gives form to an individual's daily life.[50] A certain way of doing things fits the circumstances of a certain time and place. Unexpected occurrences can break down the automatic way of doing things. On reflection, the individual can either restore or change the routine in order to respond more effectively to new circumstances or understandings. In such reflection and adaptation, the individual becomes more aware of himself and his place within a community. He can see his role in the creation of the routine where he is an agent with capacities and limitations and not simply a manipulated object. The most effective routine is one in which the agent adopts a set way of doing things as circumstances warrant. Analogously,

---

47. Lakoff and Johnson, *Philosophy in the Flesh*, p. 17.

48. Giddens ("Structuralism, Post-Structuralism and the Production of Culture," p. 214) argues, in agreement with Wittgenstein, that what cannot be articulated must be done. Human agents act and then reflect on what they have done. They are not simply determined by unconscious impulses.

49. Edmund Leach, *Culture and Communication: The Logic by Which Symbols Are Connected* (New York: Cambridge University Press, 1976), p. 62; Leonard Muellner, *The Anger of Achilles: "Mēnis" in Greek Epic* (Ithaca: Cornell University Press, 1996), pp. 27, 131.

50. John B. Thompson, "Editor's Introduction," in Pierre Bourdieu, *Language and Symbolic Power*, ed. John B. Thompson (Cambridge, Mass.: Harvard University Press, 1991), p. 17; cf. Martin Heidegger, *Being and Time* (Albany, N.Y.: SUNY Press, 1996), pp. 41-42, 56-58.

good order in a community comes about through agents responding to, adapting, and creating the structure of the community; there is an ongoing interplay between action and structure.[51]

Social and political structures are produced in order to organize a community. If traditional structures are to function properly, they must be reproduced rather than simply handed on.[52] Even though members of the royal establishment might disagree with this statement, royal authority diminished when the people were not allowed to choose to follow a king's command. Conversely, the people themselves might unknowingly forgo their role as agents in structuring the community when their own unexamined habits and practices conspired to create an unenlightened form of obedience.[53]

Even the most well-entrenched habits of obedience to a king had their limits. Unjust royal deeds would not go without a response forever. Even if people could not immediately counter unjust actions by a king, these injuries, if significant and repeated, could enter into the people's unconscious and then resurface as the opportunity presented itself. The Marxist literary critic Fredric Jameson refers to this repressed memory of struggles between the ruler and the ruled, or between classes, as "the political unconscious"; the contradictions and tensions issuing from it reveal the dialectic that lies at the heart of history.[54] While these tensions and contradictions are not directly addressed in the traditional pattern of royal authority in Homeric Greece, biblical Israel, and OB Mesopotamia, this pattern did create a platform for protest by its claim that the king was a shepherd. This traditional pattern of royal authority supported the principle that the more the people freely chose to obey the king, the greater the measure of authority the king exercised. Even though the authority structure within these monarchically organized communities was institutionalized and divinely sanctioned, the actual level of authority exercised by the king was dependent on the people's response to him. One can thus argue that this authority structure was reproduced by the people's repeated choice to obey the king.

---

51. Anthony Giddens (*The Constitution of Society: Outline of the Theory of Structuration* [Cambridge: Polity, 1984], p. 180) argues that the "facticity of social phenomena" is often equated with that of natural phenomena and thereby ignores how such phenomena have been produced by human agency.

52. Giddens, *The Constitution of Society*, p. 25.

53. Bourdieu, "The Production and Reproduction of Legitimate Language," p. 51; Rappaport, *Ritual and Religion*, p. 55.

54. Jameson, *The Political Unconscious*, p. 20.

The Legitimacy of Protest within the
Traditional Pattern of Royal Authority

The kings in Homeric Greece, biblical Israel, and OB Mesopotamia were not above criticism. The traditional pattern of royal authority promoted the image of the king as a just ruler and so opened the door for criticism. However, the more royalist sources, particularly those from Mesopotamia, give the impression that such criticism was not welcome.

The central conflict of the *Iliad* was provoked by Agamemnon's taking back a trophy awarded to Achilles. The warrior-king Agamemnon, leader of the coalition of Achaean warrior-kings in the expedition against Troy, took the woman prisoner-of-war named Briseis away from Achilles and thereby dishonored him (*Il.* 1.101-244). Achilles contended that the warrior ethic in place among the coalition did not allow the king to confiscate a trophy once it had been awarded to a warrior.[55] So, Achilles withdrew in anger from the Achaean forces, with the consequence that the forces grew so weak that they suffered heavy losses (*Il.* 9.9-28).

The narrative raises questions about the character and actions of both Agamemnon and Achilles; neither was above criticism.[56] Why did Agamemnon not devote more attention to the needs of the common effort of the Achaean forces and less to his own individual interests? Why did Achilles hold on to his anger even when it meant heavy losses for the Achaean forces? The narrative highlights the importance of human character and actions in promoting good order in a monarchically organized community. A different authority structure or more checks and balances on Agamemnon's power did not emerge as obvious solutions to the crisis in the Achaean coalition.[57] The narrative suggests that there was no substitute for discussion and reflection on the place of royal authority in the community, for such activities would have made them more aware of their obligation to discern the proper time for protest and for obedience.[58]

---

55. Vernant, *Mortals and Immortals*, p. 53; William M. Sale, "The Government of Troy: Politics in the *Iliad*," *Greek, Roman and Byzantine Studies* 35 (1994): 45; Walter Donlan, *The Aristocratic Ideal in Ancient Greece: Attitude of Superiority from Homer to the End of the Fifth Century* B.C. (Lawrence, Kan.: Coronado, 1980), p. 14; Kevin Crotty, *The Poetics of Supplication: Homer's Iliad and Odyssey* (Ithaca: Cornell University Press, 1994), p. 34.

56. Nicolai, "Gefolgschaftsverweigerung als politisches Druckmittel in der *Ilias*," p. 330; Crotty, *The Poetics of Supplication*, p. 141; Pietro Pucci, *The Song of the Sirens: Essays on Homer* (New York: Rowman & Littlefield, 1998), p. 186.

57. Giddens (*The Constitution of Society*, p. 198) differentiates "conflict" ("struggle between actors or collectivities expressed as definite social practices") from "structural contradiction" ("disjunction of structural principles of system organization").

58. Muellner, *The Anger of Achilles*, pp. 154-55. Nicolai ("Gefolgschaftsverweigerung als

It is a truism that there is no perfect form of government. Choosing one form of government in place of another may solve one set of problems but introduce another set that may be even more distressing. The account of the inauguration of kingship in Israel in 1 Samuel 8 reports that the elders requested from the judge Samuel that a king be appointed to replace the inept administration provided by Samuel's sons (vv. 1-3). In response, Samuel warned them of the potentially tyrannical ways of a king (1 Sam. 8:11-18). Although Samuel had a vested interest in the status quo of the judgeship in Israel, his skepticism about the potential of a structural change to bring about a stronger and more just social and political order was not without grounds. If, in fact, the problem with the government of the tribes was the fairness and effectiveness of Samuel's sons in their administrative roles, then perhaps a better solution than changing the structure would have been to replace the sons and keep the judgeship intact.[59] The narrative of 1 Samuel 8 posed the perennial political question about how to create the most favorable dynamic between action and structure. The elders' scrutiny of Samuel's administration indicates that the populace felt they had a role in shaping the authority structure of the community. The discernment of the question of whether or not to introduce the monarchy into Israel in 1 Samuel 8 was carried out within an assembly of the tribes where the prophet and judge Samuel called upon the Lord to decide the issue. First Samuel 8:7 reports that the Lord regarded the request for an earthly king as a rejection of his divine kingship, but nevertheless the Lord granted their request. According to this narrative, the people had a voice in the inauguration of kingship in Israel; it was not a form of government foisted upon them, but rather one reluctantly granted to them by the Lord.[60]

---

politisches Druckmittel in der *Ilias*," p. 337) notes that the Iliadic poet aimed to raise before the assembly the ethical issues surrounding the leaders of the community so that they might be attentive to them in the future; the poet did not function as a prophet who would directly confront a leader. Cf. Christos Tsagalis, "Style and Construction, Sound and Rhythm: Thetis' Supplication to Zeus (*Iliad* 1.493-516)," *Arethusa* 34 (2001): 20.

59. P. Kyle McCarter, *I Samuel*, AB 8 (Garden City, N.Y.: Doubleday, 1980), pp. 151, 160; Baruch Halpern, "The Uneasy Compromise: Israel between League and Monarchy," in *Traditions in Transformation*, ed. B. Halpern et al. (Winona Lake, Ind.: Eisenbrauns, 1981), pp. 78-79; J. J. M. Roberts, "In Defense of the Monarchy: The Contribution of Israelite Kingship to Biblical Theology," in *Ancient Israelite Religion: Essays in Honor of Frank Moore Cross*, ed. P. Miller, Jr. et al. (Philadelphia: Fortress, 1987), p. 382.

60. McCarter, *I Samuel*, p. 160; Artur Weiser, *Samuel: seine geschichtliche Aufgabe und religiöse Bedeutung*, FRLANT 81 (Göttingen: Vandenhoeck & Ruprecht, 1962), p. 32; Dennis J. McCarthy, "The Inauguration of the Monarchy in Israel: A Form-Critical Study in 1 Samuel 8–12," *Int* 27 (1973): 403; Frank Crüsemann, *Der Widerstand gegen das Königtum*, WMANT 49 (Neukirchen-Vluyn: Neukirchener Verlag, 1978), p. 83.

The Mesopotamian royal inscriptions presented the kingship as an institution sustained by the gods.[61] The court poets, who composed the inscriptions, celebrated the heroic accomplishments of the king as evidence of his divine election and so made statements that the audience was called to accept, almost as if such statements were oracles.[62] Although this genre did not try to induce debate about perennial political questions concerning the exercise of power and authority, its laudatory statements about the just king would have generated questions if the king were unjust. Still, these public documents, which sometimes were buried in the foundations of buildings and at other times were put on display and apparently read aloud to various audiences, did not record voices critical of the reigning king or of kingship as an institution.[63] For such statements critical of kings, one must look to literary works such as the *Atrahasis Epic* and the *Gilgamesh Epic* that indirectly raised questions about the impact of royal policies on a community. Even here, however, discussions focused on the place and exercise of royal authority similar to those in the narratives of 1 Samuel 8 and the *Iliad* will not be found.[64]

Were the Mesopotamian people simply mute on matters of royal policy and conduct? The royal establishment seems to have been concerned with popular perceptions of the king. The first-person speech in which the royal inscriptions were framed reveals that the king and his court wanted to promote the image of the king as one who was personally invested in the welfare of the community. Even if popular perception and public opinion were not explicitly acknowledged in royal documentation, they were not ignored in these communities where kingship was firmly entrenched. Even if the people found their voice

61. F. R. Kraus, "Das altbabylonische Königtum," in *Le palais et la royauté*, RAI 19 (Paris: Paul Geuthner, 1974), pp. 239-40; Jack Sasson, "King Hammurabi of Babylon," in *Civilizations of the Ancient Near East*, ed. Jack Sasson (New York: Scribner, 1995), p. 901; Henri Frankfort, *Kingship and the Gods* (Chicago: University of Chicago Press, 1948), pp. 237-38.

62. Cf. Grayson, "Assyria and Babylonia," pp. 163-64, 170; Henri Limet, "Reflexions sur la nature et l'efficacité d'une opposition," in *La voix de l'opposition en Mésopotamie* (Brussels: Institut des Hautes Études de Belgique, 1973), pp. 85-86.

63. Gerdien Jonker, *The Topography of Remembrance: The Dead, Tradition, and Collective Memory in Mesopotamia*, Studies in the History of Religions 68 (Leiden: Brill, 1995), p. 57; Jean Goodnick Westenholz, "Symbolic Language in Akkadian Narrative Poetry," in *Mesopotamian Poetic Language: Sumerian and Akkadian*, ed. M. Vogelzang and H. Vanstiphout, Cuneiform Monographs 6 (Groningen: Styx, 1996), p. 201; Peter Machinist ("Assyrians on Assyria in the First Millennium B.C.," in *Anfänge politischen Denkens in der Antike: Die nahöstlichen Kulturen und die Griechen*, ed. Kurt Raaflaub and Elisabeth Müller-Luckner [Munich: Oldenbourg, 1993], p. 99) argues that royal inscriptions and royal correspondence were read to the populace; cf. Rappaport, *Ritual and Religion*, p. 332.

64. Hayim Tadmor, "Monarchy and Elite in Assyria and Babylonia," in *The Origins and Diversity of Axial Civilizations*, ed. S. N. Eisenstadt (Albany, N.Y.: SUNY Press, 1986), p. 217.

ignored in deliberations on a national level, they would still have had the opportunity for political involvement at the local level,[65] and so the people's capacity for political reflection would not have atrophied simply because it was not fully exercised at the national level. They would have known that there were a time to protest and a time to refrain from protesting, for even though the royal records do not like to acknowledge that revolts against kings occurred, their reality could not always be concealed.[66]

The narratives of 1 Samuel 8, the *Iliad,* and the Mesopotamian royal inscriptions express political theologies that locate the source of royal authority in the king of the gods. This traditional theological framework places the pursuit of political, economic, and social power in a context where the desires and needs of God or the gods must be taken into account.[67] As noted earlier, 1 Samuel 8:7 states that the Lord regarded the elders' request for a king as a rejection of his divine kingship. So, the antimonarchical viewpoint woven into this narrative contended that earthly kingship in Israel was incompatible with heavenly kingship — an inversion of the typical ancient Near Eastern view that there was a symbiotic relationship between heavenly and earthly kingship.[68] However, 1 Samuel 8 as a whole relates how the Lord allowed the introduction of the kingship into Israel but warned the Israelites of the trouble that they were inviting. Within this air of skepticism about the monarchical institution, 1 Samuel 8 was grounded in the view that royal authority properly belonged to the king of the gods and could be shared only by those whom he designated.

The Iliadic narrative raised questions about how seriously Agamemnon regarded his divine election as the holder of the scepter of Argos (*Il.* 9.29-49). Agamemnon referred to Zeus as one who controlled history and could do as he wished (*Il.* 9.23-25). Was Agamemnon simply taking a fatalistic stance towards life and regarding Zeus as an anonymous power that could not be influenced? Perhaps Agamemnon revealed his own view of how a king exercised power — whether that king be human or divine — that he should be able to do what he wants or to rule absolutely without the constraints of a communal or cosmic ethical order. The traditional symbol of the just royal ruler among the Achaeans

---

65. Marc Van de Mieroop, "The Government of an Ancient Mesopotamian City: What We Know and Why We Know So Little," in *Priests and Officials in the Ancient Near East* (Heidelberg: Universitätsverlag C. Winter, 1999), pp. 143-44.

66. See the popular uprising described in the inscription of Ipiq-Ishtar of Malgium (Frayne, *RIME 4,* E4.11.1).

67. Cf. Michael Rowlands, "Centre and Periphery: A Review of a Concept," in *Centre and Periphery in the Ancient World,* ed. M. Rowlands et al. (Cambridge: Cambridge University Press, 1987), pp. 4, 8-9.

68. Crüsemann, *Der Widerstand gegen das Königtum,* p. 75.

was the scepter of Argos, but it was Odysseus rather than Agamemnon who effectively wielded this scepter in regrouping the fleeing Achaeans (*Il.* 2.186, 199, 206, 265, 268), and it was Nestor who explained most clearly the significance of the scepter (*Il.* 9.99).[69] It seems then that Agamemnon ignored the tradition's role in legitimating his authority and in practice did not regard his royal authority as anchored in and issuing from that of Zeus. As a result, he had no alternative but to lean more heavily upon the material basis of his kingship for maintaining his hold on power, which explains why he would risk alienating Achilles in order to have a war trophy.[70]

In Mesopotamia, the royal inscriptions presented the king as a pious ruler who, even though he did not refrain from self-promotion, attributed his success to the gods. The king of the gods and the king's protector deity were the authoritative and effective powers that enabled him to accomplish great deeds. So, the inscriptions typically introduce the king's heroic accomplishment by identifying and praising the king of the gods and other significant deities who commissioned him to carry out a particular deed. More attention was often given in the inscription to the identification of the gods and the king than to the description of the deed accomplished. There is no question that these inscriptions regarded the king's sovereignty as a participation in the sovereignty of the king of the gods. Yet one wonders if the idealization of the king in the inscription served to shield the king from criticism. Whether such idealization increased or decreased a king's sense of accountability most likely depended on the character of each particular king. For some kings such idealization may have tempted them to feel omnipotent, and so they ruled absolutely (e.g., Gilgamesh in the early years of his reign, tablet II, ii.10-19).[71] For others, such idealization may have triggered associations with stories in the tradition that would have made them more mindful of their indebtedness to the gods, their ancestors, and the community (e.g., the prologue and epilogue of the *Code of Hammurapi*).[72]

The traditional pattern of royal authority in Homeric Greece, biblical Israel, and OB Mesopotamia mapped out the structure and dynamics of author-

69. Peter W. Rose, *Sons of the Gods, Children of Earth: Ideology and Literary Form in Ancient Greece* (Ithaca: Cornell University Press, 1992), p. 75.

70. Pierre Carlier, *La royauté en Grèce avant Alexandre* (Strasbourg: AECR, 1984), pp. 193, 202-3.

71. Stephanie Dalley, *Myths from Mesopotamia* (Oxford: Oxford University Press, 1989), p. 52.

72. *ANET,* pp. 164-65, 177-80; Riekele Borger, *Babylonisch-assyrische Lesestücke,* AnOr 54 (Rome: Pontifical Biblical Institute, 1979), 1:5-7, 45-49; Martha Roth, *Law Collections from Mesopotamia and Asia Minor,* Writings from the Ancient World 6 (Atlanta: Scholars, 1995), pp. 76-81, 133-40.

ity in which the king of the gods, the earthly king, and the people were agents in the hierarchy spanning heaven and earth. Sovereignty properly resided in the king of the gods and was shared in by those whom he elected. When the earthly king or the people saw routines or practices of the community shifting so as to upset its equilibrium, they were empowered to try to find ways to gain a new equilibrium. An earthly tyrant could oppress a people in the short term, but he could not silence their appeals to the king of the gods. An opportunistic, rebellious people could be legitimately silenced by a king who had the physical force to do so.

The Accountability of the Earthly King to the Heavenly King and the People

The traditional pattern for legitimating royal authority promoted a dynamic of accountability: the heavenly king appointed the earthly king to shepherd his people. The metaphor of the shepherd would have communicated clearly to an agricultural people the responsibility that the king had towards the community. The sheep belonged to the divine ruler; the king was the earthly caretaker. If the king forgot the divine ownership of the sheep, he would most likely have fleeced them or used them for his own purposes. The well-known Exilic judgment speech of the prophet Ezekiel against the kings and other leaders of Israel used shepherd imagery in formulating the condemnation of their negligence:

> The word of the Lord came to me: "Son of man, prophesy against the shepherds of Israel. Prophesy and say[73] to the shepherds: 'Thus says the Lord God: Woe to the shepherds of Israel who have been pasturing themselves. Should the shepherds not pasture the sheep? You eat the fat and clothe yourselves with the wool; you slaughter the fatlings; but you do not pasture the sheep. You have not strengthened the weak ones, and you have not healed the sick. You have not bound up the injured. You have not brought back the stray, and you have not sought out the lost, but with force and violence you have herded them. They have been scattered without a shepherd and have become prey for every wild beast. My sheep have been scattered; they stray on every mountain and on every high hill. Over all the earth my sheep have been dispersed with no one to care or search for them.'" (Ezek. 34:1-6)

Shepherd imagery was also frequently used in the OB royal inscriptions to describe the appointment of the king and the responsibility he had to care for the

73. Delete *ʾălêhem* with LXX and Vg.

people.[74] Takil-ilisu (nineteenth century B.C.), the king of Malgium, referred to the source of his royal authority by saying: "When Ea [and] Damkina named my name for shepherdship of Malgium. . . ."[75] In Homer, the epithet "shepherd of the people" was applied numerous times to Agamemnon (*Il.* 2.243, etc.); it can also be inferred from the scepter of Argos that Agamemnon was expected to rule as a shepherd. However, the shepherd image was not used explicitly in the *Iliad* to emphasize Agamemnon's accountability for the welfare of the Achaeans.

The criteria for assessing whether or not a king was carrying out his mandate as a shepherd of the people would have been drawn first of all from the common experience of what a shepherd was supposed to do, and then more importantly from the model provided by the king of the gods who exercised primary shepherdship over the people. At first glance, it may appear that the traditional pattern for legitimating royal authority portrayed the relationship between the king of the gods and the king as very matter-of-fact, and so the relationship was expected to unfold in a predictable, peaceful fashion. Yet the relationship between the king of the gods and the earthly king mapped out in this pattern did not simply involve bestowal of authority by the king of the gods, to which the king responded in obedience. There was also room for conflict between the heavenly and earthly kings. Just as there was tension between the king and the people, there was also believed to be tension between the earthly king and the king of the gods. Just as humans could relate to one another with love and hate, confidence and mistrust, and mutuality and rivalry, so also was this possible between gods and humans. The relationships mapped out in the traditional pattern of royal authority reflected the ambiguities and unpredictable aspects of typical personal relationships.

In the OB royal inscriptions, the king stated that he ruled at the behest of the gods. If he later dismissed this statement as mere rhetoric, he would still have been held accountable by those who regarded any king as illegitimate who did not rule in accord with the wishes of the king of the gods.[76] If, however, the community over which the king ruled also had no regard for the king of the gods, then the king probably would not have noticed a diminution in his power by neglect of the sanctuary and the expectations of the king of the gods. The gods probably would not have had any influence in his community for some

---

74. Kraus, "Das altbabylonische Königtum," pp. 252-53, 261. Franke, *Königsinschriften und Königsideologie,* pp. 125, 196.

75. Frayne, *RIME 4,* E4.11.2.1, lines 5-8.

76. Frankfort, *Kingship and the Gods,* pp. 239-40. Rappaport (*Ritual and Religion,* p. 131) notes that the publicly enacted rituals signal the participants' acceptance of their statements regardless of their subjective attitudes.

time, for the gods of the ancient Near East were typically portrayed as silent when they were not properly invoked and honored.[77] The absence of divine power in a community would have markedly diminished the capacity of the king to act on behalf of the community;[78] such an absence would have indicated that the symbolic dimension of the king's rule was inoperative. According to the religious worldview of the ancient Near East, impiety by the king and the people curtailed the possibilities open to them.

Power first and foremost refers to the capacity to act.[79] Such a definition covers both individual and collective action. Authority overlaps with this concept of power but refers more specifically to the capacity to have one's commands obeyed for the purpose of increasing the well-being of the community.[80] Authority is the exercise of legitimate power.[81] A king increased his power — his capacity to act — not only by amassing wealth and commanding a large military force; he also grew more powerful when the community voluntarily joined together in common efforts under his leadership. A dramatic example of such common efforts that strengthened the hand of the king was the solidarity of a community in defending itself against an aggressive foe. In such a critical situation, shared concerns among the community members, particularly between the ruler and the ruled, far outweighed the differences that otherwise divided them.

Agamemnon diminished the power of the Achaean forces when he took Briseis away from Achilles. He was able to do so by force because Achilles was

---

77. F. A. M. Wiggermann, "Theologies, Priests, and Worship in Ancient Mesopotamia," in *Civilizations of the Ancient Near East*, ed. Jack Sasson (New York: Scribner, 1995), p. 1857; Jean Bottéro, "Religion and Reasoning in Mesopotamia," in *Ancestor of the West* (Chicago: University of Chicago Press, 1996), pp. 56-57. Cf. 1 Sam. 14:37-41; 28:6.

78. F. R. Kraus, *The Role of Temples from the Third Dynasty of Ur to the First Dynasty of Babylon*, Monographs on the Ancient Near East, vol. 2, fasc. 4 (Malibu, Calif.: Undena, 1990), p. 5; Carlier, *La royauté en Grèce avant Alexandre*, p. 203; cf. Giddens, *The Constitution of Society*, p. 195.

79. Giddens, *The Constitution of Society*, p. 173; Douglas Knight, "Political Rights and Powers in Monarchic Israel," *Semeia* 66 (1994): 98.

80. Arendt, *Between Past and Future*, pp. 106, 121-22; Knight, "Political Rights and Powers," p. 98; John Campbell, "The Greek Hero," in *Honor and Grace in Anthropology*, ed. J. Peristiany and J. Pitt-Rivers (Cambridge: Cambridge University Press, 1992), p. 130.

81. Ronald Cohen, "The Political System," in *Handbook of Method in Cultural Anthropology*, ed. R. Naroll and R. Cohen (New York: Columbia University Press, 1970), p. 488; idem, "Legitimacy, Illegitimacy, and State Formation," in *State Formation and Political Legitimacy*, ed. R. Cohen and J. Toland, Political Anthropology 6 (New Brunswick, N.J.: Transaction Books, 1988), pp. 71, 81-82; Talcott Parsons, "On the Concept of Political Power," *Proceedings of the American Philosophical Society* 107 (1963): 249; cf. Walter Donlan, "The Structure of Authority in the Iliad," *Arethusa* 12 (1979): 59.

restrained by his respect for the position of the king of Argos and by the intervention of Athena to stay his hand (*Il.* 1.188-222).[82] Agamemnon had the coercive and traditional power to take Briseis, but only at the price of drastically reducing the power of the coalition of Achaean forces under his command. Agamemnon's neglect of the traditional basis of his authority and his desire to increase the material basis of his status against rival warrior-kings led him to act as a tyrant who gets his commands obeyed by force (*Il.* 1.178-87). Although Agamemnon did not appeal directly to superior material force as the basis of his greater strength (*pherteros, Il.* 1.186), he clearly intended to use coercion as a means to gain Achilles' compliance to his plan to take Briseis. The fact that the other Achaean warrior-kings and the soldiers-at-large allowed Agamemnon to go forward with his threat means that they gave him a measure of authority by their acquiescence.[83] It would seem that the support of the other warrior-kings rested in no small measure upon the traditional authority of the scepter of Argos. Achilles' withdrawal had an immediate negative impact on the strength of the Achaean forces. Agamemnon soon realized that he was mistaken in his action toward Achilles (*Il.* 9.114-20).

In Israel at the beginning of the reign of Rehoboam (922-916 B.C.), the son of Solomon, the elders of the northern tribes gathered at Shechem in order to enter into covenant with the new regime in Jerusalem (1 Kings 12:1-19). The elders asked that the forced labor imposed during the years of Solomon be eliminated.[84] After consultation, Rehoboam ignored the advice of his older counselors in favor of that of the younger ones and responded to the elders' request with the arrogant claim: "My father made your yoke heavy, but I will increase the weight of your yoke. My father trained you with whips, but I will train you with scorpions" (1 Kings 12:14). The northern tribes withdrew and formed their own kingdom under Jeroboam. This episode confirms the view that self-indulgent tyrannical actions of rulers recoil on themselves and diminish the rulers' power.

In Mesopotamia, tyrannical kings also arose who overstepped traditionally established boundaries. Records of such kings are not contained in the royal inscriptions but can be inferred from some of the curses listed in the epilogue of the *Code of Hammurapi*. These curses were directed against any king who dared to abrogate the laws inscribed on Hammurapi's stele:

82. Pucci, *The Song of the Sirens,* pp. 73, 77; Donlan, "The Structure of Authority in the *Iliad,*" pp. 57-58.

83. Pucci, *The Song of the Sirens,* p. 189.

84. Moshe Weinfeld, "The Counsel of the 'Elders' to Rehoboam and Its Implications," in *Reconsidering Israel and Judah: Recent Studies on the Deuteronomistic History,* ed. G. Knoppers and J. G. McConville (Winona Lake, Ind.: Eisenbrauns, 2000), p. 537.

> May he [Enlil] stir up against him a revolt which cannot be suppressed, a rebellion which will spread ruin into his own household. (*CH* XLIX:59-63)

> May he [Shamash] overthrow his kingship. . . . May he entangle his paths. May he cause the foundations of his people to slip. May he place in his vision an evil omen concerning the removal of the foundations of his kingship and the destruction of his land. (*CH* L:20, 23-30)[85]

These sacral sanctions against a king, who from Hammurapi's perspective was lawless and impious, show that such a potentially lawless king would have rendered his rule illegitimate and so would be removed by the gods. Once a king's authority collapsed, he could rule only by force: a prospect that few kings could sustain for very long. The curses highlight the fact that royal authority was seen to have a heavenly origin and destiny; where authority was at issue, the gods were believed to be nearby.

In the communities of ancient Mesopotamia, biblical Israel, and Homeric Greece, a prevailing viewpoint of their political theologies was that truth was more fundamental than power.[86] In other words, any ruler who governed according to the principle that "might makes right" would sooner or later be punished for his transgressions. This belief in an ethical world order was not always confirmed by the community's experience. In crises such as natural disasters and invasions by powerful foes, their sense of fairness, a basis for ethical judgment more fundamental than the content of any ethical code, was challenged to make sense out of their unmerited distress.[87] Even if the only response possible for them was to lament, their outcries to the chief executive deity — the Lord in Israel, Enlil in Mesopotamia, and Zeus in Greece — underlined the fact that these communities expected a reasonable measure of justice in life: that truth is more fundamental than power.

---

85. Borger, *Babylonisch-assyrische Lesestücke,* 1:47, 48.

86. Muellner, *The Anger of Achilles,* pp. 34-35; cf. Raymond Westbrook, "Social Justice in the Ancient Near East," in *Social Justice in the Ancient World,* ed. K. D. Irani and M. Silver (Westport, Conn.: Greenwood, 1995), pp. 159-61.

87. Wolfram von Soden, *The Ancient Orient: An Introduction to the Study of the Ancient Near East* (Grand Rapids: Eerdmans, 1994), p. 185; Christoph Auffahrt, *Der drohende Untergang: "Schöpfung" in Mythos und Ritual im Alten Orient und in Griechenland am Beispiel der Odysee und des Ezechielbuches,* Religiongeschichtliche Versüche und Vorarbeiten 39 (New York: Walter de Gruyter, 1991), pp. 55, 76; cf. Bottéro, "Religion and Reasoning in Mesopotamia," p. 61.

Creating a Shared Identity between King
and People within an Interrelated Cosmos

A shared identity of the king and the people is a promise inherent in kingship that needs to be forged in the reigns of particular kings. The metaphoric identification of the king with the people, commonly labeled the royal metaphor, states that the king "is" and "is not" the people.[88] The royal metaphor suggests that unity was achieved within a monarchically organized community when the people saw their identity bound up with that of the king such that the king symbolized their corporateness. Even though the royal metaphor overlaps with the symbolic character of the king's person, the two characterizations of the king are not strictly congruent. The royal metaphor appeals directly to the people's immediate experience: Do the king's policies and actions this month confirm that the king is taking the people's well-being into account and serving them even at his own personal expense? The symbolic role of the king is one in which his role as representative of the community is more stable. Even if the king's behavior should happen to be self-serving, his person still points to the expectation of the people that they are bound together in community, and the people may strive to uphold the king's image as a symbol of the community even when his policies disconfirm his fitness for this role. Nevertheless, a tyrannical or inept king can be propped up for only so long before he is overthrown.

Some primitive peoples imagined their unity by singling out an animal as their totem.[89] The logic of the totemic practice was based on the fact that an individual animal has both a genus and a species. An individual animal belongs to a larger group without losing its specificity. By analogy, a human being could belong to a community and still retain his or her individuality. This common identity within the community was symbolized by the totem animal.[90] A similar logic appears to have been operative in the role of the king as the central symbol of the community and in the dynamics of the royal metaphor. The challenge of the royal metaphor and of the king's symbolic role was for the king and the people to find ways to promote the bonds and the well-being of the community.

Finding and establishing one's identity is a dynamic process. Just as the ongoing activity of the members is integral to the formation and maintenance of

---

88. Northrup Frye, *The Great Code: The Bible and Literature* (New York: Harcourt Brace Jovanovich, 1981), pp. 87-88; cf. Ricoeur, *The Rule of Metaphor,* pp. 247-48.

89. Hénaff, *Claude Levi-Strauss,* p. 155.

90. Hénaff, *Claude Levi-Strauss,* p. 155; Edmund Leach, "Telstar and the Aborigines or *La pensée sauvage,*" in *Sociological Theory and Philosophical Analysis,* ed. D. Emmet and A. MacIntyre (New York: Macmillan, 1970), pp. 192, 196-97.

the structures of the community, so also is such active involvement indispensable to the individual members if they are to find their place and express themselves within a community.[91] Finding and establishing one's identity is a creative process that persists throughout a lifetime. An individual's identity emerges in a relational context where care and attention are directed to the divine, human, and natural spheres.[92] As a symbol of the community, the person of the king signifies this network of relationships that not only unites humans in a community but also links this human community with the king of the gods. A person within this community seeks to find his place on this hierarchy of relationships spanning heaven and earth. His discernment takes place with this expansive, cosmic hierarchy in mind so that he does not define himself or measure himself merely in relation to others inside or outside the community. Nor does he see himself simply as occupying a slot on a static, wooden hierarchy that would be equivalent to assuming the identity of a "thing" rather than a person who is an agent with a role in the ordering of the community. A hierarchy is a grid of relationships that loses its integrity and becomes a source of oppression if the relationships are untended or distorted.[93] Paul Ricoeur differentiates *ipse,* "the unique," from *idem,* "the same," in human identity: the uniquely human identity, denoted by *ipse,* is forged by a person acting oneself into existence.[94] It is in the creative action of coming into relationship with the community that a person realizes that authority is a divine gift empowering one to find a place and a role in the hierarchy that spans heaven and earth. One acts creatively and comes to realize the richness of the event in subsequent reflection.[95]

The statement that "the king is the people" could be interpreted as giving a

91. Ricoeur ("Practical Reason," p. 203) argues for the integrative function of politics as "architectonic knowledge, that is to say, knowledge that coordinates the good of the individual with that of the community and that integrates particular abilities in a wisdom relative to the City as a whole."

92. Walter Burkert, *Creation of the Sacred: Tracks of Biology in Early Religions* (Cambridge, Mass.: Harvard University Press, 1996), pp. 80-81.

93. Giddens, *The Constitution of Society,* pp. 16-19, 51; cf. Rappaport, *Ritual and Religion,* pp. 265-66, 275.

94. Paul Ricoeur, *Oneself as Another* (Chicago: University of Chicago Press, 1992), pp. 1-3, 303-8.

95. Vico claimed that "we know what we make": i.e., in the dynamics of the creative act we are granted a type of intuitive knowledge that could not be gained otherwise; cf. Isaiah Berlin, "The Romantic Revolution," in *The Sense of Reality: Studies in Ideas and Their History,* ed. H. Hardy (New York: Farrar, Straus and Giroux, 1996), p. 185; Donald Phillip Verene, "Two Sources of Philosophical Memory: Vico versus Hegel," in *Philosophical Imagination and Cultural Memory,* ed. P. Cook (Durham, N.C.: Duke University Press, 1993), p. 50. See also Finkelberg, *The Birth of Literary Fiction in Ancient Greece,* p. 106.

warrant to the king to swallow up the people and as encouraging the people to deny themselves and accept such a condition. The royal establishment could reward heroic actions that contributed more to maintenance of the status quo rather than to the well-being of the community. Perpetuating heroic patterns without reexamining their purpose could lead to individuals spending their lives simply keeping the pattern alive and not actually benefiting the community. The unchangeability of heroic patterns could come to mirror the motionlessness of death.[96] In the sacrifices called forth from the populace, the just king would honor the individual and would not have wanted to obliterate this source of vitality in the community by rendering it motionless within a static monarchic machine.

The king and the people were inextricably tied to one another by their mutual interests. When Agamemnon dishonored Achilles, the entire Achaean coalition suffered. As Agamemnon tried to establish his identity and place in the community, he undercut the warrior ethic of the community and so displaced Achilles. The ensuing disorder involved not only humans but also the gods. The forging of one's identity, particularly that of a king, was carried out in the context of an interrelated cosmos.

The power struggles between the house of Saul and the house of David embroiled the Israelite leadership in conflicts that left little time and resources to attend to questions of the common good of the Israelite people (e.g., 2 Sam. 2:8–3:1). Later editors from the Davidic court in Jerusalem framed these stories of David's rise to power in a theological context where David's apparent self-serving actions were regarded as carrying out God's will and benefiting the Israelite people.[97] Extortion from a wealthy Judaean landowner and collaboration with the Philistines, actions that appear shadowy in isolation, were to be seen within the larger context of the well-being and security that David would bring to the Israelites. These pro-Davidic editors portrayed David in their framework and additions as a pious leader who struggled to attain the kingship in response to divine election and not out of selfish ambition.[98] These editors encouraged the Israelite people to see David's triumphs as their own. These editors were, in effect, arguing that "the king is the people": what is good for David is good for the people.

In Mesopotamia, the royal inscriptions typically celebrated heroic actions

---

96. Pucci, *The Song of the Sirens,* pp. 63-64; Jameson, *The Seeds of Time,* p. 122.

97. McCarter, *I Samuel,* pp. 27-30; Walter Brueggemann, *First and Second Samuel* (Louisville: John Knox, 1990), pp. 4-6, 181, 204; Baruch Halpern, *David's Secret Demons: Messiah, Murderer, Traitor, King* (Grand Rapids: Eerdmans, 2001), pp. 75-76.

98. McCarter, *I Samuel,* pp. 28-29; Brueggemann, *First and Second Samuel,* p. 174; Halpern, *David's Secret Demons,* pp. 283, 296.

by the king that benefited the people and so tried to link the welfare and identity of the community more closely to the king. In one of his inscriptions, Hammurapi marked the completion of his construction of a canal by naming it, "Hammurapi is the prosperity of his people."[99] This metaphorical title not only promoted a favorable image of Hammurapi in the imagination of the people but also placed an expectation on Hammurapi that he continue to bring benefits to the people. Through the identification of the well-being of the people with that of the king, these communities achieved a greater degree of centralization that enabled them to concentrate their resources on military efforts and public works projects that would scarcely have been possible otherwise. Whether such military campaigns or building projects built up or undercut the community can be answered only by assessing each initiative in its specific circumstances. In his person and actions, the king symbolized the unity of the community in a way that a material symbol, such as an emblem or a city wall, could scarcely approximate.

The royal metaphor focused on the relationship between the king and the people, or the earthly component of the cosmic hierarchy, sketched out in the traditional pattern of royal authority. However, the other part of this traditional pattern — the heavenly component — communicated a vision of royal rule in which the king and the people were to recognize that their capacity to act in concert was facilitated by the watchful care and assistance of God or the gods.[100] Human power was enhanced by divine power. The line between dream and reality and between what was possible and what usually happened was believed to shift when God or the gods became more directly involved in human affairs. The passion for the possible or pressing the boundaries of what was possible was an important dynamic in the creation of royal authority.[101] When a king acknowledged the divine source of his royal authority, he increased his sense of the stability of his rule, which in turn allowed him more room for experimentation. Conversely, the king could ignore the divine source of his authority and transgress the boundaries between the divine and the human and also those boundaries that order the human community. According to the traditions of Homeric Greece, biblical Israel, and OB Mesopotamia, the activity of God or the gods in the community was indispensable for the realization of the promise of wholeness and well-being set forth in the traditional pattern of royal authority.

99. Frayne, *RIME 4*, E4.3.6.7.
100. Burkert, *Creation of the Sacred*, pp. 93-97.
101. Muellner, *The Anger of Achilles*, p. 131; cf. Kevin J. Vanhoozer, *Biblical Narrative in the Philosophy of Paul Ricoeur: A Study in Hermeneutics and Theology* (Cambridge: Cambridge University Press, 1990), pp. 6-8.

The Role of Political Theology: To Foster Integration of the Community through Dialogue, Reflection, and Action

Tension and conflict persist in life until death. The peace and harmony we experience in life is the equilibrium gained through the balancing of competing interests. Such an agonistic view of life is not the special possession of Marxists, nor is it an invention of Heraclitus.[102] The sense that order emerges from competing forces is inherent in the dynamics of metaphor and in the constant play of the *signifier* of a symbol that is always negotiating the rich polyvalence of the *signified.* The magic of metaphor is its capacity to reveal connections between two disparate realities that would otherwise relate to one another only as isolated fragments. Yet this connection exists only as long as the tension exists.[103] The deeper connection revealed by a metaphor cannot be taken for granted; it can be lost through neglect or unavoidable change. Likewise, the power of a political or religious symbol lies in its capacity to summon diverse individuals to recognize the bonds that they have inherited or that they have promised to sustain. A symbol also may become lifeless if the bonds toward which it points have no substance and no potential.

Political theology in Homeric Greece, biblical Israel, and OB Mesopotamia consisted primarily of metaphors, symbols, and narratives and spoke about the way God or the gods influenced the political activities of the community largely by way of the tensive truth of metaphors and narratives and the play of the signifier of symbols. The creation and maintenance of the social and political hierarchy in the community so that people had a sense of belonging were not simply a matter of a one-time allocation of position and resources. The social and political hierarchy was a moving web of relationships that required vigilance if one wished to live within it.[104] The competing relationships among various individuals could have led to shifts that would have had reverberations throughout the whole structure. Kings typically tried to slow down change or prevent it if the initiative came from someone outside the king's own circle.[105] A king's efforts to maintain the social and political hierarchy and to manipulate changes to support his power drew upon the tradition of the community and its political theology.

---

102. Edward Hussey, "Heraclitus," in *The Cambridge Companion to Early Greek Philosophy,* ed. A. Long (Cambridge: Cambridge University Press, 1999), pp. 93-98; Kearney, *Modern Movements in European Philosophy,* pp. 139-41.

103. Ricoeur, *The Rule of Metaphor,* p. 248.

104. Burkert, *Creation of the Sacred,* pp. 95-96.

105. Jonker, *The Topography of Remembrance,* p. 57; cf. Rappaport, *Ritual and Religion,* pp. 274-75.

In the *Iliad*, the competition among the relatively equal warrior-kings for ascendancy in the coalition found an echo in the heavenly realm in the relations between Zeus and Poseidon. Poseidon intervened in the battle on behalf of the Achaeans, and Zeus ordered him to desist (*Il.* 15.174-83). Poseidon defended his actions by recalling the original partitioning of the cosmos into four parts: (1) the area belonging to Zeus was Olympus and the heavens, (2) Poseidon's area was the sea, (3) the underworld belonged to Hades, and (4) the earth was a neutral zone in which Zeus, Poseidon, and Hades could intervene. Poseidon claimed that Zeus had no right to prevent him from intervening to assist the Achaeans (*Il.* 15.184-99). In this particular scene, Zeus, like Agamemnon among the Achaean warrior-kings, appeared to rule as a *primus inter pares* among the gods; however, in most of the Iliadic narrative, the absoluteness of Zeus's sovereign rule was unquestioned.[106] Homer so constructed his narrative that conflicts and struggles on the earthly plane between Agamemnon and the other warrior-kings were explored further through analogues on the heavenly plane in struggles between the gods. Such reflection on the power struggles among the gods revealed how the quarrel between Achilles and Agamemnon was not an isolated instance but an example of a worldview in which conflicts between powerful individuals had repercussions throughout an interrelated cosmos.[107] When Greek audiences from the eighth to the sixth centuries B.C. listened to such episodes from the *Iliad*, they would have been invited to recognize through materials drawn from their traditions the deeper dimensions and cosmic ramifications of authority struggles in their community.[108] Such reflection could have spurred initiatives for reform or change as much as they could have generated caution about the cost of changing the status quo. Even if Homer favored the monarchical form of government, the epics themselves indicate that he placed a greater value on reflection on political issues than on promoting the party line of monarchists.[109]

In the Israelite tradition, the Lord was the absolute sovereign. Yet such a be-

---

106. Jean-Pierre Vernant, *Myth and Society in Ancient Greece* (Atlantic Highlands, N.J.: Humanities, 1980), pp. 96-97, 105; Guila Sissa and Marcel Detienne, *The Daily Life of the Greek Gods* (Stanford: Stanford University Press, 2000), pp. 101-2; Jasper Griffin, *Homer on Life and Death* (Oxford: Clarendon, 1980), p. 88.

107. Buxton, *Imaginary Greece*, pp. 141-42; William G. Thalmann, *The Swineherd and the Bow: Representations of Class in the Odyssey* (Ithaca: Cornell University Press, 1998), pp. 276-77.

108. Carlier, *La royauté en Grèce avant Alexandre*, pp. 195-204; Donlan, "The Structure of Authority in the *Iliad*," p. 63.

109. Carlier, *La royauté en Grèce avant Alexandre*, p. 201; Dean Hammer, "Who Shall Readily Obey?": Authority and Politics in the *Iliad*," *Phoenix* 51 (1997): 1-24; idem, "Politics in the *Iliad*," *Classical Journal* 94 (1998): 2-8.

lief was stretched to the breaking point by the death of Josiah in 609 B.C. and the subsequent disasters that led to the destruction of the temple in 587.[110] These events seem to be the setting for Psalm 89, a communal lament that expressed the confusion of the supporters of the Davidic monarchy over the demise of one of its idealized rulers, a tragedy that seemed to foreshadow the end of the Davidic dynasty.[111] It was commonly held in Jerusalem and Judah that the Davidic dynasty was to last forever. Psalm 89 points out how the Lord reigns as king of the gods and has promised to uphold the Davidic dynasty forever (vv. 20-38[19-37]). The concluding complaint of Psalm 89 over the demise of the current Davidic ruler expressed the confusion and distress of the community and asked the Lord for a response and assistance (vv. 39-52[38-51]). The Israelite community throughout subsequent generations prayed this psalm and engaged the questions about the Lord's apparent change of mind toward supporting the Davidic dynasty. The lament did not pretend to answer the questions about the Lord's power and fidelity raised in these circumstances; it simply brought these painful questions to expression within a communal forum where they would be faced directly. The skill with which Psalm 89 drew upon the tradition and articulated these issues of paradox in the people's relationship with God has made this lament psalm a vehicle for navigating analogous crises in later history and for shaping the imaginations of its readers on ways that the heavenly sovereign relates to the earthly one and on what impact these relationships have upon the community.[112]

In Mesopotamia, Hammurapi rebuilt the wall of Sippar and claimed in an accompanying inscription that he was able to do so because Shamash and Marduk had commissioned him.[113] Because of its indispensable role in the defense of a Mesopotamian city, the city wall was given symbolic or sacred signifi-

---

110. Hans-Joachim Kraus (*Psalms 60–150* [Minneapolis: Augsburg, 1989], p. 203) argues that Psalm 89 is to be dated between the death of Josiah in 609 B.C. and the Exile. Évode Beaucamp (*Le psautier*, 2 vols. [Paris: Gabalda, 1979], 2:92) links Psalm 89 with events at the time of the death of Josiah, but Marvin Tate (*Psalms 51–100*, WBC 20 [Dallas: Word, 1990], p. 416) sees it referring to events around the time of the deportation of Jehoiachin in 597 B.C.

111. Beaucamp, *Le psautier*, 2:85-86; Richard Clifford, "Psalm 89: A Lament over the Davidic Ruler's Continued Failure," *HTR* 73 (1980): 35-47.

112. Knut Heim, "The (God-)Forsaken King of Psalm 89: A Historical and Intertextual Enquiry," in *King and Messiah in Israel and the Ancient Near East*, ed. J. Day, JSOTSup 270 (Sheffield: Sheffield Academic Press, 1998), pp. 296-322; Gerald Wilson, *The Editing of the Hebrew Psalter*, SBLDS 76 (Chico, Calif.: Scholars, 1985), pp. 214-15; William Holladay, *The Psalms Through Three Thousand Years* (Minneapolis: Fortress, 1996), p. 78; Kraus, *Psalms 60–150*, pp. 210-11; Peter Ackroyd, *Studies in the Religious Tradition of the Old Testament* (London: SCM, 1987), pp. 41-42.

113. Frayne, *RIME 4*, E4.3.6.12.

cance; it was foundational to the life of the city.[114] In the political theology of this inscription, Hammurapi claimed that this deed was testimony to his right relationship with Shamash and Marduk and that his rule promoted good order in the community according to the divinely willed world order. The king and his court poets composed the inscription with the apparent expectation that the audience should docilely accept the testimony and cooperate with the king in his rule over the community.[115] If Hammurapi's claim appeared farfetched to some of his hearers, the traditional metaphors and symbols in this narrative would by that fact have functioned well in provoking critical reflection on the source of royal authority in Babylon and Sippar. A tradition shaped by symbols directs one's attention beyond the individual to the communal dimensions of existence, and a tradition shaped by metaphoric truth cannot easily be harnessed to a political establishment because those who are well served by the establishment will find it legitimate, but those oppressed by it will find it illegitimate.[116] Metaphoric truth has an impact to the extent that it engages the experience of those hearing the metaphor.

Political theology was compromised when it failed to take seriously the figurative level of metaphoric truth and the polyvalence of symbols. If metaphors were literalized so that their "as if" structure was banished, then the hearers were being asked to accept, at face value and without question, statements in which the metaphors were embedded. If the polyvalence of symbols was ignored, members of a community were being asked to ignore diversity and individuality in favor of uniformity. A theology stripped of metaphoric and symbolic truth became an ideology in support of a particular social or political party.[117] If such an ideology was harnessed to a royal establishment with material and military resources, it could then have been used as propaganda to generate compliance to the ruling regime.

The traditional pattern for legitimating royal rule in Homeric Greece, bib-

---

114. Marc Van de Mieroop, *The Ancient Mesopotamian City* (Oxford: Clarendon, 1997), pp. 46-47, 73-76.

115. S. N. Kramer, "Kingship in Sumer and Akkad: The Ideal King," in *Le palais et la royauté*, ed. P. Garelli, RAI 19 (Paris: Paul Geuthner, 1974), pp. 163, 175; Johannes Renger, "River, Water Courses and Irrigation Ditches and Other Matters Concerning Irrigation Based on Old Babylonian Sources (2000-1600 B.C.)," *Bulletin on Sumerian Agriculture* 5 (1990): 32; Machinist, "Assyrians on Assyria in the First Millennium B.C.," p. 102.

116. Cohen, "Legitimacy, Illegitimacy, and State Formation," p. 81.

117. Frye, *Words with Power*, p. 31; Hart, *Northrup Frye*, p. 210. Terry Eagleton (*Ideology: An Introduction* [New York: Verso, 1991], p. 188) notes: "The relationship between myth and ideology is not easy to determine. Are myths the ideologies of pre-industrial societies, or ideologies the myths of industrial ones?" He notes further that ideologies tend to be more specific and pragmatic whereas myths address more metaphysical concerns.

lical Israel, and OB Mesopotamia traced out a cosmic structure of royal author-ity that resisted being co-opted by a particular regime. Inherent in the pattern was a call to just rule in accord with the ethical world order. The king who failed to do so forfeited the legitimacy of his rule and opened the way for his over-throw. How this pattern was worked out in the messiness of the politics and power struggles of a kingdom varied according to the circumstances of the time, but the pattern itself that testified to the belief that God or the gods ruled the cosmos survived. These ancient cultures did not locate the source of sover-eignty in the earthly sphere (e.g., in the will of the people, in the state, or any other abstract entity) but rather in the heavenly one.

CHAPTER TWO

The Speech and Action of Kings: The Process of Constructing a World with Royal Power

I n times of crisis, leaders are highly valued in a community. A famine, an impending invasion by an enemy, or corruption in the government are circumstances that call for leadership to inspire and guide collective action. The individuals who rise up to meet the challenge may actually not be invested with the traditional authority of an office. Their charisma and priorities may position them to engage the community and persuade the people to follow by their speech and actions. The activities of performing good deeds and speaking inspiring words lie at the heart of authority.[1] The drama of social interaction within a community highlights the relational context within which authority arises. In the midst of rivalries and tensions, the power of the community is enhanced or diminished, and its leaders are tested. The practical wisdom of a leader is manifested not only through timely actions but also through well-chosen words.

Authoritative Speech-Acts as Enactments of the Traditional Pattern for Legitimating Royal Authority

Our English word "myth" derives from the Greek word *mythos*, "an utterance, something spoken." In his study of the language used by the heroic figures of the *Iliad*, Richard P. Martin defines *mythos* in Homer as "a speech-act indicating authority, performed at length, usually in public, with a focus on full atten-

---

1. Hannah Arendt, *The Human Condition* (Chicago: University of Chicago Press, 1958), pp. 184-85.

tion to every detail."[2] Martin differentiates this speech-act from *epos*, the Greek word from which our term "epic" derives, by defining *epos* as "an utterance, ideally short, accompanying a physical act, and focusing on message, as perceived by the addressee, rather than on performance as enacted by the speaker."[3] *Mythos* finds its proper context in Homer in public gatherings where individuals express their views on the actions that the community should take. A *mythos* focuses on what a speaker says and how he says it; in contrast, an *epos* refers to what an addressee hears. A particular word or phrase can function as a *mythos* in one context and as an *epos* in another. For example, when Odysseus tried to forestall the retreat of the warriors who were his equals, he did so with words that Martin categorizes as *epos* (*Il.* 2.188-89).[4] But when he dealt with the commoner Thersites, he did so with threats, which are categorized as *mythos* (*Il.* 2.199-200). *Mythos* is an authoritative utterance that makes a claim on another, whereas *epos* does not say anything about power or authority. *Mythos* and *epos* overlap in their usage, but *mythos* has a narrower range of meaning.[5]

As a speech-act, *mythos* can bring to light the unfinished, dialogical context in which authority arises and is maintained. Authority is an essential shaping force that contributes to good order within a community; it is a relational reality rather than a "thing" that can be passed on from one individual to another.[6] The individual who rises up to make a speech in an assembly can be seen as making a *mythos* if his words command his audience to shape either their outlook or their actions.

John Searle, in his categorization of speech-acts, defines a declarative speech-act as one that aims "to bring about a change in the world by representing it as having been changed."[7] He offers the following examples of declarative speech-acts: "'I pronounce you man and wife,' 'War is hereby declared,' 'You are fired,' and 'I resign.'"[8] Even though an individual may have thought about getting married or resigning, these intentions take on reality within the public

2. Richard P. Martin, *The Language of Heroes: Speech and Performance in the* Iliad (Ithaca, N.Y.: Cornell University Press, 1989), p. 12.

3. Martin, *The Language of Heroes*, p. 12.

4. Martin, *The Language of Heroes*, p. 22.

5. Martin, *The Language of Heroes*, pp. 28-29.

6. Hannah Arendt, *Between Past and Future: Six Exercises in Political Thought* (New York: Viking, 1961), p. 124; John Hoffman, *Sovereignty* (Minneapolis: University of Minnesota Press, 1998), p. 107; Walter Donlan, "The Relations of Power in the Pre-State and Early State Polities," in *The Development of the "Polis" in Archaic Greece*, ed. L. Mitchell and P. Rhodes (New York: Routledge, 1997), pp. 40-41.

7. John R. Searle, *Mind, Language and Society: Philosophy in the Real World* (New York: Basic Books, 1998), p. 150.

8. Searle, *Mind, Language and Society*, p. 150.

world only when they are authoritatively spoken in public. This declarative category of speech-act highlights the creative potential of language; our worlds can be decisively shaped by the solemn pronouncements that we make. Yet it is important to note that these words do not have magical power; their power issues from and functions within the social and institutional contexts that authorize this speech-act.[9] Another related category of speech-act that constructs important dimensions of the world is a commissive speech-act: "a commitment by the speaker to undertake the course of action represented in the propositional content."[10] Vows and promises are examples. Commissive and declarative speech-acts reveal that our speech does not simply take the world as it is and promote conformity; our speech, in accord with the authority granted it in its social context, has the potential to renew, reform, and build the world.

Structures of authority that minimize alienation in a community are those that are regularly produced and reproduced and avoid reification.[11] Just as one knows the rules of grammar of the language one speaks, so also one knows the rules of social life. Just as one needs to speak a language in order to maintain it, so also one needs to practice the ways of a community in order to be a part of it. The community itself remains intact only through such repeated practices that embody the rules of its social life.[12] In the act of carrying out the practices that sustain a community, the members of the community are reproducing structures that are part of their lives and so are acting themselves into existence. This reproduction is a creative act if this action is carried out in attentiveness to what the relational structure of the hierarchy spanning heaven and earth allows.[13]

Searle identifies three other categories of speech-act that can shed light on the character of ancient political leaders and their actions: (1) assertive speech-acts, which aim "to commit the hearer to the truth of the proposition," for example, statements, classifications, and explanations; (2) directive speech-acts,

9. John B. Thompson, "Introduction," in Pierre Bourdieu, *Language and Symbolic Power,* ed. John B. Thompson (Cambridge, Mass.: Harvard University Press, 1991), pp. 8-10; Jürgen Habermas, "Comments on John Searle's 'Meaning, Communication, and Representation' (1998)," in *On the Pragmatics of Communication* (Cambridge, Mass.: MIT Press, 1998), p. 269; Claude Calame, *The Craft of Poetic Speech in Ancient Greece* (Ithaca: Cornell University Press, 1995), p. 10; Armin Burkhardt, "Speech act theory — the decline of a paradigm," in *Speech Acts, Meaning and Intentions: Critical Approaches to the Philosophy of John R. Searle,* ed. A. Burkhardt (New York: Walter de Gruyter, 1990), pp. 117-18.

10. Searle, *Mind, Language and Society,* p. 149.

11. Anthony Giddens, *The Constitution of Society: Outline of the Theory of Structuration* (Cambridge: Polity, 1984), pp. 17-19, 24.

12. Giddens, *The Constitution of Society,* p. 22; Roy Rappaport, *Ritual and Religion in the Making of Humanity* (Cambridge: Cambridge University Press, 1999), p. 123.

13. Cf. Mary Louise Pratt, "Ideology and Speech-Act Theory," *Poetics Today* 7 (1986): 71.

which "try to get the hearer to behave in such a way as to make his behavior match the propositional content of the directive," for example, orders or commands; and (3) expressive speech-acts, which aim "to express the sincerity condition of the speech-act," for example, apologies, congratulations, and welcomes.[14] These categories focus on the speaker-as-agent who makes choices in describing, shaping, and adapting to the world around him.

In Homeric Greece, biblical Israel, and OB Mesopotamia, the specific speech-acts of the king provide important occasions for the manifestation of the sovereign rule of the king of the gods over the realm as mapped out in the traditional pattern of royal authority. The creative power of the speech-act, particularly a promise or a declarative statement, indicates how an individual agent can have an impact on the world in spite of the many circumstances and forces to which an individual is subject. The creativity of such a speech-act occurs within the context of a community and its social practices. Its "magic" occurs within the context of conventions and routines that shape the structure of authority in the community.

Shaping the World through Royal Speech: Episodes from the *Iliad*, 1 Samuel, and Hammurapi's Clay-Nail Inscription

The ideal king was not only strong but also eloquent. Yet most kings struggled to find the right words in a particular set of circumstances.

In Homer's *Iliad*, Odysseus made a number of strategic interventions to prevent the Achaean coalition from disintegrating (*Il.* 2.284-332; 14.82-102). The heroic code among the Achaean warriors dictated that the warrior not only be an excellent fighter but also a skilled rhetorician.[15] Among the council of warrior-kings at the head of the coalition, Agamemnon, holding the position of *primus inter pares*, was the most deficient in rhetoric.[16] One of Agamemnon's initial blunders after his quarrel with Achilles was his speech in which he encouraged the Achaean forces to withdraw to their ships and make ready to return home. This speech was apparently an exercise in reverse psychology that failed miserably, for the Achaean forces took Agamemnon at his word and began a hasty retreat to their ships.[17] It was at this point that Odysseus, at the prompting of the

14. Searle, *Mind, Language and Society*, p. 148.

15. Martin, *The Language of Heroes*, p. 27; cf. Hans Van Wees, *Status Warriors: War, Violence and Society in Homer and History* (Amsterdam: J. C. Gieben, 1992), pp. 69, 110.

16. Martin, *The Language of Heroes*, p. 123.

17. James F. McGlew, "Royal Power and the Achaean Assembly at *Iliad* 2.84-393," *Classical Antiquity* 8 (1989): 283.

goddess Athena, stepped forward, took the scepter of Argos from Agamemnon, and began to round up the fleeing forces through persuasion and coercion:

> Whichever king or distinguished man he came upon, he would stand by him and try to hold him in check with gentle words: "Man, it is not fitting to alarm you as if you were a coward. But you yourself stay here and make the other people take a seat." . . . Again when he saw a man of the people and found him shouting, he would strike him with his staff and order him with an authoritative command *(mythos):* "Man, sit still and listen to the authoritative word of others who are more powerful than you. You are lacking in aggression and strength and are not to be counted either in battle or in counsel." (*Il.* 2.188-91, 198-202)

Through assertive and directive speech-acts, Odysseus succeeded in stopping the men in their flight. The mildness in the tone of his challenge toward those who were of equal rank to him points to Odysseus's sensitivity to his audience's reaction.[18] Martin notes that a distinguishing feature of Odysseus's rhetoric was his "positioning, the stance the hero takes toward his audience and his aptitude at varying this alignment."[19] Odysseus adapted to his audience and manifested a strong interest in the dynamics of communication.

After Odysseus silenced and shamed the commoner Thersites to the delight of the Achaean forces (*Il.* 2.270-77), he addressed a lengthy *mythos* (*Il.* 2.283) to the assembled Achaeans (*Il.* 2.283-332). He began by challenging their sense of honor when he said to Agamemnon:

> Now, son of Atreus, my lord, the Achaeans wish to make you the most dishonored of all mortals, for they will not complete the undertaking which they promised you when formerly they made their way here from Argos, the pastureland suitable for horses: that is, to return home only after having crossed into strongly walled Ilios. For like little children and widowed women, they sorrowfully cry out to each other about their longing to go back home. (*Il.* 2.284-88)

Martin categorizes these words as "flyting": i.e., a verbal contest in which opponents try to outdo one another, often by hurling "cutting words" at one another or words that will shame the opponent.[20] Odysseus appealed to the pride and

---

18. Kurt Raaflaub, "Politics and Interstate Relations in the World of the Early Greek *Poleis:* Homer and Beyond," *Antichthon* 31 (1997): 17; G. S. Kirk, *The Iliad: A Commentary,* vol 1: *Books 1-4* (Cambridge: Cambridge University Press, 1985), pp. 134-38.

19. Martin, *The Language of Heroes,* p. 120.

20. Martin, *The Language of Heroes,* pp. 68, 80; Van Wees, *Status Warriors,* pp. 62, 77, 158.

integrity of Agamemnon and the Achaeans by calling to mind the dissonance between the promise that they made at the start of the campaign and their current lack of resolve.[21]

As Odysseus continued his speech, he noted that they had been on this campaign against Troy for nine years (*Il.* 2.295). This act of memory was another key rhetorical action for the Achaean hero. Nestor and Achilles were far more accomplished in the rhetorical use of memory than other Achaean heroes (*Il.* 1.259-74; 20.184-99), yet Odysseus used it effectively here to demonstrate his sympathy with the plight of the Achaean forces when he asked them to recall an earlier prophecy, "But have patience, friends, and remain a while longer until we find out whether Calchas actually uttered a prophecy or not" (*Il.* 2.299-300).[22] This command provided a segue into an extended description of a sign of a snake at Aulis with an interpretive prophecy from Calchas. The bottom line of the prophet's message was his pronouncement that the Achaeans would conquer Troy in the tenth year of the campaign (*Il.* 2.301-29). So this elaborate *mythos* of Odysseus (*Il.* 2.283-322) included the three main types of *mythos* as categorized by Martin: command, flyting, and act of recall.[23] Although he was a powerful fighter, Odysseus distinguished himself much more by his skill in communicating than by his performance on the battlefield.[24]

Odysseus exercised authority when Agamemnon stumbled. This account of the initiative by a sceptered *basileus* other than the one who held sovereign authority through the scepter of Argos exemplified Homer's way of describing the dynamics of monarchical leadership: he created scenes in which the character of particular kings and the relationships among them raised questions about the viability of this form of leadership.[25] The Homeric narratives were composed either in performance or for the purpose of performance.[26] To engage an audience in the issues raised by its narrative was an important objective of these narrative poems that were authoritative statements of the values of an

---

21. Kirk, *The Iliad*, p. 146.

22. Martin, *The Language of Heroes*, pp. 106, 238; Kevin Crotty, *The Poetics of Supplication: Homer's Iliad and Odyssey* (Ithaca: Cornell University Press, 1994), pp. 72-74; Marcel Detienne, *The Creation of Mythology* (Chicago: University of Chicago Press, 1986), pp. 38-40.

23. Martin, *The Language of Heroes*, p. 120.

24. Martin, *The Language of Heroes*, p. 120; cf. Kirk, *The Iliad*, pp. 146, 151.

25. Peter Rose, *Sons of the Gods, Children of Earth: Ideology and Literary Form in Ancient Greece* (Ithaca, N.Y.: Cornell University Press, 1992), p. 41; Martin, *The Language of Heroes*, p. 238; cf. Kurt Raaflaub, "Influence, Adaptation, and Interaction: Near Eastern and Early Greek Political Thought," in *The Heirs of Assyria*, ed. S. Aro and R. Whiting (Helsinki: Neo-Assyrian Text Corpus Project, 2000), p. 59.

26. Egbert J. Bakker, *Poetry in Speech: Orality and Homeric Discourse* (Ithaca: Cornell University Press, 1997), p. 166.

emerging Panhellenic community.[27] The task of wrestling with perennially baffling issues is one that these epic poems share with the diverse yet interlocking collection of Greek myths.[28]

In the story of David's rise to power in ancient Israel (1 Sam. 16:14–2 Sam. 5:10), there is an account of a contest between David and a wealthy landowner in Judah bearing the name of Nabal (i.e., "Fool") — most likely a name given him by the narrator (1 Sam. 25).[29] The narrator sides immediately with David and conceals any rightful claims of Nabal against the encroachments of David and his men by dismissive *ad hominem* characterizations of Nabal: harsh and ungenerous (v. 3), mean and uncommunicative (v. 17), a worthless man and a fool (v. 25).

David and Nabal never communicated face-to-face. David gave a "directive" to his men that they were (1) to give greetings of peace to Nabal (an expressive speech-act), (2) to refer to the sheepshearing festival currently under way in Nabal's household (an assertive speech-act), and (3) to describe the protection that David's men had extended to Nabal's flocks (an assertive speech-act). These expressive and assertive speech-acts by David laid the groundwork for his main request: "Please give what you can to your servants and your son David" (v. 8). David's humble, ingratiating rhetoric was snubbed by Nabal who tried to turn his communication with David into a "flyting" contest from afar when he sarcastically replied to David's men:

> Who is David? Who is the son of Jesse? Currently there are many servants who break loose from their masters. Should I take my bread, my wine, my meat that I have prepared for my own shearers, and give them to men whom I do not know where they are from? (1 Sam. 25:10-11)

When David's men reported Nabal's reply to him, David simply gave them this directive: "Let everyone gird on his sword" (v. 13). Later in the narrative, David expressed his anger at Nabal's rebuff by saying:

---

27. Jean-Pierre Vernant, *Mortals and Immortals* (Princeton: Princeton University Press, 1990), p. 58; Ian Morris, *Archaeology as Cultural History* (Oxford: Blackwell, 2000), pp. 171-72; Van Wees, *Status Warriors*, pp. 40, 58; David Tandy, *Warriors into Traders: The Power of the Market in Early Greece* (Berkeley: University of California Press, 1997), pp. 149, 152; Kurt Raaflaub, "Homer to Solon: The Rise of the *Polis:* The Written Sources," in *The Ancient Greek City-State: Symposium on the Occasion of the 250th Anniversary of the Royal Danish Academy of Sciences and Letters, July 1-4, 1992,* ed. M. H. Hansen (Copenhagen: Munksgaard, 1993), pp. 44-45.

28. Richard Buxton, *Imaginary Greece* (Cambridge: Cambridge University Press, 1994), p. 213.

29. Steven McKenzie, *King David: A Biography* (New York: Oxford, 2000), p. 100; Baruch Halpern, *David's Secret Demons: Messiah, Murderer, Traitor, King* (Grand Rapids: Eerdmans, 2001), p. 22.

So it was for nothing that I guarded all that belongs to this man in the wilderness, for nothing was missing of all that belongs to him. He has given me evil in return for good. May God do so and even more to David,[30] if in the morning I allow a male to remain among all those who belong to him. (vv. 21-22)

The oath or self-curse that David pronounced was a strong "commissive" that committed David and his men to a specific course of action, unless equally strong speech-acts were brought forward to counteract David's oath.[31]

From Nabal's perspective, David was an outlaw who was running a protection racket. Nabal did not ask David and his men to protect his flocks. Yet now, since no outsider or any of David's men had taken anything from Nabal's flocks, David expected payment for the protection services he provided.[32] Nabal's attitude may reflect that of many landowners throughout Judah's history who chafed under the burden of taxation in times of peace when the king and his army offered protection even though there was no threat to the landowners' security. A subtext to this pro-Davidic account in 1 Samuel 25 may well have been a protest against royal taxation.[33]

Not only the testimony of one of Nabal's servants who was favorable to David and critical of Nabal (vv. 14-16) but also the placating actions and words of Nabal's wife Abigail (vv. 18-19, 24-31) revealed a division within Nabal's household and suggested the imminent defection of key members to David's side. The servant warned Abigail that harm would come to their household if they did not recognize and honor the strength of David and his men (v. 16). So, Abigail gathered together abundant provisions to offer to David, but even more importantly, upon meeting David, she did obeisance to him (v. 23) and proceeded in her subsequent lengthy speech to shame Nabal and honor David with the prediction that the Lord would establish an everlasting dynasty for him (vv. 25-28). Abigail's speech and actions took on he-

---

30. Read *lĕdāwid* with LXX.

31. Jon Levenson, "1 Samuel 25 as Literature and History," *CBQ* 40 (1978): 19-20. On the significance of an oath in a tribal or segmented society for giving force to assertions, see Christoph Auffahrt, *Der drohende Untergang: "Schöpfung" in Mythos und Ritual im Alten Orient und in Griechenland am Beispiel der Odysee und des Ezechielbuches,* Religionsgeschichtliche Versüche und Vorarbeiten 39 (New York: Walter de Gruyter, 1991), p. 370.

32. Halpern, *David's Secret Demons,* pp. 22, 284; Walter Brueggemann, *First and Second Samuel* (Louisville: John Knox, 1990), p. 176.

33. Frank Crüsemann, *Der Widerstand gegen das Königtum,* WMANT 49 (Neukirchen-Vluyn: Neukirchener Verlag, 1978), p. 142; Baruch Halpern, "The Uneasy Compromise," in *Traditions in Transformation,* ed. B. Halpern and J. Levenson (Winona Lake, Ind.: Eisenbrauns, 1981), p. 79; Neils Lemche, "David's Rise," *JSOT* 10 (1978): 12.

roic proportions as she rescued her household from annihilation at the hands of David and his men.[34]

In this narrative episode of David's encounter with Nabal, direct speech by heroic characters (including assertive, directive, commissive, and expressive speech-acts) was a key factor in reshaping the landscape of authority in Judah. David's charisma and skill as a warrior and military leader were new realities in Judah that Nabal refused to recognize. Through the ensuing verbal contest and marshaling of forces, a resolution was reached that shifted the power of Nabal's household to that of David. Within this pro-Davidic edition of the story, Abigail's words that David's rise to power had been decreed by the Lord were instrumental in articulating and conferring legitimacy on this shift of power from Nabal to David.[35] Even though this narrative is not a dictation of speech-acts delivered in the Judaean desert in the early tenth century B.C., it is conceivable that verbal exchanges like this could have occurred. In this narrative that became part of the biblical tradition, it is clear that the speech of these characters was not idle; their assertive, expressive, and declarative speech-acts reshaped the world of which they were a part.

When Hammurapi (1792-1750 B.C.), the sixth king of the First Dynasty of Babylon (1894-1595 B.C.), built a wall in the city of Sippar, he followed the example of earlier Mesopotamian kings by proclaiming his accomplishment in a first-person narrative, which was preserved in the form of an inscription on a clay-nail inserted in the wall.[36] The straightforward simplicity of the narrative and the relevance of the message for Hammurapi's contemporaries are elements that strongly suggest that this written message was also communicated orally.[37] Whether in a dedication ceremony or another ritual occasion, this

---

34. Levenson, "1 Samuel 25 as Literature and History," pp. 17-20; P. Kyle McCarter, Jr., *I Samuel*, AB 8 (Garden City, N.Y.: Doubleday, 1980), p. 401. Halpern (*David's Secret Demons*, p. 77) offers another perspective on Abigail's heroism by speculating that she might have been David's sister and that this story might conceal a plot where Abigail murdered Nabal; see also McKenzie, *King David*, p. 100.

35. Levenson, "1 Samuel 25 as Literature and History," pp. 19-20; McCarter, *I Samuel*, pp. 401-2.

36. I. J. Gelb, "A New Clay Nail of Hammurapi," *JNES* 7 (1948): 267-71. Rivkah Harris (*Ancient Sippar: A Demographic Study of an Old-Babylonian City (1894-1595 B.C.)* [Istanbul: Nederlands Historisch-Archaeologisch Instituut te Istanbul, 1975], p. 7) notes that Hammurapi was repeatedly concerned about the wall of Sippar, for his twenty-third, twenty-fifth, and forty-third year-dates announce rebuilding the wall of Sippar.

37. Cf. Irene Winter, "Royal Rhetoric and the Development of Historical Narrative in Neo-Assyrian Reliefs," *Studies in Visual Communication* 7 (1981): 12-13; Peter Machinist, "Assyrians on Assyria in the First Millennium B.C.," in *Anfänge politischen Denkens in der Antike: Die nahöstlichen Kulturen und die Griechen*, ed. Kurt Raaflaub and Elisabeth Müller-Luckner

message must have been read to the populaces of Sippar and Babylon in order to persuade them to accept Hammurapi as a traditional, legitimate ruler in their cities. The inscription in cuneiform, which could be read by few outside the scribal class, carried an aura of timeless wisdom. Its encrypted message was regarded as one destined to be read by the gods and future generations.[38]

The first-person speech of the inscription would lend itself to oral proclamation.[39] This practice of composing a royal inscription in the first person was characteristic of second-millennium inscriptions, whereas the third person was dominant in the inscriptions of the third millennium. Naram-Sin (2254-2218 B.C.) was the first king to compose an inscription entirely in the first person.[40] Despite the conventional and formulaic character of much of the language of a royal inscription, the first-person speech creates the impression that one is listening to the voice of Hammurapi:

> When Shamash, the great lord of heaven and earth, the king of the gods, looked joyfully on me, Hammurapi, the prince, his favorite, with his shining face, and bestowed upon me an enduring kingship, a reign of long days [lines 1-12], (and) made firm for me, the foundation of the land which he gave me to rule (and) commanded (me with his holy decree, which does not change, to make the people of Sippar and Babylon dwell in a peaceful dwelling, (and) ordered me in a great way to build the wall of Sippar (and) to raise its top [lines 13-27], at that time, I, Hammurapi, the strong king, the king of Babylon, the pious one, the one who obeys Shamash, the beloved of Aja, who delights the heart of Marduk, his lord [lines 28-35], with the extraordinary strength which Shamash gave me, with a levy of the people of my land, raised up the tops of the foundations of the wall of Sippar with dirt like a great mountain [lines 36-44]. Indeed, I built an outstanding wall. What no king

---

(Munich: Oldenbourg, 1993), pp. 98-99; Jean Goodnick Westenholz, "Oral Traditions and Written Texts in the Cycle of Akkad," in *Mesopotamian Epic Literature: Oral or Aural?* ed. M. Vogelzang and H. Vanstiphout (Lewiston, N.Y.: Mellen, 1992), pp. 126, 138-41.

38. H. Vanstiphout, "Memory and Literacy in Ancient Western Asia," in *Civilizations of the Ancient Near East,* ed. J. Sasson (New York: Scribner, 1995), p. 2192; Peter Machinist, "On Self-Consciousness in Mesopotamia," in *The Origins and Diversity of Axial Age Civilizations,* ed. Shmuel N. Eisenstadt (Albany, N.Y.: SUNY Press, 1986), p. 193; Joan Goodnick Westenholz, "Thoughts on Esoteric Knowledge and Secret Lore," in *Intellectual Life of the Ancient Near East,* ed. Jiří Prosecký, CRRA 43 (Prague: Oriental Institute, 1998), p. 456; A. Kirk Grayson, "Assyria and Babylonia," *Or* 49 (1980): 163-64.

39. Grayson, "Assyria and Babylonia," p. 150.

40. Westenholz, "Oral Traditions and Written Texts," p. 137; Sabina Franke, *Königsinschriften und Königsideologie: Die Könige von Akkade zwischen Tradition und Neuerung* (Münster: LIT, 1995), p. 190.

among the kings had built since ancient times, I built magnificently for Shamash, my lord. The name of the wall is: "Through the command of Shamash, may Hammurapi have no enemies" [lines 45-55].[41]

Yet this voice of Hammurapi comes alive only when a reader recites the script; the inscribed tablet itself is voiceless. So Hammurapi's "I" or ego is recognized only through the voice of the reader. The script of the inscription serves as a sign pointing to Hammurapi and his accomplishment, but this script requires a reader or decoder of the signs.[42]

In the initial fifty-five lines of a total of eighty-one lines in the inscription, Hammurapi declared that he had carried out the commission given him by Shamash to build the wall of Sippar. The first part of the opening temporal clause in lines 1-12 relates the divine election of Hammurapi to the kingship of the land as a prerequisite to the construction of the wall, but yet as an event contemporaneous with its construction.[43] Both Shamash and Hammurapi are identified by titles and epithets. The second part of the temporal clause in lines 13-27 focuses on the commission to build the wall. The first part of the main clause in lines 28-35 further identifies Hammurapi with titles and epithets. Lines 36-44 describe the actual construction of the wall. In lines 45-55, Hammurapi boasts of his accomplishment and names the wall with a name that takes the form of a petition or prayer.[44] The structure of the inscription with an opening temporal clause, including the king's commission, followed by a description of his accomplishment is a form distinctive of the OB period.[45] The formulaic language of the inscription — particularly, the titles and epithets associated with the gods and the king — shows that the king was appealing to the traditions of Sippar and Babylon.[46] Hammurapi accented the greatness of his accomplishment of building the wall of Sippar, a concrete fact that he proclaimed as testimony to his divine election to the kingship, through the claim

41. Douglas Frayne, *RIME 4*, E4.3.6.2, lines 1-55.

42. See the discussion of the role of the reader of Greek inscriptions of the eighth to fifth centuries B.C. in Jesper Svenbro, *Phrasikleia: An Anthropology of Reading in Ancient Greece* (Ithaca: Cornell University Press, 1993), pp. 16-18, 41-42, 51.

43. Cf. Tikva Zadok, "The Distribution of the Temporal Sentences in the Old Babylonian Royal Inscriptions," *JANES* 24 (1996): 111, 118.

44. Victor Hurowitz ("Literary Structures in Samsuiluna A," *JCS* 36 [1984]: 203-4) identifies this sentence, which names the wall, as the center of a chiastic structure shaping the whole inscription.

45. Grayson, "Assyria and Babylonia," pp. 160-61.

46. Harris, *Ancient Sippar*, pp. 144-47; F. R. Kraus, *The Role of Temples from the Third Dynasty of Ur to the First Dynasty of Babylon*, Monographs on the Ancient Near East, vol. 2, fasc. 4 (Malibu, Calif.: Undena, 1990), p. 11; Hurowitz, "Literary Structures in Samsuilina A," p. 204.

— even though this language was formulaic — that he surpassed all his prede-cessors.[47]

Located about thirty miles north of Babylon at the northernmost reaches of lower Mesopotamia, the city of Sippar regarded its protector deity, the sun god Shamash, as the king of the gods.[48] Sippar seems to have been far enough north of Nippur to have maintained a measure of religious independence from the influence of the Ur III dynasty (2112-2004 B.C.) whose neo-Sumerian revival honored Enlil as the king of the gods and his city of Nippur as a religious center in southern Mesopotamia (i.e., Sumer).[49] In most of Hammurapi's inscrip-tions, he honored Enlil as the king of the gods, but this inscription from Sippar indicated that he was also able to respect the traditions of Sippar where Shamash was revered as the king of the gods.

The pronouncement that Shamash had commissioned Hammurapi does not state the manner in which such a message was communicated. Since there is no mention of a prophet or diviner, the inscription gives the impression that the king himself could have received direct communication from the gods.

How Hammurapi's actions were received and interpreted by the people of Sippar is difficult to decipher. In the inscription, Hammurapi claimed: "I re-moved the people of Sippar . . . from forced labor for Shamash."[50] If this libera-tion occurred at the expense of the temple establishment of Shamash, Hammurapi most likely would have strained relations with the temple person-nel by this action.[51] Later in the inscription, Hammurapi stated: "I established joy for the people of Sippar. Truly they pray for my life. . . . I established in the mouth of the people the daily recalling of my good name like a god, a custom which shall never be forgotten."[52] This statement about the practice of praying for Hammurapi does not seem to be simply an assertion that described what Hammurapi believed to be true; it also seems to have carried a directive to the people and the temple personnel in Sippar to pray daily for Hammurapi. The inscription gives the impression that the expectation to practice such prayer

47. Joan Goodnick Westenholz, *Legends of the Kings of Akkade* (Winona Lake, Ind.: Eisenbrauns, 1997), p. 264.

48. A. L. Oppenheim, *Ancient Mesopotamia: Portrait of a Dead Civilization* (Chicago: University of Chicago Press, 1977), pp. 195-96, 415; Harris, *Ancient Sippar*, pp. 144, 149.

49. Cf. W. W. Hallo, *Origins* (Leiden: Brill, 1996), p. 279; Oppenheim, *Ancient Mesopotamia*, p. 411; Piotr Steinkeller, "The Administrative and Economic Organization of the Ur III State: The Core and the Periphery," in *The Organization of Power: Aspects of Bureaucracy in the Ancient Near East*, 2nd ed., ed. M. Gibson and R. D. Biggs, Studies in Ancient Oriental Civilization 46 (Chicago: Oriental Institute, 1991), p. 23.

50. Frayne, *RIME 4*, E4.3.6.2, lines 58-59, 61.

51. Harris, *Ancient Sippar*, pp. 39-40.

52. Frayne, *RIME 4*, E4.3.6.2, lines 68-71, 74-81.

would not have been open to debate, for Hammurapi had authoritatively declared it. However, if there had been no communal consent in Sippar to such a practice, the people would hardly have felt guilty in lapsing from it.

Kings, invested with positions of authority in a community, were expected to give commands and issue decrees that would enable the community to act collectively. Hammurapi celebrated his success in wielding such authority in the construction of the wall of Sippar. Odysseus brought his rhetorical skill to the rescue of the Achaean coalition when Agamemnon failed to issue effective decrees although invested with the traditional authority of the scepter of Argos and the expectation of the Achaeans that they were to follow his lead. In his confrontation with Nabal, David was not yet the king of Judah or of Israel. He was compelled to threaten the use of force to get his commands obeyed. Authoritative speech-acts in the form of commands, assertions, and commissives functioned within these three diverse episodes from Homeric Greece, biblical Israel, and OB Mesopotamia to create royal authority. In order to exercise power legitimately, kings had to explain on the basis of the community's traditions how they had come to be leaders whose commands, declarations, and promises were bound up in the relational fabric of the community. They were not idle words spoken out of context.

The Royal Household as the Socioeconomic Basis of a King's Power

Imperative statements call for action and depend for their persuasiveness on the prestige of the one who utters them. The effectiveness and creativity of the king's speech-acts depend, in part, on the material basis of his power that is anchored in the royal household.

The picture of Odysseus in chapter 2 of the *Iliad* as a sceptered *basileus* among several other such royal figures from Greece who form a coalition to conduct a military campaign against the city of Troy in Asia Minor was the product of generations of storytelling by bards in the first half of the first millennium B.C.[53] It appears that "Homer" was a fictional poet who represents in anthropomorphic guise the tradition contained in the *Iliad* and the *Odyssey*;[54]

---

53. Gregory Nagy, *Homeric Questions* (Austin: University of Texas Press, 1996), pp. 108-111; idem, "An Evolutionary Model for the Making of Homeric Poetry," in *The Ages of Homer*, ed. Jane Carter and Sarah Morris (Austin: University of Texas, 1995), pp. 163-79.

54. Nagy, *Homeric Questions*, pp. 89-92; John Miles Foley, "Individual Poet and Epic Tradition: Homer as Legendary Singer," *Arethusa* 31 (1998): 152; Richard Seaford, *Reciprocity and Ritual: Homer and Tragedy in the Developing City-State* (Oxford: Clarendon, 1994), pp. 150-53.

in other words, "Homer" is another name for the oral tradition that produced the *Iliad* and the *Odyssey*. The Greek tradition situated the Trojan War in the thirteenth or twelfth century B.C.; Herodotus calculated the date around 1143 B.C.[55] The Homeric epics as we know them were achieving a more fixed form during the eighth to sixth centuries B.C.[56] So, the picture of Odysseus (and the other sceptered Achaean kings) purports in the first instance to be that of a Mycenaean king but reflects a royal figure influenced by the stories of Greek kings from the late Mycenaean through the Dark Age (1075-700 B.C.) into the Archaic Age (700-480 B.C.).[57] Such a traditional figure of a sceptered *basileus* would seem to have engaged a Greek audience in the city-states of the Archaic Age to imagine how a king might exercise authority, and so to have caused them to reflect on perennial issues regarding good political leadership.[58]

Kingship as an institution was sidelined in the city-states of Archaic Greece.[59] If the *basileus* still held office in a city-state, he ruled in conjunction

55. Walter Burkert, "Lydia Between East and West or How to Date the Trojan War: A Study in Herodotus," in *The Ages of Homer*, ed. Jane Carter and Sarah Morris (Austin: University of Texas Press, 1995), p. 142.

56. Nagy, *Homeric Questions*, pp. 110-11; Seaford, *Reciprocity and Ritual*, pp. 150-53.

57. The debate over the historical character of Homeric society in the epics turns on two questions: (1) Does the society reflected in the epics consist of a set of institutions and values that could realistically function? (2) If so, does this Homeric society reflect that of a particular time in Dark Age (1075-700 B.C.) or Archaic Age (700-480 B.C.) Greece? Three main positions have emerged: (1) Homeric society is realistic and reflects that of the tenth and ninth centuries B.C. (M. I. Finley, *The World of Odysseus* [New York: Viking, 1965], p. 48); (2) Homeric society is realistic and reflects that of the late ninth and early eighth century B.C. (Raaflaub, "Homer to Solon," pp. 45, 79); (3) Homeric society is an imaginative creation by the oral poet Homer shaped from traditional elements but reflecting no historical Greek society as such (Anthony Snodgrass, *Dark Age of Greece* [Edinburgh: Edinburgh University Press, 1971], pp. 389-95). For a summary of these scholarly positions, see Kurt Raaflaub, "A Historian's Headache: How to Read 'Homeric Society'?" in *Archaic Greece: New Approaches and New Evidence*, ed. N. Fisher and H. Van Wees (London: Duckworth, 1998), pp. 171-77. For the purposes of this study, which aims to present the views of the Homeric tradition and its vision of royal leadership in comparison with those of the Israelite and Old Babylonian traditions, it is not necessary to side with any one of the three positions outlined above. Such an outline helps to identify possible social and institutional contexts from which the epics emerged.

58. Pierre Carlier, *La royauté en Grèce avant Alexandre* (Strasbourg: AECR, 1984), pp. 195-201.

59. Donlan, "The Relations of Power," 44; Chester G. Starr, "The Decline of the Early Greek Kings," *Historia* 10 (1961): 129-30; John Halverson, "The Succession Issue in the *Odyssey*," *Greece and Rome* 33 (1986): 119, 126. A number of scholars do not see the *basileus* of the Dark Age as "a king" in the full sense of the term (e.g., Raaflaub, "Homer to Solon," pp. 45, 79; A. G. Geddes, "Who's Who in 'Homeric Society'?" *Classical Quarterly* 34 [1984]: 28, 36). So, Robert Drews (*Basileus: The Evidence for Kingship in Geometric Greece* [New Haven: Yale University Press,

with the heads of powerful households such that real decision-making power resided in a council of such leading men. Then, in the latter part of the sixth century B.C., it resided in the hands of tyrants.[60] So, oligarchy and then tyranny replaced monarchy as the dominant form of government in Greek communities as the *polis*[61] was emerging as a new form of political organization over the course of the Archaic Age.[62] In the fifth century B.C., in response to the rule of the tyrants, a new understanding of the status and rights of the members of the community developed: the male property holders were regarded as equals before the law *(isonomia)*. Such a view was integral to the growing authority of the popular assembly of the democratic Greek city-state of the fifth and fourth centuries B.C.[63]

Kingship in the Homeric epics exhibits a low level of institutionalization — so much so that some would argue that there really were no kings in Greece in the Dark Age or Archaic Age.[64] In the Homeric epics, there is no royal bureau-

---

1983], pp. 108-9) argues that power of the *basileus* in the Archaic Age increased over that of the *basileus* in the preceding Dark Age.

60. William M. Sale, "The Government of Troy: Politics in the *Iliad*," *Greek, Roman and Byzantine Studies* 35 (1994): 9-12; Donlan, "The Relations of Power," pp. 44-47; William G. Thalmann, *The Swineherd and the Bow: Representations of Class in the Odyssey* (Ithaca: Cornell University Press, 1998), p. 275; Rose, *Sons of the Gods, Children of Earth*, pp. 90, 102, 119.

61. With respect to the use of the term *polis*, John K. Davies ("The Origins of the Greek *Polis*: Where Should We Be Looking," in *The Development of the "Polis" in Archaic Greece*, ed. L. Mitchell and P. Rhodes [New York: Routledge, 1997], pp. 26-27) cautions that a *polis* should not be conceived according to a single model of city-state government and proposes that the term "microstate" is less likely to implant in the investigator's imagination a preconceived model of government.

62. Raaflaub ("Homer to Solon," pp. 45, 79) claims that the terms "king," "kingship," and "monarchy" should not be used to describe Homeric society since these roles and institutions did not exist in the ninth and eighth centuries B.C. This view, in my opinion, does not adequately take into account the fact that the position of *basileus* at this time was in a state of transition and not fully institutionalized, and so the outlines of this position were blurred. Dean Hammer ("The Politics of the *Iliad*," *Classical Journal* 94 [1998]: 8) explains how a structural-functional anthropology does not do justice to the political processes in the Achaean community with its low level of institutionalization. Carlier (*La royauté en Grèce avant Alexandre*, p. 145) argues that the vocabulary and data justify interpreting *basileus* as "king." The blurring of the outlines of the picture of a "king" does not mean that the position of the "king" was absent, but rather that it was under stress and countered by alternative models of leadership.

63. Moses I. Finley, *The Legacy of Greece* (Oxford: Clarendon, 1981), pp. 11, 22, 27; Paul Cartledge, "Power and the State," in *Ancient Greece*, ed. P. Cartledge (Cambridge: Cambridge University Press, 1998), p. 147.

64. Sale ("The Government of Troy," pp. 41, 50-51) identifies the *basileus* as an exclusive or superior leader, but he does not see this term as designating a permanent office within an institutional framework; see also Halverson, "The Succession Issue in the *Odyssey*," pp. 124-25. Wal-

cracy. The archaeological and textual evidence for the late Mycenaean Age testifies to a palace with a royal bureaucracy,[65] but such evidence is absent from Dark Age remains — except perhaps for some hints from recent excavations at Lefkandi.[66] Homeric kings did not tax the people within their kingdoms.[67] If a king was to have sufficient wealth to support his retainers and servants, he had to gain it through agricultural surplus (*Od.* 14.96-99) or through booty from war (*Il.* 1.366-68) or from gift exchange with other wealthy individuals (*Od.* 4.587-92; 11.355-61).[68] Reciprocity was the principle that best describes how redistribution of goods occurred in the Dark Age and into the eighth century B.C.: the people gave goods to the *basileus,* and he returned services or goods to them.[69]

The Homeric *basileus* who emerged as the leader of the kingdom can be seen as a *primus inter pares.*[70] In the late eighth century B.C., with increasing amounts of wealth entering Greek cities through growing commercial activities, the social structure in many Greek cities was shifting such that identification of an individual as an aristocrat was beginning to be grounded in the amount of wealth one possessed rather than on one's birth into this status.[71] The Homeric epics try to mask this shift by praising traditional practices of gift exchange and denigrating the trader as akin to a pirate.[72] If the most powerful *basileus* did not have an institutionalized means for getting his share of this new wealth (i.e., taxation), then he would need to be involved in the commercial activities to maintain the preeminence of his household in terms of the amount of wealth it held vis-à-vis other households in the community. If other *basilées* had more wealth,

---

ter Donlan (*The Aristocratic Ideal in Ancient Greece: Attitude of Superiority from Homer to the End of the Fifth Century B.C.* [Lawrence, Kan.: Coronado, 1980], pp. 8-9, 13-14) argues that the leading *basileus* is a chief. Raaflaub ("Homer to Solon," pp. 45, 79) argues that the term *basileus* in Homer should not be translated as "king." Geddes ("Who's Who in 'Homeric Society'?" p. 36) goes even further to claim that Homeric kingship is a literary fiction and does not reflect the social structure of any period of Greek history.

65. M. I. Finley, "Homer and Mycenae: Property and Tenure," in *The Language and Background of Homer,* ed. G. S. Kirk (Cambridge: Heffer & Sons, 1964), p. 193.

66. Morris, *Archaeology as Cultural History,* pp. 219, 228, 232.

67. Walter Donlan, "Reciprocities in Homer," *Classical World* 75 (1982): 166.

68. Finley, *The World of Odysseus,* pp. 60-62.

69. Tandy, *Warriors into Traders,* p. 101. Walter Donlan ("The Social Groups of Dark Age Greece," *Classical Philology* 80 [1985]: 304) categorizes this redistributing *basileus* as a "chief."

70. Carlier (*La royauté en Grèce avant Alexandre,* pp. 144-45, 187) rejects this position and claims that the Homeric *basileus* was a king in the full sense of the term.

71. Tandy, *Warriors into Traders,* p. 125; Morris, *Archaeology as Cultural History,* pp. 259-60; cf. Lin Foxhall, "Cargoes of the Heart's Desire: The Character of Trade in the Archaic Mediterranean World," in *Archaic Greece: New Approaches and New Evidence,* ed. Nick Fisher and Hans van Wees (London: Duckworth, 1998), p. 305.

72. Tandy, *Warriors into Traders,* p. 125.

they would have had more leverage within the community and could have displaced him. How long could the traditional basis of the authority of the *basileus* keep him in power? Were the community's values and worldview changing to the extent that the traditional language legitimating the kingship no longer resonated with them? It seems that competition among the *basilées* intensified in the late eighth century B.C. when the traditional basis of the authority of the preeminent *basileus* was eroded. Agamemnon's concern over having his share of the spoils may be a reflection of this anxiety of a late-eighth-century "king" over economic and social forces that were undermining his position.[73]

The aristocratic household was the locus from which kingship arose in Homer.[74] The dynamics of power within a royal household and a community of aristocratic households is the topic of the *Odyssey,* where the community of Ithaca acted in the extended absence of its king Odysseus.[75] The swineherd Eumaeus, who belonged to the household of Odysseus, recounted the extent of Odysseus's holdings prior to his departure for Troy:

> For sure, his livelihood was immense. No other warrior either on the dark mainland or on Ithaca itself possessed so much. Not even twenty men together had so much wealth. (*Od.* 14.96-99)

Yet Odysseus's son Telemachus did not possess the necessary strength or skills to secure his hold on the kingship over against his aristocratic rivals who were vying for the right to marry Penelope, the wife of Odysseus. His rivals were identified as *basilées* (*Od.* 18.64-65). The king in Ithaca was also a *basileus* (*Od.* 1.386-87), but he had the distinction of holding the position of "first among equals" (*Od.* 1.390-98).[76] In order to gain this position, the king-to-be had to be able to rule "by might" (*iphi, Od.* 11.284; 17.443): that is, he had to be able to get his commands obeyed (*Od.* 18.52-57, 145-56).[77] Telemachus was uncertain if he could rise to the occasion and take hold of the kingship:

---

73. Tandy, *Warriors into Traders,* p. 230; Rose, *Sons of the Gods, Children of Earth,* pp. 77-79.

74. A. H. W. Adkins, *Merit and Responsibility: A Study in Greek Values* (Oxford: Clarendon, 1960), p. 55; Seaford, *Reciprocity and Ritual,* pp. 12-13; Donlan, *The Aristocratic Ideal in Ancient Greece,* pp. 8-9, 13-14.

75. Finley, *The World of Odysseus,* p. 132; Donlan, "Reciprocities in Homer," pp. 166-167; Van Wees, *Status Warriors,* pp. 52-54.

76. Naoko Yamagata, "*Anax* and *Basileus* in Homer," *Classical Quarterly* 47 (1997): 11.

77. Finley, *The World of Odysseus,* p. 85; F. Geschnitzer, "*Basileus:* Ein terminologischer Beitrag zur Frühgeschichte des Königtums bei den Griechen," in *Festschrift Leonard C. Franz zum 70. Geburtstag,* ed. O. Menghin and H. Oberg, Innsbrucker Beiträge zur Kulturwissenschaft 11 (Innsbruck: Auslieferung durch das Sprachwissenschaftliche Institut des Leopold-Franzens-Universität, 1965), pp. 104, 108; Geddes, "Who's Who in 'Homeric Society'?" p. 28.

If Zeus bestows it [the kingship], I would like to accept it. Do you think this is the worst thing that could happen among humans? To be a king is not a bad thing. Quickly his house becomes rich, and he himself becomes more highly esteemed. But surely there are many other Achaean nobles *(basilēes)* in sea-girt Ithaca, both young and old, who could hold this office since illustrious Odysseus is dead. But I will be lord of my own household and of the slaves whom illustrious Odysseus captured for me as prisoners of war. (*Od.* 1.390-98)

The story of the *Odyssey* suggests that the suitor who gained the hand of Penelope in marriage would be in a stronger position against his other rivals to gain the kingship of Ithaca (*Od.* 2.125-28).[78] In the context of the competition among the suitors, Penelope symbolized the wealth and status of Odysseus.[79] The suitor whom she selected as her next husband was expected to be the next king in Ithaca.

Odysseus, depicted in chapter 2 of the *Iliad* in his role of regathering the fleeing Achaean forces, wielded authority because of his personal qualities, the wealth at his disposal, and the traditional position of kingship that he held in Ithaca. When Odysseus began to marshal the Achaean forces, he took the scepter of Argos from Agamemnon, the leader of the coalition or the *primus inter pares* of sceptered *basilēes* (*Il.* 2.185-87).[80] Because Agamemnon was undercutting the coalition by his blunders as leader, Odysseus stepped forward to exercise the authority that the holder of the scepter of Argos ought to have exercised within the coalition. Agamemnon's leadership of the coalition could not have rested only on the fact that he had brought the greater number of ships and soldiers to the campaign (*Il.* 2.203-6). The material requirements for assuming this leadership position were indispensable (*Il.* 2.576-80) and perhaps would have struck Greek audiences of the eighth to the sixth centuries as increasingly important; nevertheless, they did not constitute a sufficient means for Agamemnon to counter the centrifugal forces that threatened to fragment the coalition (*Il.* 1.118-87). He needed to demonstrate excellence both as a rhetorician and as a warrior.[81] Such

78. Donlan, "Reciprocities in Homer," p. 147. Carlier (*La royauté en Grèce avant Alexandre,* p. 207) maintains that the prestige gained through marriage to Penelope and the power as head of Odysseus's household was a primary goal of the competing suitors.

79. Thalmann, *The Swineherd and the Bow,* pp. 263-64; cf. Ian Morris, "The Use and Abuse of Homer," *Classical Antiquity* 5 (1986): 109-10.

80. Carlier (*La royauté en Grèce avant Alexandre,* pp. 192-93) notes that a direct, simple meaning of the scepter is that of an instrument of constraint, but the scepter of Argos was given by the gods and so carried the weight of divinely bestowed authority. See also Tandy, *Warriors into Traders,* p. 107.

81. Martin (*The Language of Heroes,* p. 62) notes that Agamemnon is the weakest rhetorician of the Achaean kings.

actions would engage the minds and wills of the Achaeans so as to create vision and momentum for the Achaeans to undertake their battle against Troy.

The weak leadership of Agamemnon paved the way for the interventions of Odysseus and other sceptered *basilēes* of the council of kings, such as Nestor (*Il.* 9.95-113) and Diomedes (9:30-49). If the *Iliad* was performed for an audience in a city-state ruled by an oligarchy, the interactions of the sceptered *basilēes* would probably have raised important questions for the ways that their leaders exercised power and responded to the needs of the city-state.[82] The Homeric epics reveal an affinity for monarchy as a form of government, but do so in a way that encourages criticism of particular kings.[83] The low level of institutionalization of the kingship may well reflect the historical situation in the tenth to the early eighth centuries B.C. in Greece, but such a low level of institutionalization may also have been furthered by the composition of the epics as they were performed for audiences throughout Greece from the eighth to sixth centuries B.C. — audiences who lived in city-states that were usually ruled by oligarchies.[84] The more pressing current issues of power and authority, sparked by an infusion of new commercial wealth, raised questions about decision making by a council of leaders that Homer perhaps felt could be framed more clearly by embedding such oligarchic practices within an institutional arrangement where monarchy was normative because of its traditional status so that the relative merits of oligarchy and monarchy could emerge through the narrative.[85] The political reflection provoked by the performance of the epics would also have been important for the Panhellenic gatherings at Athens in the sixth century B.C. that aimed to cultivate a cultural unity among the Greeks.[86]

The picture of David sketched out in the story of Nabal in 1 Samuel 25 is the product of storytellers in Judah and of writers from the Davidic court in Jerusalem. In its final form within the longer story of David's rise to power (1 Sam. 16:14–2 Sam. 5:10), this account of David's confrontation with Nabal bears an unmistakable pro-Davidic bias.[87] The final form of the narrative tries to make its case that taxes for military expenditures in peacetime were legitimate. After all, the wife and servants of Nabal deserted him when he tried to resist David, and Nabal died of what appears to have been a stroke — perhaps an

---

82. Rose, *Sons of the Gods, Children of Earth*, pp. 63-64, 107-12, 139-40; Nagy, *Homeric Questions*, pp. 39, 42; Buxton, *Imaginary Greece*, pp. 29-31.

83. Carlier, *La royauté en Grèce avant Alexandre*, pp. 194-201.

84. Tandy, *Warriors into Traders*, pp. 178-80, 189-91; Seaford, *Reciprocity and Ritual*, pp. 1-6.

85. Thalmann, *The Swineherd and the Bow*, pp. 288-98.

86. Nagy, *Homeric Questions*, pp. 39-40.

87. McCarter, *I Samuel*, pp. 28-30, 401-2; Brueggemann, *First and Second Samuel*, pp. 174, 177.

indirect statement of divine intervention on David's side. The legitimate ground for Nabal's protest, in spite of the ridicule heaped upon him, was probably not lost on generations of landowners in Judah who were expected to pay taxes to the Davidic monarchy.[88]

David's confrontation with Nabal, soon brought to a final conclusion with Nabal's death, resulted in the absorption of Nabal's household and its resources within David's household when David married Nabal's wife Abigail (1 Sam. 25:39-42). If a big man was to rise above his rivals in a community, he needed not only to have superior skills as a warrior and a leader but also to have sufficient resources to pay his bodyguard or mercenary force.[89] David began to build his power base in the Judaean desert when he fled from Saul's court as follows:

> [He] escaped to the cave of Adullam. His brothers and all his father's household heard of it, so they journeyed down there to him. Everyone who was suffering hardship, everyone who was in debt, and everyone who was embittered assembled together around him; and he became their leader. There were about four hundred men with him. (1 Sam. 22:1-2)

As David gathered about him his family and those who were alienated from Saul's regime, it was imperative that he have the resources to support them and to repay them for their services.[90] Most of their resources were to be gained through raids upon enemies of Israel (1 Sam. 30:16-25) or through exactions from the wealthy (1 Sam. 25:1-39). In spite of the additions of the pro-Davidic editors who portray David as an obedient, nonaggressive recipient of his divine election to the kingship of Israel (1 Sam. 24:7; 26:9), the core of the stories in David's rise to power reveals a charismatic, hard-nosed warrior who used his skills to establish a strong royal household.[91]

David's rival, Saul, had also been establishing his power base by gathering mercenaries about him.[92] The tradition reports that "there was hard fighting

---

88. Crüsemann, *Der Widerstand gegen das Königtum*, p. 142.

89. On the use of protection rackets in the transition toward the formation of a state, see Michael Mann, *The Sources of Social Power*, vol. 1: *A History of Power from the Beginning to A.D. 1760* (Cambridge: Cambridge University Press, 1986), pp. 58, 100.

90. H. Reviv, "The Structure of Society," in *The World History of the Jewish People*, vol. 4, part 2: *The Age of the Monarchies: Culture and Society*, ed. A. Malamat (Jerusalem: Masada, 1979), p. 130; Halpern, *David's Secret Demons*, p. 285; McKenzie, *King David*, 106.

91. Lemche, "David's Rise," pp. 8, 12, 14; Halpern, *David's Secret Demons*, pp. 284-86; McKenzie, *King David*, pp. 106-10.

92. Niels Peter Lemche ("Kings and Clients: On Loyalty between the Ruler and the Ruled in Ancient 'Israel,'" *Semeia* 66 [1995]: 12, 128-29) defines the relationship between the early Isra-

against the Philistines all the days of Saul. Whenever Saul saw any strong or valiant man, he attached him to himself" (1 Sam. 14:52; cf. 1 Sam. 22:7; 18:13). The competition between the households of Saul and David intensified and persisted beyond Saul's death at the battle of Gilboa (1 Sam. 31:1-6). Prior to the anointing of David as king by elders of the northern tribes (2 Sam. 5:1-5), there was a fierce and extended struggle between the two royal households (2 Sam. 2:12–3:1). The rivalry with Saul's household resurfaced at the time of Absalom's revolt when David was cursed by Shimei, one of Saul's relatives, as David fled from Jerusalem (2 Sam. 16:5-8), and again at the time of a drought when seven of Saul's heirs were executed on the alleged grounds that such an action was necessary to counter Saul's abrogation of an oath with the Gibeonites (2 Sam. 21:1-14).[93]

David's rhetoric in the Nabal episode revealed a leader who was willing initially to make a polite request for provisions from Nabal (1 Sam. 25:8). Yet when he was taunted by Nabal and his honor was put on the line, David was enraged and moved swiftly with force to achieve his objective (1 Sam. 25:13, 21-22).[94] Although David did not seem to be lacking in rhetorical skill, his warrior skills were the primary form of charisma demanded by his immediate circumstances. David did not hold an authoritative position in Judah or Israel. His words carried force primarily by his own strength and resources. His oath or self-curse testified that he put all of his resources and his honor on the line in order to respond to the taunt of Nabal. In these circumstances, the oath was the most effective rhetorical means for getting his will obeyed. Yet the most rhetorically skilled person in this episode in 1 Samuel 25 was Abigail. She not only knew how to soothe the angry David, but she also gave him sage advice coupled with a prediction of his future rule.[95]

The Israelite tribes had moved from a loose confederation to a monarchical form of government under Saul (1 Samuel 8–12), but the transition was still in its early stages, for the leadership of Saul resembled more that of an Israelite judge than that of a typical ancient Near Eastern king.[96] The outlines of the po-

---

elite king (or petty kings in LBA Syria and Palestine) and his subjects as that of patron and client, where the loyalty of the client was repaid by the protection provided by the patron. See also Lemche, "From Patronage Society to Patronage Society," in *The Origins of the Ancient Israelite States*, ed. V. Fritz and P. R. Davies, JSOTSup 228 (Sheffield: Sheffield Academic Press, 1996), pp. 111, 118.

93. Halpern, *David's Secret Demons*, pp. 22, 81, 84-87; McKenzie, *King David*, p. 136.

94. Brueggemann, *First and Second Samuel*, pp. 176-77; cf. Saul Olyan, "Honor, Shame, and Covenant Relations in Ancient Israel and Its Environment," *JBL* 115 (1996): 204.

95. Hans W. Hertzberg, *I & II Samuel* (Philadelphia: Westminster, 1964), pp. 203-4.

96. John Bright, *History of Israel*, 3rd ed. (Philadelphia: Westminster, 1981), p. 190.

sition of king were still blurred in this early stage of its development among the tribes of Israel. Some would categorize Saul and David as "chiefs" rather than as "kings."[97] Both Saul and David needed to create their power bases from the raw materials of manpower and material goods. The power base focused primarily upon the formation of relationships with warriors, heads of other households, and neighboring kings. Nabal was a wealthy landowner in Judah who could supply David with many of the resources he needed to reward his followers. David acted more like a big man than a chief. Even though 1 Samuel 22:1-2 states that he gathered his family about him, this same passage refers to how he attracted all the malcontents of the realm about him. He built his power base with minimal attention to a clan structure. In contrast, Saul is usually described as operating as the leader of the tribe of Benjamin. As a military leader, he initially acted like a chief, but then he began to gather mercenaries and so needed to build up the wealth of his household. Both Saul and David did not have inherited structures of monarchical power to draw upon in Israel and Judah; kingship was at a low level of institutionalization in their time.[98]

Editors of the accounts of the rivalry between David and Saul or between David and Nabal did not eliminate the viewpoints of the voice of opposition, even when they worked with a pro-Davidic bias. The Israelite tradition is polyvocal and tends to conserve dissonant, nonconforming details in its stories.[99] The narratives about Saul tend to portray him as a tragic figure. Even the most pro-Davidic narratives often sprinkle clues to the shadowy side of David's political dealings. This conservative dynamic, which does not homogenize narratives, sets the stage for debates on the place of kingship in society. Even if the audience for a narrative such as 1 Samuel 25 was an elite in Jerusalem seeking to explain David's rise to power, this narrative remained alive in the tradition and influenced the imaginations of generations of Israelites across the spectrum of society on what kings were like. It also fostered an interpretation that allowed a diversity of perspectives on perennial issues of power and authority.[100]

97. James Flanagan, "Chiefs in Israel," *JSOT* 20 (1981): 65-67; idem, *David's Social Drama: A Hologram of Israel's Early Iron Age,* Social World of Biblical Antiquity Series 7 (Sheffield: Almond, 1988), pp. 291-92; Israel Finkelstein, "The Emergence of the Monarchy," *JSOT* 44 (1989): 48.

98. Cf. Christa Schäfer-Lichtenberger, "Sociological and Biblical Views of the Early State," in *The Origins of the Ancient Israelite States,* ed. V. Fritz and P. R. Davies, JSOTSup 228 (Sheffield: Sheffield Academic Press, 1996), pp. 92, 99, 105.

99. McCarter, *I Samuel,* pp. 20-22; Halpern, *David's Secret Demons,* p. 109; idem, "The Uneasy Compromise," pp. 59-96.

100. Cf. Michael Fishbane, *Biblical Interpretation in Ancient Israel* (Oxford: Clarendon, 1985), pp. 414-18; James Brenneman, *Canons in Conflict: Negotiating Texts in True and False Prophecy* (New York: Oxford, 1997), pp. 20-27.

The picture of Hammurapi communicated through his clay-nail inscription concerning the wall of Sippar portrays a ruler who was obedient to the gods and proud of his accomplishments on behalf of the people of Sippar. Even though the courtly scribes served as Hammurapi's "speech writers" in composing this inscription, Hammurapi still had to endorse this message.[101] Because the inscription was written in the first person, the subjectivity and egocentricity of the king are a pronounced feature of the message — a feature also frequently present in Sumerian royal hymns.[102] He made a claim on the people through his beneficial actions on their behalf. Hammurapi communicated a self-image that resembles more a father figure than a detached bureaucrat — a setting in which the father was a disciplinarian as well as a protector (cf. *CH* XLVIII:20-24).[103] Even if the people of Sippar rarely saw Hammurapi, the language of the inscription aimed to communicate a sense of familiarity and oversight as one might find in an extended family. At the same time, Hammurapi emphasized his superior rank and tended to distance himself from the people through his boasting: "Indeed, I built an outstanding wall. What no king among the kings had built since ancient times, I built magnificently for Shamash."[104] Marc Van de Mieroop notes with reference to OB legal documents and royal correspondence that kings paid attention to and responded to specific requests on daily matters of those people who were associated with the palace. For those who did not have such dealings with the palace, the king probably did not have occasion to listen to them. Van de Mieroop states that on national issues the king did not seem to pay much attention to the people at large.[105]

101. Jack M. Sasson, "King Hammurabi of Babylon," in *Civilizations of the Ancient Near East,* ed. J. Sasson (New York: Scribner, 1995), p. 907; Vanstiphout, "Memory and Literacy," pp. 2188, 2190.

102. Sigmund Mowinckel, "Die vorderasiatischen königs- und fürsteninschriften: Eine stilistische Studie," in *Eucharistērion: Studien zur Religion und Literatur des Alten und Neuen Testaments für Hermann Gunkel,* vol. 1, ed. Hans Schmidt (Göttingen: Vandenhoeck & Ruprecht, 1923), pp. 297-99; Claus Wilcke, "Politik im Spiegel der Literatur, Literatur als Mittel der Politik im alteren Babylonien," in *Anfänge politischen Denkens in der Antike: Die nahöstlichen Kulturen und die Griechen,* ed. Kurt Raaflaub and Elisabeth Müller-Luckner (Munich: Oldenbourg, 1993), p. 63. On first-person speech in Greek inscriptions, see Svenbro, *Phrasikleia,* pp. 27-30, 41-42.

103. Victor Hurowitz, *Inu Anum Sīrum: Literary Structures in the Non-Juridical Sections of Codex Hammurabi,* Occasional Publications of the Samuel Noah Kramer Fund 15 (Philadelphia: University of Pennsylvania Museum, 1994), p. 34; Sasson, "King Hammurabi," pp. 907-8.

104. Frayne, *RIME 4,* E4.3.6.2, lines 45-50. Franke (*Königsinschriften und Königsideologie,* p. 192) notes that Naram-Sin (2254-2218 B.C.) used the expression "what no king among previous kings had done" to emphasize his incomparability.

105. Marc Van de Mieroop, *The Ancient Mesopotamian City* (Oxford: Clarendon, 1997), p. 119.

Hammurapi claims to have established among the people the practice of their "daily recalling my good name like a god."[106] It was apparently a mark of distinction in Hammurapi's estimation that the people come to see him as mediator of good things like a god. At some level, popular opinion was important to this OB king. This practice of recalling, which was phrased as "I have placed in the mouths of the people" (lines 80-81;[107] cf. *CH* V:22-23), seems to refer to a form of oral instruction.[108]

Even though his kingship as a form of hierarchical rule positioned him above other humans on a level closer to the gods, he still claimed to exercise a form of personal rule in which he took responsibility for the people in accord with his commission from the gods.[109] Hammurapi does not so much as hint that he will give the people a voice in decision making. Rather, according to the sequence of the narrative of the inscription, Hammurapi listens to the king of the gods and then makes the decision; after accomplishing the deed, he indicates how the gods have sanctioned this course of action.[110] Even if the people seem to be excluded from the deliberations and decision making at a national level, Hammurapi's speech-acts in his inscriptions set up expectations of his positive, personal involvement in the lives of the people in Babylon and in other Babylonian cities such as Sippar. How such involvement materialized in practice is another matter.

As the sixth king of the First Dynasty of Babylon (1894-1595 B.C.), Hammurapi (1792-1750 B.C.) inherited a royal household and a monarchical government that had held sway over the city of Babylon and its immediate environs for little more than a century.[111] Hammurapi and his predecessors in the First Dynasty of Babylon were Amorites, a West Semitic tribal group that had been immigrating into the land of Sumer and Akkad since the late third millennium.[112] In the early second millennium a number of Amorite dynas-

106. Frayne, *RIME 4*, E4.3.6.2, lines 75-81.

107. Frayne, *RIME 4*, E4.3.6.2.

108. Hurowitz, *Inu Anum Sīrum*, p. 47, n. 57; p. 61.

109. Franke (*Königsinschriften und Königsideologie*, p. 196) notes that by contrast the earlier kings of Akkad (ca. 2350-2193 B.C.) had no duties enjoined on them and were not pictured as shepherds of the people.

110. Raaflaub, "Influence, Adaptation, and Interaction," p. 56.

111. Cf. D. Charpin, "Maisons et maisonnées en babylonie ancienne de Sippar à Ur," in *Houses and Households in Ancient Mesopotamia*, ed. K. Veenhof, CRRA 40 (Leiden: Nederlands Historisch-Archaeologisch Instituut te Istanbul, 1996), p. 227.

112. Moshe Anbar, *Les tribus amurrites de Mari*, OBO 108 (Freiburg: Universitätsverlag, 1991), pp. 209-14; Dominique Charpin, "The History of Ancient Mesopotamia: An Overview," in *Civilizations of the Ancient Near East*, ed. J. Sasson (New York: Scribner, 1995), pp. 812-17; Sasson, "King Hammurabi," pp. 903-5; W. G. Lambert, "Kingship in Ancient Mesopotamia," in *King and*

ties took hold of the kingships in cities of Sumer and Akkad (for example, Kudur-Mabuk in Emutbal and Larsa).[113] The Amorites adopted the Akkadian language and the culture of Sumer and Akkad.[114] One of the features of the Amorite heritage that had a marked influence on the institution of Mesopotamian kingship was the Amorite king's emphasis upon his lineage.[115] In the prologue of his *Code*, Hammurapi identified himself as "the descendant of Sumu-la-el, the powerful son of Sin-muballiṭ" (*CH* IV:67-70).[116] In an inscription marking the opening of a canal named "Hammurapi is the prosperity of his people," Hammurapi constructed a wall nearby that he named "the wall of Sin-muballiṭ, the father who begot me" (lines 51-52); then he claimed: "I made glorious the memory of Sin-muballiṭ, the father who begot me, in the world regions" (lines 53-57).[117]

OB kingship was a revered and well-established institution with its roots reaching back into the middle part of the third millennium.[118] The kingship that Hammurapi inherited in Babylon had a relatively high level of institutionalization.[119] His royal household and government had inherited traditional ways of ruling to which he had to be attentive, as exemplified in his conformity to the expectations of the genre of the royal inscription.[120] Even if the kingship was well established, it was not a static reality that could survive if untended. Like all social and political institutions, it needed to be reproduced if

Messiah in Israel and the Ancient Near East, ed. J. Day, JSOTSup 270 (Sheffield: Sheffield Academic Press, 1998), pp. 60-61.

113. Frayne, *RIME 4*, E4.2.13a.2.

114. Charpin, "The History of Ancient Mesopotamia," p. 812; Anbar, *Les tribus amurrites de Mari*, p. 212.

115. W. G. Lambert, "The Seed of Kingship," in *Le palais et la royauté*, ed. P. Garelli, CRRA 19 (Paris: Geuthner, 1974), p. 430; Piotr Michalowski, "History as Charter: Some Observations on the Sumerian King List," in *Studies in Literature from the Ancient Near East Dedicated to Samuel Noah Kramer*, ed. J. Sasson, AOS 65 (New Haven: American Oriental Society, 1984), p. 241.

116. Rykle Borger, *Babylonische-assyrische Lesestücke*, AnOr 54 (Rome: Biblical Institute, 1979), 1:7. See also Martha Roth, *Law Collections from Mesopotamia and Asia Minor*, Writings from the Ancient World 6 (Atlanta: Scholars, 1995), p. 80.

117. Frayne, *RIME 4*, E4.3.6.7.

118. Wolfram von Soden, *The Ancient Orient: An Introduction to the Study of the Ancient Near East* (Grand Rapids: Eerdmans, 1994), p. 64; Lambert, "Kingship in Ancient Mesopotamia," pp. 55-59.

119. F. R. Kraus, "Das altbabylonische Königtum," in *Le palais et la royauté*, ed. P. Garelli, CRRA 19 (Paris: Paul Geuthner, 1974), pp. 253-60; Sasson, "King Hammurabi," pp. 905-7.

120. Vanstiphout, "Memory and Literacy," p. 2190; idem, "Some Thoughts on Genre in Mesopotamian Literature," *Keilschriftlichen Literaturen: Ausgewählte Vorträge der XXXII. Rencontre assyriologique internationale*, ed. K. Hecker and W. Sommerfeld, BBVO 6 (Berlin: Dietrich Reimer, 1986), p. 4; Hallo, *Origins*, p. 149.

it was to be a vital institution responsive to the conditions of its time.[121] Hammurapi operated from the model of a strong warrior in command of a wealthy household in which his understanding of the household was that of the extended family and clans of a Semitic chieftain where the chieftain held the collective properties.[122] Under his rule and that of other OB Amorite kings, the property controlled by the palace increased at the expense of the temple and perhaps other private landholders.[123] In Mesopotamia, however, land was an abundant resource; labor was more scarce. The capacity of the king to recruit and keep such labor organized for agricultural production would have increased his power. His capacity to draw on village networks and households was essential to his cultivation of increased holdings.[124] The OB king needed to subcontract with entrepreneurs in order to keep the labor forces intact, particularly since more were needed at sowing and harvest times.[125] His royal household was the locus from which he generated and maintained an extensive set of relationships that resulted in his rule over all of northern and southern Mesopotamia: the land of Sumer and Akkad.[126]

In the clay-nail inscription celebrating the construction of the wall of Sippar, Hammurapi noted that he relieved the people of Sippar from forced la-

121. Giddens, *The Constitution of Society,* pp. 17-19, 24. Cf. Kraus, "Das altbabylonische Königtum," pp. 252-53, 261.

122. Johannes M. Renger, "Institutional, Communal, and Individual Ownership or Possession of Arable Land in Ancient Mesopotamia from the End of the Fourth to the End of the First Millennium B.C.," *Chicago-Kent Law Review* 71 (1995): 279-83; idem, "On Economic Structures in Ancient Mesopotamia," *Or* n.s. 63 (1994): 170; I. J. Gelb, "Household and Family in Early Mesopotamia," in *State and Temple Economy in the Ancient Near East,* ed. E. Lipinski, OLA 5 (Leuven: Departement Orientalistiek, 1979), pp. 10-11.

123. Johannes M. Renger, "Das Palastgeschäft in der altbabylonischer Zeit," in *Interdependency of Institutions and Private Entrepreneurs,* MOS Studies 2 (Leiden: Nederlands Historisch-Archaeologisch Instituut te Istanbul, 2000), p. 156; cf. Kraus, *The Role of Temples,* p. 12; Van de Mieroop, *Ancient Mesopotamian City,* pp. 146-47.

124. G. van Driel, "Institutional and Non-Institutional Economy in Ancient Mesopotamia," in *Interdependency of Institutions and Private Entrepreneurs,* MOS Studies 2 (Leiden: Nederlands Historisch-Archaeologisch Instituut te Istanbul, 2000), pp. 11-15.

125. Renger, "Das Palastgeschäft in der altbabylonischer Zeit," p. 154.

126. Cf. Johannes M. Renger, "Patterns of Non-Institutional Trade and Non-Commercial Exchange in Ancient Mesopotamia at the Beginning of the Second Millennium B.C.," in *Circulation of Goods in Non-Palatial Context in the Ancient Near East,* ed. A. Archi, Incunabula Graeca 62 (Roma: Edizioni Del L'Ateneo, 1984), p. 63. On the relationship between the king and his officials in the Ur III period, see Irene Winter, "Legitimation of Authority through Image and Legend: Seals Belonging to Officials in the Administrative Bureaucracy of the Ur III State," in *Organization of Power: Aspects of Bureaucracy in the Ancient Near East,* ed. M. Gibson and R. Biggs, Studies in Ancient Oriental Civilization 46 (Chicago: Oriental Institute, 1987), pp. 90-92.

bor for Shamash.[127] This liberation reveals a clash between the temple of Shamash and the palace of Babylon. The Mesopotamian temple households in the third millennium and the Ur III period seem to have secured most of their workers from the local population and made them their dependents, whereas the palace seems to have secured most of its laborers from prisoners of war.[128] In the OB period, local laborers for the temple seem increasingly to have been hired rather than being dependents.[129] When Hammurapi liberated the temple laborers, perhaps he was shifting their status from dependents to hired laborers. However, from the perspective of the temple administrators, this was interference in their affairs and time-honored practices by a king from a neighboring city.[130] Although Hammurapi claimed in the inscription to be working in obedience to Shamash, those who were negatively impacted by his innovations no doubt had a different interpretation of his actions. On the basis of Hammurapi's royal correspondence, Rivkah Harris contends that in the middle of his reign Hammurapi began to place officials in the E-babbar temple of Sippar who referred to themselves as "servants of king *x*," *x* representing the name of the king reigning in Babylon. Previously they had referred to themselves as "servants of E-babbar" or "servants of Shamash."[131] This change Harris interprets as a transfer of control of the temple and its large holdings out of the hands of the temple hierarchy into those of Hammurapi.[132] In revamping the administration of the E-babbar temple, Hammurapi made the officials of the temple responsible to him and so strengthened the rule of his kingship in Sippar. However, this practice of replacing local administrators with those from the central administration in Babylon set the stage for sustained local dissatisfaction and resistance to his administration.[133] Johannes Renger claims that this unenlightened managerial practice by Hammurapi contributed in no small measure to the fragmentation of his empire after his death.[134]

If a king was to have his commands obeyed, he needed not only to inspire

127. Frayne, *RIME 4*, E4.3.6.2, lines 58-61.

128. Gelb, "Household and Family in Early Mesopotamia," pp. 11-12.

129. Marc Van de Mieroop, *Society and Enterprise in Old Babylonian Ur*, BBVO 12 (Berlin: Dietrich Reimer, 1992), p. 242.

130. Harris, *Ancient Sippar*, p. 40.

131. Rivkah Harris, "Some Aspects of the Centralization of the Realm under Hammurapi and His Successors," *JAOS* 88 (1968): 729.

132. Harris, "Some Aspects of the Centralization," p. 729.

133. Norman Yoffee, *The Economic Role of the Crown in the Old Babylonian Period*, Bibliotheca Mesopotamia 5 (Malibu, Calif.: Undena, 1977), p. 148.

134. Johannes M. Renger, "Interaction of Temple, Palace, and Private Enterprise," in *State and Temple Economy in the Ancient Near East*, ed. E. Lipinski, OLA 5 (Leuven: Departement Orientalistiek, 1979), p. 252.

the people but also to instill fear of him in them. The king had to be stronger than others physically and rhetorically, and he needed to be more skilled than others in providing food and security for the people. The royal household was the locus from which kings like Odysseus and Agamemnon, David and Saul, and Hammurapi and his son Samsuiluna cultivated strategic relationships and secured the material wealth that allowed them to sustain these relationships and generate new ones. Even though Hammurapi's household seems to have had greater wealth and stability relative to his community and his rivals than did that of either David or Odysseus in relation to their communities and rivals, his household was subject to a decline in fortunes just like theirs. Royal power was relational in character; the king who neglected this fact did not rule long. Nevertheless, the wealth of the royal household was significant. If the suitors in Ithaca had consumed all the substance of Odysseus's household, his kingship would have collapsed. The traditional basis of Odysseus's royal authority would have still existed, but it alone would not have been sufficient for him to receive obeisance consistently; he needed to be able to threaten the recalcitrant with physical force. If Odysseus had not been absent from Ithaca, he most likely would have tended to those conditions that would have made for a smooth succession of Telemachus to kingship over Ithaca: the inheritance practices of a typical household provided a framework for the intergenerational transfer of royal power and wealth. These principles on the importance of wealth in the maintenance of the relationships of the royal household in Homer held as well for the kingships in Israel and OB Mesopotamia.

Alliance Making: An Essential Royal Practice

As a king strove to establish his hold on power or to extend its sway, he realized that he would encounter resistance not only within his community but also from neighboring peoples and nations. Competition for scarce resources arose not only from increasing human demand but also from disequilibrium introduced into communities through famine, drought, and other natural disasters. Human rivalry and humans' contradictory relation toward nature are two significant aspects of the human condition that intensify the feeling of communities and individuals that they are "caged in."[135] When internal pressures within a community reach the boiling point, those in power must take decisive steps to prevent the disintegration or diminishment of the community.[136] Disequilib-

---

135. Mann, *The Sources of Social Power,* 1:42, 44.

136. Raaflaub, "Homer to Solon," p. 78; Susana B. Murphy, "The Notion of Moral Economy

rium in one community can lead to aggression against another community, which, in turn, can destabilize the latter community. The interrelatedness of various peoples and nations may present problems for security but, at the same time, opportunities for growth. A king in Homeric Greece, biblical Israel, or OB Mesopotamia was a key player in this balance of competing interests. His leadership in affairs at or beyond the boundaries of the kingdom were at least as important if not more so than his involvement in internal matters of the kingdom.[137]

Odysseus rallied the Achaean troops at a time when internal dissension and inept leadership threatened the dissolution of the coalition and the demise of the war effort. The ostensible purpose of the campaign against Troy was to regain Menelaus's wife Helen who had been abducted by Paris, the son of Priam, king of Troy (*Il.* 1.152-60; 2.160-62; 3.86-101, 121-28). It was a matter of honor for the Achaean warriors to redress this aggressive action carried out against their kinsman (*Il.* 2.53-83, 333-68; 9.89-90).[138] Some critics, who accept the historicity of the Trojan War, are skeptical that such a crime could have triggered and sustained a military campaign that had reached into its tenth year. They argue that a more likely historical reason for the Trojan War was a raid by the Achaeans on Troy to carry off goods and prisoners of war.[139] The coalition of Achaean warriors had carried out raids on other peoples prior to their arrival at Troy (*Il.* 1.163-68, 366-68; cf. *Od.* 10.28-47).[140] The opening chapter of the *Iliad* indicates that the quarrel between Agamemnon and Achilles was due to a problematic distribution of the spoils of war (*Il.* 1.101-88), whose value was both material and symbolic. In Homeric society, the importance of reputation, both in terms of "honor" *(timē)* as status within the community and in terms

---

in the Study of the Ancient Near East," in *Intellectual Life of the Ancient Near East,* ed. Jiří Prosecký, CRRA 43 (Prague: Oriental Institute, 1998), pp. 276-81; Moshe Weinfeld, *Social Justice in Ancient Israel and in the Ancient Near East* (Minneapolis: Fortress, 1995), pp. 33-44.

137. Mario Liverani, *Prestige and Interest: International Relations in the Near East ca. 1600-1100 B.C.* (Padova: Sargon SRL, 1990), pp. 19-24; Thalmann, *The Swineherd and the Bow,* pp. 267-68; Schäfer-Lichtenberger, "Sociological and Biblical Views of the Early State," pp. 90-92, 104-5.

138. Van Wees, *Status Warriors,* pp. 167, 198.

139. Denys Page (*History and the Homeric Iliad* [Berkeley: University of California Press, 1972], pp. 256-57) argues that the Trojan War is historical but notes that even though it is possible that the abduction of Helen triggered the conflict, the typical character of the story of the stolen princess who must be won back by her husband or lover lends credence to the contention that this story was created by the bards. Cf. Van Wees, *Status Warriors,* p. 167; Finley, *The World of Odysseus,* p. 64.

140. Raaflaub, "Politics and Interstate Relations," p. 3; idem, "Soldiers, Citizens, and the Polis," *The Development of the "Polis" in Archaic Greece,* ed. L. Mitchell and P. Rhodes (New York: Routledge, 1997), p. 51.

of "respect" *(aidōs)* within the household, made the practice of the division of spoils even more important than gift giving.[141]

Since there was no taxation within Achaean kingdoms, the primary avenue open to a warrior or a king to increase his wealth was by acquiring war booty. The raids by Achaean warriors on other lands seemed to have arisen more from the Achaean warrior's desire for self-aggrandizement than from a lack of necessary resources in the homeland.[142] The measurable, tangible quality of material goods became the primary way in which Agamemnon understood political power (*Il.* 1.118-20, 182-87; 9.119-20, 262-98).[143] Therefore, when Apollo struck the Achaean forces with a plague to punish them for not returning the daughter of Chryses, a priest in service of Apollo, to her home, Agamemnon was faced with forfeiting his prize from the previous campaign. Agamemnon feared that such a return of a war trophy would have diminished him vis-à-vis Achilles, the most highly regarded warrior of the coalition. In an attempt to shore up his rank among the Achaean warrior-kings, Agamemnon took the woman Briseis from Achilles and thereby dishonored him by violating the sense of reciprocity and solidarity undergirding the warrior code: a *modus operandi* dictating that a war prize awarded to another could not be taken back (*Il.* 9.314-22).[144] The warrior code was not a written legal document with explicit prohibitions but rather

141. Rose, *Sons of the Gods, Children of Earth*, pp. 78, 127; McGlew, "Royal Power," p. 287; Douglas Cairns, *"Aidos": The Psychology and Ethics of Honour and Shame in Ancient Greek Literature* (Oxford: Clarendon, 1993), pp. 13, 14; Van Wees, *Status Warriors*, pp. 155-56. Margalit Finkelberg (*"Timē and Aretē in Homer," Classical Quarterly* 48 [1998]: 18, 20) argues that status in the Homeric world was inherited rather than achieved by heroic deeds, and thus competitive values were not at the center of Homer's ethics; see the rejoinder by John Gould, *Myth, Ritual Memory, and Exchange: Essays in Greek Literature and Culture* (New York: Oxford, 2001), pp. 353-57.

142. McGlew, "Royal Power," p. 288; Geddes, "Who's Who in 'Homeric Society'?" p. 28; cf. Leonard Muellner, *The Anger of Achilles: "Mēnis" in Greek Epic* (Ithaca: Cornell University Press, 1996), p. 34; Elman Service, *Origins of the State and Civilization: The Process of Cultural Evolution* (New York: Norton, 1975), pp. 299-300.

143. McGlew, "Royal Power," p. 288. Louis Gernet ("'Value' in Greek Myth," in *Myth, Religion, and Society*, ed. R. L. Gordon [Cambridge: Cambridge University Press, 1981], p. 144) notes that precious objects *(agalmata)* carried an aura that promoted a kind of social power and so shaped early understandings of authority. These precious objects may have been forerunners of money. Seaford (*Reciprocity and Ritual*, p. 223) notes the paradox regarding money, which was introduced into Athens in the sixth century B.C.: it brought coherence to commodity exchange but opened the way to unlimited accumulation and thus became both an integrating and disintegrating force in this emerging city-state.

144. Vernant, *Mortals and Immortals*, p. 53; Sale, "Government of Troy," p. 45; Van Wees, *Status Warriors*, pp. 107, 110; Rose, *Sons of the Gods, Children of Earth*, pp. 61, 79; Muellner, *The Anger of Achilles*, pp. 104-6.

a way for the warriors to relate to one another that honored their commitments and sacrifices. There may not have been an explicit prohibition against Agamemnon taking Briseis, but the bonds among the warriors were undermined by this rash action.[145]

One other means by which an Achaean king could enhance his wealth through contacts with peoples beyond his borders was through gift exchange.[146] Upon his return to Ithaca after twenty years of wandering, Odysseus, disguised and unrecognized by Penelope, reported to her: "Odysseus would have been here a long time ago, but it seemed more advantageous for him to go about the wide earth and collect goods" (*Od.* 19.282-84). The gifts that Odysseus gathered in foreign lands appear to have been those regularly given to parting guest-friends.[147] When Telemachus visited Menelaus to seek information concerning the welfare and whereabouts of his father Odysseus, Menelaus promised to give Telemachus gifts upon his departure:

> But come now, remain in my halls until the eleventh or twelfth day arrives, then I will give you a fitting send-off and offer you splendid gifts, three horses and a finely crafted chariot. After that, I will give you a beautiful drinking cup so that you may make drink offerings to the immortal gods, remembering me thereby every day. (*Od.* 4.587-92)

Such gifts increased a king's wealth but more importantly strengthened the bonds between the giver and the receiver.[148] Chiefdoms were organized on reciprocal exchange where goods were circulated with the chief as the main redistributor, and so he cultivated relationships and secured his status in the exchange.[149] William G. Thalmann, however, argues that the *basileus* was not a redistributing chief

---

145. Muellner, *The Anger of Achilles*, pp. 34, 114, 136.

146. Morris, "The Use and Abuse of Homer," p. 119. Seaford (*Reciprocity and Ritual*, p. 18) notes that there was no commodity exchange among Greeks or among Trojans; the market and coinage are absent from Homeric society.

147. Finley, *The World of Odysseus*, p. 111; Tandy, *Warriors into Traders*, pp. 141-42.

148. Donlan, "Reciprocities in Homer," p. 151; Thalmann, *The Swineherd and the Bow*, pp. 261-62. Sitta von Reden ("Re-evaluating Gernet: Value and Greek Myth," in *From Myth to Reason?* ed. R. Buxton [Oxford: Clarendon, 1999], pp. 62-64) points out that the exchange value of gifts is not completely separate from the honor or affective value that gifts convey. Aristocrats and others debated the ways to assess the value of gifts in the Archaic Age.

149. Thalmann, *The Swineherd and the Bow*, p. 261. Glenn Schwartz ("Before Ebla: Models of Pre-State Political Organization in Syria and Northern Mesopotamia," in *Chiefdoms and Early States in the Near East: The Organization Dynamics of Complexity*, ed. G. Stein and M. Rotherman, Monographs on World Archaeology 18 [Madison, Wisc.: Prehistory Press, 1994], pp. 162, 164) draws a parallel between chiefs in upper Mesopotamia in the third millennium b.c. and the Homeric *basilēes* in their practice of exchanging gifts with outsiders to obtain prestige goods.

but rather a big man who exchanged gifts and honor among an elite.[150] Agamemnon transgressed the warrior code that guided the distribution of such gifts and honor. He was apparently not convinced of the value of the intangible bonds generated through gift exchange or the awarding of war trophies; for him what seemed most significant was the actual possession of goods.[151] One might say that economics was more important to Agamemnon than politics.

The negative impact of Achilles' withdrawal from the Achaean coalition forms a central element in the plot of the *Iliad*.[152] Achilles, alienated from a group in which he was highly invested, wanted the whole group to suffer for the injury done to him.[153] The anger of Achilles was vindicated as the fortunes of the Achaeans in the war grew darker and darker (*Il.* 9.9-28). The maintenance of cooperative endeavors such as alliances required sustained, sensitive efforts by the parties involved if they were to achieve their objectives. Agamemnon, who subsequently confessed to having been ruled by blindness (*atē, Il.* 9.18), allowed rivalry with Achilles to be more important than concern for the viability of the coalition.[154] Leaders who view political power merely as a matter of force forfeit the potential that comes through cooperative relationships and so diminish the vitality and well-being of their kingdoms.[155]

In the course of David's rise to power and his rivalry with Saul, David negotiated with neighboring kings to further their mutual interests. After his falling out with Saul, David took his mother and father to the king of Moab so that they might be safe (1 Sam. 22:3-4). Presumably David was allied with the king of Moab in some respect.[156] In 1 Samuel 27:1, David says:

> I will be snatched away some day by Saul. It is not good for me. Surely I should seek safety in the land of the Philistines. Then Saul will despair of searching further for me throughout the territory of Israel, and I will be safe from him.

---

150. Thalmann, *The Swineherd and the Bow*, p. 261.

151. Muellner, *The Anger of Achilles*, pp. 97-98. Charles Segal (*Singers, Heroes, and Gods in the Odyssey* [Ithaca: Cornell University Press, 1994], p. 141) notes in reference to the performance of the bard that the actual ceremony of conferring honor was significant as well as the material value of the gift itself.

152. Crotty, *The Poetics of Supplication*, p. 94; Raaflaub, "Homer to Solon," pp. 56-57.

153. Muellner, *The Anger of Achilles*, p. 137.

154. Raaflaub, "Politics and Interstate Relations," p. 23; Pietro Pucci, *The Song of the Sirens* (New York: Rowman & Littlefield, 1998), p. 205; Thalmann, *The Swineherd and the Bow*, p. 124.

155. Muellner, *The Anger of Achilles*, p. 104; cf. Giddens, *The Constitution of Society*, p. 175.

156. McCarter, *I Samuel*, p. 359; cf. Halpern, *David's Secret Demons*, p. 161. The genealogy of the line of Judah in Ruth 4:18-22 identifies the son of Boaz the Judahite and Ruth the Moabite as David's grandfather.

David became a vassal of a Philistine ruler, Achish of Gath (1 Sam. 27:5-7).[157] Since the Philistines were Israel's most feared enemy in the eleventh and tenth centuries B.C., it would seem that such cooperation with the enemy would have tarnished the image of David.[158] Not only does the biblical account make the case that David had little choice in becoming a Philistine vassal if he was to survive, it also notes that David deceived Achish by making raids against desert tribes while claiming to have plundered villages in Judah (1 Sam. 27:8-12). Also the biblical account notes that David did not participate in the battle of Gilboa (1 Sam. 29:1-11), and so David had no part in the battle against the Israelites that involved the death of Saul and his son Jonathan, the heir apparent to the throne of Israel. Despite this positive portrayal of David as a clever survivor, the reader is left with questions whether David should have been fully exonerated from the charge of opportunism in his collaboration with the Philistines at the same time that he was vying with Saul for the kingship in Israel.[159]

Another pact that David seems to have made in order to neutralize Saul's power was the one with Nahash, the king of the Ammonites. When Nahash died, David sent an embassy to Hanun, the son of Nahash, in order to renew this pact:

> Some time later the king of the Ammonites died, and Hanun, his son, took his place as king. David said, "I will be loyal to Hanun, son of Nahash, just as his father was loyal to me." So David sent servants to offer sympathy to him concerning his father. (2 Sam. 10:1-2)

The Ammonite commanders convinced Hanun that the embassy was a spying mission rather than one of friendship (2 Sam. 10:3-4). At that time, David was ruling over both the northern and the southern Israelite tribes and thus probably posed a threat to the Ammonites just as Saul had earlier. Nahash had presumably made his pact with David in order to neutralize Saul's power.[160] David subsequently defeated the Ammonite-Aramaean coalition (2 Sam. 10:8-19). The

---

157. Joseph Naveh ("Achish-Ikausu in the Light of the Ekron Dedication," *BASOR* 310 [1998]: 35) argues on the basis of a recently discovered seventh-century B.C. royal dedicatory inscription of Achish, son of Padi, that the name Achish derives from *Ik(a)yus*, which then leads to *Akhayus*, i.e., "Achaean" or "Greek."

158. Lemche, "David's Rise," pp. 12-14; McCarter, *I Samuel*, p. 416. The literary stylization of the Achish episodes as the beginning (1 Sam. 21:11-16[10-15]) and end (1 Sam. 27:1-12) of a concentric ring structure raises questions about the historicity of the accounts; cf. Cynthia Edenburg, "How (Not) to Murder a King: Variations on a Theme in 1 Sam 24; 26," *SJOT* 12 (1998): 78-79.

159. Lemche, "David's Rise," p. 14; McCarter, *I Samuel*, p. 416; P. Kyle McCarter, Jr., "The Apology of David," *JBL* 99 (1980): 500; Halpern, *David's Secret Demons*, pp. 302-6.

160. P. Kyle McCarter, Jr., *II Samuel*, AB 9 (Garden City, N.Y.: Doubleday, 1984), p. 274.

early alliances that David made with the kings of Moab, Ammon, and Philistia were important components of his strategy for wresting the kingship away from Saul.[161]

In the "History of David's Rise" (1 Sam. 16:14–2 Sam. 5:10), David was portrayed as a leader who understood well the symbolic as well as the material significance of war booty. After recovering from the Amalekites the individuals and goods taken from Ziklag (1 Sam. 30:17-20), David took care to divide the spoils among all his warriors according to the following principle: "The share of the one who goes down to battle and that of the one who remains with the baggage shall be the same; they shall share alike" (1 Sam. 30:24). This egalitarian principle of apportioning spoils was presumably matched by the expectation that all of the warriors would take their turns in going into battle. This principle is the opposite of the Homeric warrior code where the accomplishments of the hero needed to be recognized with a greater portion of the spoil. One wonders if David's warriors could function under this egalitarian system where their high risk exploits garnered no reward.[162] From the spoil taken from the Amalekites, David also made distributions to the elders of the various cities of Judah (1 Sam. 30:26-31) and so used his position as a vassal of Achish to assist the people of Judah and strengthen his bonds with them. By his gift giving, David aimed to show the people of Judah that his true loyalty lay with them rather than with Achish and the Philistines.

Kings like Hammurapi in OB Mesopotamia found it necessary to make alliances with other kings in order to check the increasing power of yet another king in their region. A celebrated letter from the Mari archives addressed to Zimri-Lim of Mari from Itur-Asdu, the governor of Nahor, points to the necessity of coalitions:

> There is no king who is powerful by himself. Ten or fifteen kings go after Hammurapi of Babylon. A like number go after Rim-Sin of Larsa, Ibalpiel of Eshnunna, or Amutpiel of Qatanum. There are twenty who go after Yarim-Lim of Yamḥad.[163]

It is clear that an ally was a partner for a specific purpose and was not necessarily a friend. Once a particular foe was countered, it was prudent for a king to look warily at his former allies to see if one of them was vying for ascendancy. In the early Old Babylonian period (ca. 2003-1765), a number of cities had the

161. Halpern, *David's Secret Demons,* pp. 161, 232, 302-6.

162. Cf. Brueggemann, *First and Second Samuel,* pp. 204-5.

163. Georges Dossin, "Les archives épistolaires du palais de Mari," *Syria* 19 (1938): 117, lines 24-27.

organization and resource base to compete with others, but they were super-seded by Isin and Larsa.[164] After 1800 B.C., Eshnunna and Babylon began to rise in influence, and so alliance making among these city-states was a particularly important political strategy.[165]

Hammurapi's rise to power over the land of Sumer and Akkad involved making and shifting a number of alliances. The middle years of his reign — the time of his twelfth to twenty-ninth year-dates[166] (1782-1765 B.C.) — were de-voted to strengthening and consolidating his power.[167] At the end of this pe-riod, Hammurapi prepared to expand that power.[168] He made a pact with Zimri-Lim of Mari in order to fend off Eshnunna, Babylon's primary foe who at that time was allied with Elam.[169] According to his thirtieth year-date (1764-1763 B.C.), Hammurapi joined a coalition that gained a victory over his north-ern rivals: Eshnunna, Elam, and Shubartu (i.e., the kingdom of Shamshi-Adad). Then he brought the middle and southern sections of Mesopotamia un-der his control.[170] Even though Hammurapi had the upper hand in his dealings with the conquered Eshnunna, the people of Eshnunna put one of their own on the throne as they sought to avoid annexation. Hammurapi negotiated a treaty with this new king, Ṣilli-Sin, and even went so far as to give him one of his daughters in marriage. Yet this arrangement did not last, for Hammurapi re-corded his victory over the army of Eshnunna in 1762-1761 B.C. in his thirty-second year-date.[171] Part of Hammurapi's strategy in conquering Larsa, which he accomplished in 1763-1762 B.C. according to his thirty-first year-date, was to cut off the waters of the Euphrates and thereby disrupt Rim-Sin's irrigation works.[172] In 1761-1760 B.C., according to his thirty-third year-date, he con-quered Mari; two years later he destroyed its walls.[173] Apparently Zimri-Lim of

---

164. Charpin, "The History of Ancient Mesopotamia," p. 813; Dietz O. Edzard, "The Old Babylonian Period," in *The Near East: The Early Civilizations*, ed. E. Cassin et al. (New York: Delacorte, 1967), pp. 191, 198.

165. Norman Yoffee, "Political Economy in Early Mesopotamian States," *Annual Review of Anthropology* 24 (1995): 299-300.

166. A. Leo Oppenheim, *ANET*, p. 270.

167. Sasson, "King Hammurabi," p. 906.

168. Hartmut Schmökel, *Hammurabi von Babylon: Die Errichtung eines Reiches* (Darmstadt: Wissenschaftliche Buchgesellschaft, 1971), p. 43.

169. Schmökel, *Hammurabi von Babylon*, pp. 40-41.

170. Sasson, "King Hammurabi," p. 906; Schmökel, *Hammurabi von Babylon*, p. 44.

171. D. Lacambre, "Hammurabi et le trône d'Ešnunna," *NABU* 8 (1994): 67-68; A. Finet, "Le trône et la rue en Mésopotamie: l'exaltation du roi et les techniques de l'opposition," in *La voix de l'opposition en Mésopotamie* (Brussels: Institut des Hautes Études de Belgique, 1973), p. 21.

172. Renger, "Institutional, Communal, and Individual Ownership," pp. 298, 300.

173. Sasson, "King Hammurabi," pp. 906-7.

Mari did not suspect Hammurapi's drive for ascendancy early enough. It seems that Zimri-Lim formed a coalition with Ishme-Dagan of Ashur just prior to Mari's downfall.[174] Obviously this coalition proved to be too little too late to resist the onslaught of Hammurapi.

When Hammurapi established his rule over the land of Sumer and Akkad (i.e., lower Mesopotamia), he still anchored his royal power in the city of Babylon. As his fortunes rose, so did those of his own city. The political unification of the land of Sumer and Akkad that he forged through his military successes led to a greater unification of the agricultural economy.[175] Until his rule, each city basically supported itself by the food from its own fields and so was relatively equal to other Mesopotamian cities.[176] However, the local resource base in wood, leather, textiles, reeds, limestone, quartz, and salt may have been greater than previously estimated and so may have provided goods for export.[177] Ashur, Sippar, Mari, Eshnunna, Der, and Dilmun were transit centers in a commercial network.[178] Although these commercial activities must have had some impact on the economy of these cities, trade itself did not lead to the kind of wealth that would elevate any one of them above their neighbors. An important factor in such undeveloped trade was the fact that the transport of food over long distances was not feasible.[179] Yet with Hammurapi's rise to power, Babylon became the center toward which taxes and tribute flowed. This resulted in shifts in the administration of the various cities and temples that gave Babylon a preeminent status among other Mesopotamian cities in the second half of the OB period (ca. 1763-1595 B.C.).

A fundamental responsibility of the king was to maintain the boundaries of the kingdom. Invasion by an enemy could mean starvation, slavery, or death for many of the people. The strongest reason for having a king was the higher degree of security that could be gained by having a standing army under the di-

174. Schmökel, *Hammurabi von Babylon*, p. 47.

175. Van de Mieroop, *The Ancient Mesopotamian City*, p. 29; idem, *Society and Enterprise*, pp. 112, 247.

176. K. Eckholm and J. Friedman, "'Capital' Imperialism and Exploitation in Ancient World Systems," in *Power and Propaganda: A Symposium on Ancient Empires*, ed. M. T. Larsen, Mesopotamia 7 (Copenhagen: Akademisk Forlag, 1979), p. 46.

177. D. T. Potts, *Mesopotamian Civilization: The Material Foundations* (Ithaca: Cornell University Press, 1997), p. 120.

178. Mogens T. Larsen, "Commercial Networks in the Ancient Near East," in *Centre and Periphery in the Ancient World*, ed. M. Rowlands et al. (Cambridge: Cambridge University Press, 1987), p. 54. See also Morris Silver, *Economic Structures of the Ancient Near East* (Totowa, N.J.: Barnes & Noble, 1985), pp. 66-68.

179. Larsen, "Commercial Networks," p. 52; Van de Mieroop, *The Ancient Mesopotamian City*, pp. 164, 190; Renger, "Patterns of Non-Institutional Trade," pp. 68, 70-72.

rection of a warrior-king. The more successful kings were those who understood the significance of building relationships with individuals and groups within the kingdom and with other kings in the region. A king who cultivated strategic relationships to rise to power needed to continue to tend to such relationships if he were to remain in power. The practice of gift giving, where relationships were cultivated through symbolic as well as material means, was essential for Homeric kings to maintain relationships with one another. David likewise used gift giving to forge new bonds with the people of Judah. David was also astute in concluding alliances with the rulers of Moab, Ammon, and Philistia as he vied with Saul for rule over Israel and Judah. Hammurapi's kingship had a higher level of institutionalization than that of either Agamemnon or David. Yet the shifting, dynamic character of his alliances with neighboring kings reveals that those alliances operated more often in the realm of competing personal relationships rather than in established patterns where one king was clearly regarded as superior. More often than not in the OB period, the opening words of the Mari letter quoted above proved true: "No king was powerful on his own."

The Voices of the Community in the Construction of the Sociopolitical World of the King

Leaders such as Agamemnon, David, and Hammurapi were uniquely positioned to bring blessings or curses to their communities. Although any human agent can influence a community through his speech and actions, the leader has an increased capacity to act because of his role and his status. The capacity to act can be defined as power.[180] While every human agent has power, the enhanced power of the leader as generated within the context of a community has greater visibility and the potential to influence a larger number of people. Nevertheless, power is always a two-way street between human agents. If one party coerces another, the coerced party may withdraw, shift priorities, or comply. The power in the relationship is shaped by the actions and responses of both parties. Coercion can legitimately be used to ensure the well-being of the community, but if a ruler relies solely on coercion to maintain control, he is not ruling with authority. Authority is legitimate power because it strengthens the matrix of relationships that constitute a community.

The drama of interactions between these human agents is the stage upon which political power is generated. In the active context of the performance of

---

180. Giddens, *The Constitution of Society,* p. 257; Mann, *Sources of Social Power,* pp. 6-7.

these interacting human agents, the social and political world is produced. The process of the performance is closer to the heart of politics than any structured products that may result from the interaction.[181] To say that politics and political thinking first began in the popular assembly of the Greek city-state where male property holders had the right to speak is too narrow and exclusive. More broadly conceived, politics is the engagement of the ruler with the ruled to form the web of relationships known as the community that resides in a particular area and can use force if necessary to keep its communal bonds intact.[182] The key question is whether or not the ruler engages the ruled so that there is an appeal to the mind and heart of the people. The obedience of the people, even if it is induced by coercion on occasions, is given by human agents and not by things. Such engagement between the ruler and the ruled can take place in the palace, the temple, the gate of the city, the mustering of troops on the battlefield, and so forth. The physical location is not the defining characteristic of politics; rather, it is the activity between ruler and ruled that generates the web of relationships known as a community resident in a particular place. When the engagement between ruler and ruled diminishes, so also does authority.

The relationship of authority between ruler and ruled builds upon the relationships that already constitute households and associations of households within the community. Although the household itself is not a political unit *per se,* the relationships of power and authority between the *paterfamilias* and the members of the household are continuous with those of a king and the members of his kingdom. The king rules over many households that are resident in a particular territory and have a common identity as residents in this political community.

The scepter of Argos, held for three generations by Agamemnon's royal household, was a symbol of the identity of the coalition of Achaean forces. As the leader who wielded this scepter in an emergency, Odysseus had to use his physical strength and persuasiveness to round up the soldiers and bring them back into the assembly. In the assembly, the decision-making power rested with the ruler who held the scepter of Argos, but the council of sceptered kings and the assembly of soldiers were called upon to listen and give advice as appropriate. Odysseus's efforts to persuade the soldiers to remain on the campaign at Troy were political acts; likewise, the soldiers' reception of his entreaties was a political act.

David began his rise to the kingship by inheriting his parent's household

---

181. Victor Turner, *Anthropology of Performance* (New York: PAJ, 1986), p. 84; Hammer, "The Politics of the *Iliad*," pp. 7-11.

182. Max Weber, *Economy and Society* (New York: Bedminster, 1968), 2:902.

and using it as a base to gather wealth and warriors. From this household base, he negotiated with the household of Nabal and took it over, as the narrative states, through marriage and inheritance. David's actions triggered responses by Abigail and the servants of Nabal's household, which led to changes in their status and roles within the changing political landscape of Judah. It was not only David's actions that enabled him to gain the kingship, but others also joined with him and shifted their identities through association with him: for example, Abigail proclaimed that David would be the king of Judah and Israel. His authority would later emerge in the full light of day, but it was now being built through the multiple interactions of individuals and their households in Judah. Because many were finding new roles and positions for themselves by associating with David and his household, political practices and structures in Judah were shifting from an association of clans to the beginning stages of a state.

Hammurapi's proclamation in his clay-nail inscription was inserted in the wall of Sippar to testify to those in Sippar who observed it that this king of the neighboring city of Babylon had carried out a beneficial deed for them. The proclamation drew upon traditional language and beliefs of the Shamash temple to persuade an audience of the divine election of Hammurapi to rule their city. Even if those who could read the inscription were limited to an elite, the wall itself was obvious to all who passed by and would have communicated a message about the power of one who was able to oversee its construction. Hammurapi's interpretation of how this wall came into existence would have been communicated orally, at least by gossip, in Sippar. This proclamation would also have had an impact on the people of Babylon, particularly those involved in the administration of his kingdom. The reception of Hammurapi's proclamation was a significant political act. Most likely, many would have rejected Hammurapi's claim; nevertheless, it is important politically that he made this effort to articulate the basis of his authority. The more persuasive Hammurapi was, the more authority he wielded, which meant that his kingship was more powerful.

Hammurapi ruled out of the locus of his royal household in Babylon. Kingship in Babylon had maintained a dynastic form for over a hundred years by the time Hammurapi began to rule. From this relatively well-established institutional position, Hammurapi was still working out of the model of the relationships of a household to extend his influence over neighboring cities. In his restructuring of the administration of the temple household of Shamash, he no doubt alienated many in the local population and diminished his authority in their eyes. Big men who ruled over wealthy households used physical and material force to increase the power of their own households, but they could not build authority in a community by such forceful means unless they also increased the well-being of the people. It is possible that Hammurapi's restructuring of the Shamash temple in Sippar decreased his authority in Sippar but increased it in Babylon, where the benefits of this restructuring were felt. The clay-nail inscription indicates that Hammurapi made an effort to persuade the people in both Sippar and Babylon to see him as their divinely appointed ruler. The proclamation of the inscription was a political act.

In the assembly of Achaean warriors, the commoner Thersites was chastised by Odysseus for speaking words critical of Agamemnon (*Il.* 2.243-77).[183] Odysseus's action won the approval of the assembly at large (*Il.* 2.270-77), which indicated that some forms of dissent could not be tolerated. Even though Thersites echoed many of the criticisms of Agamemnon voiced by Achilles, his manner was disrespectful: he did not take into account the difference in rank between himself and the sceptered kings. This episode raises questions about the place of dissent within the Homeric community. Tensions between the higher and lower ranking members of the community would have opened a crack within the aristocratic ethos dominant in the Homeric epics.[184] Upon hearing the episode of the reprimand of Thersites, the commoner in the city-states in the eighth to sixth centuries B.C. would have had an opportunity to raise questions about who had the right to speak in the assembly. In the Archaic Age (700-450 B.C.) in Greece, the male landowners were the ones who exercised the upper hand in decision making in the assemblies.[185] The Homeric narratives were capable of provoking discussions where the tensions between the center and the periphery, or between the dominant class and the subordinate class, could be expressed.

Pro- and antimonarchic viewpoints came to expression in the episode of

183. Raaflaub, "Homer to Solon," pp. 54-55. Donlan (*The Aristocratic Ideal in Ancient Greece*, p. 22) claims that the dissenting voice of Thersites probably reflects the views of the ordinary people who were primarily concerned about food and survival rather than about gaining glory.

184. For the aristocratic ethos of the epics, see Thalmann, *The Swineherd and the Bow*, pp. 275-81; Rose, *Sons of the Gods, Children of Earth*, pp. 25, 41, 55, 61, 137-40; Tandy, *Warriors into Traders*, pp. 194-96. However, Donlan (*The Aristocratic Ideal in Ancient Greece*, p. 19) does not think that there was an aristocratic class in Homer where a certain stratum of individuals had access to certain goods and privileges; rather, he contends it was a ranked society in which individuals who excelled were awarded special privileges.

185. Morris, *Archaeology as Cultural History*, pp. 114, 117, 161, 189; Paul Cartledge, "Power and the State," in *Ancient Greece*, ed. Paul Cartledge (Cambridge: Cambridge University Press, 1998), pp. 147-49; James L. O'Neil, *The Origins and Development of Ancient Greek Democracy* (Lanham, Md.: Rowman & Littlefield, 1995), pp. 1, 30-31, 135-36; Raphael Sealey, *The Justice of the Greeks* (Ann Arbor: University of Michigan Press, 1994), pp. 87-89, 152.

David and Nabal in the Judaean desert. The aggressive opportunism of David stood in tension with the ungenerous complacency of Nabal. Abigail and a servant of Nabal articulated the pro-Davidic position. The realism of the hard-nosed warrior tactics of David created a measure of ambivalence about David's motives that could have generated sympathy, at least momentarily, with Nabal. In subsequent decades, when the Jerusalem monarchy was well established, reflection on the question of royal taxation was probably provoked by this story. Royal taxation may well have been a necessity, but reflection on its legitimacy through the ongoing interpretation of passages like 1 Samuel 25 could have been a force in keeping such taxation in check.

Hammurapi's clay-nail inscription celebrated the construction of the wall of Sippar as a sign of the legitimacy of his rule over the city. The references in the inscription to shifts in the administration of corvée labor by the temple of Shamash suggest that opposing voices to the rule of Hammurapi existed in Sippar.[186] So, this royal inscription tried to remove grounds for criticizing Hammurapi through lavish praise of his person and accomplishments. As doubts about the king's perfection arose among the people either in Sippar or in Babylon, it seems that any criticism could have been expressed only in private. The image of the ruling king as an ideal was not to be tarnished. However, if people had specific questions about the justice of certain royal decisions or policies, there were avenues for them to make appeals, as evidenced repeatedly in the royal correspondence and promised in texts such as the epilogue of the *Code of Hammurapi* (XLVIII:3-58).[187]

Authority in a kingdom was centralized in the king, but he did not exercise authority alone. Such authority emerged in the interactions between the king and the people, for authority is a relational phenomenon. When ruler and ruled connected so that their common interests were augmented, then authority manifested itself. Because neither party was in control of authority, it is appropriate to speak of authority in Homeric Greece, biblical Israel, and OB Mesopotamia as a gift of the king of the gods who held sovereignty over heaven and earth.

At strategic times, a king or an aspirant to the throne had to exert force to gain compliance to measures that he believed necessary for the community. To keep the material basis of his power from slipping away, he had to keep his royal household in order, for this locus of his key relationships would weaken if it was left untended. The amount of wealth and military power at the king's dis-

---

186. Cf. Norman Yoffee, "Political Economy in Early Mesopotamian States," *Annual Review of Anthropology* 24 (1995): 301.

187. Hurowitz, *Inu Anum Sīrum*, pp. 32-37.

posal was a significant factor in his negotiations with neighboring kings, but even more significant was the way an alliance would fit into the larger network of alliances in the region where the balance of power was forged through competing and cooperating relationships among kings. In sum, the king's material power was only a tool to assist him in getting his commands obeyed and exerting influence. How he used his eloquence, wisdom, and piety in combination with his physical and material power to strengthen relationships within and outside the community was decisive in whether or not he was able to receive authority from God or the gods.

CHAPTER THREE

Centralization of the Community in the Person of the King

The world as we know it is an interpreted world. Language, with its grammar and vocabulary, is given to us along with a culture and a tradition in which language has played an indispensable role in shaping and ordering the world.[1] Our awareness of the world is mediated primarily by language. We adapt, change, and grow as we negotiate our way in a world that has been given to us and yet can never be known by us absolutely. Particularly within the practical realm of everyday life, our knowledge of people, communities, and traditions demands ongoing attentiveness if communication is to be sustained. An indispensable dimension of this communication is the use of symbols. Kings through the ages have used the crown, the scepter, and various ceremonials as symbols of royal rule where the king's person points to the unity in the community requisite for collective praxis.[2]

A symbol, a term derived from the Greek *symballein,* "to cast alongside, to throw together," is an object that stands for or represents something else. For example, the American flag symbolizes the United States. More specifically, a symbol evokes a larger whole or system of relations; so, the flag symbolizes the bonds that unite citizens of the United States. A symbol is a polyvalent sign that

---

1. Paul Ricoeur (*Time and Narrative,* vol. 1 [Chicago: University of Chicago Press, 1984], p. 57) states: "If, in fact, human action can be narrated, it is because it is always already articulated by signs, rules, and norms. It is always already symbolically mediated."

2. David Cannadine, "Introduction: Divine Rites of Kings," in *Rituals of Royalty: Power and Ceremonial in Traditional Societies* (Cambridge: Cambridge University Press, 1987), pp. 1-4; Ernst Kantorowicz, *The King's Two Bodies: A Study in Medieval Political Theology* (Princeton: Princeton University Press, 1957), pp. 4-5.

can entertain more than one meaning.[3] In contrast, the conventional sign of a red light means "stop"; this sign functions only if it has a clearly defined meaning that all drivers are aware of and accept. Unlike a sign conventionally defined to carry specific information, a symbol entertains diverse perspectives and holds them together, and thus in the political or religious sphere a symbol can unite a group without demanding uniformity.[4] For example, the crowd in a stadium can sing the national anthem where those assembled have diverse understandings of the value of patriotism.

The wall of a Greek city with its imposing physical character became a symbol for the community resident within its ramparts.[5] Likewise, the wall of the Mesopotamian city symbolized the power of the king and community resident within it.[6] The strength of the stone and the height of the wall separated hostile foes from the residents within. The pragmatic defensive function of the wall sufficiently accounted for its existence, but its prominence and durability as a boundary marker were probably characteristics that led to its additional symbolic role of helping the citizenry reflect on and distinguish between those who belonged to the community and those who did not.[7] A symbol can evoke the whole network of relationships that unites a community and calls individu-

3. Douglas McGaughey, "Ricoeur's Metaphor and Narrative Theories as a Foundation for a Theory of Symbol," *Religious Studies* 24 (1988): 431, 433; cf. John A. Lucy, "The Scope of Linguistic Relativity," in *Re-thinking Linguistic Relativity*, ed. John J. Gumperz and Stephen C. Levinson (Cambridge: Cambridge University Press, 1996), p. 40; Terry Eagleton, *Literary Theory: An Introduction*, 2nd ed. (Minneapolis: University of Minnesota Press, 1996), p. 102; John Miles Foley, *Homer's Traditional Art* (University Park: Pennsylvania State University Press, 1999), pp. 3, 13.

4. Louis-Marie Chauvet, *Symbol and Sacrament* (Collegeville, Minn.: Liturgical, 1995), p. 121.

5. Stephen Scully, *Homer and the Sacred City* (Ithaca: Cornell University Press, 1990), p. 26; cf. Kurt Raaflaub, "Homer to Solon: The Rise of the *Polis:* The Written Sources," in *The Ancient Greek City-State: Symposium on the Occasion of the 250th Anniversary of the Royal Danish Academy of Sciences and Letters, July 1-4, 1992*, ed. M. H. Hansen (Copenhagen: Munksgaard, 1993), p. 53.

6. A. L. Oppenheim, *Ancient Mesopotamia: Portrait of a Dead Civilization* (Chicago: University of Chicago Press, 1977), p. 128; Stephanie Dalley, "Ancient Mesopotamian Military Organization," in *Civilizations of the Ancient Near East*, ed. Jack Sasson (New York: Scribner, 1995), pp. 413-14.

7. Edmund Leach (*Culture and Communication: The Logic by Which Symbols Are Connected* [New York: Cambridge University Press, 1976], pp. 34-35) notes that all boundaries are artificial — they make discontinuous what is naturally continuous — and so are a source of anxiety. John R. Searle (*Mind, Language, and Society: Philosophy in the Real World* [New York: Basic Books, 1998], p. 154) states that "humans have the capacity to use one object to stand for, represent, express, or symbolize something else. It is this basic symbolizing feature of language that I take to be an essential presupposition of institutional facts."

als to reflect and act upon their bonds with one another in that community so as to keep adapting and reproducing these relationships.

The king's body functioned as a symbol for the community in Homeric Greece, biblical Israel, and OB Mesopotamia. The plot of the *Odyssey* demonstrates that the king embodies the "community principle": that is, the stronger the king, the stronger the community.[8] Without a strong king like Odysseus, the community fragments and diminishes. In biblical Israel, Psalm 20 reflects the conviction that the well-being of the community is an analogue and a consequence of the well-being of the king who is victorious in battle when the people pray:

> May he [the Lord] give what your heart seeks,
> fulfill all that you plan.
> May we rejoice in your victory
> and raise banners in the name of our God. (Ps. 20:5-6[4-5])

When Hammurapi oversaw the construction of a canal, he commemorated it in an inscription with the words: "I dug the canal (named), 'Hammurapi is the prosperity of the people,' which brings abundant waters to the lands of Sumer and Akkad."[9] The workers and resources from the community are incorporated into the king's use of the first-person pronoun: the king's body is analogous to the group of builders and represents it. The name of the canal states that the prosperity of Hammurapi is both an analogue and a cause for the prosperity of the people.

The scepter that the king held and the throne that he sat upon represented him (i.e., a metonym).[10] The flesh-and-blood reality of the king living within a community was an essential dimension of the symbolic character of the king's rule.[11] The corporeality of the king's existence included the social and psychological as well as biological dimensions of his being. If the body is the place where the "inside" and "outside" meet and where the social, cosmic, and ances-

---

8. Moses I. Finley, *The World of Odysseus* (New York: Viking, 1965), p. 106.

9. Douglas Frayne, *RIME 4*, E4.3.6.7, lines 17-22.

10. Alison Salveson, "The Trappings of Royalty in Ancient Hebrew," in *King and Messiah in Israel and the Ancient Near East*, ed. John Day, JSOTSup 270 (Sheffield: Sheffield Academic Press, 1998), pp. 131-38.

11. Although the texts of Homeric Greece, biblical Israel, and OB Mesopotamia do not explicitly state that the king's body is an analogy for the body politic, such language of European medieval political theology is implicit in the political rhetoric of these ancient cultures; cf. Kantorowicz, *The King's Two Bodies*, pp. 3-6. On the corporal or material dimension of symbols, see Paul Ricoeur, *Freud and Philosophy: An Essay on Interpretation* (New Haven: Yale University Press, 1970), pp. 12, 16-17, 45, 49.

tral are symbolically joined,[12] how much the more so was the body of the king such a dynamic locus of integration for the community.

Situated at the center of the community, the king became a reference point for structuring the relationships and practices within the community. The human and material resources of the monarchically organized community were centralized in order to strengthen the community's defense against foreign foes and to secure its livelihood through production and trade. As the primary political decision maker in the community, the king could influence not only the way in which his own household and royal court carried on their business, but also the ways in which the temple household and private entrepreneurs carried on their businesses.[13] Although coercive force to back up the king's commands was indispensable to his credibility, a more intrusive way for the king to exert influence on the people's lives was to centralize many of the practices of the community and make the people aware of his authority in their daily activities. Conversely, with greater centralization, the king set himself up to be the object of blame for conflicts and contradictions in the community, often for those for which no other explanation could be provided. Such blame was not to be expressed directly or openly, but it no doubt circulated in the workplace, the home, and private gatherings. The symbolic medium with both its benefits and its burdens for the king was essential to his capacity to structure a community and maintain its equilibrium with him at the center.[14]

The shared identity of the king and people can also be understood as the

12. Chauvet, *Symbol and Sacrament*, pp. 147-50; Robert Cummings Neville, *The Truth of Broken Symbols* (Albany, N.Y.: SUNY Press, 1996), p. 47; cf. Bryan S. Turner, "The Body in Western Society: Social Theory and Its Perspectives," in *Religion and the Body*, ed. S. Coakley, Cambridge Studies in Religious Traditions 8 (Cambridge: Cambridge University Press, 1997), pp. 15-16.

13. Marc Van de Mieroop, *The Ancient Mesopotamian City* (Oxford: Clarendon, 1997), p. 202; cf. Daniel Snell, "Trade and Commerce," in *ABD*, 6:627; Johannes Renger, "Patterns of Non-Institutional Trade and Non-Commercial Exchange in Ancient Mesopotamia at the Beginning of the Second Millennium B.C.," in *Circulation of Goods in Non-Palatial Context in the Ancient Near East*, ed. A. Archi, Incunabula Graeca 62 (Rome: Edizioni Del L'Ateneo, 1984), pp. 62-63. The Israelite tradition celebrates the trade of Solomon (1 Kings 9:26-28; 10:11-12), but the role of the merchant in Israelite society is subdued in the biblical texts (cf. Daniel Snell, "Trade and Commerce (ANE)," in *ABD*, 6:628). In spite of the increasing trade in the eighth to the sixth centuries B.C. in Greece, the Homeric epics infrequently mention traders; and, when they do, trade is seen as the occupation of pirates and lowly individuals; see David Tandy, *Warriors into Traders: The Power of the Market in Early Greece* (Berkeley: University of California Press, 1997), p. 125.

14. Victor Turner (*The Anthropology of Performance* [New York: PAJ, 1986], p. 21) promotes an examination of the dialectics of sociocultural processes where the focus is upon "changing socio-symbolic fields rather than static structures."

royal metaphor. The contention that the king "is" and "is not" the community could lead individuals to be circumspect in responding to his commands, but at the same time it could lead to a greater measure of understanding of the short-comings of the king. Metaphoric and symbolic ways of thinking, with their emphasis upon the similarities, differences, and analogies in the relationships between persons and things, are conducive to the pragmatic political task of fostering equilibrium within a community.[15] If the king were distant from most of the people and did not give them a voice in the affairs of the kingdom, the royal propaganda would try to persuade as many people as possible of the strength, benevolence, and justice of the king.[16] Symbols that call for the people to bracket their experience can lead them to make sacrifices for the community. It is conceivable that such sacrifices could be exploitation of the people by the powerful.[17] There is, however, a limit to the patience of the people. Even though symbols are conventional, this does not diminish their capacity to communicate truth; some basic truths about life are learned only in the process of creating or making something.[18] It simply means that symbols need to be seen as emerging from the interactions of people in a community. As such, they need to be rethought and reproduced just like other practices and structures in the community. Royal rhetoric drew on the traditions of the community and used symbols, metaphors, and narratives that communicated largely by resonating

15. Equilibrium is a state of balance among competing forces. In the political arena, such competing forces might be orthodoxy versus heresy or reactionary versus radical. On the dialectical character of this process, see Pierre Bourdieu, "Description and Prescription," in *Language and Symbolic Power,* ed. John B. Thompson (Cambridge, Mass.: Harvard University Press, 1991), pp. 129-32.

16. Henri Limet, "Reflexions sur la nature et l'efficacité d'une opposition," in *La voix de l'opposition en Mésopotamie* (Brussels: Institut des Hautes Études de Belgique, 1973), pp. 79, 85-86. Zdzislaw Mach (*Symbols, Conflict, and Identity: Essays in Political Anthropology* [New York: SUNY Press, 1993], pp. 108, 268-69) argues that "power structure and symbolic culture are relatively independent and shape each other." Autocratic regimes "monopolize symbolic life and do not allow the free expression of ideas." Under such tyranny, symbols generate opposition as they reveal an intolerable alienation of the majority of the population.

17. Pierre Bourdieu ("On Symbolic Power," in *Language and Symbolic Power,* ed. John B. Thompson [Cambridge, Mass.: Harvard University Press, 1991], p. 170) argues that people bracket or adapt their experience to symbols; they accept symbols by denying that the connection communicated by a symbol is arbitrary: that is, a symbol works only if people believe in it — which Bourdieu interprets as a move in which people deny the arbitrary connection between the sign and the object communicated by a symbol.

18. Paul Ricoeur, *The Rule of Metaphor: Multidisciplinary Studies of the Creation of Meaning in Language* (Toronto: University of Toronto Press, 1977), pp. 239, 306. Cf. Donald Phillip Verene, "Two Sources of Philosophical Memory: Vico versus Hegel," in *Philosophical Imagination and Cultural Memory,* ed. P. Cook (Durham, N.C.: Duke University Press, 1993), p. 50.

with the people's experience. Such royal rhetoric may have tried to hoodwink the people some of the time, but it can also be seen as trying to make intelligible the sacrifices that the king asked of them.[19] Such intelligibility, as it shaped the conscious thoughts and the political unconscious of the people, could help the community navigate difficult situations.

Semioticians and structuralists have argued that a sign or a symbol does not communicate a fixed meaning in itself; rather, its meaning is communicated in the context of its relation to other signs or symbols.[20] For example, the Israelite dietary practice of abstaining from pork may have had more to do with the way that this practice created a symbolic boundary between Israel and its neighbors than it did with responding to an economic or hygienic need. When this practice is situated within the system of clean and unclean animals, then, as Mary Douglas explains, a rationale emerges: a pig belongs to those quadrupeds that have a split hoof but do not chew the cud, which violates the characteristics of its class; as a taxonomic anomaly, the pig is unclean.[21] A structuralist sees the meaning of the dietary restriction in terms of the "wholeness" of a social structure.[22] Yet such an approach focuses upon the system itself; to the extent that the system dictates the meaning of a symbol, it detaches this meaning from the interplay of a symbol with the experience of the social actors.[23] Jacob Milgrom argues that even though there were connections between animal taxonomy and Israel's value system, Israel's dietary restriction on pork arose more from its ef-

---

19. The king, in order to ensure his preeminence in the community, may have tried to make the wagons circle around him by restructuring the community's symbol system. In these circumstances, the people may have become like sheep who placidly followed the king's statements and directions even if it meant denying their own experience. Pierre Bourdieu ("The Production and Reproduction of Legitimate Language," in *Language and Symbolic Power,* ed. John B. Thompson [Cambridge, Mass.: Harvard University Press, 1991], p. 51) refers to this manipulative use of symbols as "symbolic violence" but notes that it is carried out only on those predisposed to it. Cf. Peter W. Rose, *Sons of the Gods, Children of Earth: Ideology and Literary Form in Ancient Greece* (Ithaca: Cornell University Press, 1992), pp. 52, 55, 123-24.

20. Marcel Hénaff, *Claude Lévi-Strauss and the Making of Structural Anthropology* (Minneapolis: University of Minnesota Press, 1998), pp. 217-18. Jonathan Culler, *The Pursuit of Signs* [Ithaca: Cornell University Press, 1981], p. 40) explains that "a sign consists of the union of a signifier and signified. . . . both signifier and signifieds are purely relational entities, products of a system of differences. . . . instead of depending on the prior existence of a system of concepts, expression now depends on the prior existence of a system of signs."

21. Mary Douglas, *Purity and Danger* (London: Routledge & Kegan Paul, 1966), p. 55.

22. Walter Houston, *Purity and Monotheism: Clean and Unclean Animals in Biblical Law,* JSOTSup 140 (Sheffield: Sheffield Academic Press, 1993), p. 113; Hénaff, *Claude Lévi-Strauss,* p. 17.

23. Terry Eagleton, *Literary Theory: An Introduction,* 2nd ed. (Minneapolis: University of Minnesota Press, 1996), p. 98.

forts to differentiate its cult and dietary practices from those of the Philistines than from its view of the pig as a taxonomic anomaly.[24]

Symbols are polyvalent so that it is neither possible nor desirable to establish a clear and distinct univocal definition for the reality to which a symbol points. The symbol entertains multiple signifiers without trying to bring closure to the interpretive activity by saying that one signifier coincides fully with the signified.[25] In a symbol, as a signifier is matched with the signified, it reveals an aspect of the signified. For example, the wall of Sippar symbolizes the community resident in Sippar. What it means to be a part of that community will receive different nuances by the various members of the community, and these meanings will vary for individuals at different points in their experience.

In interpreting a symbol and allowing for the range of meanings generated by the play of the signifier, a form of binary thinking can help to unfold the polyvalence of a symbol.[26] In the dialectic between the two poles of the binary opposition, neither pole can claim more than a provisional understanding of the meaning of the symbol — although in practice such provisionality may not be acknowledged. For example, if one individual in Sippar believed that the wall of Sippar pointed to the new protection afforded by Hammurapi to the city, another may have countered by claiming that the wall pointed to the oppression that Hammurapi was causing the city. The dialectic between these two opposed interpretations continued until the contradiction between them was resolved. Another interpretation of the wall is that it is a boundary marker between those who are "inside" and "outside" the community. The opposition of "insider/outsider" is an antinomy: that is, it is not capable of a once-and-for-all solution. Political symbols facilitate political reflection by focusing upon a complex reality and allowing problematic aspects of it to be turned over in thought. This dialectic or binary thinking will lead to resolutions in some issues, but others will persist as antinomies.[27] These binary oppositions that persist — antinomies —

24. Jacob Milgrom, *Leviticus 1–16*, AB 3 (New York: Doubleday, 1991), pp. 651-52, 726.

25. Paul Ricoeur, *The Symbolism of Evil* (Boston: Beacon, 1967), pp. 350, 353-54; idem, *Freud and Philosophy*, pp. 16-18; Chauvet, *Symbol and Sacrament*, pp. 127-28.

26. Cf. G. E. R. Lloyd, *Polarity and Analogy: Two Types of Argumentation in Early Greek Thought* (Cambridge: Cambridge University Press, 1966), pp. 41-42; Saul Olyan, *Rites and Rank: Hierarchy in Biblical Representations of Cult* (Princeton: Princeton University Press, 2000), pp. 6, 12; Jean-Jacques Glassner, "The Use of Knowledge in Ancient Mesopotamia," in *Civilizations of the Ancient Near East*, ed. J. Sasson (New York: Scribner, 1995), p. 1818.

27. Culler (*The Pursuit of Signs*, p. 39) states that "the semiotics of literature . . . gives rise to a 'deconstructive movement' in which each pole of an opposition can be used to show that the other is in error but in which the undecidable dialectic gives rise to no synthesis because the antinomy is inherent in the very structure of our language, in the possibilities of our conceptual framework." Jürgen Habermas ("On the Distinction Between Poetic and Communicative Uses

characterize central issues for political reflection. Important binary oppositions for mapping out the landscape of a living, changing community are the distinctions between insider and outsider, male and female, sacred and profane, divine and human, good and evil, life and death, aristocrat and commoner, and civilized and savage. These oppositions cannot be settled once and for all without doing violence to aspects of the community's experience.[28]

The king legitimately symbolized the community as long as he remained true to the grid of relationships mapped out in the traditional pattern of authority: the king shared in the sovereign rule of the king of the gods in caring for the people. Within this larger grid of relationships, the centralizing practices of the king could strengthen the relationships in the community by including both divine and human actors. The grid of the Homeric community was shaped not only by statuses bestowed at birth but also by statuses achieved; thus, cooperative and competitive virtues had their place within the dynamics of such a community.[29] In biblical Israel, David's warriors achieved special ranks for their exploits (2 Sam. 23:8-39). Yet the final form of the tradition is subdued in its acknowledgment of the exploits of warriors or builders after the time of David and Solomon. The grid of the community in which an Israelite was to find his or her place in the community was often sketched out in genealogies in the earlier parts of Israel's history where kinship was the organizing force of the society; there status would have been ascribed more so than achieved.[30] However, in mo-

---

of Language," in *On the Pragmatics of Communication* [Cambridge, Mass.: MIT Press, 1998], pp. 393-94) cautions that the distinction between normal language and poetic language should not be covered over by using poetic language as a model for all communicative practices. The language of science, morality, and law is tested for validity in the practice of problem-solving in particular ways that art and literature are not. See also Richard Buxton, *Imaginary Greece* (Cambridge: Cambridge University Press, 1994), p. 208; Fredric Jameson, *The Political Unconscious: Narrative as a Socially Symbolic Act* (Ithaca: Cornell University Press, 1981), p. 114; idem, *The Seeds of Time* (New York: Columbia University Press, 1994), pp. 4-5, 70.

28. Jameson, *The Political Unconscious*, p. 114; John Gould, "On Making Sense of Greek Religion," in *Myth, Ritual Memory, and Exchange: Essays in Greek Literature and Culture* (New York: Oxford University Press, 2001), p. 226; Rose, *Sons of the Gods, Children of Earth*, pp. 135-36.

29. Margalit Finkelberg, "*Timē* and *Aretē* in Homer," *Classical Quarterly* 48 (1998): 18; for a critique of Finkelberg's argument on cooperative virtues as the key to the *Iliad*, see John Gould, "Addendum (2000)," in *Myth, Ritual Memory, and Exchange: Essays in Greek Literature and Culture* (New York: Oxford University Press, 2001), pp. 353-57; cf. Paul Wason, *The Archaeology of Rank* (Cambridge: Cambridge University Press, 1996), pp. 38-39.

30. Frank Moore Cross, *From Epic to Canon: History and Literature in Ancient Israel* (Baltimore: Johns Hopkins University Press, 1998), p. 7; Robert Wilson, "Genealogy, Genealogies," in *ABD*, 2:930-31; Wason, *The Archaeology of Rank*, pp. 48-49, 57, 61; cf. Baruch Halpern, *David's Secret Demons: Messiah, Murderer, Traitor, King* (Grand Rapids: Eerdmans, 2001), p. 274; David Carr, *Reading the Fractures of Genesis* (Louisville: Westminster/John Knox, 1996), p. 137.

narchical times, efforts to achieve status in the eyes of the king and of the palace and temple establishments had a prominent place as part of a stratified society.[31] In OB Mesopotamia, status was often stated to be a reality bestowed by the gods;[32] yet the hierarchy managed by the king gave opportunities for some to achieve a higher rank. Tradition and religious practices as well as economic, military, and political activities shaped the hierarchy of a particular community. In the midst of this web of intersecting forces that shaped the hierarchy of the community, the king aimed to be the central symbol of the community and to re-shape all other symbolic identifiers of the community with reference to himself — an effort that was positive for a monarchically organized community and legitimate as long as it sustained the grid of relationships mapped out in the traditional pattern of authority.[33]

The ways in which the king served as the symbolic center of the communities of Homeric Greece, biblical Israel, and ancient Mesopotamia will be examined in passages from each of these cultural traditions that address the oppositions between the civilized and the savage, nature and culture, aristocrat and commoner, divine and human, and life and death.[34] In the midst of these polarities or oppositions, the boundaries of the community were marked out and maintained. Each of these polarities can be imagined as the foci of an ellipse: for example, the tension between nature and culture creates a force field or a sphere marked out by the circumference of the ellipse. So, the boundaries of the community may be imagined as dynamic realities in the form of ellipses that intersect and overlap with the king as the common reference point of these ellipses (see the illustration on p. 108). The power and authority of the king within the community positioned him in such a way that his actions and decisions had an ongoing, decisive impact on the maintenance of the boundaries of the community.

Insiders and Outsiders: Defining the Boundaries of the Community

A primary responsibility of the king was to keep the community safe from foreign foes and invaders. He needed to maintain the boundaries of the commu-

---

31. Olyan, *Rites and Rank*, pp. 8-9; cf. Wason, *The Archaeology of Rank*, pp. 45, 57-59.

32. Jean Bottéro, *Mesopotamia: Writing, Reasoning, and the Gods* (Chicago: University of Chicago Press, 1992), p. 136; cf. Frederick Cryer, *Divination in Ancient Israel and Its Near Eastern Environment*, JSOTSup 142 (Sheffield: Sheffield Academic Press, 1994), pp. 196-97.

33. Cf. Finley, *The World of Odysseus*, p. 106.

34. The binary opposition of male-female deserves a lengthy study of its own and will not be addressed here.

The King as the Centralizing Symbol of the Community

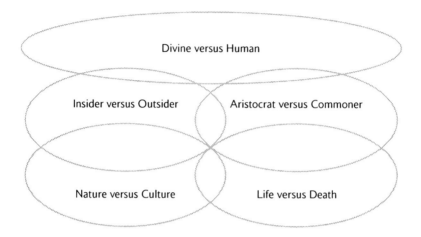

Divine versus Human

Insider versus Outsider

Aristocrat versus Commoner

Nature versus Culture

Life versus Death

nity against the forces of chaos. How the community imagined the boundaries that distinguished insiders from outsiders went beyond geographical markers to ways of life or the distinctive practices of a people.

Homer distinguished the civilized from the savage and the human from the subhuman in his account of the adventure of Odysseus and his men in the land of the Cyclopes. Homer identified humans as "eaters of bread" (*Od.* 9.89). To their horror, Odysseus and his men discovered that the Cyclopes were cannibals. In their first encounter with the giant Cyclops by the name of Polyphemus, Odysseus identified his party as followers of Agamemnon of Argos, who was now famous for his sack of Troy. Polyphemus responded by taking two of Odysseus's men, smashing them, and eating them raw, "guts, flesh and bones full of marrow" (*Od.* 9.293). This action, which Polyphemus repeated two more times on the following day (*Od.* 9.311-12, 344), situated him in the category of the subhuman or savage.[35] What people eat and what they are forbidden to eat addresses a daily repeated activity of people and so has a significant impact on the way people understand themselves and relate to one another. Sharing food and conversation at a meal is a primary way in which people cultivate relationships.[36] Polyphemus did not wish to relate to Odysseus and

35. Charles Segal, *Singers, Heroes, and Gods in the Odyssey* (Ithaca: Cornell University Press, 1994), pp. 30-32; Pierre Vidal-Naquet, *The Black Hunter: Forms of Thought and Forms of Society in the Greek World* (Baltimore: Johns Hopkins University Press, 1986), p. 8.

36. Mary Douglas, *Natural Symbols: Explorations in Cosmology* (New York: Pantheon, 1982), pp. 41, 50.

his companions by respecting their independence and difference; rather, he chose to obliterate them by devouring them.[37] Peter Rose states that Polyphemus and the Cyclopes may have served for the Archaic Greek audiences as symbols of colonists whose existence and way of life doubled back on the home cities and began to alter their social structures and practices.[38]

When Homer introduced the Cyclopes, he described them as a nonagricultural, mountain-dwelling breed: "[the Cyclopes] neither plow with their hands nor plant anything, but all grows for them without seed planting, without cultivation, wheat and barley and also the grapevines" (*Od.* 9.108-10). Polyphemus was a herder who milked his sheep and goats and made cheese (*Od.* 9.219-26, 308-10, 341-43). Earlier in his description of the land of the Cyclopes, Odysseus noted that the land itself was fit for cultivation, if the Cyclopes had chosen to do so (*Od.* 9.105-35). Homer privileged the farmer over the herder in his worldview as the one who had a more civilized way of life: an attitude that seems to reflect the increasing demarcation of space into agricultural plots at the expense of sheepherders in Greece of the eighth century B.C.[39] Sanctuaries in the rural areas served to demarcate boundaries between the civilized and the uncivilized, between plots of land and open range.[40]

The biblical tradition of Israel honored the seminomadic, shepherding way of life of its early ancestors. Although such a seminomadic lifestyle was not lived in opposition to the life of the farmer but often involved a combination of farming and herding, the biblical tradition valued a lifestyle on the margins of a state system that allowed the ancestors to carry on their way of life and to practice their family religion with integrity.[41] In the story of Cain and Abel, God preferred the sacrifice of the lamb by the herder Abel over the grain offering of the farmer Cain (Gen. 4:2-5). No clear reason is given in the story for such a preference.[42] One is left with the question why the story shows God accepting the offering of the shepherd Abel and not that of the farmer Cain. Why not vice versa? Perhaps the agricultural offering was tainted because of the curse on the

---

37. Pietro Pucci, *The Song of the Sirens* (New York: Rowman & Littlefield, 1998), p. 117.

38. Rose, *Sons of the Gods, Children of Earth*, pp. 126, 138.

39. Vidal-Naquet, *The Black Hunter*, p. 21; François de Polignac, *Cults, Territory, and the Origins of the Greek City-State* (Chicago: University of Chicago Press, 1995), pp. 34-35, 38.

40. De Polignac, *Cults, Territory, and the Origins of the Greek City-State*, p. 39.

41. Rainer Albertz, *A History of Israelite Religion in the Old Testament Period*, vol. 1: *From the Beginnings to the End of the Monarchy* (Louisville: Westminster/John Knox, 1992), p. 39; Theodore Hiebert, *The Yahwist's Landscape: Nature and Religion in Early Israel* (New York: Oxford University Press, 1996), pp. 19-22.

42. In the Jacob stories (Gen. 25:19–35:29), the narrator elevates Jacob, the shepherd, above Esau, the hunter (Gen. 25:27-28).

soil (Gen. 3:17-19).[43] The fratricide that followed was carried out by the tiller of this cursed soil.[44] Theodore Hiebert argues that the archetypal conflict in this story is not between the farmer and the herder but rather between brothers.[45] Cain was challenged to exercise restraint and not react violently toward his brother just as Adam and Eve were challenged by God's command to refrain from eating from the fruit of the tree of the knowledge of good and evil.[46] The story of the fratricide coupled with the cursing of the ground pointed to the fact that there would be trouble in living on the land as farmers.

Second Samuel 7 states that David requested to build a temple for the Lord. After giving an initial approval, the prophet Nathan reported the following nocturnal revelation that he received from the Lord:[47]

> Thus says the Lord: "Would you build me a house to reside in? I have not resided in a house from the day on which I made the Israelites go up from Egypt to the present, but I have been traveling about in a tent and a tabernacle. In all my traveling among all the Israelites, did I ever say a thing to any one of the leaders whom I appointed to shepherd my people Israel, saying: 'Why have you not built me a house of cedar?'" (2 Sam. 7:5-7)

The seminomadic, shepherding way of life is idealized in this passage as the time-honored traditional way that the Lord resided among his people. The Lord previously had not lived among the Israelites as the lord of a manor in a city.[48] David's proposal to have the Lord dwell in a "house of cedar" in the city

43. Gary Herion, "Why God Rejected Cain's Offering: The Obvious Answer," in *Fortunate the Eyes That See: Essays in Honor of David Noel Freedman in Celebration of His Seventieth Birthday*, ed. A. Beck et al. (Grand Rapids: Eerdmans, 1995), pp. 53-54, 61-62, 64; Frank Spina, "The 'Ground' for Cain's Rejection: *'ădāmāh* in the Context of Gen 1-11," *ZAW* 104 (1992): 323-24, 332.

44. Spina, "The 'Ground' for Cain's Rejection," pp. 327-28; Joseph Blenkinsopp, *The Pentateuch* (New York: Doubleday, 1992), p. 69.

45. Hiebert, *The Yahwist's Landscape*, p. 40.

46. Carr (*Reading the Fractures of Genesis*, p. 69) identified the following parallels between the stories of "Adam and Eve" and "Cain and Abel": "divine prohibition/warning (Gen. 2:17; 4:7), misdeed (3:1-6; 4:8), divine interrogations of humans (Gen. 3:8-13; 4:9-10), punishment involving alienation from the ground (3:17-19; 4:11-12), softening of condition (3:21; 4:13-15), and final expulsion of the human eastward (Gen. 3:24; 4:16)."

47. Tomoo Ishida ("*Šōpēṭ*: The Leaders of the Tribal Leagues 'Israel' in the Pre-Monarchical Period," in *History and Historical Writing in Ancient Israel: Studies in Biblical Historiography* [Leiden: Brill, 1999], p. 45) claims that the prophecy of Nathan stems from the time of David and Solomon.

48. P. Kyle McCarter, Jr., *II Samuel*, AB 9 (Garden City, N.Y.: Doubleday, 1984), p. 199; William Schniedewind, *Society and the Promise to David: The Reception History of 2 Samuel 7:1-17* (New York: Oxford University Press, 1999), pp. 38-39.

of Jerusalem threatened to send the message that settled life in the land under the rule of a king like the neighboring nations was to be accepted without question. The construction of a temple would shift an important symbol of the community and so alter the community's self-understanding. The Israelite tradition's positive estimate of the marginality of the seminomadic way of life placed a reservation on wholehearted acceptance of the monarchy.[49]

Dietary restrictions for the Israelites (Exod. 22:31; Lev. 11:2-47; Deut. 14:3-21) served to distinguish the Israelites from their neighbors. The logic of this dietary code, which forbade the consumption of land animals that did not chew the cud but had cloven hooves and of water creatures without fins and scales, appears to have been based primarily on the internal coherence of the code or system, although hygienic, economic, or cultic concerns cannot be ignored as factors shaping these dietary practices.[50] This dietary code would have helped Israel maintain its distinctiveness while accommodating to various other dimensions of city life and farming.[51]

In ancient Mesopotamia, city-life, including life both within the walls and in the surrounding countryside, was normative.[52] The antithesis to the city dwellers were mountain men who were herders, known as Gutians in popular parlance. Such roaming mountaineers were regarded as uncivilized and incapable of making progress.[53] Somewhat less barbaric, yet still stereotyped as subhuman by various Sumerian sources in the late third and early second millennium B.C., were the Amorites. These Amorites are collectively criticized as a nomadic herder in the following excerpt from "The Marriage of Martu," a Sumerian composition probably from the late Ur III or early Isin-Larsa period (ca. 2000 B.C.):[54]

A man who is clothed in a leather-sac, who. . . .
He is a tent-dweller, [*buffeted*] by wind and rain, [who offers no] prayer,
He who dwells in the mountains, [knows not] the places [*of the gods*],
A man who digs up mushrooms at the (foot of) the mountain,
 knows no submission,
He eats uncooked meat,

49. Schniedewind, *Society and the Promise to David*, pp. 48-49.

50. Douglas, *Purity and Danger*, p. 55. Milgrom (*Leviticus 1–16*, pp. 704, 726-28) argues that the dietary laws of Leviticus 11 can be understood only in the context of the total dietary system mapped out in the Priestly source.

51. Milgrom, *Leviticus 1–16*, p. 730; David Wright, "Unclean and Clean," in *ABD*, 6:740.

52. Van de Mieroop, *The Ancient Mesopotamian City*, p. 11.

53. Cf. Glassner, "The Use of Knowledge in Ancient Mesopotamia," p. 1821.

54. Jacob Klein, "The *Marriage of Martu:* The Urbanization of 'Barbaric' Nomads," in *Mutual Influences of Peoples and Cultures in the Ancient Near East*, ed. M. Malul (Haifa: University of Haifa Press, 1996), pp. 89-90.

In his lifetime has no house,
When he dies, he will not be burried (sic). (lines 132-38)[55]

As a herder who ate raw meat and who did not offer sacrifice to the gods, this Amorite resembled the Cyclopes. He was presumably also one who did not cultivate the land. However, in contrast to the Cyclopes, he was not a cannibal and did not dwell in a cave.

The contrast between city life and nomadic life was developed in the story of Enkidu in the *Epic of Gilgamesh*.[56] Enkidu was created to be the companion of Gilgamesh, the royal ruler in Uruk. The creator goddess Aruru initially placed Enkidu in the wilds as the companion of animals. Then the courtesan Shemshara initiated Enkidu into human society by having sexual relations with him. Next, shepherds taught him how to eat bread and drink beer. Later, however, when he was about to die, Enkidu cursed Shemshara for having brought him to civilization.[57] Here in the *Epic of Gilgamesh* the shepherd was situated between the animals and the city dweller. He partook of the fruits of the cultivated soil when he ate bread and drank beer. This description of the shepherd showed him to be associated with city life such as was common in the dimorphic society of most ancient Mesopotamian cities.[58]

Homeric Greece and OB Mesopotamia regarded farming and the settled

55. Translation from Jacob Klein, "Additional Notes to 'The Marriage of Martu,'" in *Kinattūtu ša darāti*, ed. A. F. Rainey (Tel Aviv: University of Tel Aviv Press, 1993), p. 20. See also Samuel N. Kramer, "The Marriage of Martu," in *Bar-Ilan Studies in Assyriology Dedicated to Pinhas Artzi*, ed. J. Klein and A. Skaist (Ramat-Gan, Israel: Bar-Ilan University Press, 1990), p. 21; Van de Mieroop, *The Ancient Mesopotamian City*, p. 43; Jean Bottéro and Samuel N. Kramer, *Lorsque les dieux faisaient l'homme: mythologie mésopotamienne* (Paris: Gallimard, 1989), p. 434, lines 132-44.

56. Frans Wiggermann, "Scenes from the Shadow Side," in *Intellectual Life of the Ancient Near East*, ed. Jirí Prosecký, CRRA 43 (Prague: Oriental Institute, 1998), p. 214; Gregory Mobley, "The Wild Man in the Bible and the Ancient Near East," *JBL* 116 (1997): 220-23.

57. Thorkild Jacobsen, "The Gilgamesh Epic: Romantic and Tragic Vision," in *Lingering over Words: Studies in Ancient Near Eastern Literature in Honor of William L. Moran*, ed. T. Abusch et al., HSM 37 (Atlanta: Scholars, 1990), pp. 234-35; Van de Mieroop, *The Ancient Mesopotamian City*, p. 44; Jonathan Z. Smith, "Wisdom's Place," in *Death, Ecstasy, and Other Worldly Journeys*, ed. John Collins and Michael Fishbane (Albany, N.Y.: SUNY Press, 1995), pp. 5-6.

58. Wolfram von Soden, *The Ancient Orient: An Introduction to the Study of the Ancient Near East* (Grand Rapids: Eerdmans, 1994), p. 77; A. Leo Oppenheim, *Ancient Mesopotamia: Portrait of a Dead Civilization* (Chicago: University of Chicago Press, 1977), pp. 113, 116; Rivkah Harris, *Ancient Sippar: A Demographic Study of an Old Babylonian City (1894-1595 B.C.)* (Leiden: Nederlands Historisch-Archaeologisch Instituut te Istanbul, 1975), pp. 10-14; Aage Westenholz and Ulla Koch-Westenholz, "Enkidu — the Noble Savage?" in *Wisdom, Gods and Literature: Studies in Assyriology in Honour of W. G. Lambert*, ed. A. R. George and I. L. Finkel (Winona Lake, Ind.: Eisenbrauns, 2000), pp. 443-44.

way of life as normative over against the herder and the seminomadic way of life. Conversely, Israel tended to idealize a seminomadic way of life insofar as it urged the community to resist absorption into a state system. Farming and shepherding coexisted in all three cultures, often with the same person cultivating crops in one season and herding in another. Nevertheless, the distinction between herder and farmer no doubt had an impact on one's place in the social hierarchy of a community in these three cultures. Royal rule supported farming as a way of life and found an important basis for its legitimacy therein.

Dietary practices also distinguished the civilized from the savage: the bread eater versus the cannibal in Homer, the one who ate bread and drank beer versus the one who grazed with the animals in OB Mesopotamia, the one who followed the Israelite dietary practices versus those who did not in biblical Israel.

Nature and Culture: The King's Responsibility for Successful Agriculture

Famine was an ever-present threat for the peoples of the ancient Near East.[59] The unpredictability of the rains and the floods was only one of the threats from nature that led to failed crops. Even though lands that received more than twelve inches of rain annually were usually guaranteed a crop, the threats from disease, pestilence, and plunder created apprehension for the farmers and reminded them that the margin between life and death was thin.[60] In lower Mesopotamia where the irrigation and flood control apparatus needed steady maintenance, the risk of crop failure was lower. However, such a mode of production was labor intensive and required ongoing coordination by community leaders.[61] Responding to crises in food production and

---

59. Christopher J. Eyre, "The Agricultural Cycle, Farming, and Water Management in the Ancient Near East," in *Civilizations of the Ancient Near East,* ed. Jack Sasson (New York: Scribner, 1995), pp. 185-88; William Shea, "Famine," in *ABD*, 2:769-70. D. T. Potts (*Mesopotamian Civilization: The Material Foundations* [Ithaca: Cornell University Press, 1997], pp. 57, 80-81) argues that agricultural production in Mesopotamia was reliable and efficient. However, Johannes Renger ("On Economic Structures in Ancient Mesopotamia," *Or* n.s. 63 [1994]: 196-97) notes that emergency loans to the poor prior to the harvest were common in the OB period. Cf. *ḥušaḥḥu,* in *CAD*, H:260-61.

60. Eyre, "The Agricultural Cycle," pp. 177-78; Oded Borowski, *Agriculture in Iron Age Israel* (Winona Lake, Ind.: Eisenbrauns, 1982), pp. 153-62; Shea, "Famine," pp. 769-73; Rose, *Sons of the Gods, Children of Earth,* pp. 130-31.

61. Johannes M. Renger, "Institutional, Communal, and Individual Ownership or Possession of Arable Land in Ancient Mesopotamia from the End of the Fourth to the End of the First Millennium B.C.," *Chicago-Kent Law Review* 71 (1995): 271; Eyre, "The Agricultural Cycle," p. 185; Potts, *Mesopotamian Civilization,* pp. 19-21.

taking measures to prevent them in the future became a primary *raison d'être* of the kingship.[62]

In the realm of fantasy in the Homeric world, the Cyclopes did not cultivate wheat or barley. Rather, such grains grew on their own and received timely rains from Zeus (*Od.* 9.109-11). The Phaeacians, a kingdom of human beings who lived in an ideal but impossible society, ate grain (*Od.* 7.104), but they did not have to till the soil.[63] They were the antithesis of the Cyclopes in their practice of hospitality, piety, feasting, and gift giving, but their society belonged to that described by Hesiod as "the age of gold," where old age and death were unknown and the earth automatically produced its fruit (*Works and Days*, lines 112-19).[64] Alcinous, king of the Phaeacians, had an orchard and a vineyard whose produce was abundant, ripe, and never withered or rotted (*Od.* 7.112-32).

In contrast to the gardens and orchards of the fantasy world of the Cyclopes and Phaeacians, the fruitful orchard of Odysseus's father Laertes in Ithaca produced regularly and abundantly, but not magically.[65] Here we see that the Homeric farmer, unlike the cunning carpenter who wrested a form from the wood, was expected to cooperate with the forces of nature.[66] On his return to Ithaca, Odysseus described to Laertes this orchard as it would have looked in Odysseus's childhood in order to prove his identity:

> Come, I will also tell you about the trees in the well-designed garden which you once gave me. When I was a child and followed along with you in the garden, I asked you about all of them. We went along among them; you named them and told me about all of them. You gave me thirteen pear trees and ten apple trees and forty fig trees. You specified fifty rows of vines to assign to me. Each bore fruit without fail; upon them were all kinds of clusters when the seasons of Zeus pressed down on them. (*Od.* 24.336-44)

Laertes' agricultural success arose through his attentiveness and care for the land and the oversight of Zeus, and such devotion to the land forged links

---

62. Gary Anderson, *Sacrifices and Offerings in Ancient Israel: Studies in Their Social and Political Importance*, HSM 41 (Atlanta: Scholars, 1987), pp. 106-16.

63. Vidal-Naquet, *The Black Hunter*, p. 29; Segal, *Singers, Heroes, and Gods*, pp. 22, 28-29.

64. Vidal-Naquet, *The Black Hunter*, p. 15; Hesiod, *Works and Days, Theogony, Shield of Heracles*, trans. Richmond Lattimore (Ann Arbor: University of Michigan Press, 1959), pp. 31-33; Raaflaub, "Homer to Solon," p. 58.

65. *Il.* 18.541-72; *Od.* 24.205-10. Vidal-Naquet, *The Black Hunter*, p. 26; cf. Buxton, *Imaginary Greece*, p. 79.

66. Margalit Finkelberg, *The Birth of Literary Fiction in Ancient Greece* (Oxford: Clarendon, 1998), pp. 109-10.

through the generations.[67] Laertes' success mirrors that of the ideal king whom the disguised Odysseus described to Penelope when he praised her:

> Lady, no mortal on the unbounded earth could reproach you, for your glory extends through the spacious heavens like that of an illustrious king who, as a god fearer, rules over many nobles and upholds good laws. The black earth bears wheat and barley; the trees are loaded with fruit; the flocks give birth without fail, and the sea provides fish. By his good leadership, the people thrive under him. (*Od.* 19.107-14)

Homer indicated that one of the fruits of just rule by a pious king was abundance from agriculture, animal husbandry, and fishing.[68] By inference, when famine beset the land, the king was expected to take responsibility for it and not simply ascribe it to bad luck. The contrast between Alcinous's garden in Phaeacia and that of Laertes in Ithaca suggests that a direct cause-and-effect relationship between the king's rule and agricultural abundance would impress itself on the observer only in the fantasy land of Phaeacia. The cause-and-effect relationship was believed to be still in force on Ithaca, but it was less direct and required more careful discernment lest one claim that the king's words and actions had a magical effect on the forces of nature. It is well to recall Odysseus's reverence for nature through his prayers and sacrifices to the Nymphs as the forces of fertility within nature to see that the Homeric king's ties with nature went beyond exploitation and magical manipulation (*Od.* 13.352-59; 17.240-46).[69]

The Israelite tradition reported that "during David's reign there was a famine of three successive years" (2 Sam. 21:1). In the ensuing narrative, David sought to find a way out of this crisis by asking the Lord to explain the cause of the famine.[70] Second Samuel 21:1 states the following response from the Lord:

---

67. Segal, *Singers, Heroes, and Gods,* p. 50.

68. Vidal-Naquet, *The Black Hunter,* p. 24; Christoph Auffahrt, *Der drohende Untergang: "Schöpfung" in Mythos und Ritual im Alten Orient und in Griechenland am Beispiel der Odysee und des Ezechielbuches,* Religiongeschichtliche Versüche und Vorarbeiten 39 (New York: Walter de Gruyter, 1991), pp. 176-77.

69. Segal, *Singers, Heroes, and Gods,* pp. 51-52; Pierre Vidal-Naquet, "Land and Sacrifice," in *Reading the Odyssey: Selected Interpretive Essays,* ed. S. Schein (Princeton: Princeton University Press, 1996), pp. 47-48; cf. Bruce Heiden, "The Ordeals of Homeric Song," *Arethusa* 30 (1997): 236-37. Laura Slatkin (*The Power of Thetis: Allusion and Interpretation in the "Iliad"* [Berkeley: University of California Press, 1991], pp. 80-81) notes that the Nymphs were local deities that lost stature in Homer's Panhellenic scheme of promoting the Olympian gods.

70. Note the parallel with the plague ravaging the Achaean forces in *Il.* 1.8-21, which was sent by Apollo for dishonor shown to one of his priests. Such divine intervention creates the circumstances that precipitate the quarrel between Agamemnon and Achilles.

"There is bloodguilt on Saul and his household because he put the Gibeonites to death." The narrative continues with David's going to the Gibeonites to ask what might be done to atone for Saul's killing a number of Gibeonites — a deed that violated an oath the Israelites had previously made. The Gibeonites asked for the ritual sacrifice of seven men from Saul's descendants (v. 6). David then handed these Saulides over to the Gibeonites who "dismembered them on the mountain before the Lord . . . at the beginning of the barley harvest" (v. 9). When the guilt was removed, the rains began to fall to open a new agricultural cycle (v. 10).[71] In the pro-Davidic cast of 2 Samuel 21:1-14, David took action to make amends for the transgression of his predecessor Saul; as king and symbolic center of the community, David was obliged to address a misdeed carried out by Saul as king.[72] Even though this narrative was designed to cover up David's execution of Saul's heirs, it is significant that the king's responsibility for successful agriculture was selected as a serious ground calling for the costly sacrifice of royal heirs.[73]

In Israel, it was believed that royal conduct had an impact on the growth of the crops. This view was also made known by Psalm 72, whose prayer combined concern for the king's administration of justice with the success of agriculture:

> O God, endow the king with your judgments,
>   the king's son with your righteousness,
> That he may judge your people rightly,
>   your lowly ones justly,
> That the mountains may produce prosperity for the people
>   and the hills abundance.[74] (vv. 1-3)

Here the just king was perceived to be a channel of the Lord's blessings of justice and agricultural abundance.[75]

In 2 Samuel 21:9-10, the seven dismembered descendants of Saul were exposed on the mountain of the Lord in Gibeon. The number "seven," the execu-

---

71. McCarter, *II Samuel,* pp. 444-45; K. C. Hanson, "When the King Crosses the Line: Royal Deviance and Restitution in Levantine Ideologies," *BTB* 26 (1996): 14; Henri Cazelles, "David's Monarchy and the Gibeonite Claim," *PEQ* 87 (1955): 166-69.

72. McCarter, *II Samuel,* pp. 444-45; Cazelles, "David's Monarchy and the Gibeonite Claim," pp. 170, 174.

73. Arvid Kapelrud, "King and Fertility: A Discussion of II Sam 21:1-14," Norsk Teologisk Tidsskrift 56 (1955): 116; Walter Brueggemann, *First and Second Samuel* (Louisville: John Knox, 1990), pp. 336-38; Halpern, *David's Secret Demons,* pp. 84-86, 313-14, 326, 328, 332, 341, 370.

74. Read *ṣĕdāqâ* with LXX.

75. Bernd Janowski, *Stellvertretung: Alttestamentliche Studien zu einem theologischen Grundbegriff* (Stuttgart: Verlag Katholisches Bibelwerk, 1997), pp. 56-58.

tion at the beginning of the barley harvest, and the display and decomposition of their corpses on the mountain were components of a ritual intended to bring about communication between the human and divine realms.[76] The costly and dramatic action of the sacrifice of seven Saulides, even if it was designed to remove potential competitors to the house of David for the throne, symbolized the repentance of the Israelite nation for breaking its oath to the Gibeonites.[77] The narrative makes the point that it was David's efforts as king to promote justice with the Gibeonites that led to the renewal of rainfall, and that the human sacrifice itself did not magically trigger the rain (cf. 2 Sam. 23:2-5).[78]

In southern Mesopotamia, in the land of Sumer, where cities arose and flourished throughout the third millennium B.C., successful agriculture was necessary for their collective existence. Hunting and fishing were also practiced, but it was the cultivation of cereal crops that allowed the population of cities to grow and its organization and diversification of occupations to develop.[79] The king played a key role in constructing and maintaining canals, catch basins, and other irrigation and drainage works necessary for conducting agriculture in the Mesopotamian plains where there was not sufficient rainfall.[80]

The grain was planted in late November at the beginning of the rainy season. The heavier rains upstream led to floods of the Tigris and Euphrates in southern Mesopotamia by April. The excessive water had to be kept away from the fields not only to prevent drowning of the crops but also to guard against the salinization of the soil that resulted from mineral deposits being left in the soil with the rapid evaporation of the flood waters in the hot climate of southern Mesopotamia. The maintenance of the flood control and irrigation devices was complicated by the large amount of silt deposited by the flood waters. The king bore a special responsibility for this collective effort.[81]

76. Robert Polzin, *David and the Deuteronomist: A Literary Study of the Deuteronomistic History, Part III, 2 Samuel* (Bloomington, Ind.: Indiana University Press, 1993), pp. 213-14. Cf. James Williams, "Sacrifice and the Beginning of Kingship," *Semeia* 67 (1994): 89-90.

77. Kapelrud, "King and Fertility," pp. 118-20; Polzin, *David and the Deuteronomist*, p. 209; Steven McKenzie, *King David: A Biography* (New York: Oxford University Press, 2000), p. 45.

78. McCarter, *II Samuel*, pp. 445, 483; Cazelles, "David's Monarchy and the Gibeonite Claim," pp. 174-75.

79. Van de Mieroop, *The Ancient Mesopotamian City*, p. 24; Eyre, "The Agricultural Cycle," p. 175; Potts, *Mesopotamian Civilization*, p. 89.

80. K. W. Butzer, "Physical Conditions in Eastern Europe, Western Asia and Egypt before the Period of Agricultural and Urban Settlement," in *CAH*, 1.1:58; Eyre, "The Agricultural Cycle," pp. 184-88; Potts, *Mesopotamian Civilization*, pp. 19-24.

81. Oppenheim, *Ancient Mesopotamia*, pp. 41-42; Johannes Renger, "River, Water Courses and Irrigation Ditches and Other Matters Concerning Irrigation Based on Old Babylonian Sources (2000-1600 B.C.)," *Bulletin on Sumerian Agriculture* 5 (1990): 32, 38-39.

Hammurapi celebrated the construction of a canal with the words:

> When Anum and Enlil gave me the land of Sumer and Akkad to rule (and) placed their halter in my hand, I dug the canal (named), "Hammurapi is the prosperity of the people," which brings abundant water to the land of Sumer and Akkad. I returned its two banks to cultivation. I repeatedly heaped up piles of grain. I established everlasting waters for the land of Sumer and Akkad. I gathered together the scattered peoples of the land of Sumer and Akkad. I procured grazing land and a watering place for them. I shepherded them with plenty and abundance. I settled them in peaceful dwellings.[82]

Hammurapi claimed that his efforts in building the canal resulted in an abundance of grain for the Mesopotamian people. He kept this accomplishment before them by naming the canal, "Hammurapi is the prosperity of the people."[83] He also urged the people to see themselves as docile, domesticated sheep to whom he gave food and water.

Since agriculture was the economic base upon which Mesopotamian cities were built, it is not surprising that other Mesopotamian kings made known their commitment to farming. For example, Lipit-Ishtar of Isin (1934-1924 B.C.) identified himself with the epithet, "the faithful cultivator of Ur."[84] Yaḫdun-Lim of Mari (1825-1810 B.C.) referred to himself as "the one who opens canals . . . the one who procures fruitfulness and abundance for his people, the one who makes everything possible exist for his people."[85] In their inscriptions, Mesopotamian kings acknowledged that they had been commissioned and supported by the gods in their public works projects. However, in the inscriptions, the kings never suggested that they had magical power over forces of nature. The Mesopotamian king was an organizer who had engineering skill and labor power at his disposal.[86] One of the king's challenges was to motivate the typical Mesopotamian family to produce beyond the subsistence level.[87] The

---

82. Frayne, *RIME 4*, E4.3.6.7, lines 10-37.

83. Renger, "River, Water Courses and Irrigation Ditches," pp. 33, 34.

84. Frayne, *RIME 4*, E4.1.5.3, lines 5-7.

85. Frayne, *RIME 4*, E4.6.8.2, lines 20, 23-25.

86. Renger, "River, Water Courses and Irrigation Ditches," pp. 38-40; G. van Driel, "Institutional and Non-Institutional Economy in Ancient Mesopotamia," in *Interdependency of Institutions and Private Entrepreneurs*, MOS Studies 2 (Leiden: Nederlands Historisch-Archaeologisch Instituut te Istanbul, 2000), p. 11.

87. G. van Driel, "Landless and Hungry? An Assessment," in *Landless and Hungry? Access to Land in Early and Traditional Societies*, ed. B. Haring and R. de Maaijer (Leiden: Research School CNWS, School of Asian, African, and Amerindian Studies, 1998), pp. 194-95; idem, "Institutional and Non-Institutional Economy in Ancient Mesopotamia," p. 12.

technical skill and labor resources devoted to agriculture had a more direct correlation with successful harvests in lower Mesopotamia than in rain-fed farming areas where the risk of crop failure was higher.[88]

The need for food reminds humans of their bodily existence and their inextricable link with nature. The Mesopotamian king could more readily celebrate his accomplishments in providing food for the people since there was less risk involved in food production and such celebration could promote the collective labor necessary for sustaining river-based farming. In the rain-based farming in biblical Israel and Homeric Greece, numerous variables needed to harmonize in order to harvest successful crops. The notion that the just rule of the king influenced harmony in nature manifests the peoples' belief in the interconnection of the moral, physical, and religious dimensions of life. To maintain social, natural, and cosmic harmony and to keep intact the boundaries against the chaotic forces of famine and death were complex tasks fraught with unpredictable problems, which the king was called upon to address in his symbolic role at the center of the community.

Aristocrat and Commoner: Negotiating Rank and Status in the Community

Within a patriarchically structured household, the parents stood at the head of the family. Below them were the sons and daughters. Those outsiders who joined the household were granted an ancillary status as servants.[89] This basic tripartite division of a household carried over into the royal household at the head of a kingdom when a monarchy was established, and then by extension into the kingdom itself.[90] The king and his family stood at the head; the king's

88. Eyre, "The Agricultural Cycle," pp. 184-88; Potts, *Mesopotamian Civilization*, pp. 19-22.

89. Von Soden, *The Ancient Orient*, pp. 72-74; Finley, *The World of Odysseus*, p. 111; Lawrence Stager, "The Archaeology of the Family in Ancient Israel," *BASOR* 260 (1985): 19-20; Fritz R. Kraus, *Vom mesopotamischen Menschen der altbabylonischen Zeit und seiner Welt* (Amsterdam: North-Holland, 1973), p. 47; Daniel Snell, *Life in the Ancient Near East: 3100-332 B.C.E.* (New Haven: Yale University Press, 1997), pp. 51-52, 60; I. J. Gelb, "Household and Family in Early Mesopotamia," in *State and Temple Economy in the Ancient Near East*, ed. E. Lipinski, OLA 5 (Leuven: Departement Orientalistiek, 1979), pp. 58, 65-68, 91-95; Max Weber, *Economy and Society*, 2 vols., ed. Guenther Roth and Claus Wittich, trans. Ephraim Fischoff et al. (New York: Bedminster, 1968), 1:359.

90. Michael Mann, *The Sources of Social Power*, vol. 1: *A History of Power from the Beginning to A.D. 1760* (Cambridge: Cambridge University Press, 1986), pp. 171-72; Weber, *Economy and Society*, 1:229-30.

army and the royal courtiers formed an elite; and the mass of the people comprised the remaining stratum of society.[91]

Evolutionary models describe the emergence of the monarchy as the movement in stages from a decentralized tribal society to a centralized chiefdom, and finally to a monarchy.[92] The gradations and distinctions of such models can bring to light significant features of Israelite, Homeric, and Mesopotamian society. However, such a taxonomic approach also has its drawbacks if the evolutionary schema sees the development of a society as a one-way process without also envisioning the possibility that a society can devolve into a less developed mode of production.[93] Changes within a society or community often mean displacements as well as advancements of individuals, and it is here that status is most poignantly experienced, here that the fragility and vulnerability of human life and human constructions become manifest.[94]

In the *Odyssey,* Eumaeus, the loyal servant of Odysseus, was described as the "noble swineherd" (*Od.* 14.3, etc.). Eumaeus told Odysseus, disguised as a wandering beggar, the story of his origins and the way in which he ended up in the house of Laertes as a servant (*Od.* 15.402-84). He was the son of Ktesias, the king of two cities in Syria (*Od.* 15.413-15). A Phoenician woman, a servant in the house of King Ktesias and the nurse of Eumaeus, schemed with a Phoenician trader to transport her to her home in Sidon. She also counseled that Eumaeus could be taken along and sold as a servant for a high price. On their departing voyage, the Phoenician woman died, and later Eumaeus was sold to Laertes (*Od.* 15.483).

91. Mann, *The Sources of Social Power,* 1:87; Leo G. Perdue, "The Israelite and Early Jewish Family: Summary and Conclusions," in *Families in Ancient Israel,* ed. L. Perdue (Louisville: Westminster/John Knox, 1997), pp. 203, 209-12; William M. Sale, "The Government of Troy: Politics in the *Iliad,*" *Greek, Roman and Byzantine Studies* 35 (1994): 50; Van de Mieroop, *The Ancient Mesopotamian City,* pp. 15-16, 146-47.

92. Elman Service, *Origins of the State and Civilization: The Process of Cultural Evolution* (New York: Norton, 1975), pp. 303-8; Wason, *The Archaeology of Rank,* pp. 17, 37-45. Robert McC. Adams (*The Evolution of Urban Society* [Chicago: Aldine, 1966], pp. 51, 110, 120) argues that palace and temple households administered food production and distribution, which led to the formation of the state; there was no tribal stage prior to the emergence of the state in Mesopotamia.

93. Mann, *The Sources of Social Power,* 1:127; William G. Thalmann, *The Swineherd and the Bow: Representations of Class in the Odyssey* (Ithaca: Cornell University Press, 1998), p. 249; Norman Gottwald, *The Politics of Ancient Israel* (Louisville: Westminster/John Knox, 2001), pp. 118, 173.

94. Saul Olyan, "Honor, Shame, and Covenant Relations in Ancient Israel and Its Environment," *JBL* 115 (1996): 204; Mann, *The Sources of Social Power,* 1:92-93; Hans van Wees, *Status Warriors: War, Violence and Society in Homer and History* (Amsterdam: J. C. Gieben, 1992), pp. 155-56; Rose, *Sons of the Gods, Children of Earth,* p. 107.

Displaced from his royal household in Syria, Eumaeus found his situation within the household of Odysseus agreeable, but he worried what the future might hold since Odysseus had been absent from Ithaca for twenty years (*Od.* 19.22, 484). Eumaeus remarked to the disguised Odysseus:

> The gods have stalled out the homeward voyage of that one who gently cared for me and would have given me possessions: a house, a plot of land, and a wife courted by many — such things as a well-disposed master gives to a servant who has produced many things and a god blesses his work as he has blessed this work of mine, at which I remain. (*Od.* 14.61-67)

Eumaeus lamented that his situation would have been so much better if Odysseus had not gone to war at Troy.[95] Eumaeus's equanimity, gratitude, and lack of bitterness testified to his nobility.[96] Yet the one characteristic that highlighted his nobility and set him in stark contrast with the suitor Antinous and with the Cyclopes was his practice of hospitality toward strangers. Eumaeus had noted earlier to Odysseus:

> Stranger, it is contrary to custom for me to dishonor a stranger, even if he be lower in rank than you. All strangers and beggars are dependent on Zeus. The gift coming from us, though small, is prized. For the way of life of the servant is always anxious when the masters who rule over him are young. (*Od.* 14.56-61)

As one who has been displaced and is anxious about the transition in leadership in the household of Odysseus, Eumaeus was sympathetic to strangers who had no household. He understood how the winds of fortune could dramatically shift one's status (*Od.* 17.322-23).[97] Eumaeus treated the wandering beggar Odysseus as if he were royalty. His capacity to entertain the double identity of Odysseus was a reflex of his own double identity as a "noble swineherd."[98] In

---

95. Cf. Ian Morris, "The Use and Abuse of Homer," *Classical Antiquity* 5 (1986): 114. Raaflaub ("Homer to Solon," p. 52) notes that the gap between free farmers and elite wealthy landowners was not great in Homeric society.

96. Segal, *Singers, Heroes, and Gods*, pp. 171-73; Thalmann, *The Swineherd and the Bow*, p. 58.

97. Thalmann, *The Swineherd and the Bow*, p. 47; Kevin Crotty, *The Poetics of Supplication: Homer's Iliad and Odyssey* (Ithaca: Cornell University Press, 1994), pp. 173-75; Irene Winter, "Homer's Phoenicians: History, Ethnography, or Literary Trope? [A Perspective on Early Orientalism]," in *The Ages of Homer*, ed. Jane Carter and Sarah Morris (Austin: University of Texas Press, 1995), pp. 28-49; Dean Hammer, "The Cultural Construction of Chance in the *Iliad*," *Arethusa* 31 (1998): 138.

98. Segal, *Singers, Heroes, and Gods*, p. 172.

Homer's view, more was required to be a noble than the possession of wealth; noble qualities could even emerge in the absence of such wealth.[99]

The primary social units in early Israel were the extended family (bêt-'āb) and the clan (mišpāḥâ). The extended family consisted of three to four generations: husband and wife, elderly parents, sons (married and unmarried), single daughters, grandchildren in the paternal line, perhaps unmarried uncles, aunts, or cousins, and also possibly slaves and retainers with their wives and children.[100] The average extended family probably had as many as fifteen persons living in a compound of two-to-four houses (Judg. 17:5, 12; Mic. 7:5-6). The more wealthy households could have had as many as fifty persons residing in them. A network of extended families in an area formed a clan (Josh. 7:14-18). The clan held title to the land. It also had to defend its member families, redeem the land, enforce the right of vengeance (2 Sam. 14:7), conduct judicial proceedings (Lev. 20:5; 25:10, 41), and carry out periodic religious festivals (1 Sam. 20:6, 29).[101]

Early Israelites identified their place in society by the local family and clan of which they were a part.[102] Living with one's relatives on the ancestral land was central to Israelite identity: that is, there was an economic substrate to the primary genealogical affiliation of the Israelites.[103] To be displaced from one's family either through debt slavery or exile threatened to undermine the identity of an Israelite. The *paterfamilias* stood at the head of the extended family. The various *patresfamilias* served as elders of the clan, but they did not unite to form an identity as an aristocratic group in distinction from the other members of their families.

The advent of the monarchy in Israel threatened to shift the wealth of the people and the land to the king to the extent that life on the land would no longer be viable.[104] The warning of Samuel to the elders at the assembly at Ramah

---

99. Thalmann, *The Swineherd and the Bow*, p. 161; Pietro Pucci, *Odysseus Polutropos* (Ithaca: Cornell University Press, 1987), pp. 185-86.

100. Karel van der Toorn, *Family Religion in Babylonia, Syria and Israel* (Leiden: Brill, 1996), p. 194; Perdue, "The Israelite and Early Jewish Family," p. 166; Stager, "The Archaeology of the Family," pp. 19-20.

101. Van der Toorn, *Family Religion in Babylonia, Syria and Israel*, p. 201.

102. Robert DiVito, "Old Testament Anthropology and the Construction of Personal Identity," *CBQ* 61 (1999): 221-25.

103. Eryl W. Davies, "Land: Its Rights and Privileges," in *The World of Ancient Israel*, ed. R. E. Clements (Cambridge: Cambridge University Press, 1987), p. 358; Carol Meyers, "The Family in Early Israel," in *Families in Ancient Israel*, ed. Leo Perdue (Louisville: Westminster/John Knox, 1997), pp. 21-22.

104. Perdue, "The Israelite and Early Jewish Family," pp. 209-12; Neils Lemche, "Kings and Clients: On Loyalty between the Ruler and the Ruled in Ancient Israel," *Semeia* 66 (1995): 130;

describes the typical ways that a king could exploit their households and undermine their way of life:

> He will take your sons and assign them to his chariots and his horses, and they will run before his chariot. He will assign them to be leaders of thousands and leaders of fifties, to plow his ground, to reap his harvest and to make his weapons and the parts of his chariots. He will take your daughters to be perfumers, cooks, and bakers. He will take the best of your fields, your vineyards, and your olive groves and will give them to his servants. He will tithe your grain and your vineyards and will give the proceeds to his officers and his servants. He will take your men-servants and your maid-servants and your choicest cattle[105] and your donkeys, and they will do his work. He will tithe your flocks, and you will become his slaves. (1 Sam. 8:11-17)

By taking the labor, the produce, and the land from the Israelite families and clans, the king would redistribute and restrict access to the wealth of the land so that there would be a distinction between the rich and the poor, the aristocrat and the commoner. The biblical tradition attests to the ongoing struggle of the Israelite people to maintain their identity as a people apart from the king and his socioeconomic innovations.[106]

Israelite tradition pays special attention to the marginalized and defenseless who fall outside of the protection of the household and the clan. The widow, the orphan, the resident alien, and the debtor were to be treated with respect and compassion (Exod. 22:20-26[21-27]). The misfortunes of war, economics, and social life could deprive people of their place in the world and so threaten to undermine their identity. Such shifts in status called for the support of the Israelite community for those who had to undergo such change.[107]

In OB Mesopotamia, the *Code of Hammurapi* referred to three "classes" or "ranks" in the society: (1) *awīlum*, "the aristocrat," (2) *muškēnum*, "middle

---

Klaus Koch, *The Prophets*, vol. 1: *The Assyrian Period* (Philadelphia: Fortress, 1982), pp. 34-35, 49-50. Cf. Borowski, *Agriculture in Iron Age Israel*, pp. 26-29.

105. Read with the LXX, *boukolia humōn* (= *bĕqarkem*), rather than with the MT, *baḥûrêkem*, "your young men."

106. P. Kyle McCarter, Jr., *I Samuel*, AB 8 (New York: Doubleday, 1980), pp. 160-62; Frank Crüsemann, *Der Widerstand gegen das Königtum*, WMANT 49 (Neukirchen-Vluyn: Neukirchener Verlag, 1978), p. 70.

107. Moshe Weinfeld, *Social Justice in Ancient Israel and in the Ancient Near East* (Minneapolis: Fortress, 1995), pp. 215-30; Morris Silver, "Prophets and Markets Revisited," in *Social Justice in the Ancient World*, ed. K. D. Irani and M. Silver (Westport, Conn.: Greenwood, 1995), pp. 19-93.

class" or "property owner," and (3) *wardum,* "slave (i.e., a debt slave or a prisoner of war)."[108] As a general principle, the strata within a society take on the character of classes when access to economic goods is determined by the stratum to which one belongs and the strata define themselves over against one another.[109] In OB Mesopotamia, property was held not only by the king and the temple but also by private individuals.[110] Individually owned private land was either farmed by the owner or leased to a tenant farmer in return for a share of the surplus grain that was to be sold to the city dwellers. In the OB period, the sale of such land is well documented in northern Mesopotamia, but not in the southern part where temples and large institutional households held title to most of the land under cultivation, which they had gained in the Ur III period (2112-2004 B.C.).[111] A person, with the apparent exception of a slave, could rise in status through an increase in wealth or through a royal appointment.[112] Throughout the third millennium, slaves were held by individuals and temples; palaces acquired slaves from prisoners of war.[113] In

---

108. *ANET,* p. 166, nn. 39, 44. F. R. Kraus, *Vom mesopotamischen Menschen,* p. 92. Von Soden (*The Ancient Orient,* pp. 77-78) notes that while there is no consensus on the definition of *muškēnum* (literally, "the one prostrating himself"), "wherever *muškēnum* stands opposite the *awīlum,* the 'free man' or 'citizen,' his status is clearly subordinated." The major positions on *muškēnum* are summarized in: F. R. Kraus, *Vom mesopotamischen Menschen,* pp. 92-125; Josef Klíma, "Im ewigen Banne der *muškēnum*-Problematic?" in *Wirtschaft und Gesellschaft im alten Vorderasien,* ed. J. Harmatta and G. Komoróczy (Budapest: Akademiai Kiado, 1976), pp. 267-74. See also Snell, *Life in the Ancient Near East,* pp. 54-55, 60.

109. Thalmann, *The Swineherd and the Bow,* pp. 21, 258; Mann, *The Sources of Social Power,* 1:10-11, 216-17; Renger, "On Economic Structures in Ancient Mesopotamia," pp. 171-72.

110. Ignace J. Gelb, "On the Alleged Temple and State Economies in Ancient Mesopotamia," in *Studi in onore di Edoardo Volterra,* vol. 6 (Milan: Giuffre, 1971), p. 137; G. van Driel, "Land in Ancient Mesopotamia," in *Landless and Hungry?* (Leider: Research School CNWS, 1998), p. 31; van de Mieroop, *The Ancient Mesopotamian City,* pp. 145-46; idem, "Old Babylonian Ur: Portrait of an Ancient Mesopotamian City," *JANES* 21 (1992): 128-29.

111. Renger, "Institutional, Communal, and Individual Ownership," p. 295; idem, "Interaction of Temple, Palace, and Private Enterprise," in *State and Temple Economy in the Ancient Near East,* ed. E. Lipinski, OLA 5 (Leuven: Departement Orientalistiek, 1979), p. 251. See also Van de Mieroop, *The Ancient Mesopotamian City,* p. 146; William W. Hallo, "God, King, and Man at Yale," in *State and Temple Economy in the Ancient Near East,* ed. E. Lipinski, OLA 5 (Leuven: Departement Orientalistiek, 1979), pp. 107-8; Ignace J. Gelb, Piotr Steinkeller, and Robert M. Whiting, Jr., *Earliest Land Tenure Systems in the Near East: Ancient Kudurrus: Text,* OIP 104 (Chicago: Oriental Institute, 1991), pp. 25-26.

112. Van der Toorn, *Family Religion in Babylonia, Syria and Israel,* pp. 103-5; von Soden, *The Ancient Orient,* p. 76.

113. Gelb, "Household and Family in Early Mesopotamia," pp. 11-12. However, von Soden (*The Ancient Orient,* p. 75) cites the absence of records of slave revolts as a reason for thinking that the state did not have slaves in the OB period.

fact, the most frequently recorded item of trade on the ancient *kudurrus* was slaves.[114]

In the Kassite period (1595-1158 B.C.) there was a marked increase in the number of royal land grants to those warriors who formed the chariot corps. It seems that many of these grants were temporary as had been the practice in OB times.[115] There is disagreement on whether or not Kassite society was feudal in character.[116] Christopher Edens claims that the stratification in the Kassite Babylonian society is more accurately described as one of status rather than of class, where status was based on inequalities of wealth. The documentation attests to a considerable transfer of wealth by the crown and provincial bureaucracies, for the state was the dominant actor in the economy, although the wealthier households did wield influence.[117]

Karel van der Toorn notes that the upper class was expected to show charity to those in need, with special reference to the following OB letter:[118]

> If you truly are my brother and are concerned about me, purchase grain from Ṣilli-Shamash at the amount of two shekels of silver, as much as he charges you, and bring it to me along with your own barley. Give me this help! Do you not recognize my intention, my experience, and my dire need? You are a noble. Come, set me free! (*AbB* 1.89, lines 19-31)[119]

The writer of this letter, Sin-uselli, referred to the addressee, Sin-bel-ili, as "my brother" and so they apparently belonged to the same family or clan.[120] However, Sin-bel-ili belonged to the upper class and had the means to assist Sin-uselli

114. Gelb, Steinkeller, and Whiting, *Earliest Land Tenure Systems,* p. 14.

115. Snell, *Life in the Ancient Near East,* pp. 70-71; William W. Hallo, *Origins: The Ancient Near Eastern Background of Some Modern Western Institutions* (Leiden: Brill, 1996), p. 283; Christopher Edens, "On the Complexity of Complex Societies: Structure, Power, and Legitimation in Kassite Babylonia," in *Chiefdoms and Early States in the Near East: The Organization of Dynamics of Complexity,* ed. G. Stein et al. (Madison, Wisc.: Prehistory Press, 1994), p. 211.

116. Von Soden (*The Ancient Orient,* p. 80) claims that "a genuine feudal system" was in place in Kassite Mesopotamia, whereas Walter Sommerfeld ("Der babylonische 'Feudalismus,'" in *Vom alten Orient zum Alten Testament,* ed. M. Dietrich and O. Loretz, AOAT 240 [Neukirchen-Vluyn: Neukirchener Verlag, 1995], pp. 488-90) is more hesitant and states that the term "feudal" needs to be qualified as more or less accurate in describing the social system evident in documents stemming from 1600-1150 B.C.

117. Renger, "On Economic Structures in Ancient Mesopotamia," p. 201; Edens, "On the Complexity of Complex Societies," pp. 211-12; cf. Gelb, Steinkeller, and Whiting, *Earliest Land Tenure Systems,* pp. 21, 24.

118. Van der Toorn, *Family Religion in Babylonia, Syria and Israel,* p. 108.

119. Fritz R. Kraus, *Briefe aus dem British Museum (CT 43 und 44),* AbB 1 (Leiden: Brill, 1964), p. 69, letter 89.

120. Cf. Gelb, "Household and Family in Early Mesopotamia," pp. 56-58, 72, 75-79.

in his poverty. Van der Toorn speculates that the aristocratic ethos was one that would have served "as a frame of reference for many ordinary people as well."[121]

The possibility of losing one's wealth or position through misfortune or sociopolitical changes threatened Mesopotamians and made them aware of the plight of the outsider. The acknowledgment of such vulnerability would seem to have made them more appreciative of the aristocratic expectation of charity toward the needy. Protection of the defenseless was also a special responsibility of the king, for Hammurapi noted in the epilogue to his *Code* that he had governed the peoples of Sumer and Akkad justly "in order that the strong might not crush the weak, that the orphan (and) the widow might receive fair treatment" (*CH* XLVII:59-62).[122] Although the distinction between the aristocrat and the commoner was based primarily upon the amount of wealth at one's disposal, it appears that in OB society such wealth carried responsibilities, the execution of which would manifest one's noble character.[123]

The clearest distinction in the hierarchy of the communities in Homeric Greece, biblical Israel, and OB Mesopotamia was that between the king and the people. An aristocratic class existed in Homeric Greece and OB Mesopotamia. A sufficiency of wealth and property was a prerequisite to aristocratic status, but such status also carried with it a particular ethos that included care for the defenseless, such as the poor and the stranger. The possibility that the misfortunes of debt or captivity in war could enslave one generated an awareness of the fragility of one's status in Homeric Greece and OB Mesopotamia as well as in biblical Israel. The safety net of the family may not have been wide enough in many cases, for the king also held a special responsibility to care for the widow, orphan, and stranger. In all three cultures, one's place in society was linked with holding property, and how such property was held and distributed was important for the individual's and family's sense of belonging. The king, as primary redistributor of material and symbolic goods, could be a threat or a blessing, for he exerted a strong influence on the place of individuals in the hierarchy of the community through his practices of taxation and gift giving.

---

121. Van der Toorn, *Family Religion in Babylonia, Syria and Israel,* p. 95.

122. Rykle Borger, *Babylonisch-assyrische Lesestücke,* AnOr 54 (Rome: Pontifical Biblical Institute, 1979), 1:46.

123. Raymond Westbrook, "Social Justice in the Ancient Near East," in *Social Justice in the Ancient World,* ed. K. D. Irani and M. Silver (Westport, Conn.: Greenwood, 1995), pp. 149-51; Snell, *Life in the Ancient Near East,* p. 60.

Life and Death: The Quest for Immortality

To the peoples of Homeric Greece, biblical Israel, and ancient Mesopotamia, the time, circumstances, and meaning of death were of greater import than the fact of death. Death was inevitable, but the form that a possible life after death might take was a matter of continuing concern. An important aspect of this afterlife was how one might live on in the memory of the family or the community. The king held a pivotal position for creating the ceremonial space (banquets, festivals, etc.) or material means (e.g., inscriptions, stelae, statues) for honoring the name and preserving the memory of individuals in the community.

In Homer, the distinctiveness of the warrior hero emerged from the high-risk exploits that brought him near to death. Achilles refused the offer of gifts from Agamemnon about which Odysseus, together with a delegation of other Achaean warrior-kings, had informed him with the following words:

> I think Agamemnon, son of Atreus, will not persuade me or the other Danaans since there was no gratitude shown for always battling endlessly against the enemies. The same allotment is given to the one who stays behind as to the one who fights intensely. Both the coward and the courageous are given the same honor. The one who works hard and the one who is lazy alike meet death. It has brought me no gain, seeing that I have suffered anguish in my heart, always to risk my life in battle. (*Il.* 9.315-22)

Achilles viewed the world from the perspective of "all or nothing."[124] It was probably such an extreme and focused attitude that carried him into the danger of battle where death threatened. From Achilles' perspective, risks on behalf of the community (*Il.* 9.326-27) were no longer honored by the Achaeans since Agamemnon had withdrawn the prize awarded to Achilles. Agamemnon offered to restore the prize to Achilles and give him numerous additional gifts (*Il.* 9.262-99), but Achilles refused the offer without hesitation. Because the high risk undertaken by the warrior in battle demanded from the warrior clear and unwavering resolve, Achilles believed that the community likewise had to be unwavering in its resolve to acknowledge and honor the heroic warrior.[125]

---

124. Jean-Pierre Vernant, *Mortals and Immortals* (Princeton: Princeton University Press, 1990), pp. 53-54; Crotty, *The Poetics of Supplication,* p. 61.

125. Vernant, *Mortals and Immortals,* pp. 53-54; Rose, *Sons of the Gods, Children of Earth,* pp. 78-79, 81-82; Leonard Muellner, *The Anger of Achilles: "Mēnis" in Greek Epic* (Ithaca: Cornell University Press, 1996), pp. 142-43. See also James Redfield, "Foreword," in Gregory Nagy, *The Best of the Achaeans: Concepts of the Hero in Archaic Greek Poetry* (Baltimore: Johns Hopkins University Press, 1979), p. ix.

When Achilles withdrew in anger from the Achaean forces, he swore an oath with the scepter in hand that he would not return to the battle until Agamemnon and the Achaeans were brought to their knees (*Il.* 1.233-37).[126]

In his response to the embassy of warrior-kings who came to persuade him to rejoin the battle, Achilles questioned the meaning of the warrior code (*Il.* 9.307-420) and began to rethink the value of the two destinies placed before him: to have either a short life with "glory" *(kleos)* or a long life with compromises (*Il.* 9.410-16).[127] The other warrior-kings criticized Achilles' inflexibility toward Agamemnon's offer of reconciliation (*Il.* 9.510-12). However, Achilles refused Agamemnon's gifts, even though they still had material worth, because he believed they had lost their symbolic value according to the currency of the warrior code: that is, Agamemnon's mode of exchanging gifts in the public forum did not honor the commitments and sacrifices of other warriors in the community.[128] Material gifts could be replaced once they were given, but the warrior gave his life, which was lost forever once it had been given. The memory of the warrior could live on only in the form of the heroic song of the community.[129] The Homeric warrior needed something more than material goods in order to risk his life for the community; as Jean-Pierre Vernant has stated, "It has nothing to do with practical calculation or with the need for social prestige. Rather, it is in a way metaphysical."[130] After Achilles' *geras*, "prize," was withdrawn, Achilles believed that he and Agamemnon operated according to two different standards of exchange.[131] Achilles cannot simply accept the gifts from Agamemnon without a corresponding commitment to establishing solidarity among the warriors in the community by honoring their commitments.[132]

The hero who died an untimely death was remembered in the song of the bards. Homer believed the "glory" *(kleos)* of the hero celebrated in bardic song to be of higher worth than the "esteem" *(timē)* which humans accorded to revered individuals in cultic and noncultic settings.[133] At death, when the *menos* ("spirit, vigor") and *thymos* ("heart") separated from the *sōma* ("corpse"), the

---

126. Gregory Nagy, *The Best of the Achaeans: Concepts of the Hero in Archaic Greek Poetry* (Baltimore: Johns Hopkins University Press, 1979), pp. 180, 188.

127. Pucci, *The Song of the Sirens*, p. 211; Christos Tsagalis, "Style and Construction, Sound and Rhythm: Thetis' Supplication to Zeus (*Iliad* 1.493-516)," *Arethusa* 34 (2001): 21-23.

128. Muellner, *The Anger of Achilles*, p. 104.

129. Segal, *Singers, Heroes, and Gods*, pp. 140-41.

130. Vernant, *Mortals and Immortals*, pp. 56-57.

131. Vernant, *Mortals and Immortals*, pp. 51-54.

132. Muellner, *The Anger of Achilles*, pp. 139-41.

133. Gregory Nagy, *Greek Mythology and Poetics* (Ithaca: Cornell University Press, 1990), pp. 136-37; Ian Morris, "Attitudes Toward Death in Archaic Greece," *Classical Antiquity* 8 (1989): 306.

psychē ("animating spirit") carried the identity of the individual. The *psychē* could reunite with the *sōma* only when the *noos* ("mind") brought them together.[134] This return brought about by the *noos* occurred through the medium of heroic poetry, such as that of the *Iliad* where the hero was immortalized.[135]

The voice counter to the heroic values championed by Achilles in the *Iliad* came to expression in the *Odyssey* during Odysseus's trip to the underworld where the shade of Achilles told Odysseus:

> Do not try to reconcile me to death, famous Odysseus. I would prefer to be a hired hand in service to another, a man without property, one who does not have many material things, rather than to rule over all the dead who have perished (*Od.* 11.488-91).

Consistent with his character in the *Iliad*, Achilles continues to be a resister; now it is against the forces of death. In contrast, Odysseus was one who accepted his fate and then used all his cleverness to carry out his desire to return home.[136] Odysseus was a new type of hero: the "man of many wiles" who remembered his family and homeland.[137] The tension between the two faces of heroism — between the all-consuming commitment to the warrior's honor by Achilles and the clever attentiveness required for survival and for return to the homeland by Odysseus — is an antinomy that persists in a synchronic reading of the Homeric epics, as does the tension between life and death in day-to-day experience. If the Achilles of the *Iliad* is an ideal type of hero through whom the Greeks sought "to socialize and civilize death,"[138] Odysseus is an ideal type who was able to rise to new life out of death-dealing circumstances.

In Israel, Saul demonstrated his charisma as a heroic leader when he mobilized the Israelites to respond to the threat of Nahash, king of the Ammonites, against the people of Jabesh-gilead, a people who had close ties with Saul's tribe of Benjamin (cf. Judg. 21:6-14).[139] Nahash demanded that the people of Jabesh-gilead seal a covenant with him by gouging out their right eyes. Enraged by the news of these treaty conditions, Saul

---

134. Nagy, *Greek Mythology and Poetics,* pp. 87-88; idem, *The Best of the Achaeans,* p. 208.

135. Nagy, *Greek Mythology and Poetics,* pp. 93, 142; Segal, *Singers, Heroes, and Gods,* pp. 87-88, 103; cf. Douglas Frame, *The Myth of Return in Early Greek Epic* (New Haven: Yale University Press, 1978), pp. ix, 86-87.

136. Karl Reinhardt, "The Adventures in the *Odyssey,*" in *Reading the Odyssey: Selected Interpretive Essays,* ed. Seth Schein (Princeton: Princeton University Press, 1996), p. 119.

137. Segal, *Singers, Heroes, and Gods,* pp. 44, 90, 102; Pucci, *The Song of the Sirens,* p. 15.

138. Jean-Pierre Vernant, "Death with Two Faces," in *Reading the Odyssey: Selected Interpretive Essays,* ed. Seth Schein (Princeton: Princeton University Press, 1996), p. 57.

139. Karel van der Toorn, "Saul and the Rise of Israelite State Religion," *VT* 43 (1993): 540.

took a yoke of oxen, cut them into parts, and sent them throughout all the territory of Israel by means of messengers with the words: "Whoever does not come out after Saul and Samuel — so it will be done to his cattle." Then the fear of the Lord fell upon the people, and they came forth like one man. (1 Sam. 11:7)

This act of terror moved the Israelite farmers and herders to assume the role of warriors in this crisis. The purpose of the campaign was to defend the people of Jabesh-gilead and to uphold justice.[140] In this episode, there was no reference to the warriors' seeking immortal fame; they went out to battle because they were afraid of what Saul would do to them if they remained at home. However, Saul is remembered in this account as a hero, which confirms that heroic exploits were highly valued in ancient Israel.

Some of the highest praise in the biblical record for Saul as warrior was given by his adversary David in his eulogy over Saul and his son Jonathan after they fell in the battle of Gilboa (2 Sam. 1:22-23).[141] In its current context in "the history of David's rise" (1 Sam. 16:14–2 Sam. 5:10), this eulogy can be seen as exonerating David from complicity in the downfall of Saul, but it also expresses David's grief and a sense of public loss over the deaths of Saul and Jonathan.[142] Even though heroic warriors may have been as highly valued in ancient Israel as in Archaic Greece, the biblical writers usually praise Israel's heroic warriors indirectly rather than immortalize them in song.

David's success as a warrior led the Israelite women who were praising the warriors returning from battle against the Philistines to sing: "Saul has slain his thousands; David, his tens of thousands" (1 Sam. 18:7). This eyewitness testimony to the jubilation over the success of the Israelite heroic warrior reflects the high value the ancient Israelites placed on the deeds of their warriors. Yet this short refrain contrasts with the typical portrayal of David as a pious warrior who refrains from self-promotion and ascribes his victories to the Lord, his protector, as seen in this excerpt from Psalm 18:

> He made my feet like those of a hind
>   and set me upon the heights.[143]
> He trained my hands for battle
>   so that my arms can bend the bronze bow.

---

140. McCarter, *I Samuel*, pp. 206-7.

141. McCarter, *II Samuel*, p. 78; Polzin, *David and the Deuteronomist*, pp. 12-14.

142. McCarter, *II Samuel*, pp. 77-79; Crüsemann, *Der Widerstand gegen das Königtum*, p. 132; Brueggemann, *First and Second Samuel*, pp. 213-18.

143. Read *bāmōt*.

You gave me the shield of your salvation,
  and your right hand supported me,
  and your promise made me great.[144]
You made room for my steps,
  and my ankles did not falter.
I pursued and overtook my enemies,
  and did not turn back until I destroyed them.
I struck them down so that they were unable to rise;
  they fell beneath my feet. (Ps. 18:34-39[33-38])

Here as a warrior, David gave thanks for his survival and success in battle. Any aspirations that he may have had of attaining immortal fame did not come to expression on his lips in the biblical record.[145]

The OB version of the *Epic of Gilgamesh* described the heroic demeanor and outlook of Gilgamesh, king of Uruk, and his companion Enkidu. When Enkidu first entered Uruk, he encountered Gilgamesh as he was on his way to marry the goddess Ishhara. Enkidu and Gilgamesh wrestled; Enkidu won but immediately praised the superior qualities and status of Gilgamesh: "To be distinctive, your mother gave birth to you. Ninsun, the wild cow of the stall, raised your head above men.[146] Enlil has assigned you kingship over the people."[147] Enkidu and Gilgamesh changed from rivals to the closest of friends. After living for some time in Uruk, Enkidu lamented that he had grown soft from the refinements of city life. Gilgamesh thus proposed that they go on an expedition to the Cedar Forest to battle Ḫuwawa. Enkidu warned of the danger posed by the "powerful and never resting Ḫuwawa."[148] Gilgamesh replied to Enkidu:

Who, my friend, can ascend to heaven?
  Only the gods live forever with Shamash.
As for humans, their days are numbered.

144. Read *wa'ănōtĕkā* with 2 Sam. 22:36.

145. Brueggemann, *First and Second Samuel*, pp. 343-44; Karl Bernhardt, *Das Problem der altorientalischen Königsideologie im Alten Testament*, VTS 8 (Leiden: Brill, 1961), pp. 281-82; David Gunn, *The Story of King David: Genre and Interpretation*, JSOTSup 6 (Sheffield: JSOT Press, 1978), p. 96.

146. Stephanie Dalley ("Gilgamesh (OBV)," in *Myths from Mesopotamia* [New York: Oxford University Press, 1989], p. 141) translates *mūtum/mutum* as "death" rather than as "men" and so reads the line as a reference to the semidivine status of Gilgamesh.

147. Text is from Morris Jastrow and Albert Clay, *Old Babylonian Gilgamesh Epic*, YOS 4 (New Haven: Yale University Press, 1920), p. 68, Pennsylvania Tablet, col. VI, lines 234-40.

148. Copy of cuneiform text in Jastrow and Clay, *Old Babylonian Gilgamesh Epic*, Yale Tablet, plate III, col. III, lines 132-33.

Whatever they accomplish is only a breath.
Now, are you afraid of death?
What has become of your mighty valor?
Let me go before you.
Let your mouth call out, "Draw near! Do not fear!"
If I should fall, I shall thereby establish my name.
They will say, "Gilgamesh went into battle with fierce Ḫuwawa!"[149]

Convinced of the fleeting character of human life and its accomplishments, Gilgamesh contended that he could win fame by dying in a contest against the legendary Ḫuwawa. This picture of the bold, daring hero in search of lasting fame describes the first of two groups of tales about Gilgamesh that were incorporated into the OB version of the *Epic of Gilgamesh* created around 1700 B.C.[150]

In contrast, the second group of tales portrays Gilgamesh as fearing the dark reality of death and trying to find a way to avoid it. When Enkidu died from illness sent by the gods as a punishment for slaying Ḫuwawa, Gilgamesh went in quest of a way to avoid death. He journeyed to the land of sunrise to find the secret of everlasting life from Utnapishtim, the primordial flood hero who had escaped death. At the end of the OB version of the *Epic of Gilgamesh*, it appears that Gilgamesh failed to pass the test of staying awake for six days and seven nights (as in the Assyrian version) and so Gilgamesh sailed off as a tragic hero with the boatman Shurshunabu.[151] The interplay between the two contrasting attitudes toward the death of the hero reveals an ambivalence toward heroic exploits that bring enduring fame.

The heroic quest for immortal fame is reflected in the epilogue of Hammurapi's *Code* where Hammurapi portrayed himself as a heroic warrior whose exploits had brought well-being to the land:

I, Hammurapi, the perfect king, was not remiss (or) negligent toward the black-headed people whom Enlil entrusted to me (and) whose shepherdship Marduk gave to me; I sought out secure places for them; I relieved terrible miseries; I caused light to go forth for them. With the strong weapon which

149. Transliteration from Wolfram von Soden, "Untersuchungen zur babylonischen Metrik, Teil I," *ZA* 71 (1981): 183, Yale Tablet, IV, 5-14; copy of cuneiform text in Jastrow and Clay, *Old Babylonian Gilgamesh Epic*, Yale Tablet, plates III-IV, col. IV, lines 140-50.

150. Jacobsen, "The Gilgamesh Epic," pp. 230-31; Gerdien Jonker, *The Topography of Remembrance: The Dead, Tradition, and Collective Memory in Mesopotamia*, Studies in the History of Religions 68 (Leiden: Brill, 1995), p. 100.

151. Jacobsen, "The Gilgamesh Epic," pp. 240-42; William Moran, "The Gilgamesh Epic," in *Civilizations of the Ancient Near East*, ed. Jack Sasson (New York: Scribner, 1995), p. 2329; Smith, "Wisdom's Place," pp. 9-12.

Zababa and Ishtar appropriated for me, with the wisdom which Ea apportioned to me, with the ability which Marduk gave me, I rooted out the enemies above and below; I did away with war; I improved the welfare of the land; I brought about the settling of the people in dwellings in the meadows; I did not allow them to have one who would terrorize them." (*CH* XLVII:9-39)[152]

Later in the epilogue, Hammurapi listed curses that he wished to be effective against anyone who might remove the words that he had placed on this stela. The stela was to make known to all future generations the name and the deeds of Hammurapi.

The epilogue gives no hint that Hammurapi was in mortal danger in these battles. Perhaps this was because the death of a Mesopotamian king in battle was regarded as an anomaly and would need to be explained.[153] In response to the death of Ur-nammu (2112-2095 B.C.) in battle, the "Poem on the Death of Ur-nammu" wrestles with the fact that the death of a king in battle is usually a fate reserved for enemy kings.[154]

Although death in its proper time was simply to be accepted, premature or unexpected death had to be explained so that its chaotic face could be domesticated. Poetry and communal ritual were the primary means of coming to terms with the anguish of early death. The bards in Greece kept alive the memory of the warrior-kings Achilles and Agamemnon; the poets in the Israelite community and royal court immortalized Saul and David in the tradition; the court poets and scribes of Mesopotamia celebrated the names of Gilgamesh and Hammurapi. The heroic exploits of warriors preserved the community in times of crisis. The double-mindedness of the Homeric epics and the *Epic of Gilgamesh* about the value of dying for one's community and about the meaning of death reflected a realistic questioning about the limits of human life and the social structures in which life unfolded. Symbolic actions such as Saul's distribution of the parts of the slaughtered oxen and Agamemnon's confiscation of Achilles' prize showed how the king decisively influenced collective actions where individuals were asked to lay down their lives for the group. In contrast to the Homeric and Mesopotamian traditions, the Israelite tradition in its final form avoids portraying its heroic figures as self-consciously striving for fame.

---

152. Borger, *Babylonisch-assyrische Lesestücke,* 1:45.
153. Hallo, *Origins,* p. 203; Jonker, *The Topography of Remembrance,* p. 97.
154. Hallo, *Origins,* pp. 229-30.

Divine and Human: Separate or Intermingling Domains?

The manifestation of the divine within human affairs was regarded as an important if not foundational event in the communities of Homeric Greece, biblical Israel, and OB Mesopotamia. The ways in which such a divine appearance was described indicated how the author negotiated the embodied yet transcendent character of the divine presence, its visible and invisible dimensions. The king's role in mediating the sovereign rule of the king of the gods demanded his attention to the religious traditions of the community.

When the Achaeans were faltering under the advance of the Trojans, Poseidon intervened to inspire the two Ajaxes. Here is an example of divine intervention that showed not only that humans were not simply victims of the whims of the gods but also that the gods responded to humans and their plight.[155] Poseidon assumed the form of the prophet Calchas, yet the god's presence was detected by Ajax, son of Oileus, who said to Ajax, son of Telamon:

> Ajax, seeing that some one of the gods who inhabit Olympus appeared as a diviner and commanded the two of us to fight alongside the ships — this is not Calchas, the seer, the interpreter of signs from birds, for I readily recognized the prints of the feet and lower legs as he went away. The gods are easily spotted. And so the heart within my chest wishes the more to engage in war and fighting; my feet below and my hands above are eager for action. (*Il.* 13.68-75)

There was a corporeality to the gods in the Homeric world that resembled but far surpassed that of humans.[156] Vernant claims that in Homer the gods were not conceived on a human model, but vice versa.[157] In other words, the Homeric gods were not anthropomorphically conceived; humans were theomorphically conceived.[158] Those rare moments when a human manifested the beauty of a vibrant, inexhaustible, perfectly integrated being were fleeting in-

---

155. Slatkin, *The Power of Thetis,* p. 113.

156. Bernard Dietrich, "From Knossos to Homer," in *What Is a God? Studies in the Nature of Greek Divinity,* ed. Alan B. Lloyd (London: Duckworth, 1997), pp. 4-5; Walter Burkert, *Greek Religion* (Cambridge, Mass.: Harvard University Press, 1985), pp. 130, 183; cf. Jack Lawson, *The Concept of Fate in Ancient Mesopotamia of the First Millennium: Toward an Understanding of Šimtu,* OBC 7 (Wiesbaden: Harrassowitz, 1994), p. 15.

157. Vernant, *Mortals and Immortals,* pp. 35-36.

158. On the view of humans as theomorphically conceived in the biblical tradition, see Johannes C. de Moor, "The Duality in God and Man: Gen. 1:26-27 as P's Interpretation of the Yahwistic Creation Account," in *Intertextuality in Ugarit and Israel,* OTS 40 (Leiden: Brill, 1998), p. 115.

stances in which a god was noticed. In the Homeric epics, the divine was regarded as continuously present in the action of the poems, but such presence became manifest primarily to the mind rather than to the eye: a mental rather than a visual phenomenon — which was still a bodily manifestation.[159] In such manifestations, the perfect, dynamic body was the superbody of a god, and this, rather than the body of a human who grows weary and disintegrates, constituted the model for imagining the gods.[160]

When gods were sighted, it was a fleeting glimpse or a revealing clue that identified them. A face-to-face encounter would have led to blindness or death.[161] The human who perceived the god often experienced an increase in energy or power, or perhaps a disquieting experience (cf. *Od.* 19.40; 20.103).[162] Bernard Dietrich claims that in the Minoan and Homeric worlds the presence of the gods was not communicated by iconic or aniconic images but rather in the mind.[163] However, Vernant emphasizes that even though in Homer it is proper to say "that the gods have a body that is not a body," the continuity of the vital forces and values shared by gods and humans should not be ruptured.[164] So, this corporeality of the gods is a fundamental characteristic of Homeric gods.

The food of Homeric gods was imperishable nectar and ambrosia, whereas the food of humans was perishable meat and grain. Vernant notes that ambrosia or spices were regarded as food for the gods because they had qualities partaking of both heaven and earth and so were thought to bring the two spheres together.[165] When the gods participated in a sacrificial banquet, they did so in order to participate in its celebratory aspect rather than to gain nourishment.[166] The bones were typically burned as the portions of the gods, whereas all the edible portions were consumed by the human participants.[167]

The Homeric warrior who did courageous deeds in battle was honored by

159. Dietrich, "From Knossos to Homer," pp. 4, 8.

160. Vernant, *Mortals and Immortals*, pp. 32-36.

161. Vernant, *Mortals and Immortals*, pp. 42-44; cf. Jane B. Carter, "Ancestor Cult and the Occasion of Homeric Performance," in *The Ages of Homer*, ed. Jane B. Carter and Sarah Morris (Austin: University of Texas Press, 1995), p. 292.

162. Walter Burkert, "From Epiphany to Cult Statue: Early Greek *Theos*," in *What Is a God? Studies in the Nature of Greek Divinity*, ed. Alan B. Lloyd (London: Duckworth, 1997), p. 21.

163. Dietrich, "From Knossos to Homer," p. 8.

164. Vernant, *Mortals and Immortals*, pp. 46-47.

165. Jean-Pierre Vernant, *Myth and Society in Ancient Greece* (Atlantic Highlands, N.J.: Humanities, 1980), p. 152.

166. Vernant, *Mortals and Immortals*, p. 35.

167. Jean-Pierre Vernant, "Myth and Divinity," in *Myth, Religion, and Society*, ed. R. L. Gordon (Cambridge: Cambridge University Press, 1977), pp. 14-15; Burkert, *Greek Religion*, p. 57.

the people at home. On the Trojan side, Sarpedon, the son of Zeus, encouraged Glaucus to go on fighting so that they might demonstrate that they were deserving of the royal prerogatives they received at home (*Il.* 12.310-28). Later, when Sarpedon was about to be killed by Patroclus, Hera restrained Zeus from intervening on behalf of his son Sarpedon and noted that Sarpedon could be carried to his homeland "where his brothers and his countrymen will treat him like a god *(tarchusousi)* with tomb and gravestone" (*Il.* 16.456-57).[168] Gregory Nagy translates *tarchuō* as "treat like a god" and argues that Homer was saying here that Sarpedon would be recognized by the people of Lycia as a local cult figure who would receive libations, sacrificial offerings, and a plot in the sacred area.[169] The kind of honor given to a divinized cult hero was *timē*, which Nagy claims could have been earned during one's lifetime and received in the cult. Such honor differed from *kleos*, the "glory" that was gained only through death and was given through the song of the bard.[170] In aristocratic circles in the Archaic Age, individuals often made offerings to ancestors and recalled their heroics in order to accent their kinship with them and so advance their own status within the social hierarchy.[171]

In the world of Archaic Greece, the gods clearly differed from humans in the fact that they did not die (*Il.* 1.352-54; 5.340-41).[172] After death, some exceptional human beings could be venerated as heroes or blessed ones in family funerary cults.[173] In Homeric Greece, these heroes and blessed ones advanced up the hierarchy above the status of humans, but whether or not a hero reached the status of a god *(theos)* probably depended on the region or local cult.[174]

In Israel, the Lord was portrayed as a deity who spoke and acted like an enthroned king and human warrior:

---

168. Vernant, *Myth and Society in Ancient Greece*, p. 105.

169. Nagy, *Greek Mythology and Poetics*, pp. 131-36; cf. Ian Morris, *Archaeology as Cultural History* (Oxford: Blackwell, 2000), p. 235.

170. Nagy, *Greek Mythology and Poetics*, p. 137; Carter, "Ancestor Cult and the Occasion of Homeric Performance," p. 307.

171. Carter, "Ancestor Cult and the Occasion of Homeric Performance," p. 304.

172. A. W. H. Adkins, "Homeric Gods and the Values of Homeric Society," *JHS* 92 (1972): 1; Jenny Strauss Clay, *The Wrath of Athena* (Princeton: Princeton University Press, 1983), p. 157; Nagy, *The Best of the Achaeans*, p. 220.

173. Carter, "Ancestor Cult and the Occasion of Homeric Performance," p. 304; Morris, *Archaeology as Cultural History*, p. 231.

174. Vernant (*Myth and Society in Ancient Greece*, p. 107) claims that it was not until the time of the philosophers that a human could be elevated to the status of a *theos*, whereas Nagy (*Greek Mythology and Poetics*, p. 133) refers to local cults in Lycia where heroes were honored as gods.

136

Yahweh said to my lord [the king]:
    Sit at my right hand,
Until I make your enemies your footstool. (Ps. 110:1)

The Lord is at your [the king's] right hand;
    he will crush kings on the day of his anger. (Ps. 110:5)

The metaphoric character of this royal imagery for the Lord in Psalm 110 is apparent when it is juxtaposed to the imagery for the Lord in the following passage concerning a theophany at Mount Sinai:

> Then Moses, Aaron, Nadab, Abihu, and seventy of the elders of Israel ascended, and they saw the God of Israel. Under his feet there appeared to be sapphire pavement, like the heavens for brightness. Yet he did not strike the Israelite leaders. After seeing God, they ate and drank. (Exod. 24:9-11)

This passage portrays the Lord as a participant in a meal with Moses and his companions.[175] The description creates the impression that the Lord is like a human — his feet are on the sapphire tilework. Yet there is no further description of the Lord, which seems to indicate that the author of this passage understood the Lord to transcend the capacity of the human imagination to picture him — even with metaphors.[176] The group who ascended the mountain were granted an exemption from the usual fate of death for anyone who looked upon the Lord.

Anthropomorphic imagery was essential for communicating the ways that the Lord interacted with humans. The limits of such imagery for picturing the Lord become apparent, particularly in theophanies such as that involving Moses, Aaron, and the seventy elders in Exodus 24:9-11.[177] Some scholars claim, on the basis of analogy with other royally supported temple cults in Palestine and fragments of iconographical evidence, that the Jerusalem temple had an anthropomorphic cult statue of YHWH.[178] However, Tryggve Mettinger frames

---

175. E. W. Nicholson, "The Origin of the Tradition in Exodus XXIV 9-11," *VT* 26 (1976): 149; Brevard Childs, *Exodus* (Philadelphia: Westminster, 1974), p. 507.

176. Childs, *Exodus*, pp. 506-7. This is an example of what Tryggve Mettinger ("Israelite Aniconism: Developments and Origins," in *The Image and the Book*, ed. K. van der Toorn, Biblical Exegesis and Theology 21 [Leuven: Peeters, 1997], p. 187) identifies as the aniconic cult of the empty throne.

177. Cf. Mettinger, "Israelite Aniconism," p. 202, n. 120.

178. Christoph Uehlinger, "Anthropomorphic Cult Statuary in Iron Age Palestine and the Search for Yahweh's Cult Images," pp. 152-53, and Karel van der Toorn, "The Iconic Book Analogies Between the Babylonian Cult of Images and the Veneration of the Torah," p. 242, and Her-

the issue of the absence of a cultic image of the Lord in terms of the wider West Semitic practice of symbolizing the deity by standing stones, and he distinguishes this practice over against the anthropomorphic cult statue of the Mesopotamian tradition. His claim that the Israelite cult was aniconic in essence from its earliest stages places the issue in the framework of centuries-old worship practices of West Semitic peoples. This practice of symbolizing the deity by aniconic standing stones undergirds the later prohibition of images of the Lord (Exod. 20:4; Deut. 5:8) that emerged in Israel's exilic efforts to clarify its identity over against that of its Mesopotamian conquerors.[179]

Israelite sacrificial offerings included burnt offerings and communion offerings. In burnt offerings, the animal or grain was completely consumed by fire and so was given without reserve to the Lord. In communion offerings, the choice fatty portions were completely burned up for the Lord, and the remainder was divided among the cultic personnel and the worshippers.[180] References in the Psalms to promises to bring burnt offerings and sacrifices to the Lord (Ps. 51:21[19]; 66:13-15) are balanced by these words of Psalm 50, where the Lord is seen to upbraid manipulative worshippers:

> Not for your sacrifices do I reproach you,
>> for your burnt offerings are before me continuously. . . .
>
> If I were hungry, I would not tell you,
>> for the world and its fullness belong to me.
> Do I eat the meat of bulls,
>> or drink the blood of goats? (Ps. 50:8, 12-13)

Here, the Israelites were warned not to think that their offerings were physical nourishment for the Lord.[181] However, the "showbread" (Lev. 24:5-9; 1 Sam. 21:5[4]), the "sweet-smelling offerings" (Num. 15:3, 7, 13, 14, etc.), and "the ta-

---

bert Niehr, "In Search of YHWH's Cult Statue in the First Temple," pp. 73-95, all in *The Image and the Book*, ed. K. van der Toorn, Biblical Exegesis and Theology 21 (Leuven: Peeters, 1997).

179. Mettinger, "Israelite Aniconism," pp. 193-202. For the view that the Israelite cult was not aniconic in essence, see Uehlinger, "Anthropomorphic Cult Statuary," pp. 152-53. Brian B. Schmidt ("The Aniconic Tradition: On Reading Images and Viewing Texts," in *The Triumph of Elohim: From Yahwisms to Judaisms*, ed. D. Edelman [Grand Rapids: Eerdmans, 1995], pp. 81, 85, 87, 103) understands the struggle over cultic images to be the adoption of the correct image of the presence of the Lord rather than the presence or absence of such images.

180. Milgrom, *Leviticus 1–16*, pp. 440-43.

181. Hans-Joachim Kraus, *Psalms 1–59* (Minneapolis: Augsburg, 1988), p. 494; Moshe Weinfeld, "The Uniqueness of the Decalogue and Its Place in Jewish Tradition," in *The Ten Commandments in History and Tradition*, ed. B.-Z. Segal (Jerusalem: Magnes, 1990), pp. 23-27, 34.

ble of the Lord" (1 Kings 7:48) are indications that the Israelites did regard the sacrificial offerings in the context of their ritual actions as food for the Lord.[182]

Whether or not Israelites regularly presented offerings to their deceased ancestors prior to the reign of Manasseh is debated. References to this ancestor cult in which the ancestors were honored and treated as divine beings who could intervene in human affairs seem to be detectable throughout the biblical tradition (e.g., Gen. 31:30; Judg. 17:5; 18:5; 1 Sam. 9:1–10:16; 20:29; Amos 6:10; Jer. 16:5-8).[183] However, Brian Schmidt has argued that such offerings to the ancestors (Jer. 16:5-8), where the ghosts of Judahite ancestors were regarded as beneficent spiritual powers (cf. 2 Kings 21:6; 23:24), became a practice in Judah at the earliest during the reign of Manasseh (687-642 B.C.) when it would have been imported from Mesopotamia.[184] Then with its strict injunctions on monolatry, the Josianic reform in the latter part of the seventh century B.C. prohibited ancestral worship and drove it underground (2 Kings 23:24).[185]

The conception of the gods from the earliest times in Mesopotamia grew out of the way the Sumerians and Akkadians related to nature and the supernatural.[186] The Mesopotamian gods, like humans, seem to have been defined by their bodies,[187] which means that a serious obligation for those who served the gods was to feed, clothe, and house these divine beings. However, Thorkild Jacobsen regards the Mesopotamian cult statue as symbol or metaphor for the god: it represents the god and paradoxically both "is" and "is not" the god. He contends that there is a spiritual dimension to the god that transcends the statue.[188] Because the Mesopotamian gods were believed to exercise power and authority over various aspects of life, it is to be expected that the way the

---

182. Anderson, *Sacrifices and Offerings in Ancient Israel*, p. 15; Niehr, "In Search of YHWH's Cult Statue in the First Temple," pp. 88-89.

183. Van der Toorn, *Family Religion in Babylonia, Syria and Israel*, p. 225; Theodore Lewis, *Cults of the Dead in Ancient Israel and Ugarit*, HSM 39 (Atlanta: Scholars, 1989), pp. 174, 176-78; idem, "Ancestor Worship," in *ABD*, 1:240-43; idem, "Banqueting Hall/House," in *ABD*, 1:581-82.

184. Brian Schmidt, *Israel's Beneficent Dead: Ancestor Cult and Necromancy in Ancient Israelite Religion and Tradition* (Winona Lake, Ind.: Eisenbrauns, 1996), pp. 275, 286-87.

185. Lewis, *Cults of the Dead*, pp. 124-27; Albertz, *A History of Israelite Religion*, 1:210-11.

186. Bottéro, *Mesopotamia*, p. 203; F. A. M. Wiggermann, "Theologies, Priests, and Worship in Ancient Mesopotamia," in *Civilizations of the Ancient Near East*, ed. Jack Sasson (New York: Scribner, 1995), p. 1869.

187. Julia M. Asher-Greve and Lawrence Asher-Greve, "From Thales to Foucault . . . and Back to Sumer," in *Intellectual Life of the Ancient Near East*, ed. Jiří Prosecký, CRRA 43 (Prague: Oriental Institute, 1998), p. 39.

188. Thorkild Jacobsen, "The Graven Image," in *Ancient Israelite Religion*, ed. P. Miller, Jr. et al. (Philadelphia: Fortress, 1987), pp. 16-20, 29.

Mesopotamians related to a king had a decisive influence on the way they imagined the gods and served them.[189]

Since the Mesopotamian gods were believed to require food and drink for their livelihood, humans, as commonly stated in Sumerian and Akkadian literature, were created to produce food and drink for the gods.[190] W. G. Lambert states that the Sumerians and Babylonians did not have the practice of sacrifice like the Hebrews, and so he translates the following lines from the *Enuma Elish* to bring to light the text's reference to the responsibility of humans to provide food and drink for the gods: "Provisioning is the need of the shrines of the gods" (IV, 11); "Henceforth you will be the provisioner of our shrines" (V, 115).[191] William Hallo notes that statistical data show that the amount of food brought into the cult equals the amount distributed to the king, the temple personnel, and certain worshippers.[192] So, even though the cultic system arranged for the food and drink offered in the cult to be consumed by humans, the religious outlook maintained that the deities consumed these provisions.[193] Within the context of Mesopotamian religious practices in which the food offered to the gods was not burnt, the anthropomorphic conception of the gods seems to have been taken more literally than was the case in the Homeric and Israelite sacrificial practices. Even if the Lord and Zeus are understood to delight in the odor of the sacrificial offerings, it is quite a different matter, as Walter Burkert has noted, to smell cooking food than to eat it.[194]

Royal ancestors who died were believed to have joined the company of the gods and so were in need of offerings of food and drink. Such a ritual setting formed the context for the recitation of the genealogy of the Hammurapi dynasty from Sumuabum (1894-1866 B.C.) to Ammiditana (1683-1647 B.C.) as known in "The Genealogy of the Hammurapi Dynasty," a text composed for Ammiditana's son, Ammiṣaduqa (1646-1626 B.C.).[195] In the *Epic of Gilgamesh*,

189. Jean Bottéro, "Introduction," in Jean Bottéro and Samuel Noah Kramer, *Lorsque les dieux faisaient l'homme: mythologie mésopotamienne* (Paris: Gallimard, 1989), p. 78.

190. W. G. Lambert, "Donations of Food and Drink to the Gods in Ancient Mesopotamia," in *Ritual and Sacrifice in the Ancient Near East,* ed. J. Quaegebeur, OLA 55 (Leuven: Peeters, 1993), p. 198.

191. Lambert, "Donations of Food and Drink," pp. 193, 198.

192. William W. Hallo, "Sumerian Religion," in *Kinattūtu ša darāti,* ed. A. F. Rainey (Tel Aviv: University of Tel Aviv Press, 1993), p. 20.

193. William W. Hallo, "The Origins of the Sacrificial Cult," in *Ancient Israelite Religion,* ed. P. Miller, Jr. et al. (Philadelphia: Fortress, 1987), p. 11. Leach (*Culture and Communication,* p. 70) claims that the code of religious language places its statements into a system where the referent is metaphysical rather than physical reality.

194. Burkert, *Greek Religion,* p. 57.

195. J. J. Finkelstein, "Genealogy of the Hammurapi Dynasty," *JCS* 20 (1966): 97, 115-16;

the people of Uruk reminded Gilgamesh as he and Enkidu were about to set out for the Cedar Forest that he had to remember to pour out water libations to Shamash and to Gilgamesh's divinized father Lugalbanda.[196] Karel van der Toorn argues that this practice of giving daily food offerings *(kispū)* to ancestors was not confined to the royal household in Mesopotamia but was also to be found in the family household where typically the *paterfamilias* was charged with overseeing these offerings.[197]

Throughout the second millennium b.c. in Mesopotamia, there was a growing consolidation of the pantheon under the rule of Marduk.[198] *Enuma Elish* VI:39-44 refers to six hundred gods assigned to their places in heaven and on earth, whereas earlier the Sumerians had worshipped over two thousand gods.[199] The Semitic gods of the second millennium were depicted as less aggressive and more refined morally than their predecessors in the Sumerian pantheon.[200] The consolidation of the pantheon seems to have occurred as part of the interplay between Sumerian and Akkadian cultural traditions, such that there were shifts and restructurings of the pantheon, but not in a linear evolutionary fashion.[201]

Mark Chavalas, "Genealogical History as 'Charter': A Study of Old Babylonian Period Historiography and the Old Testament," in *Faith, Tradition, and History: Old Testament Historiography in Its Near Eastern Context*, ed. A. R. Millard et al. (Winona Lake, Ind.: Eisenbrauns, 1994), pp. 110-20.

196. *ANET*, p. 80, tablet 3, 6.40-43. Van der Toorn, *Family Religion in Babylonia, Syria and Israel*, p. 48.

197. Van der Toorn, *Family Religion in Babylonia, Syria and Israel*, pp. 48-52; Akio Tsukimoto, "Aspekte von *Kispu(m)* als Totenbeigabe," in *Death in Mesopotamia*, ed. B. Alster, Mesopotamia 8 (Copenhagen: Akademisk Forlag, 1980), pp. 131-33; Aaron Skaist, "The Ancestor Cult and Succession in Mesopotamia," in *Death in Mesopotamia*, ed. B. Alster, Mesopotamia 8 (Copenhagen: Akademisk Forlag, 1980), pp. 126-27. D. Charpin ("Maisons et maisonnées en Babylonie ancienne de Sippar à Ur," in *Houses and Households in Ancient Mesopotamia*, ed. K. Veenhof, CRRA 40 [Leiden: Nederlands Historisch-Archaeologisch Instituut te Istanbul, 1996], p. 224) notes that the eldest son was not always designated to carry on the family line by receiving the largest share of the inheritance and taking responsibility for the offerings to the ancestors.

198. Walter Sommerfeld, *Der Aufstieg Marduks: Die Stellung Marduks in der babylonischen Religion des zweiten Jahrtausends v. Chr.*, AOAT 213 (Neukirchen-Vluyn: Neukirchener Verlag, 1982), pp. 1-2; Bottéro, "Introduction," p. 69; cf. Piotr Michalowski, "Presence at Creation," in *Lingering over Words: Studies in Ancient Near Eastern Literature in Honor of William L. Moran*, ed. T. Abusch et al., HSM 37 (Atlanta: Scholars, 1990), p. 390.

199. René Labat, *Le poème babylonien de la creation* (Paris: Libraire d'Amérique et d'Orient, 1935), p. 147; Bottéro, *Mesopotamia*, p. 216.

200. Bottéro, *Mesopotamia*, p. 217.

201. Piotr Michalowski, "The Unbearable Lightness of Enlil," in *Intellectual Life of the Ancient Near East*, ed. Jiří Prosecký, CRRA 43 (Prague: Oriental Institute, 1998), pp. 244-45; cf. Thor-

Naram-Sin (2254-2218 B.C.), grandson of Sargon (2334-2279 B.C.), delivered the city of Akkad against overwhelming odds, which led the populace to regard him as the protector deity of their city.[202] So, with Naram-Sin began the practice of a king writing his name with the divine determinative and promoting the belief that he was a god during his lifetime.[203] This practice was revived by Ur-nammu of Ur (2112-2095 B.C.), the founder of the Ur III dynasty (2112-2004 B.C.), and was promoted vigorously by his son Shulgi (2094-2047 B.C.).[204] However, only Shu-Sin (2037-2029 B.C.) among the divinized kings appears to have demanded that a sanctuary and offerings be established for him during his lifetime.[205] Hallo argues that the temple establishment responded to the divine pretensions of the Sargonids by creating a divine cultic statue in the form of a king.[206] Even though the image of a god in the form of a king had been part of the onomasticon as early as the Early Dynastic II period (ca. 2700-2600 B.C.),[207] it was apparently the struggle between the temple establishment and the palace, with its increasing power under the Sargonids, that triggered the creation of the divine cultic statue in basilomorphic form.

In the mind's eye, the people of Homeric Greece, biblical Israel, and OB Mesopotamia used imagery appropriate to humans and applied it to the gods. There was a corporeality to Homeric gods that was difficult to perceive because of their invisibility. The corporeality of the Mesopotamian gods was a presupposition of the housing and provisioning of the gods in temples. The use of anthropomorphic imagery to think and speak about the Lord is everywhere evident in the biblical tradition, but the extent to which the Lord was regarded as a God resident in a temple and served food analogous to the practices in Mesopotamian temples is yet to be established. The obligation of humans to serve the gods with food offerings or sacrifices is evident in all three cultures. Yet in Israel and Mesopotamia, the portions offered to God or the gods is burned up;

---

kild Jacobsen, *The Treasures of Darkness: A History of Mesopotamian Religion* (New Haven: Yale University Press, 1976), pp. 19-21.

202. Sabina Franke, "Kings of Akkad: Sargon and Naram-Sin," in *Civilizations of the Ancient Near East,* ed. Jack Sasson (New York: Scribner, 1995), p. 834; von Soden, *The Ancient Orient,* pp. 67-69.

203. Hallo, *Origins,* p. 152; von Soden, *The Ancient Orient,* pp. 67-69; Henri Frankfort, *Kingship and the Gods* (Chicago: University of Chicago Press, 1948), pp. 224-26.

204. William W. Hallo, *Early Mesopotamian Royal Titles, a Philologic and Historical Analysis,* AOS 43 (New Haven: Yale University Press, 1957), p. 125.

205. Hallo, "Sumerian Religion," pp. 24-25.

206. Hallo, "Sumerian Religion," pp. 18-20.

207. A. Wendell Bowes, "The Basilomorphic Conception of Deity in Israel and Mesopotamia," in *The Biblical Canon in Comparative Perspective: Scripture in Context IV,* ed. K. Younger, Jr. et al. (Lewiston, N.Y.: Mellen, 1991), pp. 240-41, 268, n. 7.

there is at least a step in the direction of a greater spiritualization of the divine in this practice. The line between gods and humans is blurred in the practice of the divinization of kings in Mesopotamia from 2250 to 1750 B.C. and of the divinization of heroes in parts of Homeric Greece. This divinizing practice may find an analog in the worship of ancestors in Israel, although this practice may have been a late importation into preexilic Israel from Mesopotamia rather than an established part of the tradition.

The King: A Centralizing Symbol within the Community

The dangers to human life posed by foreign foes, famine, social unrest, untimely death, and ennui or powerlessness form primary concerns for a human community. The legitimacy of a king's rule is closely linked to the ways in which he negotiates the dilemmas that these dangers pose to a community. Because of the symbolic and material power concentrated in the hands of the king, he can provide ways to navigate these turbulent waters or he can become part of the problem. Whether the king is viewed positively or negatively may depend on how he particularly treats individuals or segments of the community.

The boundaries of a community establishing who is a friend and who is a foe are not simply determined by geographical markers; social, ethnic, and cultural factors enter into the mix. These boundaries are thus always under negotiation. The tension or dialectic between friend and foe or human and savage is an antinomy in which a balance is sought rather than a once-and-for-all solution. A king like Odysseus in his encounter with the Cyclopes could both rescue the community from and expose the community to a dangerous foe. A ruler like David posed a threat to the seminomadic way of life in Israel through his proposal to construct a temple where the ideal in the Israelite tradition was to maintain a symbiotic relation with the city-state system without being co-opted by it. Gilgamesh found in the wild man Enkidu a worthy rival who curbed his excesses toward a tyrannical kind of rule. The interplay or tension between the civilized and the savage had its rightful place within the field of contending forces mapped out by the king as the symbolic center of the community.

The need for food alerted individuals to their ties to the environment and to a community. Laertes and Odysseus had to tend to their garden and community with care and justice in order to bring them into harmony with the natural order, whereas Alcinous in the magical kingdom of Phaeacia did not have this challenge because the Phaeacians were given harmonious relations with nature and within society. When famine struck Israel in the reign of David, the account in 2 Samuel 21:1-14 makes the point that David was responsible for agricultural success and needed to restore justice in the land so that the rains might return. Even if the account has other propagandistic motives, it nevertheless indicates that the king was expected to sustain the fertility of the land through the justice of his rule. In Mesopotamia, the king was able to demonstrate concretely the organizational superiority of monarchical rule by his capacity to oversee the construction of canals and other irrigation and flood-control projects. The persistent potential for flood, famine, and disease to cut off the food supply made this danger to a community one for which the king was expected to provide solutions.

The threat of displacement from one's home or status within the community took the form of a tension between competition and cooperation. Eumaeus, faced with what appeared to be the ascendancy of hostile suitors, saw the potential for a homestead diminishing as the suitors rose in power and the house of Odysseus diminished. The competition among households had an impact on those who were given a place within that household. In Israel, the judge Samuel in 1 Samuel 8:11-17 warned the elders that a king could confiscate their land, conscript the members of their families, and reduce them to slavery. The king could have been a blessing as a defender against foreign foes but at the same time might have taken their homes and places in the community away from them. In Mesopotamia, there were differentials in wealth that took the form of classes or ranks. One's place could shift through good or bad fortune but also through the actions of the king. Rivalry, competition, and the ups-and-downs of one's luck were realities within a community that a king could not or should not have controlled. However, his position at the top of the hierarchy meant that he would have had a marked influence on the ways that individuals moved up and down or kept their place on this grid of the community.

The threat of sudden or early death focused the issue of the meaning of life. In Homer, the warrior who died early in a dangerous battle was immortalized in the communal memory through the song of the bard. The danger that a king like Agamemnon could undercut this memory led Achilles to withdraw in anger from the campaign against Troy. In Israel, the conscious attempt of the individual to win fame as a warrior was not celebrated in the biblical tradition. Yet there are texts that indicate that the warrior-kings Saul and David operated under a form of warrior code in order to mobilize and reward their soldiers. In Mesopotamia, the king Gilgamesh sets out with Enkidu to conquer Ḫuwawa and win fame, but he is then crushed by the death of Enkidu and sets out on a second quest to find immortality. The king had a key role in inspiring and rewarding soldiers who confronted early death in battle. He could have been a blessing or a curse to the community by the way that he distributed honor.

The forces that shaped the life of the community were much larger than the king. The peoples of Homeric Greece, biblical Israel, and OB Mesopotamia understood this larger sphere as existing between the poles of heaven and earth, and being structured according to a hierarchy of gods and humans. The Homeric gods were ubiquitous and could be appealed to but not controlled by ritual means. Their excellences were imagined to set the ideal for human life. Often gods were detected in the outstanding feats of heroes. In Israel, loyalty to the Lord alone shaped the biblical tradition, particularly in its final written form. In the canonical form of the tradition, sacrifices offered to the Lord were symbolic gestures that honored rather than supplied food to the Lord. In Mesopotamia, the gods were served as individuals living in temples and so were entitled to food, clothing, and shelter from the community. The king had a role in the provisioning of temples and ritual offerings in all three cultures. In Mesopotamia from 2250 to 1750 B.C., some kings were honored with divine status prior to death. This honor of divinization resembled that accorded to a hero in the hero cults in parts of the Homeric world. This low-ranking god was believed to have the capacity to do good or ill for the community. Thus, there were cases where the movement in the hierarchy of gods and men allowed a few, select individuals to gain divine status in Mesopotamia and Homer. Such divinization is not apparent in the biblical record; furthermore, heroic ambitions that might be a means for such a rise in status are subdued or muted in the biblical record.

As a symbol of the community, the king's body can be imagined as a field upon which the primary concerns of the community were addressed and equilibrium was maintained. The polarities between friend and foe, food and famine, sense of belonging and alienation, meaning and futility, and integration and disintegration were tensions or dialectics that needed to be balanced within the analogy of the community as the king's body. This basic analogy — the community as the body of the king — created a place in which the divine and human could interact to work toward equilibrium of the polarities of the primary concerns of the community in a constructive way.

CHAPTER FOUR

The Role of Memory and Tradition in Legitimating Royal Authority

A king anchored his authority in the divine will, in realities beyond the here and now. The physical strength, material wealth, and capacity to inspire a following were concrete, tangible realities, but each of these manifestations of power signified that the king had been destined for his leadership role by forces and circumstances beyond his calculated efforts. He tried to persuade the people that he had been chosen for the kingship by the king of the gods who was revered in their tradition. Such a rhetorical effort was essential for the longevity of the king's rule.

The king of the gods held sovereignty over heaven and earth and chose a particular individual to exercise sovereignty on his behalf in the earthly sphere. The words that the king and his court used to persuade the people of his divine election needed to evoke images that the people had of their gods, their ancestors, and their identity. Words that typically would resonate with the hearts and minds of the people were those that would have been handed on through the generations in their community.[1] Such words would often have been shaped into stories that traced out the contours of a world within which the people and their ancestors resided. Thus, the traditional pattern for legitimating royal authority took concrete form within a community by drawing upon the names, attributes, and histories of the divine and human characters remembered in the community's tradition.

---

1. Paul Ricoeur, *Time and Narrative*, vol. 3 (Chicago: University of Chicago Press, 1985), pp. 113-14, 256; Norman Yoffee, "The Late Great Tradition in Ancient Mesopotamia," in *The Tablet and the Scroll: Near Eastern Studies in Honor of William W. Hallo*, ed. M. Cohen et al. (Bethesda, Md.: CDL, 1993), p. 301.

The act of remembering is essential to the integrity of an individual and a community in all times and places. By remembering individuals and events of the past, a person acknowledges his debt to his ancestors and his enduring relationship with them.[2] This act of remembering reveals aspects of individual and communal identity that can shape expectations. The experience of time as the past, the present, and the future involves the interplay between clock time and lived time, between the absolute measure of chronological time and the variable sense of durations.[3] Both forms of time are powerful factors shaping the inhabited world. They work together to give definition to the possibilities that individuals believe are open to them.

The traditions of Homeric Greece and ancient Mesopotamia claimed that an individual had a destiny or lot in life determined at birth.[4] This awareness that forces larger than life determined the course of one's life could lead to fatalism if one went so far as to believe that every significant life choice was already determined by powers outside oneself. Peoples of the ancient Near East, like peoples of all ages, wanted to know what was in store for them so that they might take steps to have a bad destiny changed and a good one implemented.[5] The notion of "destiny" *(šīmtum)* or of "one's lot or portion in life" *(moira)* made possible the fundamental awareness that an individual life is not simply a succession of "nows" but rather takes the form of a narrative with a beginning, middle, and end.[6] There is an order to an individual's life that takes the form of the plot of a story. To know the particular contents of this story of one's life is of great interest and importance to an individual. Yet apart from the certainty of death, the particulars of an individual's life story can be known in advance only

2. Ricoeur, *Time and Narrative,* 3:118; Marcel Detienne, *The Creation of Mythology* (Chicago: University of Chicago Press, 1986), pp. 38-40.

3. Paul Ricoeur, "Initiative," in *From Text to Action: Essays in Hermeneutics II* (Evanston, Ill.: Northwestern University Press, 1991), pp. 211-12; cf. Roy Rappaport, *Ritual and Religion in the Making of Humanity* (Cambridge: Cambridge University Press, 1999), pp. 176-77.

4. Jean Bottéro, *Mesopotamia: Writing, Reasoning, and the Gods* (Chicago: University of Chicago Press, 1992), p. 224; Jean-Pierre Vernant, *Mortals and Immortals* (Princeton: Princeton University Press, 1991), p. 314; Jack Lawson, *The Concept of Fate in Ancient Mesopotamia of the First Millennium: Toward an Understanding of Šimtu,* OBC 7 (Wiesbaden: Harrassowitz, 1994), pp. 127-28; Margalit Finkelberg, "*Timē* and *Aretē* in Homer," *Classical Quarterly* 48 (1998): 20.

5. Bottéro, *Mesopotamia,* pp. 141-42; Lawson, *The Concept of Fate,* pp. 128-29; Stephanie Dalley, "Occasions and Opportunities. 1. To the Persian Conquest," in *The Legacy of Mesopotamia,* ed. S. Dalley (Oxford: Oxford University Press, 1998), p. 20.

6. Ricoeur, *Time and Narrative,* 3:19-22; cf. Hans Kellner, "'As Real as It Gets': Ricoeur and Narrativity," in *Meanings in Texts and Actions: Questioning Paul Ricoeur,* ed. D. Klemme and W. Schweiker (Charlottesville: University of Virginia Press, 1993), p. 56; Donald Phillip Verene, "Two Sources of Philosophical Memory: Vico versus Hegel," in *Philosophical Imagination and Cultural Memory,* ed. P. Cook (Durham, N.C.: Duke University Press, 1993), p. 42.

as probabilities.[7] Once these particulars have occurred, they become material for remembering and so are subject to forgetting.[8]

An individual's life story cannot be remembered and told apart from the life stories of other individuals within a community, particularly those of the ancestors.[9] The interweaving of individual life stories within a community demands that the past, and not simply the present, be a factor in shaping the "horizon of expectation" of an individual and of the community as a whole.[10] This interweaving of narratives is mirrored in the making and remembering of myths. As applied narratives, the plots of the various myths influence and play off one another by complementing, supplementing, or contradicting one another.[11]

Royal Authority in the Face of Chaos or Unrest: The Importance of Recalling Past Events and Accomplishments

Critical situations upset routines and demand attention. When a crisis is anticipated, leaders try to mobilize a community to prepare for anticipated difficulties. When a crisis has overwhelmed a community, leaders try to find ways for the community to come to terms with the confusion and suffering. If the community is to make necessary adaptations to new circumstances, it needs to contextualize these changes within the memory and tradition of the community: either to reject or to continue elements of the history and identity of the community.

Nestor, the elderly sceptered king from Pylos, wielded an authority among the Achaean coalition analogous to the authority of Zeus on Olympus, for Nestor's authority went unchallenged as he delivered the largest number of *mythoi*.[12] Although Nestor stated that Agamemnon was king (*Il.* 9.69), it was

7. Achilles knows that his life is to be short and it is important for him to act in accord with this destiny *(kata aisan);* this pathway of his short life is his destiny. See Laura Slatkin, *The Power of Thetis: Allusion and Interpretation in the "Iliad"* (Berkeley: University of California Press, 1991), pp. 35-36.

8. Marcel Detienne, *The Masters of Truth in Archaic Greece* (New York: Zone, 1999), pp. 47-49; Charles Segal, *Singers, Heroes, and Gods in the Odyssey* (Ithaca: Cornell University Press, 1994), pp. 99-103; Kellner, "As Real as It Gets," p. 62.

9. Ricoeur, *Time and Narrative*, 3:213; Vernant, *Mortals and Immortals*, p. 57.

10. Ricoeur, *Time and Narrative*, 3:172; Gerdien Jonker, *The Topography of Remembrance: The Dead, Tradition, and Collective Memory in Mesopotamia*, Studies in the History of Religions 68 (Leiden: Brill, 1995), p. 176.

11. Richard Buxton, *Imaginary Greece* (Cambridge: Cambridge University Press, 1994), p. 207.

12. As stated earlier in chapter 2, *mythos* in Homer means an authoritative speech-act.

Nestor who acted like a king. He was adept in acknowledging others and their accomplishments through praise. For example, he was able to recruit volunteers for a spying mission into Troy because he not merely offered material rewards but more importantly encouraged them through words of praise (*Il.* 10.203-17).[13] In line with his strategy of offering praise to others, Nestor was also skillful in incorporating the recollection of past heroes and deeds, including his own accomplishments, into his speeches.[14] When the quarrel between Achilles and Agamemnon broke out, Nestor tried to mediate by exhorting them to obey his advice:

> But pay attention. Both of you are younger than I. In time past, I associated with men who were stronger than you and never did they slight me. I have never seen nor will I see again such men as Peirithous, and Dryas, shepherd of the people, and Caeneus and Exadius, and godlike Polyphemus and Theseus, son of Aegeus, resembling the immortals. (*Il.* 1.259-65)

Nestor went on to explain how he had fought alongside these men with whom no one currently alive could compare (*Il.* 1.266-73).[15] They belonged to the heroic world that occupied its own dimension that was neither completely human nor divine but a unique combination of both.[16] Nestor recalls his association with these heroes in his attempt to persuade Achilles and Agamemnon to pay heed to his words.

Nestor's use of authoritative utterances *(mythoi)* to persuade others had an analog on the divine plane when Zeus mediated quarrels among members of his own divine household. He sent the divine messenger Iris with the command that Athena not enter the battle between the Achaeans and the Trojans:

> For I will speak and it will come to pass: I will cripple their fast horses under the war-chariot. I will cast them from the driver's seat and shatter the war-

---

Richard P. Martin (*The Language of Heroes: Speech and Performance in the Iliad* [Ithaca: Cornell University Press, 1989], pp. 44, 48, 58) has argued that Homeric *mythos* is associated with "narrating from memory."

13. Martin, *The Language of Heroes*, pp. 108, 110.

14. Charles Segal, "Kleos and Its Ironies," in *Reading the Odyssey: Selected Interpretive Essays*, ed. Seth Schein (Princeton: Princeton University Press, 1996), p. 214; Peter W. Rose, *Sons of the Gods, Children of Earth: Ideology and Literary Form in Ancient Greece* (Ithaca: Cornell University Press, 1992), p. 57.

15. Carlo Brillante, "History and the Historical Interpretation of Myth," in *Approaches to Greek Myth*, ed. Lowell Edmunds (Baltimore: Johns Hopkins University Press, 1990), p. 102.

16. Douglas Frame (*The Myth of Return in Early Greek Epic* [New Haven: Yale University Press, 1978], pp. 80, 113) argues that Nestor held an intermediate status between god and human.

chariot. Not even in the course of ten years will they be healed of the wounds that the lightning causes, so that the bright-eyed goddess will know when it is that she fights with her father. But with Hera I am not uttering such a reproach nor am I angry, for it is always her practice to thwart me in whatever I say. (*Il.* 8.401-8)

Hera, wife of Zeus, wanted to intervene on behalf of the Achaeans who were suffering losses at the hands of the Zeus-assisted Trojans. Earlier Zeus had ordered the Olympian gods to refrain from the battle with a series of authoritative speech-acts (*mythoi*) that joined together to take the form of a narrative (*Il.* 8.5-27); the force of his commands was encapsulated in the assertion: "Then you will see how much I am the mightiest of all the gods" (*Il.* 8.17).[17] Zeus's authority was unrivaled. Even though Hera tried to get Poseidon (*Il.* 8.198-211) and Athena (*Il.* 8.350-56) to intervene in the battle on behalf of the Achaeans, Zeus understood his wife's ways and did not see her actions as a threat to his authority. Yet neither Poseidon, Zeus's brother, nor Athena, Zeus's daughter, dared to act directly against the orders of Zeus. The Olympian gods might have tested Zeus's commands and explored how serious he was in carrying out his threats, but they typically would not act in any way that directly dismissed his authority.[18]

Nestor's authority rested upon wisdom gained from experience and knowledge of the past rather than upon the physical force he could presently exert (*Il.* 2.16, 433).[19] He upbraided the Achaean warriors for their lack of courage before Hector and the Trojans and recounted how heroic ancestors such as Lycurgus of Arcadia had defeated Areithous and then handed on his armor to Ereuthalion, whom Nestor himself in his youth had defeated; therefore, he claimed that he would go forth against Hector if only he were younger (*Il.* 7.120-60). Nestor was persuasive not only because he was revered as the keeper of the traditions but also because he asked the Achaean warriors to follow his example. He was not a mere manipulator of words but an elder worthy of emulation.[20] Nestor's words of praise meant something because of who he was. His

17. Martin (*The Language of Heroes*, p. 54) claims that this stringing together of authoritative statements (*mythoi*) in narrative form is the forerunner of the later "imaginative traditional narratives" that are labeled myths. Jean-Pierre Vernant, *Myth and Society in Ancient Greece* (Atlantic Highlands, N.J.: Humanities, 1980), p. 95.

18. Martin, *The Language of Heroes*, 55. Walter Burkert (*The Orientalizing Revolution: Near Eastern Influence on Greek Culture in the Early Archaic Age* [Cambridge, Mass.: Harvard University Press, 1992], p. 106) claims that the instance of the gods trying to bind Zeus in *Il.* 1.396-406 is unique in Homer and was probably a borrowing from the Mesopotamian *Atraḥasis Epic*.

19. Margalit Finkelberg, *The Birth of Literary Fiction in Ancient Greece* (Oxford: Clarendon, 1998), p. 62.

20. Martin, *The Language of Heroes*, p. 82.

praise of contemporaries and ancestors took place within the context of the traditions of the community.

In the Israelite tradition, the composer of Psalm 89 addressed a time of crisis in the community when a Davidic king had been removed from the throne and the rule of the house of David had ceased in Jerusalem. This lengthy psalm of lament incorporated a traditional hymn of praise to the Lord (vv. 6-16[5-15])[21] and an oracular promise of an everlasting dynasty for David (vv. 20-38[19-37]) as key elements of the tradition that had shaped expectations of the people that their current tragic situation contradicted.[22] The psalmist looked to the past and narrated from memory authoritative words and actions both by the Lord and by the community about the Lord that had shaped the Israelites' identity and community.

The hymn in verses 6-16(5-15) praised the Lord as the Incomparable One who held sovereignty over divine beings and over heaven and earth:

> For who in the skies can line up opposite the Lord?
>> Who among the children of God is like the Lord,
> a God feared in the council of the holy ones,
>> great and terrible beyond all that encircle him?
> O Lord God of hosts, who is like you?
>> You are mighty and your steadiness encircles you.
> You govern the raging of the sea;
>> with the roaring[23] of its waves, you bring them to silence.
> You beat Rahab to pieces like one struck down;
>> You dispersed your enemies with your mighty arm.
> The heavens belong to you and also the earth;
>> The dry land and all that is on it, you laid their foundation. (vv. 7-12[6-11])

The hymn confidently proclaimed that the Lord's rule was firmly established and that he had no rival. This hymn was most likely used for many generations in Israelite worship prior to its incorporation into Psalm 89.[24] Its imagery of the

---

21. Claus Westermann (*Praise and Lament in the Psalms* [Atlanta: John Knox, 1981], p. 122) demarcates vv. 5-18 as the hymn of descriptive praise within Psalm 89.

22. Évode Beaucamp, *Le psautier*, 2 vols. (Paris: Gabalda, 1979), 2:85-86. For a division of Psalm 89 that regards vv. 2-38(1-37) as a unit, see Richard Clifford, "Psalm 89: A Lament over the Davidic Ruler's Continued Failure," *HTR* 73 (1980): 43-46.

23. Read *bišĕ'ôn* with the LXX.

24. Hans-Joachim Kraus, *Psalms 60–150* (Minneapolis: Augsburg, 1989), p. 201; Beaucamp, *Le psautier*, 2:86-87; Knut Heim, "The (God-)Forsaken King of Psalm 89: A Historical and Intertextual Enquiry," in *King and Messiah in Israel and the Ancient Near East*, ed. J. Day, JSOTSup 270 (Sheffield: Sheffield Academic Press, 1998), pp. 296-322.

heavenly council of gods and of the battle with Rahab, who symbolized the forces of disorder and chaos, was repeated in a number of the psalms (e.g., Ps. 74:12-17; 77:16-19) and so occupied a significant place in the mental geography of the traditional Israelite. The ancestors no doubt sang this hymn from memory in their worship, and so the testimony of one generation helped to shape that of the next.[25] The fact that this traditional hymn could be recontextualized within a lament like Psalm 89 indicated that the hymn could maintain its integrity while assuming different positions within the larger matrix of the Israelite tradition. This "intertextuality" reverenced the memory of the ancestors by narrating and renarrating it.[26]

The story line of Psalm 89 proclaimed the sovereignty of the Lord over heaven and earth (vv. 6-16[5-15]) and then linked this sovereign rule with the house of David through the divine promise of protection, worldwide rule, divine adoption of the king, and an everlasting dynasty (vv. 20-38[19-37]):

> I have placed the crown on a strong one,
>   I have lifted up a youth from the people.
> I have found my servant David;
>   with my holy oil I have anointed him;
> my hand shall be securely with him;
>   my arm shall also strengthen him. . . .
> His descendants shall continue forever,
>   and his throne shall be like the sun before me.
> It shall be secure forever like the moon,
>   a faithful witness in the skies. (vv. 20-22, 37-38[19-21, 36-37])

This oracle, recounted elsewhere in 2 Samuel 7:8-16 as a revelation to the prophet Nathan, played a central role in the political and theological traditions of Jerusalem. The promise of an everlasting dynasty in Psalm 89:20-38(19-37) was summarized earlier in verses 4-5(3-4) where it was identified as a "covenant." This solemn form of a promise did not simply commit the Lord to the Davidic house; it took on the form of a divine declaration such that the permanence of the relationship between the Lord and the Davidic house was to be taken as fact.[27] This

---

25. Frank Moore Cross, *From Epic to Canon: History and Literature in Ancient Israel* (Baltimore: Johns Hopkins University Press, 1998), pp. 38-39.

26. Michael Fishbane, *Biblical Interpretation in Ancient Israel* (Oxford: Clarendon, 1985), pp. 1-19; Ricoeur, *Time and Narrative*, 3:172.

27. Cf. William Schniedewind, *Society and the Promise to David: The Reception History of 2 Samuel 7:1-17* (New York: Oxford University Press, 1999), pp. 46-50; Jon Levenson, "The Davidic Covenant and Its Interpreters," *CBQ* 41 (1979): 217.

sovereign word of the Lord, remembered by the tradition in this oracle as delivered in the first part of the tenth century B.C., was able to exert a profound influence on the mental geography of the Israelite people while the Davidic house ruled in Jerusalem (1000-587 B.C.).[28]

Current events in Jerusalem at the time of the psalmist challenged the belief in the eternal character of the covenant. So the psalmist cried out:

> But now you have spurned and refused him;
>> you have become angry with your anointed.
> You have rejected the covenant with your servant;
>> you have defiled his crown in the dust. (vv. 39-40[38-39])

The memory of the covenant had shaped the self-understanding and the expectations of the people of Jerusalem. Using the form of a lament, the psalmist expressed the contradiction between the promise and the current reality as a plea for the Lord to intervene and show them a way forward:

> How long, O Lord? Will you hide yourself forever?
>> How long will your anger burn like fire? (v. 47[46])

The memory of the hymn regarding the Lord's sovereignty and of the promise of the everlasting covenant to David was not dismissed in these extreme circumstances that called into question the Lord's care for his people. The story line of the lament juxtaposed the promises and expectations of the past with the current confusion and asked why. Remembering was an essential component of a lament. Such remembering intensified the sense of disorientation in the present where the intent of the lament was to move God to intervene.[29]

In latter part of the second millennium B.C. in Mesopotamia, the narrative *Enuma Elish* was composed to describe the circumstances of, the reasons for, and the consequences of Marduk's rise to power as king of the gods in the Mesopotamian tradition.[30] Earlier in the OB period in the land of Sumer (southern Mesopotamia) and Akkad (northern Mesopotamia), the position of

---

28. Antii Laato, *A Star Is Rising: The Historical Development of the Old Testament Royal Ideology and the Rise of the Jewish Messianic Expectations* (Atlanta: Scholars, 1997), pp. 44-46; P. Kyle McCarter, Jr., *II Samuel*, AB 9 (Garden City, N.Y.: Doubleday, 1984), pp. 223-24.

29. Westermann, *Praise and Lament in the Psalms*, p. 215.

30. Walter Sommerfeld, *Der Aufstieg Marduks: Die Stellung Marduks in der babylonischen Religion des zweiten Jahrtausends v. Chr.*, AOAT 213 (Neukirchen-Vluyn: Neukirchener Verlag, 1982), pp. 1-2; Jean Bottéro, "Introduction," in Jean Bottéro and Samuel Noah Kramer, *Lorsque les dieux faisaient l'homme: mythologie mésopotamienne* (Paris: Gallimard, 1989), p. 69.

king of the gods was held by both Anum (the older god of the vault of the sky) and Enlil (the younger god of the moist winds). Enlil, whose sanctuary was located at Nippur, a city midway between Sumer and Akkad, was the active wielder of sovereignty, while Anum, whose sanctuary was located in Uruk, a major cultural and trade center at the end of the fourth millennium B.C., tended to be seen as semiretired.[31] With the rise of Babylon from an unknown village to the capital city of Hammurapi's kingdom, which extended its boundaries beyond the land of Sumer and Akkad, Marduk's status among the gods increased, as is evident in the opening of the following inscription of Hammurapi's son, Samsuiluna (1749-1712 B.C.):[32]

> When Anum and Enlil, the kings of heaven and earth, looked joyfully upon Marduk, the firstborn son of Ea, gave him an exalted name among the Annunaki, gave him dominion over the four regions of the world, (and) made firm for him the foundation of Babylon like (that of) heaven and earth, at that time, Marduk, the chief god of his land, the god who creates wisdom, gave to me, Samsuiluna, the king of his longing, all the lands to shepherd. Indeed he instructed me in a grand fashion to bring about the settling of the pastures of his land and lead forever his widespread people in peace.[33]

As the protector deity of Hammurapi and his successors in Babylon, Marduk was recognized as "the chief god of his land," without usurping the time-honored role of Anum and Enlil as kings over heaven and earth. In Hammurapi's regnal years of thirty to thirty-nine, Marduk was ranked among the great gods with Anum and Enlil, but Hammurapi's rise to power came from the successful completion of commissions that he claims were given to him by Anum and Enlil.[34]

The hierarchy in the Mesopotamian pantheon was stable but not static. Piotr Michalowski claims that Enlil was a relative newcomer to the Mesopotamian pantheon in the late third millennium B.C. and displaced Enki as the head of the pantheon.[35] An earlier shift such as this in the hierarchy of

31. Thorkild Jacobsen, *The Treasures of Darkness: A History of Mesopotamian Religion* (New Haven: Yale University Press, 1976), pp. 95-104. F. A. M. Wiggermann, "Theologies, Priests, and Worship in Ancient Mesopotamia," in *Civilizations of the Ancient Near East*, ed. Jack Sasson (New York: Scribner, 1995), pp. 1860, 1803-64, 1869-70; Jeremy Black and Anthony Green, *Gods, Demons and Symbols of Ancient Mesopotamia* (Austin: University of Texas Press, 1992), pp. 30, 76; Wolfram von Soden, *The Ancient Orient: An Introduction to the Study of the Ancient Near East* (Grand Rapids: Eerdmans, 1994), pp. 180-82, 212.

32. Sommerfeld, *Der Aufstieg Marduks*, pp. 87, 104.

33. Douglas Frayne, *RIME 4*, E4.3.7.5, lines 1-24.

34. Sommerfeld, *Der Aufstieg Marduks*, p. 65.

the gods would perhaps have provided a precedent for Marduk's displacement of Enlil as king of the gods, as it is discreetly narrated in the *Enuma Elish*.[36] In Mesopotamian thought, change in rulers or any other kind of activity was legitimated by downplaying its newness and accenting its rootedness in the past.[37]

The *Enuma Elish* incorporated elements from three major traditions about the gods: (1) from the Ninurta tradition originating in Nippur, the motif of the young divine hero influenced the portrayal of the young god Marduk in his courageous battle and victory over Tiamat, before whom the elder gods had retreated in fear;[38] (2) from the Enki-Ea tradition originating in Eridu, the crafty, enterprising qualities of Ea were bestowed upon Marduk by Ea whom the *Enuma Elish* designated as Marduk's father (I:80-84); and (3) from the Enlil tradition originating in Nippur, supreme executive power over heaven and earth was given to Marduk by the assembly of the gods while the *Enuma Elish* did not even mention the name of Enlil.[39] These elements are woven into a composition that begins with a new cosmogony, an account of the origin of the world unattested elsewhere in the Mesopotamian tradition.[40] The additional incorporation of anthropological, philological, and theological speculations leads H. L. J. Vanstiphout to characterize this composition as "a theological didactic poem about Marduk as the Supreme Being and his World Order."[41]

The doctrine of Marduk as king of the gods must have taken centuries to develop since Babylon first had to establish its superiority over other Mesopotamian cities.[42] The first clear evidence that Marduk was the head of

35. Piotr Michalowski, "The Unbearable Lightness of Enlil," in *Intellectual Life of the Ancient Near East*, ed. Jiří Prosecký, CRRA 43 (Prague: Oriental Institute, 1998), p. 242.

36. Jacobsen, *The Treasures of Darkness*, pp. 189-90.

37. Maria de Jong Ellis, "Mesopotamian Oracles and Prophetic Texts," *JCS* 41.2 (1989): 176.

38. W. G. Lambert, "Ninurta Mythology in the Babylonian Epic of Creation," in *Keilschriftlichen Literaturen: Ausgewählte Vorträge der XXXII. Rencontre assyriologique internationale*, ed. K. Hecker and W. Sommerfeld, BBVO 6 (Berlin: Dietrich Reimer, 1986), p. 56. Dalley ("Occasions and Opportunities," p. 65) notes that some characteristics of Tishpak, the god of Eshnunna, came to be attributed to Marduk in the *Enuma Elish*.

39. H. L. J. Vanstiphout, "Enuma Elish as a Systematic Creed: An Essay," *OLP* 23 (1992): 44-47.

40. Vanstiphout, "Enuma Elish as a Systematic Creed," p. 53. The singularity of the cosmology of the *Enuma Elish* in the Mesopotamian tradition is characterized by W. G. Lambert ("A New Look at the Babylonian Background of Genesis," in *I Studied Inscriptions from Before the Flood*, ed. R. S. Hess and D. T Tsumura, Sources for Biblical and Theological Study 4 [Winona Lake, Ind.: Eisenbrauns, 1994], p. 100) as "a sectarian and aberrant combination of mythological threads woven into an unparalleled compositum."

41. Vanstiphout, "Enuma Elish as a Systematic Creed," p. 52.

42. Bottéro, *Mesopotamia*, p. 214.

the Mesopotamian pantheon comes from a boundary stone during the reign of Nebuchadnezzar I (1126-1105 B.C.), the fourth king of the Second Dynasty of Isin (1158-1027 B.C.).[43] Thorkild Jacobsen argued that Marduk's rise in the pantheon as reflected in the *Enuma Elish* would have been officially acknowledged as early as the late OB period (ca. 1600 B.C.) and early Kassite period (ca. 1500 B.C.) when the kings of Babylon struggled with the rulers of the Sealand, a southern Mesopotamian territory that at that time included ancient Sumer with Enlil's cultic site of Nippur. If so, Enlil would have been on the side of the Sealand dynasty, Babylon's foe and the equivalent of the forces of Tiamat in the *Enuma Elish*.[44] However, the problem with this reconstruction, as Richard Clifford has pointed out, is that in the *Enuma Elish* Tiamat is associated with the fresh waters at the source of the Tigris and Euphrates and not with the salt water of the Persian Gulf near which the Sealand dynasty ruled.[45] So, it seems best to locate the acknowledgment of Marduk's rise to the position of king of the Mesopotamian gods in the latter part of the Kassite period (ca. 1150 B.C.) rather than at its beginning. Michalowski argues that by the eleventh century B.C. Marduk may well have been elevated from his position as city deity of Babylon to the level of king of the gods and head of the national pantheon so that he might be on a par with the god Assur who was the national deity of Assyria and a new political force with which to be reckoned.[46]

In the *Enuma Elish*, the crisis of impending war from Tiamat and her divine forces provoked the divine assembly under the direction of Anshar to search for a champion to deliver them from Tiamat. Anum and Nudimmud (Ea) turned back from the challenge, but Marduk volunteered on the following conditions:

> He opened his mouth and swore to me: "If I am to bring back victory for you, bind Tiamat, save your life, then form an assembly and proclaim my destiny supreme. In the divine assembly, joyfully take your places together. Let my speech determine destinies instead of yours. Do not let the life-giving

43. W. G. Lambert, "The Reign of Nebuchadnezzar I: A Turning Point in the History of Ancient Mesopotamian Religion," in *The Seed of Wisdom: Essays in Honor of T. J. Meek*, ed. W. S. McCullough (Toronto: University of Toronto Press, 1964), pp. 5-6; Victor Hurowitz, "Some Literary Observations on the Šitti-Marduk Kudurru," *ZA* 82 (1992): 48.

44. Jacobsen, *The Treasures of Darkness*, p. 190.

45. Richard Clifford, *Creation Accounts in the Ancient Near East and in the Bible*, CBQMS 26 (Washington: Catholic Biblical Association, 1994), pp. 85-86.

46. Piotr Michalowski, "Presence at Creation," in *Lingering over Words: Studies in Ancient Near Eastern Literature in Honor of William L. Moran*, ed. T. Abusch et al., HSM 37 (Atlanta: Scholars, 1990), pp. 389-90.

power that I create be destroyed. Let not my command turn back or be altered." (III:115-22)[47]

Marduk requested sovereign power from all the great gods, "the determiners of destinies" (III:130), and received it in an investiture ceremony that began as follows:

He [Marduk] took his place opposite his fathers for sovereignty. "You are the most honored among the great gods; your decree has no rival, your command is (like that of) Anum. O Marduk, you are the most honored among the great gods; your decree has no rival, your command is (like that of) Anum! Hereafter, your command cannot be altered." (IV:2-7)[48]

Even though the great gods had given Marduk the position of sovereign power, he still had to defeat Kingu, the general of Tiamat's forces who held the tablets of destinies (III:48-49). In this battle, Marduk is similar to the warrior god Ninurta who had recovered the tablets of destinies from Anzu in the Myth of Anzu.[49] Marduk did not enter the battle defenseless against Kingu, for the great gods had bestowed something akin to magical power on his words at his investiture ceremony — that is, authority or social power. The great gods had asked Marduk to test the power of his words by destroying and then restoring a constellation of stars in the heavens:

He [Marduk] spoke and at his word the constellation was destroyed; he spoke again and the constellation was restored. When the gods, his fathers, saw the effect of his speech, they rejoiced and honored him (saying), "Marduk is king!" They conferred upon him scepter, throne, and staff. They gave him unrivaled weapons that drive enemies away. (IV:25-30)[50]

The distinctive character of Marduk's sovereign rule lay in the fact that his decrees were not only effective but also unalterable. Such power was bestowed by the assembly and won in battle; it was a combination of natural and social

47. The text is from W. G. Lambert and Simon B. Parker, *Enuma Eliš: The Babylonian Epic of Creation, The Cuneiform Text* (Oxford: Clarendon, 1966), p. 19. See also René Labat, *Le poème babylonien de la création* (Paris: Libraire d'Amérique et d'Orient, 1935), p. 118; Benjamin R. Foster, *Before the Muses: An Anthology of Akkadian Literature*, vol. 1 (Bethesda, Md.: CDL, 1993), p. 371.

48. The text is from Lambert and Parker, *Enuma Eliš*, p. 21. See also Labat, *Le poème babylonien de la création*, p. 120; Foster, *Before the Muses*, p. 372.

49. Lambert, "Ninurta Mythology," pp. 58-59.

50. The text is from Lambert and Parker, *Enuma Eliš*, p. 22. See also Labat, *Le poème babylonien de la création*, p. 122; Foster, *Before the Muses*, p. 372.

power played out on the heavenly plane that led to Marduk's rise to power. The power of words to declare the existence of a reality was a key manifestation of the sovereign power of Marduk.[51] At the beginning of the *Enuma Elish,* the cosmos emerged through procreative activity (the births of Lahmu and Lahamu, Anshar and Kishar, and Anu and Nudimmud/Ea) and the building or technical activities of Ea.[52] With Marduk's heroics, human speech and political and social action rise to the level of fundamental shaping forces of the world and so contribute to the humanizing of the cosmos.[53]

The habit of looking to the past in order to get one's bearings in the present was fully in place in the communities of Homeric Greece, biblical Israel, and OB Mesopotamia. Nestor and other Homeric kings, David and the succeeding rulers of his dynasty, and Hammurapi and his successors were kings who brought intelligibility to situations by narrating from memory. Nestor used the stories of heroes of the past, emphasis on the value of gaining glory, and his own example to rouse members of the community to undertake a spying mission. The psalmist in Psalm 89 drew upon the liturgical and political traditions of the community to help the community articulate the depth of its confusion and disillusionment. The author of the *Enuma Elish* articulated a profound change in the theological traditions and the power structure of the pantheon by incorporating and reframing older traditions. Both Psalm 89 and the *Enuma Elish* appealed to primordial events to explain the present world order they espoused. The diverse genres of these texts — epic dialogue, lament psalm, and cosmological narrative — had in common the practice of narrating from memory in order to orient oneself and one's community in the present. Authoritative statements from Zeus, the Lord, or Marduk explain why the world was structured and operated the way it did. This narrative way of searching for causes helped to make the world intelligible and inhabitable.

Fame or Anonymity: The Power of Remembering or Forgetting the Name of Another

Calling to mind a friend, ancestor, notable person or a god strengthens the one who remembers and brings honor to the one remembered. If that person has

---

51. W. G. Lambert, "Technical Terminology for Creation in the Ancient Near East," in *Intellectual Life of the Ancient Near East,* ed. Jirí Prosecký, CRRA 43 (Prague: Oriental Institute, 1998), p. 192.

52. Walter Burkert, "The Logic of Cosmology," in *From Reason to Myth?* ed. Richard Buxton (Oxford: Oxford University Press, 1999), pp. 94-96.

53. Cf. Ricoeur, *Time and Narrative,* 3:213.

moved away or died, the act of recalling the person's name will resurrect images, sounds, and stories associated with the person. The power of the name to bring forth a person or a thing was evident in the creation stories of Genesis 1–2 where the act of naming separated the sun, the moon, the land animals, humans, and so on from the formlessness of chaos. To become anonymous was to reenter formlessness or chaos. So, in contrast, recalling the name of the ancestors made them a reality within the life of the community.

In the initial part of their journeys in the *Odyssey*, Odysseus and his men landed among the Lotus-eaters. These Lotus-eaters did not wish to kill Odysseus's men, but they gave them lotus to eat, which removed their desire to return home. Odysseus recounted the event as follows:

> Whoever among them ate the honey-sweet fruit of the lotus no longer wished to bear a message or return home, but wanted to remain with the lotus-eating people, to eat lotus and forget to return home. I conducted these weeping men by force back to the ships. I drew them into the hollow ships myself and tied them to the benches. Then I ordered my other faithful companions to board the swift ships quickly so that someone else might not eat the lotus and forget to return home. (*Od.* 9.94-102)

The threat of forgetting the way home was ever-present to Odysseus and his companions on their return journey.[54] Peter Rose claims that Odysseus and his companions, during their visit to the goddess Circe, forgot about home and so had to undergo a form of death by journeying to the underworld (*Od.* 10.466-95; 12.21).[55] Circe then warned Odysseus and his men upon their departure from her to shield themselves from the song of the Sirens when their ship passed by the temptresses. The men were to plug their ears with wax so as not to hear the irresistible, enchanting song. If Odysseus was to listen, he was to be bound to the masthead; if he wished to go to the Sirens upon hearing them, he was to be bound ever more firmly (*Od.* 12.37-54). When Odysseus did listen to their song, he heard the following message:

> Come here, illustrious Odysseus, great glory of the Achaeans, land the ship that you might listen to our singing, for no one yet has sailed past here in a black ship until he has heard the sweet song from our mouths. Then the one who has taken delight returns home, knowing much more. For we know ev-

---

54. Segal, *Singers, Heroes, and Gods,* pp. 33-34; Jean-Pierre Vernant, "The Refusal of Odysseus," in *Reading the Odyssey: Selected Interpretive Essays,* ed. Seth Schein (Princeton: Princeton University Press, 1996), p. 187.

55. Rose, *Sons of the Gods, Children of Earth,* p. 128.

erything that the Argives and Trojans suffered in wide Troy by divine ordinance. And we know everything that happens on the richly providing earth. (*Od.* 12.184-89)

Odysseus was addressed as "illustrious Odysseus, great glory of the Achaeans," an epithet applied to Odysseus only here in the *Odyssey* but twice in the *Iliad* (*Il.* 9.673; 10.544). This epithet exalted Odysseus's role as a heroic warrior at Troy. The carefully crafted character of this song was designed to lure Odysseus back into dwelling on his previous role as a warrior.[56] Those who listened to the Sirens did not become wiser, as the singers promised, but rather ended as rotting corpses on the beach (*Od.* 12.45-46). Odysseus longed to hear himself honored in their song, but the *Odyssey* presented such a return to the world of the *Iliad* as a temptation and a seduction.[57] These Sirens, who claimed to know all that had happened and who presented their message in melodious song, were depicted as singers like the Muses (*Il.* 2.484-93; *Od.* 8.63, 73; 24.60-62).[58] If Odysseus had dwelt on his past glories as a warrior, he would have overlooked the challenges for survival before him and would not have returned home. A typical Iliadic hero, if offered immortality as Calypso had offered Odysseus (*Od.* 5.200-13; cf. *Il.* 12.322-28), would have given up the heroic quest.[59] The true greatness of the Odysseus of the *Odyssey* lay in his remaining faithful to his household in Ithaca and in his strenuous efforts to return home.[60]

In his contest with the Cyclops, Odysseus outwitted Polyphemus by concealing his true identity. When Polyphemus was about to eat Odysseus, he asked Odysseus his name, to which Odysseus replied:

Cyclops, you ask me for my renowned name. So I will tell you. But you then, give me a guest gift just as you promised. Nobody *(outis)* is my name. My father and mother call me Nobody, and so do all my other companions. (*Od.* 9.364-67)

---

56. Pietro Pucci, *The Song of the Sirens: Essays on Homer* (New York: Rowman & Littlefield, 1998), pp. 1-4.

57. Pucci, *The Song of the Sirens*, p. 5; Segal, *Singers, Heroes, and Gods*, pp. 103, 105.

58. Pucci, *The Song of the Sirens*, pp. 6-7; Gregory Nagy, *Poetry as Performance* (Cambridge: Cambridge University Press, 1996), p. 61; cf. Egbert J. Bakker, *Poetry in Speech: Orality and Homeric Discourse* (Ithaca: Cornell University Press, 1997), p. 166; Claude Calame, *The Craft of Poetic Speech in Ancient Greece* (Ithaca: Cornell University Press, 1995), p. 71.

59. Kevin Crotty, *The Poetics of Supplication: Homer's Iliad and Odyssey* (Ithaca: Cornell University Press, 1994), p. 168.

60. Segal, *Singers, Heroes, and Gods*, p. 135.

The play on words between *outis*, "Nobody," and *mētis*, "cunning," suggests the eventual outcome of Odysseus's ruse,[61] for when Polyphemus cried out to the other Cyclopes after he was blinded by Odysseus, they asked him: "Some one *(mē tis)* is not killing you by force or treachery, is he?" (*Od.* 9.406). He answered: "Nobody *(outis)* is killing me by force or treachery" (*Od.* 9.406). His fellow Cyclopes, interpreting his response as saying that there was no visible cause for his distress, advised him to pray to Poseidon for healing. Once Odysseus had escaped from Polyphemus, he stumbled back into the ways of an Iliadic warrior by boasting:

> Cyclops, if any mortal should ask about this grievous blinding of your eye, say that Odysseus, sacker of cities, did it. He is the son of Laertes, and his home is in Ithaca. (*Od.* 9.502-5)

This unwarranted bravado would cost Odysseus his ship and his crew, for Polyphemus was then able to appeal to his father Poseidon and identify by name the one who had injured him (*Od.* 9.526-35). If the Odysseus of the *Odyssey* aimed to make a name for himself by slaying powerful foes, he would end in death and would have no survivors to sing of his memory. The new circumstances after the Trojan War required that Odysseus remember his family and household in Ithaca and the important responsibilities that he had there.[62]

In the Israelite tradition, the call "to remember" and "not to forget" occurred most frequently within the context of the relationship between the Lord and Israel.[63] Remembering was a primary way of expressing fidelity.[64] The call to remember in the psalms is often expressed to the Lord by humans who stand in need. In the lament portion of Psalm 89, the psalmist cried out: "Remember how ephemeral my life is. . . . Remember, Lord, how your servants are scorned" (vv. 48, 51[47, 50]). Conversely, the Israelites were expected to remember the Lord, a point that clearly comes to expression in the historical psalms. In Psalm 105:5, the psalmist exhorted the Israelites:

> Remember the wonders that he has done,
>   his signs, and the judgments he has spoken.

61. Segal, *Singers, Heroes, and Gods*, p. 97; Frame, *The Myth of Return in Early Greek Epic*, p. 71.

62. Segal, *Singers, Heroes, and Gods*, p. 45; Jesper Svenbro, *"Phrasikleia": An Anthropology of Reading in Ancient Greece* (Ithaca: Cornell University Press, 1993), pp. 65, 70.

63. Allen Verhey, "Remember, Remembrance," in *ABD*, 6:668; Peter Ackroyd, *Studies in the Religious Tradition of the Old Testament* (London: SCM, 1987), pp. 12-13; Joseph Blenkinsopp, "Memory, Tradition, and the Construction of the Past in Ancient Israel," *BTB* 27 (1997): 79.

64. James L. Mays, *Psalms* (Louisville: John Knox, 1994), pp. 254-55.

Psalm 106:7 states:

> Our ancestors in Egypt
>   did not understand your wonders;
> they did not remember the abundance of your kindness,
>   but rebelled against the Most High[65] at the Red Sea.
> Yet he rescued them for the sake of his name,
>   so that he might make known his power.

Israel's forgetting the Lord had consequences not only for the Israelites but also for the Lord because the Lord had linked his name and identity with the Israelites by covenant.[66] Psalm 106:7 states that the Lord rescued the Israelites from Egypt, even though they were disobedient, because it was important that the Lord reveal his power and establish his name. The same line of reasoning occurred in the prophecy of Ezekiel to account for the Lord's plan to return the Israelites from exile. Ezekiel reports that the Lord said:

> But when they entered the nations to which they came, they defiled my holy name when it was said about them, "These are the people of the Lord, but they have left their land." I took pity because of my holy name, which the house of Israel defiled among the nations to which they came. (Ezek. 36:20-21)

The Israelites were expected to remember their identity as the people of the Lord, an inherited identity that had been established during the time of their ancestors. Remembering this relationship with the Lord and reflecting His glory was to be the focal point of the Israelites' activities and existence (cf. Ezek. 36:37).[67]

The honor given to the Lord's name was to reflect his status as sovereign king of heaven and earth. In the hymn of praise in Psalm 89, the psalmist said to the Lord: "Tabor and Hermon shout with joy because of your name" (v. 13[12]). It was important that the Lord's status be acknowledged; if the Israelites ceased to sing the Lord's praises, they would have forgotten their relationship with

---

65. Read *'elyôn*.

66. Leslie Allen, *Psalms 101–150*, WBC 21 (Waco, Tex.: Word, 1983), p. 54; Mays, *Psalms*, pp. 342-43; cf. Walter Brueggemann, "Pharaoh as Vassal: A Study of a Political Metaphor," *CBQ* 57 (1995): 31. For the practice of Mesopotamians appealing to their gods on the grounds of the gods' self-interest, see Karel van der Toorn, *Family Religion in Babylonia, Syria and Israel* (Leiden: Brill, 1996), p. 140.

67. Walther Zimmerli, *Ezekiel*, vol. 2 (Philadelphia: Fortress, 1983), pp. 251-52; Moshe Greenberg, *Ezekiel 21–37*, AB 22A (New York: Doubleday, 1997), pp. 729, 735-38; Daniel Block, *The Book of Ezekiel: Chapters 25–48* (Grand Rapids: Eerdmans, 1998), pp. 347-48.

him. To the extent that the fortunes of the king of Israel reflected back upon the Lord, who protected him, it was important that the king be successful. The oracle of Psalm 89 reports the following words of the Lord:

> My faithfulness and kindness will be with him;
>   and by my name his horn will be lifted up.
> I will place his hand on the sea
>   and his right hand on the rivers.
> He will call me, "You are my father,
>   my God, and the rock of my salvation!"
> I will even make him the firstborn,
>   the highest of the kings of the earth. (vv. 25-28[24-27])

The fame of the king was to be a consequence of the power of the Lord working through him. The efforts of the king to immortalize himself in first-person speech concerning his heroic deeds did not get recorded in the Hebrew Scriptures if such boasting lacked reference to the way the Lord had empowered the king.[68] To the kinglike patriarch Abraham, the Lord promised to make his name great (Gen. 12:2); there is no passage where Abraham boasts that he is great. The promise to Abraham of future greatness is a counterpoint to the vain quest of the builders of the tower of Babel in Genesis 11:1-9 to make a name for themselves.[69] The Lord promised Abraham that collectively his descendants would be great in number and stature; the emphasis was not on Abraham's fame as an individual.[70] Yet the extent to which a name like Abraham was remembered reflected the importance and honor given to its bearer.

Mesopotamian kings sought to be remembered not only by their contemporaries but also by future generations and the gods. In their inscriptions, kings made proclamations that often took the form of first-person speech where the king boasted of his accomplishments. The stones upon which these proclamations were inscribed became "talking stones" when they were read aloud.[71]

---

68. Cf. Cross, *From Epic to Canon*, p. 27; Walter Brueggemann, *First and Second Samuel* (Louisville: John Knox, 1990), pp. 343-44.

69. David Carr, *Reading the Fractures of Genesis* (Louisville: Westminster/John Knox, 1996), pp. 187-88.

70. Claus Westermann, *Genesis 12–36* (Minneapolis: Augsburg, 1981), p. 150. On the symbolic dimension of the character of Abraham for the exiles as one who faithfully returned to his homeland, see Joseph Blenkinsopp, *The Pentateuch* (New York: Doubleday, 1992), p. 125.

71. On the characterization of Greek inscriptions from 900 to 550 B.C. as first-person performative speech-acts, see Gregory Nagy, *Homeric Questions* (Austin: University of Texas Press, 1996), p. 35; cf. Svenbro, *Phrasikleia*, p. 51.

Even though such inscriptions were literary compositions,[72] they were written to be declaimed.[73] In monumental inscriptions like that of the *Code of Hammurapi,* images of the king and the gods accompanied the text. These monuments, combining the image and voice of the king, became symbols of the king, so much so that for a foe to efface this image was to attack the king himself and not simply a representation of him.[74]

In one of his Sippar inscriptions Hammurapi proclaimed a sizable list of public works projects and social benefits that he had brought to the people of Sippar. He concluded by saying:

> Truly, they pray for my life. I have done what is pleasing to Shamash, my lord, and Aja, my lady. I established in the mouth of the people the daily recalling of my good name like a god, a custom which shall never be forgotten.[75]

The line between a king and a god tended to blur when the king accomplished heroic actions for the welfare of the community.[76] The legendary Gilgamesh typifies this royal, heroic quest for immortality by building enduring monuments and going on an expedition to the Cedar Forest.[77] Naram-Sin (2254-2218 B.C.) was the first Mesopotamian king to write his name with the divine determinative, but the practice continued for about five hundred years after him.[78] During such time, the royal courts evidenced greater literary creativity than in

---

72. Brigitte Groneberg, "Toward a Definition of Literariness as Applied to Akkadian Literature," in *Mesopotamian Poetic Language,* ed. M. Vogelzang and H. Vanstiphout, Cuneiform Monographs 6 (Groningen: Styx, 1996), pp. 59-60, 63.

73. Jean Goodnick Westenholz, "Symbolic Language in Akkadian Narrative Poetry: The Metaphorical Relationship between Poetic Images and the Real World," in *Mesopotamian Poetic Language,* ed. M. Vogelzang and H. Vanstiphout, Cuneiform Monographs 6 (Groningen: Styx, 1996), p. 201.

74. Marc Van de Mieroop, *Cuneiform Texts and the Writing of History* (New York: Routledge, 1999), p. 58; Victor Hurowitz, *Inu Anum Sīrum: Literary Structures in the Non-Juridical Sections of Codex Hammurabi,* Occasional Publications of the Samuel Noah Kramer Fund 15 (Philadelphia: University of Pennsylvania Museum, 1994), pp. 34, 40.

75. Frayne, *RIME 4,* E4.3.6.2, lines 70-81.

76. Adam Falkenstein, "Review of C. J. Gadd, *Ideas of Divine Rule in the Ancient Near East,*" *BO* 7 (1950): 56-58; Irene Winter, "'Idols of the King': Royal Images as Recipients of Ritual Action in Ancient Mesopotamia," *Journal of Ritual Studies* 6 (1992): 29-35.

77. Jeffrey Tigay, *The Evolution of the Gilgamesh Epic* (Philadelphia: University of Pennsylvania Press, 1982), pp. 6-7; Aaron Shaffer, "Gilgamesh, The Cedar Forest and Mesopotamian History," in *Studies in Literature from the Ancient Near East Dedicated to Samuel Noah Kramer,* ed. J. Sasson, AOS 65 (New Haven: American Oriental Society, 1984), p. 307.

78. William W. Hallo, *Early Mesopotamian Royal Titles, a Philologic and Historical Analysis,* AOS 43 (New Haven: Yale University Press, 1957), p. 125.

subsequent periods of Mesopotamian history as they sought to elevate the name and reputation of the Mesopotamian kings to a high level among their contemporaries.[79] Compositions such as inscriptions and hymns would seem to have been communicated to the populace at large, to an elite of the palace and temple households, and to conquered and foreign peoples not only by inscriptions on public monuments but also by public ceremonies in which various ritual means could enhance the communication of their message.[80]

As the territory of a kingdom expanded, the king probably had less time to attend to local affairs. However, Hammurapi's correspondence attests to this king's capacity for micromanaging, for he responds to issues ranging from cooking to the construction of irrigation works.[81] In the eyes of many, a king's preoccupation with international matters may have opened more space for local autonomy.[82] Household affairs and local issues associated with day-to-day life would have been a more important concern for most Babylonians than national issues. Karel van der Toorn claims that the people anchored their identities and reputations in local issues rather than in national achievements.[83] Nevertheless, the royal regimes promoted the image of the king as a world conqueror like Sargon or a just king like Hammurapi. So, the people would probably have had an image of the king in their minds and would have received some reports of his activities so that the potential was there for him to be a character in the stories of their imagination.

An important domestic practice for keeping the memory of the ancestors alive was the cult of the ancestors. The Mesopotamians believed that the ancestors continued to influence the lives of the household and needed to be fed and commemorated. A typical obligation of the eldest son or the *paterfamilias* was to bring offerings to the deceased ancestors of the family at the designated times. Within this ceremony known as the *kispum,* the invocation of the names of the dead was the central ritual. Van der Toorn notes that such commemoration molded the identity of the family around the ancestors and sustained the significance of the ancestors for the family.[84] This *kispum* ceremony was also

79. William W. Hallo, *Origins: The Ancient Near Eastern Background of Some Modern Western Institutions* (Leiden: Brill, 1996), p. 152.

80. Van de Mieroop, *Cuneiform Texts and the Writing of History,* p. 57.

81. Marc Van de Mieroop, *Society and Enterprise in Old Babylonian Ur,* BBVO 12 (Berlin: Dietrich Reimer, 1992), p. 112.

82. Marc Van de Mieroop, *The Ancient Mesopotamian City* (Oxford: Clarendon, 1997), p. 139.

83. Van der Toorn, *Family Religion in Babylonia, Syria and Israel,* p. 151.

84. Van der Toorn, *Family Religion in Babylonia, Syria and Israel,* p. 52. See also Aaron Skaist, "The Ancestor Cult and Succession in Mesopotamia," in *Death in Mesopotamia,* ed. B. Alster,

carried out in the royal household where the memory of royal ancestors was kept alive.[85]

The Mesopotamian kings intended that their inscriptions and the works they commemorated endure forever. Some OB royal inscriptions, following a pattern established in the royal inscriptions of the Old Akkadian period (2350-2193 B.C.),[86] conclude with lists of blessings for those who preserve the king's works and curses for those who would destroy them.[87] Kudur-mabuk, an early Amorite ruler of Emutbal and Larsa (second half of the nineteenth century B.C.), concluded a building inscription for a temple with the following warning:

> For the future, for later days, whoever does not strengthen that house of baked brick when it has become old, (and) does not restore its foundational wall, (and) removes its door, (and) tears out its doorposts, (and) has not returned its hinge to its place when it falls, (and) for evil reasons destroys (it), and exposes its foundations to the sun, (and) returns it to weeds, that man, be he king or lord, may Nergal, the god who created me, raging in his anger, tear out his heart. May Shamash, the lord of heaven and earth, curse him with a grievous curse.[88]

Such sacral sanctions against those who would neglect, destroy, or alter these works showed that the king wanted to be remembered, but even more so they pointed to a societal interest in maintaining continuity in its institutions and

---

Mesopotamia 8 (Copenhagen: Akademisk Forlag, 1980), pp. 126-27; Johannes M. Renger, "Institutional, Communal, and Individual Ownership or Possession of Arable Land in Ancient Mesopotamia from the End of the Fourth to the End of the First Millennium B.C.," *Chicago-Kent Law Review* 71 (1995): 298.

85. J. J. Finkelstein, "The Genealogy of the Hammurapi Dynasty," *JCS* 20 (1966): 115-16; Akio Tsukimoto, "Aspekte von *Kispu(m)* als Totenbeigabe," in *Death in Mesopotamia*, ed. B. Alster, Mesopotamia 8 (Copenhagen: Akademisk Forlag, 1980), pp. 129-33. Arguing against the belief in deceased ancestors as beneficent supernatural powers in OB times, Brian Schmidt (*Israel's Beneficent Dead: Ancestor Cult and Necromancy in Ancient Israelite Religion and Tradition* [Winona Lake, Ind.: Eisenbrauns, 1996], pp. 44, 46) claims that the commemoration of the royal ancestors in the *kispū* rites in OB Mari was aimed only at legitimating current royal rulers rather than at worshipping royal ancestors who would confer supernatural power on the royal court.

86. Sabina Franke, *Königsinschriften und Königsideologie: Die Könige von Akkade zwischen Tradition und Neuerung* (Münster: LIT, 1995), p. 238.

87. See the inscriptions of Takil-ilisu of Malgium (Frayne, *RIME 4*, E4.11.2.1), Ipiq-Ishtar of Malgium (Frayne, *RIME 4*, E4.11.1.1), and Yaḫdun-Lim of Mari (Frayne, *RIME 4*, E4.6.8.1 and E4.6.8.2).

88. Frayne, *RIME 4*, E4.2.13a.2, lines 24-51.

practices.[89] This pattern of kings rebuilding and renovating ancient sanctuaries occurred throughout the Mesopotamian tradition and was preserved in inscriptions and other documents. Within the palaces and temples of OB Mesopotamia, texts were composed to transmit valued wisdom to a wider audience and to future generations.[90]

Remembering the name of a person keeps a relationship alive. The Israelites were commanded to remember the name of the Lord. In Homer, the hero's quest for glory and immortality was equivalent to making a name for himself that would endure through the song of the bard; his name would not be stored away in a foundation deposit but would be proclaimed in public assemblies through the generations. In OB Mesopotamia, kings sought to immortalize their accomplishments through written inscriptions; the message of such writings was probably also proclaimed in public assemblies.[91] Such remembering, particularly in public assemblies, not only invoked the memory and presence of the person but also conferred honor. Remembering the names of the ancestors was also a central activity of the households in Mesopotamia and Israel; this practice was likewise carried on in the Homeric world.[92] The explicit, intentional quest of the Mesopotamian king and of the Homeric warrior for fame does not find an echo in the biblical record of Israel, which gives the impression that fame and honor were bestowed on Israelite heroes after the fact rather than as a motivation for making sacrifices for the community.

Innovation within Tradition: Change within Continuity

It is sometimes said that biography is "truer" than autobiography.[93] It is not only the desire to present a favorable image of ourselves that can influence our report, but even the way we remember can shape our account. We might think

---

89. Jonker, *The Topography of Remembrance*, pp. 15-17, 57; Hurowitz, *Inu Anum Sīrum*, p. 27, n. 40; p. 40.

90. Foster, *Before the Muses*, p. 32.

91. Westenholz, "Symbolic Language in Akkadian Narrative Poetry," p. 201; cf. A. Kirk Grayson, "Murmuring in Mesopotamia," in *Wisdom, Gods, Literature,* ed. A. R. George and I. L. Finkel (Winona Lake, Ind.: Eisenbrauns, 2000), pp. 302-7.

92. Jane B. Carter, "Ancestor Cult and the Occasion of Homeric Performance," in *The Ages of Homer,* ed. Jane Carter and Sarah Morris (Austin: University of Texas Press, 1995), p. 304; Gregory Nagy, *Greek Mythology and Poetics* (Ithaca: Cornell University Press, 1990), pp. 215-16.

93. W. H. Auden, *The Dyer's Hand and Other Essays* (New York: Random House, 1968), p. 96; Tremper Longman III, *Fictional Akkadian Autobiography: A Generic and Comparative Study* (Winona Lake, Ind.: Eisenbrauns, 1991), pp. 39-43.

that we could draw closer to the event itself if we had two or three independent accounts that we could compare. Yet with each of these accounts the reporters still recall the event from their perspectives. Certainly in recalling our own experience in an autobiography, we can narrate in the first person aspects of our own desires, expectations, and memories of experience that could not otherwise be known. However, in the process of remembering and retelling these events, we may actually remember a version told a week previously that may differ in some ways from a version told a year earlier. Events are richer than one single narrative can capture. We retain a mental image of the event that we flesh out upon reflection.[94]

Narratives involve selecting memories and configuring them in a coherent form. This complex process of selection and configuration is only imperfectly understood, yet it is shaped not only by the social location and perspective of the storyteller but also by the storyteller's skill in weaving together aspects of a rich, multifaceted event in order to engage and inform an audience.[95]

Stories of heroic figures or of gods that are well known through repeated telling resist alterations in their basic form, but variations may occur.[96] The story is readily recognizable in spite of adaptations for new audiences and changed circumstances. Myths are examples of such traditional tales with a basic "structure of sense," which seems to take on a timeless character and applies equally well to the past, present, and future.[97] The continuity of this basic "structure of sense" in a tale can become the common property of a community and can weave itself together with other stories that shape the identity of the community.

The warrior hero of the *Iliad* may have boasted of his exploits, but he did not sing his own *kleos* ("glory"). However, as part of the *Odyssey*'s counterpoint to the heroic model of the *Iliad,* Odysseus took on the role of a bard, first in the

94. Maurice E. F. Bloch, *How We Think They Think: Anthropological Approaches to Cognition, Memory, and Literacy* (Boulder, Colo.: Westview, 1998), pp. 121-24; Egbert Bakker, "Storytelling in the Future: Truth, Time, and Tense in Homeric Epic," in *Written Voices, Spoken Signs: Tradition, Performance, and the Epic Text,* ed. E. Bakker and A. Kahane (Cambridge, Mass.: Harvard University Press, 1997), p. 35.

95. Ricoeur, *Time and Narrative,* 3:122-23; Piotr Michalowski, "History as Charter: Some Observations on the Sumerian King List," in *Studies in Literature from the Ancient Near East Dedicated to Samuel Noah Kramer,* ed. J. Sasson, AOS 65 (New Haven: American Oriental Society, 1984), p. 238; Laura M. Slatkin, "Composition by Theme and the *Mētis* of the Odyssey," in *Reading the Odyssey: Selected Interpretive Essays,* ed. Seth Schein (Princeton: Princeton University Press, 1996), p. 231.

96. Brillante, "History and the Historical Interpretation of Myth," p. 120.

97. Walter Burkert, *Structure and History in Greek Mythology and Ritual* (Berkeley: University of California Press, 1979), pp. 5, 22.

utopian world of Scheria and then in Ithaca.[98] In these instances, in which Odysseus told of his adventures on his return from Troy, he crafted a picture of himself in accord with the self-identification that he gave to Alcinous and the Phaeacians: "I am Odysseus son of Laertes, one who is of interest to people for my plots, and my good repute reaches the heavens" (*Od.* 9.19-20). He left behind the epithet "sacker of cities," which he had used to describe himself to Polyphemus (*Od.* 9.504). Furthermore, he spoke longingly of his home on Ithaca when he said to his Phaeacian audience: "As for me there is no other place on earth sweeter to see" (*Od.* 9.28). Odysseus's *kleos*, "glory," took the form of his *doloi*, "wiles"; his capacity to outwit foes and escape dangers characterized his heroism in contrast to that of Achilles whose *kleos* reached its pinnacle in his giving his life for the well-being of the community.[99]

In his journeys, Odysseus survived trying and exotic experiences that, in turn, created the impression that he was semidivine. The pressing of boundaries such as that between the divine and the human was, as Leonard Muellner points out, a characteristic of epic heroes who thereby introduced a measure of ambiguity and disorder into the community.[100] Odysseus was the lover of the goddesses Circe and Calypso. Calypso offered him immortality without aging if he would stay with her and not return to Ithaca (*Od.* 5.209); his resistance contributed to his semidivine mystique.[101] He was able to blind the giant Cyclops Polyphemus (*Od.* 9.391-400) and escape Scylla and Charybdis (*Od.* 12.222-59). He figured out ways to survive against natural forces with whose power his own strength was incommensurate.[102] Yet he alone survived these ordeals; all of his companions were lost. As a survivor who remembered his homeland, Odysseus received high marks. As a military commander responsible for his forces, he was a failure.[103] Odysseus's lamentations over the trials of the heroes of Troy were appropriate (*Od.* 8.83-95, 521-34), but, as the episode of the song of the Sirens made clear (*Od.* 12.39-54, 184-91), his fate would have been death and anonymity if he had longed to hear the glory of his exploits at Troy and did not remember

---

98. Segal, "Kleos and Its Ironies," p. 204; Pietro Pucci, *Odysseus Polutropos* (Ithaca: Cornell University Press, 1987), p. 187.

99. Segal, *Singers, Heroes, and Gods*, pp. 90, 109, 114; Leonard Muellner, *The Anger of Achilles: "Mēnis" in Greek Epic* (Ithaca: Cornell University Press, 1996), p. 34.

100. Muellner, *The Anger of Achilles*, p. 131.

101. Michael N. Nagler, "Dread Goddess Revisited," in *Reading the Odyssey: Selected Interpretive Essays*, ed. Seth Schein (Princeton: Princeton University Press, 1996), pp. 155-56.

102. Karl Reinhardt, "The Adventures in the *Odyssey*," in *Reading the Odyssey: Selected Interpretive Essays*, ed. Seth Schein (Princeton: Princeton University Press, 1996), pp. 74-75; Segal, "Kleos and Its Ironies," p. 204.

103. Segal, *Singers, Heroes, and Gods*, pp. 34-35.

his fundamental commitments to household and homeland. Odysseus's pains and struggles to regain his life on Ithaca would transform him and make him the subject of the bard's song where his new form of *kleos* would endure.[104]

Odysseus first related his adventures to a human audience in the utopian land of the Phaeacians. They were the ones who conveyed him from fantasyland back to Ithaca and so were positioned midway between the world of dreams and reality.[105] Odysseus's adventures were stored away in silence in his memory until he related many of them to his loyal servant Eumaeus (*Od.* 14.191-359).[106] He could relate only portions of his stories to Penelope until he had fully disclosed his identity to her (*Od.* 23.300-344). These stories, like the guest gifts of the Phaeacians stored in a cave outside of Ithaca, were treasures to be brought forth only at the appropriate times. These stories in fantasyland were realities that had to remain submerged below consciousness until those moments when they could surface to promote greater mutual understanding with his family and confidants.[107]

Odysseus's journeys, many of which reflect typical adventures of travelers and soldiers in Archaic Greece,[108] allowed him to press significant boundaries such as those between gods and humans, between human life and the overwhelming power of nature, and between a life of pleasure and a life of many hardships.[109] Listeners to the stories of these journeys could share vicariously in them and so address a number of human longings and anxieties within their own imaginations. Fictional narratives can expand the number of possibilities open to the audience for reflecting on their experiences and thereby help them to view their experiences and understandings of the future from new perspectives.[110] People can learn from the experience of others and can explore issues reflectively without undergoing the experience itself. Odysseus's journeys became stories that allow others to see beyond the appearances and explore ways to find their place within the world of gods and humans.

---

104. Segal, *Singers, Heroes, and Gods*, pp. 33-35; John H. Finley, Jr., *Homer's Odyssey* (Cambridge, Mass.: Harvard University Press, 1978), p. 78; cf. Finkelberg, *The Birth of Literary Fiction in Ancient Greece*, p. 86.

105. Pierre Vidal-Naquet, *The Black Hunter: Forms of Thought and Forms of Society in the Greek World* (Baltimore: Johns Hopkins University Press, 1986), pp. 18, 26-29.

106. Segal, *Singers, Heroes, and Gods*, p. 30.

107. Segal, *Singers, Heroes, and Gods*, p. 30. With reference to the death of Sarpedon (*Il.* 16.454, 672, 682) Nagy (*Greek Mythology and Poetics*, p. 142) claims that "the Homeric *epos* is a repository of secrets about life and death — secrets that it will never fully reveal."

108. Finkelberg, *The Birth of Literary Fiction in Ancient Greece*, p. 150.

109. Cf. Muellner, *The Anger of Achilles*, p. 27.

110. Paul Ricoeur, *Time and Narrative*, vol. 2 (Chicago: University of Chicago Press, 1985), pp. 100, 160; Terry Eagleton, *Ideology: An Introduction* (New York: Verso, 1991), pp. 180-81.

In Israel, the prophet Ezekiel pronounced a judgment oracle against the prince *(nāgîd)*[111] of Tyre for identifying himself as a god (Ezek. 28:1-10).[112] Ezekiel quoted the prince of Tyre as saying: "I am a god; I reside in a dwelling place for gods in the heart of the seas" (Ezek. 28:2). The island fortress of Tyre, which housed the Phoenician king who headed an extensive maritime empire, was legendary for its impregnability. During Ezekiel's time (ca. 592-571 B.C.), the Babylonian king Nebuchadnezzar laid siege to Tyre for almost thirteen years (585-572 B.C.) but then withdrew.[113] It was not until the time of Alexander the Great (336-323 B.C.) that this city was finally conquered by a foreign power.[114] Ezekiel says of the prince of Tyre: "By your manifold wisdom in trade you have increased your wealth, and your heart has become haughty on account of your wealth" (Ezek. 28:5). Because of his security and wealth, it was quite possible that the prince of Tyre considered himself to be a god, far elevated above most humans. The divinelike nature of a king is a view found in the funerary literature of Egypt[115] and in compositions of court poets in Mesopotamia from about 2250 to 1750 B.C.[116] Since there were Tyrian refugees in Babylon in Ezekiel's time, it is conceivable that this judgment oracle was to be communicated to Tyrians. However, it would seem that Ezekiel composed this judgment oracle primarily for an Israelite audience to whom he wanted to teach a lesson about the distortions in self-understanding that could arise through amassing wisdom and wealth.[117] The verdict of the judgment oracle was that the Lord would bring foreign armies against the prince of Tyre:

---

111. Tomoo Ishida (*History and Historical Writing in Ancient Israel: Studies in Biblical Historiography,* Studies in the History and Culture of the Ancient Near East 16 [Leiden: Brill, 1999], pp. 61, 66-67) argues that in early Judahite history *nāgîd* means "king designate"; however, this usage of the term *nāgîd* to claim divine designation ceased with Baasha (900-877 B.C.). In Ezekiel 28, *nāgîd* is a synonym for *melek,* "king." See also Baruch Halpern, *The Constitution of the Monarchy in Israel,* HSM 25 (Chico, Calif.: Scholars, 1981), pp. 4-6.

112. Ronald M. Hals, *Ezekiel,* Forms of Old Testament Literature 19 (Grand Rapids: Eerdmans, 1989), p. 201; Walter Zimmerli, *Ezekiel,* vol. 2 (Philadelphia: Fortress, 1983), p. 76.

113. H. J. Katzenstein, "Tyre," in *ABD,* 6:690; Mario Liverani, "The Trade Network of Tyre," in *Ah, Assyria . . . Studies in Assyrian History and Ancient Near Eastern Historiography Presented to Hayim Tadmor,* ScrHier 33 (Jerusalem: Magnes, 1991), pp. 71-72, 79.

114. Douglas R. Edwards, "Tyre," in *ABD,* 6:690.

115. David Silverman, "The Nature of Egyptian Kingship," in *Ancient Egyptian Kingship,* ed. D. O'Connor and D. Silverman (Leiden: Brill, 1995), pp. 49, 60-63; John Baines, "Kingship, Definition of Culture, and Legitimation," in *Ancient Egyptian Kingship,* ed. D. O'Connor and D. Silverman (Leiden: Brill, 1995), p. 9.

116. Hallo, *Origins,* p. 152; Henri Frankfort, *Kingship and the Gods* (Chicago: University of Chicago Press, 1948), pp. 36-47.

117. Cf. Daniel I. Block, *The Book of Ezekiel: Chapters 25–48* (Grand Rapids: Eerdmans, 1998), pp. 120-21.

To the Pit they will make you descend,
and you will die a violent death in the heart of the seas.
Will you then say, "I am a god,"
before those who kill you?
You are a human and not a god
in the power of those who pierce you. (Ezek. 28:8-9)

Ezekiel defined the specific difference between gods and humans as the fact that humans suffer physical death but the gods do not. Ezekiel acknowledged, perhaps with a note of sarcasm, the wisdom of the prince of Tyre: "You are wiser than Daniel; no secret is too much for you" (Ezek. 28:3). His wisdom appeared to be a form of practical knowledge or cleverness for it led to his amassing great wealth. Yet for Ezekiel, this wisdom and wealth created an illusion for the prince of Tyre about his place in the hierarchy of the divine and human realms. The prince of Tyre had overstepped the limits between gods and humans.

Another judgment oracle follows in Ezekiel 28:11-19, which Ezekiel labeled "a lament over the king of Tyre" (v. 12).[118] The first half of this oracle pictured the king of Tyre as a privileged, blameless individual whom God had placed in the garden of Eden:

You were the signet of perfection,
filled with wisdom and perfect in beauty.
You were in Eden, the garden of God;
every precious stone was your covering,
Carnelian, chrysolite, and moonstone,
beryl, onyx, and jasper,
Lapus lazuli, turquoise, and emerald,
and gold was the working of your bracelet and your jewelry;
On the day that you were created
they were set.
With an anointed cherub as guardian
I placed you;
You were on the holy mountain of God;
among the flaming stones you walked about.
You were blameless in your ways,
from the day you were created
until wickedness was found in you. (Ezek. 28:12-15)

---

118. Hals, *Ezekiel,* p. 201; Zimmerli, *Ezekiel,* 2:89.

Ezekiel drew upon an earlier tradition of a perfect human being who had been placed in the garden of God. This person was given exceptional gifts of wisdom and beauty. The guardian cherub was apparently a symbol of the transcendent Lord present in the garden for this perfect human being.[119] The meaning of the "flaming stones" is obscure.[120]

Ezekiel used this portrayal of a primordial human to highlight the giftedness of the king of Tyre and to create a foil for the "fall" of the king of Tyre. Ezekiel located the cause of the impending demise of the king of Tyre within his trading practices: "Through the abundance of your trade you were filled with violence, and you transgressed" (Ezek. 28:16). Verse 17, echoing themes from the earlier judgment oracle in Ezekiel 28:1-10, claims that the king became enamored of his own beauty; such arrogance in turn undermined his wisdom. In this judgment oracle, Ezekiel drew upon traditional materials to help his audience see beyond appearances and imagine an idyllic garden scene for which a perfect human being had been created.[121] As applied to a king with well-established power, this garden scenario allowed Ezekiel to explore the limits of human power and to point out the dangers attendant upon possessing exceptional gifts of wisdom and wealth. Through this picture of the primordial origin and destiny of the king of Tyre, Ezekiel aimed to reconfigure the Israelites' imagination of the context in which royal power operated. The king received from God the gifts of beauty, wisdom, and wealth, gifts that the king could have used to foster an Eden-like environment of harmony and peace. Yet

---

119. Hals, *Ezekiel*, p. 200. Zimmerli (*Ezekiel*, 2:92) notes that the protective function of the cherub in blocking access to the "mountain of God" is accented here (cf. Exod. 25:20; 37:9).

120. Perhaps the "flaming stones" were an allusion to the stars as the burning heavenly bodies from which humans were believed to have originated according to early Indo-European traditions (see Nagy, *Greek Mythology and Poetics*, pp. 173-74). Robert Wilson ("The Death of the King of Tyre: The Editorial History of Ezekiel 28," in *Love and Death in the Ancient Near East*, ed. J. H. Marks and R. M. Good [Guilford, Conn.: Four Quarters, 1987], p. 216) suggests that the "flaming stones" are a reference to the burning coals of the sacrificial altar — a point that converges with his interpretation of the royal figure in the garden as patterned after the Israelite high priest. Zimmerli (*Ezekiel*, 2:93) suggests that the "flaming stones" are the heavenly inhabitants of the mountain where the gods are assembled and so are seen as creatures of light. Marvin Pope (*El in the Ugaritic Texts* [Leiden: Brill, 1955], pp. 101-2) suggests on analogy with the fire in Baal's heavenly palace *(abn brq)* that the "flaming stones" (*'abnê 'ēš*) are lightning that reflects the precious metals and jewels of the heavenly dwelling.

121. Pope, *El in the Ugaritic Texts*, pp. 98-102; Anthony J. Williams, "Mythological Background of Ezekiel 28:12-19," *BTB* 6 (1976): 54. Bernard Batto ("Paradise Reexamined," in *The Biblical Canon in Comparative Perspective: Scripture in Context IV*, ed. K. Younger, Jr. et al. [Lewiston, N.Y.: Mellen, 1991], p. 57) argues that the paradise motif was an inner biblical development that shows up in later biblical literature and was not borrowed from Mesopotamia in whose sources this motif appears to be absent.

the king took these gifts and wielded them as if he were sovereign in the areas of trade and politics. The resulting violence of the king's trade practices indicated that he was acting out of context — as if he ruled absolutely.

In Mesopotamia, when Hammurapi built a canebrake in Sippar, he described himself as "the favorite of Shamash, the beloved of Marduk."[122] When he built a storehouse for Enlil in the Enamtila temple, he described himself as "the favorite of Enlil . . . the beloved of Ninlil . . . the one who listens to Shamash, the one who delights the heart of Marduk."[123] These epithets, which proclaimed a special relationship with these deities, pointed to a deeper set of relationships than the more visible ones of Hammurapi assisting the people of Sippar and the temple personnel of Enamtila. These epithets made the claim that Hammurapi's capacity to act arose from the assistance of the gods. Here the high gods Shamash and Enlil entered into protective relationships with Hammurapi; such relationships exemplified the personal religion that was widespread through all ranks of Mesopotamian society in the third and second millennia B.C.[124] In OB Sippar, there were a number of personal names with Enlil as the theophoric element;[125] however, in the Sumerian and Akkadian onomastica of the third millennium B.C., Enlil rarely occurred as the theophoric element.[126] Van der Toorn claims that the people at large usually sought protection from lower ranking deities.[127]

The outlook promoted by the royal inscriptions was that all human initiative was made possible by the prior decisions of the gods. For example, when Samsuiluna rebuilt the wall of Kish, he announced in an inscription that this project was initiated by Enlil, who worked through Zababa and Ishtar to command and assist Samsuiluna. The inscription opens with the sentence: "Enlil, whose power is supreme among the gods, the shepherd who determines fates, looked with his holy face upon Zababa and Ishtar, the most valiant among the Igigi."[128] Samsuiluna claimed to be a legitimate ruler because of his obedient response to the commission given him by the sovereign deity Enlil. All ranks of

---

122. Frayne, *RIME 4*, E4.3.6.12, lines 37-38.

123. Frayne, *RIME 4*, E4.3.6.3, lines 7-10.

124. Jacobsen, *The Treasures of Darkness*, p. 161; Robert DiVito, *Studies in Third Millennium Sumerian and Akkadian Personal Names* (Rome: Pontificio Instituto Biblico, 1993), p. 275.

125. Rivkah Harris, *Ancient Sippar: A Demographic Study of an Old-Babylonian City (1894-1595 B.C.)* (Leiden: Nederlands Historisch-Archaeologisch Instituut te Istanbul, 1975), p. 49.

126. From the lists of personal names in the third millennium compiled by DiVito (*Studies in Third Millennium Sumerian and Akkadian Personal Names*, pp. 23-53, 128-83), I calculate that less than 3 percent of the Sumerian personal names and less than 0.5 percent of the Akkadian personal names had Enlil as the theophoric element.

127. Van der Toorn, *Family Religion in Babylonia, Syria and Israel*, p. 79.

128. Frayne, *RIME 4*, E4.3.7.7, lines 1-7.

Mesopotamian society, not just royalty, believed that their lot was marked out by the gods.[129] Such a belief, however, did not curtail their pleas to the gods to alter an evil destiny predicted by omens.[130]

The rise of Marduk to power, as narrated in the *Enuma Elish,* was anchored in events at the time of the creation of the world. The story began with the formlessness of reality:

> When the heavens above had not been named, and the earth below had not been called by name, primordial Apsu, their begetter, and mother Tiamat, the one who bore them all, mixed their waters together. A reed hut had not been woven together; marshlands were unknown. When no gods had yet been brought forth, for they had not been called by name and their destinies had not yet been determined, gods were created within them: Lahmu and Lahamu were brought forth and named. (I:1-10)[131]

The gods were brought into being by calling their names. Even when the image of birth was used for describing the origin of particular gods, the name of the new deity still communicated the reality of that deity.[132] The *Enuma Elish* stated that the firstborn son of Anum, the sky god, was Nudimmud (Enki/Ea) (I:15-16). Jacobsen notes that the *Enuma Elish* altered the earlier tradition of the Mesopotamian god list *An=Anum* by omitting Enlil as the firstborn son of Anum and the father of Nudimmud (Enki/Ea).[133] By not mentioning Enlil, the *Enuma Elish* did not allow the reality of this former king of the gods in the Mesopotamian tradition to emerge in its narrative world. The identification of Marduk as the firstborn son of Nudimmud and so as the great-grandson of Anshar, one of the two gods of the horizon, anchored Marduk's rise to power in primordial events. In the *Enuma Elish,* the cosmos was formed only after the defeat of Tiamat and according to Marduk's decrees. Marduk had secured the right to decree destinies after his defeat of Tiamat's forces and prior to the

---

129. Van der Toorn, *Family Religion in Babylonia, Syria and Israel,* p. 96; Lawson, *The Concept of Fate,* p. 92.

130. Bottéro, *Mesopotamia,* p. 124; Lawson, *The Concept of Fate,* pp. 99, 128; Frederick Cryer, *Divination in Ancient Israel and Its Near Eastern Environment,* JSOTSup 142 (Sheffield: Sheffield Academic Press, 1994), pp. 205-7.

131. The text is from Lambert and Parker, *Enuma Eliš,* p. 1. See also Labat, *Le poème babylonien de la création,* p. 76; Foster, *Before the Muses,* p. 354.

132. Jean Bottéro, "Les noms de Marduk, l'écriture et la 'logique' en Mésopotamie ancienne," in *Essays on the Ancient Near East in Memory of Jacob Joel Finkelstein,* ed. Maria de Jong Ellis, Memoirs of the Connecticut Academy of Arts & Sciences (Hamden, Conn.: Archon, 1977), p. 26; Lambert, "Technical Terminology for Creation," p. 192.

133. Jacobsen, *The Treasures of Darkness,* p. 169.

emergence of the cosmos.[134] Therefore, the authority of Marduk's commands was beyond dispute, unless one actually sought to overturn the order of the cosmos. The narrative strategy of taking the story back further than simply stating what the gods decided — as was typical of royal inscriptions — to a description of how the gods came into being and became organized under the sovereign authority of Marduk at the time of the threat posed by Tiamat recontextualized the tradition and made the omission of Enlil less obvious.[135]

The strategy of anchoring the sovereignty of an earthly king in events of prehistoric or primordial times also guided the composition of the *Sumerian King List*.[136] This composition, at least in its final form, seems to have been created by supporters of the Isin dynasty of the early OB period in order to argue that the kings of Isin were the legitimate rulers over the land of Sumer and Akkad.[137] The *Sumerian King List* divided its story of events into those that occurred before and after two major disasters: (1) the flood that occurred 28,800 years earlier and (2) the Gutian invasion. The part of the list that recounted royal rule between these two disasters began naming rulers in northern Mesopotamia, where it named forty otherwise unknown rulers of Kish before any from Akkad were mentioned. In southern Mesopotamia or Sumer, thirteen kings of Uruk, whose reigns are not mentioned by other historical records, were named. It was not until the mention of Lugal-zagesi, the fourteenth king of Uruk, that the list moved from prehistoric into historical times.[138] The purpose of this list, which drew upon the records and traditions of the cities of Mesopotamia, was to make the case that rule over the land of Sumer and Akkad, which could be held by only one city at a time, was transferred from one city to another by divine decision. No human fault or transgression triggered the transfers.[139] The list paid no attention to rivalries that most likely arose between the various cities as each sought to be designated by Enlil as the location of sovereign rule over Sumer and Akkad.

---

134. Jacobsen, *The Treasures of Darkness*, pp. 176, 178.

135. Jacobsen, *The Treasures of Darkness*, p. 191.

136. Jonker, *The Topography of Remembrance*, pp. 140-44; Norman Yoffee, "Political Economy in Early Mesopotamian States," *Annual Review of Anthropology* 24 (1995): 294.

137. Michalowski, "History as Charter," pp. 241-42; Jonker, *The Topography of Remembrance*, p. 151. Mark Chevalas ("Genealogical History as 'Charter': A Study of Old Babylonian Period Historiography and the Old Testament," in *Faith, Tradition, and History: Old Testament Historiography in Its Near Eastern Context*, ed. A. R. Millard et al. [Winona Lake, Ind.: Eisenbrauns, 1994], p. 111) summarizes the various proposed dates for the composition of the *Sumerian King List*: (1) ca. 2100 B.C. at the time of Utu-Hegal (Edzard, Jacobsen); (2) 2112-2004 B.C. in the Ur III period (Rowton); (3) ca. 1900 B.C. (F. R. Kraus); and (4) ca. 2200-2100 B.C. after the Gutian invasions (Michalowski).

138. Jonker, *The Topography of Remembrance*, p. 144.

139. Jonker, *The Topography of Remembrance*, p. 135.

Change or innovation in Homeric Greece, biblical Israel, and OB Mesopotamia was legitimate insofar as it was anchored in the will of God or the gods as articulated in the tradition. The evidence for whether or not a particular course of action is according to the divine will is often clearer in retrospect than it is at the time of deciding on a course of action. Within these traditional societies, there were both an encouragement for bold action by their leaders and a caution that such actions were not to introduce radical change into the community. Past relationships and commitments needed to be renewed and revived, but most of all sustained.

Pressing the limits of what is possible is an important practice for sustaining the relationships in a community. The adventures of Odysseus of the "many ways" and "many wiles" brought him to exotic places, but each of them imposed heavy costs on Odysseus and his crew. With the help of the gods, Odysseus was able to escape from the enchantments of fantasyland and pass through its joys and sorrows so as to return to Ithaca with expanded vision and enhanced circumspectness. His newly acquired wisdom most often could be communicated only indirectly so as to be constructive for the community in Ithaca.

Pressing the limits of what is possible involves the danger of serious transgression that undermines the hierarchy of relationships constitutive of the community. Ezekiel preached his oracles of judgment against the king of Tyre to promote among the Israelites and others who might listen to his preaching the practice of looking beyond appearances to draw closer to fundamental reality. By imagining the perfect king within Eden, Ezekiel was stretching the framework for evaluating the trade practices and self-image of the king of Tyre into the primordial era. Ezekiel made the case that the splendor and power of the king of Tyre were a gift from God, but he had forgotten this fact and claimed divine power on the basis of his beauty and mercantile achievements. A king who imagined himself to be able to do anything had set himself up for a fall. A king could press the limits of what is possible for humans constructively only if he remembered his place in the hierarchy between heaven and earth.

Traditional patterns of authority were drawn upon and updated discreetly. The inaugural act, whether it be the creation of the world or the founding of an institution, was regarded as providing a pattern of authority that promoted wholeness, integration, and community.[140] In the first part of the second millennium B.C. to support Isin's rise to supreme rule over the land of Sumer and Akkad, and in the latter part of the second millennium to support Marduk's rise to the position of king of the gods, authors created scenarios that located

---

140. Cf. Paul Ricoeur, "Thinking Creation," in *Thinking Biblically* (Chicago: University of Chicago Press, 1998), p. 49.

the authority of the kings of Isin and the origin of Marduk's sovereign authority in events of primordial or prehistoric times.

Traditional patterns of authority used memory to sustain an expansive vision. Such memory not only recalled early events according to a sense of "what must have happened" but also unfolded new dimensions of these early events through reflection on their meaning born of additional experience.[141] Such remembering, particularly in public settings, made the earlier event present and once again a source of vitality for the community. In the performance of epic poetry and other traditional compositions, the point was not so much to retrieve facts as to re-experience in the present an earlier formative experience for the community.[142]

The distinctions between the divine and the human, between nature and culture, between the savage and the civilized, and among the various ranks of divine and human beings were boundaries that were negotiated and renegotiated within the context of such a traditional pattern. The dialectic or tension between the poles of these distinctions was necessary for the vitality of the community. When a character like Odysseus pressed the edges between the divine and the human and knew that there were limits that he had to respect and negotiate as he moved among divine, human, and natural powers, it was within the tension of pressing the limits of human experience that the "larger whole" or a sense of integration emerged. As Odysseus sailed farther and farther to the East, he emerged to find himself in the West. The Oceanus on which he sailed was like a river that encircled the earth.[143] In the same way, in pressing deeper into the traditional memory, one expands one's expectations for the future that promises to bring one full circle or back again, but that equips one with the wisdom gained from a tested, rich experience. Memory and anticipation go hand in hand.[144]

Pressing the limits also meant not transgressing the limits. Ezekiel condemned the king of Tyre because he had forsaken the "larger whole" and the tension of accountability to others; he ruled as if he were absolute. He apparently had no inkling of the primordial blessed state that had been given to him by God. Mesopotamian kings undertook new building projects, new administrative arrangements in their kingdoms, and various other innovations, but they legitimated these actions by stating that the gods decreed them. The king may have cloaked his ambitions by claiming a divine origin for his initiatives,

---

141. Bloch, *How We Think They Think*, pp. 116-17.
142. Bakker, "Storytelling in the Future," p. 12.
143. Nagy, *Greek Mythology and Poetics*, p. 238.
144. Ricoeur, *Time and Narrative*, 3:213.

yet just his rhetorical attentiveness to the gods testified to his concern to keep the popular perceptions of his ambitions within the lines or limits sketched out in the tradition. There was a belief in a divinely given world order in Homeric Greece, biblical Israel, and OB Mesopotamia that leaders could transgress only at the price of great harm to themselves and their communities.

The Hierarchy of Gods and Humans: A Traditional Structure for Personal and Communal Integration

In the Homeric, Israelite, and Mesopotamian traditions, God or the gods were regarded as differing from humans by their perfection, greater power, and immortality. The divine reality left traces within the natural and human worlds that provoked diverse and sometimes competing understandings of how the divine world was organized in these three cultures.

The understanding of the gods in the Homeric world drew upon the heritage of the Minoan and Mycenaean worlds.[145] In Homer, the gods encountered humans in situations where the divine and human motivations overlapped so greatly that it was difficult to distinguish them.[146] The paradox of the identification of the god as a named agent and as an indwelling power should not be reduced. The god is both a power and a person in the story.[147] After Achilles was dishonored by Agamemnon, he grew angry and debated within himself whether or not to kill Agamemnon.

> While he was wrestling with this in his mind and heart and was drawing his great sword from its sheath, Athena came down from heaven. Earlier, the white-armed goddess Hera had sent her, for in her heart she loved and showed concern for both of them alike. She stood behind him and grasped the blond hair of the son of Peleus. She appeared to him alone and no one

145. Walter Burkert, *Greek Religion* (Cambridge, Mass.: Harvard University Press, 1985), pp. 119-21.

146. Bernard Dietrich, "From Knossos to Homer," in *What Is a God?* ed. Alan Lloyd (London: Duckworth, 1997), pp. 4-5.

147. Burkert, *Greek Religion*, pp. 182-83. J. K. Davies, "The Moral Dimension of Pythian Apollo," in *What Is a God?* ed. Alan Lloyd (London: Duckworth, 1997), p. 58) claims that the Greek gods are first power and then persons; cf. Buxton, *Imaginary Greece*, p. 145. However, Vernant (*Myth and Society in Ancient Greece*, p. 98) seems to reduce the paradoxical character of the Homeric gods when he claims that they never reach the stage where they are personal agents but rather are meaningful insofar as they constitute powers within the system of the pantheon. Yet to say that a god has a proper name and acts in a narrative is to say that this named reality is a subject that acts and so is a personal agent.

else saw her. Achilles was amazed. He turned around and at once he recognized Pallas Athena. And the eyes gleamed dreadfully. (*Il.* 1.193-200)

Athena was able to stay Achilles' hand. No one but Achilles recognized her presence. It was as if Athena appeared only within Achilles' mind.[148] While Athena functioned as a power of restraint within Achilles, she was more than that, for she is portrayed as grasping Achilles by the hair and speaking with him.[149] Athena has a name and a body. To the assembled Achaeans who did not see Athena, it could have seemed that it was only divine intervention that kept Achilles from striking Agamemnon.[150] Athena here is clearly imagined as a personal agent who empowers Achilles with restraint. Athena along with her gift of restraint could withdraw from Achilles just as quickly as she had come to him.[151]

The hierarchy of the Greek aristocratic household was mirrored in the Olympian household of Zeus. Like the patriarch of a household, Zeus was sovereign and the various members of his family had their particular spheres of influence,[152] yet the relations among the Olympians was based on "a combination of violence, deception, negotiation and reciprocity."[153] The queen Hera called upon Athena of the next generation to intervene in the quarrel between Achilles and Agamemnon. She herself refrained from entering the earthly sphere on this occasion.

Zeus's supreme rule over heaven and earth involved him in a number of areas of human concern, and thus he had a wide range of epithets applied to him.[154] The divine epithets applied to Zeus and the other gods indicated how the gods characteristically worked through individuals to incorporate them into groups and then through groups into the natural order. The gods were indispensable agents of social integration in the Homeric world.[155] Zeus, as sov-

---

148. Pucci, *The Song of the Sirens*, pp. 74, 77.

149. M. M. Willcock, "Some Aspects of the Gods in the *Iliad*," in *Essays on the Iliad*, ed. John Wright (Bloomington: Indiana University Press, 1978), pp. 66-67. Pucci (*The Song of the Sirens*, p. 197) claims that Athena functions in this episode as a "narrative device" to suspend the actual decision that Achilles made about repaying Agamemnon and so opens the way for Achilles' wrath and its consequences to unfold in the narrative. Athena is nevertheless a character that acts as a personal agent in the narrative.

150. Vernant, *Mortals and Immortals*, pp. 42-44.

151. Vernant, *Mortals and Immortals*, p. 37.

152. Vernant, *Mortals and Immortals*, p. 47; Burkert, *Greek Religion*, pp. 128-29; G. S. Kirk, *The Iliad: A Commentary*, vol. 2: *Books 5-8* (Cambridge: Cambridge University Press, 1990), pp. 9-10.

153. Buxton, *Imaginary Greece*, p. 146.

154. Burkert, *Greek Religion*, pp. 125-31.

155. Vernant, *Myth and Society in Ancient Greece*, p. 97.

ereign ruler, had the brute power to do whatever he wished and to overturn fate, but he did not do so since that would have not have respected the web of relationships and commitments that structured the social and natural orders. When Zeus pondered whether to rescue his son Sarpedon from death at the hands of Patroclus, Hera warned him:

> Most feared son of Cronus, what a bold utterance you have made! As a mortal man who was allotted such a destiny long ago, are you willing to set him free from the anguish of death? Do it, but surely we other gods do not approve. I will inform you of another matter, and you should take it to heart. If you send Sarpedon home alive, take into consideration that some other one of the gods may then wish to send his own beloved son away from the intense fighting, for many sons of the immortals are fighting around the great city of Priam. You will stir up terrible resentment among them. (*Il.* 16.440-49)

Zeus respected the existing order of rights and prerogatives that had grown up in the world around him.[156] If he did not, he would have had to bear the negative consequences: a lesson that Agamemnon learned when he took back the war prize from Achilles and therewith undercut the warrior code (*Il.* 9.115-20). By refraining from rescuing Sarpedon from death, Zeus respected the context in which he exercised his sovereignty; he did not act absolutely. The web of relationships among gods and between gods and humans would be impacted by Zeus's altering the fate of his son Sarpedon. The significance of the customary order was not to be taken lightly in the Homeric world.[157]

A *locus classicus* for the numinous appearance of the God of the Israelites is the burning bush episode. As Moses was shepherding the flocks of his father-in-law Jethro, he came to Horeb:

> The angel of the Lord appeared to him in a fire flaming out of the midst of the bush. He saw that though the bush was burning in the fire, the bush was not consumed. So Moses said, "I must go aside to see this remarkable appearance: why does the bush not burn up?" When the Lord saw that he was coming to take a look, God called to him out of the midst of the bush and said, "Moses, Moses," and he replied, "Here I am." (Exod. 3:2-4)

The contradiction of an unconsumed burning bush pointed to an event that transcended the expected, natural order.[158] It served as a sign to catch Moses'

156. Burkert, *Greek Religion*, pp. 129-30; Vernant, *Myth and Society in Ancient Greece*, p. 105.

157. Muellner, *The Anger of Achilles*, pp. 35, 129; Vernant, *Myth and Society in Ancient Greece*, pp. 103-4; cf. Crotty, *The Poetics of Supplication*, p. 87.

158. Brevard Childs, *The Book of Exodus* (Philadelphia: Westminster, 1974), p. 72; Samuel

attention.[159] The articulation of the divine will came through the words of the dialogue that followed. God identified himself as "the God of Abraham, the God of Isaac, and the God of Jacob" (Exod. 3:6). After he commissioned Moses to lead the Hebrews forth from Egypt, God further identified himself as "I will be who I will be" (Exod. 3:14). The name "God of the ancestors" was not a proper name; its specificity came from the memory of the clan deity protecting the ancestors Abraham, Isaac, and Jacob.[160] The phrase "I will be who I will be" also did not match the typical form for Hebrew proper names such as Isaac, which means "May El smile upon you." This unusual name "I will be who I will be" pointed to the distinctiveness of this God for the Hebrew people, for actions reveal a person's essence and identity most clearly.[161] This God would be faithful to them and by a promise of an enduring relationship with them would shape their horizon of expectations as a people.[162]

In the Decalogue, the Israelites were commanded to refrain from carving an image *(pesel)* of the Lord or any other god from wood or stone: "You shall not make for yourself an image or a representation of anything in the heavens above, or on the earth below, or in the waters under the earth" (Exod. 20:4). They were to be a people who communicated with the divine without the assistance of objects that aimed to visualize the divine presence.[163] The biblical record refers to the Lord as enthroned on the cherubim (1 Sam. 4:4), but the throne within the innermost part of the temple *(děbîr)* was an empty throne in terms of visual images.[164] If the prohibition against making images was not formulated until the Exilic period, it is remarkable that the Israelites refrained from making visual images of the Lord, particularly in light of the numerous

---

Terrien, *The Elusive Presence* (New York: Harper & Row, 1978), pp. 110-12; Jacobsen, *The Treasures of Darkness*, p. 6.

159. Cornelius Houtman, *Exodus*, 3 vols. (Kampen: Kok, 1993), 1:344-45

160. Gerhard von Rad, *Genesis* (Philadelphia: Westminster, 1974), p. 21; Rainer Albertz, *A History of Israelite Religion in the Old Testament Period*, vol. 1: *From the Beginnings to the End of the Monarchy* (Louisville: Westminster/John Knox, 1992), pp. 30-32.

161. Othmar Keel and Christoph Uehlinger, *God, Goddesses, and Images of God in Ancient Israel* (Minneapolis: Fortress, 1998), pp. 393-94.

162. Childs, *The Book of Exodus*, p. 76; John Durham, *Exodus*, WBC 3 (Waco, Tex.: Word, 1987), p. 39; Walter Brueggemann, *Theology of the Old Testament: Testimony, Dispute, Advocacy* (Minneapolis: Fortress, 1997), pp. 164-73; Bernhard Anderson, *Contours of Old Testament Theology* (Minneapolis: Fortress, 1999), p. 50; Terrien, *The Elusive Presence*, pp. 113-19.

163. Tryggve Mettinger, "Israelite Aniconism: Developments and Origins," in *The Image and the Book*, ed. K. van der Toorn, Biblical Exegesis and Theology 21 (Leuven: Peeters, 1997), pp. 175-78, 203; Houtman, *Exodus*, 3:21-24; Durham, *Exodus*, p. 268; cf. Keel and Uehlinger, *God, Goddesses, and Images of God in Ancient Israel*, p. 407.

164. Mettinger, "Israelite Aniconism," p. 187.

mental images of the Lord provided by the biblical tradition.[165] If the practice of refraining from making such images inhered in their West Semitic way of worship, then the repeated prophetic denunciations of idol worship can be seen as efforts to retain this way of worship, and the prohibition against making idols was the final effort to settle this issue within the pressures of the Exilic environment.[166]

The monotheistic dynamic at the heart of the Old Testament received one of its most memorable formulations in the text known as the Shema: "The Lord our God, is one Lord.[167] You shall love the Lord your God with all your heart, and with all your soul, and with all your might" (Deut. 6:4-5). This text summoned the Israelite people to focus their attention and fidelity on only one God.[168] Any other gods, whether they belonged to the people of other nations or to groups imbued with Canaanite culture, were not to be invoked, worshipped or obeyed. The drawings from a late-ninth-century B.C. military outpost, Kuntillet 'Ajrud, fifty miles south of Kadesh-barnea in the Sinai, have given rise to debates over whether or not some groups in Israel believed the Lord had a consort known as "his Asherah."[169] If such was the case, then this

165. Mettinger, "Israelite Aniconism," p. 178. Houtmann (*Exodus*, 3:23) sees both aniconic and monolatrous worship as part of Israel's early tradition. For arguments that there were cultic images of the Lord in ancient Israel, see Christoph Uehlinger, "Anthropomorphic Cult Statuary in Iron Age Palestine and the Search for Yahweh's Cult Images," pp. 152-53; Karel van der Toorn, "The Iconic Book Analogies Between the Babylonian Cult of Images and the Veneration of the Torah," p. 242; and Herbert Niehr, "In Search of YHWH's Cult Statue in the First Temple," pp. 73-95, all in *The Image and the Book*, ed. K. van der Toorn, Biblical Exegesis and Theology 21 (Leuven: Peeters, 1997).

166. Mettinger, "Israelite Aniconism," pp. 178-84.

167. Moshe Weinfeld (*Deuteronomy 1–11*, AB 5 [New York: Doubleday, 1991], p. 331) reads YHWH 'eḥād as "a noun clause, without a verb or a resumptive pronoun."

168. Yair Hoffmann, "The Concept of 'Other Gods' in the Deuteronomistic Literature," in *Politics and Theopolitics in the Bible and Postbiblical Literature*, ed. H. G. Reventlow et al., JSOTSup 171 (Sheffield: Sheffield Academic Press, 1994), pp. 79-80. Weinfeld (*Deuteronomy 1–11*, p. 338) notes that Deut. 6:4 on its own is not monotheistic, but its association with the first two commandments and other sermonic proclamations in Deuteronomy such as Deut. 10:17 provide it with a monotheistic meaning. See also Moshe Weinfeld, "The Uniqueness of the Decalogue and Its Place in Jewish Tradition," in *The Ten Commandments in History and Tradition*, ed. B.-Z. Segal (Jerusalem: Magnes, 1990), p. 20.

169. Uehlinger ("Anthropomorphic Cult," pp. 140-42, 151) suggests that the eighth century B.C. Munich terracotta is a depiction of YHWH and his Asherah and so adapts his earlier position (*God, Goddesses, and Images of God in Ancient Israel*, pp. 240-48, 370) where he held that the 'ăšērôt in the drawings at Kuntillet 'Ajrud were "cult objects in the form of a tree" and not partners of the Lord, and that such productions by caravanserai in the context of Israelite and Phoenician trade offered no evidence against the practice of monolatry in Israel. On the possibility that Asherah may have been part of both state and family worship of YHWH in Israel, see Saul

finding could exemplify the kind of worship castigated by prophets like Elijah (1 Kings 18:21), Hosea (Hos. 3:1), and Jeremiah (Jer. 2:11) and would have led them to call the people to serve the Lord alone (1 Kings 18:36, 39; Hos. 2:8-9; Jer. 3:1). The call to worship only one God who would care for all their diverse needs presented a formidable challenge to a people shaped by cultural traditions in which polytheism was the typical approach to imagining the divine world.[170]

A significant image for expressing the sovereignty of the Lord over heaven and earth was that of a king ruling over his council of vassals and administrators. This image of the heavenly council played a significant role in the hymn in Psalm 89:6-16(5-15). The comparison of the Lord with the other heavenly beings revealed the Lord's incomparability: a theological point undergirding the prohibition of making images of the Lord and other gods and the command to serve the Lord alone.[171] Since no other deities could compete with the Lord, Israel needed to focus its trust and hope in the Lord.[172] In Psalm 89:2-38(1-37), the Israelite tradition proclaimed that the Lord who ruled over the heavenly council was supreme in power and faithfulness and would manifest his incomparability in the way he related to Israel and the world through the Davidic dynasty.

By the end of the fourth millennium with the origin of cities in Mesopotamia, the gods of the Mesopotamians were transformed from nature deities into anthropomorphic deities who resided on temple estates in the cities.[173] According to the OB *Atraḫasis Epic,* human beings were created in order to care for the gods who resided in the temple estates.[174] So, one of the king's primary responsibilities was to take care of the temples. In the prologue to his *Code,* Hammurapi devoted the majority of his attention to listing the benefits he had brought to the various gods and their temple estates in the land of Sumer and

---

Olyan, *Asherah and the Cult of Yahweh in Israel,* SBLMS 34 (Atlanta: Scholars, 1988), pp. 23-38, and Mark S. Smith, *The Early History of God* (San Francisco: Harper & Row, 1990), pp. 85-94.

170. Smith, *The Early History of God,* pp. xxiii-xxv; Keel and Uehlinger, *God, Goddesses, and Images of God in Ancient Israel,* pp. 393-409.

171. Brueggemann, *Theology of the Old Testament,* pp. 139-44; Anderson, *Contours of Old Testament Theology,* p. 41; Terrien, *The Elusive Presence,* pp. 112, 118-19.

172. Bill T. Arnold, "The Weidner Chronicle and the Idea of History in Israel and Mesopotamia," in *Faith, Tradition and History,* ed. A. R. Millard et al. (Winona Lake, Ind.: Eisenbrauns, 1994), p. 147.

173. Wiggermann, "Theologies, Priests, and Worship in Ancient Mesopotamia," p. 1868; Jacobsen, *The Treasures of Darkness,* pp. 20-21; Jean Bottéro, "Religion and Reasoning in Mesopotamia," in *Ancestor of the West* (Chicago: University of Chicago Press, 1996), p. 53.

174. W. G. Lambert and A. R. Millard, *Atra-ḫasīs: The Babylonian Story of the Flood* (Winona Lake, Ind.: Eisenbrauns, 1999), pp. 57-61, tablet 1, lines 189-243; W. G. Lambert, "Donations of Food and Drink to the Gods in Ancient Mesopotamia," in *Ritual and Sacrifice in the Ancient Near East,* ed. J. Quaegebeur (Leuven: Peeters, 1993), p. 198.

Akkad.[175] In the course of the third millennium, the kinglike form of the statue of the god became the focal point of the temple cult.[176] Food offerings were placed before this cult statue twice each day. Obviously, the statue did not consume the food.[177] Yet the practices of the cult treated this statue "as if" it were a living god who did consume food.[178]

The repeated cultic practices and beliefs shaped a worldview in which the Mesopotamians understood themselves as servants of the gods. These practices evidenced a belief that their well-being depended upon the king and themselves paying heed to the gods.[179] Their knowledge of the divine world in their practice of provisioning the gods with food appeared to move away from a metaphorical understanding of the ways of the gods to what the anthropologist Edmund Leach has labeled a metonymic understanding in which religious language turns metaphors into metonyms so that the metonyms can then interrelate as signs within a system.[180] Jean Bottéro describes the world of the Mesopotamian gods as one that forms an analogy to the human world; it is an interrelated whole that reflects many of the dynamics of the human world but is transposed into the more powerful sphere where sovereignty is anchored.[181] So, when the Mesopotamians offered food to the gods, they probably knew that the gods did not eat food in the same way that humans did, but that somehow it was a valuable, nourishing offering that they were expected to give to the gods. The contradiction in the gods' requiring food and not consuming it may simply

175. Rykle Borger, *Babylonische-assyrische Lesestücke*, AnOr 54 (Rome: Pontifical Biblical Institute, 1979), 1:5-7; 2:286-88.

176. W. W. Hallo, "Sumerian Religion," in *Kinattūtu ša darāti*, ed. A. F. Rainey (Tel Aviv: University of Tel Aviv Press, 1993), p. 20.

177. Van de Mieroop, *Society and Enterprise in Old Babylonian Ur*, p. 102. Hallo ("Sumerian Religion," p. 20) notes that administrative data from the temples confirm that the amount of food brought into the cult equaled the amount distributed to the king, priests, and other participants.

178. Eiko Matsushima, "Divine Statues in Ancient Mesopotamia: Their Fashioning and Clothing and Their Interaction with the Society," in *Official Cult and Popular Religion in the Ancient Near East,* ed. E. Matsushima (Heidelberg: Universitätsverlag, 1993), p. 219; Angelika Berlejung, "Washing the Mouth: The Consecration of Divine Images in Mesopotamia," in *The Image and the Book: Iconic Cults, Aniconism, and the Rise of Book Religion in Israel and the Ancient Near East,* ed. K. van der Toorn (Leuven: Peeters, 1997), pp. 67, 72.

179. F. R. Kraus, *The Role of Temples from the Third Dynasty of Ur to the First Dynasty of Babylon,* Monographs on the Ancient Near East, vol. 2, fasc. 4 (Malibu, Calif.: Undena, 1990), p. 6.

180. Edmund Leach, *Culture and Communication: The Logic by Which Symbols Are Connected* (New York: Cambridge University Press, 1976), p. 70; cf. Graham Ward, "Biblical Narrative and the Theology of Metonymy," *Modern Theology* 7 (1991): 342-43.

181. Bottéro, *Mesopotamia,* p. 224.

have been a sign to the people that they were dealing with the metaphysical world: the code concerning food for the gods was not the same as that for humans.

The Mesopotamian pantheon, which initially took shape in the mid-third millennium, was hierarchically organized with Enlil typically designated as the king of the gods.[182] The sanctuary of Enlil at Nippur, located halfway between the lands of Sumer and Akkad, became the primary Mesopotamian sanctuary until its demise around 1720 B.C.[183] As king of the gods, Enlil ruled over an assembly of the deities of the cities of Mesopotamia. Enlil's sovereign rule was emphasized at the beginning of the following inscription that celebrated Samsuiluna's construction of a wall in Sippar for the temple of Enlil's son Zababa and his daughter Ishtar:

> Enlil, whose power is supreme among the gods, the shepherd who determines fates, looked with his holy face upon Zababa and Ishtar, the most valiant among the Igigi. His heart firmly desired to build the wall of Kish, the preeminent cultic site, their exalted dwelling, (and) to raise its head higher than before. Enlil, the great lord, whose command cannot be reversed, (whose) decrees once made cannot be changed, looked with his joyful face upon Zababa, his strong son, the one who achieves his victories, (and) upon Ishtar, his beloved daughter, a lady whose divinity is incomparable, and spoke with them words of happiness. (lines 1-29)[184]

The story line and structure of the inscription make clear the lines of authority in the divine and human worlds.[185] After stating that Enlil desired to build the wall of Kish, the inscription then quoted Enlil's words by which he commissioned Zababa and Ishtar to protect Samsuiluna and slay his enemies so that Samsuiluna might then construct the wall for their temple estate (lines 32-52). The message of this inscription supported a primary tenet of Mesopotamian temple theology for the existence of the kingship: the king was obliged to organize the people to support the temple estates of the gods.[186] This practice grew up over the course of the third millennium when the temple had extensive land holdings, an important factor underlying the picture of the Sargonic kings as

---

182. Wiggermann, "Theologies, Priests, and Worship in Ancient Mesopotamia," pp. 1860, 1869.

183. Van de Mieroop, *The Ancient Mesopotamian City*, p. 223; Hallo, *Origins*, p. 279; Bottéro, *Mesopotamia*, p. 214.

184. Frayne, *RIME 4*, E4.3.7.7, lines 1-29.

185. Hurowitz, *Inu Anum Sīrum*, p. 57.

186. Kraus, *The Role of Temples*, pp. 6, 12-13; Van de Mieroop, *Society and Enterprise in Old Babylonian Ur*, p. 96.

priests and servants of the gods.[187] In the eighteenth century B.C., this well-established royal obligation of supporting temples did not prevent Hammurapi from interfering in the administration of the temples and extracting wealth from them, but he nevertheless supported the temples and continued to cultivate his image as their patron (cf. *CH* I:50–IV:66).[188]

After describing the jubilation of Zababa and Ishtar, the inscription continued tracing out the line of authority from Enlil to Samsuiluna with a report of the words by which Zababa and Ishtar commissioned Samsuiluna (lines 70-88). These gods repeated their commission from Enlil with the command that Samsuiluna proceed with both the military campaign and the building project. The final part of the inscription recorded Samsuiluna's success in carrying out these projects. The plot of this inscription presented a common royal paradigm in Mesopotamia for the way the divine and human worlds interacted: there was one hierarchical structure for both worlds in which initiative began at the top with the king of the gods and proceeded through lower ranking gods to the human king. The religious views of the royal court, although configured in light of the desires and expectations of the king, were no doubt continuous with the religious ideas and views of the people at large. The texts from the royal archives give us more than just a picture of the religion of a Mesopotamian elite.[189]

In Homeric Greece, biblical Israel, and OB Mesopotamia, the powers that ruled the natural and human worlds were not anonymous. They were humanlike beings with names, who could be invoked. The corporeal character of the gods appears to have been most concretely conceived in humanlike terms in the cultic practices of the Mesopotamian cult. At the other extreme, the biblical tradition's prohibition of making molten and carved images of the Lord distanced the Lord from artistic and material images that might have confined him within a body. In Homer, a particular god could merge with a human so as to be identifiable primarily by the excellence of the power exhibited by the human: for example, Athena became the power of restraint within Achilles when he contemplated revenge against Agamemnon. In all three cultures, the deity bore a personal name and participated in the human world where language was a primary means of shaping reality.

---

187. Franke, *Königsinschriften und Königsideologie*, p. 37.

188. Van de Mieroop, *Society and Enterprise in Old Babylonian Ur*, pp. 245-49; Hurowitz, *Inu Anum Sīrum*, pp. 71-81; cf. Herbert Huffmon, "A Company of Prophets: Mari, Assyria, Israel," in *Prophecy in Its Ancient Near Eastern Context: Mesopotamian, Biblical, and Arabian Perspectives*, SBL Symposium Series 13 (Atlanta: SBL, 2000), p. 53.

189. Bottéro, *Mesopotamia*, p. 208; cf. A. L. Oppenheim, *Ancient Mesopotamia: Portrait of a Dead Civilization* (Chicago: University of Chicago Press, 1977), p. 181.

In these three cultures, the divine world and the human world were joined together by a hierarchical model in which rank was important. Gods and humans alike were expected to find their place within such a hierarchy fashioned according to a monarchical model. Changes within it in Mesopotamia, such as Marduk's rise to the position of king of the gods in the late second millennium, were legitimated by referring to events in primordial times and so provided a new context for seeing and maintaining the age-old hierarchical traditions. In the Homeric world, Zeus maintained his position at the head of the pantheon and often worked through the gods of his household rather than directly intervening in earthly matters. In biblical Israel, the Lord exercised a form of royal rule over heaven and earth in which the role of intermediate divine beings was much reduced in comparison to the developed polytheistic hierarchies of the Mesopotamian and Homeric religious worlds.

Formation of Communal Identity according to the Traditional Pattern for Legitimating Royal Authority

The traditional pattern for legitimating royal authority communicated a basic pattern or mental model linking the king of the gods to the king and the people. These three parties could be variously named: for example, Zeus, the Lord, or Enlil; Odysseus, David, or Hammurapi; Achaeans, Israelites, or Babylonians. The schema or mental model located sovereign rule in the king of the gods, and the earthly king was answerable to the heavenly king for the way he ruled.[190] How this schema was described depended on particular circumstances in the retelling, yet this schema had to emerge if the pattern for legitimating royal authority was to be recognized. So, this pattern functioned like a symbol: it pointed to the polyvalent reality of the king's person and rule and unfolded important but context-specific dimensions of royal rule in a community.

In communal performances of the Homeric epics, communal recitations of the Hebrew psalms, and ritual occasions for dedicating a wall or canal in Mesopotamia, the king or leaders of the assembled community would call forth in the minds of the people the schema of the pattern of legitimating royal authority. How each individual shaped the schema in his or her imagination would have drawn upon his or her own personal history, but each would have imagined, for example, how it was when Zeus sent a dream to Agamemnon or when the Lord promised David an everlasting dynasty or when Enlil commissioned Samsuiluna. In a communal setting, these memories would qualify and

---

190. Bloch, *How We Think They Think,* pp. 122-23; Bakker, *Poetry in Speech,* p. 56.

correct one another as they made present a commissioning that happened in the past and that perhaps reflected previous analogous commissionings of a king by God or the gods. In such communal gatherings, it was important that the authoritative word of the king of the gods was stated — a speech-act — that made present an earlier foundational event.[191] The presentment of such a foundational act of commissioning was the point of the assembly's remembering, much more so than the retrieval of data about some act in the past. In fact, most of those assembled would have had no experience of this foundational event, even if it had occurred only a few decades earlier. Even those events individuals experience themselves are shaped by the versions that they recount of the event, and so one recounting of the event may reflect a memory of one retelling and another of a different retelling. All these versions have validity because the original event is manifold and dimensions of it are often understood better upon subsequent reflection.[192]

The recollection of an event or a person — whether divine or human — makes that reality present. By searching through the past and bringing forth these people and events, the community honors these individuals but also expands its horizons. Homeric heroes wagered their lives on the honor that came in such communal presentments of their names. The fragility of the community and its forgetfulness would seem to have made such bardic songs a less reliable means to immortality than the inscriptions of a Mesopotamian king. In the short run, however, the Homeric performance, designed to engage the audience, would surely have created more vivid memories of a hero in the imaginations of the people than an inscription on a stone monument, no matter how impressive the iconography. Yet the eventual writing down of the Homeric epics showed that the desire for the reliability of a text triumphed over the immediacy of performance. The epics were still performed as the inscriptions were still read and the psalms recited. The essential aspect of the act of remembering was to make present what someone must have been like and what must have happened. It was the imagined person or event that reflected a communally guarded schema or pattern that was called forth in the public ceremony. Such recollection helped a community to imagine how to go forward; memory and anticipation go hand in hand.

The communal remembering of the traditional pattern for royal authority kept the king and the people accountable to the king of the gods and the tradition. Such remembering kept alive those relationships — that network of relationships essential for the community's identity. The maintenance of these rela-

191. Bakker, "Storytelling in the Future," pp. 12, 15.

192. Bloch, *How We Think They Think*, p. 124; Bakker, "Storytelling in the Future," p. 35.

tionships was not simply a human project but involved calling upon and receiving the assistance of God or the gods. God or the gods were primary agents of social order and integration. The traditions of each of these three cultures claimed that forgetfulness of the primacy of the divine could lead only to the disintegration of the community.

CHAPTER FIVE

Communication and Discernment of the Divine Will: An Essential Task for Individual and Collective Development

Fundamental to the traditional pattern for legitimating royal authority were the claims that sovereignty resided in the divine realm and that a king ruled legitimately only by obeying the king of the gods. The earthly king could increase his authority in the community by persuading the various officials and peoples within the community that he had been chosen for his role by the king of the gods. His rhetorical efforts were not mere ornamentation or ceremony that served as a supplement to the security and material prosperity he brought to the land but rather were integral to the power and stability of his reign. The court poets employed by the king aimed to communicate through their compositions the aura and the terror of the king as evidence of his divine election.[1] Their words drew upon the traditions of the community in order to make intelligible the legitimacy of the king's rule, particularly to those whose support was vital to the king's effectiveness.

The traditions that resonated with the people were rooted in the collective memory of the people and so were not simply the property of the royal court.[2]

1. Sabina Franke, *Königsinschriften und Königsideologie: Die Könige von Akkade zwischen Tradition und Neuerung* (Münster: LIT, 1995), pp. 32, 37; Claus Wilcke, "Politik im Spiegel der Literatur: Literatur als Mittel der Politik im alteren Babylonien," in *Anfänge politischen Denkens in der Antike: Die nahöstlichen Kulturen und die Griechen,* ed. K. Raaflaub and E. Müller-Luckner (Munich: Oldenbourg, 1993), pp. 63, 66.

2. Gerdien Jonker, *The Topography of Remembrance: The Dead, Tradition, and Collective Memory in Mesopotamia,* Studies in the History of Religions 68 (Leiden: Brill, 1995), pp. 17-18; John Miles Foley, "Individual Poet and Epic Tradition: Homer as Legendary Singer," *Arethusa* 31 (1998): 169-70; Frank Moore Cross, *From Epic to Canon: History and Literature in Ancient Israel* (Baltimore: Johns Hopkins University Press, 1998), pp. 50-52.

Other voices in the community offered their interpretations of the traditions and of the ways in which the divine will was communicated through them, unless the king suppressed the expression of opinions contrary to the official version. If the king was intent upon discovering the divine will, he listened to the messages and interpretations of the signs of the time offered by prophets and sages who were not part of his inner circle. In any case, such nonorthodox opinions eventually surfaced in communities as they tried to make sense out of the contradictions and paradoxes of their experience.

Just as the peoples of Homeric Greece, biblical Israel, and ancient Mesopotamia believed that the gods ruled the cosmos, so also they believed that it was possible to come to some knowledge of the divine will. The limited capacity of humans to know the inner workings of the universe did not preclude the possibility that the gods would provide significant information and strategic directives to selected individuals. The reception, discernment, and interpretation of such divine knowledge were activities enmeshed within the social and political circumstances of particular times and places. Conflict and competition over the true divine message was a familiar dimension of the communication process. These efforts to discover the divine will pointed to the belief of prophets, sages, and their communities that humans could find meaning, happiness, and vitality in life only by bringing their lives into harmony with an underlying world order created and overseen by the gods.[3]

The Need for Divine Direction in Critical Situations

The routines that structure day-to-day existence function almost invisibly unless an object breaks, an illness strikes, or some other problem impedes the normal way of doing things.[4] Like us, the peoples of Homeric Greece, biblical Is-

3. Jean Bottéro, *Mesopotamia: Writing, Reasoning, and the Gods* (Chicago: University of Chicago Press, 1992), pp. 105, 224; Gwendolyn Leick, "The Challenge of Chance: An Anthropological View of Mesopotamian Mental Strategies for Dealing with the Unpredictable," in *Intellectual Life of the Ancient Near East*, ed. Jiří Prosecký, CRRA 43 (Prague: Oriental Institute, 1998), p. 197; Jean-Pierre Vernant, *Mortals and Immortals* (Princeton: Princeton University Press, 1991), pp. 314; Gene Tucker, "Sin and 'Judgment' in the Prophets," in *Problems in Biblical Theology: Essays in Honor of Rolf Knierim*, ed. Henry T. C. Sun et al. (Grand Rapids: Eerdmans, 1997), p. 375; Leo Perdue, *Wisdom and Creation: The Theology of Wisdom Literature* (Nashville: Abingdon, 1994), p. 328; G. E. R. Lloyd, *Methods and Problems in Greek Science* (Cambridge: Cambridge University Press, 1991), p. 162.

4. Anthony Giddens, *The Constitution of Society: Outline of the Theory of Structuration* (Cambridge: Polity, 1984), pp. 16-17; John B. Thompson, "Editor's Introduction" in Pierre Bourdieu, *Language and Symbolic Power*, ed. John B. Thompson (Cambridge, Mass.: Harvard

rael, and OB Mesopotamia sought to keep the various routines of their lives in working order. Yet for problems for which there were no immediate solutions or for situations that posed substantial danger or risk, they turned to the gods who were in charge of events in heaven and on earth for direction.

The quarrel between Achilles and Agamemnon at the beginning of the *Iliad* was precipitated by a plague that was ravaging the Achaean forces (*Il.* 1.8-21). After nine days of devastation, Achilles, inspired by the goddess Hera, took the initiative to search for the cause of the plague by calling an assembly and asking a prophet to reveal the reason why Apollo had sent the plague (*Il.* 1.53-67). The Homeric community accorded the words of a prophet an objectivity that was beyond dispute, and so such a person was useful in settling disputes.[5] The prophet Calchas expressed his reluctance to speak for fear of offending Agamemnon with his message, but, after gaining the protection of Achilles in the midst of the assembly, he spoke as follows:

> He [Apollo] does not find fault because of a vow or sacrifice but rather because of the priest whom Agamemnon dishonored. He did not set free his daughter and accept the ransom. Because of this, the god skilled with the bow has given hardships and will do so further. For he will not drive away the disfiguring death from the Danaans until we return the bright-eyed young woman to her loving father without a price or a ransom. We are to take a holy offering to Chryse. Then we might persuade him and win his favor. (*Il.* 1.93-100)

The seriousness of the plague pointed to the anger of Apollo, who was traditionally associated with sending and removing illness.[6] Calchas's "inspired" explanation meant that the prize allotted to Agamemnon in a previous raid had to be retaken. Agamemnon did not question whether Calchas's words were revealed or not; rather, he attacked Calchas by insinuating that the prophet did not like him:

University Press, 1991), p. 17; cf. Martin Heidegger, *Being and Time* (Albany, N.Y.: SUNY Press, 1996), pp. 41-42, 56-58.

5. Vernant, *Mortals and Immortals*, p. 304. John Van Seters (*In Search of History: Historiography in the Ancient World and the Origins of Biblical History* [New Haven: Yale University Press, 1983], pp. 78-79) claims that the authority that these three ancient cultures gave to oracles was often a major cause of the unhistorical quality of their historical traditions. For a different interpretation of "history" in the Homeric tradition, see Pierre Vidal-Naquet, *The Black Hunter: Forms of Thought and Forms of Society in the Greek World* (Baltimore: Johns Hopkins University Press, 1986), pp. 253-54.

6. Walter Burkert, *Greek Religion* (Cambridge, Mass.: Harvard University Press, 1985), pp. 145-46, 267.

First of all, he [Agamemnon] cast a threatening glance at Calchas and said, "Seer of evil events, you have never spoken to me what is desirable. It is always to prophesy bad things that is favored in your mind. You never speak or carry out a word that is good. And now among the Danaans you prophesy and proclaim in the assembly that the god skilled in the bow brings hardships because I did not want to accept the good ransom for the young woman, the daughter of Chryses, since I very much wish to keep her in my household. (*Il.* 1.105-12)

Agamemnon did not ask for another prophet to be brought forward to give a second opinion. Rather, he proceeded to threaten the rest of the Achaeans with the process of reallocating trophies *(geras)* so that he might not be the only warrior left without one (*Il.* 1.118-20).[7] Agamemnon used the symbolic power of his position (i.e., the holder of the scepter of Argos) to retake Achilles' trophy, but in doing so he did not act like a shepherd of his people and so provided grounds for Achilles to reproach him later.[8]

According to 1 Kings 22:1-4, Jehoshaphat, king of Judah, made an alliance in the middle part of the ninth century b.c. with Ahab, king of Israel, to go to battle at Ramoth-gilead against the king of Aram to regain cities that they had lost to the king of Aram in previous battles.[9] When Jehoshaphat asked that an oracle be sought prior to battle, Ahab gathered about four hundred prophets and asked them the following question:

"Should I go to war against Ramoth-gilead or hold off?" They said, "Go up, for the Lord will put it under the king's power." Then Jehoshaphat said, "Is there still not another prophet belonging to the Lord here so that we can seek a sign from him?" The king of Israel said to Jehoshaphat, "There is still one man to seek the Lord through his sign, Micaiah son of Imlah, but I hate him for he does not prophesy good about me but rather evil." Then Jehoshaphat said, "Let not the king speak in this way." (1 Kings 22:6-8)

In seeking the war oracle, Ahab followed what seems to have been a standard procedure by posing a question that could be answered with a simple "Yes" or

---

7. Vernant, *Mortals and Immortals*, p. 53.

8. Leonard Muellner, *The Anger of Achilles: "Mēnis" in Greek Epic* (Ithaca: Cornell University Press, 1996), pp. 103-4; Pietro Pucci, *The Song of the Sirens: Essays on Homer* (New York: Rowman & Littlefield, 1998), pp. 205.

9. Simon DeVries (*Prophet Against Prophet: The Role of the Micaiah Narrative (1 Kings 22) in the Development of the Early Prophetic Tradition* [Grand Rapids: Eerdmans, 1978], p. 124) argues that the historical Israelite king in the events recorded in 1 Kings 22 was Jehoram (849-843/2 b.c.) rather than Ahab.

"No."[10] Such an approach was politically and militarily pragmatic; the situation called for decisiveness, not ambiguity. The process must have involved some form of casting of lots.[11] This decision-making procedure is analogous to the Greek rationality that distinguished issues into pairs of oppositions or antitheses insofar as it sought a politically expedient "yes" or "no" answer.[12] Yet the request for an oracle asked for a decision from a prophet who probably had not been part of earlier military strategizing. His oracle drew its authority from the divine sphere and not from dialectical reasoning. However, the time for decision in pragmatic matters often requires even the strategist to make an intuitive leap or prudent judgment since empirical data are usually inadequate to predict specific future events. The authority of the strategist in these times of decision making often comes more from his experience and rhetorical skill than from the "objectivity" of his reasoning process.

Since Jehoshaphat asked for a second opinion, he may have been following his own practice in Judah or he may have suspected that Ahab had gathered yes-men as prophets who provided him only with the answers that he sought. In this narrative Micaiah is an outsider, for he experienced opposition not only from Ahab but also from the other court prophets. It is noteworthy how closely Ahab's disdainful attitude toward Micaiah resembles that of Agamemnon toward Calchas. A king's hate for a prophet critical of his actions clearly has features that are not confined to a specific culture.

The narrative of 1 Kings 22 provokes speculation not only about the dynamics of the relationship of a king to his court prophets but also about the way court prophets relate to one another.[13] When Micaiah was summoned, the messenger encouraged Micaiah to give a message like the other court prophets (v. 13), but Micaiah claimed that he would speak only the message he would hear from the Lord. When Micaiah did answer Ahab's question about going into or refraining from battle, he surprisingly gave a response in agreement with the other prophets (v. 15). Then Ahab challenged Micaiah's honesty, which

---

10. E. Ruprecht, "*drš*, fragen nach," in *Theologishes Handworterbuch zum Alten Testament* [= *ThWAT*], 2 vols., ed. E. Jenni and C. Westermann (Munich: Chr. Kaiser Verlag, 1984), 1:468; G. Gerleman, "*š'l*, fragen, bitten," in *ThWAT*, 2:840.

11. Cf. Anne Marie Kitz, "The Hebrew Terminology of Lot Casting and Its Ancient Near Eastern Context," *CBQ* 62 (2000): 214.

12. Vidal-Naquet, *The Black Hunter*, p. 10.

13. Benjamin Uffenheimer, *Early Prophecy in Israel* (Jerusalem: Magnes, 1999), pp. 316-35; Richard Nelson, *First and Second Kings* (Louisville: John Knox, 1987), pp. 145-53; Burke O. Long, *1 Kings with an Introduction to Historical Literature*, FOTL 9 (Grand Rapids: Eerdmans, 1984), p. 236; Nadav Na'aman, "Prophetic Stories as Sources for the Histories of Jehoshaphat and the Omrides," *Bib* 78 (1997): 163-67; DeVries, *Prophet Against Prophet*, pp. 128-29, 145.

is also rather surprising in light of the fact that it is the answer that Ahab sought. Ahab's skepticism toward Micaiah's compliance may simply be a reflex of Ahab's animosity toward Micaiah or an intuition that Micaiah was setting him up for even more negative news — which of course is what happened. In response to Ahab's challenge, Micaiah immediately described a vision he had from the Lord that predicted the death of Ahab if he were to go to battle against Aram: "I saw all of Israel dispersed on the mountains, like sheep that have no shepherd; and the Lord said, 'These have no master! Let each one return home in peace'" (v. 17). Micaiah described another vision (vv. 19-23)[14] that impugned the veracity of Ahab's court prophets. One of these prophets, Zedekiah, then slapped Micaiah for implying that Zedekiah was a lying prophet.[15] Ahab concluded the episode by ordering that Micaiah be imprisoned with little to eat (v. 27). This episode demonstrates how an Israelite prophet, when called upon to deliver an oracle in a time of crisis, was enmeshed in the political and interpersonal dynamics of the decision makers. Here Micaiah and the court prophets were not simply technical specialists who were to deliver oracles when needed but were also participants in a larger rhetorical enterprise by which a king came to terms with the risks of the future.

In the latter part of the eighteenth century B.C. in Mesopotamia, Samsuiluna reported in an inscription associated with the renovation of the E-babbar temple of Shamash in Sippar that he had been successful in suppressing revolts within his kingdom:

> Then eight times within one year, all of the land of Sumer and Akkad that hated me, I killed in battle. The cities that hated me I reduced to tells and ruins. The foundation of the enemies and of the wicked I removed from the land. The whole land I put under my command.[16]

This crisis of rebellion within the kingdom formed the general background for the renovation project that was the main topic of this inscription for the E-babbar temple. This inscription follows the model of building inscriptions established in the Old Akkadian period (ca. 2350-2193 B.C.) where the war deeds of the king were only summarily reported. If such war deeds were the main focus of the inscription, then the inscription took the form of a war report.[17] The claim that Samsuiluna subdued the rebellions within one year reflected a form that was to become a topos of Assyrian inscriptions in the first

---

14. See below on p. 213.
15. Nelson, *First and Second Kings*, p. 149.
16. Douglas Frayne, *RIME 4*, E4.3.7.3, lines 39-54.
17. Franke, *Königsinschriften und Königsideologie*, p. 81.

millennium B.C. where the king's heroic war deeds were typically concentrated in one year. This typological measure of time (other examples include one day, three days, seven days, and three years) served to glorify the king's deeds much more so than dry, chronistic units would have.[18]

Upon successful completion of his military campaign and renovation activities, Samsuiluna claimed that this project had been enjoined upon him by Shamash, who also had been previously commissioned by Enlil to go forward with the project.[19] Samsuiluna praised Enlil as the initiator of the action and identified Shamash as the primary beneficiary. If indeed Samsuiluna received a divine communication inaugurating the project, then such divine commands would have had an oracular, predictive character. Yet in the narrative of the inscription itself, the divine commands appear as fulfilled prophecies whose predictive element lay in the past:

> When Enlil, the king of the gods, the great lord of the lands, looked on Shamash with his kindly face and when by his order, which cannot be changed, he commanded that the wall of Sippar, the eternal city, his sanctuary, be rebuilt, that the E-babbar temple be restored to its former condition, that the top of the ziggurat, his glorious temple tower, be raised on high like the heavens, that Shamash and Aja be brought to their holy residence with joy and happiness, then Shamash, the warrior, the hero, at the great fate which Enlil had determined for Sippar and E-babbar — (all that) became for him like a joyful festival. He (Shamash) then joyfully summoned me, Samsuiluna, the king, the work of his hand, and gave me that order.[20]

The success of the renovation project enhanced the prestige of Samsuiluna and strengthened his image as a ruler in the good graces of the gods Enlil and Shamash. For those cases in which a king believed he had received a divine commission for a project but did not complete it, he would certainly not record such subject matter for lamentation in an inscription. Royal inscriptions celebrate success: they record only those divine communications that the king carried out.[21]

In OB Mesopotamia, communications from the gods through oracles spoken by prophets are attested most prominently at Mari on the upper Euphra-

---

18. Hayim Tadmor, "History and Ideology in the Assyrian Royal Inscriptions," in *Assyrian Royal Inscriptions: New Horizons in Literary, Ideological, and Historical Analysis,* ed. F. M. Fales (Rome: Instituto per L'Oriente, 1981), p. 17.

19. Stephanie Dalley, "The Influence of Mesopotamia upon Israel and the Bible," in *The Legacy of Mesopotamia,* ed. S. Dalley (Oxford: Oxford University Press, 1998), p. 61.

20. Frayne, *RIME 4,* E4.3.7.3, lines 1-38.

21. Franke, *Königsinschriften und Königsideologie,* p. 196.

tes.[22] Abraham Malamat links this intuitive prophecy at Mari, resembling that recorded in the Bible, to the West Semitic Hanaean stratum of the population.[23] An example of such intuitive prophecy is the message which Shibtu,[24] the highest-ranking wife in the harem of king Zimri-Lim (1776-1761 B.C.), secured from a man and a woman concerning an impending battle with Ishme-Dagan, king at Ekallatum:

> For a message on the campaign which my lord is on, I waited for the signs. I asked a man and a woman for the signs. And the message is very favorable to my lord. Likewise for Ishme-Dagan I asked the man and the woman, and the word on him is not favorable. And as to the message for him, he has been placed under the foot of my lord. Thus they said: "My lord lifted up a tight hold upon Ishme-Dagan and said: 'I will overpower you with the tight hold; wrestle and I will overpower you in wrestling.'" Then I said: "Will my lord go to battle?" Thus they said: "A battle will not be fought. Right at (his) arrival, his support troops will be scattered. Then when the head of Ishme-Dagan is cut off, it will be placed under my lord's foot." (*ARM* X, 4:3-27)[25]

The oracles for the king typically addressed times of crisis and dealt with practical ways to navigate problems.[26] Prophets usually received oracles in a sanctuary and then functioned as messengers for the god to the king. Then royal deputies, accountable to the king, were responsible for conveying the message from the prophet to the king.[27] In any case, the king required that oracles be written

22. Simon Parker, "Official Attitudes Toward Prophecy at Mari and in Israel," *VT* 43 (1993): 50-51. On the Neo-Assyrian corpus of prophetic utterances, see Maria de Jong Ellis, "Mesopotamian Oracles and Prophetic Texts," *JCS* 41.2 (1989): 130-31; Herbert Huffmon, "A Company of Prophets: Mari, Assyria, Israel," pp. 47-70, and Karel van der Toorn, "Mesopotamian Prophecy between Immanence and Transcendence: A Comparison of Old Babylonian and Neo-Assyrian Prophecy," pp. 71-87, and Martti Nissinen, "The Socioreligious Role of the Neo-Assyrian Prophets," pp. 89-114, all in *Prophecy in Its Ancient Near Eastern Context: Mesopotamian, Biblical, and Arabian Perspectives*, SBL Symposium Series 13 (Atlanta: SBL, 2000).

23. Abraham Malamat, *Mari and the Bible* (Leiden: Brill, 1998), pp. 60-61; cf. Beate Pongratz-Leisten, *Herrschaftswissen in Mesopotamien*, SAAS 10 (Helsinki: Neo-Assyrian Text Corpus Project, 1999), pp. 48-49.

24. P. Artzi and A. Malamat, "The Correspondence of Šibtu, Queen of Mari in ARM X," *Or* n.s. 40 (1971): 75-76.

25. The text is from Georges Dossin, *Archives royales de Mari, X: Textes cunéiformes du Louvre XXVI, La correspondance féminine* (Paris: Imprimatur nationale, 1967), pp. 24-26. See also William L. Moran, "New Evidence from Mari on the History of Prophecy," *Bib* 56 (1969): 46-47.

26. Pongratz-Leisten, *Herrschaftswissen in Mesopotamien*, pp. 50, 63.

27. Karel van der Toorn, "Old Babylonian Prophecy between the Written and the Oral," *JNSL* 24 (1998): 57-62.

and submitted to him.[28] It is noteworthy that in *ARM* XXVI, 206:11-14 and 13:32-33 oracles were given at the city gate and before the assembly of the elders where reception of the oracle by this audience was probably a factor in the formulation of the oracle. Royal control in these instances did not require secrecy.[29] Usually a prophet had to deliver an oracle in support of the king; otherwise, the oracle was regarded as false. If, however, the prophet functioned in a sanctuary outside the direct influence of the king, oracles critical of the king arose.[30]

In critical situations with pressing dangers or potentially high risk to the well-being of the community, kings in Homeric Greece, biblical Israel, and ancient Mesopotamia sought divine assistance in the form of oracles or other means of communication with the divine so that good order might be restored to their communities. Prophets functioned within communities whose identities were shaped through interaction with the divine world. The image of the people as sheep who were cared for by the king of the gods and his representative in the person of the earthly king was recurrent in ancient Mesopotamia and biblical Israel and appeared in the Homeric world, even if less directly. There was a belief that the divine world had a vital interest in these earthly communities and could, under normal circumstances, be expected to intervene in the communities' affairs. The prophets built upon the communal belief that the gods not only were concerned for but also had particular wishes and expectations for the community. Thus, the Homeric prophet Calchas explained the plague among the Achaeans as a consequence of Agamemnon's dishonoring Chryses, the priest of Apollo. The Israelite prophet Micaiah ben-Imlah predicted Ahab's demise in an approaching battle against Aram. The OB king Samsuiluna claimed to have received divine communications to renovate Shamash's temple: an action he was able to accomplish after Shamash assisted him in quelling revolts in outlying areas of his land.

The act of communicating oracular responses should ideally be a matter of repeating to the human audience what a god has stated.[31] However, in the cases of the Homeric seer Calchas and the Israelite prophet Micaiah ben-Imlah, the narratives make clear that the way in which the human audience received the divine message had a marked impact on the content and shape of the commu-

---

28. Pongratz-Leisten, *Herrschaftswissen in Mesopotamien*, p. 66.

29. Pongratz-Leisten, *Herrschaftswissen in Mesopotamien*, p. 65; van der Toorn, "Old Babylonian Prophecy," p. 63.

30. Pongratz-Leisten, *Herrschaftswissen in Mesopotamien*, pp. 72-73. Moran, "New Evidence from Mari," pp. 18-21; Malamat, *Mari and the Bible*, p. 71; Ellis, "Mesopotamian Oracles and Prophetic Texts," pp. 134-37; Parker, "Official Attitudes Toward Prophecy," pp. 64-65.

31. Vernant, *Mortals and Immortals*, p. 314.

nication.[32] The audience's reception of a prophet's oracle, like the people's reception of a king's declarations and commands (cf. *Il.* 2.80-83), was an important factor in the power and effectiveness of the oracle in the deliberations of the king and the community. Wherever possible, it seems that the king tried to influence the kind of message a prophet would deliver. Even though the Mari texts do not raise the issue of the way the audiences' expectation influenced the shape and content of the divine message, the king's practice of having a diviner test oracles by means of extispicy and the fact that only those oracles favorable to the king were preserved demonstrate that a filtering process was operative among the Mari prophets.[33]

Divine Communication: A Glimpse into the Future

Discernment of the divine will and of the truth intended by the gods was a crucial activity shrouded in ambiguity. In biblical Israel and Homeric Greece, the fear was widespread that no one could look upon God or the gods without serious, near fatal consequences.[34] In Mesopotamia, the awesome, numinous character of the gods was augmented when they came to be imagined according to a royal model.[35] The need to find out the divine will was all-encompassing and did not rest simply with selected officials of the temple and palace or notable figures within the leading households.[36] The paradoxical closeness and elusiveness of God or the gods challenged prophets, kings, and other recipients of divine communications to speak with and about these gods and yet refrain from co-opting them through humanly constructed images and schemes.

The Homeric gods became manifest to humans obliquely.[37] Their luminos-

---

32. Cf. Robert Wilson, *Prophecy and Society in Ancient Israel* (Philadelphia: Fortress, 1980), pp. 86-88; Pucci, *The Song of the Sirens,* p. 190; Jack Sasson, "Water Beneath the Straw: Adventures of a Prophetic Phrase in the Mari Archives," in *Solving Riddles and Untying Knots: Biblical, Epigraphic, and Semitic Studies in Honor of Jonas C. Greenfield,* ed. Z. Zevit et al. (Winona Lake, Ind.: Eisenbrauns, 1995), p. 607.

33. Moran, "New Evidence from Mari," pp. 20-23; Malamat, *Mari and the Bible,* p. 79; Parker, "Official Attitudes Toward Prophecy," pp. 63-64.

34. Vernant, *Mortals and Immortals,* pp. 42-45. See Gen. 16:13; 32:30; Exod. 20:19; Judg. 6:22-23; Isa. 6:5.

35. Thorkild Jacobsen, *The Treasures of Darkness: A History of Mesopotamian Religion* (New Haven: Yale University Press, 1976), pp. 79-80; Karel van der Toorn, *Family Religion in Babylonia, Syria and Israel* (Leiden: Brill, 1996), p. 136.

36. Bottéro, *Mesopotamia,* p. 124; van der Toorn, *Family Religion in Babylonia, Syria and Israel,* pp. 136-38.

37. Vernant (*Mortals and Immortals,* pp. 42-44) notes that Homeric gods have a body, but

ity or terrible qualities could not meet the human eye directly without causing blindness (*Il.* 20.131).[38] The most explicit epiphany of a god in the *Iliad* was that of Athena, who stood behind Achilles and restrained him from killing Agamemnon (*Il.* 1.193-214). Pietro Pucci notes that "Athena seizes Achilles by the shoulders from behind, from that anterior space in which the future, for Homeric man, is symbolically situated (*Il.* 12.34; *Od.* 22.55; etc.)."[39] Because of this act of restraint, the unquenched anger of Achilles was allowed to burn on and unfold itself as the central element of the plot of the *Iliad.*[40] Athena's distinctness from Achilles as she seized him was confrontational; she was making him move toward a future that Achilles was not aware of and would have avoided if given the chance. And yet Athena, the patron of Achilles, also merged with Achilles in this passage so that it is ambiguous in the phrase "the terrible eyes shining" (*Il.* 1.200) whether the eyes belonged to Athena or Achilles.[41] This epiphany of Athena exemplified the way that the gods entered into human awareness in the Homeric world. The intervention of the gods had an impact on the motivation and accountability of the Homeric character; some things happened the way they did because of factors beyond the consciousness and control of the human actor.[42] Achilles even suggests that Zeus may have had a role in moving Agamemnon to retake Briseis from him (*Il.* 9.377; cf. 2.111).[43] Even though prophets like Calchas were called upon in critical situations to provide an interpretation of the divine intentions for the community as a whole, the individual Homeric characters were tuned into the unpredictable ways that the gods could manifest themselves in their experience. The more important aspect of the Homeric gods was their action of manifesting themselves within human experience rather than their existence in an invisible realm of superhuman splendor.[44]

Within the narrative world of the *Iliad,* Achilles' future was set from the opening scene of his quarrel with Agamemnon. His destiny was foretold by his mother, the goddess Thetis:

---

they conceal themselves when making corporeal appearances (e.g., *Il.* 1.197-200; 3.373-82; 13.62-65, 70-72).

38. Pucci, *The Song of the Sirens,* p. 70; Vernant, *Mortals and Immortals,* p. 44.

39. Pucci, *The Song of the Sirens,* p. 73.

40. Gregory Nagy, *Greek Mythology and Poetics* (Ithaca: Cornell University Press, 1990), pp. 221-22; Pucci, *The Song of the Sirens,* p. 197.

41. Pucci, *The Song of the Sirens,* pp. 73-74; cf. G. I. C. Robertson, "The Eyes of Achilleus: *Iliad* 1.200," *Phoenix* 53 (1999): 1-7.

42. Margalit Finkelberg, *The Birth of Literary Fiction in Ancient Greece* (Oxford: Clarendon, 1998), pp. 36-37, 40.

43. Pucci, *The Song of the Sirens,* pp. 186-87, 201-2.

44. Pucci, *The Song of the Sirens,* p. 76; Vernant, *Mortals and Immortals,* pp. 35-36.

Oh my! My child, giving birth to you was a calamity! Why did I raise you? If only you could remain by the ships, safe and without tears, since your apportioned life span is very short, not long at all. Now you are fated both for an early death and for misery beyond all humans. To a bad destiny, I gave birth to you in my quarters. (*Il.* 1.414-18)

In this oracular foretelling of Achilles' future, it is revealed that Achilles' life was programmed from the outset.[45] Because of his identity and the order of things, his life had to follow a particular course. True to himself, Achilles wanted the truth about the dishonor shown him by Agamemnon to come fully into the light, and so he implored Thetis to go to Zeus, her father, with the following harsh, vindictive request:

Now sit next to him and grasp his knees as you remind him of these matters in light of how he might plan to assist the Trojans and to hem in the Achaeans against the sterns of their ships and the sea as they are killed so that all might reap the fruits of their king and that the son of Atreus, Agamemnon, lord of far-reaching lands, might realize his blindness in that he did not treat the best of the Achaeans with respect. (*Il.* 1.407-12)

Thetis presented Achilles' request to Zeus, who did not answer her at first. When Thetis reiterated her request, she linked it to her honor among the gods. Christos Tsagalis argues that this framing of the request in terms of a "politics of honor" led Zeus to see the struggle between Agamemnon and Achilles as analogous to his own struggles with his rivals.[46] And so, though troubled and hesitant, Zeus granted her request. He signaled his decision by a nod of his head, which shook all of Olympus (*Il.* 1.511-30).

Within the narrative world of the *Iliad*, the plot of the *Iliad* is to be identified with the will of Zeus, where the many deaths caused by this tragic war cannot simply be traced back to the arrogance of Agamemnon or the anger of Achilles. Because Achilles had won the support of Zeus, his own anger and withdrawal from the Achaeans did not incur reciprocal anger from the gods or other humans.[47] At key points in the plot, the action is directed by the interweaving of Zeus's will with human motivation.[48] For example, the decisions

45. Pucci, *The Song of the Sirens*, pp. 227-29; Vernant, *Mortals and Immortals*, p. 314; Kevin Crotty, *The Poetics of Supplication: Homer's Iliad and Odyssey* (Ithaca: Cornell University Press, 1994), pp. 16-17, 159.

46. Christos Tsagalis, "Style and Construction, Sound and Rhythm: Thetis' Supplication to Zeus (*Iliad* 1.493-516)," *Arethusa* 34 (2001): 24.

47. Muellner, *The Anger of Achilles*, p. 121.

48. Pucci, *The Song of the Sirens*, p. 19, n. 20.

made by Agamemnon and Achilles had a far-reaching impact on the lives of thousands of Achaeans and Trojans alike (*Il.* 1.1-7), and yet the course of events was a reality far beyond the control of either of these human characters.[49]

The first of the three accounts of Saul's election to the kingship of Israel (1 Sam. 9:1–10:16; see also 10:17-27; 11:5-15) relates that Saul was searching for his father's lost donkeys and asked the seer Samuel for assistance.[50] Samuel, having been directed by the Lord to anoint Saul king of Israel (9:15-17), honored Saul at a banquet (9:22-24), anointed him ruler *(nāgîd)* on the following morning (10:1), and predicted two events as signs confirming his divine election: (1) Saul would encounter three men on their way to Bethel with gifts for him (10:3-4), and (2) Saul would meet an ecstatic band of prophets at Gibeath-elohim, and in their company the spirit of the Lord would take possession of him (10:5-6). This account highlights the divine initiative in the selection of Saul for the kingship and Saul's humility and freedom from ambition (9:21).[51]

The Lord's communication with Samuel on the day before Saul's arrival is described as: "the Lord uncovered the ear of Samuel" (1 Sam. 9:15). When Saul arrived, the text reads: "and Samuel saw Saul and the Lord let him know:[52] 'Here is the man about whom I told you: this one will rule over my people'" (9:17). Samuel alone was aware of the Lord's presence and of his communicating this message to him. The form of divination engaged in here was "intuitive": the Lord spoke within Samuel's mind.[53] Prior to this revelation, Samuel had been singled out and identified as "the man of God" (*'îš hā'elōhîm*, 9:8) and as a "seer" (*rō'eh*, 9:11), for he had gained a reputation in his village and among the tribe of Benjamin for his capacity to communicate with God (9:6).

The narrative of 1 Sam 9:1–10:16 portrayed Samuel as a seer who was granted knowledge that was hidden from ordinary humans. Samuel promised Saul that he would inform him of what was on his mind and then added that the donkeys belonging to Saul's father had already been found (9:19-20). Samuel's capacity to see beyond appearances was initially employed in this narrative to solve Saul's

---

49. Bruce Heiden, "The Ordeals of Homeric Song," *Arethusa* 30 (1997): 226-27.

50. Bruce Birch, "The Development of the Tradition on the Anointing of Saul in 1 Sam 9:1–10:16," *JBL* 90 (1971): 55-68; P. Kyle McCarter, Jr., *I Samuel*, AB 8 (Garden City, N.Y.: Doubleday, 1980), pp. 172-88; Walter Brueggemann, *First and Second Samuel* (Louisville: John Knox, 1990), pp. 69-78.

51. Wilson, *Prophecy and Society in Ancient Israel*, pp. 177-78; Brueggemann, *First and Second Samuel*, pp. 73-74; McCarter, *I Samuel*, pp. 185-86.

52. Hebrew *'ānâ* literally means "answer."

53. Klaus Koch, *The Prophets*, vol. 1: *The Assyrian Period* (Philadelphia: Fortress, 1983), p. 9; Wilson, *Prophecy and Society in Ancient Israel*, pp. 83-85, 175-78; Brueggemann, *First and Second Samuel*, pp. 72-73.

immediate problem of finding his father's donkeys, but this only set the stage for its more important function of predicting Saul's future role as king of Israel. The two signs Samuel gave to confirm Saul's divine election involved the prediction of specific events that were usually unpredictable in such detail. The narrative promotes the belief that in the divine realm the future is known before it occurs on earth.[54] The seer Samuel is portrayed as one who was granted portions of such divine knowledge to communicate to the Israelites.[55]

The second sign, which indicated that Saul would meet a prophetic band near Gibeath-elohim, was confirmed when Saul not only met them but also fell into a prophetic trance with them (1 Sam 10:10-13). The merging of the divine with the human in a trance suggested not only empowerment but also transformation: "God turned over another heart for him [Saul]" (10:9). Such possession behavior was unusual for kings; however, it finds an echo in the experience of the judges who were seized by the "spirit of God" (rûah 'ĕlōhîm, Judg. 3:10; 11:29; 13:25).[56] The sign, once confirmed, supported the view that in the divine realm the future is known. At gifted moments, the seer Samuel was portrayed as capable of transcending some constraints of time to get a glimpse of the future.

In an inscription of Samsuiluna of Babylon, the following phrases and epithets were attributed to Enlil, the king of the gods: "the one whose power is supreme among the gods, the shepherd who determines fates . . . the one whose command cannot be reversed, whose decrees once made cannot be changed."[57] In the divine economy of Mesopotamia, Enlil's decrees were of supreme value. He was believed to determine fates or destinies (mušīm šīmātim), which meant that he had primary control over the future.[58] In cities within the land of Sumer and Akkad where Nippur was the religious center in the OB period, the royal inscriptions typically identified Enlil as the one who had decreed a king's reign and had commissioned, among other tasks, a particular building project.

The first-person narrative form of an inscription made the point that it was the king, not a prophet, who had received a divine communication from

---

54. Koch, *The Prophets*, 1:5, 7-10, 18, 152-53; idem, "The Language of Prophecy," in *Problems in Biblical Theology: Essays in Honor of Rolf Knierim*, ed. H. T. C. Sun et al. (Grand Rapids: Eerdmans, 1997), pp. 218-21; Simon DeVries, *From Old Revelation to New* (Grand Rapids: Eerdmans, 1995), pp. 14-15.

55. Koch, *The Prophets*, 1:18; Peter Miscall, *1 Samuel: A Literary Reading* (Bloomington: Indiana University Press, 1986), p. 60.

56. Brueggemann, *First and Second Samuel*, pp. 75-76. Miscall (*1 Samuel*, p. 62) interprets this possession behavior as negative or demonic in light of 1 Sam. 18:10.

57. Frayne, *RIME 4*, E4.3.7.7, lines 1-3, 17-20; see also E4.3.7.3, lines 22-23; E4.3.6.2, lines 21-22.

58. Bottéro, *Mesopotamia*, pp. 124, 237.

Enlil. The communication between the king and the gods was an integral element of the king's learning and decision making in his realm.[59] If the inscription commemorated a building project carried out on behalf of another deity, then Enlil was portrayed as a distant overseer with minimal attachment to the king. For those projects that directly benefited Enlil, the inscriptions suggested the existence of a closer relationship between Enlil and the king. For example, Hammurapi identified himself as "the favorite of Enlil" (*migir* *^{d}Enlil*)[60] in an inscription commemorating his construction of a storeroom for Enlil and Ninlil. After building a canal for the land of Sumer and Akkad, Hammurapi referred to himself as "the favorite of the great gods" (*migir ilī rabûtim* [*DINGER.GAL.GAL*]).[61]

Enlil's character as developed in the Mesopotamian myths was ambiguous.[62] Claus Wilcke describes Enlil as the opposite of an ideal king, for he was neither a proven warrior nor one concerned about justice in the community.[63] In the *Atraḫasis Epic,* Enlil became upset with humans who had multiplied upon the earth:

> The land was making an uproar like a bull,
> The gods were upset at their commotion.
> Enlil heard their shouts
> And declared to the great gods,
> "The shouts of humanity have become too painful for me,
> With their commotion I am robbed of sleep.
> Sever the food supplies for the peoples,
> For their hunger, let vegetation diminish." (II, i:3-10)[64]

Enlil's decree of a famine was the second of three strategies that he devised to reduce the vitality of humans (II, i:9-10). Earlier he had tried to reduce their numbers with a plague (I, vii:360). His final effort was a flood (II, vii:44-52; II, viii:34-35). In light of this ethically ambiguous image of Enlil, it is understandable that the Mesopotamian kings usually pictured the communication

59. Pongratz-Leisten, *Herrschaftswissen in Mesopotamien,* p. 5.

60. Frayne, *RIME 4,* E4.3.6.3, line 7.

61. Frayne, *RIME 4,* E4.3.6.7, line 41.

62. Jacobsen, *The Treasures of Darkness,* p. 101; Piotr Michalowski, "The Unbearable Lightness of Enlil," in *Intellectual Life of the Ancient Near East,* ed. Jirí Prosecký, CRRA 43 (Prague: Oriental Institute, 1998), pp. 243-44; Gwendolyn Leick, "Enlil," in *A Dictionary of Ancient Near Eastern Mythology* (New York: Routledge, 1991), p. 46.

63. Wilcke, "Politik im Spiegel der Literatur," p. 70.

64. W. G. Lambert and A. R. Millard, *Atra-ḫasīs: The Babylonian Story of the Flood* (Winona Lake, Ind.: Eisenbrauns, 1999), p. 73.

process with Enlil as one in which a distant divine sovereign issued decrees rather than one in which a protector deity stood near and watched over the king.[65]

The communities of Homeric Greece, biblical Israel, and ancient Mesopotamia assumed that the gods knew the future. The communication of divine knowledge of the future to humans was unpredictable and often ambiguous. The intervention of Athena to stay Achilles' hand against Agamemnon exemplified the Homeric view that the gods manifested themselves as powers within human actions and experience. The divine intervention was a serious matter in the narrative world of the *Iliad:* the story could not have continued without it.[66] Yet the narrative also represented human experiences in the Greek world of the first millennium B.C. in which unexplainable turns of fortune occurred. The narrative provided an explanation. The revelation of Achilles' fate was in accord with the prevailing view in the Homeric world that one was given an allotted time to live *(moira)*.[67] In Achilles' case, this fate was revealed fully to him by Thetis; for most Homeric characters, it was a matter of uncovering one's fate bit by bit in the course of life.[68] In Saul's life, his encounter with the seer Samuel was marked by a sense of mystery: Samuel's actions indicated that more was going on than met the eye. Samuel's anointing conferred on Saul the position of *nāgîd* ("leader"), one designated to become a *melek* ("king").[69] The signs that Samuel gave were meant to confirm *Saul's* appointment but also to validate the authorizing words and actions of Samuel. In the narrative of 1 Samuel 9–10, the power of the divine communication was convincing, but what it actually meant for Saul still remained to be spelled out. In Mesopotamia, one sought knowledge of one's fate from the gods by deciphering signs, omens, oracles, or various ways in which the gods communicated their will to humans.[70] The king of the gods Enlil decreed destinies. The light and shadow in his character perhaps reflected the mixed character of human experience in which the balance between

---

65. Cf. van der Toorn, *Family Religion in Babylonia, Syria and Israel,* pp. 136-38.

66. Heiden, "The Ordeals of Homeric Song," pp. 224-25.

67. A. W. H. Adkins, "Values, Goals, and Emotions in the *Iliad,*" *Classical Philology* 77 (1982): 300; Pucci, *The Song of the Sirens,* pp. 227-29; Vernant, *Mortals and Immortals,* p. 314; Crotty, *The Poetics of Supplication,* pp. 16-17, 159.

68. Vernant, *Mortals and Immortals,* p. 314.

69. Baruch Halpern, *The Constitution of the Monarchy in Israel,* HSM 25 (Chico, Calif.: Scholars, 1981), pp. 4-6; idem, "Uneasy Compromise: Israel between League and Monarchy," in *Traditions in Transformation,* ed. B. Halpern and J. Levenson (Winona Lake, Ind.: Eisenbrauns, 1981), p. 72.

70. Bottéro, *Mesopotamia,* pp. 127, 136; Stephanie Dalley, "Occasions and Opportunities. 1. To the Persian Conquest," in *The Legacy of Mesopotamia,* ed. S. Dalley (Oxford: Oxford University Press, 1998), p. 20; Pongratz-Leisten, *Herrschaftswissen in Mesopotamien,* pp. 12-14.

good and ill fortune was always in question. It is significant that these ancient peoples believed that divine communication actually occurred, and so they were attentive to divine signs wherever they might appear. Their response to anxiety over the future was to find as many clues as possible about the future from God or the gods.

Discernment of the Truth of Divine Communications

Leaders must make decisions for their communities even when they are anxious about the outcome, and so they undertake various means to increase their confidence that they are making the right choice. In the high risk venture of war, Jehoshaphat of Judah requested that oracles be secured signaling divine approval. In Homer, the seer was regarded as a *dēmiourgos*, a professional like a doctor, a carpenter, or a bard; when his services were needed, he would be summoned to the household.[71] The search for oracular knowledge was common in Israel and Homeric Greece. In Mesopotamia, however, the use of other means of divination, including extispicy and hepatoscopy, was more frequent.[72] The capacity of an oracle to increase the confidence of the leader depended upon the authority granted to oracles and those who pronounced them. The authority of those who communicated oracles and other forms of divine communication was significantly shaped by the traditions and expectations of the community as well as by the struggles for power and prestige within the community.

Divine communications are by their very nature ambiguous, even in those situations where the human party longs for clear directives.[73] When a decision needed to be made so that the community might act, the leaders often framed the issue as a question requiring a "yes" or a "no" answer. For those issues that were less urgent and called for a response that applied long-term and shaped the worldview of the community, the divine communication could have been formulated with a lengthy discursive (e.g., epics, myths, poems), but it needed to be intelligible within the traditions of the community. The plot of the epic narrative, as demonstrated later by the fourth-century B.C. orator Isocrates, provided a more supple framework within which the nuances of political rela-

---

71. Vernant, *Mortals and Immortals*, p. 305; Peter W. Rose, *Sons of the Gods, Children of Earth: Ideology and Literary Form in Ancient Greece* (Ithaca: Cornell University Press, 1992), p. 113; cf. Finkelberg, *The Birth of Literary Fiction*, p. 101.

72. Bottéro, *Mesopotamia*, pp. 125-26; Joseph Blenkinsopp, *A History of Prophecy in Israel*, rev. ed. (Louisville: Westminster/John Knox, 1996), p. 32.

73. Vidal-Naquet, *The Black Hunter*, p. 257.

tionships could be unfolded than that afforded by genres whose purpose was to advise and admonish rulers.[74] The tradition could provide a framework and pointers for discerning the truth of the communication purporting to be from the divine realm. Even with the rise of the critical spirit in the sixth and fifth centuries B.C., Heraclitus still wrote in a style that has been characterized as oracular.[75] It was the orator-politicians of the fourth century who made a concerted effort to create a form of discourse based on rational foundations free from traditional religious and historical concerns.[76] They moved the battle line between poetry and prose so as to expand the sphere of prose. In contrast, contemporary literary theorists such as Derrida and Barthes, with their emphasis upon the ceaseless play of the signifier in prose as well as poetry, have moved the battle line back strongly in favor of poetry.[77]

The singer of the Homeric poems appealed to a goddess at the beginning of the *Iliad* and to the Muse at the beginning of the *Odyssey* for assistance in performing these traditional poems. The performance of the poetry of these epics was regarded as inspired, whereas later recitations of prose compositions were not.[78] In the *Iliad*, prior to the recitation of "The Catalogue of Ships" (*Il.* 2.494-877), the singer appealed to the Muses as follows:

> Tell me now, you Muses who reside on Olympus — for you are goddesses and are not only present to but also know all things, but we hear only hearsay *(kleos)* and do not know anything — who were the commanders and leaders of the Danaans. I could not describe or name the multitude even if I had ten tongues and ten mouths and a tireless voice and a will of bronze, unless the Muses of Olympus, daughters of aegis-bearing Zeus, remember all the ones who came beneath Ilios. I will now describe the leaders of the ships and all the ships. (*Il.* 2.484-93)

The task of "narrating the memory" *(mythos)* of the heroes of Troy was a process of keeping the truth alive for the community. The Greek term *alētheia,* "truth," is in effect a double negative: "not *(a-)* forgetting *(lēth-)*," where "for-

---

74. Claude Calame, "The Rhetoric of *Muthos* and *Logos*," in *From Myth to Reason?* ed. Richard Buxton (Oxford: Clarendon, 1999), p. 128.

75. Lloyd, *Methods and Problems in Greek Science,* p. 133.

76. Oswyn Murray, "Cities of Reason," in *The Greek City from Homer to Alexander,* ed. O. Murray and S. Price (Oxford: Clarendon, 1990), p. 17.

77. Cf. Jürgen Habermas, "On the Distinction between Poetic and Communicative Uses of Language," in *On the Pragmatics of Communication* (Cambridge, Mass.: MIT Press, 1998), pp. 393-94.

78. Richard Buxton, *Imaginary Greece* (Cambridge: Cambridge University Press, 1994), p. 37; Finkelberg, *The Birth of Literary Fiction,* pp. 6-9.

getting" is the negative of "remembering."[79] The Muses who "know all things" were regarded as transcending time, for they could communicate knowledge about past, present, and future events.[80] The singer called upon the Muses to help him repeat the list of the heroes of the Trojan War as well as other data about their ships. The challenge to the memory to repeat such a list would have been formidable. However, in the context of the entire Iliadic epic, memory here involved more than the mere retrieval of the names of the heroes; it also called for re-creating the griefs of these heroes so that the audiences might share in that dimension of the Trojan War.[81]

If the Muses were with the singer each time he sang the poem, then the song would achieve its purpose of proclaiming the "glory" *(kleos)* of the heroes and not mere "hearsay" (*kleos*, *Il.* 2.486).[82] However, *kleos* is not used in the pejorative sense in Homer.[83] If this play on words with *kleos* was heard by audiences in Archaic Greece, perhaps it pointed to the tendency of poetry to embrace the rich interplay between language and being where a single meaning did not capture the polyvalent reality to which it referred. In the performance of Homer, poetry was a means for communicating the essential ideas of the heroic tradition to contemporary audiences. The reality of the heroic age, in its richness, was kept alive by the memory of essential ideas that were repeated and unfolded in their polyvalent significance through engagement with the audience.[84]

The Muses are pictured as divine beings who seem to have been asked to help the singer faithfully communicate the knowledge about the Trojan War *wie es eigentlich gewesen*.[85] If the request were answered, the assistance of the

79. Marcel Detienne, *Masters of Truth in Archaic Greece* (New York: Zone Books, 1999), pp. 48-52; Gregory Nagy (*Homeric Questions* [Austin: University of Texas Press, 1996], pp. 125-27) notes that "*muthos* and *alētheia* are not opposites in Homer; in Pindar, they are opposed." When *alētheia* ("truth") became marked over against *mythos*, *mythos* not only was interpreted as "false" but also lost its original force as "authoritative utterance."

80. Pucci, *The Song of the Sirens*, p. 36; Buxton, *Imaginary Greece*, pp. 170-72.

81. Crotty, *The Poetics of Supplication*, p. xii; Egbert Bakker, "Storytelling in the Future: Truth, Time, and Tense in Homeric Epic," in *Written Voices, Spoken Signs: Tradition, Performance, and the Epic Text*, ed. E. Bakker and A. Kahane (Cambridge, Mass.: Harvard University Press, 1997), p. 11.

82. Pucci, *The Song of the Sirens*, p. 40.

83. Finkelberg, *The Birth of Literary Fiction*, p. 75.

84. Ian Morris, "The Use and Abuse of Homer," *Classical Antiquity* 5 (1986): 84-88; Pucci, *The Song of the Sirens*, p. 36; Walter Nicolai, "Gefolgschaftsverweigerung als politisches Druckmittel in der Ilias," in *Anfänge politischen Denkens in der Antike: Die nahöstlichen Kulturen und die Griechen*, ed. K. Raaflaub and E. Müller-Luckner (Munich: Oldenbourg, 1993), p. 328; Charles Segal, *Singers, Heroes, and Gods in the Odyssey* (Ithaca: Cornell University Press, 1994), pp. 130-41.

85. This phrase, "as it actually happened," was used by the nineteenth-century German his-

Muses would have freed the singer and his audience from the play of the signifier so that they could then reside securely within the fully signified.[86] According to this model, it was the singer's task to repeat, not to adapt, the tradition.[87] So, as the Homeric singer recited "The Catalogue of Ships," he would have been a channel of divine knowledge.[88] Here the Muses were asked to ensure that this basic core was preserved.[89]

The communication of knowledge free from the limitations of the human boundedness of time is impossible, yet humans often strive for a glimpse of such absolute knowledge so that it might provide benchmarks for bringing order into their worlds.[90] If memories can simply be heard and not stand in need of interpretation, then, it is contended, we stand closer to the truth.[91] This urge for timeless, unchanging knowledge resembles that of fundamentalists who want the basic truths with the subjective interpretations cordoned off. Yet in the Homeric world such a guarantee was a chimera, for the Muses could give lies to those to whom they were reluctant to tell the truth. It was only after Homer and Hesiod that the Muses were viewed as divine beings incapable of telling lies.[92]

What happens though if we listen to the Muses, get drawn into their world, and then begin asking questions of their world from the inside? A community must first remember the configuration of the plot of its story of the past if it is to reconfigure it for the present.[93] The stories of the tradition create a fabric within which new stories and divine communications can be interwoven. Margalit Finkelberg argues that the bard was responsible for remembering the *oimē*, "the pathway (of a story)" or its essential plot; then the Muses were called upon to guide the bard in the detailed creation of the epic story.[94] Once the au-

---

torian Leopold von Ranke ("The Historian's Craft," in *The Secret of World History: Selected Writings on the Art and Science of History*, ed. Roger Wines [New York: Fordham University Press, 1981], p. 58) to describe his method of empirically analyzing sources in an effort to recover the past.

86. Pucci, *The Song of the Sirens*, p. 46.

87. Cf. Finkelberg, *The Birth of Literary Fiction*, pp. 25-27.

88. Gregory Nagy, "Ancient Greek Poetry, Prophecy, and Concepts of Theory," in *Poetry and Prophecy*, ed. J. Kugel (Ithaca: Cornell University Press, 1990), p. 56.

89. Cf. Finkelberg, *The Birth of Literary Fiction*, p. 71; Claude Calame, *The Craft of Poetic Speech in Ancient Greece* (Ithaca: Cornell University Press, 1995), pp. 66, 71.

90. Paul Ricoeur, *Time and Narrative*, vol. 3 (Chicago: University of Chicago Press, 1985), pp. 202, 205-6; cf. Finkelberg, *The Birth of Literary Fiction*, p. 98.

91. Pucci, *The Song of the Sirens*, p. 46; Segal, *Singers, Heroes, and Gods*, p. 139.

92. Finkelberg, *The Birth of Literary Fiction*, pp. 157-59.

93. Paul Ricoeur, *Time and Narrative*, vol. 2 (Chicago: University of Chicago Press, 1985), p. 160; idem, *Time and Narrative*, 3:118-19.

94. Finkelberg, *The Birth of Literary Fiction*, pp. 51, 69.

dience was engaged by the plot and found its imagination caught up in the story, then it would have had to discern what was true and what was false for its particular community — a discernment that would have had to move within the play of signifiers: that is, the interplay of plural possible meanings of the reality signified.[95]

When Micaiah ben-Imlah went against the tide of opinion among Ahab's prophets and indicated that the Lord would not bring victory to Ahab and Jehoshaphat against the king of Aram, he communicated his message in the form of two visions. The first vision (1 Kings 22:17) was discussed earlier.[96] The second vision describes a scene in the Lord's heavenly court that brought into judgment the prophetic activity in the court of Ahab:

> Then he [Micaiah] said, "Therefore, hear the word of the Lord: I saw the Lord sitting upon his throne and all the heavenly attendants were standing near him to his right and to his left. And the Lord said, 'Who will deceive Ahab so that he goes up and falls at Ramoth-gilead?' One said this and another said that. Then the spirit came forth and stood before the Lord and said, 'I will deceive him.' And the Lord said, 'By what means?' He replied, 'I will go forth and become a lying spirit in the mouth of all his prophets.' Then the Lord said, 'You will deceive him and also prevail; go forth and do so.' So now, the Lord has placed a lying spirit in the mouth of all these prophets of yours. The Lord has spoken evil against you." (1 Kings 22:19-23)

The genre of the vision report signaled the reader to move beyond the constraints of the human world into the divine realm where authoritative words were enacted without hesitation.[97] The power of authoritative divine words was highlighted through the scene of the enthroned Lord with all the heavenly beings gathered around him. The shocking element in this scene was the depiction of the Lord as one who authorized false oracles for Yahwistic prophets as a way of bringing judgment against Ahab. The Lord's plan to send forth a lying spirit to trick Ahab into going into battle would have placed in doubt the indicators of spirit possession to which Ahab's prophets were accustomed. This vision revealed the possibility that a Yahwistic prophet could honestly have spoken the word of the Lord, yet that word may have brought judgment rather than success.

In this visionary scene, the Lord reformed the understanding of Yahwistic

---

95. Pucci, *The Song of the Sirens*, p. 48; Segal, *Singers, Heroes, and Gods*, pp. 140-41.

96. See p. 198 of this chapter.

97. Long, *1 Kings with an Introduction to Historical Literature*, pp. 238, 263-64; DeVries, *Prophet Against Prophet*, pp. 43-45.

prophecy to which Ahab's prophets had been accustomed by pointing out that first of all the prophet was a messenger from the Lord and not an adviser to the earthly king.[98] What appeared to be a lying spirit from the perspective of Ahab was a spirit in service of the Lord's truth. In this scene, the Lord used deception in order to bring judgment against Ahab. It thus appears that a true Yahwistic prophet could deliver oracles that carried meanings that contradicted the ordinary sense of the words; in other words, a true Yahwistic prophet could legitimately communicate lying oracles.

The addition of lying oracles to the repertoire of the true Yahwistic prophet rendered the oracles spoken by Yahwistic prophets even more ambiguous than their poetic form typically provided. Now the prophet could indeed have spoken a word of the Lord, but that word may have brought about an effect opposite to that expected by the petitioner. This account makes clear that success in one's own pursuits is not an adequate criterion for assessing the truth-value of oracles from the Lord.[99] An earthly king who believed that he had successfully co-opted a true Yahwistic prophet would have been living in deception — a deception that the Lord would allow to recoil on the king himself.

The Mesopotamians tended to view all aspects of the world as potential signs of divine activity or as signs conveying significant information about the future.[100] A privileged place for the occurrence of such signs was the entrails and livers of sacrificial animals, for it was believed that the gods placed such signs there.[101] This knowledge about the will of the gods was believed to be gained by consulting a diviner *(bārûm)*. A question phrased so as to seek a "yes" or "no" answer was posed to the diviner prior to the slaughter of sheep. Once the animal's entrails and liver were examined, the diviner could communicate the god's answer to the question.[102]

This practice reflected a belief that the gods wished to communicate with

---

98. DeVries, *Prophet Against Prophet*, pp. 45, 144-45, 150.

99. Nelson, *First and Second Kings*, p. 152; DeVries, *Prophet Against Prophet*, pp. 145, 147.

100. Bottéro, *Mesopotamia*, pp. 125-26.

101. Jack Lawson, *The Concept of Fate in Ancient Mesopotamia of the First Millennium* (Wiesbaden: Harrassowitz, 1994), p. 84; A. L. Oppenheim, *Ancient Mesopotamia: Portrait of a Dead Civilization* (Chicago: University of Chicago Press, 1977), pp. 226-27; Frederick Cryer, *Divination in Ancient Israel and Its Near Eastern Environment*, JSOTSup 142 (Sheffield: Sheffield Academic Press, 1994), pp. 134-35.

102. Jerrold Cooper, "Apodictic Death and the 'Historical' Omens," in *Death in Mesopotamia*, ed. B. Alster, Mesopotamia 8 (Copenhagen: Akademisk Forlag, 1980), p. 101; Ulla Jeyes, *Old Babylonian Extispicy: Omen Texts in the British Museum* (Leiden: Nederlands Historisch-Archaeologisch Instituut te Istanbul, 1989), p. 16; Lawson, *The Concept of Fate*, pp. 84, 86; Cryer, *Divination in Ancient Israel*, pp. 134-35; Pongratz-Leisten, *Herrschaftswissen in Mesopotamien*, p. 12.

humans. Frederick Cryer has pointed to the performative or promissory character of this process.[103] The sacrificial ritual and the declaration of the diviner shaped the present attitude and expectations of the one seeking a sign. The OB omen literature dealt most frequently with kings, yet the people at large were represented as well, for all sought the assistance of diviners on matters of hardship, sickness, and death as well as more general issues of finding their place in the scheme of things.[104] A bad omen or evil destiny could be countered by petitions to the appropriate gods.[105]

The OB diviner seems to have been an independent specialist employed by the king rather than an individual who held an office.[106] Some diviners were priests; in any case, a diviner had to have close associations with the temple cult since his service could not have been conducted without animal sacrifice.[107] The diviner at OB Mari had direct access to the king, a privilege denied later to the Assyrian diviner in the seventh century B.C.[108] The OB diviner had to swear loyalty and confidentiality in his service to the king.[109] In the royal court at OB Mari, four to seven hundred sheep were slaughtered each month so that diviners might provide answers to the various questions confronting the king and calling for action.[110] The diviner not only gave responses to "yes/no" questions by reading the livers or entrails, he also served as an adviser to the king.[111] At Mari, a diviner typically would pose the same question to two different sacrificial animals so as to validate the answer.[112] Also diviners may have performed extispicies to check one another's work.[113] The actual procedure of reading the

---

103. Cryer, *Divination in Ancient Israel*, p. 188.

104. Ulla Jeyes, "Death and Divination in the Old Babylonian Period," in *Death in Mesopotamia*, ed. B. Alster, Mesopotamia 8 (Copenhagen: Akademisk Forlag, 1980), pp. 107-9.

105. Stephanie Dalley, "Occasions and Opportunities," p. 20.

106. Pongratz-Leisten, *Herrschaftswissen in Mesopotamien*, p. 201; Cryer, *Divination in Ancient Israel*, pp. 201-3; Jeyes, *Old Babylonian Extispicy*, pp. 15-16, 21.

107. Cryer, *Divination in Ancient Israel*, p. 201. Previously Oppenheim ("Perspectives on Mesopotamian Divination," in *La divination en Mésopotamie ancienne et dans les regions voisines*, CRRA 14 [Paris: Presses Universitaires de France, 1966], p. 40) claimed that diviners were not priests but technical experts and so distanced divination from a cultic context.

108. Pongratz-Leisten, *Herrschaftswissen in Mesopotamien*, p. 201.

109. Pongratz-Leisten, *Herrschaftswissen in Mesopotamien*, pp. 150-53; Cryer, *Divination in Ancient Israel*, p. 214.

110. Pongratz-Leisten, *Herrschaftswissen in Mesopotamien*, p. 138.

111. Pongratz-Leisten, *Herrschaftswissen in Mesopotamien*, p. 154; Ivan Starr, ed., *Queries to the Sungod: Divination and Politics in Sargonid Assyria*, SAAS 4 (Helsinki: Helsinki University Press, 1990), p. xvi.

112. Pongratz-Leisten, *Herrschaftswissen in Mesopotamien*, p. 142; Jeyes, *Old Babylonian Extispicy*, p. 45.

113. Jeyes, *Old Babylonian Extispicy*, p. 34.

entrails, analogous to an autopsy on a sacrificial sheep, remained quite consistent from the OB to the Neo-Assyrian periods.[114] In the Assyrian royal court of the seventh century B.C., groups of diviners were employed who were instructed to keep searching for answers until the appropriate level of confidence for the right answer was reached. The king was the recipient of such answers, and his present need for a promise or positive declaration had to be met.[115] Scholars who interpreted celestial phenomena were sometimes less helpful as advisers than diviners since they were often unable to give a direct answer leading to action.[116]

Among the numerous forms of royal decision making involving the diviner at Mari was the verification of the credentials of intuitive prophets. The prophet was required to send the hem of a garment and a lock of hair so that the diviner might determine whether or not the prophet should be listened to (e.g., *ARM X*, 7:23-27; 8:19-28; 81:19-21).[117] It seems that the kings of Mesopotamia granted greater authority to divination through the system of reading entrails and livers of sacrificial animals than to oracles delivered by prophets.[118] However, there were times in OB Mari when intuitive prophets were called upon to explicate the findings of the diviner, which suggests that there was a complementarity of intuitive prophecy and deductive divination at Mari.[119]

A number of OB royal inscriptions state that the king of the gods determined the destinies of persons, institutions, and objects.[120] Those who accepted this message would have regarded the world as ordered and predictable if only sufficient knowledge of the will of the gods could be known. The Mesopotamians' widespread search for clues to the will of the gods attests to their conviction that the gods inscribed the destinies of persons and institutions on objects or in events.[121] If one were attentive to these signs, one could

---

114. Starr, *Queries to the Sungod*, p. xxxvi.

115. Pongratz-Leisten, *Herrschaftswissen in Mesopotamien*, pp. 200-201; cf. Starr, *Queries to the Sungod*, p. xxxv.

116. Starr, *Queries to the Sungod*, pp. xxxii-xxxiii.

117. Moran, "New Evidence from Mari," pp. 20-23; Malamat, *Mari and the Bible*, p. 79; Ellis, "Mesopotamian Oracles and Prophetic Texts," pp. 134-36.

118. Oppenheim, *Ancient Mesopotamia*, pp. 221, 226; Pongratz-Leisten, *Herrschaftswissen in Mesopotamien*, p. 14.

119. Dominique Charpin, "Mari entre l'est et l'ouest: politique, culture, religion," *Akkadica* 78 (1992): 9; Pongratz-Leisten, *Herrschaftswissen in Mesopotamien*, pp. 68-70.

120. Frayne, *RIME 4*, E4.3.7.7, lines 1-3, 17-20; see also E4.3.7.3, lines 22-23; E4.3.6.2, lines 21-22; Rykle Borger, *Babylonisch-assyrische Lesestücke*, AnOr 54 (Rome: Pontifical Biblical Institute, 1979), p. 5; *CH* I:6-7; Lawson, *The Concept of Fate*, pp. 80-81.

121. Bottéro, *Mesopotamia*, p. 127; Oppenheim, *Ancient Mesopotamia*, p. 210; cf. Cryer, *Divination in Ancient Israel*, p. 142.

learn about one's destiny or place in the divinely determined scheme of things.[122] According to an example from the omen collection known as *Šumma Ālu*, Mesopotamians practiced divination at the point of intersection of the courtyard and the house so as to symbolize the integration of the individual into the group that lived there. Divination played a role in the construction of the social hierarchy within and outside of a house.[123]

The collecting of omens began in the Akkadian period (ca. 2350-2193) and intensified in the OB period.[124] In the first millennium B.C., an elaborate system for the interpretation of signs or omens was developed.[125] The diviners drew their expertise from the interpretation of these written omens; they were scholars revered for their special knowledge.[126] The diviners were guided by manuals in which case after case was compiled to show how a general idea varied in different particular situations.[127] So, divination became a deductive "science" for predicting what might happen on the basis of signs. The system was internally coherent; it functioned as a code that rendered the world and the course of events predictable. The omen series thus came to function like "natural law," exerting a force on the lives of individuals and groups analogous to that of law codes.[128] The Assyrian kings understood the political potential of this system of divination and so promoted the collection, codification, and canonization of omens.[129] This system generated a kind of thinking in which a general principle was fleshed out in as many individual cases as could be imagined; this deductive, a priori form of reasoning survived beyond the Mesopotamians and their religious worldview.[130]

122. Oppenheim, *Ancient Mesopotamia*, pp. 226-27; Lawson, *The Concept of Fate*, pp. 87-88; Benjamin R. Foster, *Before the Muses: An Anthology of Akkadian Literature*, 2 vols. (Bethesda, Md.: CDL, 1993), 1:27; Jeyes, "Death and Divination," p. 107.

123. A. Guinan, "Social Constructions and Private Designs: The House Omens of Šumma Ālu," in *Houses and Households in Ancient Mesopotamia*, CRRA 40 (Leiden: Nederlands Historisch-Archaeologisch Instituut te Istanbul, 1996), pp. 61-63.

124. Pongratz-Leisten, *Herrschaftswissen in Mesopotamien*, p. 129; Cryer, *Divination in Ancient Israel*, pp. 139-40.

125. Oppenheim, *Ancient Mesopotamia*, pp. 210-11; Walter Farber, "Witchcraft, Magic, and Divination in Ancient Mesopotamia," in *Civilizations of the Ancient Near East*, ed. J. Sasson (New York: Scribner, 1995), p. 1904.

126. Pongratz-Leisten, *Herrschaftswissen in Mesopotamien*, pp. 290-91; Lawson, *The Concept of Fate*, pp. 88-89.

127. Bottéro, *Mesopotamia*, p. 135; Oppenheim, *Ancient Mesopotamia*, p. 211; Dalley, "Occasions and Opportunities," pp. 20-22; cf. Ellis, "Mesopotamian Oracles and Prophetic Texts," p. 159.

128. Lawson, *The Concept of Fate*, p. 83.

129. Pongratz-Leisten, *Herrschaftswissen in Mesopotamien*, p. 291.

130. Bottéro, *Mesopotamia*, p. 136.

If truth, as in the Greek linguistic realm, is interpreted primarily as "not-forgetting," then remembering the story of a community was essential to its integrity. In epic performance the bards kept alive essential ideas rather than rote memorization of names and deeds as they engaged their audiences.[131] This collective memory created a context in which the experience of the people of the Archaic Age could be interpreted: that is, what was the enduring value of the sacrifices that individuals made on behalf of the community? To what extent did Achilles or Odysseus symbolize the people's collective existence?[132] The political significance of bardic song rested upon upholding a code of honor and encouraging members of the community to make sacrifices for the common good; in doing so, the bard would earn the praise of the community. The stability of this communal memory through bardic song would have indicated whether or not *kleos* was actually undying.

The search for a divinely guaranteed knowledge upon which to assess time-bound experience existed not only in the bardic song of Homer but also in the practice of divination in biblical Israel and ancient Mesopotamia. The visions of Micaiah ben-Imlah of the enthroned heavenly king drew upon the Yahwistic traditions of Israel. The advice given by a Mesopotamian diviner garnered authority for itself by drawing upon centuries of standardized practice.

The drama associated with these divine communications centered upon the truth or falsity of their predictions. Kings commonly called upon prophets or diviners to help them make decisions in times of crisis.[133] The political relevance of oracles or signs from heaven was much more evident in situations of decision making than that of bardic song or other poetic or narrative compositions that were concerned with shaping the longer-term traditional vision. The processes by which such heavenly communications were tested in their particulars varied in each community. In the intuitive prophecy of Israel, the dynamics of the relationship between the prophet and the king and between the prophet and other prophets had an impact on the reception of the prophet's words. The intangibles such as the prophet's charisma, demeanor, and experience were most likely very important factors influencing the seriousness with which his words were taken. So, in many circumstances the Israelite prophet had to be a performer in order to communicate his message, but he probably would have been a failure if he gauged his success on gaining the approval of an audience in the manner of a bard. The Mesopotamian diviners, operating on a binary sys-

---

131. Morris, "The Use and Abuse of Homer," pp. 84-88.

132. Vernant, *Mortals and Immortals*, p. 82.

133. Hayim Tadmor, "Monarchy and Elite in Assyria and Babylonia," in *The Origins and Diversity of Axial Civilizations*, ed. S. N. Eisenstadt (Albany, N.Y.: SUNY Press, 1986), p. 209; Lawson, *The Concept of Fate*, p. 88.

tem of reading livers and then developing a complex deductive system, believed that the gods ruled over the world in a systematic fashion. The nature of this system could be discerned through attentiveness to the signs inscribed throughout the cosmos. The kings no doubt found such a system of divination more to their liking since it was more manageable than the free-wheeling activities of intuitive prophets. The kings could probably work the system in order to gain the type of advice they wanted.[134]

Reaching into the heavenly sphere for an authoritative message was a means by which these ancient peoples gained an "objective" vantage point that could provide direction leading to collective action. By analogy in contemporary settings, statistical analyses or other elaborate data-driven studies are used to organize knowledge about the past and make projections about the future. These rational approaches still do not remove the need for a leader to make a decision with its attendant risks and ambiguities. Knowledge of the past will always be incomplete and will never provide a sufficient basis for predicting the future. To cushion themselves against the unpredictability of the future, kings no doubt tried to control innovations arising outside of their immediate circle by trying to make the future conform to the status quo that upheld their power.

Heroic Models: Inspired Guidance or Distortion

The stories narrating the collective memory of the community not only shaped the outlooks of the people but also influenced the decisions they made. The accomplishments and conflicts of the gods and heroes of the community called for reflection and oftentimes for imitation.[135] The ideals and values of the community were communicated in these stories. The identity of the community members was shaped by responding to the paradigmatic individuals and events enshrined in the collective memory.

One of the most forceful statements in the *Iliad* on the challenge of facing death came from the Lycian king Sarpedon, a heroic figure in the Trojan ranks said to have been fathered by Zeus. As he was about to enter into battle, Sarpedon reflected with his fellow warrior-king Glaucus on the significance of drawing near to death:[136]

134. Oppenheim, *Ancient Mesopotamia*, pp. 226-27.

135. Vernant, *Mortals and Immortals*, p. 82.

136. G. S. Kirk (*The Iliad: A Commentary*, vol. 1: *Books 1-4* [Cambridge: Cambridge University Press, 1985], p. 262) notes that the Lycians, led by Sarpedon and Glaucus, are Troy's most important allies in the *Iliad*. Sarah Morris ("Homer and the Near East," in *A New Companion to Homer*, ed. I. Morris and B. Powell [Leiden: Brill, 1997], p. 610) identifies the Lycians as descen-

Glaucus, why is it that the two of us receive the greatest honor *(tetimēmestha)*, with a seat of honor and meats and filled drinking cups in Lycia? All regard us as gods. We hold a great plot of land by the banks of the Xanthus, land good for an orchard and for the planting of wheat. So now it is necessary that we take a position with the Lycians on the front line and take part in the heated battle so that some one of the tightly armored Lycians can say: "Certainly the ones who rule Lycia, our kings *(basilēes)*, are not without repute. They consume fat sheep and choice, honey-sweet wine, but then too their strength is outstanding when they fight with the Lycians on the front line. Friend, if we were to escape from this battle and then be about to exist forever without aging, I myself would neither fight on the front line nor send you into the fighting where honor is won. In any case, now the myriad fates of death stand facing us, which a mortal cannot escape or avoid. Let us proceed. Either we will give the boast of triumph *(euchos)* to another or another to us. (*Il.* 12.310-28)

Sarpedon expressed his conviction that the duties of a warrior were integral to the position of the king. He claimed that the honor *(timē)* and material rewards bestowed upon kings by the people obliged the king to undertake the high-risk duties of battle.[137] Departing from the usual brave front shown by Homeric warrior heroes, Sarpedon expressed his hesitation about drawing so close to death. He stated that, if it were possible, he would escape death altogether and live as an immortal. Yet the path for the Homeric warrior hero was through death and not around it. The hero won glory *(kleos)* precisely by undergoing death for the sake of the community and thus by shaping the course of events.[138]

Sarpedon, though a son of Zeus, gave voice to the frailty of his humanity. As he wrestled with his fear of death, he rehearsed in his imagination the battle scene in which the victorious warrior boasts over his slain foe. He addressed both himself and Glaucus in urging that they act so that the boast *(euchos)* of the victor be spoken by them rather than by their foes. Pucci points out that in such reflective speech Sarpedon was taking Homeric society's model of a heroic

---

dants of the Bronze Age Lukka of Anatolia. In generations prior to the Trojan War, the Greeks were linked with the Lycians through marriage and guest-friendship. So, when the Achaean Diomedes confronted the Lycian Glaucus, they recognized the pact between their grandfathers and refrained from battling one another (*Il.* 6.150-211).

137. Margalit Finkelberg, "*Timē* and *Aretē* in Homer," *Classical Quarterly* 48 (1998): 18; for a critique of Finkelberg's argument on cooperative virtues as the key to the *Iliad*, see John Gould, *Myth, Ritual Memory, and Exchange: Essays in Greek Literature and Culture* (New York: Oxford, 2001), pp. 353-57.

138. Pucci, *The Song of the Sirens*, pp. 210-11; Finkelberg, *The Birth of Literary Fiction*, p. 88.

warrior-king and accepting it as a role that he was destined to fulfill.[139] He was battling against self-doubts and persuading himself to accept this societally sanctioned image of a warrior-king, one that would take away his life but would in turn grant him immortal glory *(kleos)*. Sarpedon's ambivalence before death revealed a corresponding ambivalence about imitating an ideal that would drain his life from him. The immortalized Sarpedon would become a hero like every other hero who fulfilled the heroic pattern. As Pucci states, "What *kleos* tells of him is what can be said even before and after him."[140] Fulfilling the requirements of an ideal pattern can make one's name endure, yet it is a memory that is trimmed down to those essentials that fit the pattern.[141]

The prophet Jeremiah, legendary for the turmoil of his ministry, was remembered in the Israelite tradition as one who was called and commissioned by God before birth (Jer. 1:5). Although the narrative of his call follows a well-known pattern of commission (vv. 5, 10), objection (v. 6), reassurance (vv. 7-8), and sign (v. 9), the content of this narrative faithfully reflects the particular conflicts of his life as reported in the book of Jeremiah as a whole.[142] In his commissioning, Jeremiah reported that the Lord said:

> I have put my words in your mouth!
> See, this day I assign you over nations and kingdoms
>   to uproot and tear down,
>   to put to death and demolish,
>   to build and to plant. (Jer. 1:9-10)

As Jeremiah carried out this commission, the sacrifices demanded of him were so substantial that one could say they cost him essential aspects of life. He had no wife and children (Jer. 16:2); he was alienated from his extended family (Jer. 11:21); and people in Jerusalem mocked him for the oracles he delivered and their apparent lack of fulfillment (Jer. 17:15). A series of four laments (12:1-6;

---

139. Pucci, *The Song of the Sirens,* pp. 63-64.

140. Pucci, *The Song of the Sirens,* pp. 63-64.

141. Paul Ricoeur (*Oneself as Another* [Chicago: University of Chicago Press, 1992], pp. 1-3, 303-8) differentiates *ipse,* "the unique," from *idem,* "the same," in human identity; the uniquely human identity, denoted by *ipse,* is forged by the person acting oneself into existence in light of social expectations, whereas *idem* is mere conformity to social expectations.

142. Blenkinsopp, *A History of Prophecy in Israel,* pp. 137-38; William Holladay, *Jeremiah,* vol. 1: *A Biblical Commentary on the Book of the Prophet Jeremiah, Chapters 1–25* (Philadelphia: Fortress, 1986), pp. 36-37. Terence Collins ("Deuteronomist Influence on the Prophetical Books," in *The Book of Jeremiah and Its Reception,* BETL 128 [Leuven: University Press, 1997], p. 25) argues that the idealized prophetic figure of Jeremiah in the book of Jeremiah was shaped by post-Deuteronomistic writers in the Deuteronomic tradition who worked in Babylon after 560 B.C.

15:15-21; 17:14-18; 20:7-13) present the picture of a prophet who moved deeper and deeper into despair as he was beset with the apparent futility of his ministry and plagued by the hostility of his audience.[143] The nadir of his ministry came to expression in the final lament with these strong words:

> Lord, you have deceived me,
>   and I was deceived;
> you were too powerful for me,
>   and you prevailed.
> I have become a mockery all day long;
>   everyone ridicules me.
> For as often as I speak, I must cry out,
>   I must shout, "Violence and destruction!"
> For the word of the Lord has become for me
>   scorn and ridicule all day long. (Jer. 20:7-8)

Jeremiah made clear that he did not choose to preach a message of doom. He claimed that he had been compelled to preach this unpopular message. The high cost of this ministry led Jeremiah to feel betrayed by God.[144]

Prophets who preceded Jeremiah, such as Elijah (1 Kings 19:2-4) and Amos (Amos 7:10-15), paid a heavy price for their ministry. Yet there was no expectation that an Israelite prophet had to pass through death in order to be an authentic prophet. According to the portrait of Jeremiah sketched out in the book of Jeremiah, the critical political and social circumstances within which Jeremiah worked heightened the confrontation between Jeremiah and his audience to the point where the messenger Jeremiah came to foreshadow in his person the doom that his message from the Lord predicted would descend upon Jerusalem.[145] The pressure of such a predicament made Jeremiah cry out that the Lord had be-

---

143. Gerhard von Rad, *Old Testament Theology* (New York: Harper & Row, 1965), 2:274; Kathleen O'Connor, *The Confessions of Jeremiah: Their Interpretation and Role in Chapters 1–25*, SBLDS 94 (Atlanta: Scholars, 1988), p. 148; James Crenshaw, *A Whirlpool of Lament* (Philadelphia: Fortress, 1984), pp. 32-38. For the purposes of this study, the historicity of the experiences of Jeremiah reported in the laments is less significant than the purpose and function of the picture itself (cf. Donald Gowan, *Theology of the Prophetic Books: The Death and Resurrection of Israel* [Louisville: Westminster/John Knox, 1998], pp. 107-9; A. R. Diamond, *The Confessions of Jeremiah in Context: Scenes of Prophetic Drama*, JSOTSup 45 [Sheffield: Sheffield Academic Press, 1987], p. 145).

144. Crenshaw, *A Whirlpool of Lament*, pp. 40-41; Blenkinsopp, *A History of Prophecy in Israel*, pp. 134, 146.

145. Koch, *The Prophets*, 2:42-44; Mark S. Smith, *The Laments of Jeremiah and Their Contexts*, SBLMS 42 (Atlanta: Scholars, 1990), p. 61; Gowan, *Theology of the Prophetic Books*, p. 100.

trayed and maltreated him with such a harsh destiny. Jeremiah's own expectations and those of the people of Jerusalem of what the life of a prophet should be like were not met. By human standards, the Jeremiah portrayed in the book of Jeremiah was a failure as a prophet. The Israelite tradition celebrated Jeremiah's memory as that paradoxical failure whose life became a model for the Judahites exiled to Babylon.

Because of the practice of divinizing kings from the time of Naram-Sin (2254-2218 B.C.) through the Ur III period (2112-2004 B.C.) until about 1750 B.C. of the OB period, the death of the king presented to the royal court a problem that needed an explanation.[146] So, while the OB Babylonian king was expected to uphold the image of the king as a world-conquering military leader, he was not expected to die an untimely death in battle.[147] By the OB period, the past, as the time in which humanity and human institutions were created, became idealized as better than the present and thus a time to be replicated.[148] The king was the one who had an image to uphold.[149] The perdurance of the royal image became more important than his actual accomplishments. Thus, if a king were to fall short of the expectations that the tradition required of a king, the royal court's most important concern was that the king resolve to maintain the paradigm and the expectations of the tradition.[150] Mario Liverani notes that in the Kassite period (1595-1158 B.C.) it was more important for the Babylonian king to be perceived as ruling over all of the known world than to exercise actual dominion over distant lands. The perception of the king's rule at the center differed from what usually happened at the periphery.[151] In the first millennium B.C., the scholarly elite in Assyria and Babylon were so invested in maintaining traditional images and formulations that they would try to dissuade reforming kings from addressing social and ethical issues if this involved going against tradition.[152] The Mesopotamians put so much emphasis on the replication of an ideal past that they tended to discount and disguise the observable present to sustain that ideal past.[153]

The traditional image of the king was held up as an ideal to be imitated by the king and his court and to be revered by the society at large. Claus Wilcke

146. William W. Hallo, *Origins: The Ancient Near Eastern Background of Some Modern Western Institutions* (Leiden: Brill, 1996), pp. 203, 229.

147. Hallo, *Origins*, p. 229; Jonker, *The Topography of Remembrance*, p. 97.

148. Foster, *Before the Muses*, p. 26; Jonker, *The Topography of Remembrance*, p. 57.

149. Jonker, *The Topography of Remembrance*, p. 57.

150. Jonker, *The Topography of Remembrance*, pp. 57-60.

151. Mario Liverani, *Prestige and Interest: International Relations in the Near East, ca. 1660-1100 B.C.* (Padova: Sargon SRL, 1990), pp. 59-60.

152. Tadmor, "Monarchy and Elite in Assyria and Babylonia," p. 223.

153. Foster, *Before the Muses*, pp. 26, 43.

claims that the OB schools were the training ground for the bureaucracy.[154] Particularly in the time of Samsuiluna (1749-1712 B.C.), Sumerian literature came to occupy a large portion of the curricula of the schools. When students would copy the royal hymns, they were imbibing compositions that promoted the image of an ideal Babylonian man that they were all to imitate.[155]

The following excerpt from a hymn honoring Hammurapi probably formed part of the repertoire of texts that OB students copied:

> He has made visible the greatness of his power forever. Hammurapi (is) the king, the strong warrior, the one who slays the enemies, the flood of battles, the one who flattens the land of the foes, the one who puts an end to battles, the one who brings rebellions to silence, the one who totally destroys combatants like a clay statue, the one who eases stubborn distress. (IV:2-17)[156]

The military exploits of Hammurapi celebrated in this hymn seem to belong either to the first decade of his reign or to the time of his thirtieth to thirty-second regnal years.[157] The military strength of the king was essential to the well-being of the kingdom. Promotion of this image of the king was an important means of legitimating the king's military campaigns and expenditures. Those kings who found such expectations of them as warriors burdensome were probably advised to disguise their sentiments.

Heroic models could help to bring order to a community if society at large revered such heroic actions and if individuals, such as aristocratic warriors in Homer or members of the royal bureaucracy and court in Mesopotamia, strove to imitate them. In Mesopotamia it seems that belief in the model of an ideal, heroic king became more important than success in replicating the model in actual practice. Therefore, the king's mistakes and failures needed to be downplayed or camouflaged. The Homeric hero's resolve to win glory through death became a way for society to gain a degree of mastery over the chaos of

---

154. Wilcke, "Politik im Spiegel der Literatur," pp. 66-67; Jerrold S. Cooper, "Babbling on Recovering Mesopotamian Orality," in *Mesopotamian Epic Literature: Oral or Aural?* ed. M. E. Vogelzang and H. L. J. Vanstiphout (Lewiston, N.Y.: Mellen, 1992), pp. 112, 120.

155. Wilcke, "Politik im Spiegel der Literatur," pp. 66-67. See also Hallo, *Origins*, pp. 152, 174-75; Jonker, *The Topography of Remembrance*, p. 50; Steve Tinney, *The Nippur Lament: Royal Rhetoric and Divine Legislation in the Reign of Ishme-Dagan of Isin (1953-1935 B.C.)*, Occasional Publications of the Samuel Noah Kramer Fund 16 (Philadelphia: University of Pennsylvania Museum, 1996), p. 10.

156. Leonard C. King, *The Letters and Inscriptions of Hammurabi* (London: Luzac, 1898), n. 60.

157. Nathan Wasserman, "CT 21,40-42: A Bilingual Report of an Oracle with a Royal Hymn of Hammurabi," *RA* 86 (1982): 13.

death.[158] Even if the heroes quivered before the terror of death, such fear was not to be publicized, for it did not fit the pattern of the resolute, heroic warrior. Jeremiah's paradoxical example of anguish and failure in the midst of a committed life pointed the way for the Judahites to imagine new life after the catastrophe of the fall of Jerusalem in 587. He had to come to terms with the troubles that life sent him. The Jeremiah portrayed in the biblical record did not intentionally set out to make a name for himself as a harbinger of Judah's fate and so to lead the way in letting go of an older territorial understanding of its religion in order to be metamorphosed into a more spiritual understanding of it.[159] The biblical tradition celebrated Jeremiah's obedience to the Lord rather than any self-sacrificing efforts he may have made to make a name for himself.

Courageous, death-defying efforts to imitate these models of warrior and king brought vitality and a collective identity to the communities of Homeric Greece and OB Mesopotamia. Yet the question still lurks in the shadows of these figures whether they paid too high a price by their sacrifices. To what extent was the community sustained by draining life from its heroes, particularly those consumed with passion for fulfilling traditional models? Even where compromises were made, the model still exerted its formative influence where it was honored as an ideal. Jeremiah, even though he did not aim to be a hero, was lifted up by the tradition as a model of a faithful sufferer. Achilles, with his mad-dog approach toward winning honor in battle and defending his sense of personal honor at all costs, seems to have been too extreme to be a model for imitation; yet the celebration of his memory in story may stir up the desire to imitate him, particularly among the more resolute in spirit. The image of a godlike Mesopotamian king etched itself in the minds of aspiring royal courtiers and scribes as they copied royal inscriptions and hymns in the scribal school. The values of the Mesopotamian monarchies were perpetuated and strengthened through attention to the model of the ideal king.

Divine Guidance in the Practical Wisdom of the Trickster

When a time of crisis had passed, a community turned its attention to those activities that sustained it over the long term. Highly valued actions in a commu-

---

158. Vernant, *Mortals and Immortals,* pp. 57-58, 81-82.

159. Moshe Weinfeld, "Jeremiah and the Spiritual Metamorphosis of Israel," *ZAW* 88 (1976): 17-19. On Deutero-Isaiah's transformation of the understanding of political power in the figure of the Suffering Servant, see Rainer Albertz, *A History of Israelite Religion in the Old Testament Period,* vol. 2: *From the Exiles to the Maccabees* (Louisville: Westminster/John Knox, 1994), pp. 425-26.

nity were not confined to the warrior who went to battle and the seer who communicated the divine will. The leaders and those who advised them searched for ways to keep the community intact in the midst of the tensions and conflicts that beset ordinary life. The stories in which heroes were the marginalized who succeeded against formidable odds appealed not only to those on the margins but also to those in power who recognized that the struggles by which they came to power had to be reengaged if they were to stay in power.[160] To maintain one's rank and role often required cleverness, a species of wisdom that the peoples of these ancient cultures found praiseworthy in their heroes.

When the disguised Odysseus met with the swineherd Eumaeus on his return to Ithaca, Eumaeus prepared a meal for him at which time he asked his guest to tell the story of his identity and whereabouts (*Od.* 14.191-359). Once again within the narrative of the *Odyssey,* Odysseus took up the role of the bard. Heeding the advice that Agamemnon gave him on his visit with him in Hades (*Od.* 11.441-56), Odysseus concealed his identity as he constructed a false story about his origins in Crete, his fate at the hands of the Egyptian and Phoenician kings, and his final escape from Thesprotian slave traders near Ithaca (*Od.* 14.191-359). As the evening's storytelling around the campfire drew near its conclusion, the disguised Odysseus fabricated an episode from the Trojan War in which he was able to secure the use of another man's cloak on a cold night. In the narrated episode, the disguised Odysseus appealed to the example of the historical Odysseus at Troy who had once tricked another young soldier into running as a messenger to Agamemnon's ships and leaving behind his cloak for the historical Odysseus to use for the remainder of the night. When the disguised Odysseus finished telling this episode from Troy, he lamented his status as a beggar and wished that he could somehow gain a cloak from the swineherd (*Od.* 14.462-506). Eumaeus then replied:

> Old man, that was an excellent tale that you have told, for you have not yet spoken a profitless word or anything beyond measure. You will not lack clothing or anything else which is fitting for a sorely tried suppliant when he meets someone. It is so for now. But in the morning, you must shake out your rags again. For there are not many cloaks or changes of tunic here to put on. There is only one for each person. (*Od.* 14.508-14)

Odysseus thus succeeded in gaining a cloak by constructing a story about an imaginary episode at Troy. Odysseus as bard manipulated a memory of Troy for his immediate goal of gaining a cloak and so seemed to serve as a counterpoint to

---

160. Cf. Rose, *Sons of the Gods, Children of Earth,* pp. 121-22; Bruce Lincoln, *Theorizing Myth: Narrative, Ideology, and Scholarship* (Chicago: University of Chicago Press, 1999), p. 7.

the bard of the *Iliad,* who was expected to communicate faithfully what the Muses told him to say.[161] Where then is the wisdom of the Homeric bard located? Does he simply repeat what he is told, or does he adapt the memory of the tradition to the circumstances of the telling, even to the point of making up episodes?[162]

David, who was foreshadowed in Israel's narrative tradition by the patriarchal Jacob, was adept in using cleverness and deception in order to survive.[163] The account of Saul's pursuit of David in the Judean wilderness (1 Sam. 21:11[10]–27:1) culminates in David's escape to find protection under the Philistine ruler Achish of Gath. At the beginning of this account in 1 Samuel 21:11-16(10-15), David fled to Achish but was identified by Achish's servants as a slayer of Philistines. The narrative shows David saving his life by pretending to be a madman. At the other end of this account of Saul's pursuit of David, three episodes (27:1-12; 28:1-2; 29:1-11) explain how David again went to Achish, but this time he gained his favor.[164] The inclusion of these Achish episodes (21:11-16[10-15] and 27:1-12; 28:1-2; 29:1-11) around the account of David's flight from Saul points to the obvious apologetic intent of this account of David's flight: the historical David was associated with the Philistine ruler Achish, and such collusion with the archenemy of Israel and Judah required an explanation.[165] The narrative places the blame on Saul: David had no choice (27:1). The court writers who devised this account of David's flight from Saul were cleverly concealing facts about David just as the character David in their narrative concealed facts about himself from Achish. The clever deceptions by the court writers and David were legitimated by the fundamental need of survival.

161. Pucci, *The Song of the Sirens,* p. 95; Morris, "The Use and Abuse of Homer," pp. 88-89; Finkelberg, *The Birth of Literary Fiction,* pp. 91-93; Rose, *Sons of the Gods, Children of Earth,* pp. 115-16.

162. Louise Pratt (*Lying and Poetry from Homer to Pindar: Falsehood and Deception in Archaic Greek Poetics* [Ann Arbor: University of Michigan Press, 1993], p. 91) argues that Odysseus's lies are tactful and promote the ethical truths of the *Odyssey;* however, Finkelberg (*The Birth of Literary Fiction,* pp. 128-29) counters that even if Odysseus's lying behavior is seen as acceptable in some cases, it is never held up as paradigmatic.

163. On the trickster theme in the Jacob stories and its ideological role in relation to monarchy, see David Carr, *Reading the Fractures of Genesis* (Louisville: Westminster/John Knox, 1996), p. 267; Susan Niditch, *Underdogs and Tricksters: A Prelude to Biblical Folklore* (San Francisco: Harper & Row, 1987), pp. 124-25; Walter Brueggemann, *Genesis* (Atlanta: John Knox, 1982), pp. 251-52; Niels Peter Lemche, *Prelude to Israel's Past* (Peabody, Mass.: Hendrickson, 1998), pp. 164-65. Jacob is seen as the ancestor of royalty (Gen. 35:11) and symbolizes the people/nation of Israel (cf. Stanley Walters, "Jacob Narrative," in *ABD,* 3:608).

164. Cynthia Edenburg, "How (Not) to Murder a King: Variations on a Theme in 1 Sam 24; 26," *SJOT* 12 (1998): 79.

165. P. Kyle McCarter, Jr., "Apology of David," *JBL* 99 (1980): 500-501; Baruch Halpern, *David's Secret Demons* (Grand Rapids: Eerdmans, 2001), p. 23.

In the account of David's sojourn with Achish, David received the city of Ziklag as his own possession (1 Sam 27:5-7). Achish's trust of David and generosity toward him are astonishing, so much so that it raises questions about how long David had been associated with Achish and in what capacity.[166] How deep did David's Philistine connections reach? David resided for a year and four months among the Philistines with his wives Ahinoam and Abigail and his six hundred men (27:3-7). During that time, according to the narrative, he deceived Achish into believing that he was raiding the people of Judah when in fact he was distributing spoils to them gained from his raids on desert tribes (27:8-12). The narrative portrays David as caught in a major dilemma when the Philistines mustered for battle against the Israelites in the Jezreel Valley (29:1-2).[167] Achish expected David to go to battle against the Israelites (28:1). The objections of the Philistine commanders (29:4-5), echoing those of Achish's men to David as a slayer of Philistines in 21:11-16(10-15), compelled Achish to order David to refrain from entering the battle (29:6-7). "So David replied to Achish, 'What have I done? What have you discovered about your servant? From the time I came into your service until now, have I not gone into battle against the enemies of my lord, the king?'" (29:8). Achish accepted David's claim of loyalty (29:9-10), but to the audiences in Judah and Israel hearing this account, the referent of "my lord, the king" was not Achish, but Saul, for David repeatedly professed his reverence for Saul as the Lord's anointed in earlier accounts (24:7; 26:9). In the story, through this ambiguous statement David deceived Achish;[168] but in the tradition, with this ambiguous statement the court writers may have concealed some embarrassing facts about David and his earlier Philistine connections.

Cleverness and inventiveness qualified as significant aspects of wisdom both in Israel and in the traditions of its ancient Near Eastern neighbors.[169] As the stories about David and the patriarch Jacob (e.g., Gen. 30:25-43) show, the character who survives and prospers in his competition with others may be a trickster, but he is nonetheless a hero for his cleverness.[170] The capacity to see beyond appearances and to invent solutions to practical issues was regarded as

---

166. Halpern, *David's Secret Demons*, pp. 223-26.

167. Brueggemann, *First and Second Samuel*, pp. 197-99.

168. McCarter, *I Samuel*, p. 427.

169. Lemche, *Prelude to Israel's Past*, pp. 162-64; Jacobsen, *The Treasures of Darkness*, p. 112.

170. Gerhard Von Rad, *Genesis* (Philadelphia: Westminister, 1974), pp. 300-302; Lemche, *Prelude to Israel's Past*, p. 164. David's strategy in his retreat during Absalom's revolt (2 Sam. 15:13–17:29) demonstrated his capacity to use cunning with piety; see Brueggemann, *First and Second Samuel*, pp. 199, 309; Lemche, *Prelude to Israel's Past*, pp. 165-66; Steven McKenzie, *King David: A Biography* (New York: Oxford University Press, 2000), p. 62.

a divinely inspired form of wisdom, and thus the Israelite tradition encouraged its reception and cultivation.

The Sumerian god Enki, known as Ea in Akkadian texts and also as Nudimmud (i.e., the "image-fashioner, shaper") in the *Enuma Elish*, was the god of fresh water who was also revered as the god of wisdom.[171] Enki's association with wisdom may have arisen from observing the way in which water, streaming along a surface, is able to search out and explore all the cracks and crevices in the ground. By such an analogy then, wisdom was seen to circumvent obstacles rather than to confront them head-on.[172] One example of Enki's ingenuity and practical wisdom was his arrangement of the circumstances for the rise of Marduk to kingship in the divine assembly in the *Enuma Elish*. When the gods upset Tiamat, her lover Apsu, with the assistance of the vizier Mummu, persuaded her to have the gods eliminated. Then Ea took action:

> Preeminent in wisdom, clever, highly efficient,
> Ea, the one who notices everything, scrutinized their schemes.
> He developed and set up against them an all-encompassing plan.
> He crafted it beautifully, his excellent holy incantation.
> He recited it and called it into existence in the waters.
> Sleep flowed over him [i.e., Apsu]; he slept soundly.
> He made Apsu sleep; sleep flowed over him. (I:59-65)[173]

After Ea killed Apsu, he established his dwelling, which he named "Apsu," and therein he and his wife Damkina formed and raised Marduk, who shortly thereafter offended Tiamat. When Tiamat prepared for battle with her forces, she frightened Ea, but upon regaining his composure, Ea went to Anshar and reported the threat. When Anshar grew anxious, Ea tried to calm him. However, Anshar's confidence in Ea was dashed when Ea went forth to face Tiamat and then retreated. This apparent setback seems to have been part of Ea's all-encompassing plan: he was preparing the way for the glorious appearance of

171. Wolfram von Soden, *The Ancient Orient: An Introduction to the Study of the Ancient Near East* (Grand Rapids: Eerdmans, 1994), pp. 179-80; Jacobsen, *The Treasures of Darkness,* p. 111. S. N. Kramer and John Maier (*Myths of Enki, The Crafty God* [New York: Oxford University Press, 1989], p. 5) note how it is difficult to categorize Enki as evidenced in the range of hymns, myths, and narratives; to accent his cleverness in devising solutions, they chose the epithet of "the crafty god" over the traditional one of "lord of wisdom."

172. Jacobsen, *The Treasures of Darkness,* p. 112.

173. The text is from W. G. Lambert and Simon B. Parker, *Enuma Eliš: The Babylonian Epic of Creation, The Cuneiform Text* (Oxford: Clarendon, 1966), p. 3. See also René Labat, *Le poème babylonien de la création* (Paris: Libraire d'Amérique et d'Orient, 1935), p. 82; Foster, *Before the Muses,* p. 356.

his son Marduk.[174] At this point Ea drew Marduk aside and counseled him on how Anshar would commission him as the deliverer of the gods, for which task he was to demand in return that the assembly of the gods grant him sovereign power over all (II:129-36).[175]

The picture of Ea in the *Enuma Elish* was shaped by more than 1,500 years of reflection in the Mesopotamian tradition on the characteristic activities of this god of wisdom.[176] Jean Bottéro identifies Ea as "a super-engineer" who approached all problems as a technician.[177] His wisdom was directed toward finding solutions to problems rather than toward making decisions that would lead to collective action.[178] Ea contributed to the well-being of the heavenly and earthly spheres by bringing order and organization. He did not engage directly in politics.[179] Ea countered the power of gods such as Apsu or Tiamat by schemes and organizational plans in which he was an actor behind the scenes. His cleverness and craftiness, which were most evident in magic,[180] were usually seen to be at the service of gods and humans.[181] Walter Farber notes that magic, along with divination, was integrated into the Mesopotamian religious system and not confined to esoteric fringe groups.[182] So, Ea, the crafty one, symbolized the honored place of practical, technical wisdom within the Mesopotamian tradition.

Odysseus's skill at winning a cloak, David's strategies for staying on good terms with Achish and yet winning the support of the people of Judah, and Ea's plan for overcoming Apsu and Tiamat exemplify forms of practical wisdom that allow one to deal with reality as it actually is and survive. In Homeric Greece, biblical Israel, and OB Mesopotamia, it was believed that such clever-

---

174. Foster, *Before the Muses*, p. 361.

175. Foster, *Before the Muses*, p. 365.

176. Bottéro, *Mesopotamia*, pp. 234-36; Jacobsen, *The Treasures of Darkness*, pp. 110-16.

177. Bottéro, *Mesopotamia*, p. 239.

178. Kramer and Maier, *Myths of Enki*, p. 201.

179. Bottéro, *Mesopotamia*, p. 246; Jean-Jacques Glassner, "The Use of Knowledge in Ancient Mesopotamia," in *Civilizations of the Ancient Near East*, ed. J. Sasson (New York: Scribner, 1995), p. 1816. Michalowski ("The Unbearable Lightness of Enlil," p. 244) argues that Enki/Ea and Ninhursag were the couple associated with fertility who headed the pantheon in the fourth millennium B.C. prior to any written documents.

180. Kramer and Maier, *Myths of Enki*, p. 100.

181. Bottéro, *Mesopotamia*, p. 246; Jacobsen, *The Treasures of Darkness*, p. 116. However, W. G. Lambert ("Another Trick of Enki?" in *Marchands, diplomates et empereurs*, ed. D. Charpin and F. Joannès [Paris: Éditions recherche sur les civilisations, 1991], pp. 418-19) identifies the crafty Enki in a bilingual OB incantation from Kish as one who unfairly orders the slaughter of a noisy, sick goat.

182. Farber, "Witchcraft, Magic, and Divination," p. 1895.

ness had its place within the divine scheme of things and was bestowed upon particular human beings. It was necessary for Odysseus to conceal his identity on his return to Ithaca, and so he told stories that on the surface were not factually true. David had to pretend to be eager to enter into battle under Achish's command against the Israelites even though this would have made him a traitor to Israel and Judah; the protests of the Philistine commanders can be seen as providential. Ea used magic and a master plan to save the gods from destruction and bring them under the leadership of Marduk. These "wisdom figures" from the Homeric world, biblical Israel, and ancient Mesopotamia promoted the belief that practical wisdom puts one in touch with a divinely willed world order.

Kings such as Odysseus, David, and Hammurapi confronted foes with equal or greater strength than their own. Direct confrontation would have been costly, if not self-destructive. The capacity to assess a complex situation and devise constructive ways to survive was essential to the success of a king's rule. The focused, intense courage of a warrior like Achilles would have been useless against Scylla and Charybdis, although Odysseus was deluded into thinking he could fight against Scylla as an armed warrior (*Od.* 12.225-33). The capacity to create solutions without direct confrontation was a form of wisdom that a king could scarcely do without.

Attentiveness to Divine Communication in the Process of Constructing the World

The many-sidedness of reality resists schematization. Categories and patterns that fit in one area are inappropriate for another. The extent to which reality is malleable rather than structured is a question that is tested from different perspectives: innovators try to forge reality into new patterns, whereas traditionalists try to contain it within the old patterns. Innovating and conserving are boundary-keeping activities that demand the construction and reconstruction of patterns. In Homeric Greece, biblical Israel, and OB Mesopotamia, the sage practitioner was one who recognized this necessary tension at the boundaries and aimed to rise above crisis management to see the larger pattern where such tensions, threatening as they could be, took their place within a divinely willed order.

The first person whom Odysseus met on his return to Ithaca was Athena. He did not recognize her. Believing her to be a stranger, Odysseus fabricated a tale to explain how he had come to be cast ashore (*Od.* 13.256-86). Athena then addressed him with affection:

One would need to be shrewd and wily to get the better of you in every kind of contrivance — even if a god encountered you. Irrepressible, filled with tricks and stratagems, you, even in your own land, would not desist from your wiles and deceptive speech, for you deeply treasure them. (*Od.* 13.291-95)

Athena praised Odysseus for his cleverness *(mētis)* but then cajoled him for not having recognized her presence with him throughout his journeys (*Od.* 13.298-302). Odysseus mirrored her *mētis,* but here it is clear that he could not match its excellence.[183] J. S. Clay has argued that Athena was absent from Odysseus prior to this point in the *Odyssey* because of rivalry between them over excellence in *mētis.*[184] If such was the case, then Odysseus's arrival in Ithaca allowed him to change his attitude toward Athena from one of distrust and suspicion to one of gratitude and hope for her assistance.[185]

Odysseus was a survivor who gained family, honor, riches, and friends only to see them slip away. He remained engaged with life, displaying a wiliness in the face of the rising and falling tides of fortune. Different contexts demanded different responses, but the one constant in Odysseus's character was his wiliness.[186] A distinctive epithet applied to Odysseus in the *Odyssey* is *polutropos,* to which Pucci attributes the following three meanings: "the man of many journeys, of many turns of mind, and of many turns of language."[187] Odysseus was a protean figure whose "manyness" eludes definition. He concealed his name and identity from the Cyclopes and from family, friends, and suitors upon his return to Ithaca. If Odysseus had revealed his name, it would have limited the play of his "manyness" under disguise. Pucci notes that "the identity of Odysseus must run forever in the tracks of displacement and must be enacted by figures of speech, disguises, and riddling turnings of turns."[188] As an observant and creative individual, Odysseus's responses to new situations were predictably unpredictable.

The heroic model of Odysseus stands in creative tension with the heroic

183. Marcel Detienne, "The Sea-Crow," in *Myth, Religion, and Society,* ed. R. L. Gordon (Cambridge: Cambridge University Press, 1977), p. 26.

184. Jenny Strauss Clay, *The Wrath of Athena* (Princeton: Princeton University Press, 1983), p. 205.

185. Clay, *The Wrath of Athena,* p. 209.

186. Pucci, *The Song of the Sirens,* p. 24; Muellner, *The Anger of Achilles,* p. 130; M. I. Finley, *The World of Odysseus,* rev. ed. (New York: Viking, 1978), p. 69.

187. Pucci, *The Song of the Sirens,* p. 27; Douglas Frame, *The Myth of Return in Early Greek Epic* (New Haven: Yale University Press, 1978), p. ix; Richard Klonoski, "The Preservation of Homeric Tradition: Heroic Re-Performance in the 'Republic' and the 'Odyssey,'" *Clio* 22 (1993): 263-64.

188. Pucci, *The Song of the Sirens,* p. 27.

model of Achilles: the wily survivor in contrast to the death-defying, honor-bound warrior.[189] The interplay between these two types of characters in the Homeric poems shaped the outlook of generations of Greek audiences and moved them to reflect on their common identity as Greeks within a matrix of divine and human interaction. The wisdom inculcated by the Homeric epics was geared toward forming an outlook on life, not on providing advice for specific political decisions.[190]

King Solomon was celebrated in the Israelite tradition as the patron of wisdom. Whereas the charisma of David was military prowess, that of Solomon was wisdom.[191] According to the account of Solomon's dream at Gibeon, the Lord granted Solomon "a wise and understanding heart" (1 Kings 3:12). Solomon was praised for desiring such a gift over more self-serving gifts such as wealth and military power.[192] Solomon employed this wisdom in judicial decisions (3:16-28), in administration of the kingdom (4:1–5:8[4:28]), in building projects (5:22[5:8]–6:37), and in rhetorical and literary wisdom (5:10-12[4:30-32]; 10:1). First Kings 10:1 claims that the Queen of Sheba came to Solomon in Jerusalem "to test him with riddles." She was reported to have been overwhelmed by Solomon's abilities and accomplishments, for she said: "Look, the half was not told me; you have increased wisdom and prosperity beyond the report I heard" (10:7). Solomon's wisdom ranged from the practical to the more esoteric knowledge of lists of natural phenomena (5:13[4:33]).[193] While such knowledge required seeing beyond appearances and comprehending the bigger picture, it did not seem, on the surface, to have about it the craftiness and slipperiness characteristic of the trickster. This portrait of the wise and prosperous Solomon reflects the positive estimate that the seventh-century Deuteronomistic editor of 1 and 2 Kings had of the institution of kingship.[194] The Deuteronomist's portrait of Solomon was not uniformly positive; in particular, 1 Kings 11:4-10 describes how his many foreign wives with their gods led him to worship other gods.[195] Here the tradition shows Solomon's

---

189. Pucci, *The Song of the Sirens*, p. 23.

190. Calame, "The Rhetoric of *Muthos* and *Logos*," p. 128.

191. Andre Lemaire, "Wisdom in Solomonic Historiography," in *Wisdom in Ancient Israel: Essays in Honour of J. A. Emerton*, ed. John Day et al. (Cambridge: Cambridge University Press, 1995), pp. 117-18.

192. Nelson, *First and Second Kings*, pp. 31-33; Jerome Walsh, *1 Kings* (Collegeville, Minn.: Liturgical, 1996), pp. 76-77.

193. On the parallel with Mesopotamian list science, see Dalley, "The Influence of Mesopotamia," p. 74.

194. Gary Knoppers, "The Deuteronomist and the Deuteronomic Law of the King: A Re-examination of a Relationship," *ZAW* 108 (1996): 337-41.

195. Marvin Sweeney ("The Critique of Solomon in the Josianic Edition of the Deuteronomistic History," *JBL* 114 [1995]: 607-22) and Jerome Walsh ("The Characterization of Solomon,

courtly wisdom issuing from a position of strength, from the establishment, whereas David's cleverness was that of the young upstart who needed to form alliances with traditional enemies in order to survive and then become established.[196] Historically, Solomon was probably a local ruler of a modest-sized kingdom inherited from his father David, but the tradition chose to remember him as a wise, wealthy, established ruler.[197]

A distinguished legacy of Hammurapi's reign is what has become known as his "code of laws." This collection of judicial judgments brought together exemplary decisions rendered by wise rulers and acknowledged in the tradition as just.[198] These decisions included issues that dealt with theft, matters concerning slaves, sale and inheritance of property, bodily injury from assault, and so on. The laws were framed as cases in an "if . . ./then . . ." style. Raymond Westbrook argues that the exemplary decisions gathered in the Code of Hammurapi would have functioned first as precedents and then were placed in the framework of a code as a way of experimentally expanding the reach of these particular exemplary cases to analogous particular situations.[199] In this way, Mesopotamian legal reasoning operated on the association of particular cases rather than on the formulation of abstract statutes under which particular cases could be categorized.[200] Bottéro claims that this compilation of verdicts served as a model of how a wise and experienced ruler promoted good order in his kingdom.[201] In the epilogue to the Code, Hammurapi encouraged anyone with a complaint or a grievance to read his stela on which this compendium of exemplary royal

CBQ 57 [1995]: 482-93) interpret the Deuteronomistic portrait of Solomon in 1 Kings 3–11 as an ambivalent figure under critique throughout 1 Kings 3–10 and do not see the negative assessment confined to 1 Kings 11; cf. David Glatt-Gilad, "The Deuteronomistic Critique of Solomon: A Response to Marvin A. Sweeney," JBL 116 (1997): 700-703.

196. Walsh, 1 Kings, pp. 74-76; Nelson, First and Second Kings, p. 34.

197. J. Maxwell Miller, "Separating the Solomon of History from the Solomon of Legend," in The Age of Solomon: Scholarship at the Turn of the Millennium, ed. L. K. Handy (Leiden: Brill, 1997), p. 11; Gary Knoppers, "The Vanishing Solomon: The Disappearance of the United Monarchy from Recent Histories of Ancient Israel," JBL 116 (1997): 42.

198. Samuel Greengus, "Legal and Social Institutions of Ancient Mesopotamia," in Civilizations of the Ancient Near East, ed. J. Sasson (New York: Scribner, 1995), p. 472; Martha T. Roth, Law Collections from Mesopotamia and Asia Minor, Writings from the Ancient World 6 (Atlanta: Scholars, 1995), pp. 4-5.

199. Raymond Westbrook, "Cuneiform Law Codes and the Origins of Legislation," ZA 79 (1989): 218-19.

200. Westbrook, "Cuneiform Law Codes," pp. 218-19. On the issue of law as discretionary action as well as conformity to rules, see Sally Falk Moore, "Certainties Undone: Fifty Turbulent Years of Legal Anthropology, 1949-1999," Journal of Royal Anthropological Literature 7 (2001): 100-103.

201. Bottéro, Mesopotamia, p. 165.

cases *(dīnāt šarrim)* had been inscribed *(CH* XLVIII:8-19). The *Code* was designed to provide direction and enlightenment at the same time that it celebrated the wisdom of Hammurapi.[202]

The customary law that grew up in various parts of Mesopotamia provided the basic groundwork for the social order.[203] If conflicts arose that the customary order was ill-equipped to address, then the king would hear the case and render a decision *(ṣimdat šarrim).* These royal decisions were anchored in particular cases and not in universal principles.[204] There was no effort to create a comprehensive legal code.[205] The cases listed in Hammurapi's *Code* were meant to be exemplary and so could provide guidance in addressing analogous cases.[206] Bottéro compares the use of this compilation of royal judicial decisions to that of using paradigms in learning a language. Repetition and variation distinguished and categorized the various cases.[207]

Hammurapi had ruled for about thirty-nine years before the publication of his *Code.*[208] Touting the wisdom of an established ruler, Hammurapi likened himself to Shamash, the sun god and god of justice, for his role in bringing good order to Mesopotamia:

> At that time, Anum and Enlil appointed me to make it go well for the people, me, Hammurapi, the pious, god-fearing prince, to make justice visible in the land, to destroy the wicked and evil in order that the strong might not crush the weak, to rise up like Shamash over the dark-headed people and to give light to the land. *(CH* I:27-49)[209]

---

202. Bottéro, *Mesopotamia,* pp. 177, 183; Jonker, *The Topography of Remembrance,* p. 106; Victor Hurowitz, *Inu Anum Sīrum: Literary Structures in the Non-Juridical Sections of Codex Hammurabi,* Occasional Publications of the Samuel Noah Kramer Fund 15 (Philadelphia: University of Pennsylvania Museum, 1994), pp. 32-37, 102-3; cf. Norman Yoffee, "Context and Authority in Early Mesopotamian Law," in *State Formation and Political Legitimacy: Political Anthropology,* vol. 6, ed. Ronald Cohen and Judith Toland (New Brunswick, N.J.: Transaction Books, 1988), pp. 102-3.

203. G. R. Driver and John C. Miles, *The Babylonian Laws,* vol. 1: *Legal Commentary* (Oxford: Clarendon, 1952), p. 9; Bottéro, *Mesopotamia,* p. 180.

204. Driver and Miles, *The Babylonian Laws,* 1:19.

205. Bottéro, *Mesopotamia,* pp. 161-63.

206. Eckart Otto, "Aspects of Legal Reforms and Reformulations in Ancient Cuneiform and Israelite Law," in *Theory and Method in Biblical and Cuneiform Law: Revision, Interpolation and Development,* ed. B. Levinson, JSOTSup 181 (Sheffield: Sheffield Academic Press, 1994), pp. 162-63.

207. Bottéro, *Mesopotamia,* p. 177.

208. Jack M. Sasson, "King Hammurabi of Babylon," in *Civilizations of the Ancient Near East,* ed. J. Sasson (New York: Scribner, 1995), p. 907; Hurowitz, *Inu Anum Sīrum,* p. 102.

209. Borger, *Babylonisch-assyrische Lesestücke,* 1:5.

The wisdom contained in the *Code* aimed to promote integration of the community more so than survival of the individual. However, the particularity of the casuistic approach of the *Code* also encouraged attentiveness to the individuals caught in conflict.[210]

Individuals like Odysseus, Solomon, and Hammurapi were singled out in their cultures as figures who were endowed with an exemplary measure of wisdom. They were guided by God or the gods so as to make decisions that brought their communities into greater harmony with the world order. The wiliness of Odysseus, the organizational aptitude of Solomon, and the legal insight of Hammurapi reveal diverse aspects of practical wisdom important for the governance of a community. Although Odysseus's wiliness at first sight may appear to focus more on the survival of an individual rather than on that of a community, it is clear that the skillful navigation of changing circumstances was critical for the effective leader of a Homeric community. In the day-to-day activities of a community, the wiliness of an Odysseus was at least as important as, if not more important than, the focused self-sacrifice of Achilles. Both Solomon and Hammurapi were honored for their ability to promote unity within diversity, to see the bigger picture while attending to particular individuals and circumstances.

Knowledge within Divine Communications: Interested or Disinterested?

The claim to authority in Homeric Greece, biblical Israel, and OB Mesopotamia was expressed in terms of divine choice. Knowledge of such divine choice was tied to the interpretation of signs or oracles. Oracles most often took the form of declarative statements announcing a condition as established in the heavenly realm that was soon to manifest itself on earth. Oracles were also expressed in the form of imperatives or promises. So, the knowledge communicated by an oracle was not subject to reformulation but was rather to be accepted or rejected. Nevertheless, the oracles were usually framed in figurative language so that their interpretation was subject to debate. As authoritative statements from God or the gods, oracles communicated privileged knowledge within a community that shaped the outlook and the attitudes of the people and their leaders.

In Greece in the fifth and fourth centuries B.C., the sophists mounted a strong challenge to the authority of divination not only on the basis of an elite's claim to privileged information but also because of the passive attitudes toward

---

210. Greengus, "Legal and Social Institutions," p. 472.

knowledge generated in the people who accepted the diviners' words.[211] Yet the sophists' assessment of the process by which oracular knowledge was received was biased in favor of their own mode of gaining knowledge. They believed that if the value of the sophists' advice was to rise in Greek society, then the value of the diviners' oracles had to decline. For them it was a zero-sum game.

Oracular knowledge aimed to communicate knowledge that rose above the half-truths and limited perspectives that are part of the human condition.[212] The limitations of the human knower were to be transcended by the direct intervention of God or the gods. Such transcendent knowledge would command the attention and the obedience of the community. However, once such authoritative divine statements were accepted by the community, they had to take their place alongside other oracles, which could either complement or contradict one another. Even if a particular oracle were accepted at face value, its message could be qualified or called into question by another oracle with a contradictory message.

The *Iliad* and the *Odyssey,* as inspired by the Muses, took the form of divinely inspired knowledge, but the episode of Odysseus fabricating a story to win a cloak comically called into question whether all the stories about the heroes at Troy should be accepted at face value and as factually true. In biblical Israel, the struggle between the prophets Micaiah ben-Imlah and Zedekiah is an instance of the more general phenomenon of competition and mutual challenge among Yahwistic prophets recorded in the historical and prophetic books (e.g., the conflict between Jeremiah and Hananiah in Jer. 28:1-17). In Mesopotamia, the form of divination that carried greatest authority for the royal establishment was extispicy and hepatoscopy. For these forms of divination an elaborate system was developed for sorting out contradictory and varying messages. In all three cultures, larger narratives or collections formed frameworks for interpreting divine communications authorized by the tradition: the narratives of the Homeric epics, the canonical historical and prophetic books of the Old Testament, and the divination manuals of the Mesopotamian diviner. Such frameworks reflected the traditional values of the communities where the interests of the community embedded in such frameworks transcended the interests of a particular prophet or interpreter. So, oracles, whether in the form of declarative statements or commands or promises, had to be interpreted and contextualized. The sophists' claim that acceptance of the authority of oracles indicates a passive attitude toward knowledge applies primarily to the oral communication of isolated oracles but fails to take into account the in-

---

211. Vernant, *Mortals and Immortals,* p. 307.
212. Vernant, *Mortals and Immortals,* p. 304.

terpretive process by which oracles and collections of oracles were contextualized in a community at a particular time and place.

The stories about the reception of oracles addressed earlier in this chapter indicated that the interpretation of oracles triggered conflict and realignments within the communities: the Homeric warrior-kings countered the withdrawal of a war prize at Apollo's insistence by competing with one another in a reallocation of war prizes; the vision of Micaiah ben-Imlah regarding a lying spirit within Yahwistic prophets led to a confrontation between Micaiah and a fellow prophet Zedekiah and the subsequent confinement of Micaiah by Ahab; and the Mesopotamian practice of verifying the credentials of a prophet through the work of the haruspex showed that Mesopotamian kings took steps to counter the potentially destabilizing effects of oracles.

The truth of an oracle most often cannot be captured within a simple, straightforward statement, despite the assistance of the Muses or other divine intermediaries. The poly-vocality of the signs within the typical oracle called for its interpretation within the collective memory and the current circumstances of the community. The infused wisdom of the oracle manifested itself not simply in specific directions but also in the questions and reflections it provoked as to what the divine intention might have been for a particular time and place. Oracular knowledge could persuade a community to take a particular course of action insofar as it made sense within the context of the community's traditions and current circumstances. The proof of the divine authorship of an oracle could not have been verified before the authoritative command or exhortation in the oracle had materialized in history; therefore, the prophet had to mount a persuasive case for the veracity of the oracle through his personal authority and his credibility as a spokesperson within the tradition.

In Homeric Greece and OB Mesopotamia, heroic patterns were a particular species of "timeless" knowledge by which individuals discerned whether or not they were called to particular destinies. By faithfully answering the expectations of such a pattern, a person could have sacrificed individual expression to the point that one became identical with the pattern and one's own individuality vanished within the pattern. Clear-cut heroic patterns in Homer were countered by ambiguous heroic objectives. Was Achilles or Odysseus the better example to follow in a particular situation? If pressed too far, "timeless" knowledge could bring death where survival was called for.

The wiliness of an Odysseus and the cleverness of a David were traits that probably were not foreign to kings reputed for their wisdom, such as Solomon and Hammurapi. "Lying" or speaking indirectly seemed to hold a legitimate place in the repertoire of the kings in Homeric Greece, biblical Israel, and OB Mesopotamia. Exercising an administrative skill that verged on the charismatic meant that the king had been able to maximize diversity while maintaining unity within the community. Such a balancing act between the individual and the community required sensitivity to changing contexts while maintaining a larger, more cosmic view of the community and its issues.

CHAPTER SIX

Tension versus Equilibrium:
Essential Countervailing Dynamics
within the Exercise of Royal Authority

The claim that particular political decisions had divine support could be verified only after the advice that was given had succeeded or failed. If oracular means were used to secure divine approval, the oracles of different prophets often contradicted one another. If traditional patterns of divine direction were invoked, the way in which these patterns were to be applied to current circumstances was often subject to competing interpretations. In Homeric Greece, biblical Israel, and OB Mesopotamia, the traditional pattern for legitimating royal authority communicated the belief that the king of the gods was the supreme decision maker over heaven and earth and that this king of the gods worked through earthly kings and other human authority figures to implement divine decisions. Yet kings, like prophets and diviners, were not able to persuade everyone that they were conduits of the divine will. Docility and obedience were not automatic responses to royal decrees. Protests against particular royal decrees could have been a sign of vitality in a community where strong disagreement between the ruler and the ruled demonstrated the latter's attentiveness to justice. The diverse individuals and changing circumstances within a community demanded that the king listen carefully and consistently to the people if he wished his claim of being a just ruler to be more than an empty epithet. The king's care for the people lay at the heart of the traditional pattern for legitimating royal authority. Such care was an ethical as well as a political obligation.

The care that the king extended to the people was emphasized in the rhetoric of the royal court. The king in Israel and Mesopotamia was frequently celebrated as the shepherd of the people who made great sacrifices in order to protect and strengthen the community;[1] such shepherd imagery could also be found among the epithets applied to Homeric warrior-kings.[2] This rhetoric may have persuaded the people to be obedient, but it also raised the people's expectations that the king increase their well-being. The grandiose claims of certain kings regarding what they had accomplished created a large target for criticism once difficulties and disappointments began to surface in the community. If the king was intent on promoting justice, he needed to address these tensions in terms of both practical measures and persuasive rhetoric. If he was more intent on ruling absolutely, he focused his attention on silencing the protests. The tensions inherent in the human condition made it almost inevitable that the king would disappoint some of his subjects.[3] The way in which he responded to such tensions revealed the extent to which he was committed to caring for the people: the expectation imposed on the just ruler by the traditional pattern for legitimating royal authority.

Lament: A Creative Response to Inescapable Suffering

The traditional understanding of the way that a monarchically organized community in Homeric Greece, biblical Israel, and OB Mesopotamia fit into the larger world order was implicit in day-to-day activities. However, in those out of the ordinary situations in which the king either gained a momentous victory or suffered a crushing defeat, court poets and prophets called upon this traditional understanding to help provide explanations for the unusual state of affairs. The pattern of these traditional accounts showed that the king received his authority from the king of the gods and was held accountable for its exercise. This pattern of authority was incorporated into other genres, such as the hymn and the lament.[4] For example, the Mesopotamian royal inscription, a celebratory genre that shared many characteristics of royal hymns, typically structured its praise of the king according to this traditional pattern of authority.[5] Yet when the king was defeated in battle or there was a crop failure or an-

---

1. E.g., Ps. 78:70-72; Douglas Frayne, *RIME 4*, E4.3.7.5, lines 1-30.

2. *Il.* 2.243, etc. — applied fourteen times to Agamemnon.

3. Cf. Sally Falk Moore, "Epilogue: Uncertainties in Situations, Indeterminacies in Culture," in *Symbol and Politics in Communal Ideology* (Ithaca: Cornell University Press, 1975), p. 219.

4. Mario Liverani, "The Deeds of Ancient Mesopotamian Kings," in *Civilizations of the Ancient Near East,* ed. J. Sasson (New York: Scribner, 1995), pp. 2354-56.

5. Victor Hurowitz, *Inu Anum Sīrum: Literary Structures in the Non-Juridical Sections of Codex Hammurabi,* Occasional Publications of the Samuel Noah Kramer Fund 15 (Philadelphia:

other difficulty in the community, then the lament genre was used to raise questions about the absence of divine support for the king. Central to the lament was an appeal to a superior to understand the plight of the petitioner and to act on his behalf.[6]

In the opening chapter of the *Iliad*, Thetis, the mother of Achilles and the daughter of Zeus, appealed to Zeus to restore the honor of her son, born from her union with the mortal Peleus:

> Then she sat down before him [Zeus] and grasped his knees with her left hand; then with her right hand she took hold of him beneath the chin and entreated lord Zeus, son of Cronus, saying: "Father Zeus, if ever in time past I helped you among the immortals, either in word or in deed, carry out for me this wish. Give honor to my son, fated for an earlier death than all others. But now Agamemnon, the lord of men, has dishonored him; he has seized his trophy and taken it away. But you, Zeus of Olympus, counselor, honor him. Give strength to the Trojans until the Achaeans treat my son with respect and exalt him with honor. (*Il.* 1.500-510)

Previously Thetis had aided Zeus in suppressing a rebellion on Olympus (*Il.* 1.396-406), and so Zeus was indebted to her.[7] The severity of the crisis — a mutinous rebellion — accents the importance of Thetis's intervention and gives sufficient grounds for her mentioning this event and departing from the typical way that gods make requests of one another where they refrain from recalling past favors as an inducement for a positive response.[8] Thetis's courtly manner of beseeching Zeus — embracing his knees with her left hand and placing her

---

University of Pennsylvania Museum, 1994), pp. 14-19; Benjamin R. Foster (*Before the Muses: An Anthology of Akkadian Literature*, vol. 1 (Bethesda, Md.: CDL, 1993), pp. 37-38; Liverani, "The Deeds of Ancient Mesopotamian Kings," pp. 2356-57; Claus Wilcke, "Politik im Spiegel der Literatur: Literatur als Mittel der Politik im alteren Babylonien," in *Anfänge politischen Denkens in der Antike: Die nahöstlichen Kulturen und die Griechen,* ed. K. Raaflaub and E. Müller-Luckner (Munich: Oldenbourg, 1993), p. 63; Steve Tinney, *The Nippur Lament: Royal Rhetoric and Divine Legislation in the Reign of Ishme-Dagan of Isin (1953-1935 B.C.)*, Occasional Publications of the Samuel Noel Kramer Fund 16 (Philadelphia: University of Pennsylvania Museum, 1996), p. 25.

6. William W. Hallo, "Lamentations and Prayers in Sumer and Akkad," in *Civilizations of the Ancient Near East,* ed. J. Sasson (New York: Scribner, 1995), pp. 1871-80; Kevin Crotty, *The Poetics of Supplication: Homer's Iliad and Odyssey* (Ithaca: Cornell University Press, 1994), p. 19; Claus Westermann, *Praise and Lament in the Psalms* (Atlanta: John Knox, 1981), pp. 169-70.

7. Christos Tsagalis, "Style and Construction, Sound and Rhythm: Thetis' Supplication to Zeus (*Iliad* 1.493-516)," *Arethusa* 34 (2001): 16.

8. Laura Slatkin, *The Power of Thetis: Allusion and Interpretation in the "Iliad"* (Berkeley: University of California Press, 1991), pp. 64, 69, 102.

right hand beneath his chin — emphasized her respect for Zeus and the seriousness of her request.[9] The far-reaching effect of Zeus's affirmative reply to her request was symbolized by the impact of his nodding his head: it shook all of Olympus (*Il.* 1.530). Thetis did not request immortality for Achilles but rather a restoration of honor that would take place within the finitude of human life with all its contradictions and conflicts. Zeus's approval of Thetis's request sets in motion the plot of the *Iliad* where the embattled Achilles becomes a hero through his choices and actions in relation to others within the limitations of human life.[10] Because of Zeus's intervention, the griefs of the Trojans and Achaeans alike were multiplied, and so the *Iliad* becomes, as Kevin Crotty puts it, primarily "a story of griefs and emotions — especially *eleos* ["pity"] — roused by human suffering."[11] As a composition shaped by the poetry of lament, the *Iliad* foregrounds Achilles, whose name means "grief of the fighting men," as the most adept at lament.[12]

Thetis's supplication of Zeus at the beginning of the *Iliad* was mirrored by the Trojan king Priam's supplication of Achilles at the conclusion of the *Iliad*.[13] Such an extraordinary supplication could hardly have been possible without divine intervention: Thetis placates Achilles by informing him of Zeus's anger at Achilles' mistreatment of Hector's corpse (*Il.* 24.13-40), and Hermes transports Priam to Achilles' hut (*Il.* 24.440-67).[14] In response to Priam's supplication, Achilles notes how humans experience good and bad fortune at the hands of Zeus:

> For so the gods have assigned the lot for poor mortals: to live with troubles, while they themselves are free of troubles. Two large stone jars rest on the threshold of Zeus containing the gifts he bestows: one of evil things, the other of good things. Zeus, the one who strikes with the thunderbolt, mixes these ingredients and gives them to a person: one time, the person meets with evil,

9. Crotty, *The Poetics of Supplication*, p. 60; Guila Sissa and Marcel Detienne, *The Daily Life of the Greek Gods* (Stanford: Stanford University Press, 2000), pp. 100, 102; Tsagalis, "Style and Construction, Sound and Rhythm," p. 4.

10. Slatkin, *The Power of Thetis*, pp. 38-40; Leonard Muellner, *The Anger of Achilles: "Mēnis" in Greek Epic* (Ithaca: Cornell University Press, 1996), p. 121.

11. Crotty, *The Poetics of Supplication*, p. 59; see also Peter W. Rose, "Ideology in the *Iliad*: Polis, Basileus, Theoi," *Arethusa* 30 (1997): 192.

12. Richard P. Martin, *The Language of Heroes: Speech and Performance in the Iliad* (Ithaca: Cornell University Press, 1989), p. 86.

13. Crotty, *The Poetics of Supplication*, p. 94.

14. Muellner, *The Anger of Achilles*, pp. 171-73; Jasper Griffin, *Homer on Life and Death* (Oxford: Clarendon, 1980), pp. 23-24. On Thetis's role in helping the semidivine Achilles accept his finitude and embrace his humanity, see Slatkin, *The Power of Thetis*, pp. 44, 49.

at another time, with good. But the one to whom he gives of the painful things, he makes miserable, and an evil gadfly drives him over the shining earth, and he roams, valued neither by the gods nor by humans. (*Il.* 24:525-33)

Achilles acknowledged that sorrow was an inescapable part of life and that Zeus played a determinative role in allotting joys and sorrows to humans.[15] Achilles noted that for most humans life was a mixture of joys and sorrows, but for the more unfortunate, life was unceasing sorrow. Achilles' recognition that it was the common lot of humans to suffer rescued him from the excesses and savagery of his wrath.[16] When Priam interceded with Achilles for the return of the corpse of his son Hector, Priam asked Achilles to imagine the feelings that Achilles' father Peleus had for him so that Achilles might come to some understanding of Priam's anguish (*Il.* 24.486-92). As Achilles came to see his own suffering in that of Priam, he had pity for Priam. Achilles' pity testified to his re-entry into the human world where the suffering of others as well as one's own must be accepted and respected.[17]

In the Homeric supplication or lament, the appeal for help and the explanation of one's dire circumstances were addressed to both gods and humans to restore the suppliant to well-being. The very act of crying out built bridges between gods and humans. Even though Achilles introduced his discourse on the two urns of Zeus with the disclaimer that lamentation was ineffective (*Il.* 24.523-24), lamentation had an effect upon him that he did not anticipate.[18] His words on the common suffering of humanity revealed that he had been transformed and brought back in touch with his humanity through his encounter with the suppliant Priam.[19] So just as Thetis's supplication moved Zeus to act on Achilles' behalf, so also Priam's supplication moved Achilles to respond fa-

---

15. Crotty, *The Poetics of Supplication*, p. 78; Sissa and Detienne, *The Daily Life of the Greek Gods*, p. 111. On the deceptiveness of divine favor, see Peter W. Rose, *Sons of the Gods, Children of Earth: Ideology and Literary Form in Ancient Greece* (Ithaca: Cornell University Press, 1992), pp. 83-84. Slatkin (*The Power of Thetis*, pp. 72-73) notes that in Pindar's Isthmian 8, Zeus and Poseidon were depicted as vying for the hand of Thetis in marriage, but both gave up their strong competition for her when Themis, the guardian of the social order, warned that the offspring of Thetis and an Olympian god would surpass both Zeus and Poseidon in excellence.

16. Crotty, *The Poetics of Supplication*, pp. 10, 83; Sissa and Detienne, *The Daily Life of the Greek Gods*, p. 95.

17. Crotty, *The Poetics of Supplication*, p. 77; Richard Seaford, *Reciprocity and Ritual: Homer and Tragedy in the Developing City-State* (Oxford: Clarendon, 1994), pp. 10, 70-71, 173-76; Margalit Finkelberg, *The Birth of Literary Fiction in Ancient Greece* (Oxford: Clarendon, 1998), pp. 132-33; Muellner, *The Anger of Achilles*, p. 174.

18. Crotty, *The Poetics of Supplication*, pp. 72, 130.

19. Muellner, *The Anger of Achilles*, pp. 174-75.

vorably to Priam's request for the return of Hector's corpse. Even more significant than the response to the particular requests of these supplications was the
transformation of Achilles' character: Priam's supplication led Achilles to link
his grief over the death of Patroclus to the sorrows suffered by Priam and all the
Achaeans and Trojans in the ten lengthy years of war.[20] It is significant that
Thetis also shares in this grief that binds her son to other humans (cf. *Il.* 18.35-
37) in a world where "cosmic equilibrium is bought at the cost of human mortality."[21]

The lament of Psalm 89, stemming from the late preexilic or exilic times,
communicated the Israelites' experience of a devastating defeat — perhaps it
was the death of Josiah in 609 B.C., the deportation of Jehoiachin in 597 B.C., or
the destruction of Jerusalem in 587 B.C.[22] Psalm 89 provided language for expressing a strong sense of disappointment and confusion over the setbacks suffered by the Davidic king:

> You have broken down all his walls;
>> you have ruined his fortifications.
> All those who travel on the road plunder him;
>> he has become discredited with his neighbors.
> You have lifted up the right hand of his adversaries;
>> you have allowed all his enemies to rejoice.
> You have even turned back the press of his sword;
>> you have not upheld him in battle.
> You have brought his splendor to an end;
>> you have cast his throne to the ground.
> You have cut short the time of his youth;
>> you have wrapped him in shame. (Ps. 89:41-46[40-45])

The demise of the Davidic king as shepherd of the Israelite people entailed that
they shared in the scorn and the physical pain inflicted on the king. The fact of
military defeat with the loss of life, freedom, property, and honor is devastating,

---

20. Crotty, *The Poetics of Supplication*, pp. 48-49, 77.

21. Slatkin, *The Power of Thetis*, pp. 88, 103, 119. Ruth Scodel ("The Achaean Wall and the
Myth of Destruction," *Harvard Studies in Classical Philology* 86 [1982]: 48) has argued that the
Trojan War was interpreted in *Il.* 12.10-26 as a myth of destruction aimed at separating humans
from the gods and so drew motifs from the Mesopotamian flood myth in the *Atraḥasis Epic*.

22. Hans-Joachim Kraus (*Psalms 60–150* [Minneapolis: Augsburg, 1989], p. 203) argues that
Psalm 89 is to be dated between the death of Josiah in 609 B.C. and the Exile. Évode Beaucamp
(*Le psautier*, 2 vols. [Paris: Gabalda, 1979], 2:92) links Psalm 89 to events at the time of the death
of Josiah, but Marvin Tate (*Psalms 51–100*, WBC 20 [Dallas: Word, 1990], p. 416) sees it referring
to events around the time of the deportation of Jehoiachin in 597 B.C.

but Psalm 89 called attention to these forms of suffering as aspects of a more pressing issue: Judah's anguish over these events that seemed to disconfirm its hope that the Davidic dynasty would last forever. Verses 20-38(19-37) recall the strongly worded promise that the Lord would maintain the Davidic dynasty no matter what sins they committed, for the Lord would punish such offenses but still maintain his care for them. The abrupt change in tone between verse 38(37) and verse 39(38) accents the shock and disappointment of the Judahite community: the demise of the king juxtaposed with the promise of the everlasting Davidic dynasty left the psalmist and the community reeling.[23]

The heightened sense of disorientation in Psalm 89 led the psalmist to believe that he and the Judahite community had been abandoned by the Lord:

> How long, O Lord? Will you conceal yourself forever?
> How long will your anger burn like fire? (v. 47[46])

By means of an earlier hymn (vv. 6-16[5-15]) within Psalm 89, the psalmist had expressed his belief that the Lord was more powerful than the gods of Judah's enemies. So, the dire circumstances of Judah could then be explained only by the Lord's wrath and his turning away from his people. Even though the severity of the punishment stretched the psalmist to the breaking point, his words of lament expressed his hope that the Lord would relent and turn back to his people. The psalmist's words of supplication provided language for the Judahite community to express its grief and confusion. At the same time, the psalmist respected the fact that the severity of the defeat of the Davidic king called into question, yet did not deny, the Lord's fidelity to his covenant and also his power over neighboring gods.[24]

In this crisis situation, the foundation of the traditional account for legitimating royal authority as expressed in Psalm 89:20-38(19-37) was called into question. The form of the lament was able to engage and sustain these serious questions as the people passed through the dark night of their devastation and disappointment. Psalm 89 provided a model of faithful questioning and protest that could sustain those in dark times who had to live through the contradictions and paradoxes of experiences that had no easy answers.[25]

---

23. Kraus, *Psalms 60–150*, p. 210; Beaucamp, *Le psautier*, 2:91; Tate, *Psalms 51–100*, p. 427; Richard Clifford, "Psalm 89: A Lament over the Davidic Ruler's Continued Failure," *HTR* 73 (1980): 36, 46-47.

24. Kraus, *Psalms 60–150*, pp. 210-11; Tate, *Psalms 51–100*, p. 416; cf. Westermann, *Praise and Lament in the Psalms*, pp. 171, 177-78.

25. Tate, *Psalms 51–100*, pp. 428-30; Walter Brueggemann, *The Message of the Psalms* (Minneapolis: Augsburg, 1984), p. 52.

With the downfall of the Third Dynasty of Ur in 2004, the Ekishnugal temple of the moon god Nanna and the Agrunkug temple of his wife Ningal in Ur were destroyed.[26] As the early kings of the succeeding dynasty of Isin, Ishbi-erra (2017-1985 B.C.) and Shu-ilishu (1984-1975 B.C.), began to rebuild these temples, laments over the destruction of Ur were composed to explain how the destruction came about and to call for restoration.[27] The curses appended to the building inscriptions of temples were feared to devolve even upon the restorers who cleared away sections of the destroyed edifice in order to rebuild it. Thus, the "Lament for Ur" gave a lengthy description of the destruction of the temples in Ur in order to remove any suspicion of wrongdoing on the part of the kings of Isin so that they might proceed in their rebuilding efforts.[28]

In the "Lament for Ur," Ningal, the wife of the moon god Nanna, recalled how she had petitioned An and Enlil both in private and in the assembly of the gods to alter their decision to destroy Ur.[29] This carefully organized composition in Sumerian consists of 436 lines arranged in six-line stanzas.[30] In the section of the lament where Ningal made her appeal to the assembly, she described her efforts as follows:

> I verily clasped (?) legs, laid hold of arms,
> truly I shed my tears before An,
> truly I made supplication, I myself,
>   before Enlil:
> "May my city not be ravaged!"
>   I said to them.
> "May Ur not be ravaged!"

---

26. Thorkild Jacobsen, "Lament for Ur," in *The Harps That Once . . . . : Sumerian Poetry in Translation* (New Haven: Yale University Press, 1987), p. 447; William W. Hallo, "Lamentations and Prayers," p. 1872.

27. Jacobsen, "Lament for Ur," p. 447; Hallo, "Lamentations and Prayers," p. 1872; Wilcke, "Politik im Spiegel der Literatur," p. 36. For the earlier composition "The Lament over the Destruction of Sumer and Ur," see Piotr Michalowski, *The Lamentation over the Destruction of Sumer and Ur* (Winona Lake, Ind.: Eisenbrauns, 1989). For laments over three other cities believed to have been composed after those for Ur, see: Margaret Green, "The Eridu Lament," *JCS* 30 (1978): 127-67, and "The Uruk Lament," *JAOS* 104 (1984): 253-79; Tinney, *The Nippur Lament*, pp. 96-123.

28. Jacobsen, "Lament for Ur," p. 447; Hallo, "Lamentations and Prayers," p. 1872.

29. Samuel N. Kramer, *Lamentation over the Destruction of Ur*, Assyriological Studies 12 (Chicago: University of Chicago Press, 1940), pp. 1-6.

30. H. Vanstiphout, "Some Thoughts on Genre in Mesopotamian Literature," in *Keilschriftlichen Literaturen: Ausgewählte Vorträge der XXXII. Rencontre assyriologique internationale*, ed. K. Hecker and W. Sommerfeld, BBVO 6 (Berlin: Dietrich Reimer, 1986), p. 6; Paul W. Ferris, Jr., *The Genre of Communal Lament in the Bible and the Ancient Near East*, SBLDS 127 (Atlanta: Scholars, 1992), pp. 28-35.

I indeed said to them.
"And may end not be made
  of its people!"
I indeed said to them.

But An never bent toward those words,
and Enlil never with an "It is pleasing, so be it!"
  did soothe my heart. (lines 154-61)[31]

The divine decree marking the destruction of Ur had been made by An and Enlil as kings of the assembled Anunnaki gods. Ningal's supplication was ineffective in turning back the decreed storm of Enlil: a metaphor for the destroying armies that ravaged Ur. The downfall of the Third Dynasty of Ur may have been associated with an invasion of Amorites from Syria and Simaški from Iran, but it appears that internal economic and historical factors associated with an overly complex bureaucratic organization were the more likely causes.[32]

The definitiveness of the claim of the "Lament for Ur" that the kings of the gods decreed Ur's destruction was due in part, it would seem, to the *post factum* character of the lament's explanation.[33] The patriarchal deity An, the source of all authority, had not listened to Ningal's supplication.[34] Enlil, the wielder of executive power, was known in various myths as a god with a two-faced character — beneficent and destructive — which suited him well as the determiner of fates. Like Zeus, Enlil had almost unlimited power to apportion the good and the bad.[35] So, if an event had occurred, such as the destruction of Ur, it must

---

31. The translation is from Jacobsen, "The Lament for Ur," p. 457. The text can be found in Kramer, *Lamentation over the Destruction of Ur*, p. 33.

32. Dominique Charpin, "The History of Ancient Mesopotamia: An Overview," in *Civilizations of the Ancient Near East*, ed. J. Sasson (New York: Scribner, 1995), p. 812; Piotr Steinkeller, "On the Identity of the Toponym LU.SU(.A)," *JAOS* 108 (1988): 197-202. Michalowski (*The Lamentation over the Destruction of Sumer and Ur*, p. 9, n. 49) argues that the reason for the fall of Ur "must be sought in the complex interrelationship of historical, economic, organizational, and propagandistic factors of the Ur III state" and disagrees with H. L. J. Vanstiphout ("The Death of an Era: The Great Mortality in the Sumerian City Laments," in *Death in Mesopotamia*, ed. Bendt Alster, CRRA 26, Mesopotamia 8 [Copenhagen: Akademisk Forlag, 1980], p. 86) who claims that drought, epidemic, and famine weakened the country and left it vulnerable to foreign invasions.

33. Hallo, "Lamentations and Prayers," p. 1872.

34. Thorkild Jacobsen, *The Treasures of Darkness: A History of Mesopotamian Religion* (New Haven: Yale University Press, 1976), pp. 96-98.

35. Jacobsen, *The Treasures of Darkness*, pp. 103-4; Knut Tallqvist, *Akkadische Götterepitheta*, Studia Orientalia 7 (Hildesheim: Olms, 1974), pp. 25-26.

have been decreed by Enlil. The ethical ambiguity surrounding Enlil's exercise of power surfaced in texts such as the "flood story" in tablet XI of the *Epic of Gilgamesh*. After the flood occurred and Ea had helped Utnapishtim/Atraḥasis to survive, Ea questioned Enlil's decision to send the flood in the first place:

> You wise one among the gods, O valiant one,
>> How could you, without counsel, bring about the flood?
> Punish the offender for his sin;
>> punish the evildoer for his transgression. (XI:178-80)[36]

Ea proceeded to propose less severe punishments and thereby called into question the justice of Enlil's decree.[37] Such questions about justice were raised in the OB period without casting aside the Mesopotamians' traditional belief that Enlil was the determiner of destinies.[38]

After the destruction of Ur had been recounted in the "Lament for Ur," the poet had Ningal express her distress in an extended speech of which the following is an excerpt:

> Ah, woe is me!
>> The city has been ravaged before me,
>> and the house too
>> has been ravaged before me,
> Nanna, the temple close of Ur
>> has been ravaged before me,
>> its men killed!
> Ah, woe is me! Where can I sit me down?
>> Where can I stand?
> Ah, woe is me!
>> Out of (the debris of) my city
>> an enemy city
>> has been built! (lines 292-95)[39]

---

36. The text is taken from Rykle Borger, *Babylonisch-assyrische Lesestücke,* AnOr 54 (Rome: Pontifical Biblical Institute, 1979), 1:111. See also Stephanie Dalley, "Gilgamesh," in *Myths from Mesopotamia* (New York: Oxford University Press, 1989), p. 115; *ANET,* p. 95.

37. Wilcke, "Politik im Spiegel der Literatur," pp. 69-70.

38. Piotr Michalowski, "The Unbearable Lightness of Enlil," in *Intellectual Life of the Ancient Near East,* ed. Jiří Prosecký, CRRA 43 (Prague: Oriental Institute, 1998), p. 244; cf. Robert Oden, "Divine Aspirations in Atrahasis and in Genesis 1–11," *ZAW* 93 (1982): 203-4.

39. The translation is from Jacobsen, "Lament for Ur," p. 466; the text can be found in Kramer, *Lamentation over the Destruction of Ur,* pp. 51-53.

Through the anguish of the homeless, Ningal expressed the distress of the people of Ur — and of other peoples displaced through war. Her language could have served as a vehicle for the people of Ur to bring to expression in public liturgy the pain and disorientation they experienced with the downfall of Ur.[40] Thorkild Jacobsen claims that this lament was written soon after the events it described.[41]

Priam and Achilles suffered greatly over the deaths of Hector and Patroclus. The people of Jerusalem were devastated by the apparent cessation of the Davidic dynasty in Jerusalem. The people of Ur were distraught at the destruction of Ur. Texts from these three cultures attested that suffering was an inescapable part of life and could occur in ways that were difficult to explain within the context of a just world order. Yet, it was in such situations where negative experiences rendered the world almost unintelligible that the lament genre provided the means to navigate such trying circumstances. Not only did the lament grant legitimacy to questions about contradictory aspects of human experience, it also provided the language for seeing the similarities between one's own suffering and that of other humans. Achilles' transformation through pity and acknowledgment of the common human lot to suffer was probably mirrored in the anguish of the people of Jerusalem and the people of Ur when their cities were destroyed and they had to come to terms with their drastically altered circumstances. Questions of theodicy surfaced in each of the cultures: Where was the justice of Zeus, of the Lord, or of An and Enlil in the suffering these people had to endure? Crying out and expressing one's anguish were actions central to these lamentations. Such actions helped the individuals and communities to pass through suffering so that they could find themselves in a new space. Each of these lamentations urged people to come to terms with suffering without going so far as to ascribe a positive value to suffering itself.

Contradiction versus Antinomy: Collectively Discerning the Severity of an Injustice

People usually turn to laments when they have exhausted every other avenue to find a way out of "caged in" circumstances.[42] In this search to find a new way forward, people need to distinguish between those issues that can be addressed

---

40. Hallo, "Lamentations and Prayers," p. 1872.

41. Jacobsen, "Lament for Ur," p. 447.

42. Michael Mann, *The Sources of Social Power,* vol. 1: *A History of Power from the Beginning to A.D. 1760* (Cambridge: Cambridge University Press, 1986), pp. 42, 44.

by action to promote social, political, or environmental change and those issues that demand acceptance or adaptation by individuals or groups. Fredric Jameson refers to those issues that call for action as "contradictions" and those that call for reflection with the assistance of narratives as "antinomies."[43] An antinomy refers to the ongoing tension between two aspects of reality that must interact but cannot be fully integrated. Examples of antinomies within a monarchically organized community are the relationships between the distinct realms of the natural and those of the supernatural and between the individual and the community.[44] If a problematic issue is improperly categorized as a contradiction rather than as an antinomy, actions to ameliorate the issue can actually create more difficult problems.[45] Antinomies by definition cannot be resolved.[46] To attempt to do so will distort expectations of the members of the community and consume resources in futile efforts. An antinomy identifies an area where different categories of being or areas of life come into relationship without merging; it calls for ongoing attentiveness and for challenges to the status quo of a type that are indirect and refrain from revolt.[47] In contrast, contradictions call for action, which oftentimes takes the form of a collective effort such as a labor strike.[48]

With Odysseus absent from Ithaca for almost twenty years and the suitors consuming the substance of his household for more than three years, the youthful Telemachus summoned an assembly in Ithaca to make known to the community at large that his household was being undermined (*Od.* 2.40-79). The suitor Antinous accused Telemachus of speaking in the assembly in order to turn public opinion against the suitors (*Od.* 2.86). This occasion was the

43. Fredric Jameson, *The Political Unconscious: Narrative as a Socially Symbolic Act* (Ithaca: Cornell University Press, 1981), pp. 82-83; William G. Thalmann, *The Swineherd and the Bow: Representations of Class in the Odyssey* (Ithaca: Cornell University Press, 1998), p. 286.

44. Jean-Pierre Vernant, *Mortals and Immortals* (Princeton: Princeton University Press, 1991), p. 288.

45. Fredric Jameson (*The Seeds of Time* [New York: Columbia University Press, 1994], p. 4) states that antinomy and contradiction "stand as each other's bad conscience, and as a breath of suspicion that clings to the concept itself. To wonder whether an antinomy is not really a contradiction in disguise; to harbor the thought that what we took to be a contradiction was really little more than an antinomy."

46. Jameson, *The Seeds of Time,* p. 7.

47. Jameson (*The Seeds of Time,* pp. 7, 70) regards antinomy pejoratively: it is a "blocked mechanism" in which genuine dialectic between opposing realities or forces is absent; the two poles alternately merge into one another and do not clash so as to provoke forward movement. In contrast, an early Greek thinker like Aristotle would have taken a more conservative approach and called for caution in innovation in the political sphere (see G. E. R. Lloyd, *The Revolutions of Wisdom* [Berkeley: University of California Press, 1987], p. 82).

48. Jameson, *The Political Unconscious,* p. 83.

first time the assembly had gathered since Odysseus had left for Troy. The authority wielded by such an assembly is not made clear in the Homeric narratives, for these narratives tend to highlight the liminal character of the assembly in a community ruled by a weak monarchy.[49] The issue that Telemachus placed before the assembly involved the courtship activities of the suitors toward his mother Penelope: an issue that might be seen as more properly belonging to the private sphere of the household rather than to the public sphere of the town assembly.[50] However, the competing suitors were expected to distinguish themselves by their hospitality as well as by their high birth, strength, and character.[51] Their character and behavior had an impact on the relationships within and between households. These household relationships constituted the matrix out of which the public sphere of the *polis* eventually emerged.[52] The distinction between the public and the private should not be overdrawn, particularly in a monarchically organized community of the Homeric world where the status of the royal household had such a far-reaching effect on the whole community.[53] Telemachus's primary objective in calling the assembly was to appeal to the community's sense of justice with regard to the delinquent behavior of the suitors.[54] The potential for the community to act on Telemachus's behalf was also in the minds of the suitors.[55] Later, after the ambush of Telemachus planned by the suitors failed, the suitor Antinous expressed fear that the assembly might hear of the plot and take action against them (*Od.* 16.376-86).

Homer's promonarchical bias surfaced in the early scene of the assembly in Ithaca as he cast the suitors in a negative light (*Od.* 2.281-84) and suggested through the words of Mentor that it was in the assembly's best interests to act in

49. S. Douglas Olson, *Blood and Iron: Stories and Storytelling in Homer's Odyssey* (Leiden: Brill, 1995), pp. 187, 202.

50. Thalmann, *The Swineherd and the Bow,* p. 179; John Halverson, "The Succession Issue in the *Odyssey*," *Greece & Rome* 33 (1986): 121-25.

51. Thalmann, *The Swineherd and the Bow,* pp. 161-62.

52. Cynthia Patterson, *The Family in Greek History* (Cambridge, Mass.: Harvard University Press, 1998), p. 56.

53. Charles Segal, *Singers, Heroes, and Gods in the Odyssey* (Ithaca: Cornell University Press, 1994), p. 53; Kurt Raaflaub, "Politics and Interstate Relations in the World of the Early Greek *Poleis:* Homer and Beyond," *Antichthon* 31 (1997): 14; Mark Golden, review of Cynthia Patterson, *The Family in Greek History, Phoenix* 52 (1998): 399.

54. Walter Nicolai, "Gefolgschaftsverweigerung als politisches Druckmittel in der *Ilias*," in *Anfänge politischen Denkens in der Antike: Die nahöstlichen Kulturen und die Griechen,* ed. K. Raaflaub and E. Müller-Luckner (Munich: Oldenbourg, 1993), p. 337.

55. Olson, *Blood and Iron,* pp. 187, 189; Raaflaub, "Politics and Interstate Relations," p. 19; Rose, *Sons of the Gods, Children of Earth,* p. 101.

support of the household of Odysseus.[56] Toward the conclusion of the meeting of the assembly, Mentor rose and upbraided the people for their passivity and reluctance to intervene on behalf of Telemachus:

> But I say nothing about the bold suitors who do violent deeds by the evil schemes of their minds, for they risk their own lives by forcefully consuming the household of Odysseus. They say he will never return home. Now I am upset with you other people because you are silent and do not in any way confront the suitors and stop them, though you are many and they are few. (*Od.* 2.235-41)

The suitor Leiocritus dismissed Mentor's words and contended that the people could do nothing to stop the suitors in their feasting (*Od.* 2.242-56). At that point, the assembly broke up. It was clear that the youthful Telemachus had to be able to rule by might in order that authoritative rule might be restored in Ithaca (*Od.* 2.60-64).[57] In the narrative of the *Odyssey*, the assembly in Ithaca had not yet reached the point of filling the institutional vacuum left by an ineffective monarchy, but Mentor's speech to them indicates that the expectation for the assembly to act was there.[58] The notion of the common good was a concept present in Hector's speech about the hero who dies defending his "country" (*patrē*, *Il.* 15.496) and so saves his household at the same time. There was a continuity between the interests of the household and the network of households in a territory that can be described as the common good.[59] The concept of the common good was not completely unknown, even if not effectively acted upon by the *polis* community, prior to the mid-fifth century B.C.[60]

In the *Iliad*, the assembled warriors were expected to give support to Agamemnon as leader of the coalition. They were regarded as confirming his authority as long as they did not oppose him. When Agamemnon quarreled with Achilles in the opening chapter of the *Iliad*, he taunted Achilles with the words:

---

56. Olson, *Blood and Iron,* p. 202.

57. Moses I. Finley, *The World of Odysseus* (New York: Viking, 1965), p. 85; A. G. Geddes, "Who's Who in 'Homeric Society'?" *Classical Quarterly* 34 (1984): 30.

58. Nicolai, "Gefolgschaftsverweigerung als politisches Druckmittel in der *Ilias,*" pp. 334-35; Finley, *The World of Odysseus,* p. 80.

59. Cf. Patterson, *The Family in Greek History,* p. 45.

60. In contrast, Hans van Wees (*Status Warriors: War, Violence and Society in Homer and History* [Amsterdam: J. C. Gieben, 1992], p. 158) sharply distinguishes the informal network of power that was generated by individuals along with kindred and friends from the sense of the common good where the people at large acknowledged and acted upon shared interests. He sees this sense of obligation to the common good emerging only in the mid-fifth century B.C. when it displaced the network of personal connections and obligations.

Go home with your ships and companions; rule over the Myrmidons. I do not trouble myself about you, nor am I concerned about your wrath. But I will promise you this: since Phoebus Apollo is taking the daughter of Chryses away from me, I will escort her with one of my own ships and my own men. Then I will come to your hut and carry off the fair-cheeked Briseis, your trophy, so that you will know how much more powerful *(pherteros)* I am than you and another will shrink back from claiming to be my equal and vying with me. (*Il.* 1.179-87)

Agamemnon claimed a superior authority without appealing explicitly to any title or material force at his disposal. The authority he claimed was one that was granted to him by the assembled warriors who regarded Agamemnon as their leader.[61] The authority that Agamemnon drew upon was confirmed and acknowledged as real by the established relations of friendship and deference among the Achaean warriors. At a more fundamental level, however, the relationships among the Achaean warriors were shaped by traditions of their community that included the traditional pattern of royal authority as symbolized in the scepter of Argos.[62] At the critical moment of the altercation between Agamemnon and Achilles, the silence of the assembled warriors contributed by default a legitimacy to Agamemnon's taking Briseis.[63] On other occasions also, Agamemnon's word of command, regardless of its merit, compelled obedience because the assembled warriors granted it such authority (*Il.* 2.80-83; 14.83-102). In the short run, Agamemnon could make poor judgments and still retain his authority as leader of the coalition.

After Solomon's son Rehoboam succeeded to the kingship in Jerusalem in 922 B.C., he traveled to Shechem, a centrally important city for the northern tribes. First Kings 12:1 says that "all Israel had come to Shechem to make him king." Earlier, when David had risen to the kingship over all of Israel, he was first anointed by the southern tribes at Hebron (2 Sam. 2:4), and then later the elders of the northern tribes came to Hebron to enter into covenant with him and to anoint him as their king (2 Sam. 5:1-3). The gathering of the northern tribes at Shechem may well have been for the purpose of entering into covenant with Rehoboam.[64] It is significant that the ceremony was to take place at

61. Pietro Pucci, *The Song of the Sirens: Essays on Homer* (New York: Rowman & Littlefield, 1998), p. 189.

62. Cf. Jean-Pierre Vernant, *Myth and Society in Ancient Greece* (Atlantic Highlands, N.J.: Humanities, 1980), pp. 95-96, 98; Sissa and Detienne, *The Daily Life of the Greek Gods*, p. 107.

63. Pucci, *The Song of the Sirens*, p. 186; Muellner, *The Anger of Achilles*, pp. 139-40.

64. Dennis McCarthy, "Compact and Kingship: Stimuli for Hebrew Covenant Thinking," in *Studies in the Period of David and Solomon and Other Essays*, ed. T. Ishida (Winona Lake, Ind.:

Shechem and not at Hebron or Jerusalem; the difference in location suggests that the northerners were less interested in entering into covenant with Rehoboam than an earlier generation of northerners had been with David.[65] The assembly of the northern tribes placed a condition upon agreeing to such a covenant: "Your father made our yoke burdensome. So now you should ease up from the burdensome labor and the heavy yoke that your father imposed on us. Then we will serve you" (1 Kings 12:4).[66] Rehoboam asked for three days to consult with his advisers about the request. Rehoboam's advisers gave him conflicting advice: the older ones encouraged him to lighten the burden, but the younger ones, with excessive bravado, counseled him to increase the burden. Rehoboam listened to the younger advisers and gave the reply of a tyrant indifferent to the suffering of the northern tribes: "My father made your yoke heavy, but I will increase the weight of your yoke; my father trained you with whips, but I will train you with scorpions" (1 Kings 12:14).[67] The assembly of the northern tribes united in opposition to Rehoboam and said to him:

> "What portion is ours with David? There is no inheritance for us with the son of Jesse. To your tents, Israel! Now look to your own house, David." Then Israel went to their tents. (1 Kings 12:16)

The northern tribes subsequently anointed Jeroboam as their king and never again reunited with the southern tribes under the leadership of a Davidic king.[68] The burden imposed by the Jerusalem regime contradicted the northern tribes' sense of justice and fairness. They showed a willingness to negotiate

---

Eisenbrauns, 1982), p. 83; Baruch Halpern, "The Uneasy Compromise: Israel between League and Monarchy," in *Traditions in Transformation,* ed. B. Halpern and J. Levenson (Winona Lake, Ind.: Eisenbrauns, 1981), pp. 78, 95; Gary Knoppers, *Two Nations Under God: The Deuteronomistic History of Solomon and the Dual Monarchies,* vol. 1, HSM 52 (Atlanta: Scholars, 1993), 1:219; Jerome Walsh, *1 Kings* (Collegeville, Minn.: Liturgical, 1996), pp. 160-61; Antti Laato, "Psalm 132 and the Development of the Jerusalem/Israelite Royal Ideology," *CBQ* 54 (1992): 62.

65. Baruch Halpern, *David's Secret Demons: Messiah, Murderer, Traitor, King* (Grand Rapids: Eerdmans, 2001), pp. 351-53, 411.

66. Moshe Weinfeld (*Social Justice in Ancient Israel and in the Ancient Near East* [Minneapolis: Fortress, 1995], p. 84) identifies the northerners' request as a type of *mēšarum:* a royal edict known in OB Mesopotamia that addressed social and economic inequities.

67. Ronald Ridley ("The Saga of an Epic: Gilgamesh and the Constitution of Uruk," *Or* 69 [2000]: 361-65) reviews the parallel drawn by scholars between Rehoboam consulting with older and younger counselors and Gilgamesh consulting with two groups in Uruk in the epic *Gilgamesh and Aka* and how this relates to the issue of primitive democracy in Mesopotamia in the third millennium B.C.

68. Halpern, "The Uneasy Compromise," pp. 79-80; Knoppers, *Two Nations Under God,* p. 223.

that was not matched by the Jerusalem regime. Their refusal to enter into covenant with Rehoboam constituted, from the perspective of the Jerusalem regime, a revolt against the political arrangement that had been in place under David and Solomon. Their capacity to take a collective stand against the Davidic monarchy and its unjust policies was no doubt strengthened by their identification of themselves as outsiders to the Davidic monarchy vis-à-vis the southern tribe of Judah.[69]

The violation of the tribes' sense of justice was also the alleged reason for the elders' request for a king at an assembly at Ramah with Samuel, which the narrative of 1 Samuel 8 situates in the latter part of the period of the Judges among events believed to have occurred in the late eleventh century B.C.[70] The elders charged that Samuel's sons Joel and Abijah, whom Samuel had appointed as judges at Beersheba, were corrupt (1 Sam. 8:1-3). To correct the situation, the elders proposed that Samuel appoint a king to rule over the tribes (8:4-5). The narrative of 1 Samuel 8 characterized the elders' request as vain and ill-advised.[71] The people claimed that they wanted Israel to become like all the nations with their powerful monarchies and standing armies (8:19-20). Samuel warned them, however, of the difficulties that attended such centralized governmental and military power: they would bear heavy burdens of military service, taxation, and corvée labor and would even suffer the loss of their parcels of land and their freedom (8:11-18). The main theological point of the narrative of 1 Samuel 8 is that the elders' request for a king constituted a rejection of the Lord as their king (8:7).[72] The narrative claims that their request for a more tangible source of security in the power of an earthly king was tantamount to a lack of faith in the Lord.[73] Thus, in the Israelite tradition the monarchy as an

---

69. Halpern, "The Uneasy Compromise," pp. 89, 92; Baruch Halpern, *The Constitution of the Monarchy in Israel*, HSM 25 (Chico, Calif.: Scholars, 1981), pp. 45, 178-79.

70. Isaac Mendelsohn, "Samuel's Denunciation of the Kingship in Light of Akkadian Documents from Ugarit," *BASOR* 143 (1956): 17-22; Halpern, "The Uneasy Compromise," pp. 78-79; J. J. M. Roberts, "In Defense of the Monarchy: The Contribution of Israelite Kingship to Biblical Theology," in *Ancient Israelite Religion: Essays in Honor of Frank Moore Cross*, ed. P. Miller, Jr. et al. (Philadelphia: Fortress, 1987), p. 382.

71. P. Kyle McCarter, Jr., *I Samuel*, AB 8 (Garden City, N.Y.: Doubleday, 1980), pp. 160-61.

72. Artur Weiser, *Samuel: seine geschichtliche Aufgabe und religiöse Bedeutung*, FRLANT 81 (Göttingen: Vandenhoeck & Ruprecht, 1962), p. 32; Dennis J. McCarthy, "The Inauguration of the Monarchy in Israel: A Form-Critical Study in 1 Samuel 8–12," *Int* 27 (1973): 403; Frank Crüsemann, *Der Widerstand gegen das Königtum*, WMANT 49 (Neukirchen-Vluyn: Neukirchener Verlag, 1978), p. 83.

73. Karl Bernhardt, *Das Problem der altorientalischen Königsideologie im Alten Testament*, VTS 8 (Leiden: Brill, 1961), p. 152; Walter Brueggemann, *First and Second Samuel* (Louisville: John Knox, 1990), pp. 62-63.

institution was introduced in the midst of controversy. There was a double-mindedness about the appropriateness of an earthly kingship for Israel; such an attitude enshrined in the tradition served as an enduring basis for the legitimacy of prophetic protest in Israel.[74] The Israelite prophets did not have to contend with the aura of a divinely sanctioned monarchical institution, as was the case in Mesopotamia.[75] In light of the narrative of 1 Samuel 8, a fundamental task of the Israelite prophet like Samuel was to criticize the king and so to constitute a check upon any tendency the king might have had to absolutize his power.[76]

The political and social issues addressed by the assembly at Shechem and the assembly at Ramah as presented in the narratives of 1 Kings 12 and 1 Samuel 8 differ most noticeably by the greater concreteness and urgency of the issues of injustice at the assembly of Shechem. In 1 Kings 12, Rehoboam threatened to be a harsher tyrant than Solomon. He was a present, concrete threat, whereas in 1 Samuel 8 the threat of tyranny was only a future potentiality that might not materialize. The situation in 1 Kings 12 presented a clear contradiction to a just political order. In contrast, the case in 1 Samuel 8 for changing the form of government from a judgeship to a monarchy was much less clear and compelling. The unjust practices of Samuel's sons did not reveal unbearable contradictions within the political and social order; the case for political change in 1 Samuel 8 seemed more speculative than practical. First Samuel 12:1 reports that Samuel regarded the inauguration of the kingship in Israel as a sin. The narrative of 1 Samuel 8 raises the possibility that the elders of Israel mistakenly took action, believing that the stresses and strains of the judgeship presented contradictions that could be solved immediately through a decisive intervention rather than antinomies that needed to be negotiated over the long haul in the context of faithful trust in the Lord as king. In contrast, the revolt of the northern tribes at Shechem as narrated in 1 Kings 12 constituted a clear case of a response to an injustice that demanded quick, resolute action.

In OB Mesopotamia, it was a common practice for a king to issue a *mēšarum* edict in the first year of his reign.[77] Every king after Hammurapi in

---

74. Crüsemann, *Der Widerstand gegen das Königtum*, pp. 13-15, 247; Halpern, "The Uneasy Compromise," pp. 86-87, 94-95.

75. Thorkild Jacobsen, *The Sumerian King List*, AS 11 (Chicago: Oriental Institute, 1939), pp. 71, I:1-4; Henri Frankfort, *Kingship and the Gods* (Chicago: University of Chicago Press, 1948), p. 242.

76. Benjamin Uffenheimer, *Early Prophecy in Israel* (Jerusalem: Magnes, 1999), pp. 11, 258-59; Klaus Koch, "Die Entstehung der sozialen Kritik bei den Profeten," in *Probleme biblischer Theologie: Gerhard von Rad zum 70. Geburtstag*, ed. H. W. Wolff (Munich: Kaiser, 1971), p. 236.

77. Donald J. Wiseman, "The Laws of Hammurapi Again," *JSS* 7 (1962): 162-63; Raymond

the First Dynasty of Babylon seems to have done so in the first year of his reign, and then at other points in his reign as needed.[78] A *mēšarum* edict attempted to redress inequities and to correct imbalances in the economic order and so was adapted to particular circumstances.[79] The *mēšarum* edict issued by Ammiṣaduqa of Babylon (1646-1626 B.C.) was representative of this type of edict as one "annulling all non-commercial debts and the transactions based thereon, such as debt slavery."[80] Raymond Westbrook claims that this release from past debts was one of only three types of royal edict to appear within the context of the conservative Mesopotamian legal tradition; the other two types of royal edict were (1) the fixing of prices on goods and services and setting interest rates and (2) the reorganization of the royal administration.[81]

The earliest attested *mēšarum* edict in OB times was recorded in an inscription of Nidnusha of Der (nineteenth century B.C.) where he referred to himself as

> the just judge who oppresses no one, who provides justice for the oppressed man and woman, the one who establishes good order *(šākin mēšarim)*, the one who destroys the wicked.[82]

Various OB kings recorded in their inscriptions that they had taken actions to address questions of justice in the area of wages and prices (e.g., Nur-Adad[83]

Westbrook, "Cuneiform Law Codes and the Origins of Legislation," *ZA* 79 (1989): 214-17; Benjamin Foster, "Social Reform in Ancient Mesopotamia," in *Social Justice in the Ancient World*, ed. K. Irani and M. Silver (Westport, Conn.: Greenwood, 1995), pp. 166-68; Dominique Charpin, "Lettres et procès paléo-babyloniens," in *Rendre la justice en Mésopotamie: archives judiciare du Proche-Orient ancien (IIIe-Ier millénaires avant J.-C.)*, ed. Francis Joannès (Saint-Denis: Presses Universitaires de Vincennes, 2000), pp. 89-92.

78. G. Komoróczy, "Zur Frage der Periodizität der altbabylonischen *Mīšarum*-Erlässe," in *Societies and Languages of the Ancient Near East: Studies in Honor of I. M. Diakonoff* (Warminster, England: Aris & Phillips, 1982), pp. 197-98.

79. Fritz R. Kraus, *Ein Edikt des Königs Ammi-Ṣaduqa von Babylon*, Studia et Documenta ad Iura Orientis Antiqui Pertinentia 5 (Leiden: Brill, 1958), p. 239; Susana B. Murphy, "The Notion of Moral Economy in the Study of the Ancient Near East," in *Intellectual Life of the Ancient Near East*, ed. Jiří Prosecký, CRRA 43 (Prague: Oriental Institute, 1998), p. 278; Weinfeld, *Social Justice*, pp. 28-29.

80. Westbrook, "Cuneiform Law Codes," p. 217.

81. Raymond Westbrook, "What Is the Covenant Code?" in *Theory and Method in Biblical and Cuneiform Law: Revision, Interpolation and Development*, ed. B. Levinson, JSOTSup 181 (Sheffield: Sheffield Academic Press, 1994), pp. 24-25; idem, "Cuneiform Law Codes," pp. 216-17; cf. G. R. Driver and John C. Miles, *The Babylonian Laws*, vol. 1: *Legal Commentary* (Oxford: Clarendon, 1952), pp. 20-23.

82. Frayne, *RIME 4*, E4.12.1, lines 7-12; Dietz O. Edzard, *Die "zweite Zwischenzeit" Babyloniens* (Wiesbaden: Harrossowitz, 1957), p. 69.

83. Frayne, *RIME 4*, E4.2.8.5, lines 7-10.

and Sin-iddinam[84] of Larsa and Sin-Kashid[85] of Uruk). These kings issued decrees *(ṣimdāt šarrim)* that granted exceptions or exemptions to small producers to resolve social and economic problems in order to make the established socioeconomic system work.[86]

Voices of members of the community other than the king surface, although indirectly, on issues of justice in the OB *Atraḫasis Epic.* The narrative opens with a description of the toil that the lesser Igigi gods performed in service to the great Anunnaki gods (I, i:1-6).[87] After forty years of such excessive labor, the Igigi revolted, as related by the following excerpt that begins with the words of a leader of the Igigi who encouraged them to bring their protest to Enlil:

> "Enlil, adviser to the gods, the valiant one,
> Come, let us get him at his home!
> Now, declare war,
> Let us mix battle and attack."
> The gods listened to his words:
> They set their tools on fire,
> Their shovels they set on fire,
> And their work baskets aflame.
> They took hold of them and went
> To the gate of the shrine of the valiant one Enlil.
> It was night, at the halfway point of the watch,
> The temple was besieged, but the god did not know. (I, ii:59-71)[88]

When Enlil became aware of the uprising, he armed himself and sent for the assistance of Anum and Enki. When Enlil questioned the rebellious gods as to the one who had instigated the revolt, they joined together to claim that the revolt was a collective effort triggered by the excessive burdens of the work imposed on them. Enlil wept at their message (I, iii:166-67). This uprising of the Igigi gods most likely mirrored that of human laborers who were at times subject to the corvée in Mesopotamian kingdoms.[89]

84. Frayne, *RIME 4,* E4.2.9.6, lines 25-34, 49-69.

85. Frayne, *RIME 4,* E4.4.1.8, lines 15-22.

86. E. Bouzon, "Die soziale Bedeutung des ṣimdat-šarrim-Aktes nach den Kaufverträgen der Rim-Sin-Zeit," in *Vom Alten Orient zum Alten Testament,* AOAT 240 (Neukirchen: Neukirchener Verlag, 1995), pp. 20-21.

87. W. G. Lambert and A. R. Millard, *Atra-Ḫasīs: The Babylonian Story of the Flood* (Winona Lake, Ind.: Eisenbrauns, 1999), pp. 42-43.

88. The text is from Lambert and Millard, *Atra-Ḫasīs,* p. 47.

89. Wilcke, "Politik im Spiegel der Literatur," p. 70; Elena Cassin, "Le contestation dans le monde divin," in *Le voix de l'opposition en Mésopotamie,* ed. A. Finet (Brussels: Institut des

The *mēšarum* edict seems to have been a means for the king to release pressure within the community that might otherwise intensify to the point of revolt.[90] The repeated character of these edicts indicates that the political, social, and economic system in OB times contained contradictions that had to be resolved. The king could not expect the people to adjust their expectations and outlooks on life on some issues: especially those that dealt with the necessities of life such as sufficient nourishment and reasonable workload.[91] These issues demanded concrete action.

The silence of an assembly supports the status quo. In the face of serious injustices within a community, at what point does the assembly take action? In Ithaca, Telemachus's concerns about the suitors did not compel the assembly to unite and take action. The suitors apparently did not constitute a clear threat to the well-being of the community, for the suitors not only were part of the community but also were present as members of the assembly (*Od.* 2.50-51, 84-92).[92] The silence of the assembly allowed the suitors to continue their feasting. In contrast, the Israelite elders at Shechem and the Igigi gods in Mesopotamia saw the need for concerted action against a common threat. The case was clear. They withdrew their obedience to the status quo and collectively authorized a revolt.

The debates among the Israelite elders and the Igigi gods prior to their revolts are not narrated in the texts, but the steps leading up to their concerted actions would seem to have involved discussions about the risks of taking action and the best strategies to employ. The discussions of the assembly at Ithaca did not have to pay attention to the views of a strong monarch, as was the case in Israel and Mesopotamia. The assembly in Ithaca expressed its views through silence before Telemachus. In Israel and Mesopotamia, the views of the members of the assemblies were driven underground. Underground networking would have prepared the way for the propitious moment when the assembled people could have expressed its convictions and its intentions to take action. When the

---

Hautes Études de Belgique, 1973), p. 96; William Moran, "Some Considerations of Form and Interpretation in *Atra-Ḫasīs*," in *Language, Literature, and History: Philological and Historical Studies Presented to Erica Reiner*, ed. F. Rochberg-Halton (New Haven: American Oriental Society, 1987), p. 252.

90. Komoróczy, "Zur Frage der Periodizität der altbabylonischen *Mīšarum*-Erlässe," p. 198; Murphy, "The Notion of Moral Economy," pp. 276-78. Solon's *seisachtheia* in Athens around 594 B.C., involving a cancellation of debts, may have been inspired by the Mesopotamian *mēšarum* edict (see Stephanie Dalley and A. T. Reyes, "Mesopotamian Contact and Influence in the Greek World," in *The Legacy of Mesopotamia*, ed. S. Dalley [Oxford: Oxford University Press, 1998], p. 104).

91. Murphy, "The Notion of Moral Economy," p. 280.

92. Olson, *Blood and Iron*, p. 202.

power and authority of the central government had a negative impact on the well-being of the people, the people's need to strengthen their own networks would have become more apparent. The account of the revolt of the junior gods in the *Atraḫasis Epic* notes how the laborers' sense of justice and proportion was so severely violated that they cooperated and took action, even in the Mesopotamian kingdoms where public criticism of the king was apparently suppressed.

Resistance versus Opportunism: The Conditions for the Legitimacy of Regicide

Kings like Rehoboam of Israel refused to listen to the legitimate requests of their people. They did not understand political power as a two-way street in which the king would increase his capacity to act by increasing the capacity of the people to act.[93] Rather, the tyrannical king understands power as the unfettered effectiveness of his own commands, even though power usually requires some form of acquiescence and cannot rely completely on compulsion.[94] If compliance could be secured only through coercion, the tyrant would be willing to do so.[95] Royal resistance to the legitimate demands of the people removed the voice of the people from support of the monarchically organized community and forced this voice to operate underground.

Collective action in a monarchically organized community against a king required not only the savvy to circumvent the superior physical force at the king's disposal but also the organizational skills to bring the people to act in concert. Clearly, in a monarchically organized community there were leaders who had varying measures of independence from the royal government, such as priests, prophets, sages, and leaders of tribes or clans. Yet to lead a successful grassroots protest against a king, an individual or a group needed to be able to rally followers not only around a particular cause but also around those tradi-

---

93. Anthony Giddens, *The Constitution of Society: Outline of the Theory of Structuration* (Cambridge: Polity, 1984), p. 16.

94. Giddens, *The Constitution of Society,* p. 175.

95. Volker Fadinger ("Griechische Tyrannis und Alter Orient," in *Anfänge politischen Denkens in der Antike: Die nahöstlichen Kulturen und die Griechen,* ed. K. Raaflaub and E. Müller-Luckner [Munich: Oldenbourg, 1993], p. 266) argues that the Greek tyrants of the sixth century B.C. copied the model of monarchical rule exercised in Assyria, Persia, and Egypt in the first millennium B.C., where the ruler tried to amass sufficient force so that he did not have to pay attention to the people's opinion. See also Christian Meier, *The Greek Discovery of Politics* (Cambridge, Mass.: Harvard University Press, 1990), pp. 36-37.

tional values that called into question the king's policies.[96] If the cause for the protest was not sufficiently serious to call into question the legitimacy of a royal policy or the protest offered little promise of providing a better solution, then the organizer would probably have found it difficult to mount a sustained collective effort. If the opponents of the king wanted to displace him at any cost, regardless of the legitimacy of their actions, then they would have had to mount an effort based more on physical force than on the values of the community.[97]

Protests against royal rule could legitimate regicide if the issues of injustice and the transgression of the values of the community were sufficiently serious. Discernment of the seriousness of royal shortcomings was not a process of reasoned debate carried out free of the ambitions and fantasies of the protesters. In polemical situations the facts of the case at issue could easily be distorted. So, one justification for the king's wielding superior physical force in the community was his vulnerability to palace coups and popular uprisings, which may have been fueled more by the ambitions of the protesters than by their resolve to rectify unjust royal policies. It is little wonder that most kings tried to promote their image as just kings even if the facts of their rule belied such a claim.[98]

Upon Odysseus's return to Ithaca, he disguised himself as a begger and met the suitors in the banquet hall of his own house (*Od.* 17.336-41). Antinous, a leader of the suitors who had been plotting to kill Telemachus, was critical of the other suitors for giving generous portions to the beggar Odysseus as he made his round of the table asking for handouts. Antinous claimed that the others were so generous because they were giving away another man's possessions (*Od.* 17.450-52). When Antinous was asked for a portion, he pushed the beggar Odysseus away; and when Odysseus criticized Antinous for his meanness, Antinous threw a footstool, which struck Odysseus on the right shoulder (*Od.* 17.453-62).[99] At that point, the beggar Odysseus said to the assembled suitors:

> Listen to me, suitors of this splendid queen, that I might say the things that the heart *(thumos)* within me enjoins. Surely there is no grief or distress within the soul when a man is struck in a battle over possessions, whether

96. Giddens, *The Constitution of Society,* p. 195.

97. Paul Ricoeur, "Practical Reason," in *From Text to Action: Essays in Hermeneutics II* (Evanston, Ill.: Northwestern University Press, 1991), p. 205.

98. Keith W. Whitelam, *The Just King: Monarchical Judicial Authority in Ancient Israel,* JSOTSup 12 (Sheffield: JSOT Press, 1979), p. 219; Jean Bottéro, *Mesopotamia: Writing, Reasoning, and the Gods* (Chicago: University of Chicago Press, 1992), pp. 167-68.

99. Cf. Muellner, *The Anger of Achilles,* pp. 38-39.

over cattle or white sheep. But Antinous has struck me on account of my pitiful belly *(gastēr)*, a cursed thing, which brings humans many evils. *(Od.* 17.468-74)

Someone who is hungry has no choice but to find food. Antinous had no sympathy for the suffering of a beggar. Antinous's ambitions, which issued from his belly as much as from his heart, appeared to allow him no space for sentiments of sympathy and pity.[100]

The belly does not cease to exert its influence over human behavior even when sufficient physical nourishment is obtained. Prior to entering the banquet hall, the beggar Odysseus had remarked to the swineherd Eumaeus:

There is no way to conceal a hungry belly *(gastēr)*, a cursed thing, which brings humans many evils. Also because of it, well-equipped ships are prepared that carry evils to enemies across the barren high seas. *(Od.* 17.286-89)

Here Homer provided another perspective on the motivation for warriors going into battle: it was not simply the *thumos*, "heart," in its desire for *kleos*, "glory," that drove men into battle; the belly *(gastēr)* with its destructive hungers was also an important cause of war.[101] Perhaps class differences too had an impact on the soldier's motivation, for Walter Donlan, in light of Thersites' protest in *Iliad* 2.225-42, claims that ordinary people were more concerned about getting enough to eat and did not try to gain glory in battle.[102]

The beggar Odysseus, alienated from his own household by twenty years of wandering, was treated on his return as if he were the lowest of the low in his own house. The extended feasting of the suitors was tantamount to a gradual palace coup. The endless feasting not only satisfied the physical hungers of the suitors, it also consumed the substance of Odysseus's household and thus contributed to the strategies of ambitious suitors who longed to take over the kingship of Ithaca.[103] Antinous, who is portrayed as the most greedy and aggressive among the suitors, in effect had gone to war against the household of Odysseus where his desire for gain went unchecked.[104] The wily Odysseus knew that he

---

100. Pietro Pucci, *Odysseus Polutropos* (Ithaca: Cornell University Press, 1987), pp. 185-87; Thalmann, *The Swineherd and the Bow,* pp. 225-26; cf. Rose, *Sons of the Gods, Children of Earth,* pp. 111-12.

101. Pucci, *Odysseus Polutropos,* pp. 173-74; Crotty, *The Poetics of Supplication,* p. 136.

102. Walter Donlan, *The Aristocratic Ideal in Ancient Greece: Attitude of Superiority from Homer to the End of the Fifth Century* B.C. (Lawrence, Kan.: Coronado, 1980), p. 22.

103. Thalmann, *The Swineherd and the Bow,* pp. 187-88.

104. Pierre Carlier, *La royauté en Grèce avant Alexandre* (Strasbourg: AECR, 1984), pp. 143-44.

had to be attentive to the demands of the belly operative in his opponents as well as in himself, and so he was faced with the perennial question: When was it necessary to listen to the demands of the belly and when to resist them?[105] Odysseus through his cleverness, wisdom, and stamina was able to sublimate the desires of the belly.

As Telemachus began to come of age, the suitors devised ways to murder him so as to prevent him from succeeding his father as king in Ithaca (*Od.* 4.663-74). After Telemachus eluded their ambush on his voyage home from visiting Nestor and Menelaus (*Od.* 16.342-50), the suitors gathered to draw up a second plot on Telemachus's life, but one of their number, Amphinomous, revealed his attitude toward killing Telemachus:

> Friends, I certainly would not want to kill Telemachus. It is a dreadful thing to kill one of royal descent. But first let us seek the will of the gods. If the oracular decrees of great Zeus approve it, I myself will kill him and will urge all others to do so. But if the gods dissuade us from this course, I urge you to refrain. (*Od.* 16.400-405)

Amphinomous articulated here an important guideline in the politics of Homeric society: regicide was legitimate only if it was approved by the gods. Telemachus's escape from the suitors' first attempt at ambush would have raised questions about the gods' approval of such a plot.[106]

Amphinomous's desire to gain the approval of the gods for their plot against Telemachus was not shared by all the suitors. The duplicitous Eurymachus informed Penelope of his desire to protect Telemachus while secretly planning to murder him (*Od.* 16.434-49). Later, Eurymachus tried to lay the blame for the plot solely upon his fellow suitor Antinous when he pleaded with the warrior Odysseus who was about to kill him:

> But the one who was the cause of all this already lies dead, namely, Antinous. He instigated these actions. He did not so much wish for or aim at marriage but considered other things which the son of Cronus did not bring about: that he would ambush and kill your son and then rule as king over the community of well-built Ithaca. But now he lies dead, as was his due. (*Od.* 22.48-54)

Both Eurymachus and Antinous appear to have been driven by greed and the desire for power. After the plot failed, Eurymachus claimed that Zeus did not approve it. The narrative of the *Odyssey* does not speak of any effort by the suit-

---

105. Pucci, *Odysseus Polutropos*, p. 179.
106. Olson, *Blood and Iron*, p. 198.

ors to obtain an omen approving their plot. The definitive failure of the plot with no opportunity for a third attempt and with Odysseus threatening to kill the suitors finally seems to have convinced Eurymachus that Zeus was not in favor of it. However, these views on regicide expressed by Eurymachus do seem to echo the principle expressed earlier by Amphinomous: that regicide in the Homeric world was legitimate only if it was approved by the gods. If indeed the discernment of the divine will was only attempted *post factum*, then this process provided maximum latitude for the desires of the belly to express themselves in rivalry with opponents.[107] As the contrasting attitudes of Amphinomous and Eurymachus indicate, the extent to which the divine will was considered a serious factor in political matters varied according to the characters and the circumstances.

In Israel, when David expanded his rule over the territories of the Transjordan, he put pressure upon the human and material resources of the land of Israel.[108] The increasing centralization of the kingdom also intruded on the people's traditional ways.[109] The popular revolt that seemed to respond to these mounting pressures was instigated by David's son Absalom and so is known as Absalom's revolt. The narrative of 2 Samuel 15–19 introduces Absalom as a pretender to the throne who tried to gain the backing of the people by listening to their grievances. He stationed himself at the gate of Jerusalem and offered to hear the legal cases of Israelites from various parts of the kingdom (2 Sam. 15:1-5). Apparently, there was a need for royal judges to attend to the people's complaints that David had neglected.[110] Second Samuel 15:6 claims that through his efforts Absalom "was stealing away the loyalties of the people of Israel." The stage was set for the uprising. David's claim to be divinely elected did not mean to Absalom and the people at large that David could retain such rule under any conditions.

Dissatisfaction with David's rule was widespread. Those who remained loyal to David were the members of his court and his mercenaries (2 Sam. 15:13-18). In contrast, Absalom drew support from the northern tribes and Judah (2 Sam. 16:15; 18:6, 17; 19:8). Gilead in the Transjordan appears to have been the only Israelite area that did not join Absalom in his revolt (2 Sam. 17:24; 19:15; 19:31-32).[111] In the face of such a general uprising, David and his followers fled to the Transjordan.

---

107. Olson, *Blood and Iron*, pp. 214-15; cf. Crotty, *The Poetics of Supplication*, p. 171.

108. Crüsemann, *Der Widerstand gegen das Königtum*, p. 99; John Bright, *A History of Israel* (Philadelphia: Westminster, 1981), p. 208.

109. Halpern, *David's Secret Demons*, p. 371.

110. P. Kyle McCarter, Jr., *II Samuel*, AB 9 (Garden City, N.Y.: Doubleday, 1984), pp. 356-57; Whitelam, *The Just King*, pp. 137-42.

111. Hayim Tadmor, "Traditional Institutions and the Monarchy: Social and Political Ten-

Absalom planned to put David to death (2 Sam. 17:1-4). His justification for this drastic action against a divinely elected ruler was that David had ruled unjustly (2 Sam. 15:3-4).[112] Absalom himself felt that he had been wronged by David's failure to punish Amnon for his rape of Tamar (2 Sam. 13:20-37).[113] The unjust character of a king's rule is the rationale given by the Deuteronomist for the early demise of northern Israelite kings. For example, in 1 Kings 15:25-28 the Deuteronomist reports that: (1) Nadab became king of the northern kingdom; then (2) Nadab did evil in the sight of the Lord, which meant that he lost his legitimacy as king; and then (3) Nadab was assassinated by Baasha. The basic principle at work in this tripartite pattern is that an Israelite king can undermine the legitimacy of his rule through unjust actions and so can expect as a punishment that he will forfeit his position as king to another, usually through assassination.[114]

Absalom was able to convince the people that the Lord had turned away from David and elected him to be their new king. When he positioned himself at the gate of Jerusalem to hear the legal cases of the people, he obtained a chariot and horses and a bodyguard: symbols of a ruler who was prepared to enforce his decrees and judgments (2 Sam. 15:1-4).[115] After David fled Jerusalem, one of his advisers, Hushai, infiltrated the ranks of Absalom's advisers and pretended to switch his loyalty to Absalom. He made the following statement, whose ambiguous referent allowed Hushai to remain loyal to David while he ostensibly committed himself to Absalom: "The one whom the Lord, this people, and all the Israelites have chosen, I will belong to him, and with him I will abide" (2 Sam. 16:18).[116] This ambiguous statement by Hushai indicated, nevertheless, that the people had already acclaimed Absalom as king according to the

---

sions in the Time of David and Solomon," in *Studies in the Period of David and Solomon and Other Essays*, ed. T. Ishida (Winona Lake, Ind.: Eisenbrauns, 1982), p. 246; Crüsemann, *Der Widerstand gegen das Königtum*, p. 100; Whitelam, *The Just King*, p. 137; Robert Polzin, *David and the Deuteronomist* (Bloomington: Indiana University Press, 1993), pp. 190-91.

112. McCarter, *II Samuel*, p. 359; David Daube, "Absalom and the Ideal King," *VT* 48 (1998): 319.

113. R. N. Whybray, *The Succession Narrative: A Study of II Samuel 9–20; 1 Kings 1–2*, SBT 9, 2nd series (Naperville, Ill.: Allenson, 1968), p. 38.

114. Knoppers, *Two Nations Under God*, p. 205.

115. Cf. Polzin (*David and the Deuteronomist*, p. 150); J. P. Fokkelman, *Narrative Art and Poetry in the Books of Samuel*, vol. 1: *King David*, Studia Semitica Neerlandica 20 (Assen: Van Gorcum, 1981), pp. 166, 168.

116. McCarter, *II Samuel*, p. 390; Ludwig Schmidt, *Menschlicher Erfolg und Jahwes Initiative*, WMANT 38 (Neukirchen-Vluyn: Neukirchener Verlag, 1970), pp. 99-105, 172; Daube, "Absalom and the Ideal King," p. 323; Whybray, *The Succession Narrative*, p. 51; Fokkelman, *Narrative Art and Poetry*, 1:206.

typical ceremonial for the election of a king in which two steps occur: (1) an indication that the Lord had chosen a particular man to be king and (2) his acclamation by the people (see 1 Sam. 10:17-27).[117]

When David and his professional soldiers defeated Absalom and his army drawn from the populace, any basis for the claim to Absalom's election to the kingship by the Lord was removed.[118] Because Absalom died in the battle, the question of the legitimacy of his claim to the kingship was not pursued further in the biblical account. Instead, the account picks up again with David and his efforts to reestablish his hold on the kingship. David took steps to strengthen his ties with the tribe of Judah (2 Sam. 19:15-16), even if such measures caused disaffection among the northern tribes (2 Sam. 20:1-20).[119]

Regicide was legitimate in Israel if a king had undermined his kingship through unjust actions and if murder was a necessary means for removing him from office. Divine election was not an indelible mark imprinted on the person of the king; it could be forfeited by an unjust king. The demise of Absalom and the political astuteness of David in salvaging his rule left unanswered questions about the extent to which each man was opportunistic and the extent to which each was responding to the divine will. Such ambiguity was an inescapable, yet necessary dimension of a political arrangement in which attention was given to the intervention of the divine in the political arena.

In a number of Hammurapi's inscriptions, he or his court poets described his election to the kingship with imagery that portrayed the people as rambunctious and potentially rebellious. Court poets proclaimed that Hammurapi built the Ezida sanctuary in Borsippa "when Enlil gave him the land and the people to rule (and) placed their lead rope in his hand."[120] Hammurapi celebrated the construction of a storehouse in Babylon by claiming that he was able to do so "when Enlil gave me the people of his land so that I might exercise dominion (over them), (and when) he placed their lead rope in my hand."[121] The image of a "lead rope" (ṣerrētum) created the picture of a potentially energetic, independent animal, such as a steer or a heifer, that would run off unless closely controlled. Passive herd animals like sheep did not require lead ropes to keep them in order.

In the *Atraḫasis Epic,* the noise generated by humanity that deprived Enlil

---

117. Albrecht Alt, "The Monarchy in the Kingdoms of Israel and Judah," in *Essays on Old Testament History and Religion* (Oxford: Blackwell, 1966), p. 243; Halpern, *The Constitution of the Monarchy,* pp. 184-85.

118. Polzin, *David and the Deuteronomist,* pp. 186-87.

119. Polzin, *David and the Deuteronomist,* pp. 192-94.

120. Frayne, *RIME 4,* E4.3.6.17, lines 24-30.

121. Frayne, *RIME 4,* E4.3.6.3, lines 15-19.

of sleep (II:1-8) finds an echo in the opening section of the *Enuma Elish* in which the noise of the younger gods disturbed Tiamat. Tiamat's lover Apsu went to Tiamat and tried to persuade her to do away with the younger gods so that they, the older gods, might have peace and quiet:

> When Tiamat heard this,
> She became angry and scolded her lover,
> She cried out in distress, furious in her isolation.
> He had cast evil into her planning.
> "What? Are we going to destroy what we have made?
> Their demeanor may be annoying,
>   but we should endure it in good form." (I:41-47)[122]

The conflict between the older and younger generations of gods is one that Jacobsen has characterized as a struggle between the forces of rest and activity.[123] The metaphor of noise pointed to the positive qualities of creativity and independence. If there had been no movement, the world would not have emerged. Movement and activity are intrinsic to it. So, the *Enuma Elish* gave a privileged position to "noise" in the created order that served to legitimate the noise generated by humanity. Piotr Michalowski notes that this positive assessment of noise elevated humanity from the position of slaves of the gods to that of free, creative beings.[124] Such "noise" in *Atraḫasis* seems, however, to be interpreted as a human usurpation of divine prerogatives where rebellious, scheming humans intent on freeing themselves from their servant status to the gods challenge the divinely established hierarchy between gods and humans.[125] Humans can legitimately press the limits of what is possible for humans, but they can also overstep these limits.

In line with the image of the Mesopotamians as rambunctious cattle, a number of popular uprisings and palace coups did occur. Mesopotamian kings claimed to rule by divine right, yet such a claim did not give them the freedom to rule absolutely. Even though the texts recovered from Mesopotamian royal archives emphasize the kings' victories and downplay their setbacks, remnants of the voice of opposition to royal rule can be obtained from these texts. One royal inscription from Ipiq-Ishtar of Malgium, probably a contemporary of

---

122. The text is from W. G. Lambert and Simon Packer, *Enuma Eliš* (Oxford: Clarendon, 1966), p. 2.

123. Jacobsen, *The Treasures of Darkness*, p. 170.

124. Piotr Michalowski, "Presence at Creation," in *Lingering over Words: Studies in Ancient Near Eastern Literature in Honor of William L. Moran*, ed. Tzvi Abusch et al., HSM 37 (Atlanta: Scholars, 1990), p. 389; cf. Moran, "Some Considerations of Form," p. 252.

125. Oden, "Divine Aspirations in Atrahasis and Genesis 1–11," pp. 207-10.

Hammurapi and his son Samsuiluna,[126] records the suppression of a popular uprising in which all of the land *(mātum . . . kalûšu)* rose up as a whole *(innapḫarim)* against the king and the deity Belet-Ili:

> At that time, all of the land *(mātum . . . kalûšu)* as a whole *(innapḫarim)* went down (and) made a great uproar and committed a sacrilege. They destroyed the sanctuary, the dwelling of the great Belet-Ili, and cut down the awe-inspiring radiance of her orchard."[127]

From Ipiq-Ishtar's perspective, the populace had become outlaws by sinning against the gods and destroying the sanctuary of Belet-Ili, a deity whom he claimed was his mother. Ipiq-Ishtar believed he had the support of Anum, Enlil, Belet-Ili, and Ea in his suppression of the revolt and in his construction of a new sanctuary for Belet-Ili as well as the restoration of her previous sanctuary. The fact that the whole land rebelled strongly suggests that the people believed that the king and the temple establishment of Belet-Ili were promoting unjust practices. Even though their rebellion was foiled, this event provides an instance where Mesopotamians did not simply accept the label of passive subjects before the royal establishment but rose up in revolt when they believed circumstances warranted it.[128]

Mesopotamian kings knew that they had to guard themselves against palace coups and local uprisings. In Mari, a prophetess delivered the following message to Zimri-Lim (1782-1759 B.C.) on behalf of the goddess Annunitum:

> Zimri-Lim, you will be put to the test by a revolt. Guard yourself. Put at your side men you can trust, whom you love. Station them so that they can guard you. You must not go about by yourself. *(ARM* X, 7:8-19)[129]

The prophetess, aware of a potential palace coup, demonstrated her concern for the safety of the king, a recurring topic in the prophecies preserved in the royal archives of Mari.[130] These words of warning would no doubt have reminded

---

126. Raphael Kutscher ("Malgium," *RLA* 7 [1988]: 300-302) notes that Malgium is usually located near the mouth of the Diyala River near Kut al-'Amara.

127. Frayne, *RIME 4,* E4.11.1, lines 18-24; K. R. Veenhof, "Notes brèves," *RA* 79 (1985): 190-91.

128. Cf. Norman Yoffee, "Political Economy in Early Mesopotamian States," *Annual Review of Anthropology* 24 (1995): 302.

129. The text is from Georges Dossin and André Finet, *Archives royales de Mari, X: Textes cunéiformes du Louvre XXXI, La correspondance féminine* (Paris: Imprimatur nationale, 1967).

130. William Moran, "New Evidence from Mari on the History of Prophecy," *Bib* 51 (1969): 17-18; Abraham Malamat, *Mari and the Bible* (Leiden: Brill, 1998), pp. 70-71; Moshe Anbar, "Mari and the Origin of Prophecy," in *Kinattūtu ša darāti,* ed. A. F. Rainey (Tel Aviv: University

Zimri-Lim of the fate of his predecessors in the Lim dynasty at Mari: Yaḫdun-Lim (ca. 1825-1798 B.C.) was killed in a palace conspiracy and replaced by his son Sumu-Yamam, who in turn was killed after a three-year reign by the Assyrian usurpers Shamshi-Adad I (ca. 1830-1776 B.C.) and his son Yasmaḫ-Adad (ca. 1796-1776 B.C.).[131] Yaḫdun-Lim's claim to be divinely elected to rule by the god Dagan had not deterred the usurpers.[132] Legitimate and just rule was essential to stable royal rule, but the king also needed to be vigilant and wield sufficient physical force in order to maintain his rule. Usurpers in Mesopotamian kingdoms could make a case for the legitimacy of the regicide of their predecessors once they had been successful in gaining the throne.

Competition and disagreement between a king and his opponents in a community in Homeric Greece, biblical Israel, and OB Mesopotamia could intensify to the point of extreme polarization where regicide was regarded as legitimate. The causes for such division in the community could be diverse and range from the tyranny of the king to the ambition of opportunists within the community. The belly would have been a factor in legitimate and illegitimate uprisings: it would stir the oppressed to act for the basic requirements of life and would stir the opportunists to grasp for power. The traditions and values of the community would have been important elements in discerning the legitimacy of an uprising against a king. If the king's opponents were successful in driving him from the throne, then they could have made a case for the legitimacy of their action, such as Absalom's followers did in the early, successful part of his revolt. Force alone was insufficient to stabilize a new king's rule; he also had to be able to draw support from tradition for his rule.

If the opponents of the king were the community as a whole or a significant section of the community such as that in the Mesopotamian city of Malgium, then the organizers of such an uprising would probably have had to explain at the outset of their plotting, if the reasons were not already apparent to the people, why regicide was an appropriate and necessary action. Such a drastic action within communities where kings were divinely elected would

---

of Tel Aviv Press, 1993), p. 2; Simon Parker, "Official Attitudes Toward Prophecy at Mari and in Israel," *VT* 43 (1993): 57-59. References to conspiring servants are also found in OB omen texts; see Ulla Jeyes, *Old Babylonian Extispicy: Omen Texts in the British Museum* (Leiden: Nederlands Historisch-Archaeologisch Instituut te Istanbul, 1989), pp. 29-33.

131. Pierre Villard, "Shamshi-Adad and Sons: The Rise and Fall of an Upper Mesopotamian Empire," in *Civilizations of the Ancient Near East*, ed. J. Sasson (New York: Scribner, 1995), p. 874; J.-R. Kupper, "Jaḫdun-Lim," in *RLA*, 5:240; Y. Wu, *A Political History of Eshnunna, Mari and Assyria during the Early Old Babylonian Period* (Changchung: Institute of History of Ancient Civilizations, 1994), pp. 106-8, 328, 334, 337.

132. Frayne, *RIME 4*, E4.6.8.1, lines 9-10.

probably have required an oracle permitting regicide, as was the case with Amphinomous's request in the *Odyssey*. These extreme circumstances in which regicide would have been legitimate in Homeric Greece, biblical Israel, and OB Mesopotamia reveal that criticism and opposition to a particular king's rule took their rightful place alongside the call for the people to be obedient to the king.

The Locus of Authority: The Origin of Law and Morality

A king could not rule effectively unless his commands were obeyed. Telemachus, as heir apparent in Ithaca, could not get the suitors to obey his commands, but his lack of authority could not be solved simply by his holding the office of king; he also had to be able to rule by might. Communities confer authority on positions through customary ways of acting, traditions, and explicit decisions.[133] As discussed earlier, the Achaean coalition granted Agamemnon the authority of the leader of the coalition. His positional authority often called forth a greater measure of obedience than did the quality or content of his commands.[134] If Agamemnon were to succeed as king, he had to find ways to make decisions and give directions that were more truthful and compelling. His identity as the leader of the coalition was significant but not sufficient in itself for the success of the coalition's mission. Telemachus was youthful. Agamemnon was afflicted with "blindness" (*atē, Il.* 9.115-20) from Zeus so that he made short-sighted decisions. In the case of both would-be leaders, they had not reached the point where their own voice could command the attention and obedience that their positions demanded. There was thus a vacuum of authority both in Ithaca and in the Achaean coalition.

When the Achaean coalition had suffered serious setbacks to the point that the Achaeans had to make a special appeal to Achilles to return to battle, the elderly Nestor, in the company of the other warrior-kings, addressed Agamemnon as follows:

133. Anthony Giddens, *Central Problems in Social Theory: Action, Structure, and Contradiction in Social Analysis* (Berkeley: University of California Press, 1979), pp. 39, 59, 76; Hannah Arendt, *Between Past and Future: Six Exercises in Political Thought* (New York: Viking, 1961), p. 124; Mann, *The Sources of Social Power*, 1:67-68, 99-100; Pierre Bourdieu, *Language and Symbolic Power*, ed. John B. Thompson (Cambridge, Mass.: Harvard University Press, 1991), pp. 109-11; John N. Figgis, *Divine Right of Kings* (Cambridge: Cambridge University Press, 1934), p. 33.

134. Pucci, *The Song of the Sirens*, pp. 190, 205; Martin, *The Language of Heroes*, pp. 62, 69-71.

Son of Atreus, most distinguished one, lord of men, Agamemnon, with you I will start and with you I will conclude because you are lord of many peoples and Zeus has handed over to you the scepter *(skēptron)* and customary law *(themistes)* so that you might deliberate on their behalf. (*Il.* 9.96-99)

The *themistes* referred to established ways of acting that came by way of custom to be regarded as decreed by Zeus. There is no clear evidence in the Homeric texts that Zeus promulgated the *themistes* as specific decrees for the Achaeans to obey.[135] These orally communicated laws still had communal discussion and debate as their interpretive context. Laws did not gain a measure of independence from the oral medium until they were written on stelae placed in the marketplace or written on temple walls, from which public positions they could be read aloud.[136]

In Hesiod's *Theogony*, Themis, daughter of Gaia (lines 132-38) and married to Zeus (lines 901-4),[137] is the one who gives directives, not advice; Themis represents the fixed order of the world.[138] In the Archaic *polis*, *themis* probably referred at first to the right of every man to speak in the assembly, but then was extended to cover all the established customs of the political community.[139] Prior to 500 B.C. the Greeks regarded law as coming from an external authority; thereafter they began to regard themselves as the creators of law.[140] Nestor reminded Agamemnon that his possession of the *themistes* gave his words a distinct aura and also obliged him to rule according to the justice of Zeus.[141] Aga-

---

135. Kurt Latte, "Themis," *PW* 5.2 (2. Reihe): 1626; Carlier, *La royauté en Grèce avant Alexandre*, p. 193.

136. Karl-Joachim Hölkescamp, *Schiedsrichter, Gesetzgeber und Gesetzgebung im archaischen Griechenland*, Historia 131 (Stuttgart: Franz Steiner, 1999), pp. 278-81; Jesper Svenbro, *"Phrasikleia": An Anthropology of Reading in Ancient Greece* (Ithaca: Cornell University Press, 1993), pp. 116, 120; James Whitley, "Literacy and Law-making: The Case of Archaic Crete," in *Archaic Greece: New Approaches and New Evidence*, ed. Nick Fisher and Hans van Wees (London: Duckworth, 1998), pp. 319-20.

137. Hesiod, *Theogony*, ed. M. L. West (Oxford: Clarendon, 1966), pp. 117, 199-206; 145, 405-8.

138. Jean-Pierre Vernant, "Myth and Divinity," in *Myth, Religion, and Society*, ed. R. L. Gordon (Cambridge: Cambridge University Press, 1977), p. 1.

139. Emma Stafford, "*Themis*: Religion and Order in the Archaic *Polis*," in *The Development of the "Polis" in Archaic Greece*, ed. L. Mitchell and P. Rhodes (New York: Routledge, 1997), p. 158. See also Kurt Raaflaub, "Homer to Solon: The Rise of the *Polis*: The Written Sources," in *The Ancient Greek City-State: Symposium on the Occasion of the 250th Anniversary of the Royal Danish Academy of Sciences and Letters, July 1-4, 1992*, ed. M. H. Hansen (Copenhagen: Munksgaard, 1993), p. 63.

140. Ian Morris, *Archaeology as Cultural History* (Oxford: Blackwell, 2000), pp. 166-67.

141. William M. Sale, "The Government of Troy: Politics in the *Iliad*," *Greek, Roman and Byzantine Studies* 35 (1994): 38.

memnon's taking of the woman prisoner of war, Briseis, from Achilles constituted a breach of customary practices among the Achaean warriors: a prize once awarded to a warrior should not be retaken (*Il.* 1.182-87, 390-92; 9.314-22).[142] Agamemnon's action was an example of a king's transgression of the *themistes* that he was charged to oversee. So, Nestor challenged Agamemnon to acknowledge his fault and take steps to heal the division with Achilles (*Il.* 9.103-13). In his rivalry with Achilles, Agamemnon had used the authority of his position as leader of the coalition to strengthen his personal power rather than to serve the well-being of the coalition.[143] Only after heavy Achaean losses was Agamemnon ready to acknowledge his madness and make restitution to Achilles (*Il.* 9.115-20; cf. 1.239-44). Nestor's statement that the *themistes* came from Zeus gave them an aura and an ambiguity analogous to oracles.[144]

In the *Odyssey,* when Odysseus revealed his identity to the suitors and announced his intention to wreak vengeance on them, he said:

> You dogs, you did not expect me ever to reach home from the land of the Trojans, for you have pillaged my household and have forcefully lain with the servant women. While I was still alive, you courted my wife. You did not fear the gods who occupy the wide-reaching heavens nor the reproach of humans to come thereafter. Now over all of you the cords of destruction are fastened. (*Od.* 22.35-41)

As Odysseus prepared to slay the suitors, he proclaimed that such consequences did not come merely from humans but also from the gods. Odysseus's views on the divine role in his vengeance find an echo in the words of the suitor Eurymachus who, when faced with death at the hands of Odysseus, tried to lay the blame for the suitors' actions on the slain Antinous and stated that Zeus did not allow Antinous's plots to succeed (*Od.* 22.48-53).

Even though both Odysseus and Eurymachus noted the hand of the gods in the judgment facing the suitors, sympathy for the suitors is not absent from the narrative. The causes of the evils that befall these characters are complex, and so Odysseus's revenge is not to be understood in a narrowly moralistic way.[145] The *Odyssey* raises the issue of individual accountability over against group responsibility in ways that the *Iliad* did not in its concern with the resto-

---

142. Vernant, *Mortals and Immortals,* p. 53; Rose, *Sons of the Gods, Children of Earth,* pp. 78-79, 81-82; Muellner, *The Anger of Achilles,* pp. 34, 138-42; cf. Sale, "The Government of Troy," p. 45.

143. Pucci, *The Song of the Sirens,* p. 205.

144. Cf. Vernant, *Mortals and Immortals,* p. 307; Stafford, "*Themis,*" pp. 162-63.

145. Crotty, *The Poetics of Supplication,* p. 157.

ration of communal and cosmic order against polluting, chaotic forces.[146] The tragic nature of the suitors' involvement in the affairs of Odysseus's household is alluded to in the dream that Penelope had foreshadowing the slaying of the suitors:

> I have twenty geese at my house that feed on wheat away from the water. I am cheered when I watch them. But a large eagle with a curved beak came down from the mountain and broke all their necks and killed them. They were heaped together in the halls, but he rose up in the bright air. Then I was weeping and crying out, even though it was a dream. The fair-haired Achaean women came together around me as I wept grievously because the eagle had killed my geese. (*Od.* 19.536-43)

Within the context of this dream, Penelope seems to reveal that the presence of the suitors in the household and the attention they paid to her were not completely to her disliking.[147] Her delaying tactics had extended the time of courtship and perhaps contributed to the suitors' failure to pay their portion of the hospitality expenses of the courtship, as was customary.[148] Her mourning over their deaths, even if in the context of a dream, seems to indicate her concern for them and at the very least made the point that the suffering of the suitors deserved to be recognized as that of fellow humans.[149]

The geese as a symbol may, however, have a referent different from or in addition to the suitors. Louise Pratt interprets the twenty geese in Penelope's dream as a symbol of the twenty years of waiting for Odysseus to return. The slaughter of the geese means that the twenty years have expired, and so Penelope can expect to hear news that Odysseus has perished.[150] If, then, Penelope's weeping is linked with the end of her period of waiting, it would seem also to be related to the lamentation of the nightingale (*Od.* 19.518-24), which, as Richard Seaford has explained, manifests Penelope's liminal state of imminent transfer from Odysseus's household to that of another.[151] So, in this symbolic interpretation of the slaying of the geese, the weeping of the nightingale and the weeping over the geese pointed to a dramatic change that was about to happen in Penelope's life.

146. Muellner, *The Anger of Achilles,* pp. 37, 43.

147. Olga Levaniouk, "Penelope and the Penelops," in *Nine Essays on Homer,* ed. M. Carlisle and O. Levaniouk (Lanham, Md.: Rowman & Littlefield, 1999), p. 97.

148. Seaford, *Reciprocity and Ritual,* pp. 57-58.

149. Crotty, *The Poetics of Supplication,* p. 195.

150. Louise Pratt, "Odyssey 19.535-50: On the Interpretation of Dreams and Signs in Homer," *Classical Philology* 89 (1994): 150-52.

151. Seaford, *Reciprocity and Ritual,* p. 56.

The exercise of authority in the Homeric community wove together the divine and the human such that at times they were nearly indistinguishable. In the *Odyssey,* the Olympians do not directly intervene in human affairs as in the *Iliad;* as a result, the human characters are expected to see that the troubles they experience are ones that they bring upon themselves. However, when the *Odyssey* is viewed as a whole, it is, as S. Douglas Olson phrases it, "a tale of direct divine intervention in the world."[152] The belief that the gods were watching over the affairs of the community and that Zeus was promoting a just order reminds the reader that no matter how hard-nosed or wily the tactics of a character like Odysseus, he was acting according to an outlook that valued truth over power.[153] His strength and cleverness were not put to the service of amoral schemes in which success was the ultimate goal.[154] Odysseus was guided by the *themistes* that issued from both the tradition and the will of Zeus. Even if the interpretation and application of the *themistes* in circumstances were ensconced in the subjective desires of the Homeric characters and the contradictions of their experience, the effort to listen to the voice of the gods and the tradition testified that the characters' actions aimed to serve truth more than power. Belief in the existence of such a moral world order and its truth was challenged by the contradictions of experience that came to expression in the epics in such episodes as Hera's upsetting of the world order as guaranteed by Zeus (*Il.* 8.401-8).[155] Such truth was an embodied truth that did not deny the desires of the human actor but rather promoted such desires and transformed them as the circumstances dictated. A character like Odysseus did not sacrifice his life to an abstract truth outside of himself but rather to a transcendent truth that was in accord with his deepest wish.[156]

---

152. Olson, *Blood and Iron,* p. 215.

153. Segal, *Singers, Heroes, and Gods,* pp. 76, 83; Muellner, *The Anger of Achilles,* p. 34. Jameson (*The Political Unconscious,* p. 114) explains how Derrida demystifies binary oppositions such as presence-absence, writing-speaking, center-periphery; he emphasizes how Nietzsche identified the opposition between good and evil as the foundation for power and domination. These writers would subject the concept of truth to this hermeneutics of suspicion and demystify it. Yet, in my opinion, to criticize a conception of truth and demystify it is to alter the conception rather than to deny that there is anything to be known.

154. Crotty, *The Poetics of Supplication,* pp. 171-72; Segal, *Singers, Heroes, and Gods,* p. 54.

155. Hera and Athena favored the Achaeans in the Trojan War, but Zeus had ordered them not to assist the Achaeans in battle (*Il.* 8.5-27). With Hera's support, Athena entered the battle and Zeus made known his intent to punish her if she persisted in defying his orders. By their assistance of the Achaeans, Hera and Athena advocated the justice of the Achaeans' cause and so raised questions about the justice of Zeus's support of the Trojans to whom he granted success in order to vindicate the aggrieved Achilles. Was it the justice of Zeus's plan or his power that enabled him to prevail? See Rose, *Sons of the Gods, Children of Earth,* p. 84.

156. Crotty, *The Poetics of Supplication,* p. 169; Segal, *Singers, Heroes, and Gods,* p. 78.

When word was brought to David that his son Absalom had been killed in the battle to suppress his rebellion, it is reported that David wept and cried out: "My son Absalom, my son, my son Absalom! If only I had died instead of you, Absalom, my son, my son!" (2 Sam. 19:1[18:33]). Such anguish must have stood in tension with David's recognition that Absalom intended to kill him in order to gain the throne in Jerusalem.[157] The reader of 2 Samuel is led to believe that the depth of David's anguish would have arisen at least in part from his recognition of the negative circumstances that had beset his royal household since the time he had taken the wife of Uriah the Hittite as his wife (2 Sam. 12:11). Here he would have recognized that Absalom's rebelliousness was not simply of his own doing but part of a larger divinely supported order in which the consequences for misdeeds had to be borne.[158]

According to 2 Samuel 11–12, when David was at the height of his power, he was drawn by the beauty of Bathsheba, the wife of Uriah the Hittite (2 Sam. 11:2-5). David committed adultery with her and then took various steps to conceal the fact. When these failed, he arranged to have Uriah fall in battle. After this occurred, David brought Bathsheba into his house to be his wife. At this point, the prophet Nathan recited a parable about a rich man with many sheep who stole the only lamb belonging to a poor man in order to entertain a guest (2 Sam. 12:1-4). When Nathan asked David what should be done to the rich man, David angrily declared with the force of an oath that the man should be put to death and fourfold restitution should be made to the poor man.[159] Nathan then shocked David by saying, "You are the man!" (2 Sam. 12:7). Nathan proceeded to pronounce the divine indictment against David, who in spite of the many favors the Lord had bestowed on him had taken the wife of Uriah and arranged for Uriah's death. David himself was not to die for his sin, but the child born from his union with Bathsheba would die.[160] Furthermore, numer-

---

157. Cf. Polzin, *David and the Deuteronomist,* pp. 187-88.

158. Steven Weitzman, "David's Lament and the Poetics of Grief in 2 Samuel," *JQR* 85 (1995): 346, 355-56; Saul Olyan, "Honor, Shame, and Covenant Relations in Ancient Israel and Its Environment," *JBL* 115 (1996): 209-10; Gerhard von Rad, *Old Testament Theology,* vol. 1: *The Theology of Israel's Historical Traditions* (New York: Harper & Row, 1962), pp. 314-15; Steven McKenzie, *King David: A Biography* (New York: Oxford University Press, 2000), p. 35.

159. The fourfold restitution took the form of the deaths of four of David's sons: the child born of the union with Bathsheba (2 Sam. 12:18), Ammon (2 Sam. 13:28-29), Absalom (2 Sam. 18:15; 19:1), and Adonijah (1 Kings 2:24-25) (J. P. M. Walsh, S.J., private communication).

160. Halpern (*David's Secret Demons,* pp. 401-4) deconstructs the biblical narrative on the birth of Solomon and speculates that the child that died was a fiction created to cover over the fact that Solomon's actual father was Uriah, not David. He argues that Solomon would have strengthened his claim on the throne if he were perceived to be David's son rather than Uriah's.

ous internal troubles were to arise within his household, among which would be the revolt of his son Absalom (2 Sam. 12:7-14).[161]

The prohibitions against adultery and murder were embedded within the customs of the Israelite people. The fundamental character of these prohibitions was furthered enhanced when the tradition enshrined them within the Decalogue (Exod. 20:13-14; Deut. 5:17-18). These commonsense practical rules for maintaining a just social order were seen to be part of a larger world order decreed by the Lord.[162] The appetites and desires that issued from a human to create a vital community could also exceed their limits and so disorient the human agent. David recognized his transgression and tried to conceal it, but the prophet Nathan criticized him and pronounced the divine judgment against him.

The disorientation caused by royal transgression of the customary ways of the community was also highlighted by the ancient Israelite story of the northern king Ahab's confiscation of the parcel of land of Naboth the Jezreelite (1 Kings 21:1-16).[163] When Ahab offered to buy Naboth's property that was located next to the king's summer residence in Jezreel, Naboth refused with the words: "The Lord forbid that I should give you my fathers' inheritance" (1 Kings 21:3). It was Naboth's right to refuse the king's request according to the customs of the Israelite community. Naboth seemed to appeal to a sacred duty imposed on him to keep his ancestral inheritance within his family.[164] Even though Israelites regularly bought and sold property, it was their right to refuse such land transfer.[165] The account of 1 Kings 21 indicates that Jezebel, Ahab's Phoenician-Canaanite wife, devised underhanded judicial proceedings and succeeded in

161. Daube, "Absalom and the Ideal King," pp. 315-25; Weitzman, "David's Lament and the Poetics of Grief in 2 Samuel," pp. 348-49. Randall Bailey (*David in Love and War: The Pursuit of Power in 2 Samuel 10–12*, JSOTSup 75 [Sheffield: Sheffield Academic Press, 1990], pp. 110-11, 128) argues that Nathan's indictment of David in 2 Sam. 12:7b-12 was a later addition summarizing events related in 1 Samuel 16–2 Samuel 8 and anticipating those in 2 Samuel 12–20 according to a prophecy-fulfillment schema.

162. Terence Fretheim, *Exodus* (Louisville: John Knox, 1991), pp. 232-35.

163. Ernst Würthwein, *Die Bücher der Könige*, 2 vols., ATD 11/1-2 (Göttingen: Vandenhoeck & Ruprecht, 1977, 1984), 2:247; Walsh, *1 Kings*, pp. 326-28; Robert Martin-Achard, "La vigne de Naboth (1 Rois 21) d'après des études récentes," *ETR* 66 (1991): 1-14; Rainer Kessler, "Gott und König, Grundeigentum und Fruchtbarkeit," *ZAW* 108 (1996): 223.

164. Karel van der Toorn (*Family Religion in Babylonia, Syria, and Israel* [Leiden: Brill, 1996], p. 207) claims that the burial of family members on the same plot of land through the generations gave such property a sacred character.

165. Roland de Vaux, *Ancient Israel*, 2 vols. (New York: McGraw-Hill, 1965), 1:167. Martin Noth, *Leviticus* (Philadelphia: Westminster, 1965), pp. 188-89. Richard Nelson (*First and Second Kings* [Louisville: John Knox, 1987], p. 139) claims that Naboth refused to sell because he had put himself under oath not to sell this particular plot of land.

getting Naboth convicted of blasphemy and treason (vv. 8-14). After Naboth was executed by stoning (vv. 13-14), Ahab took possession of Naboth's vineyard (v. 16).[166] The story emphasizes Jezebel's role in removing the reluctant Naboth from the scene and thus indicts kingship, as if it were more properly a Canaanite institution, for ignoring the customs of the Israelite community and displacing Israelites from their heritage.[167] Possession of a parcel of land was fundamental to the identity of the Israelites.[168] It provided them with a place within the community that was more than a geographical space. When royal power grew in Israel, the pressure to shift land to the crown and the dependents of the crown increased. Confiscation of ancestral property was tantamount to disenfranchising an Israelite.[169]

Customary ways of doing things carry with them a memory of the sacrifices made by previous generations in constructing an environment that a people called its home.[170] The bonds created by these sacrifices and sustained by the memory of them formed the relational matrix within which certain actions were permitted and others prohibited. The murders of Uriah the Hittite and Naboth the Jezreelite were actions designed to remove the person and the memory of these individuals from their communities. The greed of the royal appetites that precipitated these murders was unjust: it transgressed both the customary and divine laws of the community. Royal efforts to disguise these transgressions revealed that these kings were aware of the power of the prohibitions against murder, adultery, and illegal land confiscation.[171] The power inhering in such prohibitions went beyond the authority of officials who could enforce them; the power of these customary and divine laws was entwined in

166. Nahum Sarna ("Naboth's Vineyard Revisited (1 Kings 21)," in *Tehillah le-Moshe: Biblical and Judaic Studies in Honor of Moshe Greenberg,* ed. Mordechai Cogan et al. [Winona Lake, Ind.: Eisenbrauns, 1997], pp. 123-26) claims that the penalty for treason was not only capital punishment but forfeiture of land to the crown. David N. Freedman (*The Nine Commandments* [New York: Doubleday, 2000], pp. 106-8, 142-44) argues that the double crime of blasphemy and treason carried the penalty not only of the death of Naboth but also of his heirs; thus, with the execution of Naboth and his heirs, his property went to the crown.

167. Würthwein, *Die Bücher der Könige,* 2:251; Martin-Achard, "La vigne de Naboth," pp. 3-7; Karel van der Toorn, "Ritual Resistance and Self-Assertion: The Rechabites in Early Israelite Religion," in *Pluralism and Identity: Studies in Ritual Behavior,* ed. J. Platvoet and K. van der Toorn, Studies in the History of Religion 67 (Leiden: Brill, 1995), pp. 238-39; Sarna, "Naboth's Vineyard Revisited (1 Kings 21)," p. 120.

168. Klaus Koch, *The Prophets,* vol. 1: *The Assyrian Period* (Philadelphia: Fortress, 1982), pp. 49-50.

169. Martin-Achard, "La vigne de Naboth," pp. 3-4, 12-13.

170. Cf. Karel van der Toorn, "Ritual Resistance and Self-Assertion," pp. 238-43.

171. Whitelam, *The Just King,* p. 180.

the fabric of the community. Efforts to change customary practices that had the force of law highlighted their sacred dimension: these practices were the result of more than merely human convention; they communicated aspects of what the community revered as the divine will.

Mesopotamian kings strove to present themselves as just rulers. From small, outlying cities to the capital cities of territorial kingdoms, the kings regularly identified themselves in their inscriptions as promoters of justice. Hammurapi's celebrated *Code* benefited from the previous codes of Ur-nammu (ca. 2100 B.C.) and Lipit-Ishtar (ca. 1930 B.C.) and one from Eshnunna (ca. 1770 B.C.).[172] It is significant that Hammurapi had his *Code* inscribed on a stone stela and placed in a public place to be seen and read (by those who could read cuneiform); the *Code* was to make known Hammurapi's efforts to bring justice and good order to the land.[173] On this black basalt stela that was originally located in Sippar but was a copy of one in Esagila in Babylon,[174] the top one-third of the stela shows Hammurapi receiving the laws from the god Shamash: a point that is also spelled out in the epilogue of the *Code of Hammurapi* (see XLVIII:95-102). By such iconography, Hammurapi made clear to illiterate and literate alike that there was divine involvement in creating or endorsing the laws.[175] However, Hammurapi was not simply a passive recipient of the laws from the divine sphere; he claimed a strong measure of ownership over the laws written on his stela, particularly in the epilogue, where he was concerned about their preservation:

> In the future days, forever, may the king who rises up in the land maintain the words of justice which I have written on my stela. May he not change the laws of the land which I decreed or the ordinances of the land which I made. May he not put aside my statutes. (*CH* XLVIII:59-74)[176]

He claimed that he had "decreed" *(diānum)* or "made" *(parāsum)* these "laws *(dīnum)*/ordinances *(purussûm)* of the land." Rather than creating these laws like a legislator, Hammurapi was an executor who sustained them and made

---

172. Martha Roth, *Law Collections from Mesopotamia and Asia Minor*, Writings from the Ancient World 6 (Atlanta: Scholars, 1995), pp. 13-35, 57-70; Westbrook, "Cuneiform Law Codes," pp. 206-12; Samuel Greengus, "Legal and Social Institutions of Ancient Mesopotamia," in *Civilizations of the Ancient Near East*, ed. J. Sasson (New York: Scribner, 1995), pp. 471-72.

173. Jack M. Sasson, "King Hammurabi of Babylon," in *Civilizations of the Ancient Near East*, ed. J. Sasson (New York: Scribner, 1995), pp. 907-8; G. R. Driver and John C. Miles, *The Babylonian Laws*, vol. 1: *Legal Commentary* (Oxford: Clarendon, 1952), pp. 27-34; cf. Tinney, *The Nippur Lament*, p. 180.

174. Hurowitz, *Inu Anum Sīrum*, p. 64.

175. Roth, *Law Collections from Mesopotamia and Asia Minor*, p. 73.

176. The text is from Borger, *Babylonisch-assyrische Lesestücke*, p. 46.

them effective.[177] These laws were probably the decisions or verdicts of particular legal cases that were incorporated into this *Code* because of their exemplary character.[178] These particular cases demonstrated how royal justice could positively intervene where customary ways no longer adequately addressed the social and political circumstances.[179]

It is important to note that the larger fabric of the social order was shaped by the traditional and customary ways of the land, which the *Code* presupposed but made no pretension of articulating.[180] Jean Bottéro notes that Mesopotamian law was largely unwritten, yet known and understood.[181] Such unwritten law emerged into writing when new problems arose requiring royal decrees. The laws of the *Code of Hammurapi* drew upon the customs of the Mesopotamian communities and the tradition of royal judicial decisions and elevated their origin to the divine sphere through the belief that Shamash had endorsed these laws.

Repetition of traditional ways and consistency of practice seem to have loomed large in the Mesopotamians' understanding of good order.[182] Hammurapi concluded his *Code* with a series of blessings and curses on future kings, which called for divine assistance in maintaining the *Code* in its current form, free of any alterations. He introduced this section as follows:

> If that man pays attention to my words which I wrote on my stela and does not cast aside my laws (and) does not distort my words (and) does not change my statutes, may Shamash make that man, like me, the king of justice, have a long reign. May he shepherd his people justly. (*CH* XLIX:2-17)

177. Norman Yoffee, "Context and Authority in Early Mesopotamian Law," in *State Formation and Political Legitimacy: Political Anthropology*, vol. 6, ed. Ronald Cohen and Judith Toland (New Brunswick, N.J.: Transaction Books, 1988), p. 106.

178. Bottéro, *Mesopotamia*, p. 165; Westbrook, "Cuneiform Law Codes," pp. 218-19.

179. Bottéro, *Mesopotamia*, p. 180; Greengus, "Legal and Social Institutions," p. 472; Yoffee, "Context and Authority," p. 104.

180. Samuel Greengus, "Some Issues Relating to the Comparability of Laws and the Coherence of the Legal Tradition," in *Theory and Method in Biblical and Cuneiform Law: Revision, Interpolation and Development*, ed. B. Levinson, JSOTSup 181 (Sheffield: Sheffield Academic Press, 1994), p. 80; cf. Yoffee, "Context and Authority," p. 102.

181. Bottéro, *Mesopotamia*, p. 179. Sophie Lafont ("Ancient Near Eastern Laws: Continuity and Pluralism," in *Theory and Method in Biblical and Cuneiform Law: Revision, Interpolation and Development*, ed. B. Levinson, JSOTSup 181 [Sheffield: Sheffield Academic Press, 1994], pp. 104-5) claims that in the practice of making legal decisions "the oral and visual tradition remains in force, while the written text has a supplementary value."

182. Westbrook, "What Is the Covenant Code?" pp. 22-24; Greengus, "Some Issues Relating to the Comparability of Laws," pp. 62-64; Gerdien Jonker, *The Topography of Remembrance: The Dead, Tradition, and Collective Memory in Mesopotamia*, Studies in the History of Religions 68 (Leiden: Brill, 1995), pp. 4, 47, 57; Foster, *Before the Muses*, p. 26.

If that man does not pay attention to my words which I wrote on my stela and disdains my curses and does not fear the curses of the gods and does away with the laws which I made, distorts my words, changes my statutes, blots out my inscribed name and inscribes his own name — (or) if he has someone else take hold (of this task) because of these curses, [then may that man be subject to all the curses that follow]. (*CH* XLIX:18-38)[183]

The "if . . . then" format of these curses follows a pattern from the time of the empire of Akkad (ca. 2350-2190 B.C.), which Sabine Franke labels an "analogy curse": for example, whoever attacks the glory of the king will experience the cutting off of his line.[184] Hammurapi noted that he did not want his own name to be removed from the stela; therefore, his own desire for immortality in the form of a remembered hero in the tradition played a significant role in his efforts to preserve the *Code* intact.[185] Yet the community was also strengthened by the stability it gained from the continuity of a set of legal guidelines from the rule of one king to the next.[186] Kings like Hammurapi, who acknowledged the importance of the gods and tradition, were quite aware of the key role that kings played in constructing the social and political order. A king typically had considerable latitude in shaping his kingdom, even when he was serious about ruling with justice according to the will of the gods and the traditions of the community. A king could make his mark and establish his reputation at the same time that he conferred an enduring benefit on the community. However, what may have appeared as a benefit to the king and to the community may have been viewed by others as exploitation and alienating changes. Thus, royal rhetoric about the just king would have seemed to them to be mere propaganda.[187]

When Hammurapi rose to power in Mesopotamia, he shaped a territorial kingdom that incorporated other Mesopotamian cities with their traditions of independence and territorial alignment.[188] His elevation of his own city of Babylon to the most important city in Mesopotamia could not have been accom-

---

183. The text is from Borger, *Babylonisch-assyrische Lesestücke*, p. 47.

184. Sabina Franke, *Königsinschriften und Königsideologie: Die Könige von Akkade zwischen Tradition und Neuerung* (Münster: LIT, 1995), pp. 240-41; cf. Hurowitz, *Inu Anum Sīrum*, pp. 37, 40-42.

185. Hurowitz, *Inu Anum Sīrum*, p. 40.

186. Greengus, "Legal and Social Institutions," pp. 471-72; Westbrook, "What Is the Covenant Code?" pp. 24-25, 28.

187. Yoffee, "Context and Authority," pp. 107-8.

188. Sasson, "King Hammurabi of Babylon," pp. 905-7; Rivkah Harris, *Ancient Sippar: A Demographic Study of an Old-Babylonian City (1894-1595 B.C.)* (Leiden: Nederlands Historisch-Archaeologisch Instituut te Istanbul, 1975), p. 7.

plished without introducing tensions with various peoples in the other cities and territories.[189] Examples of such tension in the form of tax resistance by the people at large, though sparse in the evidence recovered from Mesopotamian royal archives,[190] were recorded in the royal correspondence of the OB period. In a letter from Ammiditana (1683-1647 B.C.), the great-grandson of Hammurapi and the ninth king of his dynasty, to the leader of the merchants of Sippar-Yaḫrurum, he says:

> The collector of the goat hair reported to me as follows: "I repeatedly wrote to the leader of the merchants of Sippar-Yaḫrurum concerning the transport of the goat hair, his tax *(nēmettum)* to Babylon, but he did not have the goat hair, his tax, brought to me." Thus he reported to me. "Why did you not have the goat hair, your tax, brought to Babylon? Were you not afraid to do this? When you see this tablet of mine, have the goat hair, your tax, brought to Babylon to me." (*AbB* 2, 53:4-23)[191]

In this instance the merchants of Sippar-Yaḫrurum were going to avoid paying the impost *(nēmettum)* as long as possible. However, the king's collector brought the matter to the king's attention so that he might exert greater pressure on the merchants. In another instance, Abi-eshuḫ (1711-1684 B.C.), the grandson of Hammurapi and the eighth king of his dynasty, wrote to five men to go and make a certain merchant pay his taxes:

> To Samsuiluna-nur-matim, Awil-Nabium, Taribatum, Ibni-Marduk, and Rish-Shamash, say: Thus says Abi-eshuḫ: "Sin-iddinam, the commerce office of Sippar and the judges of Sippar wrote to me as follows: 'We wrote to Iddin-Ishtar, a merchant of Sippar, a citizen of Sippar, who lives in Kar-Shamash, to take two lambs, his tax, and come to Sippar. But he did not take the lambs, his tax, and come to Sippar.' Thus they wrote to me. When you see this tablet of mine, you should come down to Sippar with Iddin-Ishtar, the merchant of Sippar, together with the lambs, his tax, so that he might pay his tax with the lambs." (*AbB* 2, 72:1-26)[192]

These instances of delinquency in taxpaying indicate that taxpaying to a central administrative center was a burden in Mesopotamia and was evaded if possible.

189. Cf. Marc Van de Mieroop, *Society and Enterprise in Old Babylonian Ur*, BBVO 12 (Berlin: Dietrich Reimer, 1992), pp. 244, 247-48.

190. Marc Van de Mieroop, *The Ancient Mesopotamian City* (Oxford: Clarendon, 1997), p. 34; idem, *Society and Enterprise in Old Babylonian Ur*, pp. 107-8, 245, 248.

191. The text is from Rintje Frankena, *Briefe aus dem British Museum*, AbB 2 (Leiden: Brill, 1966), pp. 30-33.

192. The text is from Frankena, *Briefe aus dem British Museum*, pp. 42-43.

The Mesopotamians outside of Babylon must have believed that their own resources and those of their area were being stolen by a distant ruler. These Mesopotamians would most likely not have experienced pangs of conscience that the divinely established moral order had been transgressed through tax delinquency. Conversely, many may have felt that the moral order had been transgressed by the imposition of such taxes.[193]

The customary ways of a community in Homeric Greece, biblical Israel, and OB Mesopotamia carried an authority that could not be dismissed lightly even by the most tyrannical king or the most ambitious dissident. Even though such customary ways were subject to development and reinterpretation in new circumstances, the voices of previous generations and of the gods constituted a check upon the desires of the king or the dissident.[194] Authoritative decrees pronounced by the king or the tradition could have had an impact and endured only if they were in accord with the fundamental values of the community and with an underlying moral order of the world.[195] The locus of authority was the activity of listening to the various voices of the community, the tradition, and the gods. Authority figures were an important part of the equation insofar as they promoted the activities of discerning and decision making.

Care: The Tensive Activity That
Produces Equilibrium in a Community

The polyvalence of symbol and metaphor and the web of interpretations spawned by narrative emphasize inclusiveness and diversity at the expense of uniformity and simplicity. On the one hand, the linguistic play and rhetorical feast generated through the discussion and debate of various possibilities for action may suit the contemplative ensconced in an ivory tower but prove impractical for the leader of an unsettled community.[196] On the other hand, the

193. Murphy, "The Notion of Moral Economy," pp. 280-81.

194. For example, the kings of the first millennium B.C. respected the privileges of ancient temple cities (privileges known as *kidinnu*). See Hayim Tadmor, "Monarchy and Elite in Assyria and Babylonia," in *The Origins and Diversity of Axial Civilizations*, ed. S. N. Eisenstadt (Albany: SUNY Press, 1986), p. 217.

195. Giorgio Buccellati ("Ethics and Piety in the Ancient Near East," in *Civilizations of the Ancient Near East*, ed. J. Sasson [New York: Scribner, 1995], p. 1692) claims that even though the Mesopotamians recognized that the world order was only partially known to them, they believed that there was a predictability in such an order that humans could rely upon. For the Homeric belief in the gods' concern for the ethical world order, see Olson, *Blood and Iron*, p. 218.

196. Jürgen Habermas, "On the Distinction Between Poetic and Communicative Uses of Language," in *On the Pragmatics of Communication* (Cambridge, Mass.: MIT Press, 1998), p. 396;

care exercised by a leader who neglects the contemplative dimension of decision making will probably be constrained by shortsightedness, with a greater emphasis upon power than upon truth.[197]

In Homeric Greece, biblical Israel, and OB Mesopotamia, the limits imposed on life by the human condition were able to foster the development of better relationships within a community through sympathy and empathy. Brokenness that pressed on a human community was sometimes intensified by protest but alleviated by supplication. In other situations, supplication led to protest. Discernment of the seriousness of injustices in a community called upon the desires and wisdom of the leaders and members of a community to determine whether continuity or change was called for.

The actions of crying out and making supplication were essential, constructive steps for individuals and communities who found themselves in painful circumstances and at the end of their strength. Achilles sought to be vindicated and so implored Thetis to make supplication to Zeus on his behalf; Priam pleaded with Achilles to give the corpse of Hector to him so that he might receive an honorable burial.[198] The sympathy engendered in Achilles through Priam's heroic supplication shows how humans can be transformed by accepting the reality of suffering as part of the fabric of mortal life.[199] In Psalm 89, crying out to the Lord in the midst of confusion and anguish over the loss of the Davidic king and dynasty provided a means to come to terms with a painful reality over which there was no satisfying explanation. The Lord's previous promises of protection for the Davidic king seem to have been suspended, yet the psalmist was uncertain of this. The words of the lament helped the community to navigate changes in fundamental social and political institutions without abandoning its traditional beliefs and values. The lament over the city of Ur seems to have functioned analogously for the people of Ur. The numerous historical allusions in this composition limited its use to the specific case of the destruction at Ur, yet this narrative poem was composed for use in public liturgies. The kings of Isin apparently wanted these poems recited in order to free them from any blame before the gods for the reconstruction of the temples of the moon god Nanna and his wife Ningal. The anguish of the people of Jerusalem and Ur over the destruction brought to their cities raised questions about

---

Paul Ricoeur, *Time and Narrative*, vol. 3 (Chicago: University of Chicago Press, 1985), p. 249; Ricoeur, "Practical Reason," pp. 199, 203.

197. Habermas, "On the Distinction Between Poetic and Communicative Uses of Language," pp. 388-89, 398-99; cf. Jameson, *The Seeds of Time*, pp. 74-75.

198. Seaford (*Reciprocity and Ritual*, pp. 173-76) emphasizes that such sympathy goes beyond "fellow-feeling" to solidarity gained through participation in death ritual.

199. Muellner, *The Anger of Achilles*, pp. 164-66, 174.

the justice of the course of events. Theodicy questions also found their way into Achilles' reflections as he sought to come to terms with the loss of Patroclus and the similar anguish felt by Priam for his son Hector. The conflicts and struggles in human communities were intertwined with the cosmic world order over which the king of the gods ruled, whether it was Zeus, the Lord, or Anum and Enlil.

Some problems in a community (contradictions) call for action in order to bring about change. Other problems (antinomies) call for attention where solutions can be created within narratives in the sphere of the imagination; these problems appear to be ones in which action to bring about change would only lead to further complications. The suitors' plundering of the house of Odysseus presented a scenario that called for action by Odysseus and his household. The assembly in Ithaca was not ready to act on behalf of the royal household of Odysseus, for they did not perceive the crisis from the same perspective as did the members of Odysseus's household. The assembly of Achaean warriors was likewise passive before the crisis generated by the quarrel between Achilles and Agamemnon. Other Achaean warrior-kings intervened to shore up Agamemnon's authority and so preserve the existing structure and distribution of authority in the coalition. Unjust actions by the suitors and by Agamemnon destabilized the communities of Ithaca and the Achaean coalition. In Israel, injustices during the times of David and Solomon led to Absalom's revolt and the secession of the northern tribes from the kingship centered in Jerusalem. Rehoboam refused to make changes in response to the grievances voiced by the northern tribes, just as David had apparently turned a deaf ear to grievances by people from various parts of his realm. These revolts led to changes in the social and political arrangements in Israel, even though the Davidic dynasty stayed in power. In OB Mesopotamia, kings periodically issued *mēšarum* edicts designed to correct inequities and injustices in the economic system of the kingdom. These royal edicts released pressure that might otherwise have led to revolt. Criticism of royal rule was usually brought to expression only indirectly, but the opening scene in the *Atraḫasis Epic* of the revolt of the junior gods reveals that efforts to throw off the burdens of oppressive labor from the king were not unknown.

Regicide was legitimate in all three cultures if the gods approved it. A king's unjust actions removed the legitimacy of his authority and so were grounds for a coup. Some coups were themselves unjust since they were fueled by the opportunism of aspirants to the throne, such as Antinous and Eurymachus among the suitors at Ithaca. Even when such unjust coups were under way, the caution expressed by the suitor Amphinomous that the gods had to approve regicide may have been voiced. Absalom aimed to remove David from the throne, which most likely meant that he intended to murder him rather than merely to drive him into exile. The basis for Absalom's claim on power was the absence of effective royal justice in the realm. His claim seems to have had substance since he drew a large following from Judah and Israel, but the failure of his revolt would have called into question the legitimacy of his effort. The palace coups and popular uprisings that can be deciphered from the remains of the royal archives give a decidedly promonarchical view of these events: the grounds for such revolts were illegitimate and so were suppressed with the assistance of the gods. However, the "noise" of the populace in the *Enuma Elish* seems to point to the creativity and independence of the people that would at least indirectly give some legitimacy to popular protests.

The customary ways of a community were part of its tradition. Laws were explicitly created in order to address new circumstances that the customary ways had not yet articulated. In the *Iliad*, the *themistes*, "the customary laws," were given voice by the king who held the scepter of Argos. In Mesopotamia, the *Code* promulgated by Hammurapi stood in a tradition of such codes in Mesopotamia in the early second millennium B.C. Hammurapi's *Code* appears to be a compendium of exemplary legal decisions that served as a guide or training manual for judges and also as a statement of the vision of a community under the rule of a just Mesopotamian king. In Israel, the Torah eventually achieved the status of promulgated law in the community that incorporated it as a complement to its customary ways of life. As in the cases of Nathan's judgment of David's adultery with Bathsheba and murder of Uriah and of Ahab's confiscation of Naboth's vineyard, it is clear that a body of customary practices was in place that aimed to sustain the Israelites' identity and way of life on the land.

The king was the symbolic center of the community in Homeric Greece, biblical Israel, or OB Mesopotamia and was called to shepherd the people under his care. However, in practice the leader who exercised the greatest measure of care may have been an elder, a prophet, a priest, a sage, or another one within the ranks. At the heart of the traditional pattern for legitimating royal authority was the activity of care where the relationships within the community were nurtured in the midst of predictable and unpredictable tensions that challenged the equilibrium of the community.[200] Where care was exercised, the giver and the receiver of care were affected and often changed. Such change within the continuity of the relationships in the community enabled individuals to find their place within the divinely willed order that stretched between heaven and earth.

200. Cf. Muellner, *The Anger of Achilles*, p. 51.

CHAPTER SEVEN

The Vision of the Ideal King: Ideological Illusion or Catalyst for Authentic Praxis and Community Building

The ideal community envisioned by the traditional pattern for legitimating royal authority became a tangible reality primarily through the cultivation of relationships between the divine and human spheres. The king played a key role in enhancing or blocking the engagement with the divine. If a king attempted to exercise sovereign rule without attention to its divine source, his actions usually gave rise to conflicts and contradictions within a community that diminished its vitality and even led to its fragmentation.

The vision of the ideal king was necessarily shaped by symbols, metaphors, and narratives that created their meaning through engagement with an audience. Such a vision evoked the intuitive understanding of a larger world order. This glimpse of a "totality" — or "worldness of the world" — formed a horizon for thinking, feeling, and acting that was indispensable for the integration of individuals within a community and for collective action.[1] The polyvalence of symbols, metaphors, and narratives respected the particularities of individuals' experience; but, at the same time, engagement with the same metaphors and narratives fostered a convergence of understanding among the various individuals involved.[2] Nevertheless, it is also possible that these symbols, metaphors, and narratives, whose truth becomes manifest in the engagement provoked by

---

1. Paul Ricoeur, *Time and Narrative,* vol. 3 (Chicago: University of Chicago Press, 1985), pp. 44, 102, 213.

2. Clifford Geertz, *The Interpretation of Cultures* (New York: Basic Books, 1973), pp. 94-95; Fredric Jameson (*The Political Unconscious: Narrative as a Socially Symbolic Act* (Ithaca: Cornell University Press, 1981), p. 70; Paul Ricoeur, *Time and Narrative,* vol. 1 (Chicago: University of Chicago Press, 1984), p. 76; Richard Kearney, *Poetics of Modernity: Toward a Hermeneutic Imagination* (Atlantic Highlands, N.J.: Humanities, 1995), pp. 101-2.

the act of interpretation, could be used to manipulate the people or to create a false consciousness. Religious language is not free from ideological concerns, nor is it defined by them.

The vision of the ideal king shaped both the minds and the hearts of the members of the community not only in their speculations but also in their discernment of the best course of action. For example, the Homeric narratives about the journeying Odysseus opened up dimensions of experience urging the audience to imagine what was possible for humans, which involved not only pressing the limits between the human and the divine but also respecting them.[3]

If the person and the actions of the king were to symbolize the unity of the community, models of an ideal king could help to create a convergence of the expectations of the king and various members of the community.[4] Such models could foster accountability not only on the part of the king but also on that of the people for the well-being of the community. The sacrifices that such expectations and models called forth highlighted the seriousness of the process by which such a vision was formed. If the sacrifices were misdirected by excessive self-interest, such actions could have devoured one's life rather than transforming one. For example, Achilles' mad-dog approach to securing a warrior's honor provided an example of potent action rather than a model for imitation by members of the community.[5] It was perhaps such potency that made later Macedonian kings like Alexander look up to Achilles as a model.[6] Yet to apply Achilles' single-minded approach to all facets of a community's life would have disregarded the complexities of human experience and substituted simple solutions for situations demanding processes of careful diplomacy.[7] The model of an ideal king shaped the outlook and actions not only of a particular king but also of the people and so exercised a formative influence on the allocation of energies and resources within the community. If the model were excessively utopian, it could distort expectations and undermine commitments.[8]

---

3. Seth Schein, "Introduction," in *Reading the Odyssey: Selected Interpretive Essays*, ed. Seth Schein (Princeton: Princeton University Press, 1996), p. 15.

4. Geertz, *The Interpretation of Cultures*, pp. 99, 127.

5. James M. Redfield, "Foreword," in Gregory Nagy, *The Best of the Achaeans: Concepts of the Hero in Archaic Greek Poetry* (Baltimore: Johns Hopkins University Press, 1979), p. ix; Peter W. Rose, *Sons of the Gods, Children of Earth: Ideology and Literary Form in Ancient Greece* (Ithaca: Cornell University Press, 1992), p. 50.

6. Richard Billows, *Kings and Colonists: Aspects of Macedonian Imperialism*, Columbia Studies in the Classical Tradition 22 (Leiden: Brill, 1995), p. 66.

7. Kevin Crotty, *The Poetics of Supplication: Homer's Iliad and Odyssey* (Ithaca: Cornell University Press, 1994), p. 141.

8. Paul Ricoeur, "Initiative," in *From Text to Action: Essays in Hermeneutics II* (Evanston, Ill.: Northwestern University Press, 1991), p. 221.

The vision of the ideal king always labored under the challenge of maintaining the expanse of relationships between the divine and the human spheres mapped out by the traditional pattern for legitimating royal authority. The temptation of a king to contract this expansive vision into one that more readily served his self-interests could not be countered in a monarchical government by institutional constraints of the sort one finds in the system of constitutional democracies where there is a separation of legislative, executive, and judicial powers. Such a constitutional separation of powers may create an effective check upon a monarch or executive power and so prevent tyranny, but at the same time it fragments the decision-making leadership in the community so that no one actually exercises sovereignty.[9] In the monarchies of Homeric Greece, biblical Israel, and OB Mesopotamia, the sovereign was the king of the gods and the earthly king was his representative. As such the earthly king received his sovereignty from the heavenly realm and not from the people.[10] However, in Homeric Greece and Israel, the people acclaimed the king and were not insignificant voices in this view of political authority, which regarded sovereignty as descending from heaven.

One of the primary means for countering the king's forgetfulness of the transcendent source of his sovereignty was to cultivate practices within the community where remembering such transcendent authority was emphasized.[11] Such practices could shape attitudes and perceptions so that there was a regular order or way of being in the community that was more basic than that generated by following explicit rules. Communal practices issuing from the tradition of the community were essential to the task of proclaiming and hearing the traditional pattern for legitimating royal authority in circumstances where it too easily could have been reified into an ideology of the ruling regime. When sovereign authority was properly understood, kings promoted the relationships

9. Carl Schmitt (*Political Theology: Four Chapters on the Concept of Sovereignty* [Cambridge, Mass.: MIT Press, 1985], pp. 5, 13) contended that constitutional democracies try to configure their law to address the question of who decides once there is chaos in the polity, but this effort avoids the issue of who actually decides and reveals the fact that sovereign power goes undefined in such constitutional democracies.

10. Bertrand de Jouvenal, *Sovereignty: An Inquiry into the Political Good* (Chicago: University of Chicago Press, 1959), pp. 45, 74, 237-38. For an opposite understanding, see F. H. Hinsley (*Sovereignty*, 2nd ed. [Cambridge: Cambridge University Press, 1986], pp. 1-2), who defines sovereignty as the idea or concept of a final authority located exclusively within the community and sees it historically embodied in the state.

11. John B. Thompson, "Editor's Introduction," in Pierre Bourdieu, *Language and Symbolic Power*, ed. John B. Thompson (Cambridge, Mass.: Harvard University Press, 1991), pp. 13-14; Catherine Bell, *Ritual: Perspectives and Dimensions* (New York: Oxford University Press, 1997), p. 82.

within the community where there was a healthy tension between the individual and the community.[12]

The ways in which the communities of Homeric Greece, biblical Israel, and OB Mesopotamia incorporated and sustained the expansive vision of the traditional pattern for legitimating royal authority within their particular models of an ideal king will be examined under the following three categories: (1) models of the ideal king as mediator between heaven and earth, (2) rivalry or humility: the ideal king's engagement with the divine realm, and (3) practices for strengthening the piety of the king.

Models of the Ideal King as Mediator between Heaven and Earth

Ordinary language is peppered with expressions in the subjunctive mood. In English, such subjunctive expressions notably take the form of clauses employing the modal terms "might, may, or could" in addition to the more typical terms signifying the subjunctive, "would, should." The subjunctive highlights what *might be* or what *ought to be* the case over against the indicative mood that states what *is* the case. The notion of dialectics, where a statement generates its opposite, is contained within the subjunctive.[13] So the practice of constructing an ideal world is woven into the fabric of language.

The practice of imagining other circumstances and realities that are more perfect than those within our reach is also a consequence of the finite character of human experience: the fleeting present both in what has gone before and in what is yet to come.[14] Memory and anticipation worked together to shape a vision of an ideal king in a community. Dissatisfaction with opportunists and the rhetoric of the sophists were factors that led Plato to argue that the real world was concealed behind visible appearances and was known to humans only as shadows.[15] In contrast, many contemporary theorists emphasize appearances

12. John Hoffmann, *Sovereignty* (Minneapolis: University of Minnesota Press, 1998), pp. 96, 107.

13. Victor Turner, *The Anthropology of Performance* (New York: PAJ, 1986), p. 41.

14. Ricoeur, *Time and Narrative*, 3:19-20.

15. Jean-Pierre Vernant, *Mortals and Immortals* (Princeton: Princeton University Press, 1991), pp. 49, 171-73; Frederick Copleston, *A History of Philosophy*, vol. 1: *Greece & Rome, Part I* (Garden City, N.Y.: Doubleday, 1962), p. 154. Luc Brisson (*Plato the Myth Maker* [Chicago: University of Chicago Press, 1998], pp. 3-4) argues that Plato was aware that reason could not be freed from myth since he believed that the invisible *forms* and not visible, tangible things are the true reality — a reality that can be perceived only by reason as a faculty of the soul.

as the locus of reality and warn against the distortions inherent in imagining an invisible world of *forms* as the realm of truth.[16] Contemporary cautions about ideal models or ideal types often arise either from the suspicion that such models and types stem more from the self-interest of the theorist than from genuine insight into the essence of things or from the belief that the object of inquiry itself has an uncanny independence.[17] Such cautions demand that the text of the vision of an ideal king be examined and that the social *milieux* shaping such a vision be searched out with full awareness that such *milieux* are also complex and elusive.[18] Nevertheless, the fact that humans long for a better world is an inescapable part of the human condition. How we humans have brought such a longing to expression is a matter that requires scrutiny and discussion. The way we shape our lives depends upon it.[19]

In chapter 8 of the *Odyssey*, Alcinous, king of the Phaeacians, hosted a banquet for the wandering stranger, Odysseus. In this fantasy world of the land of Scheria, the inhabitants were human but frequently shared the company of the gods at their feasts (*Od*. 7.199-206). The Phaeacians excelled in the art of seafaring but also distinguished themselves as runners and dancers (*Od*. 8.246-53; 7.34-37). Alcinous's magical gardens revealed that food was abundant in their land (*Od*. 7.112-31); the regular feasting of the people appeared to place no pressure on the resources of the land or to create a separation between the rich and the poor (*Od*. 7.96-102).[20] Phaeacian society was hierarchically orga-

---

16. Richard Kearney, *Modern Movements in European Philosophy*, 2nd ed. (Manchester: Manchester University Press, 1994), pp. 114-16; Jonathan Culler, *The Pursuit of Signs* (Ithaca: Cornell University Press, 1981), p. 40; Anthony Giddens, "Structuralism, Post-Structuralism and the Production of Culture," in *Social Theory Today*, ed. A. Giddens and J. Turner (Cambridge: Polity, 1987), pp. 211, 214.

17. Kearney, *Modern Movements in European Philosophy*, pp. 126-29; Frank Ankersmit, "Historicism, Post-Modernism, and Epistemology," in *Post-Modernism and Anthropology: Theory and Practice* (Assen: Van Gorcum, 1995), pp. 26, 31-32; Eugene Goodhart, *The Reign of Ideology* (New York: Columbia University Press, 1997), p. 108; Christine Oravec, "Kenneth Burke's Concept of Association and the Complexity of Identity," in *The Legacy of Kenneth Burke* (Madison: University of Wisconsin Press, 1989), p. 191.

18. Ricoeur, *Time and Narrative*, 3:122-23; Joseph Gusfield, "The Bridge over Separated Lands: Kenneth Burke's Significance for the Study of Social Action," in *The Legacy of Kenneth Burke* (Madison: University of Wisconsin Press, 1989), pp. 29, 36; Giddens, "Structuralism, Post-Structuralism and the Production of Culture," p. 209.

19. Ricoeur, "Initiative," p. 221; Rose, *Sons of the Gods, Children of Earth*, pp. 25, 41, 55, 57; Richard Klonoski, "The Preservation of Homeric Tradition: Heroic Re-Performance in the 'Republic' and the 'Odyssey,'" *Clio* 22 (1993): 263-64; Fredric Jameson, *The Seeds of Time* (New York: Columbia University Press, 1994), pp. 74-75.

20. Charles Segal, *Singers, Heroes, and Gods in the Odyssey* (Ithaca: Cornell University Press, 1994), pp. 30-31. Pierre Vidal-Naquet, *The Black Hunter: Forms of Thought and Forms of*

nized.[21] Alcinous, the king, was assisted by twelve other sceptered kings who appeared to be clones of Alcinous and served as his eyes and ears to extend his care to all parts of the community (*Od.* 8.390-91).[22] The popular assembly, composed of the leaders of the Phaeacians, could call an assembly and summon Alcinous to it (*Od.* 6.53-55). Such popular initiatives may indeed have been infrequent in Phaeacia since Alcinous was inspired in the ways of the gods (*Od.* 6.12) and directed the people in ways that resonated with their hearts (*Od.* 6.11-12, 55-63, 98-102; 8.390-405). In fact, his election to the kingship, although divine in origin, seemed to be communicated through the people, as the following words of Alcinous's daughter Nausicaa indicate: "[Alcinous] holds power and might from the Phaeacians" (*Od.* 6.197).[23] Alcinous could issue decrees that made demands on the people. For example, when Alcinous wished to bestow gifts on the parting guest Odysseus, he said:

> To each of you who always drink the sparkling wine of the elders in my halls, listen to the bard. Clothing for the stranger lies in the skillfully fashioned chest, and finely crafted gold and all other gifts, as many as the Phaeacian advisors brought here. But come, let each of us give a great tripod and a basin. We in turn will pay it back through a collection from the people. It is difficult for one person to gratify another without repayment. (*Od.* 13.7-15)

The assembled Phaeacians were pleased with Alcinous's words. This redistribution of wealth by Alcinous was carried out in a way that does not seem to be onerous or impersonal.[24] He indicates that repayment will be made to those assembled — perhaps an elite — by means of a collection from the larger populace.[25] The symbolic significance of the gifts was highlighted so as to strengthen the relationship between the Phaeacians and Odysseus. Alcinous ruled in ways that respected the significance of personal relationships within and outside of

---

Society in the Greek World (Baltimore: Johns Hopkins University Press, 1986), p. 29; Pierre Carlier, *La royauté en Grèce avant Alexandre* (Strasbourg: AECR, 1984), p. 205.

21. William G. Thalmann, *The Swineherd and the Bow: Representations of Class in the Odyssey* (Ithaca: Cornell University Press, 1998), pp. 17, 40, 262.

22. Georges Vlachos, *Les sociétés politiques homériques* (Paris: Presses Universitaires de France, 1974), pp. 63, 65. Carlier, *La royauté en Grèce avant Alexandre*, pp. 145-46.

23. Vlachos, *Les sociétés politiques homériques*, p. 63.

24. Carlier, *La royauté en Grèce avant Alexandre*, p. 146.

25. Thalmann (*The Swineherd and the Bow*, p. 262) claims "that redistribution in this society is predominantly the flow of wealth upwards and then horizontally, not to any great extent back down." Cf. Edward M. Harris, "A New Solution to the Riddle of the *Seisachtheia*," in *The Development of the "Polis" in Archaic Greece*, ed. L. G. Mitchell and P. J. Rhodes (New York: Routledge, 1997), p. 109.

his realm. He is not presented as one who ruled as the distant head of a bureaucracy that taxed the people as if their only significance in the kingdom took the form of the material wealth they could provide.

The banqueting scene in which Odysseus related the adventures of his travels reflected an important social and political practice of Greek aristocrats in the Geometric (900-700 B.C.) and Archaic Ages (700-480 B.C.).[26] The gatherings presented the context for bards like Demodocus and Odysseus to compete with one another in telling stories. In the *Odyssey,* the bard would mix fiction with fact with an eye toward winning the approval of the audience. Thus, he selected and arranged his material to present a meaningful and engaging account that drew upon ancient wisdom but did not aim to provide an objective report of distant events,[27] even though the canonized versions of the Homeric epics at the Panhellenic festivals in the late sixth century B.C. did claim to give the most authoritative account of the events surrounding the Trojan War.[28] The glory *(kleos)* of the Iliadic heroes about whom the bard sang may have been based on rumor *(kleos)* as well as on fact.[29] The portion of food awarded to each bard, as ephemeral as it was, marked out and honored the excellence of the competing bards.[30] Winning the approval of those assembled at the banquet contributed to the definition of the place of the bard within the community. If the bard was supported by a king, then he was more likely to communicate truths that were not popular to the general audience.[31] The bards who sung the heroic traditions were valued by the aristocrats when they found their place in the grid of the community articulated and strengthened through such performances.[32] However, in scenes where the wandering beggar Odysseus was mistreated by the aristocratic suitors, the commoners would have found their interests promoted through criticism of the aristocrats. Homer's audience consists of both

---

26. Carlier, *La royauté en Grèce avant Alexandre,* pp. 154-57; Segal, *Singers, Heroes, and Gods,* p. 144; Pietro Pucci, *Odysseus Polutropos* (Ithaca: Cornell University Press, 1987), pp. 184-85; Jane B. Carter, "Ancestor Cult and the Occasion of Homeric Performance," in *The Ages of Homer,* ed. Jane B. Carter and Sarah Morris (Austin: University of Texas Press, 1995), p. 286; Ian Morris, *Archaeology as Cultural History* (Oxford: Blackwell, 2000), p. 182.

27. Segal, *Singers, Heroes, and Gods,* pp. 140, 149-54; Morris, *Archaeology as Cultural History,* pp. 190-91; cf. Gregory Nagy, *Homeric Questions* (Austin: University of Texas Press, 1996), pp. 39, 121, 126; Margalit Finkelberg, *The Birth of Literary Fiction in Ancient Greece* (Oxford: Clarendon, 1998), p. 152.

28. Finkelberg, *The Birth of Literary Fiction,* p. 159.

29. Segal, *Singers, Heroes, and Gods,* p. 149; Pucci, *Odysseus Polutropos,* p. 185.

30. Segal, *Singers, Heroes, and Gods,* p. 154.

31. Segal, *Singers, Heroes, and Gods,* p. 157; cf. Rose, *Sons of the Gods, Children of Earth,* pp. 113-16.

32. Thalmann, *The Swineherd and the Bow,* p. 275.

aristocrats and commoners, and he holds their interests and values in a tensive dialogue.[33]

In the banqueting scenes in Phaeacia, Alcinous, with unquestioned pre-eminence, presided over the activities. The exchange of food and drink, of songs of praise and blame, and of gifts were highly charged symbolic actions that expressed a communal understanding of the places that the individual members occupied within the community. These aristocratic banquets in the royal palace in Scheria created the setting in which Alcinous empowered the members of his community by recognizing their excellence and forged bonds with visiting dignitaries by honoring them.[34] The harmony that reigned among the Phaeacians was due not only to their freedom from material want but also to the inspired leadership of Alcinous whose distinctive attribute was his wise facilitation of relationships.

Alcinous's kingship finds an echo in the words of the disguised Odysseus as he spoke to Penelope for the first time on his return to Ithaca and compared her reputation to that of an ideal king:

> Lady, no mortal on the unbounded earth could reproach you, for your glory extends through the spacious heavens like that of an illustrious king who, as a god-fearer, rules over many nobles and upholds good laws. The black earth bears wheat and barley; the trees are loaded with fruit; the flocks give birth without fail, and the sea provides fish. By his good leadership, the people thrive under him. (*Od.* 19.107-14)

This ideal ruler resembled the image that Penelope had of the absent Odysseus. The "good laws" were customs or principles of justice that were known to the members of the community by their living in that community and developing in accord with its way of life. Law was largely an oral phenomenon through the seventh century B.C. in Archaic Greece where it was debated in the *agora*, "the assembly, marketplace" (cf. *Il.* 18.497-508).[35]

Prior to Odysseus's return, Penelope described Odysseus's way of ruling to the herald Medon in a message intended for the suitors:

---

33. Rose, *Sons of the Gods, Children of Earth*, p. 139.

34. Segal, *Singers, Heroes, and Gods*, pp. 140-41; Carlier, *La royauté en Grèce avant Alexandre*, pp. 155-56.

35. Karl-Joachim Hölkescamp, *Schiedsrichter, Gesetzgeber und Gesetzgebung im archaischen Griechenland*, Historia 131 (Stuttgart: Franz Steiner, 1999), p. 277; James Whitley, "Literacy and Law-making: The Case of Archaic Crete," in *Archaic Greece: New Approaches and New Evidence*, ed. Nick Fisher and Hans van Wees (London: Duckworth, 1998), pp. 316-17; cf. Carlier, *La royauté en Grèce avant Alexandre*, pp. 174-76.

You, the ones assembling here, pillage many goods, the property of skillful Telemachus. You did not listen to what your ancestors told you in former times when you were children, what kind of man Odysseus was among your parents, how he did not act or speak arbitrarily in public matters, which is the way of divine kings — one person they hate and another they love — but Odysseus never acted recklessly toward anyone. (*Od.* 4.686-93)

Penelope revealed her opinion that kings typically are partial to certain individuals and swayed by their own interests; nevertheless, she emphasized that the kingship as exercised by Odysseus was always fair and brought many benefits to the suitors and others in the community. Penelope gives expression to the Homeric view of the positive potential of kingship.[36]

One of the strongest statements of hope in the potential of the monarchy to bring well-being and harmony to the Israelite community occurs in the eleventh chapter of the book of the prophet Isaiah:

> A shoot will come forth from the stump of Jesse,
>   a sprout will grow from his roots.
> The spirit of the Lord will rest upon him,
>   the spirit of wisdom and discernment,
>   the spirit of counsel and strength,
>   the spirit of knowledge and of fear of the Lord.
> His pleasure will be the fear of the Lord.
> He will not judge by appearance,
>   nor will he decide by rumor.
> But he will judge the poor with justice,
>   he will decide with fairness for the humble of the land.
> He will strike the tyrant[37] with the staff of his mouth,
>   with the breath through his lips he will kill the wicked.
> Justice will be the cloth around his waist,
>   and faithfulness the cloth around his loins. (vv. 1-5)

The stump of Jesse may refer to the fortunes not only of the Davidic dynasty but also of the kingdom of Judah. If the former, it may be that Isaiah of Jerusalem feared that the Davidic monarchy itself would come to an end as a result of the Assyrian assault in 701 B.C.[38] If the latter, then the devastating event that

---

36. S. Douglas Olson, *Blood and Iron: Stories and Storytelling in Homer's "Odyssey"* (Leiden: Brill, 1995), p. 202.

37. Read *'āriṣ*.

38. Hans Wildberger, *Isaiah 1–12* (Minneapolis: Fortress, 1991), p. 469; H. G. M. William-

would fell a tree and leave a stump may have been the drastic reduction of the kingdom of Judah to Jerusalem and a few parts of Judah in the wake of the Assyrian assault.[39] However, this passage may have been the composition of a later redactor, and then the phrase the "stump of Jesse" may have referred to the threats to the monarchy in Jerusalem at the time of Josiah (640-609 B.C.)[40] or to the cessation of the monarchy in Jerusalem in 587 B.C. and the hope that it would be restored at some future time.[41] If Isaiah 11:1-5 contains an oracle from Isaiah of Jerusalem, it seems that by this vision of an ideal king Isaiah would have expressed criticism of, or even disillusionment with, the rule of Ahaz or Hezekiah and looked forward to the time when a more just and effective form of royal rule would be implemented in Jerusalem.[42] Even if Isaiah 11:1-5 came from the hand of an editor after 587 B.C., this passage indirectly expressed criticism of typical Davidic kings and described the basis upon which the monarchical institution, if properly exercised, could have brought well-being to the Israelite nation.[43]

Isaiah 11:2-5 claims that the transformation that would give rise to the new ideal king would be effected by the spirit of the Lord. The *rûaḥ,* "spirit, wind, breath," of the Lord would be a power that comes from God and would take the form of the invisible, yet perceptible realities of wisdom, discernment, counsel, strength, knowledge, and fear of the Lord.[44] Such divine empowerment would increase the capacity of the king to discern and make good judgments. His judgments would have depth that would pierce beyond partial and distorted apprehensions of the issues and facts and would communicate decisions that would be in harmony with the ethical world order (Isaiah 11:3-4).[45] The force with which this coming ideal king would deal with the recalcitrant would take

---

son, *Variations on a Theme: King, Messiah and Servant in the Book of Isaiah* (Carlisle, U.K.: Paternoster, 1998), pp. 53-55.

39. Christopher Seitz, *Isaiah 1–39* (Louisville: John Knox, 1993), p. 97.

40. Marvin Sweeney, *Isaiah 1–39 with an Introduction to Prophetic Literature,* FOTL 16 (Grand Rapids: Eerdmans, 1996), pp. 204-5. Williamson (*Variations on a Theme,* p. 53, n. 41) argues that this passage probably "would have been read with renewed hopes in Josiah's time, but that is not a sufficient argument for dating its composition then."

41. R. E. Clements, *Isaiah 1–39* (Grand Rapids: Eerdmans, 1980), pp. 121-22.

42. Wildberger, *Isaiah 1–12,* pp. 467-68. However, Seitz (*Isaiah 1–39,* p. 104) does not associate this oracle with criticism of Hezekiah's rule.

43. Joseph Blenkinsopp, *Isaiah 1–39,* AB 19 (New York: Doubleday, 2000), pp. 263-65; Brevard Childs, *Isaiah* (Louisville: Westminster/John Knox, 2001), pp. 100-101.

44. Wildberger, *Isaiah 1–12,* pp. 471-73; Childs, *Isaiah,* p. 103.

45. Wildberger, *Isaiah 1–12,* p. 473; Erich Zenger, "Die Verheissung Jesaja 11, 1-10: Universal oder Partikular?" in *Studies in the Book of Isaiah,* ed. J. Van Ruiten and M. Vervenne, BETL 132 (Leuven: Leuven University Press, 1997), pp. 146-47.

the form of an effective command. Apparently the aura of this king's strength alone would communicate the fact that he could bring about obedience to his commands through physical coercion, if necessary.[46] The Isaianic text claims that the words uttered by this king could themselves kill the wicked (Isa. 11:4).

In Isaiah 11:2, one of the distinctive gifts to be bestowed by the spirit of the Lord would be the fear of the Lord: that is, piety. The capacity of the king to take sufficient account of the Lord's care for the well-being of the kingdom of Judah would be strengthened by a divine gift. According to 2 Kings 16:7, Ahaz, king of Judah, failed to trust in the Lord's care and so took the problem of the security of his kingdom into his own hands and entered into an alliance with Tiglath-Pileser III of Assyria. This alliance led to the annexation of the Northern Kingdom into the Assyrian empire and the deportation of its population to a distant land where they were assimilated and lost their identity as Israelites. In contrast, Hezekiah, the successor of Ahaz, is presented in Isaiah 36–37 as a pious king who prayed to the Lord when Sennacherib, king of Assyria, laid siege to Jerusalem in 701 B.C. According to the narrative of Isaiah 36–37, Hezekiah's prayerful, pious actions were instrumental in effecting the miraculous deliverance of Jerusalem in 701 B.C. (Isa. 37:21).[47] However, according to Isaiah 39, Hezekiah negotiated with the Babylonians in ways that seem to indicate that he was placing more trust in this alliance making than in the protection promised by the Lord. According to Isaiah 39, as borrowed from 2 Kings 20:12-19, Isaiah criticized Hezekiah for showing the temple treasures to the Babylonian envoys in 703 B.C. and announced that as a consequence of Hezekiah's lack of trust future judgment would come upon Jerusalem.[48] The exemplary king Hezekiah of Isaiah 36–38 shows the chink in the armor of his piety in Isaiah 39.[49] It is conceivable that Isaiah 11:1-5, with its promise of the divine gift of the fear of the Lord, could have been Isaiah's response to Hezekiah's failure to trust in the Lord suffi-

---

46. Wildberger, *Isaiah 1–12*, pp. 477-78.

47. Peter R. Ackroyd, "Isaiah I–XII: Presentation of a Prophet," *Congress Volume: Göttingen, 1977*, VTSup 29 (Leiden: Brill, 1978), pp. 16-48; idem, "Isaiah 36–39: Structure and Function," in *Studies in the Religious Tradition of the Old Testament* (London: SCM, 1987), pp. 116-20; Seitz, *Isaiah 1–39*, pp. 250-52; Sweeney, *Isaiah 1–39*, pp. 457-59; Antii Laato, *Who Is Immanuel? The Rise and the Foundering of Isaiah's Messianic Expectations* (Abo: Abo Academy Press, 1988), pp. 314-15.

48. Clements, *Isaiah 1–39*, pp. 293-95; H. G. M. Williamson, *The Book Called Isaiah: Deutero-Isaiah's Role in Composition and Redaction* (Oxford: Clarendon, 1994), pp. 208-11; idem, *Variations on a Theme*, p. 88.

49. Confining the picture of the flawed Hezekiah to the presentation in 2 Kings 20:12-19, Ackroyd ("Isaiah 36–39," pp. 113-14, and "An Interpretation of the Babylonian Exile: A Study of II Kings 20 and Isaiah 38–39," in *Studies in the Religious Tradition of the Old Testament* [London: SCM, 1987], pp. 155-63), as well as Seitz (*Isaiah 1–39*, pp. 265-66) and Sweeney (*Isaiah 1–39*, pp. 510-11), contends that the Hezekiah of Isaiah 39 is still a model of piety.

ciently when faced with the opportunity to enter into alliance with the Babylonians through the embassy led by Merodach-Baladan, and so Isaiah looked forward to a coming ideal king as envisioned in Isaiah 11:1-5.

The model of the ideal king of Isaiah 11:1-5 emphasized the positive potential of the monarchical institution when it was divinely empowered and directed.[50] The responsibility of the king to make right judgments so as to bring justice and well-being into his kingdom was one that the king could not carry out by his native powers but was one that called for the king's acceptance of divine assistance according to the timing and modality chosen by the Lord. The patience and confidence demanded of an earthly king, especially in times of crisis, stretched him beyond what seemed reasonable or pragmatic. Prior to the *eschaton*, no earthly king will be able to meet this challenge of trusting in effective, timely divine intervention; the ideal king of Isaiah 11:1-5 will always be a promised future ruler.[51]

Royal inscriptions celebrated the accomplishments of Mesopotamian kings. Their rhetoric emphasized the exemplary qualities of the current ruler so as to give the impression that the ideal king was the current one. For example, when Hammurapi had built the wall of Sippar, he claimed in an inscription: "What no king among the kings had built since ancient times, I built magnificently for Shamash, my lord."[52] Hammurapi's son, Samsuiluna, used similar language to claim a unique accomplishment in an inscription celebrating the rebuilding of the wall of Sippar:

> Though Shamash had permitted this since days of old, when the brick work of E-babbar was first built, to no king from among the kings of old, so that (no king) rebuilt for him the wall of Sippar, I, Samsuiluna, the beloved of Shamash and Aja, the mighty king, the king of Babylon, the king of the four world regions, the king whose word is pleasing to Shamash and Aja, at the command of Shamash and Marduk with a work force of the people of my land in that year made bricks and raised the wall of Sippar as high as a great mountain.[53]

The language claiming that no other previous king had been able to accomplish this deed appears to be formulaic.[54] Sumerian inscriptions from the Early Dy-

---

50. Blenkinsopp, *Isaiah 1–39*, p. 265; Laato, *Who Is Immanuel?* pp. 308-9.

51. Clements, *Isaiah 1–39*, p. 122.

52. Douglas Frayne, *RIME 4*, E4.3.6.2, lines 46-50.

53. Frayne, *RIME 4*, E4.3.7.3, lines 55-81.

54. A common motif in Assyrian royal inscriptions of the first millennium is the statement that the king has accomplished what no one else has ever done. See A. Kirk Grayson, "Assyrian

nastic period (ca. 2900-2350 B.C.) had aimed to make the king's name eternal by emphasizing his incomparability.[55] Royal inscriptions praise the reigning king to make him appear as an ideal king. In his inscriptions, an OB Mesopotamian king claimed that he had been able to accomplish a particular deed for the community because he had been divinely elected. His particular accomplishments demonstrated that he had fulfilled the age-old paradigm of what a king ought to be like in a fitting matter.[56] The paradigm of the ideal was established in the past, in the beginning. All OB Mesopotamian kings were to demonstrate their legitimacy by showing how they had met the expectations of this paradigm established in primordial times.

If the rhetoric of the royal inscriptions worked effectively, it created the impression that the current king was beyond criticism, with no room for improvement.[57] Hayim Tadmor claims that the practice of idealizing the reigning Assyrian king had become so entrenched in the first millennium B.C. that the king came to be viewed as the embodiment of justice, which in turn impeded the development of a protest literature.[58] This strong investment in preserving the image of the king from criticism issued from the palace-sponsored, insular scribal culture in Assyria of the first millennium B.C.[59] By contrast, in OB times the scribal schools were not as closely linked with the palace, for many of these schools had operated from private homes.[60] Outside of scribal circles where the message of the royal inscription was communicated to the populace at large, it would seem that this audience would have understood the intent of this genre and would have made the necessary adaptations to the exaggerated claims of

---

Royal Inscriptions: Literary Characteristics," in *Assyrian Royal Inscriptions: New Horizons in Literary, Ideological and Historical Analysis*, ed. F. Fales (Rome: Instituto per L'Oriente, 1981), p. 45.

55. Sabina Franke, *Königsinschriften und Königsideologie: Die Könige von Akkade zwischen Tradition und Neuerung* (Münster: LIT, 1995), p. 82.

56. Gerdien Jonker, *The Topography of Remembrance: The Dead, Tradition, and Collective Memory in Mesopotamia*, Studies in the History of Religions 68 (Leiden: Brill, 1995), p. 57.

57. Jonker, *The Topography of Remembrance*, p. 57.

58. Hayim Tadmor, "Monarchy and Elite in Assyria and Babylonia," in *The Origins and Diversity of Axial Civilizations*, ed. S. N. Eisenstadt (Albany, N.Y.: SUNY Press, 1986), p. 223.

59. Piotr Michalowski, "Presence at Creation," in *Lingering over Words: Studies in Ancient Near Eastern Literature in Honor of William L. Moran*, ed. T. Abusch et al., HSM 37 (Atlanta: Scholars, 1990), p. 395.

60. Piotr Michalowski, "Orality and Literacy and Early Mesopotamian Literature," in *Mesopotamian Epic Literature: Oral or Aural?* ed. M. Vogelzang and H. Vanstiphout (Lewiston, N.Y.: Mellen, 1992), p. 234; Stephanie Dalley, "Occasions and Opportunities. 1. To the Persian Conquest," in *The Legacy of Mesopotamia*, ed. S. Dalley (Oxford: Oxford University Press, 1998), pp. 15-17. Nevertheless, the OB palace had a strong influence on scribal culture; cf. Douglas Frayne, "Historical Texts in Haifa: Notes on R. Kutscher's 'Brockman Tablets,'" *BO* 48 (1991): 408.

the inscriptions, much as a contemporary American audience filters the claims made in advertisements designed to sell products.

The Mesopotamian king often noted in his inscriptions not only that his glorious deed was commissioned by the gods and was pleasing to them, but also that he had been empowered by the gods to accomplish it. The ideal Mesopotamian king readily acknowledged his dependence upon the gods and tried to persuade the people that the gods whom they revered supported him. In his construction of the wall of Sippar, Hammurapi proclaimed:

> At that time, I, Hammurapi, the strong king, the king of Babylon, the pious one, the one who obeys Shamash, the beloved of Aja, the one who delights the heart of Marduk, his lord, with the extraordinary strength which Shamash gave me, with a levy of the people of my land, raised up the top of the foundations of the wall of Sippar with dirt like a great mountain.[61]

Hammurapi seemed to say that a primary manifestation of the strength that Shamash gave him was embodied in the work force raised from the people of Sippar. Divine empowerment such as this seems to have been more a form of political and organizational power than a form of physical force. As a symbol for the collective effort, Hammurapi boasts that he has built the wall. However, even the mobilization of the work force seems to have been done not simply by the royal administration but, rather, jointly with the city administration of Sippar.[62] When Samsuiluna quelled rebellions in Mesopotamia and rebuilt the wall of Kish, he included in his inscription the following passage as the words of the gods Zababa and Ishtar:

> Samsuiluna, eternal offspring of the gods, beauty of kingship, Enlil has made your fate great. He has appointed us to the task of watching over you for security. We will go at your right hand; we will kill your foes; we will place your enemies in your hand. Build the wall of Kish, our revered cultic site. Make it more imposing than before.[63]

The divine empowerment provided by Zababa and Ishtar took the form of protection and success in battle.[64] The inscription made the claim that the gods

---

61. Frayne, *RIME 4*, E4.3.6.2, lines 28-44.

62. Rivkah Harris, *Ancient Sippar: A Demographic Study of an Old-Babylonian City (1894-1595 B.C.)* (Leiden: Nederlands Historisch-Archaeologisch Instituut te Istanbul, 1975), pp. 52, 89-92.

63. Frayne, *RIME 4*, E4.3.7.7, lines 63-79.

64. Stephanie Dalley, "Ancient Mesopotamian Military Organization," in *Civilizations of the Ancient Near East*, ed. Jack Sasson (New York: Scribner, 1995), pp. 421-22; M. Weippert, "Heiliger Krieg in Israel und Assyrien," *ZAW* 84 (1972): 483-84.

Zababa and Ishtar worked so closely with Samsuiluna that they carried out the actual fighting in the battles in which he engaged.

In the foregoing inscription, Samsuiluna also proclaimed that "he made all the land of Sumer and Akkad obedient; he made the four world regions dwell under his command."[65] This claim to worldwide rule was typically expressed by Mesopotamian kings by the title, "king of the four world regions," a title introduced into the Mesopotamian royal titulary by Naram-Sin of Akkad (2254-2218 B.C.).[66] The Mesopotamians' perception of their king's rule as worldwide garnered a measure of prestige for the king that seemed to be more important than his actual exercise of such extensive dominion. Mario Liverani argues that in Kassite times (1595-1158 B.C.) the Babylonian king was more concerned about persuading the population in Babylon that he exercised worldwide dominion in order to maintain his prestige at the center of his kingdom than he was about making the peoples on the periphery obedient.[67] Even though this claim to worldwide rule had to have some basis in fact, the impression of the amount of power the king wielded was regularly exaggerated.[68]

The ideal Mesopotamian king according to the royal inscriptions was the reigning king. He had been chosen and empowered by the gods to exercise dominion over Mesopotamia and the world. Such an ideal king was regarded as standing in continuity with the tradition of royal rule established in primordial times; newness consisted in carrying out the traditional pattern in a more exceptional way. Looking to a future eschatological royal figure as in Isaiah 11 and highlighting the king's charisma for listening to the opinions of the people were expectations that did not find a place in the model of the ideal Mesopotamian king in the royal inscriptions.

The ideal Homeric king in the person of Alcinous and the ideal Israelite king in the person of the messianic ruler of Isaiah 11:1-9 were leaders attentive to the "sense of belonging" of the various members of the community. They respected and honored the members of their communities by attentive listening and fair practices that led the individuals of the community to continue working at the relationships that tied them to the community. Alcinous understood the symbolic as well as the material value of goods that were to be redistributed in the community. The ideal messianic ruler of Isaiah 11:1-9 judged the well-

---

65. Frayne, *RIME 4*, E4.3.7.7, lines 111-15.

66. William W. Hallo, *Early Mesopotamian Royal Titles, a Philologic and Historical Analysis*, AOS 43 (New Haven: Yale University Press, 1957), p. 49; Franke, *Königsinschriften und Königsideologie*, p. 193.

67. Mario Liverani, *Prestige and Interest: International Relations in the Near East ca. 1600-1100 B.C.* (Padova: Sargon SRL, 1990), p. 47.

68. Liverani, *Prestige and Interest*, p. 48.

being of the members of the community through a wisdom that penetrated beyond appearances and into harmony with the ethical world order. These ideal rulers set a high standard for royal conduct and so contributed to criticism of the rule of particular kings, whether or not such criticism was expressed openly. In Mesopotamia, the idealization of the king by the court poets and scribes seems to have been designed more to prescribe how the people (and even the king himself) should imagine the king rather than to provide criteria for assessing the king's actual performance. Nevertheless, there would seem to have been some pressure for the king to approximate the paradigm of what a Mesopotamian king was expected to be like. Such idealization promoted adherence to the status quo and tended to neutralize innovation and change.

Rivalry or Humility: The Ideal King's Engagement with the Divine Realm

If the person of the king served symbolically as the meeting place of heaven and earth, it was important that the king understood the potential and the danger of holding a position at the boundary between the divine and the human realms. If a king was to sustain his legitimacy as ruler, he needed to communicate with and be empowered by the divine realm. The king's mediation of a measure of divine power to a community could tempt the king to claim divine status and to rule as if he had transcended the limits of the human condition.

On his journeys during his return from Troy, Odysseus entered the realm of the gods and of timelessness.[69] Toward the end of his journeys prior to his landing in Phaeacia, he stayed seven years with the goddess Calypso on her island of Ogygia (*Od.* 5.55-281). She tried to persuade him to remain with her:

> Odysseus, son of Laertes, one begotten of Zeus, one with many stratagems, do you now wish to go home at once to your beloved ancestral land? May it go well for you, in any case. If you were aware of how many troubles it is your fate to traverse before reaching your ancestral land, you would remain here and watch over this house with me and be immortal, even though you want to see your wife, for whom you are pining all your days. (*Od.* 5.203-10)

Up to this point on his travels back from Troy, Odysseus had already suffered heavy losses: his companions had perished, his ship and material possessions were gone, and his physical and psychic energy had been taxed. The time with

69. John H. Finley, Jr., *Homer's Odyssey* (Cambridge, Mass.: Harvard University Press, 1978), p. 77.

Calypso was one of rejuvenation after his trip to the underworld and his deathly encounters with the Cyclopes and other dangerous beings. An Iliadic warrior like Glaucus, if offered immortality as Calypso had offered Odysseus (*Od.* 5.200-213; cf. *Il.* 12.322-28), would have given up the heroic quest and remained with her, even though escaping death meant by definition that such a warrior could no longer be a hero in the Iliadic mold.[70] Zeus frowned upon the union of a goddess with a mortal for the way in which it elevated the status of the mortal and challenged the cosmic hierarchy (*Od.* 5:104-40).[71] Yet after Athena interceded on Odysseus's behalf (*Od.* 5.7-20), Zeus decreed that Odysseus would survive and return home. With this awareness that Odysseus's lot in life was to return to Ithaca (*Od.* 5.28-42) the audience recognized in Odysseus a new type of hero: an adventurer who would survive through cleverness *(mētis)* against formidable odds.[72]

After Odysseus left Calypso, his raft was wrecked by a wave from Poseidon (*Od.* 5.313-26). To prepare him for the coming danger, the goddess Leukothea alighted on his raft in the form of a winged gannet and sympathized with him:

> Ill-fated one, why in this way does Poseidon, the earth-shaker, rage so vehemently against you, since he brings many evils against you? But he will not destroy you even though he is bitterly enraged. But act in this way. You do not seem to lack understanding. (*Od.* 5.339-42)

Then Leukothea equipped him with a magical veil and counseled him on how to reach the shore of Phaeacia (*Od.* 5.343-50).[73] For all his cleverness, Odysseus would not have survived the wrath of Poseidon had it not been his fate to do so.[74] Poseidon had become a relentless divine antagonist to Odysseus because he had blinded Poseidon's son, the Cyclops named Polyphemus (*Od.* 1.68-71).[75]

In the *Iliad,* the Achaean forces erected a wall along the sea to protect their ships and supplies from the advancing Trojan forces. In doing so, however, they had neglected to sacrifice to Poseidon, an act that would have symbolized their

---

70. Laura Slatkin, *The Power of Thetis: Allusion and Interpretation in the "Iliad"* (Berkeley: University of California Press, 1991), pp. 42-43; Crotty, *The Poetics of Supplication,* p. 168.

71. Leonard Muellner, *The Anger of Achilles: "Mēnis" in Greek Epic* (Ithaca: Cornell University Press, 1996), pp. 21-22.

72. Pucci, *Odysseus Polutropos,* p. 183; Slatkin, *The Power of Thetis,* pp. 42-43.

73. Marcel Detienne, "The 'Sea-Crow,'" in *Myth, Religion, and Society,* ed. R. L. Gordon (Cambridge: Cambridge University Press, 1977), p. 18.

74. Pucci, *Odysseus Polutropos,* p. 183.

75. Charles Segal, "Kleos and Its Ironies," in *Reading the Odyssey: Selected Interpretive Essays,* ed. Seth Schein (Princeton: Princeton University Press, 1996), p. 211; idem, *Singers, Heroes, and Gods,* p. 122.

acknowledgment of his authority over the seacoast.[76] Such an omission angered Poseidon, who then complained to Zeus:

> Father Zeus, is there any mortal on the unbounded earth who will communicate to the immortals his purpose and plan? Do you not see that the blond-headed Achaeans have built a wall for the protection of their ships and have made a ditch around it, but have not given fitting sacrifices to the gods? The fame of it will surely extend as far as the dawn spreads. They will forget the city wall which Phoebus Apollo and I built with toil for the hero Laomedon. (*Il.* 7.446-53)

Zeus assured Poseidon that his power and fame were so superior that neglect by humans could not threaten his position. This example does, however, highlight how important the practice of sacrifice was for humans in the Homeric world so that they might demonstrate their mindfulness of the power and authority of the gods.[77] When a human entered the sphere of influence of a particular god without acknowledging that god's authority, the god regarded the human as a rival.[78] The fact that human power was incommensurate with that of a Homeric god only accented the danger that humans courted when they entered a god's world.

The destruction of the Achaean wall by Poseidon and Apollo, two deities representing respectively the opposing sides of the Achaeans and Trojans, symbolized the close of the heroic age, just as did the destruction of the Phaeacian ship that, after it had transported Odysseus back to Ithaca, was turned into a cliff by Poseidon (*Od.* 13.160-64).[79] When the heroes from Troy returned, the heroic age gave way to the weaker present age of iron.[80] The experiential knowl-

---

76. Stephen Scully, *Homer and the Sacred City* (Ithaca: Cornell University Press, 1990), p. 26; cf. John Gould, "On Making Sense of Greek Religion," *Myth, Ritual Memory, and Exchange: Essays in Greek Literature and Culture* (New York: Oxford University Press, 2001), p. 216; Crotty, *The Poetics of Supplication,* p. 87.

77. Vidal-Naquet, *The Black Hunter,* p. 16; Richard Buxton, *Imaginary Greece* (Cambridge: Cambridge University Press, 1994), p. 150; Vernant, *Mortals and Immortals,* pp. 35, 280; Erwin Cook, *The Odyssey in Athens: Myths of Cultural Origins* (Ithaca: Cornell University Press, 1995), p. 119.

78. Jean-Pierre Vernant, *Myth and Society in Ancient Greece* (Atlantic Highlands, N.J.: Humanities, 1980), pp. 103-4; Karl Reinhardt, "The Adventures in the *Odyssey,*" in *Reading the Odyssey: Selected Interpretive Essays,* ed. Seth Schein (Princeton: Princeton University Press, 1996), pp. 83, 89, 131; Muellner, *The Anger of Achilles,* p. 12; Ruth Scodel, "The Achaean Wall and the Myth of Destruction," *Harvard Studies in Classical Philology* 86 (1982): 48; Jenny Strauss Clay, *The Wrath of Athena* (Princeton: Princeton University Press, 1983), p. 205.

79. Finley, *Homer's Odyssey,* p. 91; Reinhardt, "The Adventures in the *Odyssey,*" p. 131; Scodel, "The Achaean Wall and the Myth of Destruction," p. 48.

80. Finley, *Homer's Odyssey,* p. 92. Carlo Brillante, "History and the Historical Interpreta-

edge communicated through the stories of Odysseus's travels had the potential to touch the experiences of the audiences to whom the Homeric songs were sung so that this knowledge was not merely mental in character but was also formative of the hearer's self-understanding.[81] Odysseus's journeys could be shared vicariously and so could increase the hearer's understanding, but the journeys themselves were not repeatable — they belonged to the heroic age.[82]

Audiences can participate through the bard's songs in Odysseus's journeys in the realm of the gods. These journeys show how this royal figure remained faithful to household and homeland and struggled to return to earthly life from the sphere of the gods. The movement from the underworld to life, from Calypso's island to home, from Scheria to Ithaca, from sleep to the awareness that his companions had slaughtered Helios's cattle — all these experiences manifested the interplay of life and death within Odysseus's person.[83] Pietro Pucci has identified the *gastēr*, "belly," as the physiological locus in the Homeric person for this interplay of life and death in the form of pleasure and pain, fullness and deprivation, and culture and instinct.[84] Enmeshed within the human condition, subject to the demands of the belly, the Homeric king was nevertheless summoned to be a kind of savior figure who was inspired and strengthened by the divine realm in order to promote justice and well-being in a human community.[85]

The Israelite king was called to protect the Israelites and so to serve as a kind of savior figure. The royal Psalm 18 (= 2 Samuel 22) describes how the Lord equipped David and sustained him in battle:

> He made my feet like those of a hind
>   and set me upon the heights.[86]
> He trained my hands for battle
>   so that my arms can bend the bronze bow.
> You gave me the shield of your salvation,
>   and your right hand supported me,
>   and your promise[87] made me great.

---

tion of Myth," in *Approaches to Greek Myth*, ed. L. Edmunds (Baltimore: Johns Hopkins University Press, 1990), p. 102.

81. Finley, *Homer's Odyssey*, p. 95; Ian Morris, "The Use and Abuse of Homer," *Classical Antiquity* 5 (1986): 123-29.

82. Segal, *Singers, Heroes, and Gods*, p. 30.

83. Pucci, *Odysseus Polutropos*, p. 154; Reinhardt, "The Adventures in the *Odyssey*," pp. 80, 113.

84. Pucci, *Odysseus Polutropos*, p. 157.

85. Olson, *Blood and Iron*, p. 202; Carlier, *La royauté en Grèce avant Alexandre*, pp. 176-77.

86. Read *bāmōt*.

87. Read *wa'ănōtĕkā* with 2 Sam 22:36.

> You made room for my steps,
>> and my ankles did not falter.
> I pursued and overtook my enemies,
>> and I did not turn back until I destroyed them.
> I struck them so that they were unable to rise;
>> they fell beneath my feet. (Ps. 18:34-39[33-38])

David's success in battle would have made him appear godlike in comparison with other more mediocre warriors.[88] For example, in the story of David's rise to power (1 Sam. 16:14–2 Sam. 5:10), the women sang of David's excellence in his victories over the Philistines in a way that moved Saul to jealousy: "Saul has struck down his thousands; David, his tens of thousands" (1 Sam. 18:7). Most importantly, according to Psalm 18, David attributed his success as warrior to the Lord.[89] This can be seen in a number of epithets where the Lord is David's strength, his rock, his fortress, his deliverer, his shield, the horn of his salvation, and his refuge (vv. 2-3[1-2]). This psalm celebrated not only the charisma of David but also his humility and piety.[90]

The humble piety of the victorious David in Psalm 18 presents only the royalist perspective. Skepticism about the kingship, according to 1 Samuel 8, arose at the very beginning of Israel's discussion about inaugurating the kingship. According to 1 Samuel 8, kingship posed a threat to the Israelite community not only in the form of tyranny (1 Sam. 8:10-18) but also as a segue to practical atheism: that is, the Israelites would be tempted to trust more in the immediacy of the king's help rather than in the more intangible assistance of the Lord.[91] The view that earthly kingship in Israel was incompatible with the Lord's heavenly kingship came to expression forcefully in 1 Samuel 8:7, which reports that the Lord said to Samuel: "Pay heed to the people in all that they say to you. Indeed, they have not rejected you, but they have rejected me from ruling over them as king." First Samuel 8 allowed the antimonarchical voice to come to expression in its account: a voice that regarded kingship as a foreign institution that would undercut Israel's faith in the Lord and its traditional way of life.[92]

---

88. Évode Beaucamp, *Le psautier*, vol. 1 (Paris: Gabalda, 1976), pp. 97-98; Peter Craigie, *Psalms 1–50*, WBC 19 (Waco, Tex.: Word, 1983), p. 175.

89. Cf. Frank Moore Cross, *From Epic to Canon: History and Literature in Ancient Israel* (Baltimore: Johns Hopkins University Press, 1998), p. 27.

90. Walter Brueggemann, *First and Second Samuel* (Louisville: John Knox, 1990), p. 344.

91. P. Kyle McCarter, Jr., *I Samuel*, AB 8 (Garden City, N.Y.: Doubleday, 1980), p. 161; J. J. M. Roberts, "In Defense of the Monarchy: The Contribution of Israelite Kingship to Biblical Theology," in *Ancient Israelite Religion: Essays in Honor of Frank Moore Cross*, ed. P. Miller, Jr. et al. (Philadelphia: Fortress, 1987), p. 385.

92. Dennis J. McCarthy, "The Inauguration of the Monarchy in Israel: A Form-Critical

According to the narrative of 2 Samuel 11–12 when David had committed adultery with Bathsheba and had her husband Uriah the Hittite killed, his actions constituted a rebellion against the Lord (2 Sam. 11:2-27). When the child born from his union with Bathsheba became deathly ill, David entreated the Lord with complete fasting and spent nights lying on the ground. On the seventh day, the child died. David's servants did not inform him for fear that total despair would overtake him (2 Sam. 12:15-19). David's acts of petition resembled those of a mourning ritual where one symbolically enters the sphere of death.[93] When David learned of the child's death, he washed, anointed himself, and changed his clothes; then he went into the temple and worshiped;[94] finally, he went into the palace and requested food (2 Sam. 12:20). So, in the sequence of intercessory activities after his petitions were not answered, David returned to the routine of life and began to take up his typical activities. His ritual of petition and grief demonstrated his solidarity with the child and his humble acknowledgment of the Lord's sovereign rule over his life and the lives of those in his kingdom. His rising up from grief indicated his acceptance of the Lord's punishment and his willingness to return to life in the Israelite community according to the limitations and expectations mapped out by its tradition.[95]

The book of Isaiah celebrates Hezekiah as an exemplary king whose prayers of petition led not only to the deliverance of Jerusalem in 701 B.C. (Isa. 37:21) but also to the extension of his life by fifteen years in the face of a terminal illness (Isa. 38:5).[96] Hezekiah is portrayed as a king who readily listened to the prophet Isaiah; therefore, the oracle announcing his impending death is delivered as an announcement of vital information rather than as a judgment for past sins.[97] When Hezekiah learned he was about to die, he

---

Study in 1 Samuel 8–12," *Int* 27 (1973): 403; Frank Crüsemann, *Der Widerstand gegen das Königtum,* WMANT 49 (Neukirchen-Vluyn: Neukirchener Verlag, 1978), pp. 13-14, 62, 70.

93. Hans W. Hertzberg, *I & II Samuel* (Philadelphia: Westminster, 1964), p. 315; Steven Weitzman, "David's Lament and the Poetics of Grief in 2 Samuel," *JQR* 85 (1995): 347-48; Randall Bailey, *David in Love and War: The Pursuit of Power in 2 Samuel 10–12,* JSOTSup 75 (Sheffield: Sheffield Academic Press, 1990), pp. 114, 116.

94. P. Kyle McCarter, Jr. (*II Samuel,* AB 9 [Garden City, N.Y.: Doubleday, 1984], p. 302) argues that the phrase "the house of the Lord" in 2 Sam. 12:20 as a reference to the Solomonic temple is an anachronism, which was probably included by a later writer for whom it would have been customary for the king to enter the Solomonic temple for worship.

95. Brueggemann, *First and Second Samuel,* pp. 283-84; McCarter, *II Samuel,* p. 301.

96. Seitz, *Isaiah 1–39,* pp. 254-55; Childs, *Isaiah,* pp. 282-83; Samuel Balentine, *Prayer in the Hebrew Bible* (Minneapolis: Fortress, 1993), pp. 61-64.

97. Robert Cohn, "Convention and Creativity in the Book of Kings: The Case of the Dying Monarch," *CBQ* 47 (1985): 612-13.

turned his face to the wall and prayed to the Lord: "Please Lord, remember that I have behaved with fidelity and an undivided heart before you, and I have done what is pleasing in your eyes." (Isa. 38:2-3)

Soon thereafter, Isaiah delivered an oracle to Hezekiah informing him that his prayer had been answered, and then he gave Hezekiah a miraculous sign confirming the promise of healing: the sun would move back ten steps on the sun dial of Ahaz (Isa. 38:7). The account in Isaiah 38 then includes a prayer of thanksgiving as a composition of Hezekiah[98] — an insertion that accents the piety of Hezekiah and shifts the focus of this narrative on illness and recovery from the role of the prophet Isaiah, as in 2 Kings 20:1-11, to that of Hezekiah.[99] On the basis of a parallel with a Sumerian letter-prayer of Sin-iddinam of Larsa (1849-1843 B.C.) to the sun god Utu for healing, William Hallo has made the case that this psalm in Isaiah 38:9-20 could have been a letter-prayer of Hezekiah that he himself placed in the temple.[100] After petitions for healing (vv. 14-16) and a statement of confidence that this petition had been answered (v. 17), the exemplary Hezekiah of Isaiah 36–38 gives the following reason for his deliverance:

> For Sheol does not thank you,
>   death does not praise you;
> the ones who descend into the Pit do not hope
>   for your faithfulness.
> The living, the living, they give you thanks,
>   as I do today;
> fathers will inform children of your faithfulness. (Isa. 38:18-19)

For the Israelites, the underworld was a place of silence where no prayers and no remembrance of the Lord by a community came to expression.[101] Premature entry into Sheol was regarded as tragic. Likewise, on a political level in 701 B.C., the looming threat of the destruction of Jerusalem and the deportation of

---

98. Childs (*Isaiah*, p. 284) notes that most scholars regard this thanksgiving psalm, with a dominant emphasis on the lament component, as not composed for the narratives in Isaiah 36–38 but as introduced here to form a typological connection between Hezekiah's fate and that of Jerusalem. See also Ackroyd, "An Interpretation of the Babylonian Exile," p. 165; Seitz, *Isaiah 1–39*, pp. 258-61.

99. Sweeney, *Isaiah 1–39*, p. 493.

100. William W. Hallo, "The Royal Correspondence of Larsa: I. A Sumerian Prototype for the Prayer of Hezekiah," in *Kramer Anniversary Volume*, ed. B. Eichler, AOAT 25 (Kevelaer: Butzon & Bercker; 1976), pp. 212-13; Sweeney, *Isaiah 1–39*, p. 502.

101. Hans-Joachim Kraus, *Psalms 1–59* (Minneapolis: Augsburg, 1988), p. 356.

its population signaled that the Israelite community and its worship could be brought to an end — a silence analogous to that of Sheol.

Hezekiah's successful intercession for his own life paralleled that which he made for the city of Jerusalem.[102] The body of the king and the body politic of Jerusalem were given reprieves from imminent death because of the pious, faithful prayer of the king.[103] The contrast between Ahaz's refusal to trust in the Lord according to Isaiah 7 and Hezekiah's prayerful petition according to Isaiah 37–38 highlighted the seriousness of the king's relationship with the Lord for the well-being of the community. According to Isaiah 38, just as Hezekiah's healing would last only fifteen years, the future of the Davidic dynasty and of Jerusalem still hung in the balance and depended on subsequent Davidic kings following the faithful and pious example of Hezekiah.[104]

In the Mesopotamian royal inscriptions, the king typically portrayed himself as an obedient servant of the gods. In the prologue to the *Code of Hammurapi*, Hammurapi described himself as "the pious one *(na'dum)* who prays fervently to the great gods" (IV:64-66; cf. I:30), as "the reverent one" *(palḫum, I:31)* and "the humble one" *(ašrum, II:18)*, and as "one who obeys mighty Shamash" (II:23). These phrases praise Hammurapi as a king who took seriously the superior power of the gods. However, in terms of practical politics, Hammurapi had no choice but to support the temple establishments of the various cities if he ever expected to rule over the land of Sumer and Akkad. The temple establishments were a formidable political and social force within Mesopotamian cities of OB times.[105]

Statues of Mesopotamian kings were placed in sanctuaries beginning in the Early Dynastic period in Sumer (ca. 2900-2350 B.C.). The earliest examples seem to be those of deceased kings to whom intercessions were made: for example, the statue of Gilgamesh of Uruk.[106] The posthumous deification of a king

---

102. H. G. M. Williamson, "Hezekiah and the Temple," in *Texts, Temples, and Traditions: A Tribute to Menahem Haran*, ed. M. Fox et al. (Winona Lake, Ind.: Eisenbrauns, 1996), p. 52.

103. Ackroyd, "Isaiah 36–39," p. 113; Seitz, *Isaiah 1–39*, p. 257.

104. Sweeney, *Isaiah 1–39*, pp. 501-2.

105. F. R. Kraus, *The Role of Temples from the Third Dynasty of Ur to the First Dynasty of Babylon*, Monographs on the Ancient Near East, vol. 2, fasc. 4 (Malibu, Calif.: Undena, 1990), pp. 12-14; Marc Van de Mieroop, *Society and Enterprise in Old Babylonian Ur*, BBVO 12 (Berlin: Dietrich Reimer, 1992), pp. 112, 115, 208, 248; idem, *The Ancient Mesopotamian City* (Oxford: Clarendon, 1997), pp. 112, 146-47; John F. Robertson, "The Social and Economic Organization of Ancient Mesopotamian Temples," in *Civilizations of the Ancient Near East*, ed. Jack Sasson (New York: Scribner, 1995), pp. 451-52; Johannes M. Renger, "Institutional, Communal, and Individual Ownership or Possession of Arable Land in Ancient Mesopotamia from the End of the Fourth to the End of the First Millennium B.C.," *Chicago-Kent Law Review* 71 (1995): 285-86, 289, 295.

106. William W. Hallo, *Origins: The Ancient Near Eastern Background of Some Modern*

was in accord with the common Mesopotamian practice of regarding the deceased ancestors as residing among the Anunnaki gods.[107] Naram-Sin (2254-2218 B.C.) was the first living king to declare himself a deity. In the OB period (2003-1595 B.C.), statues of the divinized kings Sargon (2334-2279 B.C.) and Naram-Sin were found in numerous sanctuaries.[108] Hallo argues that the temple establishments in the late third millennium had responded to the divinization of the Sargonic kings by introducing the cult statue of the deity into the sanctuary in imitation of the royal statue.[109] So, cultic practice in the late third millennium supported the divinization of kings that was in place in Mesopotamia from 2250 to 1750 B.C. until in Babylon Hammurapi discontinued the practice of writing the king's name with the divine determinative.[110]

Those kings who claimed to be divinized still proclaimed their obedience to the great gods who exercised sovereign rule and to those deities whose protection and assistance they needed. For example, Lipit-Ishtar of Isin (1934-1924 B.C.) wrote his name with the divine determinative and regarded himself as "the son of Enlil";[111] nevertheless, he built and dedicated a storeroom in Isin in honor of the great gods Enlil and Ninlil.[112] Living divinized kings were expected to respect the hierarchy of the pantheon.[113]

The *Epic of Gilgamesh* relates an astonishing episode of the hubris of Gilgamesh and Enkidu in relation to the goddess Ishtar. Tablet six begins with a proposal of marriage from Ishtar to Gilgamesh. She promised him not only wealth but also status, for "kings, nobles, and princes will kneel before you!"

Western Institutions (Leiden: Brill, 1996), pp. 208, 229; William Moran, "The Gilgamesh Epic: A Masterpiece from Ancient Mesopotamia," in *Civilizations of the Ancient Near East,* ed. J. Sasson (New York: Scribner, 1995), p. 2327.

107. William W. Hallo, "Sumerian Religion," in *Kinattūtu ša darāti,* ed. A. F. Rainey (Tel Aviv: University of Tel Aviv Press, 1993), pp. 18-19; Karel van der Toorn, *Family Religion in Babylonia, Syria and Israel* (Leiden: Brill, 1996), p. 48.

108. Hallo, "Sumerian Religion," pp. 20-21; Hallo, *Origins,* p. 208; see also Irene Winter, "'Idols of the King': Royal Images as Recipients of Ritual Action in Ancient Mesopotamia," *Journal of Ritual Studies* 6 (1992): 29-34.

109. Hallo, "Sumerian Religion," pp. 18-19; idem, "Texts, Statues and the Cult of the Divine King," *VTSup* 40 (1988): 58-59. F. A. M. Wiggermann ("Theologies, Priests, and Worship in Ancient Mesopotamia," in *Civilizations of the Ancient Near East,* ed. J. Sasson [New York: Scribner, 1995], p. 1862) claims that even though no actual statue of a god has been recovered from the early times, such statues are depicted on art objects and described in later ritual texts.

110. Hallo, *Origins,* p. 152; idem, "Texts, Statues, and the Cult of the Divine King," p. 62.

111. Frayne, *RIME 4,* E4.1.5.3, line 5.

112. Frayne, *RIME 4,* E4.1.5.3.

113. Hallo, *Origins,* p. 203; cf. van der Toorn, *Family Religion in Babylonia, Syria, and Israel,* p. 136.

(VI:16).[114] Gilgamesh, however, described her through a series of images as a deceptive and unreliable lover (VI:42-49). He then continued his insults by naming lovers who had suffered through their association with her (VI:46-78). Enraged, Ishtar went to her father Anu and reported: "My father, Gilgamesh has repeatedly insulted me; Gilgamesh has pronounced slanderous statements against me, slanders and curses about me" (VI:84-85). She then pleaded with Anu that the Bull of Heaven be unleashed against Gilgamesh, a request to which Anu reluctantly acceded. Gilgamesh and Enkidu teamed up to slay the Bull of Heaven. After the battle, Enkidu spotted Ishtar on the walls of Uruk and hurled the thigh of the Bull of Heaven at her and cried out: "If only I could reach you, like that I would do to you" (VI:158-59). Shortly thereafter, Gilgamesh offered ointment to his father, Lugalbanda, a divinized king (VI:168). Then he and Enkidu paraded through the streets of Uruk to the adulation of the crowds (VI:171-79). After a day of celebration, they rested. Enkidu had a dream, from which he awoke and expressed the following ominous question to Gilgamesh: "My friend, why are the great gods deliberating together?" (VI:188). In that divine assembly, Enlil had decreed that Enkidu must die as a punishment for slaying the Bull of Heaven (VII:9-10).

Interaction between gods and humans was expected in the Mesopotamian world. Ishtar's offer of love to the hero Gilgamesh may reflect a practice of sacred marriage in which the reigning king, who held the priestly title of the *en* of Uruk, was espoused to Ishtar.[115] Gilgamesh's mother was the goddess Ninsun; she was the consort of Gilgamesh's father Lugalbanda who was posthumously divinized (I.33-34).[116] Therefore, Gilgamesh was identified as two-thirds divine and one-third human (I.46).[117] Gilgamesh refused Ishtar's offer in the form of a series of insults in which he charged her with badly mistreating previous lov-

---

114. The text is from Simo Parpola, *The Standard Babylonian Epic of Gilgamesh,* State Archives of Assyria Cuneiform Texts 1 (Helsinki: Vammalan Kirjapaino Oy, 1997), p. 92. Tablets I, V-IX, XI, XII of the OB version are not extant.

115. Moran, "The Gilgamesh Epic," p. 2333; Hallo, *Origins,* p. 229; Piotr Steinkeller, "On Rulers, Priests and Sacred Marriage: Tracing the Evolution of Early Sumerian Kingship," in *Priests and Officials in the Ancient Near East,* ed. K. Watanabe (Heidelberg: Universitätsverlag C. Winter, 1999), p. 131. Jerrold Cooper ("Sacred Marriage and Popular Cult in Early Mesopotamia," in *Official Cult and Popular Religion in the Ancient Near East,* ed. E. Matsushima [Heidelberg: Universitätsverlag C. Winter, 1993], p. 94) notes that the sacred marriage rite involving the reigning king seems to have ended at Isin in the early second millennium B.C.

116. Jeffrey Tigay, *The Evolution of the Gilgamesh Epic* (Philadelphia: University of Pennsylvania Press, 1982), pp. 73-74.

117. For these texts in the standard Babylonian version of the *Gilgamesh Epic,* see Parpola, *The Standard Babylonian Epic of Gilgamesh,* p. 71; an English translation is provided by Stephanie Dalley, *Myths from Mesopotamia,* rev. ed. (New York: Oxford University Press, 2000), p. 51.

ers (VI.24-79).[118] Tzvi Abusch argued that Gilgamesh refused her so vehemently because his marriage to Ishtar meant that he would die and become a king in the netherworld: a fate that he resisted as long as he could.[119]

The subsequent victory of Gilgamesh and Enkidu over the Bull of Heaven saved the land from years of famine and won the acclaim of the populace. Their victory, however, was not simply a matter of self-defense; it constituted a transgression of the divinely willed world order. For this, Enkidu had to pay with his life.[120] Rivalry with the gods frequently leads to transgressions for which humans are made aware of their mortal condition through the loss of life.[121]

Brought face to face with death, Gilgamesh set out on a journey to Utnapishtim, the primordial flood hero, to try to overcome death. His inability to pass Utnapishtim's test of conquering sleep by staying awake for six days and seven nights (XI:23-41) forced Gilgamesh to realize that he was mortal. He also came to realize that for life to be meaningful for a human, life had to be shared. So, he planned to take the plant of immortality back to Uruk to divide with others rather than to consume it immediately by himself (XI:278-83).[122]

Heroic Mesopotamian kings manifested divine qualities and were celebrated as savior figures. Nevertheless, the tradition praised such kings for their reverence for the great gods who wielded sovereignty and for their respect for the hierarchy of gods. When the divinely willed order was transgressed, even by the most heroic kings, the human transgressor was humbled and brought to recognize his place within the hierarchy of gods and humans.

In Homeric Greece, biblical Israel, and OB Mesopotamia, humans who pressed the boundaries between the human and divine were celebrated as heroes, whereas those who transgressed such boundaries were regarded as either tragic or foolish figures. In Homer, Odysseus's men all perished. Some of them appeared to be rebellious and foolish (e.g., Eurylochus in *Od.* 10.428-48), whereas others simply perished as victims of circumstances (e.g., the six men swallowed by Scylla, *Od.* 12.245-59). The failure to acknowledge the status and prerogatives of the various Homeric gods was a serious offense that threatened to upset the cosmic hierarchy; the gods defended their status jealously. In Israel,

---

118. Parpola, *The Standard Babylonian Epic of Gilgamesh,* pp. 91-92; Dalley, *Myths from Mesopotamia* (2000), pp. 78-79.

119. Tzvi Abusch, "Ishtar's Proposal and Gilgamesh's Refusal: An Interpretation of *The Gilgamesh Epic,* Tablet 6, Lines 1-79," *History of Religions* 26 (1986): 160-61.

120. Aage Westenholz and Ulla Koch-Westenholz, "Enkidu — the Noble Savage?" in *Wisdom, Gods and Literature: Studies in Assyriology in Honour of W. G. Lambert,* ed. A. R. George and I. L. Finkel (Winona Lake, Ind.: Eisenbrauns, 2000), pp. 443-44.

121. Moran, "The Gilgamesh Epic," p. 2333.

122. Nicole Vulpe, "Irony and the Unity of the *Gilgamesh Epic,*" *JNES* 53 (1994): 281.

a heroic warrior like David ascribed his strength and success to the Lord and not to himself. The king's self-understanding was a key question in the Israelite tradition as to whether the monarchy would be a blessing or curse for the people. The problem of a king forgetting his dependence on the Lord was a major reason for the antimonarchic position that viewed earthly and heavenly kingship as incompatible (1 Sam. 8:7). David's repentance after his adulterous union with Bathsheba and the planned death of her husband Uriah indicated his acceptance of limits to his power and position. Hezekiah's intercession indicated how a prayerful, pious king can increase the well-being of the community through greater reliance on the Lord's protection. Humility and piety were fundamental characteristics of an ideal Israelite king.

In Mesopotamia, the piety of the king was also important. For the first half of the OB period, a few divinized Mesopotamian kings might have been regarded as minor deities who took their place within the existing hierarchy of the pantheon. Nevertheless, these divinized kings were still obliged to care for the temples and supply them with provisions (e.g., Lipit-Ishtar of Isin, 1934-1924 B.C.).[123] The possibility of a king transgressing the boundaries mapped out in the heavenly hierarchy was related in the fictional narrative of the rivalry between Ishtar and Gilgamesh in the *Epic of Gilgamesh*. In all three cultures, the hierarchy of gods and humans had to be respected. How far one could venture into the heavenly realm without transgressing the prerogatives of the gods depended on the criteria for differentiating gods and humans held in particular historical periods in each culture.

Practices for Strengthening the Piety of the King

Any king who exercised power without paying careful attention to the people and circumstances that would be affected by his actions acted like a tyrant. The traditions of Homeric Greece, biblical Israel, and OB Mesopotamia located the source of sovereignty in the king of the gods. If an earthly king ignored this transcendent source of his authority, then the probability increased that he would make decisions that would not sufficiently take into account the needs and legitimate interests of the people he ruled. A significant check against a king's arbitrary exercise of power was the reality of God or the gods as actors in the political affairs of the kingdom. If the king were to rule in accord with the divine will, the king needed to incorporate in his routine those practices that would help him to be mindful of the divine will and to commu-

---

123. Frayne, *RIME 4*, E4.1.5.1; E4.1.5.2.

nicate with God or the gods to gain the guidance and assistance necessary to rule uprightly.

Prayer

In the *Iliad,* when the sceptered kings of the Achaeans were preparing to send an embassy to Achilles to persuade him to return to the battle, Nestor encouraged Agamemnon to choose skilled men for this assignment:

> First of all let Phoenix, beloved of Zeus, lead the way; next great Ajax and glorious Odysseus; of the heralds let Odius and Eurybates go along with them. Bring water for your hands and command them to keep ritual silence so that we may pray to Zeus, son of Cronus, that he might have mercy. (*Il.* 9.168-72)

Zeus was regarded as sovereign and was frequently entreated (*Il.* 1.394, 500; 2.371, 411-18, etc.).[124] The interaction between gods and humans in the *Iliad* was pervasive, yet the plurality of gods and their seeming indifference to the suffering of humans raised questions about how effective intercession to them could have been.[125] In the *Odyssey,* the gods appear less frequently.[126] Athena was the primary deity active on the earthly scene; however, Zeus and Poseidon were also often mentioned.[127] As Odysseus was about to enter the city of the Phaeacians to make supplication to Arete and Alcinous for conveyance back to Ithaca, he prayed to Athena and invoked her according to one of her age-old epithets, Atrytone, which seems to have referred to her untiring, persistent character:[128]

> "Pay heed to me, Atrytone, child of aegis-bearing Zeus. Listen now to me, seeing that previously you did not listen when I was shipwrecked, when the renowned Earth-shaker struck me. Allow me to come to the Phaeacians as

---

124. Donald Lateiner, "Homeric Prayer," *Arethusa* 30 (1997): 257-61.

125. Walter Burkert, *Greek Religion* (Cambridge, Mass.: Harvard University Press, 1985), p. 122. On supplication to the gods as mere ceremony, see Crotty, *The Poetics of Supplication,* p. 98.

126. Olson, *Blood and Iron,* p. 215; Schein, "Introduction," p. 14; cf. Pucci, *Odysseus Polutropos,* p. 69.

127. Detienne, "The 'Sea-Crow,'" pp. 20, 30, 34; Reinhardt, "The Adventures in the *Odyssey,*" pp. 85-86.

128. Stephanie West ("Commentary on Books I-IV," in *A Commentary on Homer's Odyssey,* vol. 1: *Introduction and Books I-VIII,* ed. S. West and J. B. Hainsworth [Oxford: Clarendon, 1988], p. 240) notes that Athena's epithet "Atrytone" is usually translated "unwearied one," but its meaning is obscure and probably is of pre-Greek origin.

one loved and pitied." So he prayed, and Pallas Athena paid heed to him. But she had not yet appeared to him face-to-face, for she feared her father's brother [Poseidon] who showed his furious anger against godlike Odysseus until he came to his own land. (*Od.* 6.324-31)

Odysseus's prayer reflects the typical pattern of prayer in Archaic poetry: (1) he invokes Athena as a deity; (2) he recalls her previous silence and the expectation that she should be attentive to him — which seems to imply that their relationship was sufficiently well-established for reciprocity to be operative; and (3) he voices the specific request of reaching the Phaeacians.[129]

Odysseus did not recognize Athena until he reached the shores of Ithaca (*Od.* 13.291-95). Her invisibility and silence toward Odysseus could be seen as her reluctance to offend the more powerful Poseidon who was angry with Odysseus.[130] Perhaps Athena kept herself out of reach because of her rivalry with Odysseus over who was more clever *(mētis)*.[131] Even though her *mētis* was clearly superior, the issue of keeping the boundary intact between human and divine excellence was an ongoing concern (i.e., an antinomy): it was important for this boundary to be pressed but not transgressed.[132] Whether it was Athena's lack of power vis-à-vis Poseidon or her antipathy to Odysseus as a rival, the result was her invisibility and distance from Odysseus throughout his journeys. The classic question of theodicy in a lament is whether the deity's silence and inaction are due to a lack of concern or to a lack of power. In the polytheistic format of the Homeric pantheon, the possibilities for constraints on the power of deities lesser than Zeus are legion. Nevertheless, the Homeric narratives offer a consolidated picture of the diverse, often conflicting traditions about the local Greek gods.[133] Within this polytheistic framework, the Homeric kings made intercession to Zeus and their protector deities.

In the Israelite tradition, David is the king most frequently depicted as engaged in prayer.[134] This is primarily a consequence of the role ascribed to him in the tradition as the patron of the temple cult and as the composer of many

129. Cf. Slatkin, *The Power of Thetis*, p. 62; Gould, "On Making Sense of Greek Religion," p. 216.

130. Reinhardt, "The Adventures in the *Odyssey*," p. 87; Vernant, *Myth and Society in Ancient Greece*, p. 103.

131. Clay, *The Wrath of Athena*, pp. 205, 209.

132. Muellner, *The Anger of Achilles*, pp. 8-15.

133. Burkert, *Greek Religion*, pp. 119-120; Jasper Griffin, *Homer on Life and Death* (Oxford: Clarendon, 1980), pp. 144, 186-87.

134. Steven McKenzie, *King David: A Biography* (New York: Oxford University Press, 2000), p. 2; cf. Kraus, *Psalms 1–59*, pp. 22-23; David M. Howard, "David," in *ABD*, 2:47A; J. M. Myers, "David," in *IDB*, 1:782A.

psalms.[135] Psalm 101, labeled by the tradition as a psalm belonging to David, is a meditative, lamentlike hymn that shows the king praying for the Lord's help and inspiration so that he might maintain an order in Jerusalem faithful to the Lord:[136]

> Of fidelity and justice I will sing;
>> to you, Lord, I will make music.
> I will seek to understand the perfect way;
>> when will you come to me?
> I will walk about with blameless heart
>> in the midst of my house.
> I will not place before my eyes
>> a hellish thing;
> I hate the rebel's deed;
>> it shall not cling to me.
> The crooked heart shall turn away from me;
>> evil I will not know.
> The one who slanders a neighbor in secret,
>> that one I will silence.
> The one of haughty looks and arrogant heart,
>> that one I cannot endure. (Ps. 101:1-5)

If David and his successors prayed this hymn, their actions would have exemplified the pious behavior of an ideal Israelite king. With this psalm, the king petitioned the Lord to be present with him in order to bring understanding, integrity, and upright behavior. The king examined his own heart at the same time he scrutinized the attitudes and behavior of those within his royal household. If the king prayed this psalm publicly at his coronation or at other occasions of communal worship, he would have created the impression that he was a pious and just king intent on carrying out the divine will.[137] Even if the impression did not accurately reflect the reality of the king's intentions and behav-

---

135. Robert North, "The Chronicler: 1-2 Chronicles, Ezra, Nehemiah," in *NJBC*, 23:40; James Kugel, "David the Prophet," in *Poetry and Prophecy*, ed. J. Kugel (Ithaca: Cornell University Press, 1990), pp. 47-50; Alan Cooper, "The Life and Times of King David According to the Book of Psalms," in *The Poet and the Historian: Essays in Literary and Historical Biblical Criticism*, HSM 26 (Chico, Calif.: Scholars, 1983), pp. 125, 129-30.

136. Sigmund Mowinckel, *The Psalms in Israel's Worship* (Oxford: Blackwell, 1962), p. 66; Otto Kaiser, "Erwägungen zu Psalm 101," *ZAW* 74 (1962): 200-203; Hans-Joachim Kraus, *Psalms 60–150* (Minneapolis: Augsburg, 1989), p. 278; Évode Beaucamp, *Le psautier*, vol. 2 (Paris: Gabalda, 1979), pp. 138-39.

137. Helen Kenik, "Code of Conduct for a King: Psalm 101," *JBL* 95 (1976): 392-93.

ior, the effort to make such an impression indicated that at least some members of the community made him pretend that piety was important.

In OB Mesopotamia, the kings were often pictured as praying to the gods. The epithets of "the reverent one" or "the obedient one" presented the image of the Mesopotamian king as attentive to and intent on communicating with the gods. Kudur-mabuk ruled over the state of Emutbal for twelve years until about 1814 B.C.[138] He installed his sons Warad-Sin (1834-1823 B.C.) and Rim-Sin (1822-1763 B.C.) in the adjoining state of Larsa to the south.[139] A cone inscription marking the construction of a temple reports the following about the pious attentiveness of Kudur-mabuk:

> With an understanding "ear," which the god gave him, he searched wisely, and in a very quiet place, a place where no foot may tread, he made forever a temple of baked brick, a holy dwelling, a repository for a stela, in whose midst sacrifices are continuous each day. He put his influential name in place.... [concerning the one who destroys this temple] May Nergal, the god who created me, raging in his anger, tear out his heart. May Shamash, the lord of heaven and earth, curse him with a grievous curse.[140]

This inscription highlights the communication between Kudur-mabuk and the deity for whom the temple was built: not only did the deity instruct him on the location, the deity also became the recipient of daily sacrifices. The stela deposited there may have had an intercessory function[141] or may have been intended to provide wise instruction, as did the *narû* texts, for kings and others who might have come there.[142] In the early second millennium B.C., Larsa was a city in which there was a well-established practice among the royalty and general populace of sending letter-prayers to deities. These letters as intercessory prayers functioned analogously to votive statues that interceded

---

138. Frayne, *RIME 4*, E4.2.13.

139. Marc Van de Mieroop, "The Reign of Rim-Sin," *RA* 87 (1993): 50-51; D. O. Edzard, "The Old Babylonian Period," in *The Near East: The Early Civilizations*, ed. J. Bottéro et al. (New York: Delacorte, 1967), p. 185.

140. Frayne, *RIME 4*, E4.2.13a.2, lines 8-21, 41-51.

141. Cf. Hallo, *Origins*, p. 233; idem, "The Royal Correspondence of Larsa," p. 210; Peter Machinist, "On Self-Consciousness in Mesopotamia," in *The Origins and Diversity of Axial Age Civilizations*, ed. S. N. Eisenstadt (Albany, N.Y.: SUNY Press, 1986), p. 193.

142. Tremper Longman III, *Fictional Akkadian Autobiography: A Generic and Comparative Study* (Winona Lake, Ind.: Eisenbrauns, 1991), pp. 147-48, 228. Jonker (*The Topography of Remembrance*, pp. 91, 95) claims that although messages written on objects were originally addressed to gods, in the case of *narû* texts these were addressed to humans when inscribed on a stela.

for an individual, but at a much lower cost of production.[143] In the latter part of the inscription above, Kudur-mabuk prayed curses against anyone in the future who would destroy or neglect the temple he had constructed. This practice of including curses at the conclusion of an inscription conformed to a basic axiom of the Mesopotamian *Weltanschauung:* the gods ruled the cosmos.

In Homeric Greece, biblical Israel, and OB Mesopotamia, kings made intercession to God or the gods. Some modern commentators on Homer are skeptical that such intercession was anything more than ceremonial, yet it is significant that words and rituals were addressed to the gods.[144] In the Israelite tradition, David was remembered as one who composed and prayed the psalms. Psalm 101 highlights how such intercession was integral to the justice of royal rule. The Mesopotamian kings demonstrated their prayerfulness and attentiveness to the gods in their temple construction and in the rationales that they provided for such construction in their inscriptions. Kings in each of the three traditions were depicted as leaders who engaged in prayer.

Attentiveness to the Traditions of the Community

At the banquet in Alcinous's palace in Scheria, the bard Demodocus sang the tales of the Achaean and Trojan warriors at Troy (*Od.* 8.63-82). The performance of these songs brought great joy to the Phaeacians but lamentation and tears to Odysseus (*Od.* 8.83-92). His grief was hidden from all the Phaeacians, except for Alcinous (*Od.* 8.93-95).[145] Odysseus wept not only for the Achaeans but also for the Trojans (*Od.* 8.578). The troubles and anguish suffered by the Achaeans and Trojans formed a bridge to the experience of the much-suffering Odysseus and created an emotional bond between Odysseus and the heroes of the past. Kevin Crotty argues that a song whose subject matter is grief has the power to transcend the self-interest of the bard, and so the bard's song can be

143. William W. Hallo, "Lamentations and Prayers in Sumer and Akkad," in *Civilizations of the Ancient Near East,* ed. J. Sasson (New York: Scribner, 1995), p. 1877; idem, "Two Letter-Prayers to Amurru," in *Boundaries of the Ancient Near Eastern World: A Tribute to Cyrus H. Gordon,* ed. M. Lubetski et al., JSOTSup 273 (Sheffield: Sheffield Academic Press, 1998), pp. 401-4; Sharon Keller, "Written Communication Between the Human and Divine Spheres in Mesopotamia and Israel," in *The Biblical Canon in Comparative Perspective: Scripture in Context IV,* ed. K. Younger, Jr. et al. (Lewiston, N.Y.: Mellen, 1991), p. 304.

144. Roy Rappaport (*Ritual and Religion in the Making of Humanity* [Cambridge: Cambridge University Press, 1999], p. 123) notes that religious rituals establish obligations and expectations that the participants accept and promise to carry out through their participation in the ritual even if they do not believe in what they are doing.

145. Segal, *Singers, Heroes, and Gods,* p. 26.

seen as communicating an "objective" truth about human experience.[146] Thus, Odysseus made authentic contact with the traditions of the heroic age through his sympathy with their griefs. In the *Iliad*, Achilles, faced with Priam in his grieving over the death of his son Hector, was able to see the similarity between his own sorrow and that of Priam. Achilles came to the conclusion that sorrows are part of the fabric of human life as shaped by the gods and thus was able to move beyond his own grief over the death of Patroclus (*Il.* 24.521-51).[147] By hearing tales of grief over heroes from the Trojan War and the heroic age, Homeric kings such as Achilles and Odysseus were able to transcend their own interests to care for other humans both within and outside their kingdoms.

The threat posed by the Sirens to Odysseus and his crew lay in the enchantment of their song (*Od.* 12.37-54, 181-200). Apparently the pleasure generated in the hearing of the Sirens' song would have tempted Odysseus and his men to yearn to be praised like immortal heroes and so to forget their identity and lose their will to live.[148] Perhaps such enchantment would not have communicated the grief of the tales and would have left them corpselike outside the human sphere where the bonds communicated through sympathy and compassion are integral.[149]

In the latter part of the seventh century and extending into the sixth century, levitical priests in Judah initiated a reform aimed ostensibly at restoring a purity of worship that reigned among the Israelite tribes in the wilderness under the leadership of Moses.[150] A document — presumably Deuteronomy 12–26 — authorizing this reform was unearthed from the Jerusalem temple (2 Kings 22:8), analogous to the function of foundation documents in Mesopotamian temples.[151] This effort at reform has been labeled the Deuteronomic reform when its goals and vision have been defined according to Deuteronomy 12–26 by the levitical priests. However, when this reform has been viewed as a religio-political program not only defined by Deuteronomy

---

146. Crotty, *The Poetics of Supplication*, pp. 120, 128, 130, 166-67.

147. Crotty, *The Poetics of Supplication*, pp. 79-80; cf. Slatkin, *The Power of Thetis*, pp. 88, 103, 119.

148. Pucci, *Odysseus Polutropos*, pp. 193-94; Crotty, *The Poetics of Supplication*, p. 204; Vernant, *Mortals and Immortals*, p. 105; cf. Finkelberg, *The Birth of Literary Fiction*, p. 97.

149. Cf. Vidal-Naquet, *The Black Hunter*, p. 23.

150. Norbert Lohfink, "The Cult Reform of Josiah of Judah: 2 Kings 22–23 as a Source for the History of Israelite Religion," in *Ancient Israelite Religion*, ed. P. D. Miller, Jr. et al. (Philadelphia: Fortress, 1987), p. 459; Bernard M. Levinson, *Deuteronomy and the Hermeneutics of Legal Innovation* (New York: Oxford University Press, 1997), pp. 16, 31.

151. Cf. Hermann Spieckermann, *Judah unter Assur in der Sargonidenzeit*, FRLANT 129 (Göttingen: Vandenhoeck & Ruprecht, 1982), pp. 74-75; Richard S. Ellis, *Foundation Deposits in Ancient Mesopotamia* (New Haven: Yale University Press, 1968), pp. 69-71, 159.

12–26 but also led by Josiah (640-609 B.C.), it has frequently been labeled the Josianic reform. The main plank of the Deuteronomic reform movement was the centralization of all Yahwistic worship in the Jerusalem temple under the watchful care of the levitical priestly reformers,[152] whereas the main purpose of Josiah's reform was the reestablishment of the temple as the ritual and symbolic center of the nation under the patronage of the Davidic king.[153]

The document recovered in the temple according to 2 Kings 22:8 presumably included Deuteronomy 16:18–18:22, which reapportioned political and religious responsibilities in the land, the most notable of which was the restriction of royal authority (Deut. 17:14-20).[154] Josiah seems to have deflected such restrictions by having his scribes present the discovery of the law as a crisis calling for national covenant renewal and celebration of the Passover under his leadership as king (2 Kings 22:3–23:20). His platform promoted his indispensable role in national and covenantal renewal.[155] Under his leadership, Josiah planned to promote elements of the rival Deuteronomic program such as the centralization of worship (Deut. 12:4-6; 2 Kings 23:8-9), the unity of Israel (Deut. 12:10-14; 2 Kings 23:16-20), and the removal of foreign cults (Deut. 13:1-19; 2 Kings 23:4-7, 10-15).[156] However, the Deuteronomic reformers wanted a king chosen by the people, one who would not acquire many horses or numerous wives. Marvin Sweeney has argued that Solomon as known in 1 Kings 3–11 was the king under criticism in Deuteronomy 17:14-17.[157] If so, it means that the Deuteronomic writers were aware of the writings of the Deuteronomists.

One significant new expectation of the king put forth by the Deuteronomic writers was the expectation that he meditate daily on the Deuteronomic law:[158]

152. Levinson, *Deuteronomy and the Hermeneutics of Legal Innovation*, pp. 31, 147-48.

153. Gary Knoppers, *Two Nations Under God: The Deuteronomistic History of Solomon and the Dual Monarchies*, vol. 2: *The Reign of Jeroboam, the Fall of Israel, and the Reign of Josiah*, HSM 53 (Atlanta: Scholars, 1994), p. 124; Levinson, *Deuteronomy and the Hermeneutics of Legal Innovation*, pp. 16, 31.

154. Erik Eynikel (*The Reform of King Josiah and the Composition of the Deuteronomistic History*, OTS 33 [Leiden: Brill, 1996], pp. 290-91) includes *sēper habbĕrît* of 2 Kings 22:8a in the redaction of the Josianic redactor (Dtr1). Patrick D. Miller, Jr., *Deuteronomy* (Louisville: John Knox, 1990), p. 141.

155. Knoppers, *Two Nations Under God*, 2:166, 173-74, 215.

156. Knoppers, *Two Nations Under God*, 2:2.

157. Marvin Sweeney, "The Critique of Solomon in the Josianic Edition of the Deuteronomistic History," *JBL* 114 (1995): 607-22. The link of Deut. 17:14-20 to Solomon is denied by Gary Knoppers, "The Deuteronomist and the Deuteronomic Law of the King: A Reexamination of a Relationship," *ZAW* 108 (1996): 337-44; David Glatt-Gilad, "The Deuteronomistic Critique of Solomon: A Response to Marvin A. Sweeney," *JBL* 116 (1997): 700-703; cf. A. D. H. Mayes, *Deuteronomy* (Grand Rapids: Eerdmans, 1979), p. 272.

158. Eynikel (*The Reform of King Josiah*, pp. 171, 186-87) claims that Deut. 17:18-19, identified

When he sits on the throne of his kingdom, he shall have a copy of this law inscribed for him in a book in the presence of the levitical priests. It shall be with him and he shall read from it all the days of his life, so that he might learn to fear the Lord his God, by keeping all the words of this law and carrying out these statutes. He shall not regard himself as higher than his kindred, nor shall he depart from the commandment to the right or the left so that he and his descendants might lengthen the days of their rule in Israel. (Deut. 17:18-20)

The main curtailment of royal authority took the form of placing the king under the authority of a document stemming from levitical priestly circles.[159] The king had always been expected to be attentive to the tradition of the Israelite community, but such tradition in oral and written forms had not been identified with a specific written document reputed to have divine authorization. The written form of this tradition as sanctioned by the levitical priests, coupled with the injunction to read it daily, signaled a shift in power from the palace to the temple. In such daily reading, the king would also serve as an example for the people to imitate.[160] A further dimension of this shift of power from the palace to the temple, as noted by Bernard M. Levinson, was the expectation that difficult legal cases were to be heard by judges appointed by the temple rather than by the king.[161]

The century of vassalage to Assyria along with the demise of the Northern Kingdom in 721 B.C. had created conditions in Judah ripe for reform. The Deuteronomic document purported to recall the central teaching and vision of the foundation of the Israelite community, but it was a document that Josiah and the royal establishment qualified and reinterpreted.[162] The tension between the Deuteronomic (priestly) and Josianic or Deuteronomistic (royal) circles was an important new phase in Israel's double-mindedness about the kingship, an essential dynamic at the heart of legitimate royal authority. The expectation that the king remember this foundational vision and teaching through daily reading is not without analogues in the ancient Near East.[163]

Hammurapi expected his successors and other Mesopotamian kings to pay attention to the laws of his *Code* (*CH* XLVIII:59-74). The practice of a king hav-

---

as Deuteronomistic by Mayes (*Deuteronomy*, p. 273), fits best with the setting of 2 Kings 23:3, 21, where both king and people are addressed, rather than with Josh. 1:8 or 1 Samuel 12, where the people, not the leader, are addressed.

159. Knoppers, *Two Nations Under God*, 2:165-66.

160. Miller, *Deuteronomy*, p. 149.

161. Levinson, *Deuteronomy and the Hermeneutics of Legal Innovation*, pp. 140-41.

162. Knoppers, "The Deuteronomist," pp. 336, 345.

163. Jonker, *The Topography of Remembrance*, pp. 102-3.

ing advice inscribed on a stela *(narû)* for the purpose of instructing subsequent rulers is a genre variously labeled by scholars as "fictional autobiography" or "*narû* literature."[164] An example of such a genre is the *Cuthean Legend,* which may have been composed by Naram-Sin of Eshnunna (ca. nineteenth century B.C.), but purports to have been narrated by Naram-Sin of Akkad (2254-2218 B.C.).[165] The speaker Naram-Sin in the *Cuthean Legend* criticized a king named Enmerkar, presumably an early king of Uruk known from Sumerian heroic epic poetry,[166] for not leaving advice to subsequent rulers concerning a military victory he had won (lines 23-30).[167] The *Cuthean Legend* speaks initially of Naram-Sin's military victories. Later, when he was surrounded by a hostile coalition, he sought an omen from the gods, who refused to allow him to counterattack. He disobeyed the gods and lost his entire army in three campaigns against the hostile coalition. Naram-Sin despaired by asking, "What is left of my reign?" (lines 84-93). The final section gives advice to later rulers:

> Whoever you are, whether governor or noble or anyone else whom the gods have called to rule over a realm, I have made for you a tablet container and have inscribed a stela *(narû)* for you. I left (them) for you in the chapel of Nergal in the Emeslam temple in Cutha. Look at this stela! Listen to the voice of this stela! Do not be confused! Do not become weak! . . . Be humble! Be obedient![168] Reply to them, "Here I am, my lord." To their hostile behavior, return goodness. . . . Do not attempt to move ahead of them. Let the wise scribes read out your stela." (lines 149-56, 170-72, 174-76)[169]

This political exhortation toward passive obedience and political isolationism was, according to Tremper Longman III, the primary message of the *Cuthean*

---

164. Longman, *Fictional Akkadian Autobiography,* pp. 47-48; Joan Goodnick Westenholz, "Heroes of Akkad," in *Studies in Literature from the Ancient Near East Dedicated to Samuel Noah Kramer,* ed. J. Sasson, AOS 65 (New Haven: American Oriental Society, 1984), pp. 327-28.

165. Longman, *Fictional Akkadian Autobiography,* p. 115; cf. Michael Astour, "Ezekiel's Prophecy of Gog and the Cuthean Legend of Naram-Sin," *JBL* 95 (1976): 572-79.

166. Joan Goodnick Westenholz, *Legends of the Kings of Akkade* (Winona Lake, Ind.: Eisenbrauns, 1997), p. 264; Bendt Alster, "Epic Tales from Ancient Sumer: Enmerkar, Lugalbanda, and Other Cunning Heroes," in *Civilizations of the Ancient Near East,* ed. J. Sasson (New York: Scribner, 1995), pp. 2315-16.

167. Longman, *Fictional Akkadian Autobiography,* p. 228; Westenholz, *Legends of the Kings of Akkade,* pp. 305-7.

168. Westenholz (*Legends of the Kings of Akkade,* p. 329) translates *lū ašrāta lū sanqāta* of line 170 as "be self-controlled, disciplined."

169. Text from Westenholz, *Legends of the Kings of Akkade,* pp. 326-30. See also O. R. Gurney, "The Sultantepe Tablets (continued): IV. The *Cuthean Legend* of Naram-Sin," *Anatolian Studies* 5 (1955): 93-113; Longman, *Fictional Akkadian Autobiography,* p. 231.

Legend.[170] This introspective tract, unique among the legends about Naram-Sin, gave antiheroic advice — be humble and turn the other cheek — because Naram-Sin had been too much of a hero by taking matters into his own hands and putting himself above the gods.[171] As a *narû* document, the *Cuthean Legend* gives an important example of how reflection on royal inscriptions developed into a didactic process for communicating the wisdom from the past.[172] Kings who read the *Cuthean Legend* would have been reminded of the importance of obeying the instructions of the gods in the omens and also would have been counseled against political expansionism.[173]

Kings in the Homeric epics, biblical Israel, and OB Mesopotamia were expected to be attentive to the traditions of the community where the divine will was discerned within the context of the memories and experiences of a particular community. Homer emphasized that listening to and narrating the tradition could draw one into sympathy with the griefs of others and so create bonds with others both living and dead. However, if the stories to be narrated celebrated oneself, such as the Sirens' songs that Odysseus heard, the temptation to glorify oneself could have led to isolation and death. In seventh-century Israel, the efforts at reform centered in attentiveness to a document recovered from the temple that provided a foundational vision for the Israelite community. The king was expected to meditate daily on this document in order to shape his understanding of himself and the community before the Lord. In Mesopotamia in the latter part of the third millennium B.C., a genre of literature developed from the royal inscriptions, known as *narû* literature or fictional autobiography, that urged kings to take note of lessons learned from the gods and from the past. By reading the *Cuthean Legend,* a king was expected to be more attentive to the omens given by the gods, for neglect had led to disaster for the ruler Naram-Sin, as cited in the *Legend.*

Sacrifice and Temple Patronage

In Homer, sacrifice was the ritual act by which an animal was slaughtered and then the meat was consumed in a communal meal. Prior to setting out to bat-

---

170. Longman, *Fictional Akkadian Autobiography,* p. 116.

171. Westenholz, "Heroes of Akkad," p. 333; idem, *Legends of the Kings of Akkade,* pp. 264, 266.

172. Westenholz, *Legends of the Kings of Akkade,* p. 266; Machinist, "On Self-Consciousness in Mesopotamia," p. 193; Jonker, *The Topography of Remembrance,* pp. 102-3; cf. Victor Hurowitz, "Some Literary Observations on the Šitti-Marduk Kudurru," *ZA* 82 (1992): 57.

173. Jonker, *The Topography of Remembrance,* pp. 102-3; Sabina Franke, "Kings of Akkad: Sargon and Naram-Sin," in *Civilizations of the Ancient Near East,* ed. J. Sasson (New York: Scribner, 1995), pp. 838-39.

tle, Agamemnon offered an ox to Zeus, and various Achaeans made animal of-ferings to their deities (*Il.* 2.398-404). The shedding of blood was a dreadful event that evoked the terrors of death, but the banquet that followed brought renewed life. Walter Burkert claims that the collective action of the commu-nity in slaughtering the animal created solidarity from a psychological point of view because the members all shared in the act of aggression and guilt.[174] This mediation between life and death and the bonding among the members of a community were activities to which the gods drew near. In Homeric sacri-fice, only the thigh bones were burned as the gods' portion (*Il.* 2.427; *Od.* 3.9); so, almost the entire animal was given over to human consumption (*Il.* 2.421-32).[175] This ritual action took place in the midst of an assembled community; there was no demarcated sacred space that preceded or endured beyond the ritual action.[176]

The noble swineherd Eumaeus offered sacrifice and prayers to the gods as he extended hospitality to the disguised Odysseus (*Od.* 14.418-38). In contrast, the suitors, with their endless feasts, never offered sacrifice.[177] Eumaeus, situ-ated on the margins of Ithacan society during the twenty years of Odysseus's absence, maintained the practice of sacrifice that was central to civilized life in the Homeric world. In the orderly kingdoms of Pylos and Sparta, sacrifice was regularly carried out (*Od.* 3.5-9, 380-84, 418-63; 4.352-53, 472-79, 581-83). The crisis in the society of Ithaca, symbolized by the absence of sacrifice among the suitors, brought to light the close link between sacrifice and communal life. Without a means of mediating between what is human and what is not human and also among human beings, the equilibrium requisite to civilized life could not be maintained.[178]

In the fantasy world of Odysseus's journeys, the Cyclopes did not sacrifice (*Od.* 9.275-79).[179] Odysseus attempted to offer sacrifice with the sheep that he had taken from the flocks of the Cyclopes; however, he reported that Zeus did not accept this offering (*Od.* 9.551-53). Pierre Vidal-Naquet indicates that Zeus rejected the sacrifice because the sheep belonged to Polyphemus and because it

---

174. Burkert, *Greek Religion*, p. 58.

175. Burkert, *Greek Religion*, p. 57; François de Polignac, *Cults, Territory, and the Origins of the Greek City-State* (Chicago: University of Chicago Press, 1995), p. 35.

176. De Polignac, *Cults, Territory, and the Origins of the Greek City-State*, p. 16.

177. Vidal-Naquet, *The Black Hunter*, pp. 24-25; Cook, *The Odyssey in Athens*, p. 148; Rich-ard Seaford, *Reciprocity and Ritual: Homer and Tragedy in the Developing City-State* (Oxford: Clarendon, 1994), pp. 30, 51.

178. Vidal-Naquet, *The Black Hunter*, p. 25.

179. Pietro Pucci, *The Song of the Sirens: Essays on Homer* (New York: Rowman & Littlefield, 1998), p. 117.

was offered on nonhuman territory.[180] In the idealized heroic society of Phaeacia, the practice was the polar opposite of that among Cyclopes, for sacrifice was regularly offered (*Od.* 7.191), analogous to what was found in the earthly kingdoms of Pylos and Sparta.

When Odysseus and his companions landed on the island of the sun god Helios, Odysseus warned them that they should not slaughter the cattle and sheep of Helios. However, they were marooned on the island so long that their provisions ran out and they had to turn to hunting to secure food.[181] In these circumstances, one of the companions, Eurylochus, persuaded the others, while Odysseus was asleep, to ignore Odysseus's earlier warning:

> All forms of death are dreadful to poor mortals, but to die from hunger and so to meet one's fate is the most miserable. But come, after we drive off the best of Helios' cattle, we will offer sacrifice to the immortals who inhabit the wide heaven. If we ever come to Ithaca, our ancestral land, we will immediately build a rich temple for Helios Hyperion, and in it we will place many excellent offerings. If he is provoked to anger in any way because of his straight-horned cattle and wants to destroy our ship and the other gods concur, I would rather perish from life once for all by drowning in a wave than to be drained continually over a long period on a desert island. (*Od.* 12.341-51)

The men proceeded to slaughter cattle from Helios's herd. The enraged Helios appealed to Zeus in the company of the other gods, who then destroyed the men's ship because of this sacrilege. The promise to build a temple on their return is one of the few references to temples in Homer (see also *Od.* 6.9), which reflects the fact that temples were first introduced into Greek society with the rise of the *polis* in the eighth century B.C. but spread rapidly in the seventh century.[182]

The Israelite king was not a regular official in the cult, but there were certain occasions on which he performed some priestly functions (2 Sam. 6:13, 17-

---

180. Vidal-Naquet, *The Black Hunter,* p. 20.

181. Cook (*The Odyssey in Athens*, pp. 120, 127) states that the Thrinakia episode is based on an etiological myth describing the origin of sacrifice; he notes that the crews' unorthodox sacrifice effaces the distinction between the wild and the domestic.

182. Walter Burkert, "Greek *Poleis* and Civic Cults: Some Further Thoughts," in *Studies in the Ancient Greek "Polis"* (Stuttgart: Franz Steiner, 1995), p. 205; Kurt Raaflaub, "Homer to Solon: The Rise of the *Polis*: The Written Sources," in *The Ancient Greek City-State: Symposium on the Occasion of the 250th Anniversary of the Royal Danish Academy of Sciences and Letters, July 1-4, 1992,* ed. M. H. Hansen (Copenhagen: Munksgaard, 1993), p. 52; de Polignac, *Cults, Territory, and the Origins of the Greek City-State,* pp. 8, 152-54; Morris, *Archaeology as Cultural History,* pp. 273-74.

18; 1 Kings 3:4, 15; 8:5, 62-64; 9:25; 12:33).[183] In Psalm 20, the king offered sacrifice while the people were making intercession for him:

> May the Lord answer you on the day of trouble,
> may the name of the God of Jacob protect you.
> May he send you help from the sanctuary,
> and from Zion may he support you.
> May he remember all your cereal offerings,
> and accept[184] your burnt offering. (Ps. 20:2-4[1-3])

The *Sitz im Leben* of this psalm was most likely a liturgy preceding the king's setting out for battle,[185] and so his sacrificial role was probably an offshoot of his role as military commander (cf. 1 Sam. 13:8-10).

The pious, faithful Israelite king was one who acknowledged that his sovereignty was a participation in the sovereignty of the Lord, that his power as a warrior was a result of the protection given by the Lord, and that his kingdom and empire were sustained by the Lord. According to Psalm 132, David wished to make known his vassalage to the Lord by bringing the Ark as the primary symbol of the Lord's presence into Jerusalem, and so David was remembered as speaking the following words of promise:[186]

> I will not enter my dwelling,
> I will not go up to my bed.
> I will not allow sleep for my eyes,
> slumber for my eyelids,
> Until I find a place for the Lord,
> a dwelling for the Mighty One of Jacob. (Ps. 132:3-5)

According to an oracle toward the end of this psalm, the Lord acceded to David's request and made known his desire to dwell on Zion (Ps. 132:13-16). Da-

---

183. Roland de Vaux, *Ancient Israel*, 2 vols. (New York: McGraw-Hill, 1965), 1:113-14.

184. I emend the anomalous *-eh* of *yĕdaššĕneh* to the suffixal form *-ehā* to read *yĕdaššĕnehā* (see GKC 48d). A word-for-word translation of v. 4b(3b) reads: "And your burnt offering may he regard it as fat." The fat upon the entrails was designated as the portion to be given to God (Lev. 3:14-16). Therefore, in my translation I interpret the Lord's regarding the burnt offering as fat as his accepting it.

185. Hans-J. Kraus, *Die Psalmen*, 2nd ed., BKAT 15/1-2 (Neukirchen-Vluyn: Neukirchener Verlag, 1961), p. 163.

186. C. L. Seow, *Myth, Drama, and the Politics of David's Dance*, HSM 44 (Atlanta: Scholars, 1989), pp. 146-50; P. Kyle McCarter, Jr., "The Ritual Dedication of the City of David in 2 Samuel 6," in *The Word Shall Go Forth: Essays in Honor of David Noel Freedman in Celebration of His Sixtieth Birthday*, ed. C. L. Meyers and M. O'Connor (Winona Lake, Ind.: Eisenbrauns, 1983), p. 276.

vid's actions were seen as fundamental to the foundation of Zion as a sanctuary and to its continued maintenance.[187]

Solomon built and dedicated the temple in Jerusalem (1 Kings 8). In the eyes of the late preexilic editor of the history of the monarchy, known as the Deuteronomist, the temple became a key institution for maintaining fidelity to the Lord.[188] The Israelites were expected to turn toward the temple when they prayed (1 Kings 8:29-30, 44-45, 48). The king, in the eyes of the Deuteronomist, had a pivotal role to play in the welfare of the temple, an institution whose cultic practices the Torah supported and guided in order to promote fidelity to the Lord.[189]

In accord with the practices of previous Mesopotamian kings,[190] Hammurapi claimed in the prologue to his *Code* that he carried out ritual duties in various temples. He stated that he was "the one who regularly performs the great rites of Ishtar" in the temple of Hursagkalama in Kish (*CH* II:63-65), "the one who keeps intact the purification rites of Eabzu" (*CH* I:66–II:1), which was the temple of Ea in Eridu, and "the one who offers the great bread offerings for Eninnu" (*CH* III:43-46), which was the temple of Ningirsu at Girsu.[191] Whatever the nature of Hammurapi's role in these cultic activities, the occasions for his participation were most likely ceremonial ones where he could demonstrate to the temple personnel and the local populace his reverence for the deity who resided there.[192] One of Hammurapi's early contemporaries, Yaḫdun-Lim, king of Mari (1825-1810 B.C.), recorded that "he offered his great royal libation *(nīqum)* at the Great Sea [i.e., the Mediterranean]."[193] At the completion of this phase of his military and commercial expedition to the

187. McCarter, "The Ritual Dedication of the City of David," pp. 275-76; Carol Meyers, "David as Temple Builder," in *Ancient Israelite Religion*, ed. P. D. Miller, Jr. et al. (Philadelphia: Fortress, 1987), pp. 262-63; Antti Laato, "Psalm 132 and the Development of the Jerusalem/Israelite Royal Ideology," *CBQ* 54 (1992): 64-66. For a postexilic dating of Psalm 132 and an interpretation of this psalm as invoking the memory of David to inspire the rebuilding of the temple, see Corrine Patton, "Psalm 132: A Methodological Inquiry," *CBQ* 57 (1995): 643-54.

188. A. D. H. Mayes, *The Story of Israel between Settlement and Exile* (London: SCM, 1983), pp. 108-10.

189. Knoppers, *Two Nations Under God*, 2:121.

190. Cf. Van de Mieroop, *Society and Enterprise in Old Babylonian Ur*, p. 115; Robertson, "The Social and Economic Organization of Ancient Mesopotamian Temples," p. 452.

191. G. R. Driver and John Miles, *The Babylonian Laws* (Oxford: Clarendon, 1952), 2:134-35.

192. Kraus, *The Role of Temples from the Third Dynasty of Ur to the First Dynasty of Babylon*, p. 7; idem, "Das altbabylonische Königtum," in *Le palais et la royauté*, RAI 19 (Paris: Paul Geuthner, 1974), pp. 240-41; cf. Robertson, "The Social and Economic Organization of Ancient Mesopotamian Temples," p. 452; Jack M. Sasson, "King Hammurabi of Babylon," in *Civilizations of the Ancient Near East*, ed. J. Sasson (New York: Scribner, 1995), p. 907.

193. Frayne, *RIME 4*, E4.6.8.2, lines 48-49.

Mediterranean coast, Yaḫdun-Lim marked this moment with a significant ritual action; the libation appears to have been offered to the Great Sea.[194]

In the prologue to his *Code,* Hammurapi portrayed himself as a patron of the temples of cities throughout Mesopotamia. Victor Hurowitz has labeled this list of accomplishments "the piety register" (*CH* I:50–IV:66), which included twenty-four cities divided into the following groups: (1) the cities of Nippur, Eridu, Babylonia, Ur, Sippar, Larsa, Uruk (*CH* I:50–II:47); (2) cities in central Babylonia (*CH* II:48–III:35); (3) cities on the eastern periphery (*CH* III:36–IV:22); and (4) cities to the north (*CH* IV:23-66).[195] Foremost among Hammurapi's accomplishments was his renovation of temples. For example, Hammurapi claimed to be "the one who raised on high the temple of Ebabbar" (*CH* II:29-30) for Shamash, a temple in Sippar that had originally been constructed by Naram-Sin of Akkad (2254-18 B.C.).[196] He also claimed to be "the one who raised up the head of Eanna" (*CH* II:42-43), the temple of Ishtar in Uruk. Hammurapi's patronage did not end with building projects, however; he also attended to the general needs of temples and provided them with provisions. For example, he stated that he was "the reverent one who provides for Ekur" (*CH* I:60-62), the temple of Enlil in Nippur. He also paid special attention to the temple of his protector god Marduk, and so he claimed to be "the one who attends to Esagila all his days" (*CH* II:10-12). Hammurapi's beneficent actions toward these temples publicly signaled his respect and reverence for the primary deities of the Mesopotamian cities.[197]

The most important symbol of an OB Mesopotamian city was the cultic statue.[198] The collective identity of the people of the city was communicated through the symbols of the temple cult of the city's tutelary deity.[199] If Hammurapi was to make a credible case that the city's deity supported his rule, then he had to cultivate his relationship with the temple establishment of that

194. Abraham Malamat, "The Divine Nature of the Mediterranean Sea in the Foundation Inscription of Yaḫdunlim," in *Mari in Retrospect: Fifty Years of Mari and Mari Studies,* ed. Gordon Young (Winona Lake, Ind.: Eisenbrauns, 1992), p. 215.

195. Victor Hurowitz, *Inu Anum Ṣīrum: Literary Structures in the Non-Juridical Sections of Codex Hammurabi,* Occasional Publications of the Samuel Noah Kramer Fund 15 (Philadelphia: University of Pennsylvania Museum, 1994), pp. 72-89.

196. Erich Ebeling, "Ebabbara," in *RLA,* 2:263.

197. Kraus, *The Role of Temples from the Third Dynasty of Ur to the First Dynasty of Babylon,* pp. 12-13.

198. Wiggermann, "Theologies, Priests, and Worship in Ancient Mesopotamia," p. 1862; Benjamin R. Foster, *Before the Muses: An Anthology of Akkadian Literature,* vol. 1 (Bethesda, Md.: CDL, 1993), p. 33.

199. Kraus, *The Role of Temples from the Third Dynasty of Ur to the First Dynasty of Babylon,* pp. 5-6. Cf. van der Toorn, *Family Religion in Babylonia, Syria, and Israel,* pp. 87-88.

city. Cultic actions lay at the heart of Mesopotamian religion; such actions communicated important social and political messages at the same time that they paid reverence to the gods.[200]

As a central symbol of the community, the king played a key role in the community's relations with the gods. Offering sacrifice was the primary cultic activity in Israel and Homer. In Homer, the thigh bones were burnt as the gods' portion, whereas in Israel it was the choice, fatty portions that belonged to the Lord. In Mesopotamia, the food was simply given to the gods and was not burnt. Kings offered sacrifice or carried out ceremonial roles in the cult only on special occasions, such as the dedication of Solomon's temple or Agamemnon's offering of sacrifice to Zeus at a critical point in the campaign against Troy. The king's support for the temples of God or the gods was emphasized in Israel and Mesopotamia. Noteworthy were the construction and dedication of Solomon's temple and Hammurapi's renovation and patronage of various temples throughout the land of Sumer and Akkad. In Archaic Age Greece, temples were only beginning to be established in the late eighth century B.C. and had only a minimal influence on the shape of the Homeric world; their potential in the Greek world would unfold in the context of the Greek *polis*.

Maintaining Order in the Land according to the Divine Will

Two important customary rights were not able to be upheld effectively in Ithaca during Odysseus's absence: the right of the guest stranger to hospitality and the right to speak in the assembly. When Odysseus returned to Ithaca disguised as a beggar, he was received by the noble swineherd Eumaeus but mistreated by a number of the suitors (*Od.* 14.30-89; 17.410-80). The contrast between the aristocratic suitors and the noble swineherd highlighted the contradiction in Ithacan society that those with material means were lacking in hospitality and compassion.[201] When the stage had been set for Odysseus's final confrontation with the suitors in the banquet hall, Penelope, inspired by Athena, challenged the suitors to string a bow belonging to Odysseus and kept in storage for twenty years, and use it to shoot an arrow through twelve axes (*Od.* 21.1-4, 67-79). She promised to marry the one who would win the contest. There was a tension in this contest between competition and hospitality, for the guests at this banquet were asked to compete with one another. William G. Thalmann speculates that

200. Thorkild Jacobsen, *The Treasures of Darkness: A History of Mesopotamian Religion* (New Haven: Yale University Press, 1976), pp. 14-17.

201. Rose, *Sons of the Gods, Children of Earth,* p. 106.

this may have functioned as a ritual or ordeal by which an outsider became a member of a group.[202]

The bow was a gift to Odysseus from Iphitus, a man from Ithaca whom he had met in Messenia in his youth on a mission to recover livestock lost to a Messenian raiding party. Iphitus had gone in search of his lost mares; Odysseus, still a youth, had been commissioned by his father and the elders of Ithaca to recover three hundred sheep and their shepherds. Iphitus gave the bow to Odysseus, but he subsequently was murdered by Heracles of Messenia, who was supposed to offer Iphitus protection and hospitality, as typically extended to guest friends (*Od.* 21.18-41). Heracles' mother was the human Alcmene, but his father was Zeus (*Il.* 14.324; *Od.* 11.268). Heracles was married to Zeus's daughter Hebe (*Od.* 11.601-4). Heracles' skill as an archer went beyond that of the typical human, but Homer regarded him as a ruthless murderer (*Od.* 11.605-15; 21.26-30). Odysseus never took the bow from Iphitus into battle since it carried for him the memory of his friend killed while a guest stranger.[203]

Telemachus volunteered to be the first contestant so that, if victorious, he would keep his mother from departing from his household (*Od.* 21.101-17). His inability to bend the bow indicated that he did not have the physical strength necessary for the kingship (*Od.* 21.118-35); however, in the subsequent debate over whether the beggar Odysseus should be allowed a chance to bend the bow, Telemachus insisted that he rather than Penelope should have the authority to decide who could participate in the contest: his newfound courage to speak authoritatively perhaps indicated that he was coming of age (*Od.* 21.343-53).[204] When Telemachus had Eumaeus take the bow to Odysseus, the stage was set for Odysseus's restoration of order in Ithaca, an order that would uphold the *themistes* supported by Zeus, such as the rights of the guest stranger.

In the course of the battle against the suitors, the exits from the banquet hall were blocked so that no one could escape. One of the suitors Agelaus had cried out:

> Friends, will not someone go out through a side door and inform the people so that there will be an outcry as soon as possible? Soon this man will have shot his bow for the last time. (*Od.* 22.132-34)

The role that the people at large in Ithaca could play in promoting order in the community has lurked in the background through most of the *Odyssey.*[205]

---

202. Thalmann, *The Swineherd and the Bow,* pp. 141-45.
203. Segal, *Singers, Heroes, and Gods,* pp. 53-54; cf. Olson, *Blood and Iron,* p. 200.
204. Segal, *Singers, Heroes, and Gods,* pp. 55-56.
205. Olson (*Blood and Iron,* p. 189) claims that the community consciousness of the people

When Telemachus took the scepter in hand and spoke to the popular assembly at the beginning of the *Odyssey,* he lamented that the people had not acted to keep the suitors from destroying his household (*Od.* 2.60-79). His right to speak in the assembly, symbolized by the scepter, was without consequence since the political context in Ithaca had no effective means of enforcing the laws and customs of the community. If there was no king to enforce ethical and moral order in the community, then the populace would have had to fill the vacuum. From the perspective of Odysseus's household (i.e., Homer's promonarchical view) the populace did not act to uphold the laws and customs of the community. S. Douglas Olson claims that Homer saw the revenge that Odysseus brought on the suitors to have been a consequence of the people's inaction (*Od.* 2.229-41; 24.454-60).[206] The people of Ithaca seem to have either sympathized with the suitors or been indifferent to the trouble besetting Odysseus's house. The force of public opinion in Ithaca was not negligible, for when Odysseus and Telemachus planned the battle against the suitors, they were concerned about the fallout with the people (*Od.* 24.489-501). In the end, Odysseus's victory demonstrated a central point of the *Odyssey:* the potential for an effective monarchy to bring about justice in accord with the will of Zeus (*Od.* 24.528-48).

A key responsibility of the Israelite king was to protect the defenseless:

> For he will deliver the needy when he cries out,
>   and the afflicted man who has no helper.
> He will have pity on the poor and the needy,
>   and the lives of the poor ones he will save.
> From oppression and violence he will save their lives,
>   and precious in his eyes shall be their blood. (Ps. 72:12-14)

The widow, the fatherless, and the sojourner were three significant categories of unfortunate people who stood in need of aid from others.[207] While the sojourner *(gēr)* fell outside the network of families and clans, the widow and the fatherless were usually able to appeal to relatives.[208] Israelite law defended the rights of the widow, the fatherless, and the sojourner (Exod. 22:20-23[21-24];

---

of Ithaca can be detected in their worrying about what others will think (*Od.* 16.376-82; 22.216-23; 24.426-38, 463-68).

206. Olson, *Blood and Iron,* p. 202.

207. Leo Perdue, "The Israelite and Early Jewish Family: Summary and Conclusions," in *Families in Ancient Israel,* ed. L. Perdue (Louisville: Westminster/John Knox, 1997), pp. 193-95, 198-99; Bernd Janowski, *Stellvertretung: Alttestamentliche Studien zu einem theologischen Grundbegriff* (Stuttgart: Verlag Katholisches Bibelwerk, 1997), pp. 50-54.

208. Perdue, "The Israelite and Early Jewish Family," pp. 198-99.

23:6-9). They were placed directly under the Lord's protection (Ps.146:9; Mal. 3:5). An oracle of Jeremiah to the king of Judah points to the fact that the kings were not always mindful of their responsibility toward the unfortunate ones among their people:

> Do what is just and upright. Deliver the one who has been robbed from the power of the oppressor. Do no wrong or violence to the sojourner, the fatherless, or the widow. You must not shed innocent blood in this place. (Jer. 22:3)

A king who oppressed or neglected the defenseless would, according to the laws of the Israelite tradition, bring down God's judgment on himself and the nation. The king's capacity to bring weal or woe to the land was integrally linked to the reign of justice in the land.

The promise to enforce justice in the land forms the conclusion to the royal Psalm 101:

> My eyes are on the faithful of the land
>> to dwell with me.
> Anyone who walks on the perfect way
>> shall serve me.
> That one shall not dwell within my house
>> who practices deceit.
> The one who utters lies shall not stand firm
>> before my eyes.
> Each morning I will destroy
>> all the evil ones of the land,
> cutting off from the city of the Lord
>> all doers of evil. (Ps. 101:6-8)

The king who confessed his integrity of heart and fidelity to the covenant expected that those in his kingdom would do likewise. The king saw it as his duty to enforce fidelity to the covenant, even with physical force.[209]

The reform movement led by Josiah in the late preexilic period addressed not only cultic concerns but also political and social ones.[210] The picture of this reform sketched by the promonarchical Deuteronomist in 2 Kings 22–23 highlights the potential of the kingship to restore a just and good order to the land of Israel. Second Kings 23:25 celebrates Josiah's incomparability:

---

209. Kenik, "Code of Conduct for a King," p. 398.
210. Lohfink, "The Cult Reform of Josiah of Judah," pp. 465-69.

There was no king before him who turned to the Lord as he did with his whole heart and with his whole soul, and with all his might according to all the law of Moses. And after him no one like him rose up.

In the face of his tragic early death and the controversial nature of his reforms, Josiah left a legacy of hope to those in the Deuteronomistic movement that a future ideal king would usher in the utopian social program outlined in Deuteronomy 12–28.[211]

The Mesopotamian king regarded himself as the defender of the downtrodden.[212] In the epilogue of his *Code,* Hammurapi stated that he inscribed his laws on the stela "in order that the strong might not crush the weak, that the orphan (and) the widow might receive fair treatment" (*CH* XLVII:59-62). In the OB royal inscriptions, the kings who most frequently claimed to have promoted justice in their lands were the kings of Isin and Larsa. For example, Enlil-bani of Isin (1860-1837 B.C.) proclaimed that he had "established justice in the land of Sumer and Akkad"[213] and had "established justice and righteousness in Nippur";[214] in Larsa, Nur-Adad (1865-1850 B.C.),[215] Sin-iddinam (1849-1843 B.C.),[216] and Warad-Sin (1834-1823 B.C.)[217] each refers to himself as "the shepherd of righteousness." Hammurapi continued the tradition attested in Isin and Larsa of the king's commitment to justice by: (1) naming the second year-date of his reign as one in which "he had established justice in his land," (2) dedicating a "statue of Hammurapi (as) king of justice" as his twenty-second year-date, and (3) declaring a *mēšarum* edict upon taking over the throne of Larsa, according to the thirty-first year-date.[218]

The dominant picture of himself that Hammurapi presented in the prologue and epilogue of his *Code* was that he was both the mouthpiece of the law received from the god Shamash and the enforcer of such laws:

> I wrote my valuable words on my stela and put it in place before my statue, the king of justice, in order to facilitate the legal process in the land and to make decisions according to the decrees of the land, and to allow the op-

211. Knoppers, *Two Nations Under God,* 2:226-27.

212. Samuel Greengus, "Legal and Social Institutions of Ancient Mesopotamia," in *Civilizations of the Ancient Near East,* ed. J. Sasson (New York: Scribner, 1995), pp. 471-72; Sasson, "King Hammurabi of Babylon," pp. 907-8.

213. Text and translation from Frayne, *RIME 4,* E4.1.10.9, lines 10-11.

214. Text and translation from Frayne, *RIME 4,* E4.1.10.1001, lines V:10-12.

215. Frayne, *RIME 4,* E4.2.8.3, line 2.

216. Frayne, *RIME 4,* E4.2.9.14, line 3.

217. Frayne, *RIME 4,* E4.2.13.18, line 3.

218. *ANET,* pp. 269-70; Sasson, "King Hammurabi of Babylon," p. 907.

pressed to receive fair treatment. . . . I, Hammurapi, am the just king to whom Shamash entrusted the laws *(kinātim)*. My words are singled out; my deeds have no rival. (*CH* XLVII:70-78; XLVIII:95-102)[219]

As a mouthpiece and enforcer of the laws, Hammurapi mirrored the status and role of the god Shamash as described in an inscription of Yaḫdun-Lim:

> For Shamash, the king of heaven and earth, the judge of gods and humans, the one whose office is (the dispensation of) justice *(mēšarum)*, the one to whom the laws *(kinātum)* were entrusted as a gift.[220]

This inscription indicated that the *kinātum*, "laws, truths, correct procedures," were regarded as transcending even the god Shamash. In this respect, the *kinātum* resembled "fate" *(moira)* in the Homeric world, which appeared to be something like "a fixed order rather than a power."[221] In OB times, the ideal Mesopotamian king presented himself as one who was obedient to the gods and attentive to an ethical world order.[222]

In Homeric Greece, biblical Israel, and OB Mesopotamia, one of the king's primary functions was to maintain justice in the community by upholding its customs and laws as sanctioned by the gods. This communal order was perceived to be in harmony with the ethical world order supported by the king of the gods. Odysseus's slaughter of the suitors championed the interests of the royal household over that of the suitors, and so the moral ambiguity of the action emerged when viewed from the perspective of the suitors' families, which was allowed to come to expression but was not supported by the narrator. The king's role of defending the vulnerable parties in the society was evident in the Homeric custom of hospitality to strangers, and such an expectation was also enjoined upon the Israelite and Mesopotamian kings. The king's capacity to use force to gain compliance for his commands meant that portions of the community did not agree with his directives. If he were to win their obedience and support in the long run, he had to validate the justice of his directives and explain how they converged with the customs and laws of the community and the divinely willed world order.

---

219. Rykle Borger, *Babylonisch-assyrische Lesestücke,* AnOr 54 (Rome: Pontifical Biblical Institute, 1979), 1:46-47.

220. Frayne, *RIME 4,* E4.6.8.2, lines 1-6.

221. William C. Greene, *Moira: Fate, Good, and Evil in Greek Thought* (Cambridge, Mass.: Harvard University Press, 1944), pp. 13-14. See also Clay, *The Wrath of Athena,* p. 156.

222. Jean-Jacques Glassner, "The Use of Knowledge in Ancient Mesopotamia," in *Civilizations of the Ancient Near East,* ed. J. Sasson (New York: Scribner, 1995), p. 1821.

The Ideal King: The Influence of Dream on Practice

Images and models of an ideal king were important for creating collective efforts in the communities of Homeric Greece, biblical Israel, and OB Mesopotamia. The king with an expansive vision in which he took seriously the heavenly origin of his sovereign authority would have been more apt to respect the limits of his power while at the same time pressing the limits of such power. The traditional pattern for legitimating royal authority presumed a symbiotic relationship between heavenly and earthly kingship, but the relationships between the king and the gods and between the king and the people were tensive in character: the precise shape of the relationship emerged in decisions and actions. The expansiveness of the vision required for just royal rule was modeled by Homer's king Alcinous, the spirit-endowed messianic king of Isaiah 11, and the paradigmatic Mesopotamian king of the OB royal inscriptions. All of these ideal royal rulers claimed special assistance and favors from the gods: it was such divine assistance that enabled them to accomplish heroic deeds for their communities. A common reservation about ideal models has been that they may be abstract and frozen and so could drain the life out of would-be imitators. The divine empowerment of kings described in these models was integral to their credibility.

The ideal king in Israel and Homeric Greece did not simply try to maintain the status quo by repeating what already existed; he tried to explore the boundaries of what was possible. The adventures of Odysseus marked by his tension with Poseidon and David's confident trust in the Lord's protection in the midst of battle indicated that the boundary between life and death had to be approached if the vitality and security of the kingdom were to be maintained. In practice in Mesopotamia, the adventures of Gilgamesh and Enkidu seemed to be part of most kings' rule even though the model for the Mesopotamian king mapped out in the royal inscriptions tended to see all danger in the past tense: thus the reigning king was the ideal king who had already striven to live up to the model established in primordial times. In actuality, change and development occurred in the Mesopotamian kingdoms, and their traditional mind-set served only to slow the rate of change, not to stop it. Heroic kings such as Odysseus, David, and Gilgamesh pressed the boundary between gods and humans, but such a boundary could have been safely crossed only insofar as the king respected the hierarchy in place between gods and men. Israelites had feared the inauguration of kingship because of the temptation for the king himself and the people to come to expect the king to act like a god. In Mesopotamia prior to the time of Hammurapi, a lengthy tradition of divinizing kings had grown up. If any king, semidivine or merely human, transgressed against divine prerogatives or prohibitions, he paid a heavy price, whether it was the death of Enkidu in the case of Gilgamesh or the death of Odysseus's crew in his blinding of Polyphemus or the death of the infant born from David's union with Bathsheba.

The traditional pattern for legitimating royal authority claimed that the king could rule more effectively if he took seriously the divine source of his authority. Practices designed to keep the king attentive to the gods were prayer, mindfulness of the tradition, and sacrifice and attention to the temples and sanctuaries of the gods. Crying out to the gods in lament or intercession was common in all three cultures. Agamemnon prayed while offering sacrifice in hope of gaining Zeus's support; the Davidic king prayed Psalm 101 to gain divine assistance in ruling with integrity; Kudur-mabuk of Emutbal built a temple and erected a stela to make intercession or to communicate wisdom to visitors to the sanctuary. Not only calling upon the gods but also paying attention to the traditions of the community was formative of the king's outlook and judgment as a ruler. Listening to the tragic songs of the Achaean and Trojan warriors moved Odysseus to share in their sorrows; meditating daily on the Torah was a way for the Israelite king to imbue himself with a sense of the divinely willed ways of the Israelite community; the recitation of the *Cuthean Legend* was an example of a practice that Mesopotamian kings could pass on to their successors so that they might pay more attention to the omens of the gods and not strictly follow their own judgments. The other significant practice that kept kings mindful of the divine origin of their authority was sacrifice and patronage of the temples and sanctuaries. Sacrifice was a central cultic activity in Homeric Greece and Israel, whereas provisioning of the gods through food offerings was enjoined upon Mesopotamian kings. The care of temples in Israel and Mesopotamia was an expected royal duty, whereas in Homeric Greece, temples were only beginning to dot the landscape as the epics were composed.

The authoritative king in Homeric Greece, biblical Israel, and OB Mesopotamia was a just king. He had to be attentive to the customs and laws of the community so that he ruled not only in accord with the needs of the people but also in accord with the will of God or the gods and the ethical world order. In Mesopotamia, in an inscription of Yaḫdun-Lim of Mari, the laws were even regarded as transcending Shamash. The sense of a world order that was integral to creation was also reflected in the Torah (cf. Psalm 19) and in the order of the world or fate that Zeus was reluctant to transgress when he was tempted to rescue his son Sarpedon from imminent death. The king was expected to uphold the customs and laws of the community, particularly in his concern for the vulnerable and defenseless. Oftentimes, the king had to use force in order to fend off chaotic forces from within or without the community: Odysseus defeated the suitors; the king in Psalm 101 vowed to remove evildoers from Jerusalem;

Hammurapi claimed in the epilogue to his *Code* that he would keep the strong from oppressing the weak.

The social location of the ones who shaped the visions of the ideal king had a formative effect on their efforts, yet such visions also situated themselves within the traditions of the community. The more dissatisfied the creator of the vision was with the status quo, the more the ideal ruler would have been seen as a future ruler. The more enmeshed the creator of the vision was within the status quo, the more the current ruler would have been described as approximating the ideal.

CONCLUSION

Royal Authority — a Divine
Gift for the Integration
of the Community

Authority, a gift from God or the gods, is essential for the common life. From the close-knit family to the multiple constituencies of a territorial kingdom, the exercise of authority is integral to collective action. Authority is a relational reality that sustains and increases the well-being and vitality of a community. It becomes manifest in a community through the speech and actions of individuals commissioned according to traditional patterns for legitimating leaders. The traditional pattern for appointing an individual as king and assessing his performance bears a number of important similarities in the three cultures of Homeric Greece, biblical Israel, and OB Mesopotamia, yet the particular circumstances and histories of each community make the implementation of such a pattern of authority distinctive not only cross-culturally but also individually in the rule of particular kings in each culture. The aim of this comparative study has been an examination of: (1) the relational dynamics operative within the traditional pattern for legitimating royal authority and (2) the similar and divergent ways this traditional pattern contributed to the creation of royal authority in Homeric Greece, biblical Israel, and OB Mesopotamia.

The Relational Dynamic at the Heart of Royal Authority

This study has focused on the relational dynamics fostered by the traditional pattern for legitimating royal authority, for it was in such interpersonal processes that authority was manifested. The stability of authoritative relationships required the repeated engagement of the ruler and the ruled in addressing the particularities of the lives of the community members so as to prevent the alienation

341

of individuals from the life of the community. A perfect exercise of authority was fully sketched out by Homer in the rule of the imaginary king Alcinous of the utopian kingdom of Phaeacia. Alcinous was inspired by the gods to know what the various members of the community needed so that his commands resonated with their deepest desires. Obedience seemed almost effortless in this community that was blessed with abundant crops, talented people, and excellences of various kinds. Alcinous strengthened his royal authority when he recognized and honored not only visitors but also members of his community. He also acknowledged the superior status of the gods through regular sacrifice. Through these actions, Alcinous demonstrated his respect both for the cosmic hierarchy between gods and humans and for the social hierarchy within the community. The equilibrium within the Phaeacian community indicated that relationships there were in harmony with the underlying ethical world order, an order to which even the gods were attentive. Alcinous set an impossibly high standard for any mortal king. Yet a king inspired by the gods could approximate various aspects of Alcinous's harmonious rule where the cultivation of relationships took precedence over the accumulation of means of coercion or physical force.

An individual came to exercise authority in a community in Homeric Greece, biblical Israel, or OB Mesopotamia because he had been commissioned for such a role by God or the gods. The speech and actions of a Homeric, Israelite, or Mesopotamian king required the creativity and sacrifices of an individual king, but these were enacted within contexts where structures and traditions were already in place. The king was given a stage upon which his words and actions could be effective for the community, yet this was an empty stage unless he performed. His leadership was authoritative to the extent that he brought the community to obedience to the will of the king of the gods. This authoritative leadership, in turn, manifested the underlying ethical world order in that the community came to realize its place in the scheme of things under the leadership of an upright king.

The exercise of authority was a creative act, but not *creatio ex nihilo*. The king's commands received a hearing because the people recognized the legitimacy of the role of the king within their community. A particular king increased or decreased the amount of authority he wielded within this communal or institutional matrix by the quality of his leadership. He did not begin with a *tabula rasa,* nor did he act in a vacuum. The material and symbolic resources that shaped the community and its traditions set the stage for the king to be able to enhance the well-being of the community. The wisdom and the strength to lead the community were regarded as gifts from God or the gods. The more excellent the king's leadership the more he was seen to participate in the divine realm or to be blessed by the gods.

The king who ignored the tradition and the gifts of the community with which he had been entrusted ruled as a tyrant, for he would have had no choice but to rule by coercion rather than by authority. The tyrant valued power over truth. Even if he secured his hold on power in the short run, eventually the opposition to his rule mounted and he was overthrown. Each king made decisions that fell somewhere on a continuum between the authoritative and the tyrannical. His capacity to make his commands more authoritative depended on how he responded to the challenge of sustaining the relationships mapped out in the traditional pattern for legitimate royal authority.

The anchoring of royal authority in the sovereignty of the king of the gods called on the king to look beyond himself to discern the divine will. The invisibility of God or the gods and the ambiguity inherent in most divine communication made questions about the validity of such divine communication inevitable. Yet the seriousness with which such divine communication was pursued determined whether the king ruled authoritatively or tyrannically. The temptation to doubt the validity of such divine communication repeatedly prompted kings to take matters into their own hands and judge the best course of action on the basis of the data at hand. How the king discerned the divine will was of utmost practical importance. The king himself claimed to receive divine messages or oracles, but more often such messages were communicated via prophets, diviners, priests, or sages. When the messages of these other authority figures conflicted with one another, the king needed to have the means for judging among them. For those royal judgments that proved beneficial to the community, a case could be made that they were inspired.

The king had to be pragmatic. He had to make decisions and issue commands that led to action. The larger framework that he drew upon for guidance in making decisions was communicated through the tradition. If his decisions were to transcend his own interests and be attentive to the well-being of the community, then he had to carry out various practices that kept him attentive to the traditional order. In the Homeric world, the bard communicated the tradition by singing the exploits of heroes who, accompanied by the gods, carried out death-defying feats on behalf of the community. In Israel, the prophets, priests, and people remembered the wondrous deeds of the Lord by which the community was called into being and sustained. In Mesopotamia, the king and his court poets proclaimed in hymns and inscriptions the heroic deeds that the king, commissioned by the gods, was able to accomplish for the people. Such acts of remembering honored God or the gods or heroes and at the same time provided guidance for the king. While such traditional accounts may not have provided specific directions to a king for pressing problems, they mapped out the larger terrain of the community's character and place in the scheme of things — a kind of mental and spiritual geography.

A more intense practice that encapsulated this attentiveness of the king to the tradition was the daily reading of the Torah enjoined on the king in Jerusalem by the Deuteronomic reformers in the late seventh century B.C. Even if this practice proved to be impractical for the typical king, it nevertheless communicated the important lesson that imbibing the tradition was a daily practice that promised to shape the king's imagination and so have an impact on his judgments. The Homeric epics served as an introduction to the emerging mind-set of the Panhellenic community for peoples of the various Greek city-states. In Mesopotamia, the *Code of Hammurapi,* the royal inscriptions, and traditional stories communicated the Mesopotamian worldview in terms of a set of intersecting narratives rather than as a systematic statement of its beliefs and values. Such a narrative approach characterizes Israelite and Homeric traditions as well.

Royal authority belonged to God or the gods. The king exercised it on their behalf. It was given in trust, and eventually the king was called to account for its exercise. This chain of command and accountability was succinctly expressed by the metaphor of the king as the shepherd of the people. The shepherd metaphor for the king is frequently found in the OB royal inscriptions and is prominent in a number of OT texts. However, in Homer, it appears only in the genealogy of the scepter of Argos and in epithets for Agamemnon and a few other Achaean warrior-kings. In the plots of the *Iliad* and the *Odyssey,* due to the weakness of Agamemnon and the absence of Odysseus, the exercise of such divinely bestowed shepherdship was in danger of becoming a thing of the past. According to the shepherd metaphor in these three cultures, the people obeyed the king's commands because he had been given authority by the gods. If the king forgot the divine source of his authority, he fell into self-centered, fearful, greedy actions, such as those of Agamemnon in his quarrel with Achilles, which diminished the well-being of the community. The judgment against the shepherds of Israel in Ezekiel 34 indicates that Israelite kings often came up short in meeting the demands of their divine commissioning as kings. The same assessments of royal leadership were no doubt made in Mesopotamian kingdoms such as Malgium where a popular uprising occurred in the nineteenth century B.C. It appears that the royal establishment suppressed criticism of Mesopotamian kings, for the few records of such criticism preserved in royal archives present their negative assessments of the king obliquely and from a royalist perspective. Nevertheless, the fact that the shepherd metaphor lived on in the rhetoric shaping the image of the OB king indicates that the populace was given the means for judging whether the king was attentive to the common good or only intent upon his own profit. Royal authority in Homeric Greece, biblical Israel, and OB Mesopotamia was hardly intelligible unless it was linked to the underlying ethical world order where the king's decrees were assessed according to their capacity to bring the community into greater harmony with the cosmos.

The king was the chief redistributor of symbolic value in the community. Such a role was often more significant than his corresponding role as redistributor of material goods. It is obvious that humans have basic needs for food and shelter that cannot be overlooked without unrest. However, the issues that frequently sparked rivalries and competition among the members of the community were measured symbolically. The way that these issues were sorted out signaled the extent to which one's life was invested in a particular community. Public recognition of the ways that individuals had given their lives to build up a community took the form of symbolic gifts and ceremonials. Agamemnon's retaking the trophy previously given to Achilles indicates that such acts of dying on behalf of the community were not valued by Agamemnon as king of the Achaean coalition. However, because of his leadership position, Agamemnon was not free to redistribute trophies as if he were simply a warrior in competition with other warriors for the trophies; he was entrusted with the higher responsibility of keeping the coalition intact, even if such a responsibility demanded that he be diminished in his wealth and symbolic capital and be made to appear less powerful in the face of his rivals. Such an honor system — although portrayed as less competitive in nature — was also operative in OB Mesopotamia. Although the examples of heroes celebrated in the royal inscriptions were the kings themselves and not their subordinates, the practice of granting land to soldiers is described in Article 26 of the *Code of Hammurapi* (IX:66–X:12) and indicates that such practices of public recognition of status took place in OB times. In the biblical tradition of Israel, the honoring of heroic figures was regularly carried out in the past tense when the heroes were recognized posthumously (e.g., Saul and Jonathan in 2 Sam. 1:19-27), and in such accounts the honor was regularly ascribed to God who enabled a hero such as the warrior David to succeed (cf. 2 Sam. 22:2-51 = Psalm 18).

Symbols call attention to actions that nurture relationships integral to the well-being of the community. By calling to mind previous heroic actions, symbols signal the need for such actions to recur in the future. The corporeality of a symbol contributes a sense of durability to a relationship without reifying the relationship or reducing it to a thing that an individual can control without further engagement and investment of self. A symbol can remain meaningful only within a community and a tradition that values it. A king who neglected his role as chief distributor of symbolic value was either a weak ruler or a tyrant, for if a king neglected the symbolic dimension of his power, the community diminished in vitality and freedom and the king was able to get his commands obeyed only through his capacity to manipulate material goods or inflict bodily harm for noncompliance.

A monarchic community with an authority structure anchored in the heavens presented a picture of a web of moving relationships that cried out for a stability that could be won only through fidelity and other-directed attentiveness. The relationships between the king, the king of the gods, and the people had to be negotiated and renegotiated within the particularities of day-to-day existence. The embodiment of divine power in the community was manifest primarily in the relationships between the king and the people and among the people. Rivalry among humans or of humans with the divine could lead to shifts in rank or status but also could lead to hubris or transgression. Because of the dangers associated with shifts in status or other changes in the structure of the community and because of the fragility inherent in political relationships, those with investments in the status quo tried to slow the rate of change in the community.

Repetition of primordial heroic patterns and celebration of the beginning of practices or institutions as the ideal are ways in which traditional societies have maintained the status quo and resisted innovation. Developments do occur in traditional societies, but significant innovations could be cloaked in the guise of structures or practices decreed in the primordial era. For example, the *Enuma Elish* recounts the rise of Marduk to the position of king of the gods, which means that Marduk replaced Enlil in this position. Yet the narrative states that Marduk won this position through his defeat of Tiamat at the time of the creation of the world and the conferral of supreme sovereignty on him by the assembly of the gods at that time. No mention of Enlil is given in the account. The narrators described this "palace coup" in heaven indirectly to avoid giving the impression that a palace coup could be legitimate. Also in Mesopotamia, the royal inscriptions frequently referred to Enlil as the "determiner of destinies"; there was a belief that the future had been determined by the gods and that humans should try to find out their destinies in order either to accept them or to petition the gods to alter unfavorable ones. In Homer, there is the notion that the *moira*, "the fate," of an individual was decreed. However, the specific content of such decreed fate seemed to be revealed only in special circumstances to specific individuals. So, in reality typical Homeric individuals had much room to make decisions that would impact their future and the future of their community. In the tradition of biblical Israel, the memory of the acts of God held a central place in Israel's imagination and self-understanding. Yet the God of Israel was one who engaged the Israelites and so honored the decisions that they made. If something was decreed for the future, it was usually not seen as something that had been set in primordial times only to be worked out in historical time. So, although both Israelite and Homeric society placed a high value on the past and the tradition, the practice of reduplicating the past such that the future was robbed of its meaning did not prevail in these two cultures. Nevertheless, the rate of social and political change in Israelite and Homeric societies was slowed by their emphasis upon tradition as providing the benchmarks for identity and self-understanding.

The traditional pattern for legitimating royal authority created a field or space in which people could find grounds for acting collectively under royal leadership or for withdrawing from such leadership. The symbolic and rhetorical space created by such a traditional pattern gave permission to the dissenting voice in the community because the pattern made royal rule accountable to the standards of the ethical world order. Even though such a world order was known primarily through the intuitions of experience, the credibility of such experiential knowledge was increased by the metaphors and narratives of the traditional accounts legitimating royal authority. People knew when a king was fleecing them and not acting like a shepherd; the traditional accounts gave them a communal language for expressing and validating their grievances. If a tyrannical king suppressed such protests, then he added one more reason to the legitimacy of his overthrow. Apart from those extreme cases that called into question the legitimacy of a particular king's rule, the traditional accounts also created the space in which perennial questions about the vitality and well-being of the community could be reviewed. The assembly of the Greek city-state of the sixth century B.C. in which political decisions were regularly made was prefigured in the councils of the Achaean warrior-kings in the *Iliad* and to some extent in the larger assemblies of the warriors in the *Iliad* and of the people of Ithaca in the *Odyssey*. Assemblies in Israel at the time of the inauguration of the kingship in 1 Samuel 8 and the assembly at Shechem in 1 Kings 12, which led to the secession of the northern tribes from union with Jerusalem, attest to the reality and potency of the popular voice in ancient Israel's history. In Mesopotamia, scenes in the *Atraḥasis Epic* and the *Enuma Elish* refer to the revolts of lesser gods against senior or older gods. These scenes of revolt most likely reflect experiences in Mesopotamian cities in which members of the populace rose up in protest against particular royal policies. The collective action of such groups could hardly have arisen without the development of a common mind on particular political and social issues. Although we do not have records of the populace as a whole deliberating on particular issues as part of royal decision making in Mesopotamia or in Israel, various Mesopotamian literary works and Israelite narratives indicate that these peoples reflected on issues of the proper and just ordering of their communities.

A docile audience is expected to listen attentively. Even though a docile people may give the benefit of the doubt to the ruling king or despair of taking action against him, such a nonrevolutionary stance does not mean that the people were unreflective or incapable of political reflection. These ancient peoples, even if only in the quiet and safety of their homes, could not have avoided asking questions about many of the following recurring political issues: about their place within the community, about the possibility or right of possessing a plot of land, about the significance of going to battle on behalf of the community, on the way in which the leaders of the community kept or did not keep their promises, on the wisdom of making heroic sacrifices for the community, on the understanding of the divine will for the community, on the plight of the vulnerable and defenseless, and on the dangers or opportunities posed by ambition and greed. Reflection on such issues occurs in the texts of the traditions of Homeric Greece, biblical Israel, and OB Mesopotamia. This reflection did not take the form of debate in a popular assembly vested with decision-making power, but the social grouping of the popular assembly was not a prerequisite for political reflection. The issues listed above refer to ways in which power and authority had an impact on the day-to-day lives of the populace — as such, these issues were preeminently political in character.

Similar and Contrasting Aspects of Royal Authority in Homeric Greece, Biblical Israel, and OB Mesopotamia

The following five aspects of kingship are threads that run through the texts from Homer, biblical Israel, and OB Mesopotamia. The format of an outline communicates well the logic of the comparative exercise undertaken in this study: the main items of the outline (e.g., #1 and #1a) identify aspects of royal rule shared by each of the three cultural traditions of royal rhetoric; then the subordinate items (e.g., #1a1, 1a2, and 1a3) give specific instances of this aspect in each culture. It is in the latter category of subordinate items that the distinctive features of kingship in each culture come to the fore.

1. **The king was the chief redistributor of material and symbolic goods in the community.**

   a. Rivalry among aspirants to the kingship was more apparent in communities where the reigning king was weak.

      (1) In the *Iliad*, rivalry among warriors was prized. These warriors were potential leaders of the coalition so that the line distinguishing the honor of a warrior from the glory of the king could be blurred. This

348

seems to have been a major reason why Agamemnon vied with Achilles and took Briseis, the woman prisoner of war, away from Achilles. The negative aspects of opportunism and rivalry were also evident with the suitors in the *Odyssey*.

(2) Saul and David vied for the kingship. In their rise to power they secured the loyalty of family, friends, soldiers, and advisers and set the stage for enduring competition between their households.

(3) The Mesopotamian royal inscriptions did not report rivalry among aspirants for the kingship. They tried to idealize the reigning king as a ruler raised high above all rivals. Nevertheless, such rivalry occasionally surfaced as a subtext in a number of inscriptions, as well as in material from royal letters and myths.

b. The king occupied a social position empowering him to confer honor on individuals in the name of the community. A trophy had material value that was further enhanced by the symbolic value bestowed upon the recipient through its public conferral.

(1) Alcinous rewarded the bard Demodocus with a greater portion of meat for his performance. The transitory character of an individual performance was matched by the fleeting character of the food portion. Ironically, this transitory poetic performance of the bard was to be the means by which the hero's aspirations for immortality were to be realized. The power of these communal symbols was evident in Agamemnon's public stripping away of Achilles' trophy. This created an almost irreparable breach between Achilles and Agamemon that resulted in Achilles' withdrawal from the coalition.

(2) Reports of the Israelite king honoring others in the community who are still alive are rare in the Israelite tradition.

(3) A Mesopotamian king typically celebrated collective accomplishments as ones done in his own name.

c. The king used property as a material means of exchange or as a symbolic means of conferring status on an individual. Such redistribution could have had an impact on the rank of individuals within the community.

(1) Eumaeus regarded the expected gift of property from his master Odysseus as a conferral of status.

(2) Naboth regarded the proposed purchase of his ancestral property as a threat to disenfranchise or excommunicate him.

(3) The property given to soldiers in the *Code* testified to the reward or compensation given to them for their service.

d. The king strengthened or weakened the center of the community by the way in which he redistributed material and symbolic goods.

(1) Alcinous gave gifts to Odysseus to honor him as a distinguished guest. This practice indicated how good relations among the leaders of various peoples were cultivated in the Homeric world. He asked the leaders to contribute freely with the promise that they would be repaid. Taxation was not an established practice in Homeric kingdoms.

(2) David concluded alliances with Nahash, king of the Ammonites, but was dishonored by Nahash's son Hanun and provoked to war (2 Samuel 10). The king's collection of taxes was likely to be regarded as extortion in peacetime (cf. 1 Sam. 8:11-18; 25:9-13. Symbolic gift giving had its place, but not as a primary means of enhancing the wealth of the center.

(3) OB kings concluded alliances, exacted tribute from captive peoples, and extracted taxes on various goods in the land. OB kings held title to extensive crown lands and worked the economy to maintain the wealth at the center. Symbolic gift giving had a place in OB times but was not a primary means of amassing wealth.

2. **The king was a symbol centralizing the community.**

a. The king had a special responsibility for maintaining the bonds of the community and preventing fragmentation.

(1) In the *Iliad,* Odysseus used the scepter of the king of Argos to prevent the departure homeward of the fleeing Achaean forces. In the *Odyssey,* Odysseus stopped his ears from hearing the exploits of the Achaean heroes as sung by the Sirens and strove to return home to Ithaca where he was needed in his household and community. His tears at hearing these exploits sung by Demodocus bonded him with the Achaean community and its heroes through shared suffering.

(2) David placed self-interest above communal interest in his affair with Bathsheba and so brought dissension and revolt into his household and kingdom.

(3) The OB king claimed in his inscriptions to accomplish great deeds for the community. The community members who contributed to

the accomplishment of these deeds must have seen the king's claims as an affirmation of their collective efforts. How the king faltered through self-interest or weakness in promoting collective efforts is not recorded in the inscriptions and seems to be missing from the materials of the royal archives that tend to idealize the king and cover over shortcomings.

b. Self-promotion by the king was a practice that aimed to create an image of the king as a participant in both the divine and human realms.

(1) Agamemnon claimed to be more powerful than Achilles even though he acknowledged Achilles' excellence as a warrior. Achilles was revered by Homer as semidivine, for his mother Thetis was a goddess. Both Agamemnon and Achilles claimed to be godlike.

(2) David claimed excellence as a warrior but attributed his skill and success to YHWH as his protector.

(3) The OB king was portrayed in royal inscriptions and hymns as praising his own accomplishments, which accorded with the practice of court etiquette in a number of Mesopotamian cities between 2250 and 1750 B.C. where the king's name was written with the divine determinative: that is, the practice of divinizing the king.

3. **The king was expected to be attentive to the divine world.**

a. The way in which a community understood the source of sovereign rule in their community had a strong impact on the way a king understood the limits of his decision-making power and his mode of exercising it.

(1) The *Iliad* portrayed Agamemnon as a king who neglected to utilize authority vested in him by the divinely wrought scepter of the king of Argos, which symbolized his participation as king in the sovereignty of Zeus over the Achaeans. As a result, he often attempted to exercise sovereignty as if it originated with himself.

(2) In the Israelite tradition, kingship did not carry the aura of unquestioned divine support but rather was suspected of being an institution whose proponents might eventually treat it as the source of sovereignty rather than as a participant in the sovereignty of YHWH (1 Samuel 8).

(3) Kingship in Mesopotamia was regarded as a divinely sanctioned institution such that in their inscriptions kings emphasized their divine election to this well-established office.

b. The way in which a community imagined the divine world to be structured shaped the character of its response to God or the gods.

    (1) In the Homeric world, Zeus exercised sovereignty over the course of events yet his brother Poseidon and the other deities of his Olympian household were active forces for weal and woe within the earthly sphere. Zeus was enthroned on Olympus and was seen to intervene in events by such means as a thunderbolt rather than in anthropomorphic form, as Athena typically did. Humans were expected to pay heed to a number of gods who sometimes held contradictory positions.

    (2) In Israel where YHWH was believed to rule over the course of events, misfortune was regarded either as a consequence of human sin or as a subject for lamentation addressed to YHWH: that is, a crying out born of confusion and need. In the final form of the biblical tradition, the imperative for obedience to YHWH in this aniconic, monolatrous faith was clear and focused.

    (3) In OB Mesopotamia, Enlil as king of the gods did not function as a protector deity for a king like Hammurapi; rather, this protector function was carried out by Marduk, the chief god of Hammurapi's city of Babylon. The division of labor within the Babylonian pantheon created the possibility for understanding misfortune or chaos as a consequence of conflict among the gods. Marduk and Enlil were conceived in basilomorphic form both in linguistic images and in artistically wrought images for the temple cult. Here also the requirement that a king obey a number of gods presents a king with a situation in which divine expectations stood in tension with one another.

c. The hierarchy between gods and humans needed to be acknowledged by practices such as sacrifice, prayer, and attentiveness to the divine will.

    (1) Homeric kings offered prayer and sacrifice on numerous occasions, but they were not patrons of temples since temples were foreign to Greece prior to the eighth century B.C.

    (2) In Israel, kings such as David and Solomon aspired to be patrons of the Jerusalem temple and were remembered as praying and offering sacrifice on special occasions.

    (3) In OB Mesopotamia, Hammurapi celebrated his patronage of temples in various Mesopotamian cities in the prologue to his *Code*. Such attention to the gods and their cults was a standard expectation for OB kings.

4. The justice of royal rule became manifest insofar as it was in accord with the ethical world order.

    a. Successful agriculture was regarded as a consequence of the justice of the king's rule.

        (1) In the *Odyssey,* Penelope praised the ideal just king as one whose reign brought forth agricultural abundance.

        (2) In Psalm 72, the petition is voiced that the king rule with justice so that the crops might flourish. The drought reported in 2 Samuel 21 was regarded as a punishment for Saul's breaking an oath to the Gibeonites and so attested to the perceived connection between royal justice and agricultural success.

        (3) In OB Mesopotamia, kings typically proclaimed that their success in constructing canals and other devices essential to agriculture was evidence of their divine election. Success in river-fed agriculture was more predictable than in rain-fed agriculture; nevertheless, the OB king acknowledged that the gods initiated and oversaw such success.

    b. The king was expected to promote the well-being of his kingdom by ruling in accord with a world order shaped by God or the gods.

        (1) In the *Iliad,* the scepter of the king of Argos is accompanied by *themistes,* "customary laws." The king was expected to be attentive to the will of Zeus and the customs of the community.

        (2) In biblical Israel, the king was not portrayed as a promulgator of laws; for the various corpora of biblical law, this function was attributed to Moses. Clearly, the Israelite king made executive decrees and other forms of positive law (cf. 1 Sam. 30:24), but he was not imagined to be a lawgiver in the biblical tradition.

        (3) In OB Mesopotamia, Hammurapi etched his name into history by promulgating his law code and having it inscribed on stelae. He claimed to be acting on behalf of the god Shamash as he promulgated his laws, which were probably exemplary legal decisions sifted through the practices of the community.

5. The prophet and the popular assembly challenged the king and his policies and so helped to promote just royal rule.

    a. Kings sought the advice of intermediaries such as prophets and diviners in making important political and military decisions.

(1) In the *Iliad,* Achilles demanded that a prophet be consulted to learn the cause of the plague ravaging the Achaean forces. The message from the prophet Calchas that Apollo was punishing the Achaeans for their abduction of the daughter of his priest Chryses helped to create the circumstances that led to the quarrel between Achilles and Agamemnon.

(2) The Israelite prophet played a fundamental leadership role in the Israelite community as a messenger from the court of YHWH, the true sovereign over Israel and the nations. As such, the prophet could challenge the king if he saw the king's actions diverging from what he discerned to be the will of YHWH.

(3) The primary intermediary in Mesopotamia was the diviner who practiced extispicy and hepatoscopy. Oracular prophets functioned in Mari and a few other places in the OB period, but even in these cities their authority in the eyes of the king needed to be validated by a diviner.

b. The assembly of the people or of their representatives played a subordinate role within a monarchically organized community.

(1) In the *Iliad,* the assembly of Achaean soldiers listened to the scepter-bearing kings Agamemnon and Odysseus. Their ridicule of the protester Thersites indicated that popular opinion had an impact. In the *Odyssey,* the assembly chose not to express its support for Telemachus against the suitors, despite the urging of Mentor.

(2) In Israel, an assembly of tribal elders requested the inauguration of the kingship (1 Samuel 8) and anointed David king over Judah (2 Sam. 2:4) and over Israel (2 Sam. 5:3). Later, an assembly of northern elders led the revolt and secession of the northern tribes from the Davidic kingdom.

(3) In Mesopotamia, evidence of a popular assembly uniting to make a decision appears indirectly in the literary narratives of *Atraḫasis* and *Enuma Elish* where the assembly consisted of gods who were protesting against the policies of Enlil as king of the gods. As expected, the functioning of a popular assembly was not recorded in royal inscriptions.

Royal Authority: Its Promise of Stability and Harmony

A king was called upon to promote the integration of the various dimensions of a community. In his words and example, the king was expected to place the needs of the community ahead of his own needs. The traditional pattern for legitimating royal authority in Homeric Greece, biblical Israel, and OB Mesopotamia emphasized the divine election of the king for rule and his accountability for the ways he carried out that commission. This pattern assumed that the gods ruled the cosmos. The king stepped onto a stage that had been shaped by the gods in interaction with human communities. The king was able to speak and act authoritatively only if he worked with the people of the community in respect for the traditions and in accord with the material resources he had been given. The king was obliged not to forget the "givenness" of the world in which he exercised authority, for this understanding undergirded his call to attentiveness to God or the gods, the people, and the tradition.

The traditional pattern of authority traced out a line of command and accountability without specifying who gave the command and what the content of the command was. Each culture identified its sovereign deity from whom all decision making gained its legitimacy. What courses of action this sovereign deity decreed for a community could be discerned only in particular circumstances. Thus, the pattern itself was flexible and open-ended on specifics. Its main contention was that humans were subject to God or the gods and were not autonomous. If the king took this contention seriously, he would devote time, attention, and resources to discerning the divine will.

Ambiguity in divine communications engaged the king, prophets, priests, sages, and the people to ferret out the divine intention for their particular circumstances. The obedience, questioning, and criticism that arose in interpreting oracles were communicative actions that had the potential to strengthen or weaken relationships in the community. Such engagement and reflection indicated that a privileged locus for revelation of the divine will was the speaking and acting of the community. In a monarchical community, the king and his advisers often made decisions without consultation with the masses. When crises occurred, however, such as the impending withdrawal of Achilles from the coalition, kings were likely to summon the community or its representatives to describe the threatening circumstances. When the people had grievances, they expected a hearing from the king; if denied, they would probably have judged his rule to be unjust and would legitimately have moved to overthrow him. Acts of communication created the setting in which people tried to find and refind their place within the community and the larger world order. According to the traditional pattern for legitimating royal authority, communication that promoted integration and harmony within the community needed to include the voices of God or the gods, the king, and the people. If any of these parties were excluded from the conversation, harmony would disappear.

Social mobility in the hierarchical societies of Homeric Greece, biblical Israel, and OB Mesopotamia was rare. People were born into certain families. In Mesopotamia and Homeric Greece, it was contended that one was fated for a certain place in life by the gods or the world order. Nevertheless, the place on the hierarchy was symbolized by the amount of honor shown to a person and not simply by the material goods at one's control. Those points at which one could rise or fall in the social hierarchy were particular tension points that could upset the equilibrium of the community and as such called for the king's involvement. The boundaries between classes and nations needed to be negotiated and renegotiated so as to provide valid definition of one's place in the scheme of things.

The heroic quest for honor could channel an individual's energy toward an important communal enterprise. Yet if this heroic pattern were not questioned and adapted, it could have created expectations calling for imitation of a model that would have sustained itself but would have been less conducive to what the community actually needed in particular circumstances. Imitating such a pattern could have drained the life from an individual and allowed only the pattern to manifest itself. Such misdirected self-giving would have been carried out on behalf of the pattern and not for the good of the community. Heroic actions inspired and guided by traditional patterns were essential to the life of the community, but such energies could have been squandered if the patterns guiding such heroic actions were not repeatedly evaluated. The examples of Achilles and Odysseus raised important questions about what a hero ought to be, but neither provided a model for heroic action that was to be imitated directly.

The charisma of a king pointed to his divine election. The responsibility of fostering harmony and integration in a community exceeded the mortal capacities of any king. It was little wonder that these ancient cultures celebrated agricultural success as a sign of divine favor to a just king: such success was vital to the livelihood of the community, and yet so many variables were beyond human control. The king who distributed symbolic and material goods so as to promote harmony and integration within the community could have celebrated these accomplishments as evidence of his divine election and so have increased the effectiveness of his commands in the future. Royal authority was a participation in divine authority. The extent to which a king was able to maximize such participation determined how well he was able to keep a dynamic community intact and growing.

BIBLIOGRAPHY

The following bibliography is divided into sections on Theory, Hermeneutics, and General Background; Homeric Greece; Ancient Israel; and Ancient Mesopotamia. Within each section, the entries are arranged alphabetically according to author. For multiple entries for an author, books are listed alphabetically by title, followed by articles in books, journals, dictionaries, etc., listed alphabetically by title.

Theory, Hermeneutics, and General Background

Adams, Robert McC. *The Evolution of Urban Society.* Chicago: Aldine, 1966.

Ankersmit, Frank. *History and Tropology: The Rise and Fall of Metaphor.* Berkeley: University of California Press, 1994.

⸻. "Historicism, Post-Modernism and Epistemology." In *Post-Modernism and Anthropology: Theory and Practice.* Edited by Karen Geuijen et al., pp. 21-51. Assen: Van Gorcum, 1995.

Arendt, Hannah. *Between Past and Future: Six Exercises in Political Thought.* New York: Viking, 1961.

⸻. *The Human Condition.* Chicago: University of Chicago Press, 1958.

Auden, W. H. *The Dyer's Hand and Other Essays.* New York: Random House, 1968.

Baker, Keith Michael. "Introduction." In *The French Revolution and the Creation of Modern Political Culture.* Vol. 1, *The Political Culture of the Old Regime.* Edited by Keith Baker, pp. xii-xiii. New York: Pergamon, 1987.

Bell, Catherine. *Ritual: Perspectives and Dimensions.* New York: Oxford University Press, 1997.

Berlin, Isaiah. *The Sense of Reality: Studies in Ideas and Their History.* Edited by Henry Hardy. New York: Farrar, Straus and Giroux, 1996.

357

Billows, Richard. *Kings and Colonists: Aspects of Macedonian Imperialism.* Columbia Studies in the Classical Tradition 22. Leiden: Brill, 1995.

Bloch, Marc. "Two Strategies of Comparison." In *Comparative Perspectives: Theories and Methods.* Edited by Amitai Etzioni and Fredric Dubow, pp. 39-41. Boston: Little, Brown and Company, 1970.

Bloch, Maurice E. F. *How We Think They Think: Anthropological Approaches to Cognition, Memory, and Literacy.* Boulder, Colo.: Westview, 1998.

Bourdieu, Pierre. *Language and Symbolic Power.* Edited by John B. Thompson. Cambridge, Mass.: Harvard University Press, 1991.

Brillante, Carlo. "History and the Historical Interpretation of Myth." In *Approaches to Greek Myth.* Edited by Lowell Edmunds, pp. 93-138. Baltimore: Johns Hopkins University Press, 1990.

Burkhardt, Armin. "Speech act theory — the decline of a paradigm." In *Speech Acts, Meaning and Intentions: Critical Approaches to the Philosophy of John R. Searle.* Edited by Armin Burkhardt, pp. 91-128. New York: Walter de Gruyter, 1990.

Cannadine, David. "Introduction: Divine Rites of Kings." In *Rituals of Royalty: Power and Ceremonial in Traditional Societies,* pp. 1-19. Cambridge: Cambridge University Press, 1987.

Chauvet, Louis-Marie. *Symbol and Sacrament: A Sacramental Reinterpretation of Christian Existence.* Collegeville, Minn.: Liturgical, 1995.

Cohen, Ronald. "The Political System." In *Handbook of Method in Cultural Anthropology.* Edited by Raoul Naroll and Ronald Cohen, pp. 484-99. New York: Columbia University Press, 1970.

Culler, Jonathan. *The Pursuit of Signs.* Ithaca: Cornell University Press, 1981.

Douglas, Mary. *Natural Symbols: Explorations in Cosmology.* New York: Pantheon, 1982.

Eagleton, Terry. *Ideology: An Introduction.* New York: Verso, 1991.

———. *Literary Theory: An Introduction.* 2nd ed. Minneapolis: University of Minnesota Press, 1996.

Figgis, John N. *Divine Right of Kings.* Cambridge: Cambridge University Press, 1934.

Frye, Northrup. *The Great Code: The Bible and Literature.* New York: Harcourt Brace Jovanovich, 1981.

———. *Words with Power.* San Diego: Harcourt Brace Jovanovich, 1990.

Geertz, Clifford. *The Interpretation of Cultures.* New York: Basic Books, 1973.

Giddens, Anthony. *Central Problems in Social Theory: Action, Structure, and Contradiction in Social Analysis.* Berkeley: University of California Press, 1979.

———. *The Constitution of Society: Outline of the Theory of Structuration.* Cambridge: Polity, 1984.

———. "Sructuralism, Post-Structuralism and the Production of Culture." In *Social Theory Today.* Edited by Anthony Giddens and Jonathan Turner, pp. 195-223. Cambridge: Polity, 1987.

Goodhart, Eugene. *The Reign of Ideology.* New York: Columbia University Press, 1997.

Gumperz, John, and Stephen Levinson. "Introduction: Linguistic Relativity Reexamined." In *Rethinking Linguistic Relativity*. Edited by John Gumperz and Stephen Levinson, pp. 1-18. Cambridge: Cambridge University Press, 1996.

Habermas, Jürgen. "Actions, Speech Acts, Linguistically Mediated Interactions, and Lifeworld." In *On the Pragmatics of Communication*, pp. 215-55. Cambridge, Mass.: MIT Press, 1998.

————. "Comments on John Searle's 'Meaning, Communication, and Representation' (1988)." In *On the Pragmatics of Communication*, pp. 257-75. Cambridge, Mass.: MIT Press, 1998.

————. "On the Distinction Between Poetic and Communicative Uses of Language." In *On the Pragmatics of Communication*, pp. 383-401. Cambridge, Mass.: MIT Press, 1998.

Heidegger, Martin. *Being and Time*. Albany, N.Y.: SUNY Press, 1996.

Hénaff, Marcel. *Claude Lévi-Strauss and the Making of Structural Anthropology*. Minneapolis: University of Minnesota Press, 1998.

Hinsley, F. H. *Sovereignty*. 2nd ed. Cambridge: Cambridge University Press, 1986.

Hoffman, John. *Sovereignty*. Minneapolis: University of Minnesota Press, 1998.

Humphreys, Sally C. "Diffusion, Comparison, Criticism." In *Anfänge politischen Denkens in der Antike: Die nahöstlichen Kulturen und die Griechen*. Edited by Kurt Raaflaub and Elisabeth Müller-Luckner, pp. 1-11. Munich: Oldenbourg, 1993.

————. "Dynamics of the Greek Breakthrough: The Dialogue between Philosophy and Religion." In *The Origins and Diversity of Axial Age Civilizations*. Edited by S. N. Eisenstadt, pp. 92-110. New York: SUNY Press, 1986.

Hussey, Edward. "Heraclitus." In *The Cambridge Companion to Early Greek Philosophy*. Edited by A. A. Long, pp. 93-98. Cambridge: Cambridge University Press, 1999.

Jameson, Fredric. *The Political Unconscious: Narrative as a Socially Symbolic Act*. Ithaca: Cornell University Press, 1981.

————. *The Seeds of Time*. New York: Columbia University Press, 1994.

Jouvenal, Bertrand de. *Sovereignty: An Inquiry into the Political Good*. Chicago: University of Chicago Press, 1959.

Kantorowicz, Ernst. *The King's Two Bodies: A Study in Medieval Political Theology*. Princeton: Princeton University Press, 1957.

Kearney, Richard. *Modern Movements in European Philosophy*. 2nd ed. Manchester: Manchester University Press, 1994.

————. *Poetics of Modernity: Toward a Hermeneutic Imagination*. Atlantic Highlands, N.J.: Humanities, 1995.

Kellner, Hans. "As Real as It Gets: Ricoeur and Narrativity." In *Meanings in Texts and Actions: Questioning Paul Ricoeur*. Edited by David Klemme and William Schweiker, pp. 49-56. Charlottesville: University of Virginia Press, 1993.

Leach, Edmund. *Culture and Communication: The Logic by Which Symbols Are Connected*. New York: Cambridge University Press, 1976.

————. "Telstar and the Aborigines or *La pensée sauvage*." In *Sociological Theory and Philosophical Analysis*. Edited by Dorothy Emmet and Alasdair MacIntyre, pp. 183-203. New York: Macmillan, 1970.

Lincoln, Bruce. *Theorizing Myth: Narrative, Ideology, and Scholarship*. Chicago: University of Chicago Press, 1999.

Lloyd, G. E. R. *Demystifying Mentalities*. New York: Cambridge University Press, 1990.

Lohmeyer, Ernst. "The Right Interpretation of the Mythological." In *Kerygma and Myth: A Theological Debate*. Edited by Hans W. Bartsch, pp. 124-37. New York: Harper & Brothers, 1961.

Lucy, John A. "The Scope of Linguistic Relativity." In *Rethinking Linguistic Relativity*. Edited by John Gumperz and Stephen Levinson, pp. 37-69. Cambridge: Cambridge University Press, 1996.

Mach, Zdzislaw. *Symbols, Conflict, and Identity: Essays in Political Anthropology*. New York: SUNY Press, 1993.

Malul, Meir. *The Comparative Method in Ancient Near Eastern and Biblical Legal Studies*. AOAT 227. Neukirchen-Vluyn: Neukirchener Verlag, 1990.

Mann, Michael. *The Sources of Social Power*. Vol. 1, *A History of Power from the Beginning to A.D. 1760*. Cambridge: Cambridge University Press, 1986.

McGaughey, Douglas. "Ricoeur's Metaphor and Narrative Theories as a Foundation for a Theory of Symbol." *Religious Studies* 24 (1988): 415-37.

Meier, Christian. *The Greek Discovery of Politics*. Cambridge, Mass.: Harvard University Press, 1990.

Mitchell, W. J. T. "Ekphrasis and the Other." In *Picture Theory: Essays on Verbal and Visual Representation*, pp. 151-81. Chicago: University of Chicago Press, 1994.

Moore, Sally Falk. "Certainties Undone: Fifty Turbulent Years of Legal Anthropology, 1949-1999." *Journal of Royal Anthropological Literature* 7 (2001): 95-115.

Neville, Robert Cummings. *The Truth of Broken Symbols*. Albany, N.Y.: SUNY Press, 1996.

Ong, Walter. *Orality and Literacy: The Technologizing of the Word*. New York: Methuen, 1982.

Oravec, Christine. "Kenneth Burke's Concept of Association and the Complexity of Identity." In *The Legacy of Kenneth Burke*. Edited by Herbert Simons and Trevor Melia, pp. 174-95. Madison: University of Wisconsin Press, 1988.

Parsons, Talcott. "On the Concept of Political Power." *Proceedings of the American Philosophical Society* 107 (1963): 232-62.

Pratt, Mary Louise. "Ideology and Speech-Act Theory." *Poetics Today* 7 (1986): 59-72.

Ranke, Leopold von. "The Historian's Task." In *The Secret of World History: Selected Writings on the Art and Science of History*. Edited by Roger Wines. New York: Fordham University Press, 1981.

Rappaport, Roy. *Ritual and Religion in the Making of Humanity*. Cambridge: Cambridge University Press, 1999.

Ricoeur, Paul. *Freud and Philosophy: An Essay on Interpretation*. New Haven: Yale University Press, 1970.

———. *From Text to Action: Essays in Hermeneutics II*. Evanston, Ill.: Northwestern University Press, 1991.

———. *Oneself as Another*. Chicago: University of Chicago Press, 1992.

————. *The Rule of Metaphor: Multidisciplinary Studies of the Creation of Meaning in Language.* Toronto: University of Toronto Press, 1977.

————. *The Symbolism of Evil.* Boston: Beacon, 1967.

————. *Time and Narrative.* 3 vols. Chicago: University of Chicago Press, 1984, 1985.

————. "Thinking Creation." In André Lacoque and Paul Ricoeur, *Thinking Biblically,* pp. 31-67. Chicago: University of Chicago Press, 1998.

Scarborough, Milton. *Myth and Modernity: Postcritical Reflections.* Albany, N.Y.: SUNY Press, 1994.

Schmitt, Carl. *Political Theology: Four Chapters on the Concept of Sovereignty.* Cambridge, Mass.: MIT Press, 1985.

Searle, John R. *Mind, Language and Society: Philosophy in the Real World.* New York: Basic Books, 1998.

Service, Elman. *Origins of the State and Civilization: The Process of Cultural Evolution.* New York: Norton, 1975.

Smith, Jonathan Z. "Wisdom's Place." In *Death, Ecstasy, and Other Worldly Journeys.* Edited by John Collins and Michael Fishbane, pp. 3-13. Albany, N.Y.: SUNY Press, 1995.

Thompson, John B. "Editor's Introduction." In Pierre Bourdieu, *Language and Symbolic Power.* Edited by John B. Thompson, pp. 1-31. Cambridge, Mass.: Harvard University Press, 1991.

Turner, Bryan S. "The Body in Western Society: Social Theory and Its Perspectives." In *Religion and the Body.* Edited by Sarah Coakley, pp. 15-41. Cambridge Studies in Religious Traditions 8. Cambridge: Cambridge University Press, 1997.

Turner, Victor. *The Anthropology of Performance.* New York: PAJ, 1986.

Vanhoozer, Kevin J. *Biblical Narrative in the Philosophy of Paul Ricoeur: A Study in Hermeneutics and Theology.* Cambridge: Cambridge University Press, 1990.

Vansina, Jan. *Oral Tradition as History.* Madison: University of Wisconsin Press, 1985.

Verene, Donald Phillip. "Two Sources of Philosophical Memory: Vico versus Hegel." In *Philosophical Imagination and Cultural Memory.* Edited by Patricia Cook, pp. 40-61. Durham, N.C.: Duke University Press, 1993.

Weber, Max. *Economy and Society.* 2 vols. Edited by Guenther Roth and Claus Wittich. Translated by Ephraim Fischoff et al. New York: Bedminster, 1968. Translation of *Wirtschaft und Gesellschaft.* 4th ed. Edited by J. Winckelmann. Tübingen: J. C. B. Mohr, 1956.

Homeric Greece

Adkins, A. W. H. *Merit and Responsibility: A Study in Greek Values.* Oxford: Clarendon, 1960.

————. "Homeric Gods and the Values of Homeric Society." *JHS* 92 (1972): 1-19.

————. "Values, Goals, and Emotions in the *Iliad.*" *Classical Philology* 77 (1982): 292-326.

Auffahrt, Christoph. *Der drohende Untergang: "Schöpfung" in Mythos und Ritual im Alten Orient und in Griechenland am Beispiel der Odysee und des Ezechielbuches.* Religiongeschichtliche Versüche und Vorarbeiten 39. New York: Walter de Gruyter, 1991.

Bakker, Egbert J. *Poetry in Speech: Orality and Homeric Discourse.* Ithaca: Cornell University Press, 1997.

———. "Storytelling in the Future: Truth, Time, and Tense in Homeric Epic." In *Written Voices, Spoken Signs: Tradition, Performance, and the Epic Text.* Edited by Egbert Bakker and Ahuvia Kahane, pp. 11-36. Cambridge, Mass.: Harvard University Press, 1997.

Brisson, Luc. *Plato the Myth Maker.* Chicago: University of Chicago Press, 1998.

Burkert, Walter. *Creation of the Sacred: Tracks of Biology in Early Religions.* Cambridge, Mass.: Harvard University Press, 1996.

———. *Greek Religion.* Cambridge, Mass.: Harvard University Press, 1985.

———. *The Orientalizing Revolution: Near Eastern Influence on Greek Culture in the Early Archaic Age.* Cambridge, Mass.: Harvard University Press, 1992.

———. *Structure and History in Greek Mythology and Ritual.* Berkeley: University of California Press, 1979.

———. "From Epiphany to Cult Statue: Early Greek *Theos.*" In *What Is a God? Studies in the Nature of Greek Divinity.* Edited by Alan Lloyd, pp. 15-34. London: Duckworth, 1997.

———. "Greek *Poleis* and Civic Cults: Some Further Thoughts." In *Studies in the Ancient Greek Polis,* pp. 201-10. Stuttgart: Franz Steiner, 1995.

———. "The Logic of Cosmology." In *From Reason to Myth?* Edited by Richard Buxton, pp. 87-106. Oxford: Oxford University Press, 1999.

———. "Lydia Between East and West or How to Date the Trojan War: A Study in Herodotus." In *The Ages of Homer.* Edited by Jane Carter and Sarah Morris, pp. 139-48. Austin: University of Texas Press, 1995.

Buxton, Richard. *Imaginary Greece.* Cambridge: Cambridge University Press, 1994.

Cairns, Douglas. *"Aidos": The Psychology and Ethics of Honour and Shame in Ancient Greek Literature.* Oxford: Clarendon, 1993.

Calame, Claude. *The Craft of Poetic Speech in Ancient Greece.* Ithaca: Cornell University Press, 1995.

———. "The Rhetoric of *Muthos* and *Logos.*" In *From Myth to Reason?* Edited by Richard Buxton, pp. 119-43. Oxford: Oxford University Press, 1999.

Carlier, Pierre. *La royauté en Grèce avant Alexandre.* Strasbourg: AECR, 1984.

Carter, Jane. "Ancestor Cult and the Occasion of Homeric Performance." In *The Ages of Homer.* Edited by Jane Carter and Sarah Morris, pp. 285-312. Austin: University of Texas Press, 1995.

Cartledge, Paul. "Power and the State." In *Ancient Greece.* Edited by Paul Cartledge, pp. 139-65. Cambridge: Cambridge University Press, 1998.

———. "Writing the History of Archaic Greek Political Thought." In *Archaic Greece:*

New Approaches and New Evidence. Edited by Nick Fisher and Hans van Wees, pp. 379-99. London: Duckworth, 1998.

Clay, Jenny Strauss. *The Wrath of Athena.* Princeton: Princeton University Press, 1983.

Cline, Eric H. *Sailing the Wine-Dark Sea: International Trade and the Late Bronze Age Aegean.* BAR International Series 591. Oxford: Tempus Reparatum, 1994.

Cook, Erwin. *The Odyssey in Athens: Myths of Cultural Origins.* Ithaca: Cornell University Press, 1995.

Crotty, Kevin. *The Poetics of Supplication: Homer's Iliad and Odyssey.* Ithaca: Cornell University Press, 1994.

Davies, John K. "The Moral Dimension of Pythian Apollo." In *What Is a God? Studies in the Nature of Greek Divinity.* Edited by Alan Lloyd, pp. 43-64. London: Duckworth, 1997.

———. "The Origins of the Greek *Polis:* Where Should We Be Looking." In *The Development of the Polis in Archaic Greece.* Edited by Lynette G. Mitchell and P. J. Rhodes, pp. 24-37. New York: Routledge, 1997.

Detienne, Marcel. *The Creation of Mythology.* Chicago: University of Chicago Press, 1986.

———. *The Masters of Truth in Archaic Greece.* New York: Zone, 1999.

———. "The 'Sea-Crow.'" In *Myth, Religion, and Society.* Edited by Raymond L. Gordon, pp. 16-42. Cambridge: Cambridge University Press, 1977.

Dietrich, Bernard. "From Knossos to Homer." In *What Is a God? Studies in the Nature of Greek Divinity.* Edited by Alan Lloyd, pp. 1-13. London: Duckworth, 1997.

Donlan, Walter. *The Aristocratic Ideal in Ancient Greece: Attitude of Superiority from Homer to the End of the Fifth Century* B.C. Lawrence, Kans.: Coronado, 1980.

———. "Reciprocities in Homer." *Classical World* 75 (1982): 166.

———. "The Relations of Power in the Pre-State and Early State Polities." In *The Development of the Polis in Archaic Greece.* Edited by Lynette G. Mitchell and P. J. Rhodes, pp. 39-48. New York: Routledge, 1997.

———. "The Social Groups of Dark Age Greece." *Classical Philology* 80 (1985): 293-308.

Drews, Robert. *"Basileus": The Evidence for Kingship in Geometric Greece.* New Haven: Yale University Press, 1983.

Fadinger, Volker. "Griechische Tyrannis und Alter Orient." In *Anfänge politischen Denkens in der Antike: Die nahöstlichen Kulturen und die Griechen.* Edited by Kurt Raaflaub and Elisabeth Müller-Luckner, pp. 263-316. Munich: Oldenbourg, 1993.

Finkelberg, Margalit. *The Birth of Literary Fiction in Ancient Greece.* Oxford: Clarendon, 1998.

———. "*Timē* and *Aretē* in Homer." *Classical Quarterly* 48 (1998): 14-28.

Finley, M. I. *The Legacy of Greece.* Oxford: Clarendon, 1981.

———. *The World of Odysseus.* New York: Viking, 1965.

———. "Homer and Mycenae: Property and Tenure." In *The Language and Background of Homer.* Edited by Geoffrey S. Kirk, pp. 133-59. Cambridge: Heffer & Sons, 1964.

Foley, John Miles. *Homer's Traditional Art.* University Park: Pennsylvania State University Press, 1999.

————. "Individual Poet and Epic Tradition: Homer as Legendary Singer." *Arethusa* 31 (1998): 149-78.

Foxhall, Lin. "Cargoes of the Heart's Desire: The Character of Trade in the Archaic Mediterranean World." In *Archaic Greece: New Approaches and New Evidence*. Edited by Nick Fisher and Hans van Wees, pp. 295-309. London: Duckworth, 1998.

Frame, Douglas. *The Myth of Return in Early Greek Epic*. New Haven: Yale University Press, 1978.

Geddes, G. "Who's Who in 'Homeric Society'?" *Classical Quarterly* 34 (1984): 17-36.

Gentili, Bruno. *Poetry and Its Public in Ancient Greece: From Homer to the Fifth Century*. Baltimore: Johns Hopkins University Press, 1988.

Gernet, Louis. "'Value' in Greek Myth." In *Myth, Religion, and Society*. Edited by Raymond L. Gordon, pp. 111-46. Cambridge: Cambridge University Press, 1981.

Geschnitzer, F. "*Basileus*: Ein terminologischer Beitrag zur Frühgeschichte des Königtums bei den Griechen." In *Festschrift Leonard C. Franz zum 70. Geburtstag*. Edited by Osmund Menghin and Hermann Oberg, pp. 99-112. Innsbrucker Beiträge zur Kulturwissenschaft 11. Innsbruck: Auslieferung durch das Sprachwissenschaftliche Institut des Leopold-Franzens-Universität, 1965.

Golden, Mark. Review of Cynthia Patterson, *The Family in Greek History*. *Phoenix* 52 (1998): 399.

Gould, John. "Homeric Epic and the Tragic Moment." In *Myth, Ritual Memory, and Exchange: Essays in Greek Literature and Culture*, pp. 158-73. New York: Oxford University Press, 2001.

————. "On Making Sense of Greek Religion." In *Myth, Ritual Memory, and Exchange: Essays in Greek Literature and Culture*, pp. 203-34. New York: Oxford University Press, 2001.

Greene, William C. *Moira: Fate, Good, and Evil in Greek Thought*. Cambridge, Mass.: Harvard University Press, 1944.

Griffin, Jasper. *Homer on Life and Death*. Oxford: Clarendon, 1980.

Halverson, John. "The Succession Issue in the *Odyssey*." *Greece and Rome* 33 (1986): 119, 126.

Hammer, Dean. "The Cultural Construction of Chance in the *Iliad*." *Arethusa* 31 (1998): 124-48.

————. "The Politics of the *Iliad*." *Classical Journal* 94 (1998): 1-30.

————. "Who Shall Readily Obey? Authority and Politics in the *Iliad*." *Phoenix* 51 (1997): 1-24.

Hansen, Mogens Herman. "Introduction: *Polis* as a Citizen-State." In *The Ancient Greek City-State*. Edited by Mogens H. Hansen, pp. 7-29. Copenhagen: Munksgaard, 1993.

Harris, Edward M. "A New Solution to the Riddle of the *Seisachtheia*." In *The Development of the "Polis" in Archaic Greece*. Edited by Lynette G. Mitchell and P. J. Rhodes, pp. 103-12. New York: Routledge, 1997.

Heiden, Bruce. "The Ordeals of Homeric Song." *Arethusa* 30 (1997): 221-39.

Hesiod. *Theogony*. Edited by Martin L. West. Oxford: Clarendon, 1966.

————. *Works and Days, Theogony, Shield of Heracles.* Translated by Richmond Lattimore. Ann Arbor: University of Michigan Press, 1959.

Hölkescamp, Karl-Joachim. *Schiedsrichter, Gesetzgeber und Gesetzgebung im archaischen Griechenland.* Historia 131. Stuttgart: Franz Steiner, 1999.

Homer. *Homeri Opera: Iliad I-XII* and *Iliad XIII-XXIV.* Edited by David B. Monro and Thomas W. Allen. 3rd ed. Oxford: Clarendon, 1920.

————. *Homeri Opera: Odyssey I-XII* and *Odyssey XIII-XXIV.* Edited by Thomas W. Allen. 2nd ed. Oxford: Clarendon, 1917, 1919.

————. *Iliad.* Translated by A. T. Murray. Revised by William F. Wyatt. Loeb Classical Library. 2 vols. Cambridge: Harvard University Press, 1999.

————. *Odyssey.* Translated by A. T. Murray. Revised by George E. Dimock. Loeb Classical Library. 2 vols. Cambridge: Harvard University Press, 1995.

Jaeger, Werner. *Paideia: The Ideals of Greek Culture.* 2nd ed. 3 vols. New York: Oxford University Press, 1945.

Janko, Richard. "The Homeric Poems as Oral Dictated Texts." *Classical Quarterly* 48 (1998): 1-13.

Kirk, G. S. *The Iliad: A Commentary.* Vol. 1, *Books 1-4.* Cambridge: Cambridge University Press, 1985.

————. *The Iliad: A Commentary.* Vol. 2, *Books 5-8.* Cambridge: Cambridge University Press, 1990.

Klonoski, Richard. "The Preservation of Homeric Tradition: Heroic Re-Performance in the 'Republic' and the 'Odyssey.'" *Clio* 22 (1993): 251-72.

Lateiner, Donald. "Homeric Prayer." *Arethusa* 30 (1997): 241-72.

Levaniouk, Olga. "Penelope and the Penelops." In *Nine Essays on Homer.* Edited by Miriam Carlisle and Olga Levaniouk, pp. 95-136. Lanham, Md.: Rowman & Littlefield, 1999.

Lloyd, G. E. R. *Methods and Problems in Greek Science.* Cambridge: Cambridge University Press, 1991.

————. *Polarity and Analogy: Two Types of Argumentation in Early Greek Thought.* Cambridge: Cambridge University Press, 1966.

————. *The Revolutions of Wisdom.* Berkeley: University of California Press, 1987.

Martin, Richard P. *The Language of Heroes: Speech and Performance in the* Iliad. Ithaca: Cornell University Press, 1989.

McGlew, James F. "Royal Power and the Achaean Assembly at *Iliad* 2.84-393." *Classical Antiquity* 8 (1989): 283-95.

Meier, Christian. "Emergence of an Autonomous Intelligence among the Greeks." In *The Origins and Diversity of Axial Age Civilizations.* Edited by S. N. Eisenstadt, pp. 65-91. Albany, N.Y.: SUNY Press, 1986.

Morris, Ian. *Archaeology as Cultural History.* Oxford: Blackwell, 2000.

————. "The Use and Abuse of Homer." *Classical Antiquity* 5 (1986): 81-138.

Morris, Sarah. "Homer and the Near East." In *A New Companion to Homer.* Edited by Ian Morris and Barry Powell, pp. 599-623. Leiden: Brill, 1997.

Mosse, Claude. "Inventing Politics." In *Greek Thought: A Guide to Classical Knowledge*, pp. 147-62. Cambridge, Mass.: Harvard University Press, 2000.

Most, Glenn. "From *Mythos* to *Logos*." In *From Myth to Reason?* Edited by Richard Buxton, pp. 25-47. Oxford: Oxford University Press, 1999.

———. "The Poetics of Early Greek Philosophy." In *The Cambridge Companion to Early Greek Philosophy*. Edited by A. A. Long, pp. 332-62. Cambridge: Cambridge University Press, 1999.

Muellner, Leonard. *The Anger of Achilles: "Mēnis" in Greek Epic*. Ithaca: Cornell University Press, 1996.

Murray, Oswyn. "Cities of Reason." In *The Greek City from Homer to Alexander*. Edited by Oswyn Murray and Simon Price, pp. 1-25. Oxford: Clarendon, 1990.

Naddaf, Gerard. "Translator's Introduction." In Luc Brisson, *Plato the Myth Maker*, pp. vii-xi. Chicago: University of Chicago Press, 1998.

Nagler, Michael N. "Dread Goddess Revisited." In *Reading the Odyssey: Selected Interpretive Essays*. Edited by Seth Schein, pp. 141-62. Princeton: Princeton University Press, 1996.

Nagy, Gregory. *The Best of the Achaeans: Concepts of the Hero in Archaic Greek Poetry*. Baltimore: Johns Hopkins University Press, 1979.

———. *Greek Mythology and Poetics*. Ithaca: Cornell University Press, 1990.

———. *Homeric Questions*. Austin: University of Texas Press, 1996.

———. *Poetry as Performance*. Cambridge: Cambridge University Press, 1996.

———. "Ancient Greek Poetry, Prophecy, and Concepts of Theory." In *Poetry and Prophecy*. Edited by James Kugel, pp. 56-66. Ithaca: Cornell University Press, 1990.

———. "An Evolutionary Model for the Making of Homeric Poetry: Comparative Perspectives." In *The Ages of Homer*. Edited by Jane Carter and Sarah Morris, pp. 163-79. Austin: University of Texas Press, 1995.

Naveh, Joseph. "Achish-Ikausu in the Light of the Ekron Dedication." *BASOR* 310 (1998): 35.

Nicolai, Walter. "Gefolgschaftsverweigerung als politisches Druckmittel in der *Ilias*." In *Anfänge politischen Denkens in der Antike: Die nahöstlichen Kulturen und die Griechen*. Edited by Kurt Raaflaub and Elisabeth Müller-Luckner, pp. 317-41. Munich: Oldenbourg, 1993.

Olson, S. Douglas. *Blood and Iron: Stories and Storytelling in Homer's Odyssey*. Leiden: Brill, 1995.

O'Neil, James L. *The Origins and Development of Ancient Greek Democracy*. Lanham, Md.: Rowman & Littlefield, 1995.

Page, Denys. *History and the Homeric Iliad*. Berkeley: University of California Press, 1972.

Patterson, Cynthia. *The Family in Greek History*. Cambridge, Mass.: Harvard University Press, 1998.

Polignac, François de. *Cults, Territory, and the Origins of the Greek City-State*. Chicago: University of Chicago Press, 1995.

Pratt, Louise. *Lying and Poetry from Homer to Pindar: Falsehood and Deception in Archaic Greek Poetics*. Ann Arbor: University of Michigan Press, 1993.

————. "Odyssey 19.535-50: On the Interpretation of Dreams and Signs in Homer." *Classical Philology* 89 (1994): 147-52.

Pucci, Pietro. *Odysseus Polutropos*. Ithaca: Cornell University Press, 1987.

————. *The Song of the Sirens*. New York: Rowman & Littlefield, 1998.

Raaflaub, Kurt. "A Historian's Headache: How to Read 'Homeric Society'?" In *Archaic Greece: New Approaches and New Evidence*. Edited by Nick Fisher and Hans van Wees, pp. 169-93. London: Duckworth, 1998.

————. "Homer and the Beginnings of Political Thought." *Proceedings of the Boston Area Colloquium in Ancient Philosophy* 4 (1988): 1-25.

————. "Homer to Solon: The Rise of the *Polis*: The Written Sources." In *The Ancient Greek City-State: Symposium on the Occasion of the 250th Anniversary of the Royal Danish Academy of Sciences and Letters, July 1-4, 1992*. Edited by Mogens H. Hansen, pp. 41-105. Copenhagen: Munksgaard, 1993.

————. "Influence, Adaptation, and Interaction: Near Eastern and Early Greek Political Thought." In *The Heirs of Assyria*. Edited by Sanna Aro and R. M. Whiting. Helsinki: Neo-Assyrian Text Corpus Project, 2000.

————. "Politics and Interstate Relations in the World of the Early Greek *Poleis*: Homer and Beyond." *Antichthon* 31 (1997): 1-27.

————. "Soldiers, Citizens, and the *Polis*." In *The Development of the Polis in Archaic Greece*. Edited by Lynette G. Mitchell and P. J. Rhodes, pp. 49-59. New York: Routledge, 1997.

Reden, Sitta von. "Re-evaluating Gernet: Value and Greek Myth." In *From Myth to Reason?* Edited by Richard Buxton, pp. 51-70. Oxford: Clarendon, 1999.

Redfield, James. "Foreword." In Gregory Nagy, *The Best of the Achaeans: Concepts of the Hero in Archaic Greek Poetry*, pp. ix-xi. Baltimore: Johns Hopkins University Press, 1979.

Reinhardt, Karl. "The Adventures in the *Odyssey*." In *Reading the Odyssey: Selected Interpretive Essays*. Edited by Seth Schein, pp. 63-132. Princeton: Princeton University Press, 1996.

Robertson, G. I. C. "The Eyes of Achilleus: *Iliad* 1.200." *Phoenix* 53 (1999): 1-7.

Rose, Peter. *Sons of the Gods, Children of Earth: Ideology and Literary Form in Ancient Greece*. Ithaca: Cornell University Press, 1992.

————. "Ideology in the *Iliad*: Polis, Basileus, Theoi." *Arethusa* 30 (1997): 151-99.

Russo, Joseph. "Oral Theory: Its Development in Homeric Studies and Applicability to Other Literatures." In *Mesopotamian Epic Literature: Oral or Aural?* Edited by Marianna E. Vogelzang and H. L. J. Vanstiphout, pp. 7-21. Lewiston, N.Y.: Mellen, 1992.

Sale, William. "The Government of Troy: Politics in the *Iliad*." *Greek, Roman and Byzantine Studies* 35 (1994): 5-102.

Schein, Seth. "Introduction." In *Reading the Odyssey: Selected Interpretive Essays*. Edited by Seth Schein, pp. 3-32. Princeton: Princeton University Press, 1996.

367

Scodel, Ruth. "The Achaean Wall and the Myth of Destruction." *Harvard Studies in Classical Philology* 86 (1982): 33-50.

Scully, Stephen. *Homer and the Sacred City.* Ithaca: Cornell University Press, 1990.

Seaford, Richard. *Reciprocity and Ritual: Homer and Tragedy in the Developing City-State.* Oxford: Clarendon, 1994.

Sealey, Raphael. *The Justice of the Greeks.* Ann Arbor: University of Michigan Press, 1994.

Segal, Charles. *Singers, Heroes, and Gods in the Odyssey.* Ithaca: Cornell University Press, 1994.

—————. "Kleos and Its Ironies." In *Reading the Odyssey: Selected Interpretive Essays.* Edited by Seth Schein, pp. 201-22. Princeton: Princeton University Press, 1996.

Sissa, Guila, and Marcel Detienne. *The Daily Life of the Greek Gods.* Stanford: Stanford University Press, 2000.

Slatkin, Laura. *The Power of Thetis: Allusion and Interpretation in the "Iliad."* Berkeley: University of California Press, 1991.

—————. "Composition by Theme and the *Mētis* of the Odyssey." In *Reading the Odyssey: Selected Interpretive Essays.* Edited by Seth Schein, pp. 223-38. Princeton: Princeton University Press, 1996.

Snodgrass, Anthony. *Dark Age of Greece.* Edinburgh: University Press, 1971.

Stafford, Emma. "*Themis:* Religion and Order in the Archaic *Polis.*" In *The Development of the "Polis" in Archaic Greece.* Edited by Lynette G. Mitchell and P. J. Rhodes, pp. 158-66. New York: Routledge, 1997.

Starr, Chester G. "The Decline of the Early Greek Kings." *Historia* 10 (1961): 129-30.

Svenbro, Jesper. *"Phrasikleia": An Anthropology of Reading in Ancient Greece.* Ithaca: Cornell University Press, 1993.

Tandy, David. *Warriors into Traders: The Power of the Market in Early Greece.* Berkeley: University of California Press, 1997.

Thalmann, William G. *The Swineherd and the Bow: Representations of Class in the Odyssey.* Ithaca: Cornell University Press, 1998.

Tsagalis, Christos. "Style and Construction, Sound and Rhythm: Thetis' Supplication to Zeus (*Iliad* 1.493-516)." *Arethusa* 34 (2001): 1-29.

Vernant, Jean-Pierre. *Mortals and Immortals.* Princeton: Princeton University Press, 1990.

—————. *Myth and Society in Ancient Greece.* Atlantic Highlands, N.J.: Humanities, 1980.

—————. "Death with Two Faces." In *Reading the Odyssey: Selected Interpretive Essays.* Edited by Seth Schein, pp. 55-62. Princeton: Princeton University Press, 1996.

—————. "Myth and Divinity." In *Myth, Religion, and Society.* Edited by Raymond L. Gordon, pp. 1-15. Cambridge: Cambridge University Press, 1977.

—————. "The Refusal of Odysseus." In *Reading the Odyssey: Selected Interpretive Essays.* Edited by Seth Schein, pp. 185-90. Princeton: Princeton University Press, 1996.

Vidal-Naquet, Pierre. *The Black Hunter: Forms of Thought and Forms of Society in the Greek World.* Baltimore: Johns Hopkins University Press, 1986.

—————. "Land and Sacrifice." In *Reading the Odyssey: Selected Interpretive Essays.* Edited by Seth Schein, pp. 33-54. Princeton: Princeton University Press, 1996.

Vlachos, Georges. *Les sociétés politiques homériques*. Paris: Presses Universitaires de France, 1974.

Wade-Gery, Henry. *The Poet of the Iliad*. Cambridge: Cambridge University Press, 1952.

Waldbaum, Jane C. "Greeks *in* the East or Greeks *and* the East? Problems in the Definition and Recognition of Presence." *BASOR* 305 (1997): 1-17.

Wason, Paul. *The Archaeology of Rank*. Cambridge: Cambridge University Press, 1996.

Wees, Hans van. *Status Warriors: War, Violence and Society in Homer and History*. Amsterdam: J. C. Gieben, 1992.

West, Martin. "The Date of the *Iliad*." *Museum Helveticum* 52 (1995): 151-72.

West, Stephanie. "Commentary on Books I-IV." In Alfred Heubeck, Stephanie West, and J. B. Hainsworth. *A Commentary on Homer's Odyssey*. Vol. 1, *Introduction and Books I-VIII*, pp. 48-245. Oxford: Clarendon, 1988.

Whitley, James. *Style and Society in Dark Age Greece: The Changing Face of a Pre-literate Society 1100-700 BC*. Cambridge: Cambridge University Press, 1991.

———. "Literacy and Law-making: The Case of Archaic Crete." In *Archaic Greece: New Approaches and New Evidence*. Edited by Nick Fisher and Hans van Wees, pp. 311-31. London: Duckworth, 1998.

Willcock, M. M. "Some Aspects of the Gods in the *Iliad*." In *Essays on the Iliad*. Edited by John Wright, pp. 58-69. Bloomington: Indiana University Press, 1978.

Winter, Irene. "Homer's Phoenicians: History, Ethnography, or Literary Trope? [A Perspective on Early Orientalism]." In *The Ages of Homer*. Edited by Jane Carter and Sarah Morris, pp. 247-71. Austin: University of Texas Press, 1995.

Yamagata, Naoko. "*Anax* and *Basileus* in Homer." *Classical Quarterly* 47 (1997): 1-14.

Ancient Israel

Ackroyd, Peter. *Studies in the Religious Tradition of the Old Testament*. London: SCM, 1987.

———. "Isaiah I-XII: Presentation of a Prophet." In *Congress Volume: Göttingen 1977*, pp. 16-48. VTSup 29. Leiden: Brill, 1978.

Albertz, Rainer. *A History of Israelite Religion in the Old Testament Period*. Vol. 1, *From the Beginnings to the End of the Monarchy*. Louisville: Westminster/John Knox, 1992.

———. *A History of Israelite Religion in the Old Testament Period*. Vol. 2, *From the Exiles to the Maccabees*. Louisville: Westminster/John Knox, 1994.

Allen, Leslie. *Psalms 101–150*. WBC 21. Waco, Tex.: Word, 1983.

Alt, Albrecht. *Essays on Old Testament History and Religion*. Garden City, N.Y.: Doubleday, 1968.

Anderson, Bernhard. *Contours of Old Testament Theology*. Minneapolis: Fortress, 1999.

Anderson, Gary. *Sacrifices and Offerings in Ancient Israel: Studies in Their Social and Political Importance*. HSM 41. Atlanta: Scholars, 1987.

Arnold, Bill T. "The Weidner Chronicle and the Idea of History in Israel and Mesopotamia." In *Faith, Tradition and History*. Edited by A. R. Millard et al., pp. 129-48. Winona Lake, Ind.: Eisenbrauns, 1994.

Astour, Michael. "Ezekiel's Prophecy of Gog and the Cuthean Legend of Naram-Sin." *JBL* 95 (1976): 567-79.

Bailey, Randall. *David in Love and War: The Pursuit of Power in 2 Samuel 10–12*. JSOTSup 75. Sheffield: Sheffield Academic Press, 1990.

Baines, John. "Kingship, Definition of Culture, and Legitimation." In *Ancient Egyptian Kingship*, pp. 3-47. Leiden: Brill, 1995.

Balentine, Samuel. *Prayer in the Hebrew Bible*. Minneapolis: Fortress, 1993.

Barstad, Hans. "Comparare necesse est? Ancient Israelite and Ancient Near Eastern Prophecy in Comparative Perspective." In *Prophecy in Its Ancient Near Eastern Context: Mesopotamian, Biblical, and Arabian Perspectives*, pp. 3-11. SBL Symposium Series 13. Atlanta: Society for Biblical Literature, 2000.

———. "No Prophets? Recent Developments in Biblical Prophetic Research and Ancient Near Eastern Prophecy." *JSOT* 57 (1993): 39-60.

Batto, Bernard. "Paradise Reexamined." In *The Biblical Canon in Comparative Perspective: Scripture in Context IV*. Edited by K. Lawson Younger, Jr. et al., pp. 33-66. Lewiston, N.Y.: Mellen, 1991.

Beaucamp, Évode. *Le psautier*. 2 vols. Paris: Gabalda, 1979.

Bernhardt, Karl. *Das Problem der altorientalischen Königsideologie im Alten Testament*. VTSup 8. Leiden: Brill, 1961.

Birch, Bruce. "The Development of the Tradition on the Anointing of Saul in 1 Sam 9:1–10:16." *JBL* 90 (1971): 55-68.

Blenkinsopp, Joseph. *A History of Prophecy in Israel*. Rev. ed. Louisville: Westminster/John Knox, 1996.

———. *Isaiah 1–39*. AB 19. New York: Doubleday, 2000.

———. *The Pentateuch*. New York: Doubleday, 1992.

———. "Memory, Tradition, and the Construction of the Past in Ancient Israel." *BTB* 27 (1997): 76-82.

Block, Daniel I. *The Book of Ezekiel: Chapters 25–48*. Grand Rapids: Eerdmans, 1998.

Borowski, Oded. *Agriculture in Iron Age Israel*. Winona Lake, Ind.: Eisenbrauns, 1982.

Brenneman, James. *Canons in Conflict: Negotiating Texts in True and False Prophecy*. New York: Oxford University Press, 1997.

Brettler, Marc. "Biblical Literature as Politics: The Case of Samuel." In *Religion and Politics in the Ancient Near East*. Edited by Adele Berlin, pp. 71-92. Bethesda: University Press of Maryland, 1996.

Bright, John. *History of Israel*. 3rd ed. Philadelphia: Westminster, 1981.

Brueggemann, Walter. *First and Second Samuel*. Louisville: John Knox, 1990.

———. *The Message of the Psalms*. Minneapolis: Augsburg, 1984.

———. *Theology of the Old Testament: Testimony, Dispute, Advocacy*. Minneapolis: Fortress, 1997.

———. "Pharaoh as Vassal: A Study of a Political Metaphor." *CBQ* 57 (1995): 27-51.

Carr, David. *Reading the Fractures of Genesis*. Louisville: Westminster/John Knox, 1996.

Cazelles, Henri. "David's Monarchy and the Gibeonite Claim." *PEQ* 87 (1955): 165-75.

Childs, Brevard. *Exodus*. Philadelphia: Westminster, 1974.

———. *Isaiah*. Louisville: Westminster/John Knox, 2001.

Clements, R. E. *Isaiah 1–39*. Grand Rapids: Eerdmans, 1980.

Clifford, Richard. *Creation Accounts in the Ancient Near East and in the Bible*. CBQMS 26. Washington: Catholic Biblical Association, 1994.

———. "Psalm 89: A Lament over the Davidic Ruler's Continued Failure." *HTR* 73 (1980): 35-47.

Cohn, Robert. "Convention and Creativity in the Book of Kings: The Case of the Dying Monarch." *CBQ* 47 (1985): 603-16.

Collins, Terence. "Deuteronomist Influence on the Prophetical Books." In *The Book of Jeremiah and Its Reception*. Edited by A. H. W. Curtis and Thomas Römer, pp. 15-26. BETL 128. Leuven: University Press, 1997.

Cooper, Alan. "The Life and Times of King David According to the Book of Psalms." In *The Poet and the Historian: Essays in Literary and Historical Biblical Criticism*, pp. 125, 129-30. HSM 26. Chico, Calif.: Scholars, 1983.

Craigie, Peter. *Psalms 1–50*. WBC 19. Waco, Tex.: Word, 1983.

Crenshaw, James. *A Whirlpool of Lament*. Philadelphia: Fortress, 1984.

Cross, Frank Moore. *From Epic to Canon: History and Literature in Ancient Israel*. Baltimore: Johns Hopkins University Press, 1998.

Crüsemann, Frank. *Der Widerstand gegen das Königtum*. WMANT 49. Neukirchen-Vluyn: Neukirchener Verlag, 1978.

Cryer, Frederick. *Divination in Ancient Israel and Its Near Eastern Environment*. JSOTSup 142. Sheffield: Sheffield Academic Press, 1994.

Daube, David. "Absalom and the Ideal King." *VT* 48 (1998): 315-25.

Davies, Eryl W. "Land: Its Rights and Privileges." In *The World of Ancient Israel*. Edited by Ronald E. Clements, pp. 349-57. Cambridge: Cambridge University Press, 1987.

DeVries, Simon. *From Old Revelation to New*. Grand Rapids: Eerdmans, 1995.

———. *Prophet Against Prophet: The Role of the Micaiah Narrative (1 Kings 22) in the Development of the Early Prophetic Tradition*. Grand Rapids: Eerdmans, 1978.

Diamond, A. R. *The Confessions of Jeremiah in Context: Scenes of Prophetic Drama*. JSOTSup 45. Sheffield: Sheffield Academic Press, 1987.

DiVito, Robert. "Old Testament Anthropology and the Construction of Personal Identity." *CBQ* 61 (1999): 217-38.

Douglas, Mary. *Purity and Danger*. London: Routledge & Kegan Paul, 1966.

Durham, John. *Exodus*. WBC 3. Waco, Tex.: Word, 1987.

Edenburg, Cynthia. "How (Not) to Murder a King: Variations on a Theme in 1 Sam 24; 26." *SJOT* 12 (1998): 64-85.

Edwards, Douglas R. "Tyre." In *ABD*, 6:690-91.

Eynikel, Erik. *The Reform of King Josiah and the Composition of the Deuteronomistic History*. OTS 33. Leiden: Brill, 1996.

Ferris, Paul W., Jr. *The Genre of Communal Lament in the Bible and the Ancient Near East*. SBLDS 127. Atlanta: Scholars, 1992.

Finkelstein, Israel. "The Emergence of the Monarchy in Israel: The Environmental and Sociological Aspects." *JSOT* 44 (1989): 43-74.

Fishbane, Michael. *Biblical Interpretation in Ancient Israel*. Oxford: Clarendon, 1985.

Flanagan, James. *David's Social Drama: A Hologram of Israel's Early Iron Age*. Social World of Biblical Antiquity Series 7. Sheffield: Almond, 1988.

———. "Chiefs in Israel." *JSOT* 20 (1981): 647-73.

Fokkelman, J. P. *Narrative Art and Poetry in the Books of Samuel*. Vol. 1, *King David*. Studia Semitica Neerlandica 20. Assen: Van Gorcum, 1981.

Freedman, David Noel, with Jeffrey C. Geoghegan and Michael M. Homan. *The Nine Commandments: Uncovering a Hidden Pattern of Crime and Punishment in the Hebrew Bible*. Edited by Astrid Beck. New York: Doubleday, 2000.

Fretheim, Terence. *Exodus*. Louisville: John Knox, 1991.

Glatt-Gilad, David. "The Deuteronomistic Critique of Solomon: A Response to Marvin A. Sweeney." *JBL* 116 (1997): 700-703.

Greenberg, Moshe. *Ezekiel 21–37*. AB 22A. New York: Doubleday, 1997.

Gottwald, Norman. *The Politics of Ancient Israel*. Louisville: Westminster/John Knox, 2001.

Gowan, Donald. *Theology of the Prophetic Books: The Death and Resurrection of Israel*. Louisville: Westminster/John Knox, 1998.

Gunn, David. *The Story of King David: Genre and Interpretation*. JSOTSup 6. Sheffield: JSOT Press, 1978.

Halpern, Baruch. *The Constitution of the Monarchy in Israel*. HSM 25. Chico, Calif.: Scholars, 1981.

———. *David's Secret Demons: Messiah, Murderer, Traitor, King*. Grand Rapids: Eerdmans, 2001.

———. "The Uneasy Compromise: Israel Between League and Monarchy." In *Traditions in Transformation*. Edited by Baruch Halpern and Jon Levenson, pp. 59-96. Winona Lake, Ind.: Eisenbrauns, 1981.

Hals, Ronald M. *Ezekiel*. FOTL 19. Grand Rapids: Eerdmans, 1989.

Hanson, K. C. "When the King Crosses the Line: Royal Deviance and Restitution in Levantine Ideologies." *BTB* 26 (1996): 11-25.

Heim, Knut. "The (God-)Forsaken King of Psalm 89: A Historical and Intertextual Enquiry." In *King and Messiah in Israel and the Ancient Near East*. Edited by John Day, pp. 296-322. JSOTSup 270. Sheffield: Sheffield Academic Press, 1998.

Herion, Gary. "Why God Rejected Cain's Offering: The Obvious Answer." In *Fortunate the Eyes That See: Essays in Honor of David Noel Freedman in Celebration of His Seventieth Birthday*. Edited by Astrid Beck et al., pp. 52-65. Grand Rapids: Eerdmans, 1995.

Hertzberg, Hans W. *I & II Samuel*. Philadelphia: Westminster, 1964.

Hoffmann, Yair. "The Concept of 'Other Gods' in the Deuteronomistic Literature." In *Politics and Theopolitics in the Bible and Postbiblical Literature*. Edited by H. G. Reventlow et al., pp. 66-99. JSOTSup 171. Sheffield: Sheffield Academic Press, 1994.

Holladay, William. *Jeremiah 1: A Biblical Commentary on the Book of the Prophet Jeremiah Chapters 1–25.* Philadelphia: Fortress, 1986.

―――. *The Psalms Through Three Thousand Years.* Minneapolis: Fortress, 1996.

Houston, Walter. *Purity and Monotheism: Clean and Unclean Animals in Biblical Law.* JSOTSup 140. Sheffield: Sheffield Academic Press, 1993.

Houtman, Cornelius. *Exodus.* 3 vols. Kampen: Kok, 1993.

Howard, David M. "David." In *ABD*, 2:41-49.

Ishida, Tomoo. *History and Historical Writing in Ancient Israel: Studies in Biblical Historiography.* Leiden: Brill, 1999.

Janowski, Bernd. *Stellvertretung: Alttestamentliche Studien zu einem theologischen Grundbegriff.* Stuttgart: Verlag Katholisches Bibelwerk, 1997.

Kaiser, Otto. "Erwägungen zu Psalm 101." *ZAW* 74 (1962): 195-205.

Kapelrud, Arvid. "King and Fertility: A Discussion of II Sam 21:1-14." *Norsk Teologisk Tidsskrift* 56 (1955): 113-22.

Katzenstein, H. J. "Tyre." In *ABD*, 6:686-90.

Keel, Othmar, and Christoph Uehlinger. *God, Goddesses, and Images of God in Ancient Israel.* Minneapolis: Fortress, 1998.

Keller, Sharon. "Written Communication Between the Human and Divine Spheres in Mesopotamia and Israel." In *The Biblical Canon in Comparative Perspective: Scripture in Context IV.* Edited by K. Lawson Younger, Jr. et al., pp. 299-313. Lewiston, N.Y.: Mellen, 1991.

Kenik, Helen. "Code of Conduct for a King: Psalm 101." *JBL* 95 (1976): 391-403.

Kessler, Rainer. "Gott und König, Grundeigentum und Fruchtbarkeit." *ZAW* 108 (1996): 214-32.

Kitz, Anne Marie. "The Hebrew Terminology of Lot Casting and Its Ancient Near Eastern Context." *CBQ* 62 (2000): 207-14.

Knight, Douglas. "Political Rights and Powers in Monarchic Israel." *Semeia* 66 (1994): 93-117.

Knoppers, Gary. *Two Nations Under God: The Deuteronomistic History of Solomon and the Dual Monarchies.* 2 vols. HSM 52/53. Atlanta: Scholars, 1993, 1994.

―――. "The Deuteronomist and the Deuteronomic Law of the King: A Reexamination of a Relationship." *ZAW* 108 (1996): 329-46.

―――. "Introduction." In *Reconsidering Israel and Judah: Recent Studies on the Deuteronomistic History.* Edited by Gary Knoppers and J. G. McConville, pp. 1-18. Winona Lake, Ind.: Eisenbrauns, 2000.

―――. "The Vanishing Solomon: The Disappearance of the United Monarchy from Recent Histories of Ancient Israel." *JBL* 116 (1997): 19-44.

Koch, Klaus. *The Prophets.* Vol. 1, *The Assyrian Period.* Philadelphia: Fortress, 1982.

―――. "Die Entstehung der sozialen Kritik bei den Profeten." In *Probleme biblischer Theologie: Gerhard von Rad zum 70. Geburtstag.* Edited by Hans W. Wolff, pp. 236-57. Munich: Kaiser, 1971.

―――. "The Language of Prophecy." In *Problems in Biblical Theology: Essays in Honor of Rolf Knierim*. Edited by Henry T. C. Sun et al., pp. 210-21. Grand Rapids: Eerdmans, 1997.

Kraus, Hans-Joachim. *Psalms 1–59*. Minneapolis: Augsburg, 1988.

———. *Psalms 60–150*. Minneapolis: Augsburg, 1989.

Kugel, James. "David the Prophet." In *Poetry and Prophecy*. Edited by James Kugel, pp. 45-55. Ithaca: Cornell University Press, 1990.

Laato, Antii. *A Star Is Rising: The Historical Development of the Old Testament Royal Ideology and the Rise of the Jewish Messianic Expectations*. Atlanta: Scholars, 1997.

———. *Who Is Immanuel? The Rise and the Foundering of Isaiah's Messianic Expectations*. Abo: Abo Academy Press, 1988.

———. "Psalm 132 and the Development of the Jerusalem/Israelite Royal Ideology." *CBQ* 54 (1992): 49-66.

———. "Second Samuel 7 and Near Eastern Royal Ideology." *CBQ* 59 (1997): 244-69.

Lemaire, André. "Wisdom in Solomonic Historiography." In *Wisdom in Ancient Israel: Essays in Honour of J. A. Emerton*. Edited by John Day et al., pp. 106-18. Cambridge: Cambridge University Press, 1995.

Lemche, Neils. "David's Rise." *JSOT* 10 (1978): 2-25.

———. "From Patronage Society to Patronage Society." In *The Origins of the Ancient Israelite States*. Edited by Volkmar Fritz and Philip R. Davies, pp. 106-20. JSOTSup 228. Sheffield: Sheffield Academic Press, 1996.

———. "Kings and Clients: On Loyalty between the Ruler and the Ruled in Ancient Israel." *Semeia* 66 (1995): 119-32.

Levenson, Jon. "1 Samuel 25 as Literature and History." *CBQ* 40 (1978): 11-28.

———. "The Davidic Covenant and Its Interpreters." *CBQ* 41 (1979): 205-19.

Levinson, Bernard M. *Deuteronomy and the Hermeneutics of Legal Innovation*. New York: Oxford University Press, 1997.

———. "The Reconceptualization of Kingship in Deuteronomy." Forthcoming.

Lewis, Theodore. *Cults of the Dead in Ancient Israel and Ugarit*. HSM 39. Atlanta: Scholars, 1989.

———. "Ancestor Worship." In *ABD*, 1:240-42.

———. "Banqueting Hall/House." In *ABD*, 1:581-82.

Liverani, Mario. "The Trade Network of Tyre." In *Ah, Assyria . . . Studies in Assyrian History and Ancient Near Eastern Historiography Presented to Hayim Tadmor*, pp. 65-79. ScrHier 33. Jerusalem: Magnes, 1991.

Lohfink, Norbert. "The Cult Reform of Josiah of Judah: 2 Kings 22–23 as a Source for the History of Israelite Religion." In *Ancient Israelite Religion*. Edited by Patrick D. Miller, Jr. et al., pp. 459-75. Philadelphia: Fortress, 1987.

Long, Burke O. *1 Kings with an Introduction to Historical Literature*. FOTL 9. Grand Rapids: Eerdmans, 1984.

Martin-Achard, Robert. "La vigne de Naboth (1 Rois 21) d'après des études récentes." *ETR* 66 (1991): 1-14.

Mayes, A. D. H. *Deuteronomy*. Grand Rapids: Eerdmans, 1979.

———. *The Story of Israel between Settlement and Exile*. London: SCM, 1983.

Mays, James L. *Psalms*. Louisville: John Knox, 1994.

McCarter, P. Kyle, Jr. *I Samuel*. AB 8. Garden City, N.Y.: Doubleday, 1980.

————. *II Samuel*. AB 9. Garden City, N.Y.: Doubleday, 1984.

————. "The Apology of David." *JBL* 99 (1980): 500.

————. "The Ritual Dedication of the City of David in 2 Samuel 6." In *The Word Shall Go Forth: Essays in Honor of David Noel Freedman in Celebration of His Sixtieth Birthday*. Edited by Carol Meyers and M. O'Connor, pp. 273-78. Winona Lake, Ind.: Eisenbrauns, 1983.

McCarthy, Dennis J. "Compact and Kingship: Stimuli for Hebrew Covenant Thinking." In *Studies in the Period of David and Solomon and Other Essays*. Edited by Tomoo Ishida, pp. 75-92. Winona Lake, Ind.: Eisenbrauns, 1982.

————. "The Inauguration of the Monarchy in Israel: A Form-Critical Study in 1 Samuel 8–12." *Int* 27 (1973): 401-12.

McKenzie, Steven. *King David: A Biography*. New York: Oxford University Press, 2000.

Mendelsohn, Isaac. "Samuel's Denunciation of the Kingship in Light of Akkadian Documents from Ugarit." *BASOR* 143 (1956): 17-22.

Mettinger, Tryggve. "Israelite Aniconism: Developments and Origins." In *The Image and the Book*. Edited by Karel van der Toorn, pp. 173-204. Biblical Exegesis and Theology 21. Leuven: Peeters, 1997.

Meyers, Carol. "David as Temple Builder." In *Ancient Israelite Religion*. Edited by Patrick D. Miller, Jr. et al., pp. 262-63. Philadelphia: Fortress, 1987.

————. "The Family in Early Israel." In *Families in Ancient Israel*. Edited by Leo Perdue, pp. 1-47. Louisville: Westminster/John Knox, 1997.

Milgrom, Jacob. *Leviticus 1–16*. AB 3. New York: Doubleday, 1991.

Miller, J. Maxwell. "Separating the Solomon of History from the Solomon of Legend." In *The Age of Solomon: Scholarship at the Turn of the Millennium*. Edited by Lowell Handy, pp. 1-24. Leiden: Brill, 1997.

Miller, Patrick D., Jr. *Deuteronomy*. Louisville: John Knox, 1990.

Miscall, Peter. *1 Samuel: A Literary Reading*. Bloomington: Indiana University Press, 1986.

Mobley, Gregory. "The Wild Man in the Bible and the Ancient Near East." *JBL* 116 (1997): 217-33.

Moor, Johannes C. de. "The Duality in God and Man: Gen. 1:26-27 as P's Interpretation of the Yahwistic Creation Account." In *Intertextuality in Ugarit and Israel*, pp. 112-25. OTS 40. Leiden: Brill, 1998.

Mowinckel, Sigmund. *The Psalms in Israel's Worship*. Oxford: Blackwell, 1962.

Myers, J. M. "David." In *IDB*, 1:782A.

Na'aman, Nadav. "Prophetic Stories as Sources for the Histories of Jehoshaphat and the Omrides." *Bib* 78 (1997): 153-73.

Nelson, Richard. *First and Second Kings*. Louisville: John Knox, 1987.

Nicholson, Ernest. *Pentateuch in the Twentieth Century: The Legacy of Julius Wellhausen*. Oxford: Clarendon, 1998.

————. "The Origin of the Tradition in Exodus XXIV 9-11." *VT* 26 (1976): 148-60.

Niditch, Susan. *Underdogs and Tricksters: A Prelude to Biblical Folklore.* San Francisco: Harper & Row, 1987.

Niehr, Herbert. "In Search of YHWH's Cult Statue in the First Temple." In *The Image and the Book.* Edited by Karel van der Toorn, pp. 73-95. Biblical Exegesis and Theology 21. Leuven: Peeters, 1997.

North, Robert. "The Chronicler: 1-2 Chronicles, Ezra, Nehemiah." In *New Jerome Biblical Commentary* (1990), 23:40.

Noth, Martin. *Leviticus.* Philadelphia: Westminster, 1965.

O'Connor, Kathleen. *The Confessions of Jeremiah: Their Interpretation and Role in Chapters 1–25.* SBLDS 94. Atlanta: Scholars, 1988.

Oden, Robert. "Divine Aspirations in Atrahasis and in Genesis 1–11." *ZAW* 93 (1982): 197-216.

Olyan, Saul. *Asherah and the Cult of Yahweh in Israel.* SBLMS 34. Atlanta: Scholars, 1988.

———. *Rites and Rank: Hierarchy in Biblical Representations of Cult.* Princeton: Princeton University Press, 2000.

———. "Honor, Shame, and Covenant Relations in Ancient Israel and Its Environment." *JBL* 115 (96): 201-18.

Otto, Eckart. "Aspects of Legal Reforms and Reformulations in Ancient Cuneiform and Israelite Law." In *Theory and Method in Biblical and Cuneiform Law: Revision, Interpolation and Development.* Edited by Bernard Levinson, pp. 160-96. JSOTSup 181. Sheffield: Sheffield Academic Press, 1994.

Parker, Simon. "Official Attitudes Toward Prophecy at Mari and in Israel." *VT* 43 (1993): 50-68.

Patton, Corrine. "Psalm 132: A Methodological Inquiry." *CBQ* 57 (1995): 643-54.

Perdue, Leo. *Wisdom and Creation: The Theology of Wisdom Literature.* Nashville: Abingdon, 1994.

———. "The Israelite and Early Jewish Family: Summary and Conclusions." In *Families in Ancient Israel.* Edited by Leo Perdue, pp. 163-222. Louisville: Westminster/John Knox, 1997.

Polzin, Robert. *David and the Deuteronomist: A Literary Study of the Deuteronomistic History, Part III, 2 Samuel.* Bloomington: Indiana University Press, 1993.

Pope, Marvin. *El in the Ugaritic Texts.* Leiden: Brill, 1955.

Rad, Gerhard von. *Genesis.* Philadelphia: Westminster, 1974.

———. *Old Testament Theology.* Vol. 1, *The Theology of Israel's Historical Traditions.* New York: Harper & Row, 1962.

Reviv, H. "The Structure of Society." In *The World History of the Jewish People.* Vol. 4, Part 2, *The Age of the Monarchies: Culture and Society.* Edited by Abraham Malamat, pp. 125-46. Jerusalem: Masada, 1979.

Roberts, J. J. M. "In Defense of the Monarchy: The Contribution of Israelite Kingship to Biblical Theology." In *Ancient Israelite Religion: Essays in Honor of Frank Moore Cross.* Edited by Patrick D. Miller, Jr. et al., pp. 377-96. Philadelphia: Fortress, 1987.

Rogerson, John. *Myth in Old Testament Interpretation.* BZAW 114. New York: Walter de Gruyter, 1974.

376

Salveson, Alison. "The Trappings of Royalty in Ancient Hebrew." In *King and Messiah in Israel and the Ancient Near East.* Edited by John Day, pp. 119-41. JSOTSup 270. Sheffield: Sheffield Academic Press, 1998.

Sarna, Nahum. *Genesis.* New York: JPS, 1989.

———. "Naboth's Vineyard Revisited (1 Kings 21)." In *Tehillah le-Moshe: Biblical and Judaic Studies in Honor of Moshe Greenberg,* pp. 119-26. Winona Lake, Ind.: Eisenbrauns, 1997.

Schäfer-Lichtenberger, Christa. "Sociological and Biblical Views of the Early State." In *The Origins of the Ancient Israelite States.* Edited by Volkmar Fritz and Philip R. Davies, pp. 78-105. JSOTSup 228. Sheffield: Sheffield Academic Press, 1996.

Schmidt, Brian. *Israel's Beneficent Dead: Ancestor Cult and Necromancy in Ancient Israelite Religion and Tradition.* Winona Lake, Ind.: Eisenbrauns, 1996.

———. "The Aniconic Tradition: On Reading Images and Viewing Texts." In *The Triumph of Elohim: From Yahwisms to Judaisms.* Edited by Diana Edelman, pp. 75-105. Grand Rapids: Eerdmans, 1995.

Schmidt, Ludwig. *Menschlicher Erfolg und Jahwes Initiative.* WMANT 38. Neukirchen-Vluyn: Neukirchener Verlag, 1970.

Schniedewind, William. *Society and the Promise to David: The Reception History of 2 Samuel 7:1-17.* New York: Oxford University Press, 1999.

Seitz, Christopher. *Isaiah 1–39.* Louisville: John Knox, 1993.

Seow, C. L. *Myth, Drama, and the Politics of David's Dance.* HSM 44. Atlanta: Scholars, 1989.

Seters, John van. *In Search of History: Historiography in the Ancient World and the Origins of Biblical History.* New Haven: Yale University Press, 1983.

———. "The Creation of Man and the Creation of the King." *ZAW* 101 (1989): 333-42.

Shea, William. "Famine," In *ABD,* 2:769-73.

Silver, Morris. "Prophets and Markets Revisited." In *Social Justice in the Ancient World.* Edited by K. D. Irani and Morris Silver, pp. 179-98. Westport, Conn.: Greenwood, 1995.

Silverman, David. "The Nature of Egyptian Kingship." In *Ancient Egyptian Kingship.* Edited by David O'Connor and David Silverman, pp. 49-92. Leiden: Brill, 1995.

Smith, Mark S. *The Early History of God.* San Francisco: Harper & Row, 1990.

———. *The Laments of Jeremiah and Their Contexts.* SBLMS 42. Atlanta: Scholars, 1990.

Spieckermann, Hermann. *Judah unter Assur in der Sargonidenzeit.* FRLANT 129. Göttingen: Vandenhoeck & Ruprecht, 1982.

Spina, Frank. "The 'Ground' for Cain's Rejection: *'ǎdāmāh* in the Context of Gen 1–11." *ZAW* 104 (1992): 319-32.

Stager, Lawrence. "The Archaeology of the Family in Ancient Israel." *BASOR* 260 (1985): 1-36.

Starbuck, Scott. *Court Oracles in the Psalms: The So-Called Royal Psalms in Their Ancient Near Eastern Context.* SBLDS 172. Atlanta: Scholars, 1999.

Sweeney, Marvin. *Isaiah 1–39 with an Introduction to Prophetic Literature.* FOTL 16. Grand Rapids: Eerdmans, 1996.

————. "The Critique of Solomon in the Josianic Edition of the Deuteronomistic History." *JBL* 114 (1995): 607-22.

Tadmor, Hayim. "Traditional Institutions and the Monarchy: Social and Political Tensions in the Time of David and Solomon." In *Studies in the Period of David and Solomon and Other Essays.* Edited by Tomoo Ishida, pp. 239-57. Winona Lake, Ind.: Eisenbrauns, 1982.

Tate, Marvin. *Psalms 51–100.* WBC 20. Dallas: Word, 1990.

Terrien, Samuel. *The Elusive Presence.* New York: Harper & Row, 1978.

Toorn, Karel van der. *Family Religion in Babylonia, Syria and Israel.* Leiden: Brill, 1996.

————. "The Iconic Book Analogies Between the Babylonian Cult of Images and the Veneration of the Torah." In *The Image and the Book.* Edited by Karel van der Toorn, pp. 229-48. Biblical Exegesis and Theology 21. Leuven: Peeters, 1997.

————. "Ritual Resistance and Self-Assertion: The Rechabites in Early Israelite Religion." In *Pluralism and Identity: Studies in Ritual Behavior.* Edited by Jan Platvoet and Karel van der Toorn, pp. 229-60. Studies in the History of Religion 67. Leiden: Brill, 1995.

————. "Saul and the Rise of Israelite State Religion." *VT* 43 (1993): 519-42.

Tucker, Gene. "Sin and 'Judgment' in the Prophets." In *Problems in Biblical Theology: Essays in Honor of Rolf Knierim.* Edited by Henry T. C. Sun et al., pp. 373-88. Grand Rapids: Eerdmans, 1997.

Uehlinger, Christoph. "Anthropomorphic Cult Statuary in Iron Age Palestine and the Search for Yahweh's Cult Images." In *The Image and the Book.* Edited by Karel van der Toorn, pp. 97-155. Biblical Exegesis and Theology 21. Leuven: Peeters, 1997.

Uffenheimer, Benjamin. *Early Prophecy in Israel.* Jerusalem: Magnes, 1999.

Vaux, Roland de. *Ancient Israel.* 2 vols. New York: McGraw-Hill, 1965.

Verhey, Allen. "Remember, Remembrance." In *ABD,* 5:667-69.

Walsh, Jerome. *1 Kings.* Collegeville, Minn.: Liturgical, 1996.

————. "The Characterization of Solomon." *CBQ* 57 (1995): 471-93.

Ward, Graham. "Biblical Narrative and the Theology of Metonymy." *Modern Theology* 7 (1991): 335-49.

Weinfeld, Moshe. *Deuteronomy 1–11.* AB 5. New York: Doubleday, 1991.

————. *Social Justice in Ancient Israel and in the Ancient Near East.* Minneapolis: Fortress, 1995.

————. "Jeremiah and the Spiritual Metamorphosis of Israel." *ZAW* 88 (1976): 2-55.

————. "The Uniqueness of the Decalogue and Its Place in Jewish Tradition." In *The Ten Commandments in History and Tradition.* Edited by B.-Z. Segal, pp. 1-44. Jerusalem: Magnes, 1990.

Weippert, Manfred. "Heiliger Krieg in Israel und Assyrien." *ZAW* 84 (1972): 459-93.

Weiser, Artur. *Samuel: seine geschichtliche Aufgabe und religiöse Bedeutung.* FRLANT 81. Göttingen: Vandenhoeck & Ruprecht, 1962.

Weitzman, Steven. "David's Lament and the Poetics of Grief in 2 Samuel." *JQR* 85 (1995): 341-60.

Westermann, Claus. *Praise and Lament in the Psalms.* Atlanta: John Knox, 1981.

Whitelam, Keith W. *The Just King: Monarchical Judicial Authority in Ancient Israel.* JSOTSup 12. Sheffield: JSOT Press, 1979.

Whybray, R. N. *The Succession Narrative: A Study of II Samuel 9–20; 1 Kings 1–2.* SBT 9. 2nd series. Naperville, Ill.: Allenson, 1968.

Wildberger, Hans. *Isaiah 1–12.* Minneapolis: Fortress, 1991.

Williams, Anthony J. "Mythological Background of Ezekiel 28:12-19?" *BTB* 6 (1976): 49-61.

Williams, James. "Sacrifice and the Beginning of Kingship." *Semeia* 67 (1994): 73-92.

Williamson, H. G. M. *The Book Called Isaiah: Deutero-Isaiah's Role in Composition and Redaction.* Oxford: Clarendon, 1994.

———. *Variations on a Theme: King, Messiah and Servant in the Book of Isaiah.* Carlisle, U.K.: Paternoster, 1998.

———. "Hezekiah and the Temple." In *Texts, Temples, and Traditions: A Tribute to Menahem Haran.* Edited by Michael Fox et al. Winona Lake, Ind.: Eisenbrauns, 1996.

Wilson, Gerald. *The Editing of the Hebrew Psalter.* SBLDS 76. Chico, Calif.: Scholars, 1985.

Wilson, Robert. *Prophecy and Society in Ancient Israel.* Philadelphia: Fortress, 1980.

———. "The Death of the King of Tyre: The Editorial History of Ezekiel 28." In *Love and Death in the Ancient Near East: Essays in Honor of Marvin H. Pope.* Edited by John H. Marks and Robert M. Good, pp. 211-18. Guilford, Conn.: Four Quarters, 1987.

———. "Genealogy, Genealogies." In *ABD,* 2:929-32.

Wright, David. "Unclean and Clean." In *ABD,* 6:729-41.

Würthwein, Ernst. *Die Bücher der Könige.* 2 vols. ATD 11/1-2. Göttingen: Vandenhoeck & Ruprecht, 1977, 1984.

Zenger, Erich. "Die Verheissung Jesaja 11,1-10: Universal oder Partikular?" In *Studies in the Book of Isaiah.* Edited by J. van Ruiten and M. Vervenne, pp. 137-47. BETL 132. Leuven: Leuven University Press, 1997.

Zimmerli, Walter. *Ezekiel 2.* Philadelphia: Fortress, 1983.

Ancient Mesopotamia

Abusch, Tzvi. "Ishtar's Proposal and Gilgamesh's Refusal: An Interpretation of *The Gilgamesh Epic,* Tablet 6, Lines 1-79." *History of Religions* 26 (1986): 143-87.

Alster, Bendt. "Epic Tales from Ancient Sumer: Enmerkar, Lugalbanda, and Other Cunning Heroes." In *Civilizations of the Ancient Near East.* Edited by Jack Sasson, pp. 2315-16. New York: Scribner, 1995.

Anbar, Moshe. *Les tribus amurrites de Mari.* OBO 108. Freiburg: Universitätsverlag, 1991.

———. "Mari and the Origin of Prophecy." In *Kinattūtu ša darāti.* Edited by Anson F. Rainey, pp. 1-5. Tel Aviv: University of Tel Aviv Press, 1993.

Artzi, P., and A. Malamat. "The Correspondence of Šibtu, Queen of Mari in ARM X." *Or* n.s. 40 (1971): 75-89.

Asher-Greve, Julia M., and Lawrence Asher-Greve. "From Thales to Foucault . . . and Back to Sumer." In *Intellectual Life of the Ancient Near East.* Edited by Jiří Prosecký, pp. 29-40. CRRA 43. Prague: Oriental Institute, 1998.

Berlejung, Angelika. "Washing the Mouth: The Consecration of Divine Images in Mesopotamia." In *The Image and the Book.* Edited by Karel van der Toorn, pp. 45-72. Leuven: Peeters, 1997.

Black, Jeremy, and Anthony Green. *Gods, Demons and Symbols of Ancient Mesopotamia.* Austin: University of Texas Press, 1992.

Borger, Rykle. *Babylonisch-assyrische Lesestücke.* AnOr 54. Rome: Pontifical Biblical Institute, 1979.

Bottéro, Jean. *Mesopotamia: Writing, Reasoning, and the Gods.* Chicago: University of Chicago Press, 1992.

———. "Les noms de Marduk, l'écriture et la 'logique' en Mésopotamie ancienne." In *Essays on the Ancient Near East in Memory of Jacob Joel Finkelstein.* Edited by Maria de Jong Ellis, pp. 5-28. Memoirs of the Connecticut Academy of Arts & Sciences. Hamden, Conn.: Archon, 1977.

———. "Religion and Reasoning in Mesopotamia." In *Ancestor of the West,* pp. 3-66. Chicago: University of Chicago Press, 1996.

Bottéro, Jean, and Samuel Noah Kramer. *Lorsque les dieux faisaient l'homme: mythologie mésopotamienne.* Paris: Gallimard, 1989.

Bouzon, E. "Die soziale Bedeutung des simdat-šarrim-Aktes nach den Kaufverträgen der Rim-Sin-Zeit." In *Vom Alten Orient zum Alten Testament,* pp. 11-30. AOAT 240. Neukirchen-Vluyn: Neukirchener Verlag, 1995.

Bowes, Wendell. "The Basilomorphic Conception of Deity in Israel and Mesopotamia." In *The Biblical Canon in Comparative Perspective: Scripture in Context IV.* Edited by K. Lawson Younger, Jr. et al., pp. 235-75. Lewiston, N.Y.: Mellen, 1991.

Buccellati, Giorgio. "Ethics and Piety in the Ancient Near East." In *Civilizations of the Ancient Near East.* Edited by Jack Sasson, pp. 1685-96. New York: Scribner, 1995.

Butzer, K. W. "Physical Conditions in Eastern Europe, Western Asia and Egypt before the Period of Agricultural and Urban Settlement." In *CAH,* 1.1:58.

Cassin, Elena. "La contestation dans le monde divin." In *La voix de l'opposition en Mésopotamie.* Edited by André Finet, pp. 89-110. Brussels: Institut des Hautes Études de Belgique, 1973.

Charpin, Dominique. "The History of Ancient Mesopotamia: An Overview." In *Civilizations of the Ancient Near East.* Edited by Jack Sasson, pp. 807-29. New York: Scribner, 1995.

———. "Lettres et procès paléo-babyloniens." In *Rendre la justice en Mésopotamie: archives judiciare du Proche-Orient ancien (IIIe-Ier millénaires avant J.-C.).* Edited by Francis Joannès, pp. 69-111. Saint-Denis: Presses Universitaires de Vincennes, 2000.

———. "Maisons et maisonnées en Babylonie ancienne de Sippar à Ur." In *Houses and*

Households in Ancient Mesopotamia. Edited by Klaas Veenhof, pp. 221-35. CRRA 40. Leiden: Nederlands Historisch-Archaeologisch Instituut te Istanbul, 1996.

————. "Mari entre l'est et l'ouest: politique, culture, religion." *Akkadica* 78 (1992): 1-10.

Chavalas, Mark. "Genealogical History as 'Charter': A Study of Old Babylonian Period Historiography and the Old Testament." In *Faith, Tradition, and History: Old Testament Historiography in Its Near Eastern Context*. Edited by A. R. Millard et al., pp. 103-28. Winona Lake, Ind.: Eisenbrauns, 1994.

Cooper, Jerrold. "Apodictic Death and the 'Historical' Omens." In *Death in Mesopotamia*. Edited by Bendt Alster, pp. 99-105. Mesopotamia 8. Copenhagen: Akademisk Forlag, 1980.

————. "Babbling on Recovering Mesopotamian Orality." In *Mesopotamian Epic Literature: Oral or Aural?* Edited by Marianna E. Vogelzang and H. L. J. Vanstiphout, pp. 103-22. Lewiston, N.Y.: Mellen, 1992.

————. "Sacred Marriage and Popular Cult in Early Mesopotamia." In *Official Cult and Popular Religion in the Ancient Near East*. Edited by E. Matsushima, pp. 81-96. Heidelberg: Universitätsverlag C. Winter, 1993.

Dalley, Stephanie. *Myths from Mesopotamia*. Oxford: Oxford University Press, 1989.

————. *Myths from Mesopotamia*. Rev. ed. New York: Oxford University Press, 2000.

————. "Ancient Mesopotamian Military Organization." In *Civilizations of the Ancient Near East*. Edited by Jack Sasson, pp. 413-22. New York: Scribner, 1995.

————. "The Influence of Mesopotamia on Israel and the Bible." In *The Legacy of Mesopotamia*. Edited by Stephanie Dalley, pp. 57-83. Oxford: Oxford University Press, 1998.

————. "Occasions and Opportunities. 1. To the Persian Conquest." In *The Legacy of Mesopotamia*. Edited by Stephanie Dalley, pp. 9-33. Oxford: Oxford University Press, 1998.

Dalley, Stephanie, and A. T. Reyes. "Mesopotamian Contact and Influence in the Greek World." In *The Legacy of Mesopotamia*. Edited by Stephanie Dalley, pp. 85-106. Oxford: Oxford University Press, 1998.

DiVito, Robert. *Studies in Third Millennium Sumerian and Akkadian Personal Names*. Rome: Pontifical Biblical Institute, 1993.

Dossin, George. *Archives royales de Mari, X. Textes cunéiformes du Louvre XXVI, La correspondance féminine*. Paris: Imprimatur nationale, 1967.

————. "Les archives épistolaires du palais de Mari." *Syria* 19 (1938): 105-26.

Driel, G. van. "Institutional and Non-Institutional Economy in Ancient Mesopotamia." In *Interdependency of Institutions and Private Entrepreneurs*, pp. 5-23. MOS Studies 2. Leiden: Nederlands Historisch-Archaeologisch Instituut te Istanbul, 2000.

————. "Land in Ancient Mesopotamia." In *Landless and Hungry? Access to Land in Early and Traditional Societies*. Edited by B. Haring and R. de Maaijer, pp. 19-49. Leiden: Research School CNWS, School of Asian, African, and Amerindian Studies, 1998.

————. "Landless and Hungry? An Assessment." In *Landless and Hungry? Access to Land in Early and Traditional Societies*. Edited by B. Haring and R. de Maaijer, pp. 190-98.

Leiden: Research School CNWS, School of Asian, African, and Amerindian Studies, 1998.

Driver, G. R., and John C. Miles. *The Babylonian Laws.* 2 vols. Oxford: Clarendon, 1952.

Ebeling, Erich. "Ebabbara." In *RLA,* 2:263.

Eckholm, K., and J. Friedman. "'Capital' Imperialism and Exploitation in Ancient World Systems." In *Power and Propaganda: A Symposium on Ancient Empires.* Edited by Mogens T. Larsen, pp. 41-58. Mesopotamia 7. Copenhagen: Akademisk Forlag, 1979.

Edens, Christopher. "On the Complexity of Complex Societies: Structure, Power, and Legitimation in Kassite Babylonia." In *Chiefdoms and Early States in the Near East: The Organization of Dynamics of Complexity.* Edited by Gil Stein et al., pp. 209-23. Madison: Prehistory Press, 1994.

Edzard, Dietz O. *Die "zweite Zwischenzeit" Babyloniens.* Wiesbaden: Harrossowitz, 1957.

———. "The Old Babylonian Period." In *The Near East: The Early Civilizations.* Edited by Elena Cassin et al., pp. 171-231. New York: Delacorte, 1967.

Ellis, Maria de Jong. "Mesopotamian Oracles and Prophetic Texts." *JCS* 41.2 (1989): 127-86.

Ellis, Richard S. *Foundation Deposits in Ancient Mesopotamia.* New Haven: Yale University Press, 1968.

Eyre, Christopher J. "The Agricultural Cycle, Farming, and Water Management in the Ancient Near East." In *Civilizations of the Ancient Near East.* Edited by Jack Sasson, pp. 175-88. New York: Scribner, 1995.

Falkenstein, Adam. Review of C. J. Gadd, *Ideas of Divine Rule in the Ancient Near East. BO* 7 (1950): 56-58.

Farber, Walter. "Witchcraft, Magic, and Divination in Ancient Mesopotamia." In *Civilizations of the Ancient Near East.* Edited by Jack Sasson, pp. 1895-1909. New York: Scribner, 1995.

Finet, André. "Le trône et la rue en Mésopotamie: l'exaltation du roi et les techniques de l'opposition." In *La voix de l'opposition en Mésopotamie.* Edited by André Finet, pp. 2-27. Brussels: Institut des Hautes Études de Belgique, 1973.

Finkelstein, J. J. "Genealogy of the Hammurapi Dynasty." *JCS* 20 (1966): 95-118.

Foster, Benjamin R. *Before the Muses: An Anthology of Akkadian Literature.* Vol. 1. Bethesda, Md.: CDL, 1993.

———. "Social Reform in Ancient Mesopotamia." In *Social Justice in the Ancient World.* Edited by K. D. Irani and Morris Silver, pp. 165-77. Westport, Conn.: Greenwood, 1995.

Franke, Sabina. *Königsinschriften und Königsideologie: Die Könige von Akkade zwischen Tradition und Neuerung.* Münster: LIT, 1995.

———. "Kings of Akkad: Sargon and Naram-Sin." In *Civilizations of the Ancient Near East.* Edited by Jack Sasson, pp. 831-41. New York: Scribner, 1995.

Frankena, Rintje. *Briefe aus dem British Museum.* AbB 2. Leiden: Brill, 1966.

Frankfort, Henri. *Kingship and the Gods.* Chicago: University of Chicago Press, 1948.

Frayne, Douglas. *The Royal Inscriptions of Mesopotamia. Early Periods.* Vol. 4, *Old Babylonian Period (2003-1595 BC).* Toronto: University of Toronto Press, 1990.

———. "Historical Texts in Haifa: Notes on R. Kutscher's 'Brockman Tablets.'" *BO* 48 (1991): 378-409.

Gelb, Ignace J. "Household and Family in Early Mesopotamia." In *State and Temple Economy in the Ancient Near East.* Edited by Edward Lipinski, pp. 1-97. OLA 5. Leuven: Departement Orientalistiek, 1979.

———. "A New Clay Nail of Hammurapi." *JNES* 7 (1948): 267-71.

———. "On the Alleged Temple and State Economies in Ancient Mesopotamia." In *Studi in onore di Edoardo Volterra.* Vol. 6, pp. 138-54. Milan: Giuffre, 1971.

Gelb, Ignace J., Piotr Steinkeller, and Robert M. Whiting, Jr. *Earliest Land Tenure Systems in the Near East: Ancient Kudurrus: Text.* OIP 104. Chicago: Oriental Institute, 1991.

Glassner, Jean-Jacques. "The Use of Knowledge in Ancient Mesopotamia." In *Civilizations of the Ancient Near East.* Edited by Jack Sasson, pp. 1815-23. New York: Scribner, 1995.

Grayson, A. Kirk. "Assyria and Babylonia." *Or* 49 (1980): 140-94.

———. "Assyrian Royal Inscriptions: Literary Characteristics." In *Assyrian Royal Inscriptions: New Horizons in Literary, Ideological and Historical Analysis.* Edited by Frederick M. Fales, pp. 35-47. Rome: Instituto per L'Oriente, 1981.

———. "Murmuring in Mesopotamia." In *Wisdom, Gods, Literature.* Edited by A. R. George and I. L. Finkel, pp. 301-8. Winona Lake, Ind.: Eisenbrauns, 2000.

Green, Margaret. "The Eridu Lament." *JCS* 30 (1978): 127-67.

———. "The Uruk Lament." *JAOS* 104 (1984): 253-79.

Greengus, Samuel. "Legal and Social Institutions of Ancient Mesopotamia." In *Civilizations of the Ancient Near East.* Edited by Jack Sasson, pp. 469-84. New York: Scribner, 1995.

———. "Some Issues Relating to the Comparability of Laws and the Coherence of the Legal Tradition." In *Theory and Method in Biblical and Cuneiform Law: Revision, Interpolation and Development.* Edited by Bernard Levinson, pp. 60-87. JSOTSup 181. Sheffield: Sheffield Academic Press, 1994.

Groneberg, Brigitte. "Toward a Definition of Literariness as Applied to Akkadian Literature." In *Mesopotamian Poetic Language.* Edited by Marianna E. Vogelzang and H. L. J. Vanstiphout, pp. 59-84. Cuneiform Monographs 6. Groningen: Styx, 1996.

Guinan, A. "Social Constructions and Private Designs: The House Omens of Šumma Ālu." In *Houses and Households in Ancient Mesopotamia,* pp. 61-68. CRRA 40. Leiden: Nederlands Historisch-Archaeologisch Instituut te Istanbul, 1996.

Gurney, O. R. "The Sultantepe Tablets (continued): IV. The *Cuthean Legend* of Naram-Sin." *Anatolian Studies* 5 (1955): 93-113.

Hallo, William W. *Early Mesopotamian Royal Titles, a Philologic and Historical Analysis.* AOS 43. New Haven: Yale University Press, 1957.

———. *Origins: The Ancient Near Eastern Background of Some Modern Western Institutions.* Leiden: Brill, 1996.

———. "God, King, and Man at Yale." In *State and Temple Economy in the Ancient Near*

East. Edited by Edward Lipinski, pp. 99-111. OLA 5. Leuven: Departement Orientalistiek, 1979.

———. "Lamentations and Prayers in Sumer and Akkad." In *Civilizations of the Ancient Near East.* Edited by Jack Sasson, pp. 1871-81. New York: Scribner, 1995.

———. "The Origins of the Sacrificial Cult." In *Ancient Israelite Religion.* Edited by Patrick D. Miller, Jr. et al., pp. 3-13. Philadelphia: Fortress, 1987.

———. "The Royal Correspondence of Larsa: I. A Sumerian Prototype for the Prayer of Hezekiah." In *Kramer Anniversary Volume.* Edited by Barry Eichler, pp. 211-24. AOAT 25. Kevelaer: Butzon & Bercker; 1976.

———. "The Royal Inscriptions of Ur: A Typology." *HUCA* 33 (1962): 1-43.

———. "Sumerian Religion." In *Kinattūtu ša darāti.* Edited by Anson F. Rainey, pp. 15-35. Tel Aviv: University of Tel Aviv Press, 1993.

———. "Texts, Statues and the Cult of the Divine King." *VTSup* 40 (1988): 54-66.

———. "Two Letter-Prayers to Amurru." In *Boundaries of the Ancient Near Eastern World: A Tribute to Cyrus H. Gordon.* Edited by Meir Lubetski et al., pp. 397-410. JSOTSup 273. Sheffield: Sheffield Academic Press, 1998.

Harris, Rivkah. *Ancient Sippar: A Demographic Study of an Old-Babylonian City (1894-1595 B.C.).* Leiden: Nederlands Historisch-Archaeologisch Institut te Istanbul, 1975.

———. "Some Aspects of the Centralization of the Realm under Hammurapi and His Successors." *JAOS* 88 (1968): 729.

Huffmon, Herbert. "A Company of Prophets: Mari, Assyria, Israel." In *Prophecy in Its Ancient Near Eastern Context: Mesopotamian, Biblical, and Arabian Perspectives,* pp. 47-70. SBL Symposium Series 13. Atlanta: Society for Biblical Literature, 2000.

Hurowitz, Victor. *Inu Anum Sīrum: Literary Structures in the Non-Juridical Sections of Codex Hammurabi.* Occasional Publications of the Samuel Noah Kramer Fund 15. Philadelphia: University of Pennsylvania Museum, 1994.

———. "Literary Structures in Samsuiluna A." *JCS* 36 (1984): 191-205.

———. "Some Literary Observations on the Šitti-Marduk Kudurru." *ZA* 82 (1992): 39-59.

Jacobsen, Thorkild. *The Harps That Once. . .: Sumerian Poetry in Translation.* New Haven: Yale University Press, 1987.

———. *The Sumerian King List.* Assyriological Studies 11. Chicago: Oriental Institute, 1939.

———. *The Treasures of Darkness: A History of Mesopotamian Religion.* New Haven: Yale University Press, 1976.

———. "The Gilgamesh Epic: Romantic and Tragic Vision." In *Lingering over Words: Studies in Ancient Near Eastern Literature In Honor of William L. Moran.* Edited by Tzvi Abusch et al., pp. 231-49. HSM 37. Atlanta: Scholars, 1990.

———. "The Graven Image." In *Ancient Israelite Religion.* Edited by Patrick D. Miller, Jr. et al., pp. 15-32. Philadelphia: Fortress, 1987.

Jastrow, Morris, and Albert Clay. *Old Babylonian Gilgamesh Epic.* YOS 4. New Haven: Yale University Press, 1920.

Jeyes, Ulla. *Old Babylonian Extispicy: Omen Texts in the British Museum.* Leiden: Nederlands Historisch-Archaeologisch Instituut te Istanbul, 1989.

―――. "Death and Divination in the Old Babylonian Period." In *Death in Mesopotamia.* Edited by Bendt Alster, pp. 107-21. Mesopotamia 8. Copenhagen: Akademisk Forlag, 1980.

Jonker, Gerdien. *The Topography of Remembrance: The Dead, Tradition, and Collective Memory in Mesopotamia.* Studies in the History of Religions 68. Leiden: Brill, 1995.

King, Leonard C. *The Letters and Inscriptions of Hammurabi.* London: Luzac, 1898.

Klein, Jacob. "Additional Notes to 'The Marriage of Martu.'" In *Kinattūtu ša darāti.* Edited by Anson F. Rainey, pp. 93-106. Tel Aviv: University of Tel Aviv Press, 1993.

―――. "The *Marriage of Martu:* The Urbanization of 'Barbaric' Nomads." In *Mutual Influences of Peoples and Cultures in the Ancient Near East.* Edited by Meir Malul, pp. 83-96. Haifa: University of Haifa Press, 1996.

―――. "On Writing Monumental Inscriptions in the Ur III Scribal Curriculum." *RA* 80 (1986): 1-7.

Klíma, Josef. "Im ewigen Banne der *muškēnum*-Problematic?" In *Wirtschaft und Gesellschaft im alten Vorderasien.* Edited by J. Harmatta and G. Komoróczy, pp. 267-74. Budapest: Akademiai Kiado, 1976.

Komoróczy, G. "Zur Frage der Periodizität der altbabylonischen *Mīšarum*-Erlässe." In *Societies and Languages of the Ancient Near East: Studies in Honor of I. M. Diakonoff,* pp. 196-205. Warminster, England: Aris & Phillips, 1982.

Koschaker, Paul. "Zur staatlichen Wirtshaftsverwaltung in altbabylonischer Zeit, insbesondere nach Urkunden aus Larsa." *ZA* 47 (1942): 135-80.

Kramer, Samuel N. *Lamentation over the Destruction of Ur.* Assyriological Studies 12. Chicago: University of Chicago Press, 1940.

―――. "The Marriage of Martu." In *Bar-Ilan Studies in Assyriology Dedicated to Pinhas Artzi.* Edited by Jacob Klein and Aaron Skaist, pp. 11-27. Ramat-Gan, Israel: Bar-Ilan University, 1990.

Kramer, S. N., and John Maier. *Myths of Enki, the Crafty God.* New York: Oxford University Press, 1989.

Kraus, Fritz R. *Briefe aus dem British Museum (CT 43 und 44).* AbB 1. Leiden: Brill, 1964.

―――. *Ein Edikt des Königs Ammi-Saduqa von Babylon.* Studia et Documenta ad Iura Orientis Antiqui Pertinentia 5. Leiden: Brill, 1958.

―――. *The Role of Temples from the Third Dynasty of Ur to the First Dynasty of Babylon.* Monographs on the Ancient Near East. Vol. 2, Fasc. 4. Malibu, Calif.: Undena, 1990.

―――. *Vom mesopotamischen Menschen der altbabylonischen Zeit und seiner Zeit.* Amsterdam: North-Holland, 1973.

―――. "Das altbabylonische Königtum." In *Le palais et la royauté.* Edited by Paul Garelli, pp. 235-61. CRRA 19. Paris: Paul Geuthner, 1974.

Kupper, J.-R. "Jaḫdun-Lim." In *RLA,* 5:239-40.

Kutscher, Raphael. "Malgium." In *RLA,* 7:300-304.

Labat, René. *Le poème babylonien de la création.* Paris: Libraire d'Amérique et d'Orient, 1935.

Lacambre, D. "Hammurabi et le trône d'Ešnunna." *NABU* 8 (1994): 67-69.

Lafont, Sophie. "Ancient Near Eastern Laws: Continuity and Pluralism." In *Theory and Method in Biblical and Cuneiform Law: Revision, Interpolation and Development.* Edited by Bernard Levinson, pp. 92-118. JSOTSup 181. Sheffield: Sheffield Academic Press, 1994.

Lambert, W. G. "Another Trick of Enki?" In *Marchands, diplomates et empereurs.* Edited by Dominique Charpin and Francis Joannès, pp. 415-19. Paris: Éditions recherche sur les civilisations, 1991.

―――. "Donations of Food and Drink to the Gods in Ancient Mesopotamia." In *Ritual and Sacrifice in the Ancient Near East.* Edited by Jan Quaegebeur, pp. 191-201. OLA 55. Leuven: Peeters, 1993.

―――. "Kingship in Ancient Mesopotamia." In *King and Messiah in Israel and the Ancient Near East.* Edited by John Day, pp. 54-70. JSOTSup 270. Sheffield: Sheffield Academic Press, 1998.

―――. "A New Look at the Babylonian Background of Genesis." In *I Studied Inscriptions from Before the Flood.* Edited by Richard S. Hess and David T. Tsumura, pp. 96-111. Sources for Biblical and Theological Study 4. Winona Lake, Ind.: Eisenbrauns, 1994.

―――. "Ninurta Mythology in the Babylonian Epic of Creation." In *Keilschriftlichen Literaturen: Ausgewählte Vorträge der XXXII. Rencontre assyriologique internationale.* Edited by Karl Hecker and Walter Sommerfeld, pp. 55-60. BBVO 6. Berlin: Dietrich Reimer, 1986.

―――. "The Reign of Nebuchadnezzar I: A Turning Point in the History of Ancient Mesopotamian Religion." In *The Seed of Wisdom: Essays in Honor of T. J. Meek.* Edited by William S. McCullough, pp. 3-13. Toronto: University of Toronto Press, 1964.

―――. "The Seed of Kingship." In *Le palais et la royauté.* Edited by Paul Garelli, pp. 427-40. CRRA 19. Paris: Geuthner, 1974.

―――. "Technical Terminology for Creation in the Ancient Near East." In *Intellectual Life of the Ancient Near East.* Edited by Jirí Prosecký, pp. 189-93. CRRA 43. Prague: Oriental Institute, 1998.

Lambert, W. G., and A. R. Millard. *Atra-Ḫasīs: The Babylonian Story of the Flood.* Winona Lake, Ind.: Eisenbrauns, 1999.

Lambert, W. G., and Simon B. Parker. *Enuma Eliš: The Babylonian Epic of Creation, The Cuneiform Text.* Oxford: Clarendon, 1966.

Larsen, Mogens T. "Commercial Networks in the Ancient Near East." In *Centre and Periphery in the Ancient World.* Edited by Michael Rowlands et al., pp. 47-56. Cambridge: Cambridge University Press, 1987.

Lawson, Jack. *The Concept of Fate in Ancient Mesopotamia of the First Millennium: Toward an Understanding of Šimtu.* OBC 7. Wiesbaden: Harrassowitz, 1994.

Leick, Gwendolyn. "The Challenge of Chance: An Anthropological View of Mesopotamian Mental Strategies for Dealing with the Unpredictable." In *Intellectual Life of the Ancient Near East.* Edited by Jirí Prosecký, pp. 195-98. CRRA 43. Prague: Oriental Institute, 1998.

———. "Enlil." In *A Dictionary of Ancient Near Eastern Mythology,* pp. 45-47. New York: Routledge, 1991.

Limet, Henri. "Reflexions sur la nature et l'efficacité d'une opposition." In *La voix de l'opposition en Mésopotamie.* Edited by André Finet, pp. 79-86. Brussels: Institut des Hautes Études de Belgique, 1973.

Liverani, Mario. *Prestige and Interest: International Relations in the Near East ca. 1600-1100 B.C.* Padova: Sargon SRL, 1990.

———. "The Collapse of the Near Eastern Regional System at the End of the Bronze Age: The Case of Syria." In *Centre and Periphery in the Ancient World.* Edited by Michael Rowlands et al., pp. 66-73. Cambridge: Cambridge University Press, 1987.

———. "The Deeds of Ancient Mesopotamian Kings." In *Civilizations of the Ancient Near East.* Edited by Jack Sasson, pp. 2353-66. New York: Scribner, 1995.

Longman III, Tremper. *Fictional Akkadian Autobiography: A Generic and Comparative Study.* Winona Lake, Ind.: Eisenbrauns, 1991.

Machinist, Peter. "Assyrians on Assyria in the First Millennium B.C." In *Anfänge politischen Denkens in der Antike: Die nahöstlichen Kulturen und die Griechen.* Edited by Kurt Raaflaub and Elisabeth Müller-Luckner, pp. 77-104. Munich: Oldenbourg, 1993.

———. "On Self-Consciousness in Mesopotamia." In *The Origins and Diversity of Axial Age Civilizations.* Edited by S. N. Eisenstadt, pp. 183-202. Albany, N.Y.: SUNY Press, 1986.

Malamat, Abraham. *Mari and the Bible.* Leiden: Brill, 1998.

———. "The Divine Nature of the Mediterranean Sea in the Foundation Inscription of Yaḫdunlim." In *Mari in Retrospect: Fifty Years of Mari and Mari Studies.* Edited by Gordon Young, pp. 211-15. Winona Lake, Ind.: Eisenbrauns, 1992.

Matsushima, Eiko. "Divine Statues in Ancient Mesopotamia: Their Fashioning and Clothing and Their Interaction with the Society." In *Official Cult and Popular Religion in the Ancient Near East.* Edited by Eiko Matsushima, pp. 209-19. Heidelberg: Universitätsverlag, 1993.

Michalowski, Piotr. *The Lamentation over the Destruction of Sumer and Ur.* Winona Lake, Ind.: Eisenbrauns, 1989.

———. "History as Charter: Some Observations on the Sumerian King List." In *Studies in Literature from the Ancient Near East Dedicated to Samuel Noah Kramer.* Edited by Jack Sasson, pp. 237-48. AOS 65. New Haven: American Oriental Society, 1984.

———. "Orality and Literacy and Early Mesopotamian Literature." In *Mesopotamian Epic Literature: Oral or Aural?* Edited by Marianna E. Vogelzang and H. L. J. Vanstiphout, pp. 227-45. Lewiston, N.Y.: Mellen, 1992.

———. "Presence at Creation." In *Lingering over Words: Studies in Ancient Near Eastern Literature in Honor of William L. Moran.* Edited by Tzvi Abusch et al., pp. 381-96. HSM 37. Atlanta: Scholars, 1990.

—. "Sumerian Literature: An Overview." In *Civilizations of the Ancient Near East.* Edited by Jack Sasson, pp. 2279-91. New York: Scribner, 1995.

—. "The Unbearable Lightness of Enlil." In *Intellectual Life of the Ancient Near East.* Edited by Jirí Prosecký, pp. 237-47. CRRA 43. Prague: Oriental Institute, 1998.

Mieroop, Marc Van de. *The Ancient Mesopotamian City.* Oxford: Clarendon, 1997.

—. *Cuneiform Texts and the Writing of History.* New York: Routledge, 1999.

—. *Society and Enterprise in Old Babylonian Ur.* BBVO 12. Berlin: Dietrich Reimer, 1992.

—. "The Government of an Ancient Mesopotamian City: What We Know and Why We Know So Little." In *Priests and Officials in the Ancient Near East.* Edited by Kazuko Watanabe, pp. 139-61. Heidelberg: Universitätsverlag C. Winter, 1999.

—. "Old Babylonian Ur: Portrait of an Ancient Mesopotamian City." *JANES* 21 (1992): 119-30.

—. "The Reign of Rim-Sin." *RA* 87 (1993): 47-69.

Moran, William. "The Gilgamesh Epic: A Masterpiece from Ancient Mesopotamia." In *Civilizations of the Ancient Near East.* Edited by Jack Sasson, pp. 2327-36. New York: Scribner, 1995.

—. "New Evidence from Mari on the History of Prophecy." *Bib* 56 (1969): 15-56.

—. "Some Considerations of Form and Interpretation in *Atra-Ḥasīs*." In *Language, Literature, and History: Philological and Historical Studies Presented to Erica Reiner.* Edited by Francesca Rochberg-Halton, pp. 245-55. New Haven: American Oriental Society, 1987.

Mowinckel, Sigmund. "Die vorderasiatischen königs- und fürsteninschriften: eine stilistische Studie." In *Eucharistērion: Studien zur Religion und Literatur des Alten und Neuen Testaments für Hermann Gunkel.* Vol. 1. Edited by Hans Schmidt, pp. 278-322. Göttingen: Vandenhoeck & Ruprecht, 1923.

Murphy, Susana B. "The Notion of Moral Economy in the Study of the Ancient Near East." In *Intellectual Life of the Ancient Near East.* Edited by Jirí Prosecký, pp. 269-81. CRRA 43. Prague: Oriental Institute, 1998.

Nissinen, Martti. "The Socioreligious Role of the Neo-Assyrian Prophets." In *Prophecy in Its Ancient Near Eastern Context: Mesopotamian, Biblical, and Arabian Perspectives,* pp. 89-114. SBL Symposium Series 13. Atlanta: Society for Biblical Literature, 2000.

Oppenheim, A. L. *Ancient Mesopotamia: Portrait of a Dead Civilization.* Chicago: University of Chicago Press, 1977.

—. "Perspectives on Mesopotamian Divination." In *La divination en Mésopotamie ancienne et dans les regions voisines,* pp. 35-43. CRRA 14. Paris: Presses Universitaires de France, 1966.

Parpola, Simo. *The Standard Babylonian Epic of Gilgamesh.* State Archives of Assyria Cuneiform Texts 1. Helsinki: Vammalan Kirjapaino Oy, 1997.

Pongratz-Leisten, Beate. *Herrschaftswissen in Mesopotamien.* SAAS 10. Helsinki: Neo-Assyrian Text Corpus Project, 1999.

Potts, D. T. *Mesopotamian Civilization: The Material Foundations*. Ithaca: Cornell University Press, 1997.

Renger, Johannes. "Das Palastgeschäft in der altbabylonischer Zeit." In *Interdependency of Institutions and Private Entrepreneurs*. Edited by A. C. V. M. Bonegaar, pp. 153-83. MOS Studies 2. Leiden: Nederlands Historisch-Archaeologisch Instituut te Istanbul, 2000.

———. "Institutional, Communal, and Individual Ownership or Possession of Arable Land in Ancient Mesopotamia from the End of the Fourth to the End of the First Millennium B.C." *Chicago-Kent Law Review* 71 (1995): 269-319.

———. "Interaction of Temple, Palace, and Private Enterprise." In *State and Temple Economy in the Ancient Near East*. Edited by Edward Lipinski, pp. 249-56. OLA 5. Leuven: Departement Orientalistiek, 1979.

———. "Königsinschriften B. Akkadisch." In *RLA*, 6:65-76.

———. "On Economic Structures in Ancient Mesopotamia." *Or* n.s. 63 (1994): 157-208.

———. "Patterns of Non-Institutional Trade and Non-Commercial Exchange in Ancient Mesopotamia at the Beginning of the Second Millennium B.C." In *Circulation of Goods in Non-Palatial Context in the Ancient Near East*. Edited by Alfonso Archi, pp. 31-123. Incunabula Graeca 82. Rome: Edizioni del L'Ateneo, 1984.

———. "River, Water Courses and Irrigation Ditches and Other Matters Concerning Irrigation Based on Old Babylonian Sources (2000-1600 B.C.)." *Bulletin on Sumerian Agriculture* 5 (1990): 31-46.

Ridley, Ronald. "The Saga of an Epic: Gilgamesh and the Constitution of Uruk." *Or* 69 (2000): 341-67.

Robertson, John F. "The Social and Economic Organization of Ancient Mesopotamian Temples." In *Civilizations of the Ancient Near East*. Edited by Jack Sasson, pp. 443-54. New York: Scribner, 1995.

Roth, Martha. *Law Collections from Mesopotamia and Asia Minor*. Writings from the Ancient World 6. Atlanta: Scholars, 1995.

Sasson, Jack M. "King Hammurabi of Babylon." In *Civilizations of the Ancient Near East*. Edited by Jack Sasson, pp. 901-15. New York: Scribner, 1995.

———. "Water Beneath the Straw: Adventures of a Prophetic Phrase in the Mari Archives." In *Solving Riddles and Untying Knots: Biblical, Epigraphic, and Semitic Studies in Honor of Jonas C. Greenfield*. Edited by Ziony Zevit et al., pp. 599-608. Winona Lake, Ind.: Eisenbrauns, 1995.

Schwartz, Glenn. "Before Ebla: Models of Pre-State Political Organization in Syria and Northern Mesopotamia." In *Chiefdoms and Early States in the Near East: The Organization Dynamics of Complexity*. Edited by Gil Stein et al., pp. 153-74. Monographs on World Archaeology 18. Madison: Prehistory Press, 1994.

Shaffer, Aaron. "Gilgamesh, the Cedar Forest and Mesopotamian History." In *Studies in Literature from the Ancient Near East Dedicated to Samuel Noah Kramer*. Edited by Jack Sasson, pp. 307-13. AOS 65. New Haven: American Oriental Society, 1984.

Silver, Morris. *Economic Structures of the Ancient Near East*. Totowa, N.J.: Barnes & Noble, 1985.

Skaist, Aaron. "The Ancestor Cult and Succession in Mesopotamia." In *Death in Mesopotamia*. Edited by Bendt Alster, pp. 123-28. Mesopotamia 8. Copenhagen: Akademisk Forlag, 1980.

Snell, Daniel. *Life in the Ancient Near East: 3100-332 B.C.E.* New Haven: Yale University Press, 1997.

———. "Trade and Commerce." In *ABD*, 6:627.

Soden, Wolfram von. *The Ancient Orient: An Introduction to the Study of the Ancient Near East*. Grand Rapids: Eerdmans, 1994.

———. "Untersuchungen zur babylonischen Metrik, Teil I." *ZA* 71 (1981): 161-204.

Sommerfeld, Walter. *Der Aufstieg Marduks: Die Stellung Marduks in der babylonischen Religion des zweiten Jahrtausends v. Chr.* AOAT 213. Neukirchen-Vluyn: Neukirchener Verlag, 1982.

———. "Der babylonische 'Feudalismus.'" In *Vom Alten Orient zum Alten Testament*. Edited by Manfried Dietrich and Oswald Loretz, pp. 467-90. AOAT 240. Neukirchen-Vluyn: Neukirchener Verlag, 1995.

Starr, Ivan, ed. *Queries to the Sungod: Divination and Politics in Sargonid Assyria*. SAAS 4. Helsinki: Helsinki University Press, 1990.

Steinkeller, Piotr. "The Administrative and Economic Organization of the Ur III State: The Core and the Periphery." In *The Organization of Power: Aspects of Bureaucracy in the Ancient Near East*. 2nd ed. Edited by M. Gibson and R. D. Biggs, pp. 19-41. Studies in Ancient Oriental Civilization 46. Chicago: Oriental Institute, 1991.

———. "On Rulers, Priests and Sacred Marriage: Tracing the Evolution of Early Sumerian Kingship." In *Priests and Officials in the Ancient Near East*. Edited by Kazuko Watanabe, pp. 103-37. Heidelberg: Universitätsverlag C. Winter, 1999.

———. "On the Identity of the Toponym LU.SU(.A)." *JAOS* 108 (1988): 197-202.

Tadmor, Hayim. "History and Ideology in the Assyrian Royal Inscriptions." In *Assyrian Royal Inscriptions: New Horizons in Literary, Ideological, and Historical Analysis*. Edited by Frederick M. Fales, pp. 13-33. Rome: Instituto per L'Oriente, 1981.

———. "Monarchy and Elite in Assyria and Babylonia." In *The Origins and Diversity of Axial Civilizations*. Edited by S. N. Eisenstadt, pp. 203-24. Albany, N.Y.: SUNY Press, 1986.

Tallqvist, Knut. *Akkadische Götterepitheta*. Studia Orientalia 7. Hildesheim: Olms, 1974.

Tigay, Jeffrey. *The Evolution of the Gilgamesh Epic*. Philadelphia: University of Pennsylvania Press, 1982.

Tinney, Steve. *The Nippur Lament: Royal Rhetoric and Divine Legislation in the Reign of Ishme-Dagan of Isin (1953-1935 B.C.)*. Occasional Publications of the Samuel Noah Kramer Fund 16. Philadelphia: University of Pennsylvania Museum, 1996.

Toorn, Karel van der. "Mesopotamian Prophecy between Immanence and Transcendence: A Comparison of Old Babylonian and Neo-Assyrian Prophecy." In *Prophecy in Its Ancient Near Eastern Context: Mesopotamian, Biblical, and Arabian Perspectives*, pp. 71-87. SBL Symposium Series 13. Atlanta: Society for Biblical Literature, 2000.

————. "Old Babylonian Prophecy between the Written and the Oral." *JNSL* 24 (1998): 55-70.

Tsukimoto, Akio. "Aspekte von *Kispu(m)* als Totenbeigabe." In *Death in Mesopotamia.* Edited by Bendt Alster, pp. 129-38. Mesopotamia 8. Copenhagen: Akademisk Forlag, 1980.

Vanstiphout, H. L. J. "The Death of an Era: The Great Mortality in the Sumerian City Laments." In *Death in Mesopotamia.* Edited by Bendt Alster, pp. 83-89. CRRA 26. Mesopotamia 8. Copenhagen: Akademisk Forlag, 1980.

————. "Enuma Elish as a Systematic Creed: An Essay." *OLP* 23 (1992): 37-61.

————. "Memory and Literacy in Ancient Western Asia." In *Civilizations of the Ancient Near East.* Edited by Jack Sasson, pp. 2181-96. New York: Scribner, 1995.

————. "Some Thoughts on Genre in Mesopotamian Literature." In *Keilschriftlichen Literaturen: Ausgewählte Vorträge der XXXII. Rencontre assyriologique internationale.* Edited by Karl Hecker and Walter Sommerfeld, pp. 1-11. BBVO 6. Berlin: Dietrich Reimer, 1986.

Veenhof, Klaus R. "Notes brèves." *RA* 79 (1985): 190-91.

Villard, Pierre. "Shamshi-Adad and Sons: The Rise and Fall of an Upper Mesopotamian Empire." In *Civilizations of the Ancient Near East.* Edited by Jack Sasson, pp. 873-83. New York: Scribner, 1995.

Vulpe, Nicola. "Irony and the Unity of the *Gilgamesh Epic.*" *JNES* 53 (1994): 275-83.

Wasserman, Nathan. "CT 21,40-42. A Bilingual Report of an Oracle with a Royal Hymn of Hammurabi." *RA* 86 (1982): 1-18.

Westbrook, Raymond. "Cuneiform Law Codes and the Origins of Legislation." *ZA* 79 (1989): 201-22.

————. "Social Justice in the Ancient Near East." In *Social Justice in the Ancient World.* Edited by K. D. Irani and Morris Silver, pp. 149-63. Westport, Conn.: Greenwood, 1995.

————. "What Is the Covenant Code?" In *Theory and Method in Biblical and Cuneiform Law: Revision, Interpolation and Development.* Edited by Bernard Levinson, pp. 15-36. JSOTSup 181. Sheffield: Sheffield Academic Press, 1994.

Westenholz, Aage, and Ulla Koch-Westenholz. "Enkidu — the Noble Savage?" In *Wisdom, Gods and Literature: Studies in Assyriology in Honour of W. G. Lambert.* Edited by A. R. George and I. L. Finkel, pp. 437-51. Winona Lake, Ind.: Eisenbrauns, 2000.

Westenholz, Joan Goodnick. *Legends of the Kings of Akkade.* Winona Lake, Ind.: Eisenbrauns, 1997.

————. "Heroes of Akkad." In *Studies in Literature from the Ancient Near East Dedicated to Samuel Noah Kramer.* Edited by Jack Sasson, pp. 327-36. AOS 65. New Haven: American Oriental Society, 1984.

————. "Oral Traditions and Written Texts in the Cycle of Akkad." In *Mesopotamian Epic Literature: Oral or Aural?* Edited by Marianna E. Vogelzang and H. L. J. Vanstiphout, pp. 123-54. Lewiston, N.Y.: Mellen, 1992.

————. "Symbolic Language in Akkadian Narrative Poetry: The Metaphorical Relationship between Poetic Images and the Real World." In *Mesopotamian Poetic Lan-*

guage: Sumerian and Akkadian, pp. 183-206. Cuneiform Monographs 6. Groningen: Styx, 1996.

———. "Thoughts on Esoteric Knowledge and Secret Lore." In *Intellectual Life of the Ancient Near East*. Edited by Jirí Prosecký, pp. 451-62. CRRA 43. Prague: Oriental Institute, 1998.

Wiggermann, F. A. M. "Scenes from the Shadow Side." In *Intellectual Life of the Ancient Near East*. Edited by Jirí Prosecký, pp. 207-26. CRRA 43. Prague: Oriental Institute, 1998.

———. "Theologies, Priests, and Worship in Ancient Mesopotamia." In *Civilizations of the Ancient Near East*. Edited by Jack Sasson, pp. 1857-70. New York: Scribner, 1995.

Wilcke, Claus. "Politik im Spiegel der Literatur, Literatur als Mittel der Politik im älteren Babylonien." In *Anfänge politischen Denkens in der Antike: Die nahöstlichen Kulturen und die Griechen*. Edited by Kurt Raaflaub and Elisabeth Müller-Luckner, pp. 29-75. Munich: Oldenbourg, 1993.

Winter, Irene. "'Idols of the King': Royal Images as Recipients of Ritual Action in Ancient Mesopotamia." *Journal of Ritual Studies* 6 (1992): 13-42.

———. "Legitimation of Authority Through Image and Legend: Seals Belonging to Officials in the Administrative Bureaucracy of the Ur III State." In *Organization of Power: Aspects of Bureaucracy in the Ancient Near East*. Edited by McGuire Gibson and Robert Biggs, pp. 69-93. Studies in Ancient Oriental Civilization 46. Chicago: Oriental Institute, 1987.

———. "Royal Rhetoric and the Development of Historical Narrative in Neo-Assyrian Reliefs." *Studies in Visual Communication* 7 (1981): 3-28.

Wiseman, Donald J. "The Laws of Hammurapi Again." *JSS* 7 (1962): 161-72.

Wu, Y. *A Political History of Eshnunna, Mari and Assyria during the Early Old Babylonian Period*. Changchung: Institute of History of Ancient Civilizations, 1994.

Yoffee, Norman. *The Economic Role of the Crown in the Old Babylonian Period*. Bibliotheca Mesopotamia 5. Malibu, Calif.: Undena, 1977.

———. "Context and Authority in Early Mesopotamian Law." In *State Formation and Political Legitimacy*. Edited by Ronald Cohen and Judith Toland, pp. 95-113. Political Anthropology 6. New Brunswick, N.J.: Transaction Books, 1988.

———. "The Late Great Tradition in Ancient Mesopotamia." In *The Tablet and the Scroll: Near Eastern Studies in Honor of William W. Hallo*. Edited by M. Cohen et al., pp. 300-308. Bethesda, Md.: CDL, 1993.

———. "Political Economy in Early Mesopotamian States." *Annual Review of Anthropology* 24 (1995): 281-311.

Zadok, Tikva. "The Distribution of the Temporal Sentences in the Old Babylonian Royal Inscriptions." *JANES* 24 (1996): 111-18.

405